T0202937

Lecture Notes in Computer Science   14182

Founding Editors

Gerhard Goos
Juris Hartmanis

Editorial Board Members

Elisa Bertino, *Purdue University, West Lafayette, IN, USA*
Wen Gao, *Peking University, Beijing, China*
Bernhard Steffen ⓘ, *TU Dortmund University, Dortmund, Germany*
Moti Yung ⓘ, *Columbia University, New York, NY, USA*

The series Lecture Notes in Computer Science (LNCS), including its subseries Lecture Notes in Artificial Intelligence (LNAI) and Lecture Notes in Bioinformatics (LNBI), has established itself as a medium for the publication of new developments in computer science and information technology research, teaching, and education.

LNCS enjoys close cooperation with the computer science R & D community, the series counts many renowned academics among its volume editors and paper authors, and collaborates with prestigious societies. Its mission is to serve this international community by providing an invaluable service, mainly focused on the publication of conference and workshop proceedings and postproceedings. LNCS commenced publication in 1973.

Jérémie Guiochet · Stefano Tonetta ·
Erwin Schoitsch · Matthieu Roy ·
Friedemann Bitsch

Editors

Computer Safety, Reliability, and Security

SAFECOMP 2023 Workshops

ASSURE, DECSoS, SASSUR, SENSEI, SRToITS, and WAISE
Toulouse, France, September 19, 2023
Proceedings

 Springer

Editors
Jérémie Guiochet 🆔
University of Toulouse
Toulouse, France

Stefano Tonetta 🆔
Fondazione Bruno Kessler
Trento, Italy

Erwin Schoitsch 🆔
Austrian Institute of Technology GmbH
Vienna, Austria

Matthieu Roy
LAAS-CNRS
Toulouse, France

Friedemann Bitsch 🆔
Thales Deutschland GmbH
Ditzingen, Germany

ISSN 0302-9743   ISSN 1611-3349 (electronic)
Lecture Notes in Computer Science
ISBN 978-3-031-40952-3   ISBN 978-3-031-40953-0 (eBook)
https://doi.org/10.1007/978-3-031-40953-0

This Springer imprint is published by the registered company Springer Nature Switzerland AG
The registered company address is: Gewerbestrasse 11, 6330 Cham, Switzerland

Paper in this product is recyclable.

Preface

The SAFECOMP workshops preceding the SAFECOMP conference have become more attractive since they publish their own proceedings in the Springer LNCS series (LNCS vol. 14182, the book in your hands; the main conference proceedings are LNCS 14181). This meant adhering to Springer's guidelines, i.e., the International Program Committee of each workshop had to make sure that at least three independent reviewers reviewed the papers carefully. Reviews were single-blind. The selection criteria differed from those of the main conference since authors were encouraged to submit workshop papers on work in progress or controversial topics. In total, 35 regular papers (out of 49) were accepted. There were a few invited papers and talks, which were not all included in the proceedings. All workshops had an introduction written by the chairs. The workshops were organized as hybrid events to allow participation in case of travel restrictions.

This year, eight workshops had been proposed: one was cancelled, two shared jointly the workshop day (ASSURE 2023 and SASSUR 2023), and one (MASCA 2023) did not publish papers:

- ASSURE 2023 – 8th International Workshop on Assurance Cases for Software-Intensive Systems, chaired by Ewen Denney, Ibrahim Habli, and Ganesh Pai.
- DECSoS 2023 – 18th Workshop on Dependable Smart Embedded and Cyber-Physical Systems and Systems-of-Systems, chaired by Erwin Schoitsch and Amund Skavhaug.
- SASSUR 2023 – 10th International Workshop on Next Generation of System Assurance Approaches for Critical Systems, chaired by Jose Luis de la Vara and Barbara Gallina.
- SENSEI 2023 – 2nd International Workshop on Security and Safety Interactions, chaired by Christina Kolb, Milan Lopuhaä-Zwakenberg, and Elena Troubitsyna.
- SRToITS 2023 – 1st International Workshop on Safety/ Reliability/ Trustworthiness of Intelligent Transportation Systems, chaired by Ci Liang, Nour-Eddin El Faouzi, and Mohamed Ghazel.
- WAISE 2023 – 6th International Workshop on Artificial Intelligence Safety Engineering, chaired by Simos Gerasimou, Orlando Avila-García, Mauricio Castillo-Effen, Chih-Hong Cheng, and Zakaria Chihani.

The workshops provide a truly international platform for academia and industry.

It has been a pleasure to work with the SAFECOMP conference chair Jérémie Guiochet, the Program chair Stefano Tonetta, the workshop co-chair Matthieu Roy, the publication chair Friedemann Bitsch, the web chair Joris Guerin, the workshop chairs, the Program Committees, the local organization, and the authors. Thank you all for your cooperation and excellent work!

September 2023   Erwin Schoitsch

Organization

EWICS TC7 Chair

Francesca Saglietti   University of Erlangen-Nuremberg, Germany

General Chair

Jérémie Guiochet   LAAS-CNRS, Université de Toulouse, France

Conference Program Co-chairs

Stefano Tonetta   Fondazione Bruno Kessler, Italy
Jérémie Guiochet   LAAS-CNRS, Université de Toulouse, France

General Workshop Co-chairs

Erwin Schoitsch   AIT Austrian Institute of Technology, Austria
Matthieu Roy   LAAS-CNRS, France

Position Papers Chair

António Casimiro   University of Lisbon, Portugal

Publication Chair

Friedemann Bitsch   GTS Deutschland GmbH, Germany

Publicity Chair

Barbara Gallina   Mälardalen University, Sweden

Industry Chair

Magnus Albert   SICK AG, Germany

Web Chair

Joris Guerin   Espace-Dev, IRD, Univ. Montpellier, France

Local Organization Committee

Marie Laure Pierucci   LAAS-CNRS, France
Isabelle Lefebvre   LAAS-CNRS, France
Karama Kanoun   LAAS-CNRS, France

Workshop Chairs

ASSURE 2023

Ewen Denney   KBR/NASA Ames Research Center, USA
Ibrahim Habli   University of York, UK
Ganesh Pai   KBR/NASA Ames Research Center, USA

DECSoS 2023

Erwin Schoitsch   AIT Austrian Institute of Technology, Austria
Amund Skavhaug   Norwegian University of Science and Technology,
                                 Norway

SASSUR 2023

Jose Luis de la Vara   Universidad de Castilla-La Mancha, Spain
Barbara Gallina   Mälardalen University, Sweden

SENSEI 2023

Christina Kolb	University of Edinburgh, UK
Milan Lopuhaä-Zwakenberg	University of Twente, The Netherlands
Elena Troubitsyna	KTH Royal Institute of Technology, Sweden

SRToITS 2023

Ci Liang	Harbin Institute of Technology, China
Nour-Eddin El Faouzi	Université Gustave Eiffel, France
Mohamed Ghazel	Université Gustave Eiffel, France

WAISE 2023

Simos Gerasimou	University of York, UK
Zakaria Chihani	CEA-List, France
Òrlando Avila-García	ARQUIMEA Research Center, Spain
Chih-Hong Cheng	Fraunhofer Institute of Cognitive Systems, Germany
Mauricio Castillo-Effen	Lockheed Martin, USA

Gold Sponsor

SICK AG

IMAGINARY

Silver Sponsor

Critical Systems Labs Inc.

Supporting Institutions

European Workshop on Industrial
Computer Systems

Technical Committee 7 on Reliability,
Safety and Security

Laboratory for Analysis and
Architecture of Systems, Carnot
Institute

Université de Toulouse

Université Toulouse III Paul Sabatier

Fondazione Bruno Kessler

AIT Austrian Institute of Technology

GTS Deutschland GmbH

Lecture Notes in Computer Science
(LNCS), Springer Science + Business
Media

Technical Group ENCRESS in GI and
ITG

European
Network of
Clubs for
REliability and
Safety of
Software

Gesellschaft für Informatik (GI)

Inside Industry Association

Informationstechnische Gesellschaft
(ITG) im VDE

Austrian Computer Society

Electronics and Software Based
Systems (ESBS) Austria

European Research Consortium for
Informatics and Mathematics

Austrian Software Innovation
Association

Contents

**10th International Workshop on Next Generation of System
Assurance Approaches for Critical Systems (SASSUR 2023)**

**2nd International Workshop on Security and Safety Interaction
(SENSEI 2023)**

8th International Workshop
on Assurance Cases
for Software-Intensive Systems
(ASSURE 2023)

8th International Workshop on Assurance Cases for Software-Intensive Systems (ASSURE 2023)

Ewen Denney[1], Ibrahim Habli[2], and Ganesh Pai[1]

[1] KBR/NASA Ames Research Center, Moffett Field, CA 94401, USA
{ewen.denney,ganesh.pai}@nasa.gov
[2] University of York, York YO10 5DD, UK
ibrahim.habli@york.ac.uk

1 Introduction

This volume contains the papers presented at the 8th International Workshop on Assurance Cases for Software-intensive Systems (ASSURE 2023), collocated this year with the 42nd International Conference on Computer Safety, Reliability, and Security (SAFECOMP 2023), in Toulouse, France.

As with the previous seven editions of ASSURE, the workshop this year aims to provide an international forum for presenting emerging research, novel contributions, tool development efforts, and position papers on the foundations and applications of assurance case principles and techniques. The workshop goals are to: (i) explore techniques to create and assess assurance cases for software-intensive systems; (ii) examine the role of assurance cases in the engineering lifecycle of critical systems; (iii) identify the dimensions of effective practice in the development/evaluation of assurance cases; (iv) investigate the relationship between dependability techniques and assurance cases; and, (v) identify critical research challenges towards defining a roadmap for future development.

This year, the workshop program contains a diverse selection of assurance case research: how a safety case can aid in driving the development process; modifying assurance cases to manage potentially malicious behavior emerging from safety vulnerabilities; security cases constructed from formal verification; how assurance in timing properties for automotive time-sensitive networks is established; and an assurance case framework for dependability of autonomous driving.

2 Acknowledgements

We thank all those who submitted papers to ASSURE 2023 and congratulate those authors whose papers were selected for inclusion into the workshop program and proceedings. We especially thank our distinguished Program Committee members who provided useful feedback to the authors:

- Simon Burton, Fraunhofer IKS, Germany
- Chih-Hong Cheng, Fraunhofer IKS, Germany

- Martin Feather, NASA Jet Propulsion Laboratory, USA
- Yoshiki Kinoshita, Kanagawa University, Japan
- Philippa Ryan Conmy, University of York, UK
- Daniel Schneider, Fraunhofer IESE, Germany
- Irfan Šljivo, KBR/NASA Ames Research Center, USA
- Kenji Taguchi, National Institute of Informatics, Japan
- Alan Wassyng, McMaster University, Canada
- Sean White, Health and Social Care Information Centre, UK

Their efforts have resulted in a successful eighth edition of the ASSURE workshop series. Finally, we thank the organizers of SAFECOMP 2023 for their support of ASSURE 2023.

Using Assurance Cases to Prevent Malicious Behaviour from Targeting Safety Vulnerabilities

Victor Bandur$^{(\boxtimes)}$ (iD), Mark Lawford (iD), Sébastien Mosser (iD), Richard F. Paige (iD), Vera Pantelic (iD), and Alan Wassyng (iD)

McMaster Centre for Software Certification, McMaster University, Hamilton, Canada
{bandurvp,lawford,mossers,paigeri,pantelv,wassyng}@mcmaster.ca

Abstract. We discuss an approach to modifying a safety assurance case to take into account malicious intent. We show how to analyze an existing assurance case to reveal additions and modifications that need to be made in order to deal with the effects of malicious intent aimed at safety critical applications, and where to make them.

1 Overview

In 2018 researchers in the McMaster Centre for Software Certification (McSCert) published a paper on safe and secure over-the-air software updates [2].

In the paper, we presented an assurance case (AC) we developed based on ISO 26262 [4] for functional safety, and on SAE J3061 [9] for cybersecurity. We were looking for a way to integrate safety and security. The top-level of that AC is shown in Fig. 1, in a GSN-like notation.

The approach was reasonably successful in that it helped us find a vulnerability in the implementation of the Uptane framework (see [1]). Later, we began to question our integration of safety and security as equals in the AC and in hazard analyses. The reason we began to doubt that strategy is captured in Fig. 2.

The figure shows how malicious acts, including cybersecurity threats, can bypass safety mitigations built into a system.

From this grew the idea that we may be able to protect the safety of a system from malicious intent without a general cybersecurity analysis and mitigation. This is the first component of this research – explore using the safety argument to identify security concerns. Future work will include comparison with a more traditional approach that deals with safety and security as equals.

2 A Fast Food Coffee Cup Example

The following coffee cup example originated in McSCert, with an early version of the top-level of the AC published in 2020 [3]. We explored ACs that did not include software since we wanted to focus on safety (freedom from loss/harm), irrespective of the nature of the system. Everything we had analyzed up till

J. Guiochet et al. (Eds.): SAFECOMP 2023 Workshops, LNCS 14182, pp. 5–14, 2023.
https://doi.org/10.1007/978-3-031-40953-0_1

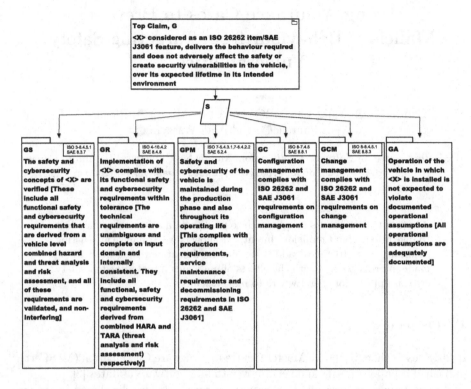

Fig. 1. Top-Level of an Assurance Case for Over-the-Air Software Updates - from [2]

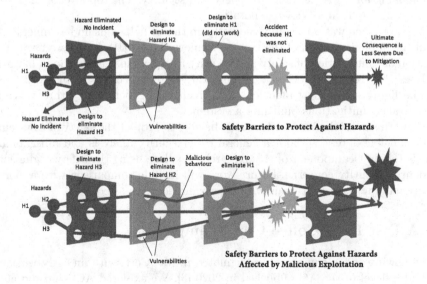

Fig. 2. Malicious Exploitation of Safety Vulnerabilities

then included software as a major component of the system. We chose this as the example to use for this analysis to highlight that we are interested in all malicious activities and are not restricted to cybersecurity. Examples of such cups are those deployed in fast food enterprises.

Figure 3 shows the top-level of the coffee cup AC. The top-level of the previously developed safety AC is analyzed to determine which assumptions, claims

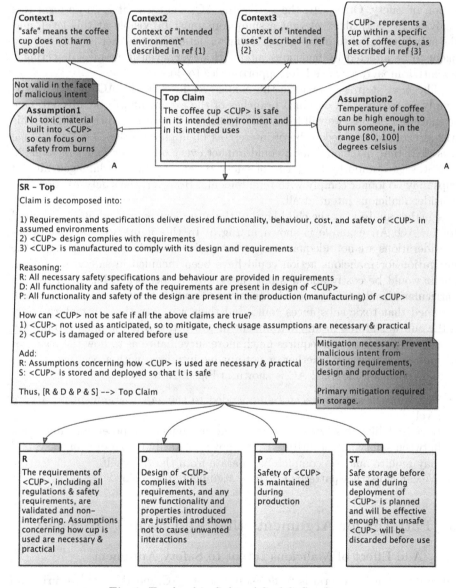

Fig. 3. Top-level in Safety AC of Coffee Cup

and evidence could be affected by malicious intent. The red notes in the figure show the results of this initial analysis.

Most of the effects of malicious intent will be detected at lower levels of the AC. However, even at the top-level, Fig. 3, one of the items of interest, if we consider security, is that the overall assumption that toxic material is not built into the cup may not be valid in the face of malicious intent. This, and other items, have implications for the analysis at the lower levels.

This is the first step in including the effects of malicious intent in the preservation of safety. Obviously, the better the AC, the easier it is to perform this analysis. In particular, relevant assumptions must be visible at this level, and the subclaims need to have enough detail to determine whether or not they are likely to be affected by malicious intent. However, even if we miss detecting a potential impact, we have later opportunities to do so.

The next step is to analyze the next lower level in the AC. Again, this is simply an exploration of which branches of the argument will be affected. Due to space limitations, we will focus only on the "ST" branch, shown in Fig. 4. This was already determined to be of interest as highlighted in Fig. 3. At this stage it is clear that malicious intent could impact every one of the four subclaims in ST. Storage is important in terms of safety, because weakened/damaged/altered cups may no longer comply with requirements. However, the safety AC does not consider malicious intent at all.

Further analysis at the child level of the argument reveals additions required to the AC. An example is shown in Fig. 5. In this figure we see that safety considerations are not adequate to prevent against malicious action. Some of the mitigation for malicious action could have been included in safety mitigation, but it would be costly and was not thought to be necessary, based on risk. In particular, the check on toxic substances when malicious intent was not included, assumed that toxic substances could find their way into the cup material only if the cup was stored in an environment in which this could happen. To protect against malicious intent requires much more surveillance as to how the packages of cups are stored and whether or not anyone interferes with a package.

The resulting modified AC is shown in Fig. 6. Note that:

- The *security* argument can be appended to the *safety* argument on a local level
- Localized like this, we can analyze the argument for potential interaction between safety and security – this is not necessarily trivial or even easy, and may require analysis completely separate from the AC itself
- We can construct patterns for these arguments (see below)

3   Patterns for Arguments that Add Security to Safety

3.1   Add Effect of Malicious Intent to Safety Argument

Since our plan in general is to develop a safety AC and then add security, an obvious initial pattern for this is to simply add conjunctive security claims to

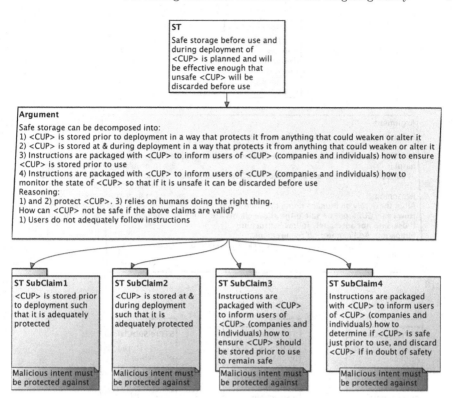

Fig. 4. Storage Branch in Safety AC of Coffee Cup

the existing safety claims – as in Fig. 6. This works in general, and it is simple. However, there are serious drawbacks to this approach. The most critical drawback is that this results in localized silos – one for safety and another for security. Based on our previous experience, this is something we had decided to avoid. First, there is obvious duplication in the different branches if we do this, which impacts maintenance of the AC. More importantly, there is less chance of analyzing interactions. Separating safety and security exacerbates the problems that GSN-like notations have in coping with cross-cutting concerns.

To avoid this, we should explore alternatives. Readers will have noticed that our *Strategy* nodes contain brief reasoning as to what subclaims and/or evidence are necessary to support the parent claim (sometimes included in Justification nodes in GSN). We believe the search for alternative claim structure starts here.

3.2   Re-Analyze the Local Argument

In the example in Fig. 6, the *Default safety plus security argument* is:

- <CUP> is stored so that moisture, pressure and toxic substances do not harm it

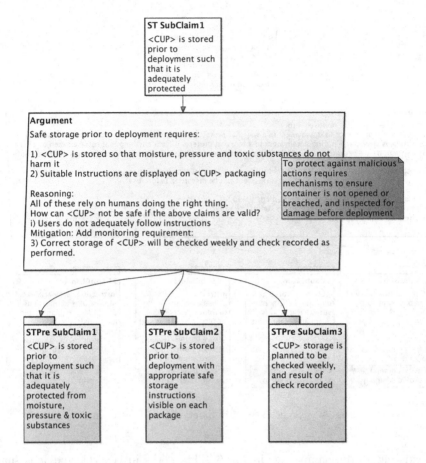

Fig. 5. Storage Pre-Deployment Branch in Safety AC of Coffee Cup

- Suitable instructions are displayed on <CUP> packaging
- Correct storage of <CUP> will be checked weekly and check recorded as performed
- Access to storage is restricted, and monitored
- Stored packages are protected from tampering
- People with access to storage are vetted

We notice immediately that there is a simple difference between the safety and security arguments: safety clauses refer to <CUP> and a security clause to packages of cups. The focus on packaging is vital to the security argument. The focus on <CUP> was natural in the safety argument and did not raise any concerns. However, the argument could easily have referred to packages of cups if necessary. With this in mind, and looking for ways to integrate this better, an *improved argument* may be:

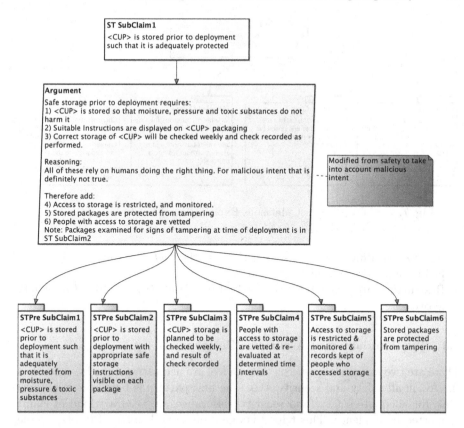

Fig. 6. Storage Pre-Deployment Branch in Safe & Secure AC of Coffee Cup

- Packages containing <CUP>s are stored in a restricted and monitored storage area, in such a way that moisture, pressure, and toxic substances cannot harm the <CUP>s by accident or malicious action
- People with access to the storage area are vetted for access
- Suitable instructions are displayed on packages containing <CUP>s and cannot be removed or altered without leaving a noticeable trace
- Correct storage of packages containing <CUP>s will be checked for damage and/or tampering weekly, by at least two people, and the check immutably recorded as performed with names of the checkers (durations and number of people are placeholders here in lieu of more detailed analysis).

This results in the modified claim structure shown in Fig. 7.

This shows how we can integrate safety and security at a particular level in the AC. A simple process view of it, for a particular claim decomposition, is:

1. Analyze the safety argument to identify where malicious intent affects safety, and add that to the argument (in the example this is shown in Figs. 3, 4, 5 and resulted in Fig. 6)

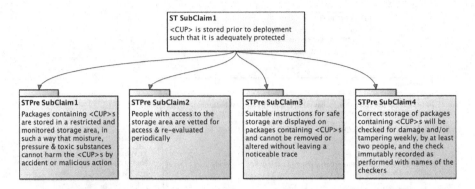

Fig. 7. Protecting Against Malicious Exploitation of Safety Vulnerabilities

2. Analyze wording in the reasoning clauses (the *Default argument*, above) to facilitate integrating safety & security
3. Restructure argument based on revised argument (the *Improved argument*, above)

3.3 Two Fundamental Assurance Patterns

There are two structural patterns that we feel are necessary at the lower levels of the AC in all safety and security ACs. The first pattern is based on an old idea that, for adequate safety (and security) assurance, we need a tripod of claims supported by evidence. This tripod is based on 3-Ps, Product/Process/People, as shown in Fig. 8. For example, SubClaim1 in the right part of Fig. 9 should be supported by claims that all relevant hazards, including mitigations are documented, that the hazard analysis method was appropriate, and that the team that performed the hazard analysis was competent to do so.

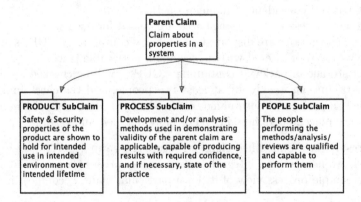

Fig. 8. Tripod Pattern of Product/Process/People

The second pattern is used to deal with a never-ending problem in assuring safety and security – completeness. This pattern is simple, but difficult to implement sufficiently well. It is shown in the left part of Fig. 9 with an example to its right. SubClaim2 is the added component of the argument.

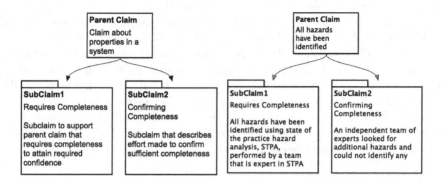

Fig. 9. Completeness Pattern and Example Instantiation

4   Related Work

There has been some related work on providing integrated assurance of safety and security. Some of this work focuses on considering security concerns within specific safety analyses, e.g., security-aware HAZOPs [8] or secure FTA [7]. Other approaches include security-aware STPA [11], or modeling approaches such as UMLsec [6] or security profiles associated with SysML, or the security annexe for AADL. Of additional note is SSAF [5], which attempts co-assurance of security and safety with checkpoints for ensuring no conflicts.

5   Conclusion

We are advocating that an effective way of dealing with the effect of security on the safety of a system, is to (surprisingly) first conduct the safety analysis and develop a safety Assurance Case Template (see [10]), which is constructed prior to system development. Then, by analyzing the safety AC for vulnerability to malicious intent, it is possible to integrate security assurance into the AC. It is important to note that the techniques we presented above apply equally well to cybersecurity threats as they do to the software-free coffee cup, and that this is not a full security analysis. It results in an AC that analyzes safety primarily, but takes into account how malicious activity can adversely affect the safety of the system. We believe the security "story" starts with a careful analysis of the assumptions and reasoning at every level of the safety AC though this technique does not apply to those argument segments in the AC that are confined to the application of a safety process, such as safety-only hazard analysis. We also reuse patterns that were developed for safety ACs, that are just as useful when malicious intent is introduced. Based on this initial security focused exploration of the safety AC, we believe it is possible to develop a systematic approach, based on an initial safety AC, to analyze the potential for malicious attacks on safety critical systems. Again, this is planned future work.

We do not completely agree with the view that says malicious behaviour is no different from inadvertent behaviour, and that if we cope with inadvertent behaviour it will be sufficient. We believe there is a real difference. For instance, we have a requirement that protects against inadvertently spilling the coffee. One mitigation is to design a lid that has safeguards built in so that accidentally knocking over the cup will not result in a spill. However, malicious behaviour could potentially damage the safeguard mechanism and not be obvious to a user. Inspecting the safety AC with respect to how malicious activity can adversely affect the safety argument helps to identify this "security" concern.

References

1. Uptane: Securing Software Updates for Automobiles. https://uptane.github.io/. Accessed 25 Apr 2023
2. Chowdhury, T., et al.: Safe and secure automotive over-the-air updates. In: Gallina, B., Skavhaug, A., Bitsch, F. (eds.) SAFECOMP 2018. LNCS, vol. 11093, pp. 172–187. Springer, Cham (2018). https://doi.org/10.1007/978-3-319-99130-6_12
3. Chowdhury, T., Wassyng, A., Paige, R.F., Lawford, M.: Systematic evaluation of (safety) assurance cases. In: Casimiro, A., Ortmeier, F., Bitsch, F., Ferreira, P. (eds.) SAFECOMP 2020. LNCS, vol. 12234, pp. 18–33. Springer, Cham (2020). https://doi.org/10.1007/978-3-030-54549-9_2
4. ISO: 26262: Road vehicles-Functional safety. International Standard ISO/FDIS (2018)
5. Johnson, N., Kelly, T.: Devil's in the detail: through-life safety and security co-assurance using SSAF. In: Romanovsky, A., Troubitsyna, E., Bitsch, F. (eds.) SAFECOMP 2019. LNCS, vol. 11698, pp. 299–314. Springer, Cham (2019). https://doi.org/10.1007/978-3-030-26601-1_21
6. Jürjens, J.: UMLsec: extending UML for secure systems development. In: Jézéquel, J.-M., Hussmann, H., Cook, S. (eds.) UML 2002. LNCS, vol. 2460, pp. 412–425. Springer, Heidelberg (2002). https://doi.org/10.1007/3-540-45800-X_32
7. Kordy, B., Piètre-Cambacédès, L., Schweitzer, P.: Dag-based attack and defense modeling: don't miss the forest for the attack trees. Comput. Sci. Rev. **13–14**, 1–38 (2014)
8. Macher, G., Sporer, H., Berlach, R., Armengaud, E., Kreiner, C.: SAHARA: a security-aware hazard and risk analysis method. In: Nebel, W., Atienza, D. (eds.) DATE 2015, pp. 621–624. ACM (2015)
9. SAE Vehicle Electrical System Security Committee, et al.: SAE J3061-Cybersecurity Guidebook for Cyber-Physical Automotive Systems. SAE-Society of Automotive Engineers (2016)
10. Wassyng, A., et al.: Can product-specific assurance case templates be used as medical device standards? IEEE Des. Test **32**(5), 45–55 (2015)
11. Young, W., Leveson, N.G.: Systems thinking for safety and security. In: Jr., C.N.P. (ed.) ACSAC 2013, pp. 1–8. ACM (2013)

Constructing Security Cases Based on Formal Verification of Security Requirements in Alloy

Marwa Zeroual[1,2(✉)], Brahim Hamid[2], Morayo Adedjouma[1],
and Jason Jaskolka[3]

[1] Université Paris-Saclay, CEA, List, 91120 Palaiseau, France
{marwa.zeroual,morayo.adedjouma}@cea.fr
[2] IRIT, Université de Toulouse, CNRS, UT2, 118 Route de Narbonne,
31062 Toulouse Cedex 9, France
brahim.hamid@irit.fr
[3] Carleton University, Ottawa, ON, Canada
jason.jaskolka@carleton.ca

Abstract. Assuring that security requirements have been met in design phases is less expensive compared with changes after system development. Security-critical systems deployment requires providing security cases demonstrating whether the design adequately incorporates the security requirements. Building arguments and generating evidence to support the claims of an assurance case is of utmost importance and should be done using a rigorous mathematical basis, namely formal methods. In this paper, we propose an approach that uses formal methods to construct security assurance cases. This approach takes a list of security requirements as input and generates security cases to assess their fulfillment. Furthermore, we define security argument patterns supported by the formal verification results presented using the GSN pattern notation. The overall approach is validated through a case study involving an autonomous drone.

Keywords: Formal methods · Assurance case · Argument pattern · Security requirements · Security case

1 Introduction

Security-critical systems are prone to failure and security violations. Vulnerabilities can be caused by many factors: poor requirement specifications, underestimating the threat, and malicious exploitation of all the above by an attacker. Consequently, security engineers are required to provide assurance cases containing evidence and arguments to prove the security property of the system. Assurance cases are bodies of evidence organized in structured arguments that justify specific claims about a system property hold [12]. When assurance cases aim to demonstrate the security of a system, they are known as security cases. Formal model-based security cases are the ones that contain a formal model from

J. Guiochet et al. (Eds.): SAFECOMP 2023 Workshops, LNCS 14182, pp. 15–25, 2023.
https://doi.org/10.1007/978-3-031-40953-0_2

which evidence for the top-level claims is derived. Formal methods are applicable in specifying and verifying critical systems from various industrial domains [3]. Despite this, there are limitations to formalizing large-size systems, such as ensuring that the program works correctly with the hardware and operating system and the complexity involved in creating formal definitions of semantics for language constructs and software system components [2]. Building security cases to document and demonstrate that a system design meets the primary security requirements (SRs) is challenging, especially because sufficient evidence is needed to support assurance claims and traceability for compliance checks. In this paper, we propose an approach for demonstrating the compliance of SRs at the design level in the form of security cases. First, we assume a complete list of SRs that are determined following a secure development methodology. Next, we formalize the system model and the SRs using Alloy language. Then, we verify the SRs compliance and the system model. Afterward, security cases are defined and supported by the formal verification results. This is followed by the derivation of re-utilizable security argument pattern.

The remainder of this paper is organized as follows. Section 2 presents some definitions and the illustrative example. Section 3 details the proposed approach. Section 4 presents the proposed security argument patterns and exemplifies their application. Section 5 reviews related works. Finally, Sect. 6 concludes with future work directions.

2   Background

2.1   Overview of Alloy

Alloy is a lightweight formal modeling language based on first-order relational logic. An Alloy model comprises a set of signatures, each defining a set of atoms. There are several ways to specify constraints in the model. One is to treat them as *facts* that should always hold. Another is to treat them as *predicates* defined in the form of parameterized formulas that can be used elsewhere and as *assertions* that are intended to follow from the facts of a model. The semantics of Alloy is defined using *instances*. An instance is a binding of values to variables (e.g., signatures, signatures fields). *A core instance* is an instance associated with the model's facts, and the implicit constraints in the signature *declarations*. We can instruct Alloy Analyzer to verify whether the property *prop* of the system design holds, with the command: **check** *prop* **for** *n*, which would exhaustively explore every model instance within *n* atoms typed by each signature. If the property does not hold, the analyzer generates a counterexample we can visualize. The absence of counterexamples guarantees that the property holds in the modeled system within the specified scope. As claimed in [7], most counterexamples are found in a reasonably small scope.

2.2   Goal Structuring Notation

There are several notations and existing tools for developing and documenting assurance cases, and the most popular of these is *Goal Structuring Notation*

(GSN). GSN is a graphical notation that can be used to visualize arguments that assure critical properties: safety, security, and resilience of systems, services, or organizations. This paper adopts the GSN pattern notation (an extension of core GSN [6]) to visualize and present the argument structure. A summary of the graphical elements of the GSN Pattern Notation is provided in Fig. 1.

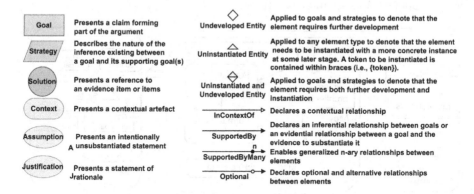

Fig. 1. Principal elements of the GSN Pattern Notation

2.3   Illustrative Example

We illustrate our contributions using an example from ACAS Xu [8], a collision avoidance system for drones. The scenario involves two drones. One called the "ownship". The system is visualized in Fig. 2. The ownship's sensors collect data about other drones, which is then processed to determine an appropriate avoidance strategy. A planner generates a trajectory to navigate, and the actuator executes actions to follow the planned trajectory. The system's security is compromised if an attacker can modify messages sent to the processor, leading to decisions that result in a collision.

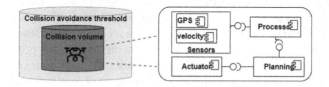

Fig. 2. Architecture of ACAS Xu

We extract from the work [1] a selection of SRs that impose requirements to design a secure ACAS Xu: (*SR1* :) The GPS messages are genuine and have not been intentionally altered, (*SR2* :) The processor must receive data only from valid sensors, and finally (*SR3* :) The system should employ mechanisms to mitigate unauthorized disclosure of the planning information.

3   General Overview of the Methodology

We propose constructing security cases from the SRs via their formal specification and verification in Alloy. Our approach runs in parallel to and is informed by the system development process. Each activity of our approach recovers artifacts from system development and provides a security case to ensure and demonstrate the development and assurance activities.

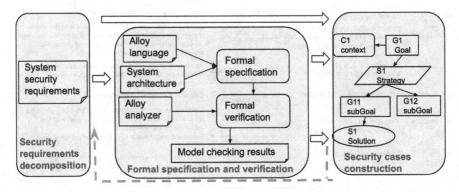

Fig. 3. Generating security cases from formal specification and analysis of SRs

As visualized in Fig. 3, we distinguish two main processes that influence the construction of security cases: (1) elicitation of security requirements, (2) representation of formalised system security requirements in formal models. Note that the construction of security cases is done by applying argument patterns reporting on the formal specification of the system and the SRs. If we can not build security cases, we revisit and improve the formalization of the requirements and the system. The grey shows this dependence dashed line in Fig. 3. The elicitation of the SRs is out of the scope of this paper.

3.1   Formal Specification and Analysis of SRs in Alloy

The formal method Alloy provides a structured way to specify the system model and its SRs. Subsequently, the formal verification provides strong evidence that a system is secure and meets its SRs. We formalize security objectives, as an implementation of SRs at the architecture level. The output of this process includes two main elements: the formal specification results (which consist of the system architecture model and the formalization of security objectives) and the formal verification results. These two elements correspond, respectively, to the first and second arrows from the formalization to the security cases construction top to bottom. To do so, we rely on works from [10] where, first, we adopt a metamodel to describe the architecture and capture (1) the functional architecture in terms of components and connectors, and (2) the behavioral aspects of the architectural elements. The modeling is done in the context of component-based architecture (CBA) while adopting the message passing paradigm for the communication. Formally speaking, a subset of these elements is specified in Listing 1.1.

```
1  sig Component {   uses: set Port}
2  sig Msg extends CommunicationStyle {    sent: one Tick,
3           received: Component -> lone Tick,   payload: one Payload    }
       ........
```

Listing 1.1. Declarations of some architecture elements

The metamodel enables us to describe the objectives: each objective is associated with a representative property that is defined as a Predicate constraint. After that, these properties are used in the realization of the objectives through model checking: we define assertions to check that the properties are not violated. Alloy Analyzer detects the violation of an objective due to the violation of the assertion by finding a counterexample. For example, the predicate *payloadIntegrity* showed in Listing 1.2 is a representative property associated with the payload integrity objective and the assertion *integrityNotHold* is used to detect the violation of this objective. The objective is defined as follows: "if some component c_2 is able to get the payload p of m then p is the accurate payload of m (has not been altered)." Formally speaking:

```
1  pred payloadIntegrity {  all m:Msg, c:Component, p:Payload |
2                     E_get_pld[c,m,p]   implies once sent_with[m,p] }
3  assert integrityNotHold {
4    all c1,c2: Component, m:Msg| payloadIntegrity[c1,c2,m] }
```

Listing 1.2. Payload Integrity property

Alloy Analyzer finds a counterexample related to the violation of the *payloadIntegrity* property. Consequently, an appropriate security requirement is added to codify a security mechanism to satisfy the payload integrity objective. The *intg* requirement is defined as a predicate on the connector that guarantees that the sender's payload is the same payload received by the receiver through this connector.

```
1  pred Connector.intg {
2       all m:Msg, t:Tick, c:Component, d:Payload |
3       m in this.buffer.t   implies E_set_pld[c,m,d,t]
4       implies some al:AllowedSetPld | al.msg = m and al.comp = c
5       all c:Component, t:Tick | E_inject[c,m,t]
6       implies some al:AllowedSetPld | al.msg = m and al.comp = c }
7  assert integrityHold {  (all c:Connector | c.intg)
8       implies all c1, c2 : Component , d:Payload | payloadIntegrity
         [c1,c2,d] }
```

Listing 1.3. Payload Integrity solution

Finally, we check if the added requirement *intg* implies the satisfaction of the assertion violated previously. According to Alloy, no counterexample was found. The satisfaction of *intg* property allows the fulfillment of the corresponding security requirement to realize the payload integrity, as shown in Listing 1.3.

3.2 Construction of Security Cases

We build the security cases by applying argument patterns. We derive these patterns from the previous approach processes. First, the formal model development requires an argument about the well-definedness of the system model upon which we applied the formal method. It is the role of (P1). Building this argument is based on Alloy semantics provided in 2.1 and which shows the necessary conditions for a model to be well-defined.

Moreover, the formal methods involve building security cases by providing evidence elements and guiding the arguing process according to the formal language elements used for the property specification as shown in (P2). The strategies used are mainly inspired by the formal specification and verification of the requirements. Regarding the evidence elements, we use the results of the formal verification. In summary, the outputs of the approach provide reusable security argument patterns: an argument pattern for the well-definedness of the system model (P1), and an argument pattern for the satisfaction of SR (P2). The following section will present these three argument patterns in detail.

4   Security Argument Patterns

This section presents the argument patterns derived from the approach presented in Sect. 3 and their application on the case study presented in Sect. 2.3.

4.1   Pattern for the Well-Definedness of the System Model (P1)

The goal of this pattern in Fig. 6 is to claim the well-definedness of the system model according to Alloy language semantics. A consistent model has at least one instance that resolves all the facts and the declarations. The system model describes assumptions about the world in which a system operates, requirements that the system is to achieve, and a design to meet those requirements. The root

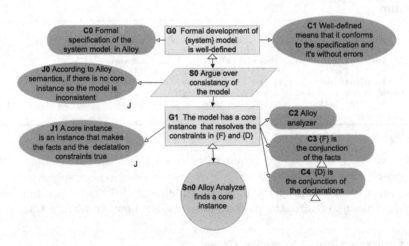

Fig. 4. Pattern for the well-definedness of the system model (P1)

claim in (G0) resumes the main goal of the pattern in the context (C0, C1). According to Alloy language rules (C2), a model is inconsistent if it does not have any core instances (S0,J0,J1). The goal (G1) claims that the model has an instance that resolves constraints formed by the conjunction of the facts (C3) and the declarations (C4). The analysis results (Sn0) form the evidence to support the claim. On one side, the set of declarations regroups all implicit constraints in the signatures, mainly type and multiplicity ones. Listing 1.1 depicts some examples of declarations constraints used for the specification of the CBA metamodel from [11]. On the other side, a subset of the conjunction of the facts used to build the CBA metamodel from [11] is presented in Listing 1.4 (Fig. 4).

```
1  fact ComponentsConnectorFacts {
2     no disj m,m': Msg | some m.payload and m'.payload
3     all m: Msg | origin_sender != receiver   ... }
```

Listing 1.4. Examples of facts

We illustrate the application of this pattern (see Fig. 5). First, we define the components and the connectors connecting them based on the metamodel shown in Listing 1.1. Then, we have to formally show that the ACAS Xu model is consistent. We use particularly the facts from 1.4 as the context in the node (C3). The metamodel is built with all the constraints, we will not add new facts to describe the ACAS Xu architecture. However, we add new declarations as shown in Listing 1.5 to instantiate the context node (C4).

```
1  sig Processor extends Component {} {uses = PortPlanOut + PortSenIn}
2  sig Sensors extends Component {} { uses = PortSenOut } ....
```

Listing 1.5. Some declarations used to describe ACAS Xu

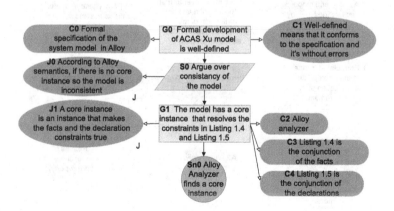

Fig. 5. P1 instantiation example

4.2 Argument Pattern for the Satisfaction of SRs (P2)

The goal of (P2) is to provide a convincing argument about using Alloy as a formalization language to formalize and verify the SRs. The structure of (P2) is shown in Fig. 6. The root claim (G2) of the pattern is about the satisfaction of the requirement {security requirement}. We refer to the requirement in the node (C5). Context node (C6) provides extra details about the system model and describes the operating environment in which the system operates securely. Since the pattern claims that the system model realizes the SR, it is wise to assume that the system model is well-defined in Alloy (A0) and reflects the true system (A1). The pattern (P1) represents an argument to develop this assumption (A0). The proposed strategy (S1) involves arguing through formal specification and verification of the security requirement presented as model property. The argument implies that if the sub-claims (G3, G4) are satisfied, then the system satisfies the requirement. Sub-claim (G3) claims that the proposed formalization *property* (C7) is the proper formalization of the requirement. We rely on domain and formalization experts' inspection (Sn1) as evidence that the formulated expression is the proper specification of the requirement and is well-defined according to restrictions imposed in Alloy. According to claim (G4), the model satisfies the property {property}. This claim is supported by the results of model checking on *property*: Alloy Analyzer (C8) doesn't find a counterexample. We assume that the tool support (Alloy Analyzer) is correct (A2) (i.e., analysis parameters (e.g., scope analysis) are well defined).

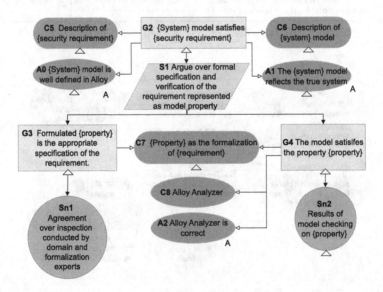

Fig. 6. Argument pattern for the satisfaction of security requirement (P2)

We illustrate the application of this pattern (Fig. 7). We refer to the system in nodes (G2, C5, A0, A1). For the sake of simplicity, we only showcase one instance of (P1) for the satisfaction of the security requirement (SR1). First, we refer to the requirement (SR1) in the context node (C5). SR1 is prescribing the need for a mechanism to realize the message integrity objective. Recall that Listing 1.2 shows the formalization of the integrity objective of any message's payload exchanged between all the components. Particularly, for messages exchanged between GPS sensors and the processor. Consequently, the property *GPSMsgIntegrity* shown in Listing 1.6 is the formal specification of the requirement and is referred to in nodes (C5, G3, G4, Sn2). We follow the same steps to instantiate (P1) for the realization of SR2 and SR3.

```
1   assert GPSMsgIntegrity{ payloadIntegrity [Sensors,Processor]}
2   check GPSMsgIntegrity for 3
```

Listing 1.6. Formal specification of SR1

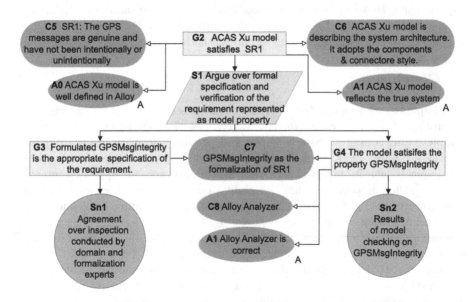

Fig. 7. P2 instantiation example

5   Related Works

Several approaches suggest mapping the activities from the security cases construction process to those of the secure system development process. Activities from different stages of the secure system development process help create either of the two parts (viz., argumentation strategies and evidence) of security cases or both. The work in [5] proposes to use Architecture Analysis and Design Language (AADL) and annex it with Resolute language to specify the system architecture, safety rules, and security claims. The analysis leads to the generation of fragments of assurance cases. This approach, like ours, avoids inconsistencies between a design and its assurance cases, thanks to automated model transformation. However, it needs to show how to assemble these fragments since each fragment is separately arguing about one component from the AADL metamodel. In [9], the authors introduce security assurance cases and present an expansion to the agile development process that entails the construction of these documents. They extract from the security procedures execution the evidence and argumentation needed to support the assurance case. The approach only applies to modular software, where security claims are associated with specific components. Unlike this, we formalized security requirements involving more than one component. Another work in [4] proposes embedding the Isabelle proof assistant and SACM (Structured Assurance Case Model) to generate safety cases. The requirements are expressed using High Order Logic, which allows for specifying more advanced requirements. However, the paper needs more argumentation about model correctness and well-definedness, which is mandatory for model-based development in general, and development using formal methods in particular.

6   Conclusion

In this paper, we propounded a formal model-based approach for the rigorous generation of a security case for critical systems. The approach takes a set of complete and consistent SRs as input and produces security cases for realizing these requirements, along with a well-defined system model. Our work in this paper is security-oriented and Alloy-aware, however, the approach remains valid for other properties (safety, reliability, etc.) and uses other formal methods. However, using the approach in different domains requires basic knowledge of formal modeling, requirements engineering, and assurance cases construction. The argument patterns generated by the approach can be expressed in various notations and have the potential for re-usability. In future work, we aim to develop a tool to facilitate the use of these patterns and instantiate them for constructing error-free security assurance cases. Furthermore, future work includes developing additional argument patterns to support consistency and completeness assessments of identified security requirements, aiming to enhance the confidence in the security case.

References

1. Altawy, R., Youssef, A.M.: Security, privacy, and safety aspects of civilian drones: a survey. ACM Trans. Cyber-Phys. Syst. 1(2), 1–25 (2016). https://doi.org/10. 1145/3001836
2. Batra, M.: Formal methods: benefits, challenges and future direction. J. Global Res. Comput. Sci. 4(5), 21–25 (2013)
3. ter Beek, M.H., Larsen, K.G., Ničković, D., Willemse, T.A.: Formal methods and tools for industrial critical systems. Int. J. Softw. Tools Technol. Transfer 24(3), 325–330 (2022)

4. Foster, S., Nemouchi, Y., Gleirscher, M., Wei, R., Kelly, T.: Integration of formal proof into unified assurance cases with Isabelle/SACM. Formal Aspects Comput. **33**(6), 855–884 (2021)
5. Gacek, A., Backes, J., Cofer, D., Slind, K., Whalen, M.: Resolute: an assurance case language for architecture models. ACM SIGAda Ada Lett. **34**(3), 19–28 (2014)
6. Habli, I., Kelly, T.: A safety case approach to assuring configurable architectures of safety-critical product lines. In: Giese, H. (ed.) ISARCS 2010. LNCS, vol. 6150, pp. 142–160. Springer, Heidelberg (2010). https://doi.org/10.1007/978-3-642-13556-9_9
7. Jackson, D.: Software Abstractions: Logic, Language, and Analysis. MIT press, Cambridge (2012)
8. Manfredi, G., Jestin, Y.: An introduction to ACAS Xu and the challenges ahead. In: 2016 IEEE/AIAA 35th Digital Avionics Systems Conference (DASC), pp. 1–9. IEEE (2016)
9. ben Othmane, L., Angin, P., Weffers, H., Bhargava, B.: Extending the agile development process to develop acceptably secure software. IEEE Trans. Depend. Secure Comput. **11**(6), 497–509 (2014)
10. Rouland, Q., Hamid, B., Bodeveix, J.P., Filali, M.: A formal methods approach to security requirements specification and verification. In: 2019 24th International Conference on Engineering of Complex Computer Systems (ICECCS), pp. 236–241. IEEE (2019)
11. Rouland, Q., Hamid, B., Jaskolka, J.: Specification, detection, and treatment of stride threats for software components: modeling, formal methods, and tool support. J. Syst. Architect. **117**, 102073 (2021)
12. Weinstock, C.B., Lipson, H.F., Goodenough, J.: Arguing security-creating security assurance cases. Carnegie Mellon University, Technical report (2007)

Assurance Cases for Timing Properties of Automotive TSN Networks

Ryan Kapinski, Vera Pantelic(✉) ⓘ, Victor Bandur ⓘ, Alan Wassyng ⓘ,
and Mark Lawford ⓘ

McMaster Centre for Software Certification, McMaster University,
Hamilton, ON, Canada
{kapinsra,pantelv,bandurvp,wassyng,lawford}@mcmaster.ca

Abstract. The problem of configuring an Automotive TSN (Time-Sensitive Networking) Ethernet network with desired timing properties consists of several individual complex problems, each with its own solution landscape. When the chosen solutions come together in the implementation of timing guarantees on these networks, presenting the argument and evidence for the correct behaviour of the network with respect to the timing requirements itself becomes a difficult problem. In this paper, we present work in progress on demonstrating the use of assurance cases in making this argument explicit for an example TSN Ethernet timing requirement for an automotive powertrain network.

Keywords: Assurance case · Automotive Ethernet · Time-Sensitive Networking (TSN) · Timing properties

1 Introduction

The automotive engineering landscape is undergoing a revolution. The rise in demand for ADAS functions, autonomous vehicles, connectivity, and mobility is driving the need for new in-vehicle networking technologies to support high-bandwidth data. Automotive Ethernet is widely touted as the communication backbone of future vehicles [1,7]. Several approaches have been proposed to enable real-time and safety critical communication over automotive Ethernet, including, most prominently, Time-Sensitive Networking (TSN) [5]. TSN standards offer time synchronization, bounded low-latency communication, redundancy for safety-critical applications, *etc.*

The analysis of real-time properties of networks in cyber-physical systems has been widely studied [3]. Further, work exists that leverages structured arguments such as assurance cases for reasoning about software timing properties (*e.g.*, [4]). However, to the best of the authors' knowledge, assurances cases have not yet been applied to TSN networks. Assurance cases (ACs) explicitly present reasoning that a system satisfies a property. In this paper, we present work-in-progress on using ACs for assuring timing requirements of systems containing automotive TSN Ethernet networks. We envision the small AC slice we build

J. Guiochet et al. (Eds.): SAFECOMP 2023 Workshops, LNCS 14182, pp. 26–31, 2023.
https://doi.org/10.1007/978-3-031-40953-0_3

in this paper to be expanded to a full AC to guide developers in understanding which mechanisms should be employed to achieve timing requirements in systems relying on TSN mechanisms, as well as what evidence needs to be provided to assure the timing properties of such systems. Also, the AC can be leveraged as part of larger ACs assuring properties of systems to which the networks belong. For example, we expect the AC to be part of safety cases of modern automotive systems employing automotive Ethernet.

2   TSN Ethernet

The system to be analysed in this work is an automotive TSN Ethernet network used for real-time communication. A simplified form is shown in Fig. 1. The network is made up of only *end nodes* and *switches*. End nodes are devices with a single port that can source or sink messages in the form of Ethernet packets. Switches are devices with multiple ports that forward packets from one port to another depending on the destination MAC (Media Access Control) address of the packet, and a forwarding table that associates MAC addresses with outgoing ports. Each port can be connected to exactly one other port, and each port has a unique MAC address. While the use of multiple switches depicted here may seem unnecessary, a safety-critical application would use such switch chaining due to communications path redundancy requirements [2].

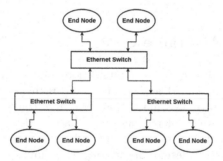

Fig. 1. A simplified block diagram representing a switched Ethernet Network.

In TSN, the *Time Aware Shaper (TAS)* [6] uses the fact that Ethernet devices can queue outgoing packets separately based on information in their headers. Each egress (outgoing) port of every Ethernet device in a TSN network has eight queues. Flows in the network (unidirectional streams of Ethernet packets between end nodes) are organized into traffic classes that are used to isolate flows into separate queues based on their requirements. Whenever an Ethernet device's egress port is available for transmission, one of its eight queues is selected, a packet is taken from it and sent out. The TAS employs the traditional TDMA (Time-Division Multiple Access) scheme by enabling and disabling the egress queues according to a schedule. This schedule executes periodically with the schedule *hyperperiod*, and is composed of smaller time slots that define the queue states (enabled or disabled) at a specific phase and for a specific duration relative to the hyperperiod. The schedule is executed relative to a clock that is assumed to be synchronized with all other devices in the network, allowing the network as a whole to orchestrate designated times for specific traffic classes to flow. A simplified block diagram of a typical Ethernet interface with TAS features is shown in Fig. 2.

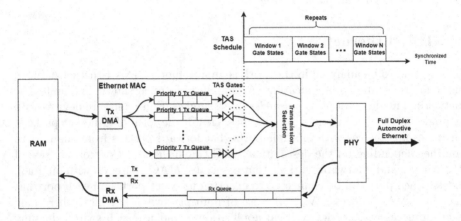

Fig. 2. Block diagram of a typical Ethernet MAC with a TAS. Rx and Tx paths of packets between system RAM and physical Ethernet media are denoted by arrows.

3   Building an Assurance Case

Terminology. The unidirectional communication from an end node to another through the network is called a *flow*. Here, the realization of a flow will be periodic packets of a static size and format, typical of traditional control system applications. The flows considered here have hard real-time requirements. To meet these requirements, specifications regarding communications timing are determined during system design. Specifically, the timing specification includes upper bounds for the *end-to-end latency* and *jitter*, as well as a *period* for packets contained in this flow.

Top Level Claim. A top-down approach is used to construct this assurance case, and the argumentation will be represented in the core Goal Structuring Notation (GSN) [9] syntax. The assurance case is shown in Fig. 3. The top-level claim refers to a specific flow and its associated timing specification, *FLOW_X* and *TSPEC_X*, respectively. The top level claim, *G1*, is stated as follows: "All messages in communication flow *FLOW_X* satisfy the timing specification *TSPEC_X*." The associated context (*C1*, *C2*, and *C4*) presents necessary definitions and network-related assumptions.

Satisfying the Timing Specification. The top level goal can be decomposed into subclaims that individually address latency (*G2*), jitter (*G3*), and period (*G4*).

Arguing Upper Bound on Latency. We focus on **G2** and leave the jitter and period subclaims as undeveloped goals. Arguing this claim involves analyzing the strategy used for achieving bounded latency in the network. The strategy is based on TSN mechanisms being configured on all devices, and on constraints regarding the timing of packet transmissions. This network achieves bounded latency by scheduling packets from flows to be sent and forwarded through the network at specific time intervals. This ensures that packets from other flows do not interact with each other, by using a TDMA scheme.

Using TAS to Achieve Bounded Latency. The TAS as described in standard [6] only gives the structure and behavior of the mechanism itself. The standard does not specify how the TAS should be used to achieve the bounded latency. It is up to the designer to configure the TAS such that it achieves a bounded latency for specific traffic. Creating a schedule is not a simple task [8] and it requires tool support. In addition to analyzing the constraints on the schedule itself, the AC also exposes the requirements on other participating devices in the network. For example, if the schedule design assumes that a node will transmit a packet at a specific time, this should be captured in the argument, since the argument of bounded latency (below) relies on this behaviour.

Bounded Latency Strategy. The strategy is to assign each flow a time slot in which no other traffic in the network can be forwarded. This means that during the time slot dedicated to *FLOW_X*, only packets from *FLOW_X* will be transmitted throughout the network. However, each traffic class can contain several flows. But the TAS is limited to isolating only traffic classes, and not the flows within the classes. This means that if a particular flow's packet is not transmitted, forwarded, and received within its scheduled time slot, it can not only affect its own timing, but the timing of other flows in its traffic class. As such, it is up to the transmitting nodes to ensure that they transmit at the correct time. This particular approach is wasteful of bandwidth, but makes the AC easy to understand.

Bounded Latency Argument. Assuming a system designed according to the strategy defined above, the claim that the latency of *FLOW_X* is bounded within specification can be decomposed into sub-claims. The supporting subclaims will follow the structure of the constraints in the strategy above, in which the packets of *FLOW_X* are assigned specific time slots within the TAS schedule. In Fig. 3, **S1** states this approach. The TSN strategy is then analyzed to extract what implicit claims are stated in the design. This approach makes implicit claims of the design explicit in the assurance case, to allow for more structured argumentation that the design achieves its goal of a bounded latency. For example, this TSN strategy is dependant on all end nodes transmitting precisely when they are allowed to according to the network schedule. This dependency is explicit in the assurance case, and ensures that the reasoning also contains an argument that the end nodes will indeed transmit precisely when allowed.

When decomposing **G2** according to **S1**, the TSN design was found to be dependant on the three subclaims **G5**, **G6**, and **G7**. We next focus on **G6**.

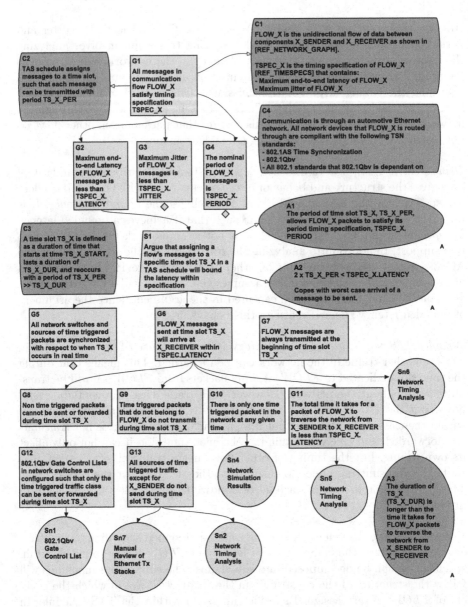

Fig. 3. Argument for the TSN network's ability to satisfy the timing requirements of a specific flow in the network. This argument in its current state is not complete and serves more as a pattern than a complete argument.

G6 requires that *FLOW_X* messages sent at the correct time will arrive within the specified latency. *G6* can be further decomposed into a series of supporting goals *G8*, *G9*, *G10*, and *G11*. *G8* states that time triggered traffic is isolated temporally from non time triggered traffic during *TS_X*. This isolation is directly supported by the gate control list of the TAS, and can be verified to show that during TS_X only $FLOW\_X$ traffic can be forwarded and sent. **G9** is needed for similar reasons as **G8**, but is more complicated as the TAS does not isolate messages within the same traffic class, which in this case is time triggered packets. It is then up to all sources of time triggered packets that they do not send any packets during TS_X, which is a process that can be controlled by either SW or HW on every time triggered node. To support **G9**, **G13** states that it is up to the transmitting nodes to ensure that they do not transmit during TS_X. For the sake of this argument, **G13** is supported by an empirical timing analysis (**Sn2**) to show that the nodes do not transmit when they should not, and a manual review of the HW/SW stack (**Sn7**) to ensure that the mechanism that does not allow them to transmit at the wrong time accomplishes this task.

4   Conclusions

We envision this work to inform the development of patterns and templates for reasoning about timing properties of cyber-physical systems using TSN mechanisms, as part of larger ACs reasoning about vehicle properties at a system level. This is an important part of compliance with existing software safety standards, and also aids incremental certification.

References

1. Bandur, V., Selim, G., Pantelic, V., Lawford, M.: Making the case for centralized automotive E/E architectures. IEEE Trans. Veh. Technol. **70**(2), 1230–1245 (2021). https://doi.org/10.1109/TVT.2021.3054934
2. Bandur, V., Pantelic, V., Tomashevskiy, T., Lawford, M.: A safety architecture for centralized E/E architectures. In: 2021 51st Annual IEEE/IFIP International Conference on Dependable Systems and Networks Workshops (DSN-W). IEEE (2021). https://doi.org/10.1109/dsn-w52860.2021.00022
3. Geyer, F., Carle, G.: Network engineering for real-time networks: comparison of automotive and aeronautic industries approaches. IEEE Commun. Mag. **54**(2), 106–112 (2016). https://doi.org/10.1109/MCOM.2016.7402269
4. Graydon, P., Bate, I.: Realistic safety cases for the timing of systems. Comput. J. **57**(5), 759–774 (2014). https://doi.org/10.1093/comjnl/bxt027
5. IEEE: Time-sensitive networking task group (2017). https://www.ieee802.org/1/pages/tsn.html. Accessed 29 Oct 2019
6. IEEE 802.1 Time-Sensitive Task Group: IEEE 802.1Qbv-2015 - IEEE Standard for Local and Metropolitan Area Networks - Bridges and Bridged Networks - Amendment 25: Enhancements for Scheduled Traffic. Technical report IEEE 802.1Qbv, IEEE (2015)
7. Matheus, K., Königseder, T.: Automotive Ethernet, 1st edn. Cambridge University Press, USA (2015). https://doi.org/10.1017/CBO9781107414884
8. Stüber, T., Osswald, L., Lindner, S., Menth, M.: A survey of scheduling algorithms for the time-aware shaper in Time-Sensitive Networking (TSN) (2023). https://doi.org/10.48550/arXiv.2211.10954
9. The Assurance Case Working Group: Goal Structuring Notation Community Standard Version 3 (2021)

Toward Dependability Assurance Framework for Automated Driving Systems

Yutaka Matsuno[1]([✉])(iD), Toshinori Takai[2], Manabu Okada[3],
and Tomoyuki Tsuchiya[3]

[1] College of Science and Technology, Nihon University, Funabashi City, Japan
matsuno.yutaka@nihon-u.ac.jp
[2] Change Vision, Inc., Tokyo, Japan
toshinori.takai@change-vision.com
[3] TIER IV, Inc., Tokyo, Japan
{manabu.okada,tomoyuki.tsuchiya}@tier4.jp

Abstract. Automated driving systems are advancing towards practical use, and commercial use has already begun in limited environments. Automated driving is a technology that will have a wide-ranging impact on our lives, making it crucial to form consensus on the dependability of automated driving systems among various stakeholders encompassing the general public. Since 2022, we have been conducting joint research and development with an automated driving technology startup, toward developing a framework for assuring the dependability of automated driving systems, using assurance cases. This position paper reports our goals and the current status of our work.

Keywords: automated driving system · assurance cases · continuous assurance argument · dependability

1 Introduction

Automated driving systems are advancing towards practical use, and commercial use has already begun in limited environments. Automated driving is a technology that will have a wide-ranging impact on our lives, making it crucial to form consensus on the dependability of automated driving systems among various stakeholders encompassing the general public.

Toward making consensus building among the society for the dependability of automated driving systems, since 2022, we have been conducting joint research and development with TIER IV [1], an automated driving technology startup, on methods, tools, and frameworks for assuring the dependability of automated driving systems, using *assurance cases*. This paper reports our goals and the current status of our work.

---

[1] https://tier4.jp/en/.

© The Author(s), under exclusive license to Springer Nature Switzerland AG 2023
J. Guiochet et al. (Eds.): SAFECOMP 2023 Workshops, LNCS 14182, pp. 32–37, 2023.
https://doi.org/10.1007/978-3-031-40953-0_4

TIER IV has a vision of "democratizing automated driving" and aims to build an ecosystem where anyone can contribute to the development of technology by leading the development of the world's first open-source automated driving OS, "Autoware[2]". With the aim of solving social issues such as reducing traffic accidents and labor shortages, the company has collaborated with many partners to develop the technology and has accumulated a track record of more than 100 demonstrations of automated driving in Japan and overseas.

From 2022 (and continuing through 2030), TIER IV has started a national project called "Creation of collectively scalable automated driving systems", as a part of "Development of on-board computing and simulation technologies for energy conservation in electric vehicles and similar platforms" funded by New Energy and Industrial Technology Development Organization (NEDO), Japan. The grant is about 190 million US dollars.

The project has the following four research and development goals, and our research is in goal 3.

1. To develop adaptive algorithms for enabling the combination of various technical components to meet customer requirements.
2. To develop critical real-time system software for guaranteeing compliance with maximum latency requirements even when various technical components are combined under given power constraints.
3. To assure the dependability/safety of the automated vehicle system, and provide a means to explain the dependability/safety to stakeholders even when various technical components are combined, based on assurance cases.
4. To develop edge-oriented agile CI/CD pipelines, for reducing the time and data volume required to verify and validate automated driving functions, even when various technical components are combined.

One of the features of this project is that our research on assurance cases is conducted in parallel with the three other technical research and development activities related to automated driving. This research structure allows not only for the description of assurance cases as models in our system assurance research, but also for the demonstration, through tool integration, that the contents of these descriptions match the actual behavior of the automated driving systems.

The structure of the paper is as follows. Section 2 discusses an initial design of the dependability framework. Section 3 shows our current trial of describing an assurance case for automated driving system. Section 4 concludes the paper.

2   Toward Dependability Assurance Framework for Automated Driving Systems

There are various definitions of dependability, and in our project, the following definition [2] will be referred to.

Dependability is ability to perform as and when required.

---

[2] https://github.com/autowarefoundation/autoware.

For a system to be dependable, it must not only be safe but also satisfy other attributes such as availability. While safety is paramount and the focus of this paper, dependability is crucial for a new technology like automated driving to be accepted by society. Therefore, our project aims to assure the dependability of automated driving systems.

The dependability framework for developing and operating automated driving systems consists of processes, methods, and tools. Currently, the content of these is under consideration, and the following items are being discussed.

- Processes: Stakeholder agreement process, architecture description process, implementation process, and operational process.
- Methods: Safety analysis such as STAMP/STPA [5], Trade-off analysis methods for dependability attributes, stakeholder analysis, and continuous system assurance methods throughout development and operation.
- Tools: Assurance case tools, modeling tools, and a parameter repository (discussed below), and their integration with Autoware.

Currently we have been defining the top level process depicted in Fig. 1.

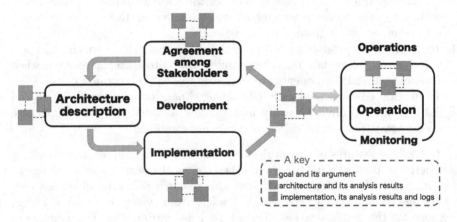

Fig. 1. An Abstract Process for Assuring Automated Driving Systems

The rationale of the abstract process in Fig. 1 is as follows. Automated driving system shall be assured to achieve "Absence of unreasonable risk" ([3,4]). The evidence of achieving the goals shall be demonstrated qualitatively and quantitatively along with an assurance framework. For example, safety evidence such as evaluation of risk identification has reviewed through the holistic safety approach which is based on functional safety [3] and SOTIF [4]. Another example is that the acceptance criteria (sometimes known as safety metrics). The acceptance criteria comprise validation targets that are both reasonably defined and theoretically sound. Once these validation criteria are met with quantitative evidence, they are continuously monitored for the assurance argument during operation. Furthermore, automated driving systems need to respond to a greater number of unknowns [4], changes, and their combinations than previous systems. To cope with these unknowns and changes, we observe that (1) within a process where development and operation are integrated, and (2) it is necessary to share and agree on dependability and safety goals and arguments that should be achieved at each point in time among stakeholders. Next, (3) in order to share and agree on assurance cases among stakeholders, it is necessary to describe and update the model of the system architecture throughout development and operation. Moreover, to verify whether the description in the assurance cases is being realized in the actual system, (4) the whole system should be designed to always be able to obtain values of parameters related to dependability and safety in the system and environment, and to monitor these values during operation.

Also, we are designing a parameter repository that extracts parameters related to dependability and safety from the system architecture model and manages their values. The parameter repository retrieves parameters such as the maximum speed and acceleration defined in the automated vehicle from source repository such, as well as the distance to other vehicles and their speeds during the operation of the automated vehicle using various sensors on the road. These parameters appear in the assurance case using GSN [1]. Currently, we are designing a tool-chain that integrates the system modeling tool Astah*[3] and D-Case Communicator [6], which is a web-based GSN tool.

3   A Use Case of the Dependability Assurance Framework

While defining the dependability assurance framework, we are also conducting trial descriptions of assurance cases for TIER IV 's automated driving shuttle service whose systems include Level 4 driving automation. The automated driving system primarily operates on predefined routes. The operating environment is one of the largest logistics hubs in Japan, where TIER IV 's automated vehicles are used to efficiently transport workers around the nearly 700,000 m^2 logistics hub. One of examples of the assurance cases is in Fig. 2, using GSN notation. The GSN diagram is created by an safety engineer of TIER IV.

The top goal is "The Automated driving shuttle service achieves absence of unreasonable risk". To argue the top-goal, the top goal is decomposed into two sub goals via the strategy node "Demonstrate and ague by each location at the logistics hub". For the strategy node, context C10 "The definition of {routes} and {intersection point} list of the logistics hub" is attached. The argument whether the list of routes and intersection points is sufficient is in Assurance Claim Point ([1]) ACP-S1-C.

The left part of the argument is shown in Fig. 3. The sub goal is "The automated driving shuttle bus ensures that the system satisfies the acceptance criteria and evaluates the residual risks to each scenario that is considered in the intersection point".

---

[3] https://astah.net/.

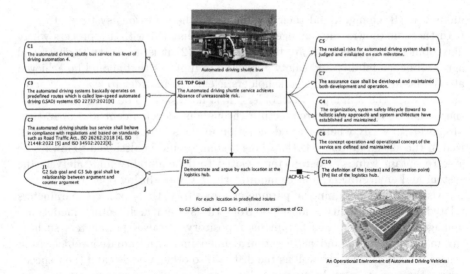

Fig. 2. Top Structure of Assurance Cases for Automated Driving Systems

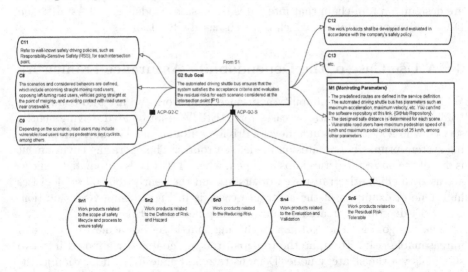

Fig. 3. Argument for Satisfying Criteria

The right part of the argument is shown in Fig. 4. The sub goal is "The auto-mated driving shuttle bus have admittedly limitations of the systems behaviors or performance to satisfy the acceptance criteria in the intersection points, how-ever the counter measures of them have been planned and implemented to main-tain system safety". The argument is an example of how to cope with unknowns.

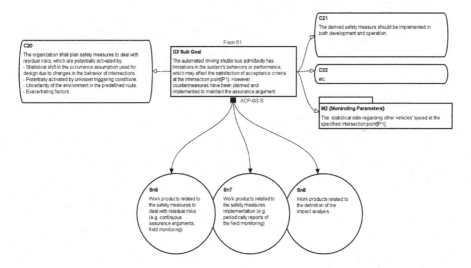

Fig. 4. An Example of Top Structure of Assurance Cases for automated Driving Systems

4   Concluding Remarks

In this position paper, we presented the direction of a framework for assuring the dependability of automated driving systems using assurance cases, a joint research with TIER IV. Currently, we are detailing the proposed process and designing the toolchain. We also continue trial descriptions and patternization of assurance cases for automated driving systems.

Acknowledgments. This paper is based on results obtained from a project subsidized by the New Energy and Industrial Technology Development Organization (NEDO), Japan.

References

1. Assurance Case Working Group: Goal structuring notation community standard version 3 (2021). https://scsc.uk/r141C:1?t=1
2. ISO: ISO 9000:2015 Quality management systems - Fundamentals and vocabulary (2015)
3. ISO: ISO 26262:2018 road vehicle - functional safety -, part 1 to part 10 (2018)
4. ISO: ISO 21448:2022 Road vehicles - Safety of the intended functionality (2022)
5. Leveson, N.G., Thomas, J.P.: STPA Handbook (2018)
6. Matsuno, Y.: D-case communicator: a web based GSN editor for multiple stakeholders. In: Tonetta, S., Schoitsch, E., Bitsch, F. (eds.) SAFECOMP 2017. LNCS, vol. 10489, pp. 64–69. Springer, Cham (2017). https://doi.org/10.1007/978-3-319-66284-8_6

18th International ERCIM/EWICS Workshop on Dependable Smart Embedded Cyber-Physical Systems and Systems-of-Systems

18th International Workshop on Dependable Smart Cyber-Physical Systems and Systems-of-Systems (DECSoS 2023)

European Research and Innovation Projects in the Field of Dependable Cyber-Physical Systems and Systems-of-Systems

(supported by EWICS TC7, ERCIM and Horizon2020/Horizon KDT JU projects' work)

Erwin Schoitsch[1] and Amund Skavhaug[2]

[1] Center for Digital Safety and Security, AIT Austrian Institute of Technology GmbH, Vienna, Austria
`Erwin.Schoitsch@ait.ac.at`
[2] Department of Mechanical and Industrial Engineering, NTNU (The Norwegian University of Science and Technology), Trondheim, Norway
`Amund.Skavhaug@ntnu.no`

1 Introduction

The DECSoS workshop at SAFECOMP follows already its own tradition since 2006. In the past, it focussed on the conventional type of "dependable embedded systems", covering all dependability aspects as defined by Avizienis, Lapries, Kopetz, Voges and others in IFIP WG 10.4. To put more emphasis on the relationship to physics, mechatronics and the notion of interaction with an unpredictable environment, massive deployment and highly interconnected systems of different type, the terminology changed to "cyber-physical systems" (CPS) and "Systems-of-Systems" (SoS). The new megatrend IoT ("Internet of Things") as super-infrastructure for CPS as things added a new dimension with enormous challenges. "Intelligence" as a new ability of systems and components leads to a new paradigm, "Smart Systems", with embedded AI (Artificial Intelligence) inside. Collaboration and co-operation of these systems with each other and humans, and the interplay of safety, cybersecurity, privacy, and reliability, together with cognitive decision making, are leading to new challenges. Another rather new aspect becoming increasingly important is the necessity to take ethical, societal and human-centred concerns into account ("Society 5.0"). These aspects are also part of all recommendations around "Trustworthy AI", from standards, computer associations, up to national actions, the EC and UNESCO. Verification, validation and certification/qualification with respect to trustworthiness, an extension of the conventional paradigms of safety and security considering all stakeholders concerns are even more challenging now, as these systems operate in an unpredictable environment and are open, adaptive and even (partly) autonomous. Examples are e.g., the smart power grid, highly automated transport systems, advanced manufacturing systems ("Industry 4.0/5.0"), mobile co-operating autonomous vehicles and robotic systems, smart health care, and smart buildings up to smart cities.

Society depends more and more on CPS and SoS - thus it is important to consider trustworthiness (dependability (safety, reliability, availability, security, maintainability, etc.), privacy, resilience, robustness and sustainability), together with ethical aspects in a holistic manner. These are targeted research areas in Horizon Europe and public-private partnerships such as the KDT JU (Joint Undertaking) (Key Digital Technologies), which will transform to the new "Chips JU", covering an even broader area of topics than before. The public part in these Joint Undertakings are the EC and the national public authorities of the participating member states, the private partners the three Industrial Associations INSIDE (formerly ARTEMIS), AENEAS and EPOSS. Funding comes from the EC and the national public authorities ("tri-partite funding": EC, member states, project partners). Besides KDT, some other JTIs (Joint Technology Initiatives), who organize their own research & innovation agenda and manage their work as separate legal entities according to Article 187 of the Lisbon Treaty, are: Innovative Medicines Initiative (IMI), Fuel Cells and Hydrogen (FCH), Clean Sky, Bio-Based Industries, Shift2Rail, Single European Sky Air Traffic Management Research (SESAR).

Besides these Joint Undertakings there are many other so-called contractual PPPs, where funding is completely from the EC (via the Horizon Europe program), but the work program and strategy are developed together with a private partner association. e.g., Robotics cPPP SPARC with euRobotics as private partner. Others are e.g., Factories of the Future (FoF), Energy-efficient Buildings (EeB), Sustainable Process Industry (SPIRE), European Green Vehicles Initiative (EGVI), Photonics, High Performance Computing (HPC), Advanced 5G Networks for the Future Internet (5G), the Big Data Value PPP and the cPPP for Cybersecurity Industrial Research and Innovation.

The landscape of PPPs was updated in the context of the next EC Research Programme "HORIZON Europe" (2021–2027), where re-organized Jus have been established (e.g. ECS-KDT (Electronic Components and Systems, Key Digital Technologies) as ECSEL successor), including additional key themes like photonics and software, advanced computing technologies, bio-sensors and flexible electronics), besides new PPPs. Due to the COVID-19 crises and other negotiations within the EC, the new Programmes were delayed, e.g., the first Call for KDT started December 2021, the first new projects were decided June 2022.

But this will not be the end of the story – the climate crises and the Ukraine war have demonstrated the vulnerability of European economy. The European Commission reacted by the "Green Deal" and measures to mitigate the energy and chip respectively other resources' shortness. KDT JU as research programme will be extended and become the "Chips Joint Undertaking" to ensure European digital sovereignty and to make us "future fit". Billions will be invested in course of the European Chips Act with the aim of jointly creating a state-of-the-art European chip ecosystem from production to security of supply, so developing a new arena for groundbreaking European technologies, while remaining true to the policy objectives for digital transformation, sustainability and the Green Deal.

This year, the first series of Horizon Europe-KDT JU projects has started, and still ongoing H2020/ECSEL and nationally funded projects are "co-hosting" scientifically the DECSoS Workshop via contributions from supported partners, some of the reports covering contributions from more than one project such achieving synergetic effects. Of course, the organizations of the authors have to be recognized as supporter of the work presented as well. Some examples are (see also acknowledgements in the papers and at the end of the introduction):

- **SECREDAS** ("Product Security for Cross Domain Reliable Dependable Automated Systems"), (https://www.ecsel.eu/projects/secredas), contributing to ECSEL Lighthouse Cluster "Mobility.E").
- **AI4CSM** (Automotive Intelligence for Connected, Shared Mobility, https://www.ait.ac.at/en/research-topics/dependable-systems-engineering/projects/ai4csm; https://ai4csm.automotive.oth-aw.de/) (project no. 101007326-2. Electric, Connected, Automated and Shared Mobility build together the European approach to mitigate climate change and environmental degradation in the transport and mobility domain, thus fulfilling goals of the European Green Deal, the European implementation of the UN SDG (Sustainable Development Goals). Functional architectures, embedded intelligence and functional virtualization for connected and shared mobility developing and using advanced electronic components, trustworthy AI for decision making, systems for advanced perception, efficient propulsion and batteries, advanced connectivity, new integration and platform concepts, implemented in use cases (demonstrators). Demonstrators on system-integration-level include:

  - Smart, connected and shared mobility for urban areas,
  - Electric vehicle development on AI-inside based components and functions (fault detection, analysis and mitigation, highly automated driving, AI enabled perception and sensor fusion platforms etc.),
  - Particular aspects are the evaluation of the achievements with respect to the "Green Deal" (climate neutrality, zero pollution, sustainable transport, transition towards circular economy), of the ethical/societal aspects of decision making, and standardization activities.

- **Comp4Drones** (Framework of key enabling technologies for safe and autonomous drones' applications, https://artemis-ia.eu/project/180-COMP4DRONES.html; started October 2019) (project no. 826610).
- **TEACHING** (A computing toolkit for building efficient autonomous applications leveraging humanistic intelligence, EU-H2020, GA no. 871385)
  The TEACHING project focuses on mission-critical, energy-sensitive autonomous systems and the development of technology bricks for humanistic AI concepts. To enhance the development of the technology bricks, the building of a dependable engineering environment to support the development of a self-adaptive artificial humanistic intelligence in a dependable manner is intended. For details see also short description of papers (5) and (6) of "This Year's Workshop".
- **AIMS5.0** (Artificial Intelligence in Manufacturing leading to Sustainability and Industry5.0, EU HORIZON-KDT JU no. 101112089):

AIMS5.0 aims at European digital sovereignty in comprehensively sustainable production, by adopting, extending, and implementing AI tools & methods and chip technology across the whole industrial value chain to further increase the overall efficiency. In essence, the project will deliver:

- AI-enabled electronic components & systems for sustainable production
- AI tools, methods & algorithms for sustainable industrial processes
- SoS-based architectures & micro-services for AI-supported sustainable production
- Semantic modelling & data integration for an open access productive sustainability platform
- Acceptance, trust & ethics for industrial AI leading to human-centered sustainable manufacturing.

20 use cases in 10 industrial domains resulting in high TRLs will validate the project's findings in an interdisciplinary manner. A professional dissemination, communication, exploitation, and standardization will ensure the highest impact possible. AIMS5.0 will result in lower manufacturing costs, increased product quality through AI-enabled innovation, decreased time-to-market and increased user acceptance of versatile technology offerings. They will foster a sustainable development, in an economical, ecological, and societal sense and act as enablers for the Green Deal and push the industry towards Industry5.0.

National Programmes funding DECSoS projects, were for example:

- **ADEX** Autonomous-Driving Examiner, (Austrian Research Promotion Agency, Programme "ICT for the Future", Grant Agreement 880811). ADEX aims at developing a trustworthy examiner for controllers of self-driving vehicles. The project will adopt a scenario-based approach, combining techniques from artificial intelligence and traffic accident analysis to generate concrete challenging scenarios. Following a human-centered iterative design approach the developed automated verification and testing methodology will be transparent and provide user understandable. The project results will be evaluated both in virtual (simulation) and physical environments. Project outcomes will help to significantly increase the trust of design engineers and regulatory bodies in autonomous-driving controllers.

Results of these projects are partially reported in presentations at the DECSoS-Workshop. Some presentations refer to work done within companies or institutes, not referring to particular public project funding.

This list is of course not complete, it considers only projects which provided contributions to the work and papers of the authors and co-authors directly or indirectly via the work within their organizations and companies. Short descriptions of the projects, partners, structure and technical goals and objectives are described on the project- and the ECSEL/KDT websites, see also the Acknowledgement at the end of this introduction and https://www.kdt-ju.europa.eu/projects.

2 This Year's Workshop

The workshop DECSoS 2023 provides some insight into an interesting set of topics to enable fruitful discussions. The focus is on system-of-systems resilience, safety and cybersecurity of (highly) automated and critical systems analysis, development, validation and applications (mainly in the mobility area). Presentations are mainly based on ECSEL, Horizon 2020, new KDT-JU projects and nationally funded projects, and on experiences of partners' companies and universities. In the following explanations the projects are mentioned, which at least partially funded the work presented.

The session starts with an introduction and overview to the DECSoS Workshop, setting the scene for European Research and Innovation and co-hosting projects and organizations ERCIM, EWICS and ECSEL JU/KDT JU and Horizon 2020 (Austria), throwing highlights on projects like AI4CSM, TEACHING, ADEX and others, like AIMS5.0, a recently started KDT JU project on "Smart Manufacturing" (see short description before and Acknowledgements).

The first session on **"System-of-Systems Resilience"** comprises one presentation:

(1) **A Quantitative Approach for System of Systems' Resilience Analyzing Based on Archimate**, *by Huanjun Zhang, Yutaka Matsubara, and Hiroaki Takada.*
Two significant characteristics of SoS, the independence of the "constituent systems" and the involvement of multiple stakeholders, are ignored when attacking the issue of resilience for SoS. The paper proposed a quantitative method for analysing the resilience of SoS by visual modelling using the EA tool ArchiMate, evaluating and designing resilience from multiple stakeholders' perspectives. A case study on "Mobility as a Service" (MaaS) is presented.

The second session focusses on Cybersecurity and Safety of complex critical applications:

(2) **Towards DO-178C Compliance of a Secure Product,** *by Lijun Shan.*
To integrate certified secure products in an airborne system is a common approach. The paper shows the evaluation of a COTS-secure product certified against Common Criteria against DO-178C which poses new challenges because of different focusses in the standards. The insights obtained are presented. ECSEL projects SECREDAS and AMASS are referenced when addressing cross-concern reuse of certification/qualification artefacts.

(3) **The Need for Threat Modelling in Unmanned Aerial Systems**, by Abdelkader *Magdy Shaaban, Oliver Jung, and Christoph Schmittner.*
To identify cybersecurity vulnerabilities in Unmanned Aerial Systems is necessary for safe operation of such UAS. It is challenging to automate this work for such complex systems. In this paper, the tool ThreatGet is used to for threat modelling and for identifying cybersecurity vulnerabilities. Furthermore, a novel ontology-based threat modelling approach is developed and its effectiveness examined. The EU-projects "Labyrinth" (https://labyrinth2020.eu) and AIMS5.0 (started recently, for continuing work) are referenced and acknowledged.

(4) **Using Runtime information of controllers for safe adaptation at runtime**: a Process Mining approach, *by Jorge Da Silva, Miren Illarramendi, and Asier Iriarte.* Systems working in critical or autonomous scenarios need continuous verification during runtime after deployment to ensure long-term correct functioning, a fact that is considered e.g., in the upcoming Automated Driving Systems standards like ISO TS 5083. The paper presents a tool CRESCO, especially the improvements of the existing tool, to perform periodic checks effectively. The system allows then to automatically generate new code files from the traces of the log-file for replacement in case of a faulty scenario to occur. More robustness is the result.

The afternoon session dedicated to "Dependability of AI systems", managed and moderated by the TEACHING project (a H2020 project, see Acknowledgements at the end of the introduction):

(5) **Safety and Robustness for Deep Neural Networks: An Automotive Use Case**, *by Davide Bacciu, Antonio Carta, Claudio Gallicchio, and Christoph Schmittner.*
AI systems in context of automated driving are a critical issue because of the safety requirement to review these building blocks according to functional safety standards, which is not possible in the conventional way for Deep Neural Networks. In the Teaching project, the stress factor of the driver/user of an automated vehicle is measured and the driving style is adapted to reduce stress. Since this is not directly acting on the control of the vehicle, it is only safety related if the driver should be able to perform according to an automatically requested "Take over" by the vehicle or intentionally, and the chosen automated driving style is inadequate because the stress assessment was wrong. The possible situations have been analyzed according to the upcoming ISO/IEC TR 5469, Functional safety and AI, thus experimentally applying this standard.

(6) **Towards Dependable Integration Concepts for AI-based Systems**, *by Georg Macher, Romana Blazevic, Omar Veledar, and Eugen Brenner.*
This paper serves as introduction to a workshop triggered by the TEACHING project. It provides an overview of the concepts related to dependability issues of autonomous systems, particularly automated driving systems. The analysis of dependability of AI-based systems covers policies, political influences, economic and sociological influences, technology and standardization aspects, legal and environmental aspects, as well as technological factors and research, e.g., XAI (explainable AI9, interpretability, controllability, etc. This article laid the groundwork for an expert workshop where business leaders, academics, and decision-makers may join together to create the future of dependable AI-based autonomous systems. By addressing the challenges and exploring potential solutions, to pave the way for the development of trustworthy and resilient systems.

As chairpersons of the DECSoS workshop, we want to thank all authors and contributors who submitted their work, the SAFECOMP Publication Chair Friedemann Bitsch, the SAFECOMP conference chair Jérémie Guiochet, the Program chair Stefano Tonetta, the workshop co-chair Matthieu Roy, the web chair Joris Guerin, the Program Committee and the local organization. Particularly we want to thank the EC and national public funding authorities who made the work in the research projects possible. We do not want to forget the continued support of our companies and organizations, of ERCIM, the European Research Consortium for Informatics and Mathematics with its Working Group on Dependable Embedded Software-intensive Systems, and EWICS TC7, the creator and main sponsor of SAFECOMP, with its chair Francesca Saglietti and the sub-groups, who always helped us to learn from their networks.

We hope that all participants will benefit from the workshop, enjoy the conference and will join us again in the future!

Acknowledgements. Part of the work presented in the workshop received funding from the EC (H2020/ECSEL Joint Undertaking) and the partners National Funding Author-ities ("tri-partite") through the projects SECREDAS (nr. 783119), Comp4Drones (nr. 826610), AI4CSM (nr. 101007326). The AIMS5.0 project. Funded by the HORIZON-KDT-JU-2022-1-IA, project no. 101112089 and national funding authorities of the part-ners. The project ADEX is funded by the national Austrian Research Promotion Agency FFG in the program "ICT for Future" (FFG, BMK Austria) (no. 880811). The TEACH-ING project is funded by the EU Horizon 2020 research and innovation programme under GA n.871385, the LABYRINTH2020 project was funded under GA 861696.

This list does not claim to be complete, for further details check the papers.

International Program Committee 2023

Friedemann Bitsch	GTS Deutschland GmbH, Germany
Jens Braband	Siemens AG, Germany
Bettina Buth	HAW Hamburg, Germany
Peter Daniel	EWICS TC7, UK
Barbara Gallina	Mälardalen University, Sweden
Denis Hatebur	University of Duisburg-Essen, Germany
Miren Illarramendi Rezabal	Mondragon University, Spain
Willibald Krenn	SAL – Silicon Austria Labs, Austria
Erwin Kristen	AIT Austrian Institute of Technology, Austria
Georg Macher	Graz University of Technology, Austria
Helmut Martin	Virtual Vehicle Competence Center, Austria
Tristan Miller	Research Studios Austria FG, Austria
Peter Puschner	Vienna University of Technology, Austria
Francesca Saglietti	University of Erlangen-Nuremberg, Germany
Christoph Schmittner	AIT Austrian Institute of Technology, Austria
Christoph Schmitz	Zühlke Engineering AG, Switzerland
Daniel Schneider	Fraunhofer IESE, Kaiserslautern, Germany
Erwin Schoitsch	AIT Austrian Institute of Technology, Austria
Amund Skavhaug	NTNU Trondheim, Norway
Lorenzo Strigini	City University London, UK
Markus Tauber	Research Studios Austria, Austria

A Quantitative Approach for System of Systems' Resilience Analyzing Based on ArchiMate

Huanjun Zhang[✉], Yutaka Matsubara[✉], and Hiroaki Takada

Graduate School of Informatics, Nagoya University, Nagoya, Aichi 464-8601, Japan
imbacracy1@gmail.com, yutaka@ertl.jp

Abstract. With the development of IT technology and the increasing demand for service integration, the widespread application of System of Systems (SoS) is inevitable in the era to come. Among numerous key issues related to SoS, analyzing the resilience of SoS is a challenging problem. Although many studies and discussions for system engineering have provided solutions for this problem, two significant characteristics of SoS, which are the independence of Constituent systems (CSs) and the involvement of multiple stakeholders, are ignored. Based on these two characteristics, this paper proposed a quantitative method for analyzing the resilience of SoS. The method includes visual modeling of the SoS using the EA tool ArchiMate, quantitatively simulating the model based on defining the value of service capacities of the CSs and evaluating and designing resilience from multiple stakeholders' perspectives. Finally, a case study based on Mobility as a Service (MaaS) is presented. By analyzing resilience of MaaS, the critical node is identified, and by resilience redesign, the resilience of the SoS is improved after enhancement.

Keywords: System of systems · Resilience · ArchiMate

1 Introduction

In ISO 21841, System of systems is defined as a set of systems or system elements that interact to provide a unique capability that none of the constituent systems can accomplish on its own [1]. Its characteristics include the operational independence of individual systems, managerial independence of the systems, geographical distribution, emergent behavior, evolutionary development, and represents a higher level of abstraction than "system" [2]. Moreover, a more significant factor is hidden beneath the surface features of the SoS, which are the multitude of stakeholders. Conflicting interests among them make it difficult to implement management measures. These pose significant challenges for engineers concerned with the security of SoS.

Traditional risk management primarily focuses on assessing the probability and impact of potential disruptions, aiding engineers in identifying and preventing issues [3]. However, for SoS, it is impossible to prevent all malicious events, and these errors can be magnified by the interdependence of internal elements. For example, the Suez Canal obstruction in 2021 took six days to restore due to a lack of contingency plans,

© The Author(s), under exclusive license to Springer Nature Switzerland AG 2023
J. Guiochet et al. (Eds.): SAFECOMP 2023 Workshops, LNCS 14182, pp. 47–60, 2023.
https://doi.org/10.1007/978-3-031-40953-0_5

leading to global supply chain disruptions and losses of approximately USD$15 to 17 billion [4]. This case demonstrates that "black swan" events can cause significant losses that are difficult to bear for a system. Therefore, designing systems with resilience should also be an important part of ensuring system security. Resilience is ability to absorb and adapt to a changing environment [5] and is currently applied to different fields, such as organizational, social, economic, and engineering [6].

The resilience exhibited by SoS is more difficult to understand and evaluate than resilience in traditional fields due to the complexity of SoS. Its nature is an emergent behavior, which means that the mechanism from underlying behavior to the final manifestation of resilience cannot be depicted by mathematical models. Therefore, resilient design needs to be implemented from the top-down starting from the requirements and architecture phase, rather than in the underlying technology details design phase. So, the issue this paper aims to explore is how to quantitatively evaluate and design the resilience of SoS during the architecture phase.

In response to the issue, a resilience evaluation methodology for SoS based on the EA modeling language ArchiMate is proposed. The contribution of this paper is outlined as follows:

1. An SoS visualized modeling method based on ArchiMate is introduced. In this approach, SoS is abstracted as a topological structure consisting of multiple CS interfaces and their serving relationships, enabling the generalization and standardization of the method to different types of SoS.
2. A stakeholder-centric quantitative resilience analysis method is proposed. In this approach, service capacity, relation dependency, and disruption, which are quantitative, are introduced for quantifying SoS resilience and determining critical CSs. Also, in quantifying process, multiple stakeholders' requirements were considered.
3. A case study for MaaS is implemented. The paper abstracted the MaaS as an SoS model and conducted a resilience evaluation and design, demonstrating the effectiveness of the proposed approach.

2 Related Works

The initial phase of SoS analysis is typically based on architecture, which is derived from systems engineering in the military domain. In 2001, scholars utilized the Department of Defense Architecture Framework (DoDAF) to establish models for combat SoS [7]. Li et al. proposed an executable SoS architecture based on the DoDAF 2.0 metamodel [8]. Furthermore, architecture tools from the software engineering field are also commonly used to model SoS. Michael et al. [9] used UML to establish SoS topologies and implemented a simulation using OMNeT++. Bondar [10] utilized the Zachman framework to model SoS for agile development, reducing the development cycle of SoS architecture. In addition to architectural methods, simulation tools from other fields have also been applied to SoS, including Discrete Event System Specification (DEVS) [11], System Dynamics [12, 13], Bayesian network [14], Petri-Nets [15], and agent-based modeling (ABM) [16].

In the field of SoS resilience, some approaches employ Bayesian networks to evaluate the resilience of SoS and get result in a probability form [14, 17]. Other approaches indirectly reflect the resilience by defining other indicators, such as Uncertainty [18] and Criticality [19]. These indicators do not characterize resilience, but rather indicate the direction for designing resilience by identifying vulnerable nodes. Some approaches define quantitative resilience as a linear combination of measurable SoS attributes (the system performance at specific time points) [20]. Other methods consider the entire process from the occurrence of the disruption to its recovery, defining resilience as a function of measurement of performance (MOP), often integrating the MOP curve [21]. More methods consider additional details based on the MOP curve. For example, Emanuel [22] incorporated considerations for time horizon, endogenous preferences, and intertemporal substitutability into resilience. Didier [23] simultaneously considered both the MOP curve and demand curve in resilience calculations. However, these methods have not considered multiple stakeholders.

3 Proposed Approach

The proposed resilience evaluation and design approach involves four processes: Archi-Mate modeling, simulation, resilience evaluation, and resilience redesign, as shown in Fig. 1.

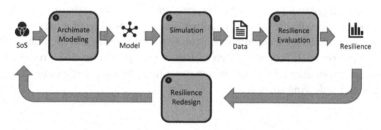

Fig. 1. Overview of the proposed approach.

3.1 ArchiMate Modeling

The modeling language, ArchiMate, based on The Open Group Architecture Forum (TOGAF) ensures uniform standards, methods, and communication among enterprise architecture experts, and provides a visual model topology for non-expert stakeholders. To avoid potential misunderstandings arising from conceptual abstractions, at the beginning of the method, the real-world SoS is abstracted to the conceptual SoS architectures and matched with the concepts in the TOGAF architecture, as illustrated in Fig. 2. The core architecture of ArchiMate consists of three layers: the Business layer, Application layer, and Technology layer, which respectively correspond to the SoS layer, CS layer, and System elements layer in the SoS architecture. Each layer includes an interface layer that provides services outwardly and an implementation layer that implements services internally. The internal composition of the CS and their lower-level elements fall under

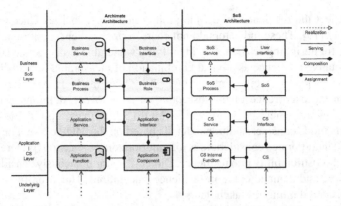

Fig. 2. The Correspondence between SoS Architecture and ArchiMate Architecture

the scope of systems engineering research due to the independence of the CS, and therefore are omitted in the illustration, despite ArchiMate providing corresponding concepts to match them.

According to the corresponding relationships described above, an SoS can be abstract to an ArchiMate model, as shown in Fig. 3. SoS is abstracted as a standard topology structure consisting of four elements: SoS process and CS service as two nodes, and Flow-Relationship and Serving-Relationship as two links. The process of a user enjoying an SoS service is achieved by sequentially executing SoS processes and spending a certain amount of time on each process. When a user is in a particular SoS process, it will occupy the corresponding CS service, which constitutes the basic logic of the simulation described in the following sections.

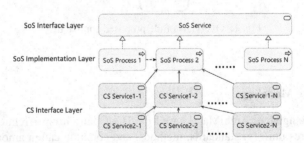

Fig. 3. Example SoS-ArchiMate model

3.2 Simulation

The simulation for evaluating the SoS resilience involves generating a certain number of user requests for SoS services, and observing the changes in the parameters, status, and service quality of the SoS under the disruptions. Capacity is a commonly used concept in this section, indicating the number of requests a service interface can fulfill per unit time. It is the basis for quantifying simulation in this method.

Simulation Assumptions

Assumption 1: Disruption Model. Resilience mainly targets low-frequency, high-impact disruptions [3], Therefore, the disruption model, as shown in Fig. 4, is proposed. t_0 represents the start time of the simulation, t_s represents the time when the disruption occurs, and t_f represents the end time of the simulation. Disruptions can occur at any CS service node and have an impact on the entire SoS, and it does not address the causes of disruptions but rather focuses solely on their negative impacts. This model predicts that CS services affected by disruptions will experience an immediate drop in their capacity to a low level (*LowCapacity*), which will last for a period (*RespondTime*). Afterward, it will take some time (*RecoverTime*) for the capacity to gradually recover to its initial level. The specific values for *LowCapacity*, *RespondTime*, and *RecoverTime* need to be set in the simulation.

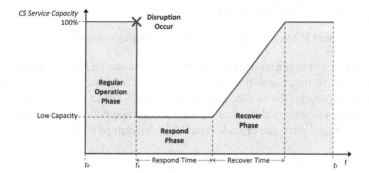

Fig. 4. An example of a disruption model.

Assumption 2: User Agent. In this simulation, the user is assumed to be an agent with three different states. The agent imitates the behavior of users when using SoS services, starting from the first SoS process and executing each subsequent process until the final one. During each SoS process, the agent will request the corresponding CS services. If the CS service is available, meaning that there is remaining capacity, the agent will enter the running state and occupy the capacity at the current time. Otherwise, the agent will enter the blocking state. Whenever one SoS process is completed, the agent will enter the ready state for the next SoS process. The total simulation time (*SimulationTotalTime*) and the number of users generated per unit time (*UserGenerateSpeed*) need to be set in the specific simulation.

Assumption 3: Redundancy. Investors often hope that the services provided exactly match the user demand [24]. However, in actual production, a certain percentage of redundancy is usually set. Therefore, it is assumed that all CS services have a capacity that is a certain percentage higher than normal-operating demand. This percentage (*Redundancy*) needs to be set in the specific simulation.

Identification of Nodes and Links' Properties. This section defines the properties that belong to the SoS model elements and how the values of these properties are determined in the simulation.

The Serving-Relationship has a property, Serving Dependability (*ServingD*), which refers to the probability that the target of the Serving-Relationship requests the service from the source, and its value is between 0 and 1. The value of *ServingD* is determined by the architect and domain experts in the target SoS based on past data and experience, and it will not change during a single simulation.

CS service has two properties, CS Service Self Capacity (*ServiceSC*) and CS Service Real Capacity (*ServiceRC*).

ServiceSC refers to the number of user requests that can be fulfilled within a unit of time when external resources are abundant, subject only to the limitations of its own capabilities. According to assumption 3, the initial value of *ServiceSC* needs to consider both services demanded (*ServiceD*) and redundancy. *ServiceD* can be obtained through stress testing, where the peak demand for each CS service obtained during the test is its *ServiceD*. During runtime, disruptions directly affect the corresponding *ServiceSC*. So, the value of *ServiceSC* is shown in Eq. 1.

$$ServiceSC(t) = ServiceD \cdot (1 + Redundancy) \cdot Disruption(t) \tag{1}$$

ServiceRC refers to the number of user requests that can be fulfilled within a unit of time, affected by its own capabilities and the *ServiceRC* of other services it depends on. This property represents the service capability of the CS service provided to the others. Figure 5A shows an enlarged view of a parent CS service node in the example model shown in Fig. 3, and the value of its *ServiceRC* is determined by Eq. 2

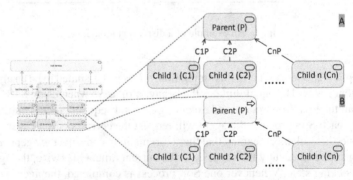

Fig. 5. A parent node relies on other child CS service nodes.

$$ServiceRC_P(t) = min\left(ServiceSC_P(t), \frac{ServiceRC_{C1}(t)}{Dependability_{C1P}}, \cdots, \frac{ServiceRC_{Cn}(t)}{Dependability_{CnP}} \right) \tag{2}$$

The parent node P depends on the child nodes $C_1, C_2, \ldots C_n$, with the *ServingD* of the Serving-Relationships between them, denoted as $C_1P, C_2P, \ldots C_nP$, respectively. Equation 2 indicates that the *ServiceRC$_P$*, depends on the weakest point, which could be its own capacity, *ServiceSC$_P$*, or the service capacity of other dependencies, *ServiceRC$_{Cn}$*.

SoS process has two properties, SoS process Regular Time (*ProcessRT*) and SoS process Capacity (*ProcessC*).

ProcessRT refers to the time required to complete the target SoS process in the absence of any disruptions. The property is derived from the average time taken to complete the SoS process and remains constant throughout the simulation.

ProcessC refers to the number of users allowed for the current step, determined by *ServiceRC$_{Cn}$* of the dependent CS service. Figure 5B shows an enlarged view of a parent SoS process node in the example model of Fig. 3. And the value of its *ProcessC* is determined by Eq. 3.

$$ProcessC_P(t) = min\left(\frac{ServiceRC_{C1}(t)}{Dependability_{C1P}}, \cdots, \frac{ServiceRC_{Cn}(t)}{Dependability_{CnP}} \right) \tag{3}$$

Simulation Outputs. The output for each CS service disruption's simulation includes:

- Ending time (*UserET*), planned time (*UserPT*), and used time (*UserUT*) for each user.
- Available service capacity (*ServiceRC*) and the number of services used (*ServiceU*) for each CS service at each simulation time.
- The number of users currently in running (*SoSR*) and the number of users waiting in the blocking queue (*SoSW*) within the entire SoS.

3.3 Resilience Evaluation and Design

Based on the SoS architecture, Stakeholders are identified as three types: SoS organizers, who focus on the operating condition of the SoS, CS providers, who focus on the overall profit of the CS, and users, who focus on the quality of individual services.

SoS organizers' MOP is defined as Eq. 4, reflecting the congestion status of the SoS. CS providers' MOP is defined as Eq. 5, reflecting the average utilization rate of all CSs. n represents the number of CSs. And users' MOP is defined as Eq. 6, reflecting the average on-time rate. k represents the number of users whose *UserET* is t.

$$MOP_{SoS}(t) = \frac{SoSR(t)}{SoSR(t) + SoSW(t)} \tag{4}$$

$$MOP_{CS}(t) = \frac{1}{n}\sum_{i=1}^{n} \frac{ServiceU_i(t)}{ServiceSC_i(t)} \tag{5}$$

$$MOP_U(t) = \frac{1}{k(t)}\sum_{i=1}^{k(t)} \frac{UserPT_i}{UserUT_i} \tag{6}$$

Here, MOP plays a bridging role between stakeholder requirements and the resilience of the SoS. On one hand, it reflects the stakeholder-based performance of the SoS, while on the other hand, it serves as the cornerstone for measuring the resilience of the SoS. According to the sensitivity analysis result in reference [22], this paper represents the resilience of the target SoS when disruption occurs on CS service i using the Eq. 7. $MOP_0(t)$ represents the MOP when no disruption occurs.

$$Resilience_i = \frac{\int_{t_f}^{t_0}\left(MOP_{SoS,i}(t) + MOP_{CS,i}(t) + MOP_{U,i}(t)\right)dt}{3\int_{t_f}^{t_0}MOP_0(t)dt} \tag{7}$$

The indicators that demonstrate the resilience of an SoS have been defined as:

$$SoSResilience = \frac{1}{n}\sum_{i=1}^{n}Resilience_i \tag{8}$$

Equation 7 and Eq. 8 illustrate that the SoS resilience is characterized as the average resilience demonstrated by each CS services node during disruption testing. The resilience exhibited by each disrupted node is calculated based on the mean of the MOP for users, SoS organizers, and CS providers.

If the stakeholders are not satisfied with *SoSResilience*, critical nodes in the SoS model need to be strengthened for improving resilience.

How to Identify Critical Nodes? Sort the $Resilience_i$ values. $Resilience_i$ represents the resilience of the CS service$_i$ when subjected to disruption, and a lower value indicates a greater impact on SoS resilience. Therefore, this service interface should be given priority during design to enhance the overall SoS resilience.

How to Enhance Critical Nodes? There are five specific measures.

- Increase the *Redundancy*.
- Reduce the *ServingD* of relationship from other services on the target nodes.
- Reduce disruption's *RespondTime* by improving response capacity.
- Reduce disruption's *RecoverTime* by improving recovery capacity.
- Increase disruption's *LowCapacity* by improving absorb capacity.

4   Case Study: Mobility as a Service

4.1   MaaS Introduction

This paper takes MaaS as a case study for the evaluation and design of SoS resilience. MaaS can be defined as the integration of various transport modes, such as public transit, ride sharing, and biking into a single service, accessible on demand, via a seamless digital planning and payment application [25]. Therefore, MaaS can be seen as an SoS, and the systems it integrates are CSs. In case study, MaaS is divided into six seamless processes: Log in, Plan, Order, Authenticate, Travel and Pay.

- Log in: MaaS verifies user identity and payment account.
- Plan: An information integration process. MaaS provides users travel options by integrating map information, vehicle information, and transportation schedules.

- Order: A booking integration process. MaaS provides users with a one-stop ticketing service by integrating the ticketing systems of various transportation platforms.
- Authenticate: MaaS checks passengers' identity upon boarding.
- Travel: A transportation integration process. MaaS integrates various means of transportation to provide users with transportation, and navigation service.
- Pay: A payment integration process. MaaS allows for multiple payment methods, and internally allocates revenue to various CSs.

4.2 Model and Parameters

According to Sect. 3, an ArchiMate model of the MaaS is established, as shown in Fig. 6. The left two columns of the figure depict the interaction between the user and MaaS at the business layer. The right blue columns demonstrate how CS realizes the business processes by providing services through interfaces. Table 1 presents assumption parameters of simulation.

After setting the assumption parameters and initial properties, the MaaS model was simulated. The modeling software is ArchiMate Version: 4.10.0. The simulation was run on a personal computer with a 12th Gen Intel(R) Core (TM) i7-12700H 2.30 GHz processor and 32 GB of RAM.

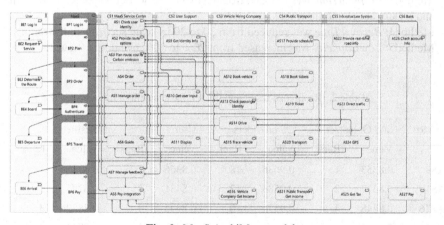

Fig. 6. MaaS ArchiMate model

4.3 Resilience Analysis

According to Sect. 3.3, the resilience of MaaS was evaluated and the results are presented in Table 2. The three categories of stakeholders provide evaluations of MaaS resilience for each disrupted CS service. The average of them, denoted as Resilience$_i$, is listed in the last column of the table. A higher rank in the Resilience$_i$ indicates a more critical node, where disruptions occurring on that node would have a greater impact on the overall resilience of the SoS. Finally, the SoS resilience of the MaaS model established in Sect. 4.2 is evaluated as 0.8997.

Table 1. Parameters of assumptions for MaaS simulation

	Parameters	Value
Assumption 1	*LowCapacity*	20%
	RespondTime	15
	RecoverTime	30
Assumption 2	*SimulationTotalTime*	300
	UserGenerateSpeed	20
Assumption 3	*Redundancy*	20%

To enhance the resilience of the SoS, the methods outlined in Sect. 3.3 were used to strengthen the most critical node, 'AS9 Get Identity Info'.

- Control Group (CG): Simulation set as Sect. 4.2.
- Method1: *Redundancy* was increased from 20% to 50% by scaling up servers.
- Method2: *ServingD* of the relationship relied on 'AS9' was reduced 25% by increasing local servers.
- Method3: *RespondTime* was reduced from 15 to 9 by network congestion monitoring and DDOS attack monitoring.
- Method4: *RecoverTime* was reduced from 30 to 20 by team security skills training.
- Method5: *LowCapacity* was increased from 20% to 30% by adding firewalls.

Table 2. Resilience result and CS service criticality ranking

service	SoS Organizer		CS providers		User		Resilience$_i$	
	Value	Rank	Value	Rank	Value	Rank	Value	Rank
AS9	0.8353	1	0.9636	18	0.8366	1	0.8785	1
AS10	0.8372	2	0.9583	12	0.8431	2	0.8795	2
AS26	0.8448	4	0.9571	10	0.8445	3	0.8822	3
AS11	0.8427	3	0.9559	9	0.8482	4	0.8823	4
AS1	0.8496	6	0.9514	6	0.8494	5	0.8835	5
AS7	0.8525	12	0.9523	7	0.8520	6	0.8856	6
AS3	0.8502	8	0.9474	1	0.8623	9	0.8866	7
AS5	0.8479	5	0.9587	15	0.8538	7	0.8868	8
AS15	0.8505	9	0.9508	4	0.8626	10	0.8880	9
AS17	0.8505	10	0.9508	5	0.8626	11	0.8880	10
AS22	0.8512	11	0.9507	3	0.8633	12	0.8884	11
AS24	0.8500	7	0.9575	11	0.8622	8	0.8899	12

(continued)

Table 2. (*continued*)

service	SoS Organizer		CS providers		User		Resilience$_i$	
	Value	Rank	Value	Rank	Value	Rank	Value	Rank
AS14	0.8633	13	0.9657	20	0.8745	13	0.9012	13
AS20	0.8633	14	0.9657	21	0.8745	14	0.9012	14
AS6	0.8640	16	0.9657	19	0.8751	16	0.9016	15
AS23	0.8633	15	0.9726	22	0.8745	15	0.9035	16
AS2	0.8816	21	0.9477	2	0.8946	26	0.9080	17
AS12	0.8789	17	0.9584	13	0.8916	22	0.9097	18
AS18	0.8789	18	0.9584	14	0.8916	23	0.9097	19
AS4	0.8822	22	0.9556	8	0.8946	27	0.9108	20
AS13	0.8807	19	0.9616	16	0.8917	24	0.9113	21
AS19	0.8807	20	0.9616	17	0.8917	25	0.9113	22
AS8	0.8840	25	0.9890	23	0.8860	19	0.9197	23
AS16	0.8837	23	0.9924	24	0.8857	17	0.9206	24
AS21	0.8837	24	0.9924	25	0.8857	18	0.9206	25
AS27	0.8849	27	0.9924	26	0.8869	20	0.9214	26
AS25	0.8849	26	0.9925	27	0.8869	21	0.9214	27
SoSResilience: 0.8997								

The improvement results are shown in Table 3. And Fig. 7. Methods 1 through 5 all improved the SoS resilience and reduced the criticality of AS9. This demonstrates the sensitivity of the SoS resilience metric proposed in this paper to different disruptions and countermeasures, effectively reflecting the system's ability to withstand disruptions.

To assess the significance of critical nodes, we applied the same resilience enhancement methods to the "AS20 Transport" and "AS25 Get tax" nodes, which are ranked 14th and 21st, respectively, in terms of resilience criticality as shown in Table 2. The comparative results are presented in Table 4, showing that the same method applied to different service nodes yields varying improvements in the overall resilience of the SoS. The application of the method to AS9 (ranked first in importance) resulted in higher efficiency compared to AS20 (ranked in the middle), whereas its application to AS25 (ranked last in importance) showed the lowest efficiency.

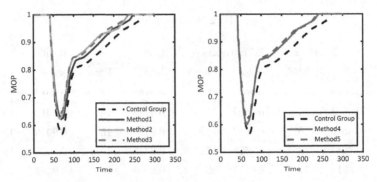

Fig. 7. The MOP curve after enhancing AS9 using the five methods.

5 Conclusion

The method proposed in this paper can be used for the quantitative evaluation and design of SoS resilience. First and foremost, SoS is abstracted into a topology structure of business processes and application services by EA tool ArchiMate which is not only beneficial for agile development but also facilitates understanding and communication among stakeholders. The model treats the underlying CS as uncontrollable black boxes to simulate the independence of CS. Moreover, the capability of CS service and relationship between services are quantified to simulate the model. Based on the data recorded during the simulation related to SoS organizer, CS providers, and users, the SoS resilience based on demands of multi-stakeholders is calculated. At last, the proposed method is applied to the case study of MaaS for demonstrating the effectiveness of the proposed method. Table 5 compares the characteristics of this paper and several existing studies.

In the future, more in-depth research can be conducted to address the limitations of current studies, including designing additional disruption models and intelligent user agent to validate the assumptions of simulation, studying stakeholder games and resilience-cost efficiency to optimize resilience evaluating and redesign methods, and using real-world accident cases to validate the feasibility of proposed methods.

Table 3. The SoS Resilience after enhancing AS9 using the five methods.

	SoS Organizer		CS providers		User		Resilience$_i$		SoSResilience
	Value	Rank	Value	Rank	Value	Rank	Value	Rank	
CG	0.8353	1	0.9636	18	0.8366	1	0.8785	1	0.8997
Method1	0.8681	16	0.9708	21	0.8691	12	0.9027	15	0.9006
Method2	0.8874	27	0.9746	22	0.8887	21	0.9169	22	0.9010
Method3	0.8826	22	0.9730	22	0.8838	16	0.9131	22	0.9009
Method4	0.8741	16	0.9703	21	0.8751	16	0.9065	16	0.9007
Method5	0.8790	18	0.9730	22	0.8804	16	0.9108	20	0.9008

Table 4. The comparison of the resilience enhancement applied to nodes AS9, AS20, and AS25

| | AS9 Get Identity Info | AS20 Transport | AS25 Get tax |
	SoSResilience	SoSResilience	SoSResilience
Method1	0.9006	0.9004	0.9002
Method2	0.9010	0.9007	0.9006
Method3	0.9009	0.9007	0.9005
Method4	0.9007	0.9003	0.9003
Method5	0.9008	0.9006	0.9002

CG SoSResilience: 0.8997

Table 5. Comparison of this research and some existing studies on SoS resilience engineering

	Quantitative metric	Guide resilience design	Sensitivity to change	Consider multi-stakeholders
Proposed Method	Quantitative	✓	High	✓
Indirect Method [26, 27]	Semi-quantitative	✓	Low	✗
Possibility Method [20, 28]	Semi-quantitative	✓	High	✗
Point Method [29]	Quantitative	✗	Low	✗
Period Method [30–32]	Quantitative	✗	High	✗

References

1. International Organization for Standardization. ISO/IEC/IEEE 21841 Systems and software engineering—Taxonomy of systems of systems (2019)
2. Sage, A.P., Cuppan, C.D.: On the systems engineering and management of systems of systems and federations of systems. Inf. Knowl. Syst. Manag. **2**, 325–345 (2001)
3. Uday, P., Marais, K.B.: Designing resilient systems-of-systems: a survey of metrics, methods, and challenges. Syst. Eng. **18** (2015)
4. Lee, J., Wong, E.Y.: Suez Canal blockage: an analysis of legal impact, risks and liabilities to the global supply chain. In: MATEC Web of Conferences (2021)
5. International Organization for Standardization. ISO 22300 Security and resilience—Vocabulary (2021)
6. Hosseini, S., Barker, K., Ramírez-Márquez, J.E.: A review of definitions and measures of system resilience. Reliab. Eng. Syst. Saf. **145**, 47–61 (2016)
7. Stanilka, S., Dagli, C.H., Miller, A.: 1.3.4 object-oriented development for DoDAF system of systems. In: INCOSE International Symposium, vol. 15 (2005)

8. Li, L., Dou, Y., Ge, B., Yang, K., Chen, Y.: Executable system-of-systems architecting based on DoDAF meta-model. In: 2012 7th International Conference on System of Systems Engineering (SoSE), pp. 362–367 (2012)
9. Michael, J.B., Shing, M., Miklaski, M.H., Babbitt, J.D.: Modeling and simulation of system-of-systems timing constraints with UML-RT and OMNeT++. In: 2004 Proceedings. 15th IEEE International Workshop on Rapid System Prototyping, pp. 202–209 (2004)
10. Bondar, S., Hsu, J.C., Pfouga, A., Stjepandić, J.: Agile digital transformation of system-of-systems architecture models using Zachman framework. J. Ind. Inf. Integr. **7**, 33–43 (2017)
11. Mittal, S., Risco-Martín, J.L.: Model-driven systems engineering for netcentric system of systems with DEVS unified process. In: 2013 Winter Simulations Conference (WSC), pp. 1140–1151 (2013)
12. Wang, J., Yuan, H.: System dynamics approach for investigating the risk effects on schedule delay in infrastructure projects. J. Manag. Eng. **33**, 04016029 (2017)
13. Watson, B.C., Chowdhry, A., Weissburg, M.J., Bras, B.: A new resilience metric to compare system of systems architecture. IEEE Syst. J. **16**, 2056–2067 (2022)
14. Hosseini, S., Khaled, A.A., Sarder, A.: general framework for assessing system resilience using Bayesian networks: a case study of sulfuric acid manufacturer. J. Manuf. Syst. **41**, 211–227 (2016)
15. Rao, M., Ramakrishnan, S., Dagli, C.H.: Modeling and simulation of net centric system of systems using systems modeling language and colored Petri-nets: a demonstration using the global earth observation system of systems. Syst. Eng. **11**, 203–220 (2008)
16. Silva, R., Braga, R.T.: Simulating systems-of-systems with agent-based modeling: a systematic literature review. IEEE Syst. J. **14**, 3609–3617 (2020)
17. Yodo, N., Wang, P.: Resilience modeling and quantification for engineered systems using Bayesian networks. J. Mech. Des. **138**, 031404 (2016)
18. Zhou, Z., Matsubara, Y., Takada, H.: Resilience analysis and design for mobility-as-a-service based on enterprise architecture modeling. Reliab. Eng. Syst. Saf. **229**, 108812 (2022)
19. Ed-daoui, I., Itmi, M., Hami, A.E., Hmina, N., Mazri, T.: A deterministic approach for systems-of-systems resilience quantification. Int. J. Crit. Infrastruct. **14**, 80–99 (2018)
20. Dessavre, D.G., Ramírez-Márquez, J.E., Barker, K.: Multidimensional approach to complex system resilience analysis. Reliab. Eng. Syst. Saf. **149**, 34–43 (2016)
21. Uday, P., Marais, K.B.: Resilience-based system importance measures for system-of-systems. In: Conference on Systems Engineering Research (2014)
22. Emanuel, R.: Hybrid resilience framework for systems of systems incorporating stakeholder preferences (2018)
23. Didier, M., Broccardo, M., Esposito, S., Stojadinović, B.: A compositional demand/supply framework to quantify the resilience of civil infrastructure systems (Re-CoDeS). Sustain. Resilient Infrastruct. **3**, 102–186 (2018)
24. Ng, I.C., Wirtz, J., Lee, K.S.: The strategic role of unused service capacity. Int. J. Serv. Ind. Manag. **10**, 211–244 (1999)
25. Muller, M., Park, S., Lee, R., Fusco, B., Correia, G.H.: Review of whole system simulation methodologies for assessing mobility as a service (MaaS) as an enabler for sustainable urban mobility. Sustainability **13**, 5591 (2021)

Towards DO-178C Compliance of a Secure Product

Lijun Shan[✉]

Internet of Trust SAS, 77 Avenue Niel, 75017 Paris, France
lijun.shan@internetoftrust.com

Abstract. An approach to enhancing the cybersecurity of airborne systems is integrating certified secure products, given that the secure products demonstrate their compliance to the airworthiness standards. We conduct an evaluation of a COTS (Commercial Off The Shelf) secure product against DO-178C, so that it can be certified once integrated into an airborne system. Although the secure product has been certified under Common Criteria (CC), certifying it against DO-178C poses new challenges to the developer due to the different focuses of the two certification standards. While CC primarily focuses on evaluating the security features of a product, DO-178C places greater importance on ensuring the integrity of development assurance processes. This paper presents the insights that we obtained while addressing the challenges encountered during the evaluation under DO-178C.

Keywords: Cybersecurity · Airworthiness · DO-178C Compliance · COTS software · Secure Product

1 Introduction

While aircrafts are increasingly software-intensive and inter-connected, the aviation industry is increasingly recognizing cybersecurity as a critical aspect. An approach to enhancing cybersecurity of airborne systems is to integrate mature security products, especially security-certified ones. In order to be approved of the usage in aircraft, however, the security products have to conform to aviation regulations and standards. DO-178C/ED-12C [1], titled *Software Considerations in Airborne Systems and Equipment Certification*, is the *de facto* standard by which the certification authorities such as US Federal Aviation Administration (FAA), European Union Aviation Safety Agency (EASA), and Transport Canada approve airborne software.

We conduct an evaluation of a COTS (Commercial Off The Shelf) secure product, called TOE (Target Of Evaluation) in the sequel, against DO-178C. Despite that TOE has been certified under Common Criteria (CC)[1], certifying the product against DO-178C poses new challenges to the developer. While CC primarily evaluates the products' security features as well as the development process, DO-178C places greater emphasis on ensuring the integrity of development assurance processes.

---

[1] https://www.commoncriteriaportal.org/cc/.

J. Guiochet et al. (Eds.): SAFECOMP 2023 Workshops, LNCS 14182, pp. 61–72, 2023.
https://doi.org/10.1007/978-3-031-40953-0_6

62   L. Shan

The paper presents the ongoing work and the insights that we obtained while addressing the challenges encountered during the evaluation. Through the practice, we gained a comprehension of DO-178C requirements, especially the rigor of the processes and the interplay between the processes. We are conducting complementary activities and working out missing artefacts to meet the requirements. Moreover, we identified a needed role change from a COTS software developer to an airborne software supplier, and a necessary culture shift towards the safety-in-design approach. The significance of this project surpasses the certification of a single product. It drives organizational and procedural changes for higher maturity in assuring software quality, including to invest in more resources on safety assurance activities, to strengthen collaboration within the organization, and to strive for continuous improvement.

2 Related Work

The cybersecurity of airborne systems has become a critical issue due to the increasing use of digital technologies in aviation. In [2], the authors compare DO-178C and aviation software cybersecurity standards, including DO-326A/ED-202A *Airworthiness Security Process Specification*, DO-356A *Airworthiness Security Methods and Considerations*, and DO-355 *Information Security Guidance for Continuing Airworthiness*.

Guidelines on aviation computer systems' safety and cybersecurity and related certification processes are discussed in [3]. An overview is given on current guidelines, developed by Radio Technical Commission for Aeronautics (RTCA) in the U.S., and European Organization for Civil Aviation Equipment (EUROCAE) in Europe, as well as advisory circulars and orders from the U.S. Federal Aviation Administration (FAA).

Addressing the reuse of certification artifacts between security and safety critical domains, EU projects e.g. AMASS[2] and SECREDAS[3] studied cross-concern reuse of qualified or certified CPS (Cyber Physical System) products. The notion of security-informed safety oriented process line was introduced in [4–6]. In comparison to the existing research on methodologies which facilitate reusing certification artifacts, our work reported in this paper aims to identify the difference between the CC and DO-178C in terms of their requirements on engineering activities.

In spite of the variety of security products, there is a lack of research reported in the literature regarding the certification of security products under DO-178C, as far as we know. The most related work is presented in [7], which aims to certify PikeOS separation kernel under CC, given that the product has undergone certification for DO-178B. This work is similar to ours but takes the opposite direction.

3 DO-178C Overview

This section summarizes the core concepts of DO-178C and the expected artefacts, to set a background for the discussion.

---

[2] https://www.amass-ecsel.eu.
[3] https://secredas-project.eu.

3.1 Core Concepts

DO-178C takes a lifecycle approach to software development. A core concept is Lifecycle Process. All activities throughout the software development lifecycle are organized into three groups of lifecycle processes: Planning Processes, Development Processes, and Integral Processes.

Software Level, also known as Design Assurance Level (DAL), indicates the safety-criticality, i.e. the degree to which the software's failure can cause harm or loss of life. It is determined from a system lifecycle process, called System Safety Assessment Process.

Objectives are statements which define what must be achieved during a lifecycle process. The higher the DAL of a software system, the more objectives are required.

3.2 Expected Output from the Processes

Planning Processes: The planning processes are used to establish the plans at the beginning of a software project, including:

- Plan of Software Aspect of Certification (PSAC): An overall plan for the project. This plan is a summary of all other plans.
- Plan for the Development Processes: Software Development Plan (SDP).
- Plans for the Integral Processes: Software Verification Plan (SVP), Software Configuration Management Plan (SCMP), Software Quality Assurance Plan (SQAP).

Development Processes: These processes include requirements development, design, implementation, and integration. The output artefacts include:

- Software High-Level Requirements (HLRs).
- Software Design, including Low-Level Requirements (LLRs) and Software Architecture.
- Software Implementation, including source code and executable object code.

Integral Processes: These processes include software verification, lifecycle process verification, configuration management, and quality assurance. The output artefacts include:

- Software Verification Results
- Software Quality Assurance Results
- Software Configuration Management Results.

4 Objectives of the Project

The project aims to conduct an evaluation of the TOE against DO-178C and to construct a *certification kit*, i.e. a collection of artefacts which demonstrates the compliance to DO-178C. Certifying the TOE against the aviation security standard DO-326A is also in progress, but is beyond the scope of this paper.

The TOE was developed as a COTS software product. Due to business confidentiality, details of the TOE as well as its CC Evaluation Assurance Level (EAL) and the targeted

DO-178C DAL level cannot be revealed. Nevertheless, the research presented in this paper can be applied to any CC-certified COTS product targeting at any DO-178C DAL level.

Different from CC certification where a COTS software product can be certified as an individual product independent of the context of its usage, the subject of a DO-178C certification has to be an airborne system which integrates software and hardware. The responsibility of a software developer is to build a certification kit, i.e. a collection of artefacts including documents, code, test reports, etc., called *software lifecycle data* in DO-178C. The certification kit will be delivered to a system integrator, who is responsible for integrating the hardware and software components into a system, building the evaluation evidence of the system based on the certification kits of the components, and submitting a certification request to the authority. Note that in the context of DO-178C, *system* only means an airborne system which consists of software and hardware, despite that *software*, *system* and *software system* are often used interchangeably in the context of software engineering.

For the TOE to be integrated into an airborne system, typically a customized development is necessary for adapting the TOE to the specific hardware platform. The integrator may also have specific requirements on functionality, security or safety. Given the client requirements, the developer may need to configure the TOE or develop new features.

In addition to produce the certification kit, this project also serves to cultivate the project team with safety engineering methodologies and lifecycle processes, and to equip them with techniques and tools for DO-178C compliance. The experience gained through this project prepares the project team to adhere to DO-178C in future customized development.

5 Reusing CC Artefacts

Since the TOE was developed previously and certified under CC, we expect to reuse the existing artefacts in constructing DO-178C certification kit. The first question we posed is: can CC artefacts be reused for building DO-178C certification kit? To answer this question, we conducted a gap analysis by comparing DO-178C with CC requirements, identified the reusable artefacts as well as the missing ones, and envisaged the actions to take in order to bridge the gap.

5.1 Gap Analysis: CC VS. DO-178C

Common Criteria (ISO/IEC 15408) is the *de facto* standard for cybersecurity certification around the world. It provides a framework for evaluating and certifying the security capabilities of IT products and systems with standardized evaluation criteria and assurance levels. CC defines a standardized terminology for specifying security functional requirements (SFRs) and security assurance requirements (SARs) in a Protection Profiles (PPs) for a group of similar products. The vendor of a product can make claims about the product's security attributes in a Security Target (ST) which strictly or partially conforms to one or multiple PPs. Then testing laboratories can evaluate the products to determine if they actually meet the claims.

The comparison of DO-178C and CC showed their different focuses: while CC primarily focuses on evaluating the security features of a product, DO-178C places greater emphasis on ensuring the integrity of development assurance processes.

Take requirement specification as an example. There are two essential differences between CC and DO-178C in terms of software requirements: the content of the requirements, and the role of the requirements in the certification of a product. Firstly, the content of the product requirements concerned by CC is different from that evaluated by DO-178C. CC evaluation addresses only the security requirements, while the other aspects of product requirements are out of the scope of a product certification. In contrast, DO-178C requires to specify all aspects of software requirements, including functional, safety, performance and security ones.

Secondly, the role of requirement specification in CC evaluation differs a lot from that in DO-178C. CC certification aims to verify if a product meets the security requirements that it declares in its Security Target, while the elicitation and the specification of the security requirements are not the focus of CC evaluation of a product. In practice, the security requirements definition is usually formulated in a Protection Profile, which is neutralized to specific products. The CC-certified Protection Profiles are then used as templates of security requirements in specific products' Security Target. In contrast, under DO-178C, software requirements are important artefacts produced during the product's lifecycle. Requirements-related activities, including requirement elicitation, formulation, quality assurance and verification, are defined in the three groups of lifecycle processes:

- **Planning Processes:** Software Requirement Standard and Software Design Standard should prescribe project-specific criteria and guideline for the formulation of software requirements.
- **Development Processes:** Software HLRs and Software Design should document the software requirements at various abstraction levels, their rationality and traceability, and the verification methods for each requirement.
- **Integral Processes:** Software Requirement Verification Results on HLRs and LLRs should document the reviews and analysis of the requirements.

In summary, DO-178C imposes dedicated processes for specifying and ensuring the quality of software requirements. In contrast, under CC, requirement specification and the related assurance activities are typically conducted during the construction of Protection Profiles, not within a product's lifecycle.

5.2   Reusable and Missing Artefacts

The difference in the focus of the two certifications raises the question that to which extent the CC evidences can be reused in the DO-178C evaluation. The question can only be answered via a detailed examination of the DO-178C guideline on each engineering activity and the corresponding lifecycle data one-by-one.

Through this gap analysis, we identified the reusable artefacts for each group of lifecycle processes, as summarized in Table 1. Through the construction of the DO-178C artefacts, however, we realized that the reusing of CC artefacts is limited to a smaller level

Table 1. CC Evaluation Evidences VS. DO-178C Lifecycle Data

	DO-178C artefact	Reusable CC artefacts
Planning Processes	Plan of Software Aspect of Certification (PSAC)	Lifecycle Description
	Software Development Plan (SDP)	Tools and Technique
	Software Verification Plan (SVP)	Lifecycle Description
	Software Configuration Management Plan (SCMP)	Configuration Management Capabilities
Development Processes	Software High Level Requirements (HLR)	- Security Target - Lifecycle Requirements
	Software Design: - Software Architecture - Low Level Requirements	- Security Architecture, - Functional Specification, - TOE Design, - TOE Security Functionality Internals
Integral Processes	Software Verification Results	Test Documentation
	Software Quality Assurance Results	Lifecycle Description
	Software Configuration Management Results	Configuration Management Capabilities

of granularity. This is primarily due to the differences between the requirements of DO-178C and CC. Even in cases where certain CC artefacts can be reused, it is necessary to construct a DO-178C artefact by synthesizing pertinent information from CC artefacts, internal engineering documents, and developers' undocumented knowledge. When an artefact is missing, it means that some DO-178C lifecycle process was incomplete or insufficiently documented.

Planning Processes: The plans required by DO-178C are missing for the TOE, as CC does not cover planning processes. The construction of the Plans, however, may reuse existing CC artefacts, including *Lifecycle Description*, *Configuration Management Capabilities*, and the code standard in *Tools and Technique.*

Development Processes: Software requirements, design and implementation were produced for the TOE in compliance to CC and can be reused. But constructing the artefacts for DO-178C still needs a significant amount of rework.

- **Software Requirements:** The CC artefacts corresponding to software requirements are *Security Target* and *Lifecycle Requirements*, both presenting only security requirements. For the DO-178C certification kit, the other aspects of software requirements, including functional, safety and performance ones, have to be constructed through a step-wise refinement from *System Requirements*.

- **Design:** The CC artefacts corresponding to Design include *Security Architecture, Functional Specification, TOE (Target of Evaluation) Design, TOE Security Functionality Internals.* Again, they address only the security features. For the DO-178C certification kit, the other aspects of the design have to be constructed, including software structure, data flow, control flow, resource management, etc.

Integral Processes: Integral processes comprise of various types of processes, including configuration management, quality assurance, software verification, and process verification. Among them, configuration management and software verification were documented during the development of the TOE, and the CC artefacts can be reused. The other processes need to be complemented following the DO-178C guideline.

5.3 Bridging the Gap

This project consists of two types of activities: **Reusing CC artefacts:** for the lifecycle processes which have been conducted, this project constructs DO-178C software lifecycle data based on existing artefacts; **Complementing lifecycle processes:** for the lifecycle processes which were incomplete with respect to DO-178C, this project complements them and produce required artefacts.

Although reusing existing CC artifacts to achieve DO-178C compliance may seem like an attractive goal, through this project we learned that the reuse has to be carried out at a very detailed level. Given the considerable disparity between the two standards, it's nearly impossible to generate a DO-178C lifecycle data item by merely reusing CC artifacts at a high level of granularity, such as a document or a chapter. Instead, we have to synthesize, refine, and enrich the existing artifacts. The following two sections present the lessons learned in complementing the lifecycle processes, notably the Planning Processes and the Development Processes.

6 Planning Processes

The planning processes are used to establish the plans for the other lifecycle processes, including Development Processes and Integral Processes.

As identified in Sect. 5, the plans were not covered by the CC artefacts and should be produced in this project. Despite that each plan addresses a specific lifecycle process, the person responsible for a specific lifecycle process is not able to produce the plan by himself. Instead, establishing a plan requires a sufficient understanding of the interplay between all the three groups of lifecycle processes, and an intensive collaboration between various roles of the team. Take Software Development Plan (SDP) as an example.

6.1 Understanding DO-178C Guideline: The Role of SDP

SDP includes three standards: Software Requirements Standard, Software Design Standard, and Software Code Standard. Note that *standard* here means a set of guidelines and criteria established by the organization for a specific project, not in the sense of ISO standards or FAA standards. The three Standards in the SDP impose consistent criteria for various development stages, for all members of the team, and for all components of the software under development.

Each of the three Standards in SDP plays two roles: for the development processes, the Standards provide guideline for developers to create requirements, design and code, respectively; for the software verification, the Standards are used as review criteria by reviewers to verify if the lifecycle data satisfy the Objectives defined in DO-178C. The standards should be as concrete and operational as possible, so that the developers can apply them in their daily work, and the reviewers can use them to create review checklist for each lifecycle data. The establishment of the Standards, therefore, requires a consensus-building involving project members with different roles.

6.2 Proposed Solution

For the three Standards to be practical and applicable, we refined the corresponding Objectives of DO-178C lifecycle processes into specific criteria. For instance, the Software Requirements Standard that we created includes the following aspects of criteria and guidance:

- Quality attributes of requirements: criteria for effective and implementable requirements. For example, a requirement should be atomic, verifiable, traceable.
- Representation of document: criteria for document layout, numbering scheme, identifying and using tables, identifying graphics and using symbols, etc.
- Traceability: instructions on building traceability matrix, either manually or with tool support.

In our project, all the plans are constructed after the product development. The standards should be established with the considerations from three aspects:

- Since the product and some artefacts already exit, the Standards should reflect the practice. For instance, code standard was chosen before the development of the TOE, and it is kept in the Code Standard.
- New standards, i.e. Software Requirements Standard and Software Design Standard, should promote best-practices compliant to DO-178C. For instance, both standards should impose criteria for the lifecycle data to be verifiable.
- The new standards should be easy to be followed by the developers in the future customized development of the product. For instance, the criteria of *verifiable* should impose the developers to indicate the verification methods, e.g. functional testing or real-time analysis, for each requirement in Software Requirements and Software Design.

Our approach to converging the different considerations is to revise the SDP through iterations by conducting the three types of lifecycle processes:

(1) Planning Processes: To establish a 1st version SDP.
(2) Development Process: To partially develop Software Requirements and Software Design based on existing artefacts.

(3) Integral Process: To develop Review Checklists based on the Standards in the SDP, and apply such checklists when reviewing Software Requirements and Software Design. The utilization of the Standards confirms their practicability for this project, including the sufficiency and necessity of the criteria in the Standards.

(4) Confirmation of SDP: To revise the SDP with the feedback from the Integral process.

To summarize, creating the SDP in the Planning Processes needs to involve various roles within the project team to conduct various lifecycle processes. Similarly, to produce any other plan also needs to consider its role in the entire project, including when it will be used, by whom, and how.

7 Development Processes

The development processes are used to specify and refine the requirements, and implement the software to satisfy the requirements. The processes include requirements development, design, implementation, and integration.

As identified in Sect. 5, software security requirements were specified in the CC artefacts. The other aspects of software requirements, including those on functionality, safety, and performance need to be produced in this project. At the design level, the non-security aspects of the design have to be constructed via reverse engineering of the TOE.

7.1 Understanding DO-178C Guideline: Relations Between the Requirements

According to DO-178C, the input to the Development Processes includes System Requirements and System Safety Assessment, both are the output of a system lifecycle process named System Safety Assessment Process. This system-level process also determines the Software Level for the software via a hazard assessment. The software HLRs should be defined via a top-down decomposition of system requirements: firstly, allocating System Requirements to hardware and software; then, producing software HLRs by refining the System Requirements allocated to the software. The software HLRs are then refined into design, and finally implementation.

7.2 Defining System Requirements

For a COTS software, however, System Requirements and System Safety Assessment Process are unavailable, since the software was designed out of the context of its usage. How to construct the System Requirements as the input to the Software Development Processes is the first challenge that we met before building the Development Processes data.

For our project, a potential user has conceived the conceptual model of an airborne system which integrates the TOE, but not yet fully designed the system. We have received from the potential user a suggested Software Level for the TOE, and a high-level system description in terms of the functionality, the architecture and the required security features. Our approach to establishing presumed System Requirements is to combine the existing system description with a set of general System Safety Requirements. The presumed System Requirements can be adjusted as soon as the system requirements from a system integrator is available.

The major missing part for constructing System Requirements is system safety requirements, which is the output of System Safety Assessment process according to DO-178C. Conducting a system hazard assessment is, however, not yet possible at the current stage of our project, and also out of the capacity of a software developer. A trade-off solution that we took is to cite the general airborne system safety requirements from FAA "Computing System Safety" [8], where Annex A provides a set of sample general safety requirements for flight computing systems.

We examined these general safety requirements and classified them into two groups: requirements on engineering process and requirements on computing systems. The first group, **requirements on engineering process**, are all covered by the DO-178C guideline. An example from [8] is "*A.1.1 Computer systems shall be validated for operation in the intended use and environment*". This requirement is also stated in DO-178C Software Verification Process, which states "*Selected tests should be performed in the integrated target computer environment*" [1]. This group of requirements is automatically achieved by a project conforming to DO-178C. The second group, **requirements on computing systems**, include requirements on computer system performance, fault tolerance, resource management, etc. An example from [8] is "*A.1.2 Under maximum system loads, CPU throughput shall not exceed 80 percent of its design value*". We incorporated the second group of general safety requirements from Annex A [8] into the System Safety Requirement in our project. In addition, we identified a set of project-specific safety requirements from the high-level system description provided by the potential user.

In summary, we constructed the System Requirements by taking two steps: (1) specifying System Functional Requirements and System Security Requirements based on the high-level system description provided by the potential user; (2) specifying System Safety Requirements based on a set of general safety requirements from FAA "Computing System Safety" [8].

A presumed requirement allocation is then performed, where the System Requirements are assigned to hardware, the TOE or the other software. The part of System Requirements allocated to the TOE becomes the input to the Software Development Processes in our project.

7.3 Defining Software HLRs

Given the System Requirements allocated to the TOE, the first process in Software Development Processes is specifying software HLRs. The challenge is to decompose System Requirements into measurable criteria against which the software can be evaluated.

While refining System Requirements to HLR, we discovered the necessity of re-categorizing of the requirements. System-level safety is achieved through multiple aspects of concerns, including real-time performance, robustness, redundancy in terms of architecture design, etc. Through the decomposition of system safety requirements to HLRs, we transformed system-level safety requirements into software-level functional requirements, security requirements, and performance requirements. The re-categorization facilitates to identify the verification methods for each requirement.

Table 2 shows examples of re-categorization of requirements through the decomposition of system safety requirements. For instance, a system safety requirement states that the system shall fail-safe and fail-secure. When we transform this safety requirement to software HLR, it becomes a functional requirement on the degraded operations of the software, whose implementation can be verified via functional tests. In contrast, a system safety requirement on the maximum CPU throughout, when transformed to a software HLR, becomes a performance requirement which can be verified via performance analysis. In summary, when mapping System Requirements to HLRs, some requirements may need to be re-categorized with the consideration on the verification method for each software requirement.

Table 2. CC Evaluation Evidences VS. DO-178C Lifecycle Data

System Safety Requirement	Software HLR on the TOE	Verification Method for HLR
Fail-safe and fail-secure	Functional requirement: degraded operations	Functional test
CPU throughput shall not exceed 80 percent of its design value	Performance requirement	Performance analysis
System shall ensure memory isolation	Security requirement: memory partitioning against illegal access	Analysis by reasoning

7.4 Software Design

In DO-178C terminology, Software Design consists of two complementary artefacts: LLRs and Software Architecture. Both of them refine software HLRs.

The challenge for developing LLRs lies in the structure of information and the abstraction level. LLRs should be detailed enough so that the source code can be directly implemented without further information. Our on-going work tries to specify multi-level LLRs through step-wise refinement, due to the complexity of the TOE.

Software Architecture should present the software design from multiple perspectives, including software structure, data structure, data flow, control flow, resource management, partitioning methods, etc. These design artefacts are to be used in the Software Verification as evaluation criteria. The challenge for specifying Software Architecture also comes from the complexity of the TOE.

8 Conclusion

The paper presents the ongoing work for building a DO-178C certification kit, and the insights we obtained while addressing the challenges encountered in the project. Integral Processes will be discussed in future work.

Reusing of CC artefacts helps to build the DO 178C certification kit, since CC artefacts contain detailed and rigorously specified information regarding the product design and development process. However, the primary challenge lies in identifying the absent information and carrying out the necessary engineering activities to address those gaps.

Through the evaluation, we identified a need of role change from COTS software developer to airborne software supplier. The role change necessitates an increase in the rigor of software engineering activities, more collaboration within the organization, and continuous improvement of safety assurance capabilities.

References

1. RTCA Inc. (Radio Technical Commission for Aeronautics) and EUROCAE (European Organization for Civil Aviation Equipment). DO-178C/ED-12C Software Considerations In Airborne Systems And Equipment Certification (2012)
2. Torens, C.: Safety versus security in aviation, comparing DO-178C with security standards. In: AIAA Scitech 2020 Forum, p. 0242 (2020)
3. Zalewski, J., Kornecki, A.: Trends and challenges in the aviation systems safety and cybersecurity. TASK Quart. 23(2), 159–175 (2019). https://doi.org/10.17466/tq2019/23.2/a
4. Gallina, B.: Quantitative evaluation of tailoring within spice-compliant security-informed safety-oriented process lines. J. Softw.: Evol. Process 32(3), e2212 (2020)
5. Gallina, B., Kashiyarandi, S., Zugsbratl, K., Geven, A.: Enabling cross-domain reuse of tool qualification certification artefacts. In: Bondavalli, A., Ceccarelli, A., Ortmeier, F. (eds.) SAFE-COMP 2014. LNCS, vol. 8696, pp. 255–266. Springer, Cham (2014). https://doi.org/10.1007/978-3-319-10557-4_28
6. Gallina, B., Fabre, L.: Benefits of security-informed safety-oriented process line engineering (2015)
7. Blasum, H., Tverdyshev, S.: From a DO-178B certified separation kernel to common criteria security certification. SAE Technical Paper (2011)
8. U.S. Department of Transportation Federal Aviation Administration. Computing System Safety, no. AC 450.141-1A (2021)

The Need for Threat Modelling in Unmanned Aerial Systems

Abdelkader Magdy Shaaban$^{(\boxtimes)}$ (ID), Oliver Jung (ID), and Christoph Schmittner (ID)

AIT Austrian Institute of Technology GmbH - Center for Digital Safety & Security, Giefinggasse 4, 1210 Vienna, Austria
{abdelkader.shaaban,oliver.jung,christoph.schmittner}@ait.ac.at
https://www.ait.ac.at

Abstract. Detecting cybersecurity vulnerabilities in Unmanned Aerial Systems (UAS) is essential to ensure the safe operation of drones. This supports the determination of cybersecurity objectives and the description of security requirements needed to achieve these objectives. However, it is challenging to automate this process to identify potential cyber threats and ensure the correctness of the applied security requirements, especially in a complex system such as a UAS network. In this work, we use ThreatGet as a threat modelling tool to identify potential cyber threats in UAS and highlight existing security vulnerabilities. This assists in determining the appropriate security requirements that could be implemented to achieve our security goal. We then develop a novel ontology-based threat modelling approach to infer a set of security threats based on the applied security requirements and then check the effectiveness of these requirements against threats to ensure these requirements are fulfilled.

Keywords: Cybersecurity · Potential Threats · Security Requirements · Threat Modelling · Unmanned Aerial Systems

1 Introduction

Today's Unmanned Aerial Vehicles (UAVs) are equipped with multiple components fully connected to other network terminals to accomplish specific tasks in the air. Drones with smart components are highly needed to act and track objects to accomplish complex missions [1]. The rising demand for Internet connectivity in drone components increases the necessity for cybersecurity. Cybersecurity plays an essential role in the Unmanned Aerial Systems (UAS) domain. It aims to protect all data transmitted between connected points within the UAS network and to protect critical drone components responsible for controlling and managing the drone maneuver [2]. However, cybersecurity is considered a challenging issue in drone technology. A cyber attack against a drone could make the drone act as a flying weapon. The absence of security measures in the UAS design could lead to unanticipated outcomes [3]. Well-established cybersecurity measures and correctly implemented security requirements are essential to

J. Guiochet et al. (Eds.): SAFECOMP 2023 Workshops, LNCS 14182, pp. 73–84, 2023.
https://doi.org/10.1007/978-3-031-40953-0_7

establishing a secure UAV system. However, it is challenging to identify existing security vulnerabilities to detect any potential cyber threats. In addition, it is crucial to ensure that the applied security requirements are fulfilled, especially when considering multiple security issues in a complex system such as a UAS network.

Threat modeling is considered an applicable cybersecurity approach in multiple domains, including the UAS sector. In this paper, we deploy this approach to ensure the implementation of security measures and requirements, guaranteeing security by design in the UAS domain. Consequently, we use the ThreatGet[1] tool to identify the main security issues in the UAS in the early stages of the development of the UAS, which helps to determine the primary security goals. According to our mapping approach, described in [2], we establish an applicable set of security requirements based on the security standard IEC 62443 [4]. We also introduce a novel ontology-based threat modelling approach to support the assessment of the correctness and effectiveness of the applied security requirements against potential cyber incidents for each system component. This approach generates a test case and details the investigation process for evaluating applied security requirements. It then suggests a new set of security requirements that could be incorporated into the system design to address and resolve the existing security gaps.

2 Threat Modelling in the UAS Domain

Threat modelling is a method for identifying, analyzing, and prioritizing potential risks in various technical domains, such as automotive, railways, Internet-of-Things (IoT), and Cyber-Physical-Systems (CPS). This method is crucial in the UAS domain for automatically tracking interconnected components in the UAS network and identifying potential cyber incidents that could be triggered within the network. In this work, threat modelling is conducted for risk analysis purposes and to assess the correctness of the applied security requirements, ensuring these requirements are fulfilled.

2.1 Threat Modelling for Risk Analysis

As part of our cybersecurity investigation in the Labyrinth EU project[2], we developed a threat Knowledge-Base (KB) that contains a wide range of cyber threats based on state of the art [5–12]. A knowledge representation is used to describe the behavior of these threats, as discussed in [2]. The KB is part of our threat modelling tool, ThreatGet. ThreatGet is developed to investigate possible cybersecurity threats in the system model for UAS and other domains as introduced in [13–17]. The outcomes of the ThreatGet tool provide a clear understanding of which security mechanisms need to be implemented to mitigate cyber risks. The tool automates risk analysis and evaluates identified risks to detect cybersecurity vulnerabilities that require further attention.

---

[1] https://www.threatget.com.
[2] https://labyrinth2020.eu.

2.2   Threat Modelling for Checking Security Requirements

Threat modelling can be used in different phases of a system development lifecycle. For example, when more information about security measures for a system becomes available, threat modelling can be utilized to determine the appropriate security requirements [18]. However, ensuring the correctness of the applied security requirements is crucial. The approach used for that purpose should consider all system components, potential threats, and applied security requirements to guarantee satisfactory results. In Labyrinth, we developed a novel ontology-based threat modelling approach to automate the testing process and ensure the correctness of the applied security requirements in UAS models. This approach performs a reverse action, infers potential security issues (i.e., threats) from the existing security solutions (i.e., applied security requirements) to assess the effectiveness of these requirements against threats. Figure 1 illustrates the structure of the proposed ontology-based approach.

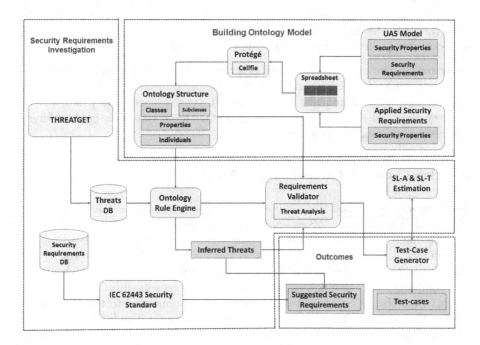

Fig. 1. The Structure of the Proposed Ontology-Based Threat Modelling Approach

The Figure illustrates the main building blocks of the proposed ontology-based threat modelling approach.

Building Ontology Model: The proposed approach aims to build a comprehensive knowledge domain for a UAS model. This includes multiple elements such as classes, subclasses, properties, individuals, and relationships. These elements represent necessary information, including security requirements, security properties, components, and communication channels. However, constructing an ontology hierarchy can be challenging due to the large amount of information that needs to be described ontologically. Therefore, all necessary details are defined in a spreadsheet. Then, we utilize Protegé [19] and its plugin Cellfie [20] to automatically import and translate the content of the spreadsheet into an ontology form.

Security Requirements Investigation: The "Ontology Rule Engine" processes the ontology model and infers a set of potential threats that could propagate through the system network. The "Requirements Validator" checks the effectiveness of these requirements against newly inferred threats by matching the common security characteristics between threats (e.g., violation of properties, risk severities, etc.) and the applied security requirements. The proposed approach calculates the Achieved Security Level (SL-A), which describes the security level reached after applying the security requirements. It compares this with the actual Target Security Level (SL-T), which describes the goal that needs to be achieved, aiming to demonstrate whether the applied security requirements have been fulfilled. The unaddressed threats or unfulfilled requirements are identified as security gaps in the system design that require additional security concerns.

Outcomes: The ontology approach generates a test case for each component, providing more detailed insight into the investigation process for evaluating applied security requirements. Our proposed approach suggests a new set of security requirements that could be integrated with the system design to address and resolve existing security gaps.

3   Use Case: A Generic UAS Model

In this work, we utilized the components catalogue from ThreatGet to model a high-level diagram of a UAS example, as shown in Fig. 2.

The diagram consists of multiple components representing a high-level UAS system model, as depicted in the lower part of the model. As shown in the figure, the Ground Control Station (GCS) communicates with the UAV through a wireless communication channel, enabling the UAV to receive direct commands or signals from the GCS. These two components are connected to the Unmanned Traffic Management (UTM) server via a cellular network. The UTM server handles all flight-related data, including location and sensor data from the UAV and other information related to UAV operations. Each component is modelled within a boundary or a security zone (i.e., Server Zone, UAV Zone, and GCS Zone). Security zones are described by the IEC 62443 security standard, which consists of logical or physical system components that share corresponding security requirements.

Each system component has a more detailed structure that describes the internal data flow among the interconnected components. ThreatGet provides the ability to model the internal structure of each system component in depth as sub-diagrams, as illustrated in the upper part of Fig. 2.

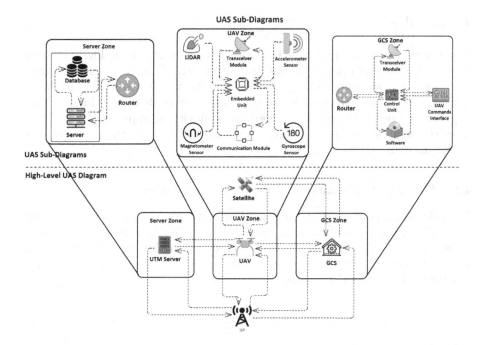

Fig. 2. A Generic UAS Model

UAV Zone: This zone represents the drone itself, encompassing multiple sensors (e.g., LiDAR, Magnetometer, Gyroscope, and Accelerometer) for data collection. These sensors transmit the gathered data to an onboard Electronic Control Unit (ECU) for processing. This data can then be transferred to other connected components (e.g., GCS) via a communication module.

GCS Zone: This is the GCS zone; it comprises components necessary to manage the operation of the UAV, including the User Interface, Embedded Control Unit, and Router device for communicating with other terminals in the UAS network.

Server Zone: This zone includes the server, which accommodates a database for storing collected data about the UAV flight, and a router device for managing data transmission with other terminals in the UAS network.

Each component and communication channel has security mechanisms defined as protections against cyber attacks. The threat modelling approach leverages these mechanisms to inspect potential security vulnerabilities that could lead to cyber incidents, as presented in Sect. 4.1. In addition, Sect. 4.2 presents the results of our proposed ontology-based threat modelling approach, which checks for correct implementation of the applied security requirements in our UAS example.

4   Results

Based on the previously presented UAS model (i.e., Fig. 2), we employ ThreatGet to identify potential cyber risks within that model. From the results obtained via ThreatGet, we define the appropriate security requirements that should be implemented to meet the primary security goal that needs to be achieved. Subsequently, we utilize the ontology-based threat modelling approach to verify the effectiveness of the applied security requirements and ensure their accuracy for mitigating cyber risks.

4.1   ThreatGet: Identifying Security Vulnerabilities

The rule engine of ThreatGet is essential in examining the violation of security properties and detecting potential cyber threats. We apply the threat analysis process to the system model to check how potential threats could be trigged within the system network. Figure 3 illustrates all threats identified by Threat-Get for the high-level UAS model.

Threat Analysis Results(1)   □ ×

Threat List

| Show All... | | Search ... | | **139 of 139 Threats** | | | | Summary | Print Report |

Title	Source	Target	Impact	Likelihood	Risk	Category
Malicious UAS communications attacks			Major	Medium	3	Tampering
Malicious UAS communications attacks			Major	Medium	3	Tampering
Malicious UAS communications attacks			Major	Medium	3	Tampering
Malicious UAS communications attacks			Major	Medium	3	Tampering
Malicious UAS communications attacks			Major	Medium	3	Tampering
Malicious UAS communications attacks			Major	Medium	3	Tampering
Malicious UAS communications attacks			Major	Medium	3	Tampering
Malicious UAS communications attacks			Major	Medium	3	Tampering
ADS-B message Modification			Severe	High	5	Tampering
Compromise communication everywhere			Severe	High	5	Tampering
Communication interference			Severe	Medium	4	Denial of Service
Communication interference			Severe	Medium	4	Denial of Service
Communication interference			Severe	Medium	4	Denial of Service
Unauthorized UAV-control			Major	Medium	3	Tampering
Compromise data confidentiality			Moder...	Low	2	Information Disclosure
Wireless APN-Flood			Moder...	Low	2	Denial of Service
Wireless APN-Flood			Moder...	Low	2	Denial of Service
Lawful interception			Moder...	Low	2	Denial of Service
Lawful interception			Moder...	Low	2	Denial of Service
Lawful interception			Moder...	Low	2	Denial of Service
Machine to machine fragility			Major	Low	2	Denial of Service
Machine to machine fragility			Major	Low	2	Denial of Service
Machine to machine fragility			Major	Low	2	Denial of Service
Compromise eNodeB/Femtocell/Microcell			Moder...	Low	2	Denial of Service
Compromise eNodeB/Femtocell/Microcell			Moder...	Low	2	Denial of Service
Access to wireless interface to impersonate parts of the net...			Negligi...	Medium	1	Spoofing
Access to wireless interface to impersonate parts of the net...			Negligi...	Medium	1	Spoofing
Access to wireless interface to impersonate parts of the net...			Negligi...	Medium	1	Spoofing

Fig. 3. A List of all Identified Threats by ThreatGet

ThreatGet identifies 139 threats in our UAS example; each threat violates a specific set of security properties. ThreatGet classifies these property violations based on the STRIDE categories [21] (i.e., **S**poofing violates **authentication**, **T**ampering violates **integrity**, **R**epudiation violates **non-repudiation**, **I**nformation Disclosure violates **confidentiality**, **D**enial of Service violates **availability**, and **E**levation of Privilege violates **authorization**). This classification assists in determining the main security goal that needs to be achieved and in selecting the appropriate set of security requirements to fulfil those objectives.

4.2 Ontology-Based Approach: Security Requirements Checking

Based on the outcomes presented in Sect. 4.1, we apply security requirements to each system component. These requirements provide guidance on how to protect each system component from potential cyber threats. These requirements are defined based on our previously developed mapping approach, as introduced in [2]. The mapping technique aims to establish a clear correlation between cyber threats and security requirements in accordance with the security standard IEC 62443 part 4-2 [4]. Table 1 illustrates a simple example of the selected security requirements for the UAV component.

Table 1. Set of Selected Security Requirements for the UAV Component

Foundational Requirements (FRs)					
IAC	UC	SI	DC	TRE	RA
CR_1_10	CR_2_1	CR_3_8	CR_4_1	CR_6_2	CR_7_1
CR_1_14	CR_2_1_1	CR_3_2	CR_4_2_1	CR_6_1	CR_7_6
CR_1_11	CR_2_3	EDR_3_11			
CR_1_5	CR_2_1_3	CR_3_5			
CR_1_12		EDR_3_2			
5	4	5	2	2	2

Approximately 20 security requirements have been identified as the primary requirements for the UAV component in our UAS example. These requirements are either from the CR or EDR classes. The standard [4] categorizes each security requirement according to the type of a specific component (i.e., CR, EDR, NDR, HDR, and SAR). These categories are defined as follows:

- **CR: Component Requirements:** Describes security requirements for a system component without specifying the type of component.
- **EDR: Embedded Device Requirements:** Outlines the set of requirements for embedded devices.
- **HDR: Host Device Requirements:** Similar to EDR, but these requirements are more dedicated to host devices, such as servers.
- **NDR: Network Device Requirements:** Includes requirements for network devices such as communication modules and router devices.

- **SAR: Software Application Requirements:** A set of requirements related to software components.

These categories are described in a Foundational Requirements (FRs) set, as described in IEC 62443 standard [4]. They are defined as follows [2]:

- **Identification and Authentication Control (IAC):** Supports authentication and manages spoofing issues.
- **Use Control (UC):** Provides authorization and handles violations of privileges in system components.
- **System Integrity (SI):** Supports data integrity and assists in managing related tampering issues.
- **Data Confidentiality (DC):** Ensures the confidentiality of data.
- **Timely Response to Events (TRE):** Assists in handling various repudiation attacks.
- **Resource Availability (RA):** Ensures the availability of system components.

These requirements should be integrated with the UAV to protect this component from cyber threats. It is essential to ensure these requirements are capable of addressing any potential cyber threats. Further, we use the ontology-based threat modelling approach (as presented and discussed in Sect. 2.2) to verify the correctness of the applied security requirements. As input for this ontology-based approach, we construct a comprehensive ontology model that incorporates all details described in the UAS model (i.e., ThreatGet's model, as illustrated in Fig. 2), considering security properties defined for each component. In addition, we combined all data related to the chosen security requirements listed in Table 1 and described them in an ontology form to determine whether they were satisfied. The ontology-based approach then investigates the correctness of these requirements by inferring a set of potential threats that could propagate within the system network and checking if any of the applied security requirements are sufficient to address these threats. The outputs of the proposed ontology-based threat modelling approach are depicted in the User-Interface (UI) of our proposed approach in Fig. 4.

The figure presents the results of the ontology-based threat modelling approach that was utilized to investigate the protection of the system components (as listed in label 1) with considering all of the applied security requirements of our UAS example, as specified in label 2. This approach performs inference actions to evaluate the effectiveness of all applied security requirements on the potential threats. Therefore, a set of potential threats is identified (label 3) with all related information regarding these threats, such as likelihood, impact, risk, and STRIDE category. Then determines which requirements have been fulfilled. The X symbols in Fig. 4 indicate that a specific security requirement has been assessed and confirmed to have effectiveness (as "true" in the Validity column) in addressing one or more inferred threats, as labeled in 4. An overview of the evaluation process of all applied security requirements is defined in label 5, where

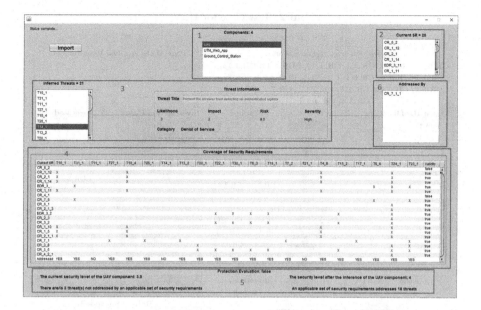

Fig. 4. Outcomes of the Proposed Ontology-Based Threat Modelling Approach

more information is defined in the form of test cases. A test case for each system component is generated; each test case contains a more detailed investigation and preliminary calculations of the current security level to highlight if any security issues need more security concern. A sample of the generated test case is presented in Table 2. As discussed in Sect. 2.2, our proposed approach suggested additional security requirement(s) to address any identified security gaps; these requirement(s) are listed in the UI (as specified in label 6), that should be part of the system design for protecting a system component (in our case is the UAV component), for addressing a particular threat "T4_1" (i.e., "Prevent the receiver from detecting un-authenticated signals").

The test case provides information emphasizing the correctness of the applied security requirement while also providing details if any security gaps are detected. As described in this test case, there are 20 security requirements applied to the UAV; the ontology inferred 21 different threats (as shown in Fig. 4) and then tested whether any of these requirements could mitigate the inferred threats. Based on that, the test case determines the TRUE (valid) security requirement or FALSE (invalid). Our approach provides a set of suggested requirements that could be used to fill any security gaps or could be considered as a set of recommended security requirements for improving the overall applied security in our system. For example, all selected security requirements cannot address threat T14_1; therefore, evaluating that threat is defined as false, and the ontology approach suggested applying security requirement CR_7_1_1 to mitigate that risk. Then, this approach calculates the effectiveness rate of all applied security requirements to the UAV, where about 90% of these require-

Table 2. Test Case for UAV

Test Case for UAV						
Applied Security Requirements					Rate of the Applied Requirements	
CR_6_2, CR_1_12, CR_2_1, CR_1_14, EDR_3_11, CR_1_11, CR_4_1, CR_7_6, CR_6_1, CR_2_1_3, EDR_3_2, CR_2_3, CR_3_2, CR_1_10, CR_1_5, CR_2_1_1, CR_7_1, CR_3_8, CR_3_5, CR_4_2_1					20	
#	Threat ID	Likelihood	Impact	Severity	Applied	Investigation Result	Suggested
1	T20_1	4	4	Critical	CR_3_8, CR_3_5	TRUE	EDR_3_14
2	T14_1	3	3	High	NA	FALSE	CR_7_1_1
3	T4_8	3	3	High	CR_1_12, CR_2_1, CR_1_14, CR_1_11, CR_1_10, CR_1_5, CR_2_1_1	TRUE	EDR_3_12, EDR_3_13
4	T36_1	1	1	Low	EDR_3_14_1, CR_3_1_1, CR_1_9_1, CR_1_14, CR_1_5_1, CR_2_1, CR_1_5, CR_1_9, EDR_3_12, CR_1_10	TRUE	EDR_2_4_1, EDR_3_13, EDR_3_12, EDR_3_14_1, EDR_3_10_1
...	....	....	....	.....	......	....	.....
Average Severity Level			3	Investigation Result		FALSE	
Suggested Security Requirements					Rate of Suggested Requirements	
EDR_2_4_1, EDR_3_13, EDR_3_12, EDR_3_14_1, EDR_3_10_1, EDR_3_11, CR_7_1_1, CR_7_1, CR_3_3, CR_3_3_1, EDR_3_14, EDR_3_2, EDR_2_4, EDR_2_13, EDR_3_11_1, CR_3_4_2, CR_3_4, CR_3_5					18	
Security Requirement Reduction Rate					10.00%	
Effective Rate					90.00%	
Security Level (Current State)					Level - 3	
Security Level (After suggested security requirements)					Level - 4	

ments are successfully validated to address the identified threats. As described in the table, the average severity level of all identified threats is estimated as High. The current security level (i.e., security level estimation according to the applied security requirements) is estimated to be Level-3. However, the system designer should follow the suggested security requirements for each unaddressed threat to ensure that all potential cyber threats are covered.

The suggested security requirements might be applicable as security solutions for addressing these threats. Therefore, the test case also indicates all suggested security requirements and estimates the reduction achieved by selecting these requirements, which is about a 10% reduction in security requirements compared to the previously selected ones (as presented in Table 1).

5 Summary, Conclusion, and Future Work

Cybersecurity is an essential topic that needs increased attention in the UAS domain. It protects data transmitted between connected components in the UAS network and critical safety components responsible for controlling UAV operations. In this paper, we used ThreatGet as a threat modelling tool to investigate potential cyber threats propagating within the UAS network. This creates a clear image of which security requirements should be defined to achieve specific security goals. However, it is essential to evaluate whether these requirements are fulfilled. Therefore, we developed a novel ontology-based threat modelling approach to investigate all applied security requirements in a UAS example and demonstrate whether any requirements could effectively reduce cyber risks. We tested both modelling approaches, i.e., ThreatGet and the ontology-based one, in a simple UAS example. The outcomes of ThreatGet guide us in determining which security requirements could be a part of our UAS model. Following our mapping approach, as presented in [2], we defined which security requirements should be selected for identified threats. We then built a complete ontology model for the UAS example, containing all applied security requirements. Next, we applied the ontology-based threat modelling approach to evaluate all applied requirements and identify existing security gaps by inferring a set of potential threats that could impact any component within the system. This approach creates a test case for each system component, providing more details about each component, applied security requirements, and how any applied requirements could address the inferred threats. Finally, the ontology approach suggests a set of security requirements that could potentially fill any gaps in a system model.

This work suggests that threat modelling could be a promising method for enhancing cybersecurity in the UAS sector. Our findings show that threat modelling can help identify security vulnerabilities and potential cyber threats that might propagate within the system network. Additionally, it can be utilized to evaluate whether security requirements are being met.

The findings of this paper were based on a UAS example to demonstrate the importance of incorporating threat modelling into the UAS sector. However, as part of the AIMS5.0 project, we plan to delve deeper, broaden the scope of this work, examine the threat modelling methodology more thoroughly, and compare it with similar approaches through future research and practical applications.

Acknowledgements. This work is accomplished as a part of the AIMS5.0 project. The project is selected for funding from the HORIZON-KDT-JU-2022-1-IA, project no. 101112089 and national funding authorities of the partners.

References

1. Genc, H., Zu, Y., Chin, T.-W., Halpern, M., Reddi, V.J.: Flying IoT: toward low-power vision in the sky. IEEE Micro **37**(6), 40–51 (2017)
2. Shaaban, A.M., Jung, O., Fas Millan, M.A.: Toward applying the IEC 62443 in the UAS for secure civil applications. In: Haber, P., Lampoltshammer, T.J., Leopold, H., Mayr, M. (eds.) Data Science - Analytics and Applications. Springer, Wiesbaden (2022). https://doi.org/10.1007/978-3-658-36295-9_7
3. Shaaban, A.M., Jung, O., Schmittner, C.: A proposed X.800-based security architecture framework for unmanned aircraft system, pp. 389–397. Trauner Verlag (2022). Artwork Size: 479 pages Medium: PDF

4. IEC. Security for industrial automation and control systems - part 4-2: Technical security requirements for IACS components. Technical report, International Standard (2019)
5. Javaid, A.Y., Sun, W., Devabhaktuni, V.K., Alam, M.: Cyber security threat analysis and modeling of an unmanned aerial vehicle system. In: 2012 IEEE Conference on Technologies for Homeland Security (HST), pp. 585–590 (2012)
6. Lattimore, G.L.: Unmanned aerial system cybersecurity risk management decision matrix for tactical operators. Technical report, Naval Postgraduate School, Monterey, CA, USA (2019)
7. Walters, S.: How to set up a drone vulnerability testing lab (2016). https://medium.com/@swalters/how-to-set-up-a-drone-vulnerability-testing-lab-db8f7c762663. Accessed 12 June 2023
8. Manesh, M.R., Kaabouch, N.: Cyber-attacks on unmanned aerial system networks: detection, countermeasure, and future research directions. Comput. Secur. **85**, 386–401 (2019)
9. Kristen, E., et al.: D2.3 Architecture Requirements and Definition (v2). Technical report, AFarCloud deliverable (2020)
10. Macaulay, T.: The 7 deadly threats to 4G: 4G LTE security roadmap and reference design, vol. 25, p. 2017 (2013)
11. United Nations Economic Commission for Europe UNECE. CSOTA ad hoc "Threats 2" (2017). https://wiki.unece.org/pages/viewpage.action?pageId=45383725. Accessed 11 June 2023
12. Kotapati, K., Liu, P., Sun, Y., LaPorta, T.F.: A taxonomy of cyber attacks on 3G networks. In: Kantor, P., et al. (eds.) ISI 2005. LNCS, vol. 3495, pp. 631–633. Springer, Heidelberg (2005). https://doi.org/10.1007/11427995_82
13. Schmittner, C., Chlup, S., Fellner, A., Macher, G., Brenner, E.: ThreatGet: threat modeling based approach for automated and connected vehicle systems. In: AmE 2020-Automotive meets Electronics; 11th GMM-Symposium, pp. 1–3. VDE (2020)
14. Schmittner, C., Schrammel, B., König, S.: Asset driven ISO/SAE 21434 compliant automotive cybersecurity analysis with ThreatGet. In: Yilmaz, M., Clarke, P., Messnarz, R., Reiner, M. (eds.) EuroSPI 2021. CCIS, vol. 1442, pp. 548–563. Springer, Cham (2021). https://doi.org/10.1007/978-3-030-85521-5_36
15. Shaaban, A.M., Schmittner, C.: Threatget: new approach towards automotive security-by-design (2020)
16. Schmittner, C., Shaaban, A.M., Macher, G.: ThreatGet: ensuring the implementation of defense-in-depth strategy for IIoT based on IEC 62443. In: 2022 IEEE 5th International Conference on Industrial Cyber-Physical Systems (ICPS), pp. 1–6. IEEE (2022)
17. Chlup, S., Christl, K., Schmittner, C., Shaaban, A.M., Schauer, S., Latzenhofer, M.: THREATGET: towards automated attack tree analysis for automotive cybersecurity. Information **14**(1), 14 (2023)
18. Ma, Z., Schmittner, C.: Threat modeling for automotive security analysis. Adv. Sci. Technol. Lett. **139**, 333–339 (2016)
19. Protégé. Protégé Framework. https://protege.stanford.edu. Accessed 10 June 2023
20. Johardi. Cellfie (2018). https://github.com/protegeproject/cellfie-plugin. Accessed 10 June 2023
21. Shostack, A.: Threat Modeling: Designing for Security. Wiley, Hoboken (2014). OCLC: ocn855043351

Using Runtime Information of Controllers for Safe Adaptation at Runtime: A Process Mining Approach

Jorge Da Silva, Miren Illarramendi$^{(\boxtimes)}$, and Asier Iriarte

MGEP Mondragon Goi Eskola Politeknikoa S. Coop, Gipuzkoa, Spain
{jorge.dasilva,asier.iriarte}@alumni.mondragon.edu,
millarramendi@mondragon.edu

Abstract. The increasing complexity of current Software Systems is generating the urge to find new ways to check the correct functioning of models during runtime. Runtime verification helps ensure that a system is working as expected even after being deployed, essential when dealing with systems working in critical or autonomous scenarios. This paper presents an improvement to an existing tool, named CRESCO, linking it with another tool to enable performing periodical verification based on event logs. These logs help determine whether the functioning of the system is inadequate or not after the last periodic check. If the system is determined to be working incorrectly, new code files are automatically generated from the traces of the log file, so they can be replaced when a faulty scenario is to occur. Thanks to this improvement, the CRESCO components are able to evaluate their correctness and adapt themselves at runtime, making the system more robust against unforeseen faulty scenarios.

Keywords: Runtime adaptation · Process Mining · Runtime fault detection

1 Introduction

Testing, validation and adaptation of deployed software is an important necessity, due to the increasing complexity and variety of current Software Systems (SS). Given that the consequences of failure of these systems can turn into a catastrophe, ensuring that SS operation is always as expected is essential, especially for systems located in critical scenarios. If the functioning is not the expected one, it is also important to provide a method which helps the system return to its expected working flow.

One of them is verification, which is a dynamic analysis technique used to determine whether the running behaviour of a system satisfies a previously defined correctness property, as stated in [13]. It can be obtained by following a Model Driven Engineering (MDE) approach. The application of this technique is beneficial because it reduces the learning curve by designing systems

J. Guiochet et al. (Eds.): SAFECOMP 2023 Workshops, LNCS 14182, pp. 85–94, 2023.
https://doi.org/10.1007/978-3-031-40953-0_8

using graphical elements that directly link to a familiar domain. It also lets a broader range of subject experts to understand the system and ensure that it meets the needs of the user [30]. Different techniques for designing MDEs exist, among which Unified Modelling Language State-Machines (UML-SM) constitute a widely spread formalism.

However, MDE techniques need to be integrated into a runtime perspective. To achieve that, one of the possibilities consists on following runtime verification and adaptation according to the models@runtime approach. As long-running SSs used in critical scenarios need to safely adapt to the changes of their execution environment, it is usually inconvenient to take them offline to apply such changes, so these actions need to be done at runtime with the least human intervention possible [7,9].

In this paper, we present an approach to make a SS adapt automatically when failures are detected, avoiding malfunctioning and faulty scenarios. The main contribution provides the following benefits:

1. Automatic runtime adaptation is performed, thus when a failure is detected, there is no necessity for a developer to get involved to try solve the detected point of failure, providing the SS the capacity to run without supervision.
2. Adaptation is based on the previous functioning of the system: it will adapt to correct malfunctioning taking into account the previous valid executions.

The paper is organized as follows. Section 2 details the work's background. Section 3 details the work done during the study. In Sect. 4 the related work is presented. Finally, conclusions and future work are provided in Sect. 5.

2   Background

In this section, we will define some concepts that will help understand the work presented in this document.

One way to perform runtime verification is to observe the runtime information (traces) sent by the software controller to the externalized runtime checker/ adapter. Since correct traces will be finite and predefined in the checker/adapter, when the received trace is not defined as a correct one, the checker/adapter comes to a state that a Trace-Violation has been detected.

Runtime Adaptation is a technique prevalent to long-running, highly available software systems, whereby system characteristics (e.g., its structure, locality ...) are altered dynamically in response to runtime events (e.g., detected hardware faults or software bugs, changes in system loads), while causing limited disruption to the execution of the system [9].

In [15] is proposed an "externalized" runtime adaptation system that is composed of external components that monitors the behaviour of the software component of the running system. These external components are responsible for determining when a software component's behaviour is within the envelope of acceptable system parameters. When the software component's behaviour fall outside of the expected limits, the external components start the adaptation process. To accomplish these tasks, the externalized mechanisms maintain one or more system models, which provide an abstract, global view of the running system, and support reasoning about system problems and repairs. DevOps is a development methodology aimed at bridging the gap between Development and Operations. To do so, emphasis is established on different aspects, such as communication and collaboration, quality assurance, continuous integration and automatically deployed delivery [22]. As stated in [6], "DevOps is a set of practices intended to reduce the time between committing a change to a system and the change being placed into normal production, while ensuring high quality". The DevOps methodology was created as a counterpart to the V-Model, where the process is linear and, once finished, does not feedback itself. In DevOps, instead, the process is continuous, as it can be observed in Fig. 1.

Tests done during the development of SW are tasks of high importance. In DevOps, however, the tests are not only done in the development phase, but also in the operation phase. Monitoring is performed as well during this phase, verifying the correct functioning of the SW, i.e., runtime verification is used to ensure the correctness of the system. This last process makes it possible for a safe adaptation to be performed whenever an error is detected, i.e., a runtime adaptation is carried out to correct the error.

One way to perform runtime verification in DevOps is by observing the runtime information – also known as traces – sent by a software controller to an externalized runtime checker, obtaining two different SSs. Correct traces will be finite and predefined in the checker. Therefore, when the received trace is not correct, the checker will notify that a Trace-Violation has been detected.

Process mining is a technique oriented towards discovering, monitoring and improving real processes using the event logs recorded by information systems [33]. One of the many tools that allows to perform process mining is ProM, which is developed by the Eindhoven University of Technology [2]. The logs employed act as the foundation for finding valuable patterns using different methods, one of which is the Directly Follows Graph (DFG). As explained in [25], this type of graph can be derived from the log and represents which activity follows another one directly.

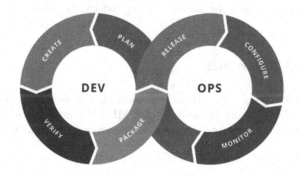

Fig. 1. Entire process of the DevOps methodology [21].

As mentioned earlier, adapting at runtime is an important part of the DevOps methodology. To provide a high-quality runtime adaptation, one of the possibilities is to use automatic code generation, which is a method centered around creating executable code by an executing process. This technique permits programs to create specialized instruction sequences based on the information obtained at runtime [12]. Embracing the usage of automatic code generation is significantly important, as it enables the code to optimize itself, obtaining better results than with only once compiled programs.

This work is based on [20]. In this work, a framework named CRESCO is used for the generation of reflective software components, which provide information regarding the internal status of UML-SM element-based components. These components communicate with a Runtime Safety Properties Checker (RSPC), which ensures that the observable actions to be taken by the CRESCOs are valid. If they are not, the CRESCO machines are warned.

In the implementation of this work, we have dockerized the framework to easily use it in different use cases (both CRESCO and the RSPC).

2.1 The CRESCO Framework

The CRESCO framework is the C++ implementation of the RESCO metamodel [19]. RESCO is a metamodel composed of two packages: (1) a design package oriented towards modeling the application-specific part and (2) a runtime package that enables a UML-SM based software component to reflect the model it comes from.

Any specific application is modeled using the design package and its main goal is to describe a State Machine (SM). A component named the Executor contains the implementation of the reactions that need to be triggered whenever an action occurs in the SM. Both the SM and the Executor components are generated automatically from the UML-SM model defined by the designer (i.e. by the Acceleo tool [1]).

The runtime part, which is generic for all components and applications created with RESCO, is modelled using the runtime package. It includes generic elements oriented towards providing runtime model observation capabilities. The runtime elements are used for implementing the execution semantics of state machines.

3 Proposed Approach

The aim of the following subsections is presenting the details of the process of periodically checking the correctness of the UML-SM components, as well as the steps to adapt their behaviour dynamically whenever an unexpected situation is addressed.

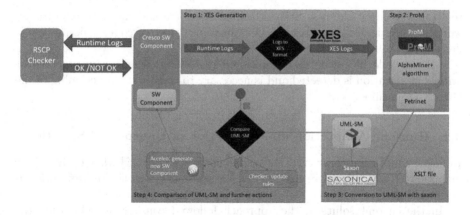

Fig. 2. Process for runtime adaptation of the CRESCO SS

3.1   Periodical Verification of the CRESCO Components

Figure 2 presents a graphical representation of the process and the tools involved
on it.

First, each CRESCO component periodically sends the log where the transitions performed by the component are stored to an external program. Then,
the log format is adapted to the one needed to import the information to ProM
(Extensible Event Stream (XES)), which is a standard defined for specifying, as
stated in [16].

The second step is performed using the ProM tool. The previously adapted
log is imported to this tool, and it transforms the logs to a PetriNet. Even if ProM
can generate more types of diagrams, some of those cannot be exported, or the
data displayed is not adequate to be used later. However, using the AlphaMiner+
algorithm to generate the PetriNet, it is possible to attain something similar to
a UML-SM with what the log represents. This is because the AlphaMiner+
algorithm is based on the directly follows graph (DFG). A DFG is a graph
where activities (nodes) and its directly-follows relationships (directed edges)
are represented.

This can be translated to UML-SMs, as the nodes and directly-follows relationships of the DFG will resemble the states and transitions of the UML-SMs,
respectively.

After the PetriNet has been generated, it is necessary to conduct a transformation, so a properly generated UML-SM is obtained. For that, a Extensible
Stylesheet Language Transformation (XSLT) file is created. The purpose of this
type of files is to enable the transformation of XML files into other XML files.
This was achieved with saxon [29].

The obtained UML-SM is then compared to the one currently running, to
ensure that the transitions between states remain the same. If a change in the
relations of the states of the UML-SM is detected, the Acceleo [1] tool is used to
generate the new files of code that will rule the CRESCO machine. The Acceleo

tool takes as input the new State Machine diagrame and the CRESCO framework, automatically generates the aforementioned files of code. This process is described in [19].

All the code files generated are stored to be used when an unexpected or erroneous situation is detected and is necessary to correct the functioning of the CRESCO machine.

3.2 Runtime Adaptation upon Detection of Unexpected Situations

Runtime adaptation constitutes a possible method to be used when ensuring the maintenance of a SS. Ensuring that the SS retain their continuous execution is essential.

In the current solution, the approach followed consists on rebuilding the CRESCO machines and the checker whenever an unexpected erroneous situation is detected. To do that, both the CRESCOs and the checker are replaced by the newly generated code files, which are stored in a folder. Afterward, the new deployment of the systems is activated and initialized from the point where the error was detected. This is to ensure that the flow of the CRESCO systems is continued through different executions.

3.3 Result

A video with an example has been prepared to show the process. The example is based on a Train Traction and Door controller (Fig. 3) and it can be found on https://github.com/millarramendi/Safecomp.git

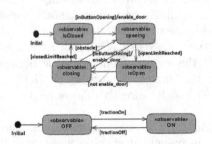

Fig. 3. Door and Traction UML-SM controllers

4 Related Work

Several other successful works exist in the frame of runtime adaptation. Thus, it is the goal of this section to briefly highlight the features of those works and their differences with the work presented in this paper.

Creating a runtime checker for checking system level safety properties is an important research problem. Existing approaches to runtime verification require specifications that not only define the property to monitor, but also contain details of the implementation, sometimes even requiring the implementation to add special variables or methods for monitoring [28], that is code instrumentation.

In [18], they defined a generic SW monitoring model and analyzed different existing monitors. Depending on the programming language used and the formalism used to express the properties, different implementations of monitors have been proposed [24], among others CoMA [5], RV-MONITOR [10] and AspectC++ [32], BEE++ [8], DN-Rover [11], HiFi [4] etc. The abstraction level of specification and monitoring of the above solutions is the same: specifications and the monitor's checking properties are at the component or class level.

One of the first works exploring the idea of generating monitors from a specification and developing a tool chain for it was the MaC (Monitoring and Checking) framework [23]. They presented a tool that uses the specification information to generate the checker. It is a debugging tool, designed to supplement testing. While the MaC framework showed the effectiveness of monitoring systems for compliance with specification, the framework's target was primarily for software systems with instrumented code, requiring modifications to the source code and making it unsuitable for usage in safety-critical embedded applications. In contrast to our approach, this framework is not isolated from the target system.

In the same direction, ConSerts [31] framework monitors the system's conformance with its certificates during execution. The solution is focused on the Safety Integrity Level (SIL) of the different components that are part of the system. This approach works at a system requirement level and not in detecting errors. In this regard, the approaches might be complementary to the present work.

ModelPlex [27], checks cyber-physical systems (CPSs) in model terms. It uses the KeYmaera proof engine to verify the safety of a CPS model, and generates monitors to check system traces for compliance with the model. It requires a high degree of user expertise both to write the original model in Dynamic Logic (the KeYmaera mathematical language) and to guide the proof engine towards a formal proof of the property. Our approach is a solution designed to check system level safety properties in model terms but without required expertise in formal methods.

LuMiNous [28] framework's target is the same area as the checker presented in this paper: system level specifications are checked by components' level information. The contribution of this framework relies on the translation of high-level specifications into runtime monitors but, in this case, their solution is for Java (AspectJ based solution), which is not suitable for embedded systems.

In [14], an idea is proposed to achieve fault tolerance in critical features of software functionalities of modern cars, using the Plug&Play technique to integrate new components in a Runtime Environment (RTE), which contains safety-related mechanisms like health monitoring.

The Plug&Play methodology explained in [14] is specifically designed to achieve correctness in critical systems thanks to its Electrics and Electronics (E/E) architecture, which provides built-in mechanisms to achieve fault tolerance. However, the main intention of the technology is to have the possibility to add new functionalities to a complex system (in this case a car).

In [26], a solution is proposed to tackle divide-by-zero and null-deference errors, where a component for *recovery shepherding* detects these errors and its further occurrences during the execution of a program and avoids them to ensure the correct functioning of the application even after the failure happened.

The proposed solution, however, only takes into account two errors, as the subsequent errors that are corrected are also of one of those types. Applying this methodology in a critical system could be dangerous, as the faulty scenario needs to be correctly analyzed and treated, and not only dodged, because otherwise the system could suffer unaffordable losses.

In [17], a lightweight solution to runtime error recovery is proposed, where the errors of interest are detected by the system, and then a copy of the state of the program before the buggy state is done, in order to check in a *sandbox-like* situation different solutions, picking the best of them to overcome the error.

Even though this solution provides an appropriate way to handle the errors generated during runtime, as the solution is only applied once (as this solution considers the context of the execution), this could lead to serious problems in critical scenarios, where faulty configurations need to be avoided the next time they happen without the need to redo the process again.

5   Conclusions and Future Work

The paper presents a periodical check process to verify the correctness of the UML-SM of a SS. In the case of detecting discrepancies between both UML-SMs, corrections of the currently running UML-SM are generated based on event logs, which are stored until a unexpected scenario happens. This adaptation is done on top of the CRESCO framework, which is designed to provide runtime observable components.

The main conclusion is that the defined methodology to adapt when a faulty scenario is detected is capable of maintaining the CRESCO machines working, retaining the expected functionality.

Another conclusion is that the process of periodically checking if the functioning of the CRESCO machine is correct based on the log of the UML-SM provides little overhead to the SS. This enables to effectively maintain a good response time, demonstrating that the method used is adequate for working in critical scenarios.

Some limitations in the process exist too. For example, as explained in [3], the naive use of DFGs may cause several problems:

- Possibility to lead to Spaghetti-like DFGs, generating loops even when activities are executed at most once.

– Information mapped onto DFGs can be misleading the average time reported between two activities as it needs to be taken into account that only the situations where they directly follow each other are considered.

Nevertheless, this limitation would be solved by selecting another algorithm that addresses the problems presented by DFGs, being adequate to be integrated into the process proposed.

In the future, we would like to evolve the method followed to achieve run-time adaptation, so that CRESCO software systems do not lose communication with their control system during run-time adaptation. This would make the solution much more realistic and suitable for efficient integration into CPS.

References

1. Acceleo. Technical report (2016). https://www.eclipse.org/acceleo/
2. Prom tools. Technical report (2020). https://www.promtools.org/doku.php
3. van der Aalst, W.M.: A practitioner's guide to process mining: limitations of the directly-follows graph (2019)
4. Al-Shaer, E.S.: A hierarchical filtering-based monitoring architecture for large-scale distributed systems. Old Dominion University (1998)
5. Arcaini, P., Gargantini, A., Riccobene, E.: CoMA: conformance monitoring of java programs by abstract state machines. In: Khurshid, S., Sen, K. (eds.) RV 2011. LNCS, vol. 7186, pp. 223–238. Springer, Heidelberg (2012). https://doi.org/10.1007/978-3-642-29860-8_17
6. Bass, L., Weber, I., Zhu, L.: DevOps: A Software Architect's Perspective. Addison-Wesley Professional (2015)
7. Blair, G., Bencomo, N., France, R.B.: Models@ run.time. Computer 42(10), 22–27 (2009). https://doi.org/10.1109/MC.2009.326
8. Bruegge, B., Gottschalk, T., Luo, B.: A framework for dynamic program analyzers. In: ACM SIGplan Notices, vol. 28, pp. 65–82. ACM (1993)
9. Cassar, I., Francalanza, A.: Runtime adaptation for actor systems. In: Bartocci, E., Majumdar, R. (eds.) RV 2015. LNCS, vol. 9333, pp. 38–54. Springer, Cham (2015). https://doi.org/10.1007/978-3-319-23820-3_3
10. Daian, P., Guth, D., Hathhorn, C., Li, Y., Pek, E., Saxena, M., Şerbănuţă, T.F., Roşu, G.: Runtime verification at work: a tutorial. In: Falcone, Y., Sánchez, C. (eds.) RV 2016. LNCS, vol. 10012, pp. 46–67. Springer, Cham (2016). https://doi.org/10.1007/978-3-319-46982-9_5
11. Diaz, M., Juanole, G., Courtiat, J.P.: Observer-a concept for formal on-line validation of distributed systems. IEEE Trans. Software Eng. 20(12), 900–913 (1994)
12. Engler, D.R., Proebsting, T.A.: DCG: an efficient, retargetable dynamic code generation system. ACM SIGPLAN Not. 29(11), 263–272 (1994)
13. Falcone, Y., Havelund, K., Reger, G.: A tutorial on runtime verification. Eng. Dependable Softw. Syst. 141–175 (2013)
14. Frtunikj, J., Rupanov, V., Camek, A., Buckl, C., Knoll, A.: A safety aware run-time environment for adaptive automotive control systems. In: Embedded Real-Time Software and Systems (ERTS2) (2014)
15. Garlan, D., Schmerl, B.: Model-based adaptation for self-healing systems. In: Proceedings of the First Workshop on Self-healing Systems, pp. 27–32. ACM (2002)

94   J. Da Silva et al.

16. Group, X.W.: IEEE standard for extensible event stream (XES) for achieving inter-operability in event logs and event streams. IEEE Std 1849-2016, pp. 1–50 (2016). https://doi.org/10.1109/IEEESTD.2016.7740858
17. Gu, T., Sun, C., Ma, X., Lü, J., Su, Z.: Automatic runtime recovery via error handler synthesis. In: 2016 31st IEEE/ACM International Conference on Automated Software Engineering (ASE), pp. 684–695. IEEE (2016)
18. Guo, C.G., Zhu, J., Li, X.L.: A generic software monitoring model and feature analysis. J. Softw. **6**(3), 395–403 (2011)
19. Illarramendi, M., Etxeberria, L., Elkorobarrutia, X., Sagardui, G.: Runtime observable and adaptable UML state machines: models@ run. time approach. In: Proceedings of the 34th ACM/SIGAPP Symposium on Applied Computing, pp. 1818–1827. ACM (2019)
20. Illarramendi, M., Etxeberria, L., Larrinaga, F., Sagardui, G.: Cresco framework and checker: automatic generation of reflective UML state machine's C++ code and checker. In: 2020 IEEE International Symposium on Software Reliability Engineering Workshops (ISSREW), pp. 25–30. IEEE (2020)
21. Industriees, B.: Devops (2021). https://www.bigindustries.be/blog/6-proven-steps-to-become-a-devops-engineer. Accessed 10 May 2023
22. Jabbari, R., bin Ali, N., Petersen, K., Tanveer, B.: What is devops? A systematic mapping study on definitions and practices. In: Proceedings of the Scientific Workshop Proceedings of XP2016, pp. 1–11 (2016)
23. Kim, M., Viswanathan, M., Kannan, S., Lee, I., Sokolsky, O.: Java-MaC: a runtime assurance approach for java programs. Formal Methods Syst. Design **24**(2), 129–155 (2004)
24. Laboratory, F.S.: Monitoring oriented programming. http://fsl.cs.illinois.edu/index.php/MOP
25. Leemans, S.J., Fahland, D., Van der Aalst, W.M.: Scalable process discovery and conformance checking. Softw. Syst. Model. **17**(2), 599–631 (2018)
26. Long, F., Sidiroglou-Douskos, S., Rinard, M.: Automatic runtime error repair and containment via recovery shepherding. ACM SIGPLAN Not. **49**(6), 227–238 (2014)
27. Mitsch, S., Platzer, A.: ModelPlex: verified runtime validation of verified cyberphysical system models. Formal Methods Syst. Design **49**(1–2), 33–74 (2016)
28. Pezzé, M., Wuttke, J.: Model-driven generation of runtime checks for system properties. Int. J. Softw. Tools Technol. Transf. **18**(1), 1–19 (2016). https://doi.org/10.1007/s10009-014-0325-2
29. Saxonica: Developers of the saxon processor for XSLT, XQuery, and XML schema, including the only XSLT 3.0 conformant toolset (2022)
30. Schmidt, D.C.: Model-driven engineering. Comput.-IEEE Comput. Soc. **39**(2), 25 (2006)
31. Schneider, D., Trapp, M.: A safety engineering framework for open adaptive systems. In: 2011 Fifth IEEE International Conference on Self-Adaptive and Self-Organizing Systems (SASO), pp. 89–98. IEEE (2011)
32. Spinczyk, O., Gal, A., Schröder-Preikschat, W.: AspectC++: an aspect-oriented extension to the C++ programming language. In: Proceedings of the Fortieth International Conference on Tools Pacific: Objects for Internet, Mobile and Embedded Applications, pp. 53–60. Australian Computer Society, Inc. (2002)
33. Van Der Aalst, W.: Process mining. Commun. ACM **55**(8), 76–83 (2012)

Safety and Robustness for Deep Neural Networks: An Automotive Use Case

Davide Bacciu[1], Antonio Carta[1(✉)] [iD], Claudio Gallicchio[1] [iD], and Christoph Schmittner[2]

[1] Department of Computer Science, University of Pisa, Pisa, PI, Italy
{davide.bacciu,antonio.carta,claudio.gallicchio}@unipi.it
[2] Austrian Institute of Technology, Vienna, Austria
christoph.schmittner@ait.ac.at

Abstract. Current automotive safety standards are cautious when it comes to utilizing deep neural networks in safety-critical scenarios due to concerns regarding robustness to noise, domain drift, and uncertainty quantification. In this paper, we propose a scenario where a neural network adjusts the automated driving style to reduce user stress. In this scenario, only certain actions are safety-critical, allowing for greater control over the model's behavior. To demonstrate how safety can be addressed, we propose a mechanism based on robustness quantification and a fallback plan. This approach enables the model to minimize user stress in safe conditions while avoiding unsafe actions in uncertain scenarios. By exploring this use case, we hope to inspire discussions around identifying safety-critical scenarios and approaches where neural networks can be safely utilized. We see this also as a potential contribution to the development of new standards and best practices for the usage of AI in safety-critical scenarios. The work done here is a result of the TEACHING project, an European research project around the safe, secure and trustworthy usage of AI.

Keywords: recurrent neural networks · adversarial robustness · human-in-the-loop · automotive · dependability

1 Introduction

The rapid advancements in artificial intelligence (AI) and machine learning (ML) have enabled the development of sophisticated deep neural networks (DNNs) that can perform complex tasks with great accuracy. However, the use of DNNs in safety-critical applications, such as autonomous driving, is still a topic of debate. While DNNs have shown great promise in improving the safety and efficiency of automotive systems, their usage in safety-critical scenarios remains a concern due to the difficulty in ensuring robustness to noise, domain drift, and uncertainty quantification.

This research was supported by TEACHING, a project funded by the EU Horizon 2020 research and innovation programme under GA n. 871385.

J. Guiochet et al. (Eds.): SAFECOMP 2023 Workshops, LNCS 14182, pp. 95–107, 2023.
https://doi.org/10.1007/978-3-031-40953-0_9

Currently, automotive safety standards recommend avoiding the use of DNNs in safety-critical scenarios, given the potential risks associated with their usage. We argue that there are scenarios where DNNs can be used safely, provided that their actions are restricted and monitored. In this paper, we present a scenario where a DNN is used to adapt the driving style to minimize the user's stress. In this scenario, only certain actions of the DNN are safety-critical, allowing for greater control over the model's behavior.

To ensure the safety of the DNN, we propose a mechanism based on robustness quantification and a fallback plan. This ensures that the DNN can minimize user stress in safe conditions while avoiding unsafe actions in uncertain scenarios. By exploring this use case, we hope to inspire discussions around identifying safety-critical scenarios where DNNs can be safely utilized. This could influence the development of new standards and best practices for the usage of AI in safety-critical automotive applications.

The objectives of the paper are:

1. We show that current standards suggest to avoid the use of DNNs (Technology class III) in safety-critical scenarios;
2. we argue that DNN can be used in scenarios where there is a minimal safety risk (Usage Level C) and the model can be easily restricted to a subset of safe actions;
3. we describe a Level C use case which uses recurrent networks where we quantify the adversarial robustness and ensure safety by restricting the actions in any unsafe setting.

The work presented here was done in TEACHING, short for "A computing Toolkit for building Efficient Autonomous appliCations leveraging Humanistic INtelliGence". TEACHING is an European Union-funded research project aimed at designing a comprehensive computing platform and associated software toolkit. This platform and toolkit are intended to support the development and deployment of autonomous, adaptive, and dependable Cyber-Physical Systems of Systems (CPSoS) applications. The project focuses on enabling these applications to leverage sustainable human feedback to drive, optimize, and personalize the provisioning of their services.

The TEACHING project revolves around four key concepts:

- Distributed Edge-oriented and Federated Computational Environment: The project aims to create an integrated computational environment that seamlessly combines heterogeneous resources, including specialized edge devices, general-purpose nodes, and cloud resources. One important aspect is the utilization of edge devices equipped with specialized hardware to execute AI, cybersecurity, and dependability components of autonomous applications.
- Runtime Dependability Assurance of CPSoS: TEACHING focuses on developing methods and tools to ensure runtime dependability assurance for CPSoS. This includes the establishment of systematic engineering processes for designing both conventional and AI-based runtime adaptive systems. These approaches will be applied in both cloud and edge environments to

guarantee continuous assurance throughout the software life cycle, incorporating AI methodologies tailored towards a cognitive security framework.

- Software-level Abstraction of the Computing System: The project aims to realize a software-level abstraction of the computing system, enabling the easy and coordinated deployment of different application components onto suitable CPSoS resources. This concept also involves orchestrating application components to optimize resource efficiency, minimize energy consumption, and meet the dependability requirements of the application.
- Synergistic Human-CPSoS Cooperation: TEACHING emphasizes the collaboration between humans and CPSoS in the spirit of Humanistic Intelligence. It explores AI methodologies and continuous monitoring of human physiological, emotional, and cognitive (PEC) states to facilitate applications with unprecedented levels of autonomy and flexibility. This collaboration maintains the required dependability standards for safety-critical systems operating with humans in the loop.

By focusing on these four main concepts, the TEACHING project aims to advance the development and deployment of efficient and dependable autonomous applications within CPSoS, while leveraging humanistic intelligence and ensuring safety-critical operations.

In Sect. 2, we will describe the current automotive standards with a focus on recommendations regarding safety and AI. Section 3.4 provides an overview of the deep neural network literature relevant for our system. Both sections cover the relevant state of the art, from a standardization and technical point of view. In Sect. 3 we describe our scenario in more detail, discuss the challenges associated with using DNNs in safety-critical scenarios, and propose our mechanism for ensuring the safety of the DNN. Finally, we discuss the potential implications of our work and how it could contribute to the development of safer and more efficient automotive systems (Sect. 4).

2   Automotive Standards for Dependability

Functional safety standards for automotive applications (road vehicles) are in the focus of ISO TC22 SC32, WG08. This group has created the basic functional safety standard for road vehicles, ISO 26262 (Ed.2, not considering nominal performance issues; now preparing for Ed 3, also including new technologies like AI and SotiF-related issues) and ISO 21448 SotiF, Safety of the intended Functionality, considering uncertainties of environment and functional insufficiencies impacting even vehicles safety fulfilling ISO 26262 functional safety requirements). Automated Driving Systems safety is handled in TR 4804, which is published as "Safety and cybersecurity for automated driving systems - Design, verification and validation" and will be superseded by TS 5083, "Safety for automated driving systems". The following figure shows the interrelationships between these standards (Fig. 1). These standards focus on dependability for road vehicles considering also the impact of AI systems integrated and nominal performance issues caused by functional insufficiencies. In the TEACHING project, the safe functioning of the ADS is assumed. The ASIL safety integrity levels include also as part of the assessment the controllability by the driver, The role of the human is also part of some of the trustworthiness standards which development recently started, e.g., like ISO/IEC PWI 18966: Artificial Intelligence (AI) - (human) Oversight of AI systems, and other human-related or ethics and governance related standards. In automated driving, when, particularly in case of an identified failure during operation or if the vehicle leaves the ODD (Operational Design Domain) for which it was designed (due to an unexpected mismatch of environment or situational conditions), the ADS has to request a takeover to the driver or passenger, the human reaction will become safety-relevant. How this has to be taken into account when assessing the functional safety of the AI system monitoring human health and awareness (alertness) conditions will be discussed during our presentation of the scenario.

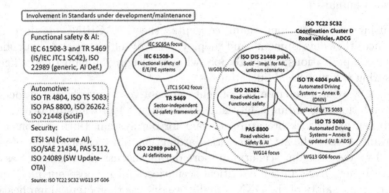

Fig. 1. Automotive standardization landscape on functional safety and AI (source: ISO TC22/SC32 WG13).

2.1   Current AI Standards Recommendations on Robustness and Functional Safety

ISO and IEC created a Joint Technical Committee (JTC1) aiming for harmonized standardization in the AI-sector. The ISO/IEC JTC1 SC42 Standardization Committee for "Artificial Intelligence" has published already 17 ISO/IEC standards under its own responsibility and is developing (in different stages of development) 30 new standards. The most important WG is WG03, Trustworthiness. ISO/IEC JTC1 SC42, WG03, "Trustworthiness", started together in cooperation with the maintenance team of IEC 61508-3, the basic functional safety standard, SW part, to develop TR 5469 "Functional safety and AI systems". The approach taken, in short, was to classify AI technology classes and usage classes. The following figure tries to map these and provide recommendations:

AI Technology Classes

Class I developed and reviewed using existing functional safety methods and standards.

Class II cannot be fully developed and reviewed using existing functional safety methods and standards, but it is still possible to identify a set of available methods and techniques satisfying the properties (e.g., additional V&V). to achieve the necessary risk reduction

Class III cannot be developed and reviewed using existing functional safety methods and international functional safety standards and it is also not possible to identify a set of available methods and techniques satisfying the functional safety properties.

AI Application and Usage Classes

A1. Used in safety relevant E/E/PE system and automated decision making possible.

A2. Used in safety relevant E/E/PE system and no automated decision making (e.g., for uncritical diagnostics). B1: Used to develop safety relevant E/E/PE systems (offline support tool). Automated decision making of developed function is possible.

B2. Used to develop safety relevant E/E/PE systems (offline support tool). No automated decision making of the developed function is possible.

C. AI technology is not part of a safety function in the E/E/PE system. Has potential indirect impact on safety (e.g., increase demand placed on a safety system).

D. AI technology is not part of a functional safety function in the E/E/PE system, but can have indirect impact on the function (e.g., increase demand placed on a safety system).

3 Automotive Use Case

In this section, we describe the use case. It is a use case where a module of the system continuously predicts the stress of the user. The prediction is made via a pre-trained Recurrent Neural Network [7], which is a deep neural network designed to process time series.

In this use case, the system continuously monitors the stress of the users. In safe condition, it tries to minimize the user's stress by controlling the driver profile. For example, some users may become more stressed because the current driving style is too slow, while others may be stressed due to the high acceleration and speeds. An adaptive model learn the user's preference and adaptive the driving profile for them automatically.

The user's stress is also monitored to control the activation of some driving profiles. In some settings, the profile may only be allowed if the user is ready to take action in case of emergency (ISO TS 5083). If the user is deemed too stressed, some of the driving profiles may be temporarily disabled until the stress

AI Technology Class => AI application and usage level	AI technology Class I	AI technology Class II	AI technology Class III
Usage Level A1 (1)	Application of risk reduction concepts of existing functional safety International Standards possible	Appropriate set of requirements (3)	At the time of writing this document no appropriate set of properties with related methods and techniques is known to achieve sufficiently reduction of risk
Usage Level A2 (1)		Appropriate set of requirements (3)	
Usage Level B1 (1)		Appropriate set of requirements (3)	
Usage Level B2 (1)		Appropriate set of requirements (3)	
Usage Level C (1)		Appropriate set of requirements (3)	
Usage Level D (2)	No specific functional safety requirements for AI technology, but application of risk reduction concepts of existing functional safety International Standards		

1 Static (offline) (during development) teaching or learning only

2 Dynamic (online) teaching or learning possible

3 The appropriate set of requirements for each usage level can be established by application of risk reduction concepts of existing functional safety International Standards and additional consideration of Clauses 8, 9, 10 and 11 of this document. Examples are provided in Annex B. Defining detailed requirements for each usage level is beyond the Scope of this document.

Fig. 2. Recommendations for usage of AI technology classes in certain usage levels. (Source: DTR 5469, which is already in an advanced stage).

level is reduced. Notice that the stress is monitored only for the purpose of the automated driving system. The user can always disable the system and take over the control of the car. This is in accordance with the German Ethics guidelines, which state that the driver should always be allowed to take over the automated systems (Fig. 2).

3.1 Use Case Description

In the scenario, the user is a passenger in a car driven by an autonomous driving system. The driving system supports different driving styles, such as a relaxed mode and a sport mode. We assume that the relax mode is fully autonomous. In contrast, the sport mode may have restrictions, such as geofencing some areas where the user must take the wheel, or allowing usage in some settings only if the user is awake, alert, and unstressed. The system monitors the passenger stress level and selects the driving mode that maximizes the user's comfort and minimizes stress with an adaptive model. As a result, there is a continuous interaction between the human passenger and the autonomous system.

Overall, the system is made of four components that interact in a closed loop:

Passenger. The passenger is part of the system because its stress is a result of the surrounding environment, such as the car temperature, its speed, or the traffic. The passenger also produces outputs, its physiological data, that is used by the rest of the system to inform the autonomous decisions, possibly resulting in a change in the driving style. In case fitness and alertness are required (see take-over case as explained before) this data may be also safety-relevant.

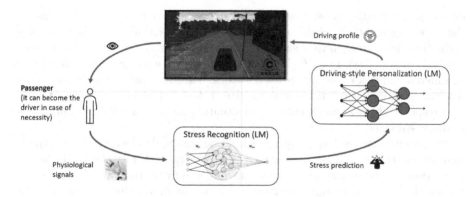

Fig. 3. Stress recognition use case.

Stress prediction. The physiological data of the passenger, such as electrodermal activity and heart rate, are continuously monitored via sensors. These signals are fed as input to a *stress prediction module*, a Recurrent Neural Network (RNN) module that predicts the *stress of the passenger* given its physiological data. The output of this module is a time series of the stress predictions.

Driving style personalization. The driving style personalization is a module that takes as input the stress predictions and the environmental data (state of the car and input from its sensors) and determines whether the driving style must be changed or not. The driving style model is a deep neural network.

Autonomous driving system. Finally, a change in the autonomous driving system changes the state of the car (e.g. its speed) and as a result affects the stress of the user, closing the interaction loop.

A diagram of the entire system is shown in Fig. 3.

3.2   Usage Level C and Deep Neural Networks

An initial analysis of the use case shows that the application class (driver monitoring, but not controlling the automated vehicle) is Usage Level D, which is uncritical from the viewpoint of the automated vehicle's behaviour and safety. In ISO TS 5083, "Automated Driving Systems", an evolving standard, there is a subgroup E10 ("Post deployment phase") that addresses the deployment and operation phase. In this subgroup, it is stated that in the event of a failure of the Automated Driving System (ADS) or when the Operational Design Domain (ODD) for which the vehicle was designed is exceeded, there may be a requirement to include the driver, passenger, or remote operator interaction. This scenario is comparable to the situation of an airline passenger seated next to the emergency exit. In the event of an emergency, this passenger is required to take certain actions. Therefore, it is necessary to inquire if the passenger is physically capable of fulfilling this responsibility. If the passenger is unable to do so, an alternative passenger will need to occupy that seat. In this case, a risk of wrong detection of drivers/passengers fitness and alertness because of a high-stress level may have a safety impact. This case has to be studied separately, being of Usage Level C. In this case, appropriate requirements have to be considered and risk reduction measures taken. This may include strong signaling if within a defined short timeframe the driver does not react properly by taking over respectively the vehicle changes to situation-based degraded motion modes as discussed later.

If the autonomous driving system would be able to drive everywhere without limitations, this would be a Usage Level D use case. A mistake in the stress prediction or driving style personalization models may result in a higher stress for the user but it will not cause safety-critical issues, assuming that the autonomous driving system is a safe component.

However, due to law and safety regulations, there may be many requirements that would limit the usage of the autonomous system and therefore result in a Usage Level C use case, which requires a more attentive design in the two predictive models.

For example, there are some situations where the passenger or user of a vehicle or transportation system must be prepared to take action in case of an emergency. In these instances, it is essential that the passenger remains alert and ready to assume control of the vehicle or perform certain actions, such as opening emergency doors, if necessary. Suppose that the self-driving system is fully autonomous when driving at slower speeds, but may require the user's help in certain situations when driving at faster speeds. For instance, a sport driving mode may be available in certain areas only if the user remains alert, relaxed, and firmly grasping the steering wheel, prepared to take over control of the vehicle if an emergency arises.

In this scenario, the stress and driving style modules are part of a safety-critical system because the stress prediction module must determine if the user is too stressed and therefore the sport mode should be disabled. Conversely, the driving style module must never allow a driving style that is forbidden in the current setting.

This is a Usage Level C because activating the sport mode even if the user is stressed will increase the demand on the safety system. The same is valid for the cases mentioned before when alertness is required (TS 5083, post-deployment phase): fitness to react properly is endangered if the stress level had become too high and no proper action had been taken.

3.3   Stress Module Robustness

In this section, we focus on the problem of assessing the robustness of the stress predictor. As a robustness measure, we would like to quantify the robustness of the model to perturbations of the input specifically crafted to break it. These are the worst-case perturbations and can be measures via adversarial robustness [12] methods.

The stress prediction model takes as input a sequence of sensor measurements $x(1), \ldots, x(t)$, where $\mathbf{x}(t) \in \mathbb{R}^{N_X} \in \mathbb{R}^{N_H}$, where we denote as $\mathbf{x}^t$ the current measurement. The chosen model for the stress predictor is a Recurrent Neural Network (RNN), which is a model that keeps an internatl state $\mathbf{h}(t) \in \mathbb{R}^{N_H}$ and updates it at each timestep as

$$\mathbf{h}(t) = \tanh\left(\mathbf{W}_{in}\mathbf{x}(t) + \hat{\mathbf{W}}\mathbf{h}(t-1)\right), \tag{1}$$

where $\mathbf{W}_{in} \in \mathbb{R}^{N_H \times N_X}$ is the input-to-recurrent parameter matrix, and $\hat{\mathbf{W}} \in \mathbb{R}^{N_H \times N_H}$ the recurrent matrix. We omit biases from the previous and the following equations to simplify the notation. The stress predictor outputs $\mathbf{y}(t) \in \mathbb{R}^{N_Y}$ with a linear layer on top of the hidden state as

$$\mathbf{y}(t) = \mathbf{W}\mathbf{h}(t), \tag{2}$$

where $\mathbf{W} \in \mathbb{R}^{N_Y \times N_H}$ is a hidden-to-output matrix. The network can be trained end-to-end via backpropagation-through-time. Alternatively, we can initialize the RNN parameters separately and train only the final classifier, which can be trained with a closed-form equation. This approach is known as reservoir computing [10]. An interesting consequence of partial training is that we could initialize the RNN parameters to improve its adversarial robustness. This an open question and a promising research direction.

Adversarial Robustness Quantification. There are several methods to computed adversarial robustness bounds, such as POPQORN [12] and CertRNN [6]. Given a reference dataset of sequences $\mathbf{X} = \{\mathbf{x_0}, \ldots, \mathbf{x_n}\}$, a model F and its predictions on the reference dataset $\mathbf{Y} = \{\mathbf{y_0}, \ldots, \mathbf{y_n}\}$ and an l_p ball with radius ϵ, robustness quantification methods provide an upper and lower bound for the RNN's output for each sequence in $\mathbf{X}$ when subject to noise with radius ϵ. Therefore, given a target accuracy, we can find the maximum perturbation ϵ that achieves the target accuracy. We can use methods such as POPQORN to quantify the robustness of our trained model before deployment. This functionality is implemented in a learning module of the TEACHING platform [2]. According to ISO/IEC TR 24029-1:2021 definition, POPQORN is an empirical method.

The resulting method requires three parameters, each of which is critical for safety:

trained model. The architecture of the model, its hyperparameters, training algorithm, and training data all affect the robustness of the method.

reference dataset. The robustness quantification is an empirical method that relies on a curated dataset. Particular care must be taken to ensure that the dataset is as extensive as possible.

required accuracy. Any amount of noise will result in a accuracy drop. Therefore, there must be a minimal required accuracy that must be guaranteed by the model even for the largest amount of noise.

Automotive standards and best practices should inform the creation of the dataset. The largest amount of operating conditions, such as types of roads, countries, weather conditions, must be represented in the dataset to ensure robustness in any given setting. The reference dataset is a test dataset used only for evaluation. To guarantee a fair evaluation, it must not be used during any step of the model training, such as the hyperparameter selection or preprocessing (e.g. computing normalization constants), or feature selection. If the reference dataset is used in any capacity, the resulting robustness bounds will be an overestimate of the actual robustness on new data.

Finally, every application must define a target accuracy. Given that we use a machine learning model, we cannot expect perfect accuracy, and we expect the accuracy for large perturbations to be even lower. The application must guarantee safety even when using an imperfect model, up to a certain target accuracy. The models can also be made more robust by ensembling different models.

The robustness quantification assesses whether the system accuracy is adequate and robust, and therefore deemed safe for each specific operating condition. For example, a system may be certified only in some specific settings, such as specific city zones, weather conditions, or road types. The system may fail to certify in specific conditions either due to lack of reference data, target accuracy, or target robustness. The fallback system ensures safety even in these scenarios.

Fallback System. An interesting property of our use case is that only some of the choices are safety-critical (i.e., the sport mode under some specific conditions). As a result, it is always possible to make the model safer by excluding the safety-critical choices from the possible actions. This results effectively in a conversion of our Level C use case into a Level D, where no choice would result in harm to the user. A fallback mechanism can be used, where the safety-critical choices are possible only for the samples that are deemed close enough to the regions of interest where the network reaches the target accuracy. In case of uncertainty, the safety-critical choices can always be disabled to ensure the safety of the system even when an unsafe model is used.

Overall, the robustness quantification and fallback system work together to ensure safety. If the system detects a known and safe operating condition it enables all the driving modes, reverting to safe choices in unknown and unsafe scenarios. Detection of unsafe conditions can be measure offline via robustness quantification and implemented online by explicitly enabling the safe conditions with simple signals, e.g. via geofencing. Be default, an unknown operating condition is deemed unsafe, restricting the usage to the safe driving modes.

3.4 Related Work on Adversarial Robustness for Deep Neural Networks

It is well known that deep neural networks are susceptible to adversarial attacks [4]. An adversarial example is an input that has been modified to fool the DNN to make an incorrect classification by adding a small amount of well-crafted noise. To the human eye, an adversarial example is often indistinguishable from the original data.

Adversarial attacks are a practical issue that strongly limits the deployment of DNN in autonomous vehicles. [13] shows that it is possible to add a sticker to an object, such as a road signals, such that the object will be consistently misclassified by the DNN classifier. There are also universal attacks which are able to make the DNN fail on all possible objects. For example, [13] shows that you can place a sticker over a camera to misclassify all the objects of a certain class. Such attacks are known as universal perturbations.

[1] identifies the problem of obfuscated gradients.

Adversarial training consists in the training of a network with the original and adversarial examples during training. By training on adversarial examples directly, the model can become more robust to adversarial noise. [3] provides a taxonomy and a review of existing methods.

While many work propose defenses to improve adversarial robustness, most are quickly broken by new attacks or due to weaknesses in their defense evaluation [4].

[5] shows that unlabeled data can be used to significantly improve adversarial robustness in semisupervised learning.

While most work on adversarial examples focuses on images, our scenario uses Recurrent Neural Networks (RNNs) to process time series. POPQORN is a certification methods that allow to estimate robustness bounds for RNN models such as the Long Short-Term Memory (LSTM) [11]. More recently, CertRNN proposed a general framework for certifying the robustness of RNNs, providing an exact formula for the computation of bounding planes [6]. The computation results in a tighter bound that outperforms POPQORN.

Research on adversarial robustness is still very active, and it is an open question whether it is possible to fully fix robustness issues. [9] establishes fundamental limits on the robustness of some classifiers in terms of a distinguishability measure between the classes. Unlike previous works, [15] claims that it is possible to train robust and accurate models. The paper shows that regular adversarial examples leave the manifold, even though on-manifold adversarial examples exist, and they correspond to generalization errors. As a result, increasing the accuracy will increase the robustness and the two objectives are not necessarily contradicting goals. [8] proposes contrastive learning through the lens of robustness enhancement and proposes AdvCL, an adversarial contrastive pretraining framework which enhances cross-task robustness transferability. [14] introduce a novel regularizer that encourages the loss to behave linearly in the vicinity of the training data, thereby penalizing gradient obfuscation while encouraging robustness.

4   Conclusion

In this paper, we describe an automotive use case with a human in the loop, as studied by the TEACHING project. This is a usage level C use case that can be solved using recurrent neural networks. However, current standards prevent the usage of deep neural networks for level C use cases, except when appropriate mitigation measures are taken. We argue that our use case provides an example where neural networks can be applied, and encourage more discussion on the topic. In particular, technical solutions need to be developed to address both the robustness quantification, uncertainty estimation, and the development of fallback mechanisms. Extremely conservative fallback mechanisms can already be used today, but there is a need for more effective solutions. On the other hand, regulatory bodies and standards commitees must explore the consequences of the usage of neural networks in level C use cases, with a particular focus on the specification of robustness and accuracy targets, the curation of reference datasets, and best practices to develop effective fallback mechanisms.

References

1. Athalye, A., Carlini, N., Wagner, D.: Obfuscated Gradients Give a False Sense of Security: Circumventing Defenses to Adversarial Examples (2018). https://doi.org/10.48550/arXiv.1802.00420
2. Bacciu, D., et al.: TEACHING - trustworthy autonomous cyber-physical applications through human-centred intelligence. In: 2021 IEEE International Conference on Omni-Layer Intelligent Systems (COINS), pp. 1–6 (2021). https://doi.org/10.1109/COINS51742.2021.9524099
3. Bai, T., Luo, J., Zhao, J., Wen, B., Wang, Q.: Recent Advances in Adversarial Training for Adversarial Robustness (2021). https://doi.org/10.48550/arXiv.2102.01356
4. Carlini, N., et al.: On Evaluating Adversarial Robustness (2019). https://doi.org/10.48550/arXiv.1902.06705
5. Carmon, Y., Raghunathan, A., Schmidt, L., Duchi, J.C., Liang, P.S.: Unlabeled data improves adversarial robustness. In: Advances in Neural Information Processing Systems, vol. 32. Curran Associates, Inc. (2019)
6. Du, T., et al.: Cert-RNN: Towards Certifying the Robustness of Recurrent Neural Networks, South Korea, p. 19 (2021)
7. Elman, J.L.: Finding structure in time. Cogn. Sci. **14**(2), 179–211 (1990)
8. Fan, L., Liu, S., Chen, P.Y., Zhang, G., Gan, C.: When does contrastive learning preserve adversarial robustness from pretraining to finetuning? In: Advances in Neural Information Processing Systems, vol. 34, pp. 21480–21492. Curran Associates, Inc. (2021)
9. Fawzi, A., Fawzi, O., Frossard, P.: Fundamental limits on adversarial robustness
10. Gallicchio, C., Micheli, A., Pedrelli, L.: Deep reservoir computing: a critical experimental analysis. Neurocomputing **268**, 87–99 (2017). https://doi.org/10.1016/J.NEUCOM.2016.12.089
11. Hochreiter, S., Schmidhuber, J.: Long short-term memory. Neural Comput. **9**(8), 1–32 (1997). https://doi.org/10.1144/GSL.MEM.1999.018.01.02
12. Ko, C.Y., Lyu, Z., Weng, L., Daniel, L., Wong, N., Lin, D.: POPQORN: quantifying robustness of recurrent neural networks. In: Proceedings of the 36th International Conference on Machine Learning, pp. 3468–3477. PMLR (2019)
13. Li, J., Schmidt, F.R., Kolter, J.Z.: Adversarial camera stickers: a physical camera-based attack on deep learning systems. arXiv:1904.00759 [cs, stat] (2019)

14. Qin, C., et al.: Adversarial robustness through local linearization. In: Advances in Neural Information Processing Systems, vol. 32. Curran Associates, Inc. (2019)
15. Stutz, D., Hein, M., Schiele, B.: Disentangling adversarial robustness and generalization. In: Proceedings of the IEEE/CVF Conference on Computer Vision and Pattern Recognition, pp. 6976–6987 (2019)

Towards Dependable Integration Concepts for AI-Based Systems

Georg Macher[(⊠)], Romana Blazevic, Omar Veledar, and Eugen Brenner

Graz University of Technology, Graz, Austria
{georg.macher,romana.blazevic,omar.veledar,brenner}@tugraz.at

Abstract. AI-based methods are currently on the rise for multiple applications, therefore also their application for autonomous or trustworthy embedded systems is discussed more frequently.

There are various ways that can leverage AI-based technologies, but since AI has the potential to affect the key system properties of trustworthy embedded systems, a far higher level of maturity and dependability is required for the implementation of emerging AI-based technologies in safety-critical domains (such as an autonomous vehicle).

The TEACHING project focuses on mission-critical, energy-sensitive autonomous systems and the development of technology bricks for humanistic AI concepts. To enhance the development of the technology bricks, the building of a dependable engineering environment to support the development of a self-adaptive artificial humanistic intelligence in a dependable manner is intended.

The paper establishes the body of knowledge and fundamental ground for a workshop discussion on engineering methods and design patterns that can be used to develop dependable and AI-based autonomous system development.

The assurance of dependability continues to be an open issue with no common solution yet. Therefore, the expert discussion on multiple perspectives related to all factors of the PESTEL analysis (political, environmental, social, technological, economic, and legal) should provide an updated common view of the diverse fields of expertise and exchange between domain experts during the workshop.

Keywords: AI · dependable systems · CPSoS · dependability

1 Introduction

Dependability engineering of adaptive, cloud-based and/or AI-based systems is a topic for which common grounds and best practices are yet established. First concepts and agreeable approaches still need to be instantiated [16].

Therefore, this work focuses on triggering a workshop and open discussion on engineering methods and design patterns that can be used to develop dependable

Supported by the H2020 project *TEACHING* (n. 871385) - www.teaching-h2020.eu.

J. Guiochet et al. (Eds.): SAFECOMP 2023 Workshops, LNCS 14182, pp. 108–117, 2023.
https://doi.org/10.1007/978-3-031-40953-0_10

and AI-based autonomous system development. Engineering methods and design patterns that support the development of dependable AI-based autonomous systems shall be discussed, as well as other factors of the PESTEL analysis of AI-based trustworthy embedded systems development.

The related body of knowledge origins from the TEACHING project and considers dependable architectural concepts and dependability engineering concepts for their applicability to different scenarios of evolving AI-based Cyber-Physical Systems of Systems (CPSoS) in the automotive domain [2]. The paper shines the light on the current state of practice and provides a fundamental ground for a workshop discussion on engineering methods and design patterns that can be used to develop dependable and AI-based autonomous system development [15].

The intention is to trigger an expert discussion on multiple perspectives related to all factors of the PESTEL analysis (political, environmental, social, technological, economic, and legal) to update the common view of the diverse involved fields of expertise and exchange between domain experts.

The intention of the workshop is to discuss the different factors of AI-based trustworthy embedded systems development and cover a comprehensive set of methods, tools, and engineering approaches to establish trust in these novel systems. AI-based concepts raise new challenges through the embracing of non-deterministic components and their no strict correctness characteristics. With currently established engineering concepts, the necessary development evidence and standard compliance measures can not be achieved. Therefore, several questions arise concerning dependability and standard compliance, including process and technical engineering aspects.

For dependable system integration, in most cases, an assumption of deterministic function assures always the same output for a given input and a possible prediction and determining of the system behaviour under all considered circumstances during development time. This assumption is the basis for the construction of state-of-the-art assurance argumentation based on evidence for appropriate process engineering.

But with AI-based systems, the traditional processes and engineering approaches can no longer guarantee this system behaviour under all considered circumstances. Even more to consider, it is not possible to state the necessary requirements and pledge their correct implementation by evidence that would be needed for appropriate safety assurance.

The TEACHING project focuses on autonomous applications running in distributed and highly heterogeneous environments with AI-based concepts. The results are exploited in the automotive and avionics domains, which both pose an autonomous challenge with high dependability needs for these systems.

To structure the way of thinking for the workshop, the discussion could be aligned around four central conceptual approaches from the TEACHING project to ensure dependability features (e.g., safety or security) of AI-based systems. Table 1 provides an overview of the concepts and intention.

Aside from this structuring, the workshop further focuses on the automotive sector, which is confronted by the main trends related to technology, legal,

Table 1. Overview of concepts and main intentions

	Concept	Main Intention
I	support of operator	human is supported by AI-based system and takes decisions, traditional safety measures may guarantee system safety, system operation not autonomously, but operator takes decisions
II	selection between policies	policy-based decision-making ensures deterministic system behaviour, traditional safety measures may apply, but only restricted AI algorithm capabilities due to finite set of policies
III	AI-based system with monitoring	AI decisions are compared with classic supervisor system, monitor may meet classic safety requirements, AI limited by monitor functionalities, two nearly equally sophisticated systems needed
IV	AI to enhance system dependability	conventional system works without AI intervention, AI acts as a monitor for the system to increases reliability, AI must understand normal vs. abnormal behaviour of system

and societal challenges, nevertheless, the other factors of the PESTEL analysis should be considered and discussed. In the following sections, initial inputs to the current state of the PESTEL factors will be given.

2 PESTEL Analysis of Dependability of AI-Based Systems

In this section, an initial analysis of the PESTEL factors (political, economic, sociological, technological, legal and environmental) of AI-based CPSoS for dependability application is given to support the expert workshop discussion.

The PESTEL analysis is a strategic framework for assessing the business environment of a given context. The primary influencing factors are examined, which also include the political, economic, sociological, technological, legal, and environmental spheres. This analysis can be applied in a variety of situations to direct making strategic decisions or analyse the given context in a structured manner.

2.1 Political Influences on Dependable AI-Based Systems

Political influences on the engineering of AI-based dependable embedded systems are mainly related to regulations and policies regulating the use of such systems.

Governments are increasingly recognizing the importance of AI-based embedded systems and are enacting regulations and policies to govern their development and deployment. Regulations cover areas such as data privacy, security, algorithmic transparency, accountability, and ethical considerations [30]. More information is to be followed in the standardization overview section.

Additional influencing factors are related to funding and investment, where the European Union puts high priorities and allocate resources to support the development of these specific types of systems. These investments naturally accelerate advancements and drive engineering efforts in these areas.

2.2 Economic Influences on Dependable AI-Based Systems

Current information.

AI-based and embedded systems have been experiencing continuous and significant growth due to increasing demand and adoption across various industries [25]. The attractiveness and market potential of AI-based embedded systems have attracted investments and supported innovation in many industries [1]. Nevertheless, the dependability of these systems is yet rather a road blocker in this endeavour.

Funding has been directed towards startups, research and development, infrastructure, and talent acquisition, but yet the economic risks for autonomous AI-based systems have rarely been taken.

An additional economic impact to consider, is the creation of new or changed job and Workforce skills. While automation and AI adoption create new job opportunities in development, system integration, and data analysis, the upskilling and reskilling of the workforce have to be an important consideration [24].

2.3 Sociological Influences on Dependable AI-Based Systems

Sociological factors reflect the broader impact of technologies on society and encompass various dimensions. One of the most important influences here is the perception of trust in AI-based systems [3,4]. Political debates and public discourse around AI's ethical and societal implications can majorly influence the adaptation of AI-based system approaches. Societal factors play a significant role in shaping the uptake and acceptance of AI-based embedded systems.

Ethical considerations and concerns surrounding AI and embedded systems are additional influences on the engineering of these systems. Issues, such as algorithmic bias, transparency, fairness, and accountability are critical to be aligned and agreed [13].

Additionally, AI-based embedded systems often rely on large amounts of data, which implies raising concerns about privacy and data protection. Societal expectations in the European context for the securing and privacy of personal information are having a huge impact on data collection and usage. Therefore, compliance with data protection regulations and privacy-preserving techniques are essential building blocks. Digital equality and accessibility, as well as, cultural and social norms can majorly shape the deployment and usage of AI-based embedded systems.

2.4 Technological Influences on Dependable AI-Based Systems

Technological influence factors will be detailed in a separate section of this paper, but shall be mentioned here too for completeness reasons. These factors encompass the technical aspects that influence the development, design, and deployment of these systems.

Here, the selection and development of AI algorithms and models have a significant impact on the performance and capabilities of embedded systems [5]. Consider factors shall include accuracy, efficiency, scalability, interpretability, and adaptability when choosing or designing AI algorithms. The advancing of AI-based algorithms is massively shaped by hardware and computing Infrastructure, data collection and processing features, and connectivity and Communication possibilities. For dependable embedded systems, real-time constraints and dependability features (such as security and safety) are essential [17].

Furthermore, software engineering and development practices shape modular design, code quality, software testing, debugging, version control, and documentation, and thus enable a broader acceptance and uptake [23]. Engineers therefore shall ensure interoperability with other devices, platforms, or services in the ecosystem to further support the acceptance.

2.5 Legal Influences on Dependable AI-Based Systems

Political and legal influence factors, which will be related to standardization and legislation activities [21], will be detailed in a separate section of this paper.

Legal influences on dependable AI-based systems are significant not only due to governance and regulatory actions, but also frameworks such as the European Union's General Data Protection Regulation (GDPR) and similar rules for the collection, storage, and use of personal data are crucial legal factors. Additionally, issues related to liability and accountability for AI-based systems, and intellectual property (IP) considerations are important in AI-based systems.

2.6 Environmental Influences on Dependable AI-Based Systems

Environmental influences on the dependability of AI-based embedded systems are in this context not related to the physical or surrounding conditions in which these systems operate.

Although maybe also be exposed to various harsh environments, this part of the analysis shall focus on sustainability and its impact on the environment. Modern computation systems shall be designed to minimize energy consumption, utilize eco-friendly materials, consider minimal ecological footprint, and the potential consequences throughout their lifecycle.

In this context, AI-based systems challenge key aspects like energy efficiency, environmentally friendly materials, usage of rare earth, and e-waste management. E-waste, generated from the disposal of electronic devices, poses significant environmental challenges. For AI-based embedded systems, e-waste considerations may also include data centres and their efficiency, as well as the carbon footprint of training data (often involving extensive computational resources and rework iterations).

3 Regulation and Standardization Activities

In this section, regulations and domain activities are briefly summarized and given as an overview for discussion. In general, standards represent the agreed state of the art within a particular domain. They are not legally binding but offer the agreed design and development practices. This synopsis shall trigger discussions related to resulting challenges for dependable AI-based embedded systems.

The legal basis for type approval is provided by the United Nations Economic Commission for Europe ('UNECE') [28], which European manufacturers need to comply with. The UNECE Regulations contain (a) administrative procedures, (b) performance-oriented test requirements, (c) conformity of production, and (d) mutual recognition of type approvals. The regulations related to the automotive sector come from UNECE world forum for harmonisation of vehicle regulations (WP.29)[1].

The most prominent automotive standards that shall always be considered are: (a) ISO 26262 [7] intended for the functional safety of embedded automotive systems, (b) ISO 21448 [12] related to the safety of the intended functionality (SotIF), and (c) ISO SAE 21434 [9] considering cybersecurity engineering. Additionally, ISO DTR 4804 - Road Vehicles, Safety and cyber-security for Automated Driving Systems Design, Verification and Validation [8] provides recommendations and guidance steps for developing and validating automated driving systems.

UNECE WP.29 released an informal document (WP.29-175-21) about artificial intelligence and vehicle regulation, focusing on (a) HMI enhancements for infotainment and (b) development of self-driving functionalities.

Additionally, the European Commission has been actively studying AI and its impact on citizens' lives [25]. The high-level expert group involved released a set of guidelines for AI-based systems and a concept to create a unique 'ecosystem of trust'. The proposed framework defines a risk-based approach which clearly differentiates between the different AI applications and the related risk involved by the system.

For high-risk AI-based systems, the high-level requirements that shall be assessed for conformity and compliance are:

- Training data should be sufficiently broad and cover all relevant safety scenarios

---

[1] https://unece.org/wp29-introduction.

- Data and record-keeping, data related to potentially problematic actions or decisions by AI systems should be traced back and verified
- Clear information must be provided as to the AI system's capabilities and limitations
- Robustness and accuracy of AI systems shall be reproducible; adequately dealing with errors or inconsistencies during all life cycle phases; AI systems shall be resilient; mitigating measures shall be taken
- Human oversight shall ensure that the output of the AI system does not become effective unless it has been previously reviewed and validated by a human
- Other specific requirements for certain particular AI applications

The ISO PAS 8800 [10] has the objective to provide industry-specific guidance on the use of safety-related Artificial Intelligence/Machine Learning (AI/ML)-based functions in road vehicles. It will address any gaps in ISO 26262 specifically related to the safe implementation of AI components and support processes of development and validation of AI-based functions. The document is built upon guidance contained within ISO/IEC CD TR 5469 - Artificial Intelligence—Functional Safety and AI systems (still under development) [11], maintaining consistency with it when possible.

4   Technological Factors and Research Activities

The conflicting effects of privacy, safety, and security are becoming more dominant in many domains, including automotive. To ensure safety, vehicles need to exchange information and work with available data. For security reasons, certain mechanisms need to enable verification and ensure data integrity, which also implies dismissal or mistrust in certain information. For privacy, anonymity is preferable, and data exchange for tracking and profiling reasons shall be generally avoided or reduced. Therefore, the automotive industry faces a few unique challenges for transforming research results into standards and economical productions while integrating safety and security [22].

Data-driven engineering (DDE) seems to be a promising approach for AI software development, focusing on data quality, preparation, training, testing, and validation of the AI-based system in its operational design domain (ODD) [19]. AI software development requires additional development considerations, focusing on which data set is used in different phases. However, achieving sufficient data quality is a non-trivial task. There should be a use-case-oriented gathering of data. In this context, a strong enabler of DDE could be the concept of a digital twin, entailing information, models, and data from all phases of the lifecycle [27].

Another technical concept is related to explainable AI (XAI). Transparent and understandable decision-making of AI-based systems shall improve the dependability and trust of an AI-based system in this context [18]. Currently, there is no standard and generally accepted definition of explainable AI. Actually, the XAI term tends to refer to the movement, initiatives, and efforts made in response to AI transparency and trust concerns, more than to a formal technical concept. Tocchetti et al. [26] summarize human-centred perspectives on challenges and opportunities in this context.

Besides these publications, several survey and overview papers [6,14,20,23] provide perspectives and descriptions of the AI and safety landscape [5]. However, there is no common approach to protect the systems against wrong decisions and possible harm to the environment, determination of safety measures for AI-based systems or generic pattern for the AI-based system applications.

For dependable system integration, different challenges apply to deterministic and non-deterministic functions. When integrating a deterministic function, it can be assured that the function will always produce the same output for a given input. Therefore, it is possible to design a system for which the system behaviour can be predicted and determined under all considered circumstances. This assumption is the basis for the construction of sufficiently safe products and state-of-the-art safety argumentation based on evidence for appropriate process engineering during design, development, implementation, and testing.

On the other hand, non-deterministic functions deliver different outputs to the same inputs at different runs. Therefore, it is not possible with traditional processes and engineering approaches to design a system that predicts the system's behaviour under all considered circumstances.

Finally, the concept of resilience engineering shall also be mentioned in this context. Resilience Engineering (RE) focuses on establishing systems that can manage occurring issues during the operation time and coping with them in a dependable manner [29]. Therefore, resilience is balancing between the stability of the system and adaptation to change needed by the given context. Additionally, it is also related to the ability to return to normal operation after experiencing unusual conditions.

5   Outlook for the Workshop

The ongoing rise of AI-based methods across various applications has sparked discussions about their integration also into autonomous and trustworthy embedded systems. The unique characteristics of AI, however, have prompted questions about the dependability and maturity needed to apply these technologies in safety-critical sectors. In response, the TEACHING project concentrates on creating technological building blocks for concepts of humanistic AI in mission-critical autonomous systems.

The discussion will centre on the PESTEL analysis provided, which examines political, environmental, social, technological, economic, and legal factors. This analysis will facilitate an updated common view on engineering methods and concepts suitable for the development of dependable and AI-based autonomous systems.

This article lays the groundwork for an expert workshop where business leaders, academics, and decision-makers may join together to create the future of dependable AI-based autonomous systems. By addressing the challenges and exploring potential solutions, to pave the way for the development of trustworthy and resilient systems that embrace the transformative power of AI while upholding the highest standards of dependability.

Acknowledgments. The presented work is partially supported by TEACHING, a project funded by the EU Horizon 2020 research and innovation programme under GA n.871385.

References

1. Armengaud, E., Peischl, B., Priller, P., Veledar, O.: Automotive meets ICT—enabling the shift of value creation supported by European R&D. In: Langheim, J. (ed.) Electronic Components and Systems for Automotive Applications. Lecture Notes in Mobility, pp. 45–55. Springer, Cham (2019). https://doi.org/10.1007/978-3-030-14156-1_4
2. Bacciu, D., et al.: Teaching – trustworthy autonomous cyber-physical applications through human-centred intelligence (2021)
3. Clement, P., Danzinger, H., Veledar, O., Koenczoel, C., Macher, G., Eichberger, A.: Measuring trust in automated driving using a multi-level approach to human factors (2021)
4. Clement, P., et al.: Enhancing acceptance and trust in automated driving trough virtual experience on a driving simulator. Energies 15(3), 781 (2022)
5. Hernández-Orallo, J.: AI safety landscape from short-term specific system engineering to long-term artificial general intelligence. In: 2020 50th Annual IEEE/IFIP International Conference on Dependable Systems and Networks Workshops (2020)
6. Hinrichs, T., Buth, B.: Can AI-based components be part of dependable systems? In: 2020 IEEE Intelligent Vehicles Symposium (IV), pp. 226–231 (2020)
7. ISO - International Organization for Standardization. ISO 26262 Road vehicles Functional Safety Part 1–10 (2011)
8. ISO - International Organization for Standardization. ISO/TR 4804:2020 Road vehicles—Safety and cybersecurity for automated driving systems—Design, verification and validation (2020)
9. ISO - International Organization for Standardization. ISO/SAE 21434 Road Vehicles - Cybersecurity engineering (2021)
10. ISO - International Organization for Standardization. ISO/AWI PAS 8800 Road Vehicles—Safety and artificial intelligence, work-in-progress
11. ISO - International Organization for Standardization. ISO/IEC CD TR 5469 Artificial intelligence—Functional safety and AI systems, work-in-progress
12. ISO - International Organization for Standardization. ISO/WD PAS 21448 Road vehicles - Safety of the intended functionality, work-in-progress
13. Leslie, D.: Understanding artificial intelligence ethics and safety: a guide for the responsible design and implementation of AI systems in the public sector (2019)
14. Ma, Y., Wang, Z., Yang, H., Yang, L.: Artificial intelligence applications in the development of autonomous vehicles: a survey. IEEE/CAA J. Autom. Sinica 7(2), 315–329 (2020)
15. Macher, G., et al.: Dependable integration concepts for human-centric AI-based systems. In: Habli, I., Sujan, M., Gerasimou, S., Schoitsch, E., Bitsch, F. (eds.) SAFECOMP 2021. LNCS, vol. 12853, pp. 11–23. Springer, Cham (2021). https://doi.org/10.1007/978-3-030-83906-2_1

16. Macher, G., Diwold, K., Veledar, O., Armengaud, E., Römer, K.: The quest for infrastructures and engineering methods enabling highly dynamic autonomous systems. In: Walker, A., O'Connor, R.V., Messnarz, R. (eds.) EuroSPI 2019. CCIS, vol. 1060, pp. 15–27. Springer, Cham (2019). https://doi.org/10.1007/978-3-030-28005-5_2

17. Macher, G., Seidl, M., Dzambic, M., Dobaj, J.: Architectural patterns for integrating AI technology into safety-critical systems. In: 26th European Conference on Pattern Languages of Programs, EuroPLoP 2021. Association for Computing Machinery, New York (2022)

18. Nanda, V., Speicher, T., Dickerson, J.P., Gummadi, K.P., Zafar, M.B.: Unifying model explainability and robustness via machine-checkable concepts (2020)

19. Petersen, P., et al.: Towards a data engineering process in data-driven systems engineering. In: 2022 IEEE International Symposium on Systems Engineering (ISSE) (2022)

20. Houben, S., et al.: Inspect, understand, overcome: A survey of practical methods for AI safety. CoRR, abs/2104.14235 (2021)

21. Schmittner, C., Macher, G.: Automotive cybersecurity standards - relation and overview. In: Romanovsky, A., Troubitsyna, E., Gashi, I., Schoitsch, E., Bitsch, F. (eds.) SAFECOMP 2019. LNCS, vol. 11699, pp. 153–165. Springer, Cham (2019). https://doi.org/10.1007/978-3-030-26250-1_12

22. Schoitsch, E., Schmittner, C., Ma, Z., Gruber, T.: The need for safety and cybersecurity co-engineering and standardization for highly automated automotive vehicles. In: Schulze, T., Müller, B., Meyer, G. (eds.) Advanced Microsystems for Automotive Applications 2015. Lecture Notes in Mobility, pp. 251–261. Springer, Cham (2016)

23. Martínez-Fernández, S., et al.: Software engineering for AI-based systems: a survey. CoRR, abs/2105.01984 (2021)

24. Stolfa, J., et al.: Automotive engineering skills and job roles of the future? In: Yilmaz, M., Niemann, J., Clarke, P., Messnarz, R. (eds.) EuroSPI 2020. CCIS, vol. 1251, pp. 352–369. Springer, Cham (2020). https://doi.org/10.1007/978-3-030-56441-4_26

25. The European Commission. White Paper on Artificial Intelligence: a European approach to excellence and trust. European Commission (2020)

26. Tocchetti, A., et al.: A.I. robustness: a human-centered perspective on technological challenges and opportunities (2022)

27. Trauer, J., Schweigert-Recksiek, S., Onuma, L., Spreitzer, K., Mörtl, M., Zimmermann, M.: Data-driven engineering - definitions and insights from an industrial case study for a new approach in technical product development (2020)

28. UNECE. Task force on Cyber Security and (OTA) software updates (CS/OTA). https://wiki.unece.org/pages/viewpage.action?pageId=40829521. Accessed 07 Sept 2019

29. Veitch, E., AndreasAlsos, O.: A systematic review of human-AI interaction in autonomous ship systems. Saf. Sci. **152**, 105778 (2022)

30. Veledar, O., et al.: Steering drivers of change: maximising benefits of trustworthy IoT. In: Yilmaz, M., Clarke, P., Messnarz, R., Reiner, M. (eds.) EuroSPI 2021. CCIS, vol. 1442, pp. 663–674. Springer, Cham (2021). https://doi.org/10.1007/978-3-030-85521-5_45

10th International Workshop on Next Generation of System Assurance Approaches for Critical Systems (SASSUR 2023)

10th International Workshop on Next Generation of System Assurance Approaches for Critical Systems (SASSUR 2023)

Jose Luis de la Vara[1] and Barbara Gallina[2]

[1] Department of Computing Systems, Universidad de Castilla-La Mancha, Albacete, Spain
`joseluis.delavara@uclm.es`
[2] Division of Computer Science and Software Engineering, Mälardalen University, Västerås, Sweden
`barbara.gallina@mdu.se`

1 Introduction

System assurance and certification are amongst the most expensive and time-consuming tasks in the development of critical systems, e.g., safety-critical, security-critical, privacy-critical, explainability-critical, mission-critical, and business-critical ones. Assurance and certification of critical systems require the execution of complex and labour-intensive activities, such as the management of compliance with hundreds or thousands of criteria defined in standards, the management of a large volume of assurance evidence artefacts, or the provision of convincing and valid justifications that a system is dependable. Therefore, the companies developing critical systems or components, as well as the companies assessing them, need approaches that facilitate these activities and ideally increase their efficiency. The challenges arising from system assurance and certification are further growing as a result of the technological advancements of critical systems, such as new connectivity, autonomy, adaptation, and learning features.

Since 2012, the SASSUR workshop has been intended to explore new ideas on assurance and certification of critical systems. It provides a forum for thematic presentations and in-depth discussions about specification, analysis, reuse, composition, and combination of compliance criteria, assurance arguments, assurance evidence, and contextual information about critical products and processes, in a way that makes assurance and certification more cost-effective, precise, and scalable. SASSUR aims at bringing together experts, researchers, and practitioners from diverse communities, such as safety, privacy, and security engineering, the recently coined explainability engineering, certification processes, model-based engineering, software and hardware design, and application communities (transport, healthcare, industrial automation, robotics, nuclear, defence, etc.).

2 This Year's Workshop

The program of SASSUR 2023 consists of three high-quality papers (in alphabetical order):

- A Methodology for the Qualification of Operating Systems and Hypervisors for the deployment in IoT devices, *by Irene Bicchierai, Enrico Schiavone, Massimiliano Leone Itria and Lorenzo Falai*
- Computer-Aided Generation of Assurance Cases, *by Timothy E. Wang, Chanwook Oh, Matthew Low, Isaac Amundson, Zamira Daw, Alessandro Pinto, Massimiliano L. Chiodo, Guoqiang Wang, Saqib Hasan, Ryan Melville and Pierluigi Nuzzo*
- RACK: A Semantic Model and Triplestore for Curation of Assurance Case Evidence, *by Abha Moitra, Paul Cuddihy, Kit Siu, David Archer, Eric Mertens, Daiel Russell, Kevin Quick, Valentin Robert and Baoluo Meng*

We hope that all the authors and participants will benefit from the workshop, enjoy the workshop, and join us again in the future!

Acknowledgements. We are grateful to the SAFECOMP organization committee and collaborators for their support in arranging SASSUR, especially to Erwin Schoitsch and Matthieu Roy as Workshop Chairs and to Friedemann Bitsch as Publication Chair. We also thank all the authors of the submitted papers for their interest in the workshop, and the program committee for its work. Finally, the workshop is supported by the 4DASafeOps (Sweden's Software Center), ET4CQPPAJ (Sweden's Software Center), iRel4.0 (H2020-ECSEL ref. 876659; MCIN/AEI ref. PCI2020-112240; NextGen.EU/PRTR), REBECCA (HORIZON-KDT ref. 101097224; MCIN/AEI ref. PCI2022-135043-2; NextGen.EU/PRTR), VALU3S (H2020-ECSEL ref. 876852; MCIN/AEI ref. PCI2020-112001; NextGen.EU/ PRTR), and ETHEREAL (MCIN/AEI ref. PID2020-115220RB-C21; ERDF) projects, and by the Ramon y Cajal Program (MCIN/AEI ref. RYC-2017-22836; ESF).

Organization

Workshop Committees

Organization Committee

Jose Luis de la Vara   Universidad de Castilla-La Mancha, Spain
Barbara Gallina   Mälardalen University, Sweden

Programme Committee

Morayo Adedjouma	CEA LIST, France
Clara Ayora	University of Castilla-La Mancha, Spain
Fabien Belmonte	Alstom, France
Markus Borg	CodeScene, Sweden
Carmen Cârlan	Edge Case Research, Germany
John Favaro	Intecs, Italy
Brahim Hamid	IRIT - University of Toulouse, France
Jason Jaskolka	Carleton University, Canada
Garazi Juez	BMW, Germany
Georg Macher	Graz University of Technology, Austria
Johnny Marques	Aeronautics Institute of Technology (ITA), Brazil
Thor Myklebust	SINTEF, Norway
Nuria Quintano	Tecnalia, Spain
Philippa Ryan Conmy	University of York, UK
Christoph Schmittner	Austrian Institute of Technology (AIT), Austria
Irfan Šljivo	National Aeronautics and Space Administration (NASA), USA
Fredrik Warg	Research Institutes of Sweden (RISE), Sweden
Marc Zeller	Siemens, Germany

A Methodology for the Qualification of Operating Systems and Hypervisors for the Deployment in IoT Devices

Irene Bicchierai[✉] ⓘ, Enrico Schiavone ⓘ, Massimiliano Leone Itria,
Andrea Bondavalli ⓘ, and Lorenzo Falai

ResilTech S.R.L., Pontedera, PI, Italy
{irene.bicchierai,enrico.schiavone,massimiliano.itria,
andrea.bondavalli,lorenzo.falai}@resiltech.com

Abstract. In an increasingly interconnected world, where critical infrastructures strongly depend on software applications there is the need to rely on software with demonstrated guarantees of reliability, availability, safety and security. Above all, Operating Systems (OSs) used in critical contexts must have specific characteristics to ensure the correct functioning of software applications and to protect from accidental and malicious failures that could lead to catastrophic consequences. To ensure a secure application layer, applications must run on OSs that possess specific properties, adequate quality and high robustness.

This paper presents an OS qualification methodology, which helps designers to select an operating system (or hypervisor) suitable for being employed in a specific critical context. The methodology includes quality, safety, and security evaluations, according to the desired OS properties and the specific context of use. For each evaluation, the procedure is described through the application of different standards (e. g. ISO/IEC 25040, EN50128, ISO26262, ISO/IEC 15408, etc.), thus considering all the necessary aspects with respect to today's technical and regulatory needs. Finally, an application of the qualifying methodology is presented, showing the safety and security evaluation of a Xen Hypervisor integrated in a railway infrastructure.

Keywords: Software Qualification · Operating Systems · Hypervisors · Safety · Security · Quality

1 Introduction

Managing resilience of critical systems [1] such as railway systems, automotive systems, power plants, health management systems, defense systems, requires the adoption of extremely reliable processes, technologies, systems and sensors. Some application areas require electronic systems based on wireless technology, sensors, real-time video images, cloud computing and machine-to-machine communications. In these scenarios, Internet

---

Enrico Schiavone is actually with ALSTOM Ferroviaria S.p.A.

J. Guiochet et al. (Eds.): SAFECOMP 2023 Workshops, LNCS 14182, pp. 123–134, 2023.
https://doi.org/10.1007/978-3-031-40953-0_11

of Things (IoT) systems [3] take on particular relevance, due to its diffusion. The term IoT refers to the process of connecting, through Internet, devices such as medical devices, smart meters for energy distribution, sensors in critical infrastructure, aircraft control systems, and so on.

Design of IoT critical systems has to face multiple issues that depend on software system and hardware on which the software operates. Indeed, in critical systems, software and hardware are closely related as the choice of a software as an Operating System (OS) implies the adoption of a particular hardware and vice versa. In addition, it is not enough that the software at the application level is robust to ensure system protection, but applications must in turn be managed correctly by a reliable OS. In critical contexts, the concepts of safety and security are also strongly correlated, because security vulnerabilities can have severe consequences in terms of safety. Indeed, the railway standard EN 50129 [2] recognizes security threats as safety hazards. This means that all aspects security of OSs should be taken into consideration for designing safety-critical systems. Given their wide diffusion in IoT systems, also Hypervisors (HVs), (i.e., systems capable of virtualizing OSs on a single machine) must be considered together with the OSs thanks to their particular security-oriented architecture.

This paper defines a methodology for OSs and HVs qualification for being applied in IoT critical context. The work is organized as follows: in Sect. 2 a landscape of existing methodologies for qualifying OSs is traced. Some of the referenced works are not specifically aimed to OSs, but they are applicable to OSs being applicable in general to software. Then, Sect. 3.1 introduces software qualification and software standards that guide software development. The specific application domain and emergent IoT technology for facing issues in critical systems are described in Sects. 3.2 and 3.3. Section 4 describes the OS qualification methodology, Sect. 5 reports the application of the methodology to the evaluation of a Xen Hypervisor integrated in a railway infrastructure, and finally Sect. 6 draws conclusions and future works.

2 Related Work

In recent years, various research projects have addressed issues of software qualification and certification, proposing various solutions to optimize verification and validation activities in different domains. The AMBER project [4] examined railway software standards in order to indicate how the aspects of assessing reliability and resilience are addressed in the standards.

The CEMSIS project [5], referring in particular to the domain of nuclear energy, proposes different cost-effective approaches and techniques to demonstrate that a given safety instrumented system containing Commercial Off The Shelf (COTS) products, not specifically designed for industry nuclear, is suitable for supporting safety-important functions. The projects cited above [4, 5] does not address specifically OSs, but software in general.

OSs are addressed instead in [6], in which a methodology is proposed to isolate safety-related services or programs from COTS OSs failures through design and detection techniques. [6] considers the IEC 61508 [25], DO-178B [24] and CENELEC EN50128 [11] safety standards. A further study [7] has conducted to evaluate the level of security and integrity of the Linux OS in railway context. [7]concludes that Linux would, in general terms, be suitable for many safety-related applications and that its safety certification may be possible.

Another interesting work is [8], although a bit outdated today because it dates back to 2001. It examines the practical methods available for assessing the integrity level of COTS-based systems with the IEC 61508 standard. The authors of [8] explain the benefits and the disadvantages of techniques such as: stress tests (i.e., verification of system or application performance in conditions that exceed the threshold of the level used by load tests), statistical tests (black-box methods) or the use of tools for static code analysis, data flow analysis and fault injection (white-box methods). In [8] the limitations of these methods are presented, namely: the lack of data on failures that the manufacturer reserves the right to provide, the difficulty in calculating the test results without automated mechanisms, the problem of optimizing tests that take time, the difficulty of covering a wide range of software errors. Furthermore, the authors of [8] propose a hybrid approach for the safety certification of a system based on COTS that combines analytical modeling and measurements. A modeling step is first used to identify the components that represent safety issues in the COTS software. A mitigation strategy is proposed for these components, which is then validated in an experimental phase conducted on the real system.

3 Introduction to Software Qualification

A software product can be certified according to a specific standard if it is possible to rigorously document its compliance with the given standard. In European safety critical contexts (e.g., railway, industry, automotive, energy...) standard certifications are required by current legislation. Unlike certification, software qualification is instead a more streamlined process that disregards governance aspects, but provides proof that a software is suitable to perform its task correctly in the environment in which it is intended. Software qualification is based on guidelines provided by software standards.

3.1 Software Standards

Software standards represent a guide for development throughout the software product lifecycle. Many standards for software quality, safety and security, have been analysed with the aim to select and adopt the main suitable concepts for the OS/HV qualification methodology described in the next section. For brevity, only the software standard adopted are mentioned herein.

Software quality refers to the extent to which a software meets a certain number of expectations with respect to its functioning and internal structure. The quality standard considered for the qualification methodology is the ISO/IEC 25000 [10] standard family, also known as SQuaRE (System and Software Quality Requirements and Evaluation). It aims to create a framework for evaluating the quality of the software product.

Regarding safety, standards are aimed at guiding the development and subsequent activities of a software and hardware product, guaranteeing the required safety levels. Each standard refers to its own product life cycle model which includes design, risk analysis, installation, maintenance, dismantling and disposal. Verifying the compliance of a software with a precise standard for safety means carrying out a set of evaluation actions of all phases of the life cycle, proving that these phases have been managed as recommended by the standard.

Among many safety standards available for various sectors, the methodology proposed in this paper adopts three different standards for addressing three different sectors (i.e., railway, automotive, general industrial systems). The European safety standard EN 50128 [11] has been chosen for addressing railway domain. Regarding the automotive sector, the methodology is based on the ISO 26262 [12] that is an international standard for the functional safety of electrical and/or electronic (E/E) systems for automobiles. ISO 26262 uses a series of steps to regulate product development at the system, hardware and software level. Finally, the IEC 61508 [25] standard has been followed for general applications in industrial sectors. This covers the functional safety of systems using electrical, electronic and programmable electronic technologies (E/E/PE). Finally, for security aspects, the methodology is based on ISO/IEC 15408 [13] Common Criteria (CC) standard for the certification of the security of IT products, which allows to compare the results of product security assessments.

3.2   The Application Domain

The application domains comprise all the application areas that require a new type of in-vehicle and ground-based electronic systems based on wireless technology, sensors, real-time video images, cloud computing and machine-to-machine communications. Among them, we report the example of railway and automotive domain.

In the railway domain, recent services use driverless trains equipped with remote monitoring of speed and braking through automated signals, such as the access rolling stock data remotely system [14]. Other systems are able to monitor the operation of automatic doors (e.g., the Siemens [15] system) or control air conditioning (e.g., Toshiba [16]). In Netherlands, rail operators are already monitoring the number of passengers to control to the occupation of platforms and train stations [17]. In other cases, sensors installed on the wheels and brakes of a train can detect abnormal vibrations and prevent accidents, while sensors in the railway infrastructure allow to detect changes in temperature, weather conditions and even natural disasters such as earthquakes [18].

In the automotive sector, IoT technologies are now highly widespread. They include, for example, GPS communication of modern vehicles, automatic emergency calls in case of accident, virtual cockpit and infotainment in cars. In this context, the use of Real Time Operating Systems (RTOS) and HV systems can improve the level of safety and security by isolating safety-related applications from non-safety-related ones.

3.3   Applicability of the Qualification Methodology

The OS/HV qualification methodology has been designed to be applicable in any domain. In particular the railway and automotive domains have been considered, but it is possible to consider other domains by referring to the procedure based on IEC 61508. The qualification methodology is applicable to both COTS OS/HV, including Ready to

Use Software Product (RUSP), as well as open-source ones. It consists of three fundamental procedures, whose task is to evaluate three fundamental attributes respectively: quality, safety and security. Each procedure is carried out by the evaluator, who has the information and documents necessary for carrying out the required verification and validation activities. Some of this information is often provided by the OS/HV manufacturer (e.g., OS/HV functionalities, security functions, hardware requirements, software requirements and library dependencies, user manual).

4   Methodology for OS and Hypervisor Qualification

The first step of the proposed methodology consists in examining the characteristics of the application domain and producing a plan for the OS/HV qualification called Qualification Plan. This plan defines the sequence of the steps to be performed. The steps depend on the need for safety, quality or security of the specific context. As shown in Fig. 1, if safety is required, the safety evaluation procedure has to be performed, if not, the quality evaluation procedure has to be performed. If security is required, the security evaluation procedure has to be carried on. If neither safety nor security are required, only the quality evaluation procedure is performed. The Qualification Plan therefore defines which procedures must be performed, why and in what order.

In safety critical contexts, demonstrating compliance with safety requirements is always needed for OS running on IoT devices. According to the proposed methodology, in case the safety is demonstrated, evaluation of quality is not needed because quality is considered implicitly guaranteed by safety. On the other hand, if the demonstration of safety is not required, the methodology foresees, as a first step, the quality evaluation, and subsequently the security evaluation (if it is required). The procedure to be followed is documented in the Qualification Plan.

The final result of the qualification activity is a document called *Qualification Report*, which includes the results of the procedures performed and an appropriately motivated final verdict of suitability. The evaluation procedure includes requirement verification activities that should be supported by techniques and tools aimed at reducing human evaluation errors and time costs. Some of these supporting techniques and tools are: Software Failure Modes and Effects Analysis (SFMEA) [19], Static Code Analysis [20], Fault Injection Test [21], Control Flow Analysis, robustness test. Furthermore, each evaluation procedure of the methodology is not performed if the OS/HV is already certified with the required standard. In this case, the evaluator reports evidence of the certification in the *Qualification Report* and proceeds to the next step.

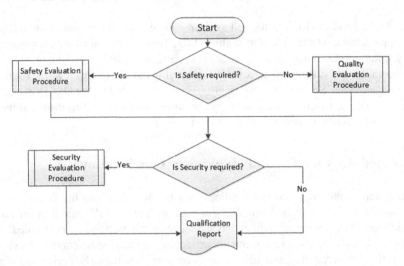

Fig. 1. Methodology for Qualification of Operating Systems and Hypervisors

4.1 Quality Evaluation

The first step of the quality evaluation is to distinguish the cases in which the OS/HV is open-source or COTS software. This influences the evaluation procedure since, typically, the code of a COTS software is not available and it is accessible only by the development team. In order to properly deal with the two different cases, the ISO/IEC 25051 standard is used for defining requirements for COTS OS/HV, while the ISO/IEC 25030 for defining requirements for the open-source OS/HV. As depicted in Fig. 2, the next step is *Establish the Evaluation Requirement* activity prescribed by ISO/IEC 25040 [26] which refers to the evaluation requirements included in ISO/IEC 25051 or ISO/IEC 25030 according to the OS/HV type. This activity defines the objective of the evaluation, the parts of the product to be evaluated and identifies related evaluation measures considering information available from the development of the OS.

Then, the evaluator carries out in sequence three tasks foreseen by ISO/IEC 25040: i) *Specify the Evaluation*: an evaluation model is chosen by establishing the measures that influence quality with appropriate metrics and associated thresholds; ii) *Plan the Evaluation*: evaluation activities are planned; iii) *Execute the Evaluation*: the planned activities are carried out by applying the decision criteria to the quality measures. The evaluator checks whether the result of the evaluation is as expected.

Once the assessment has been carried out, the evaluator updates the Qualification Report and checks if the quality of the analyzed OS is acceptable considering the coverage of the requirements obtained. If so, the evaluator goes to the next step of the methodology if it is required by the procedure in Fig. 1. Otherwise, the OS must be considered unsuitable for the purpose for which the qualification is being performed.

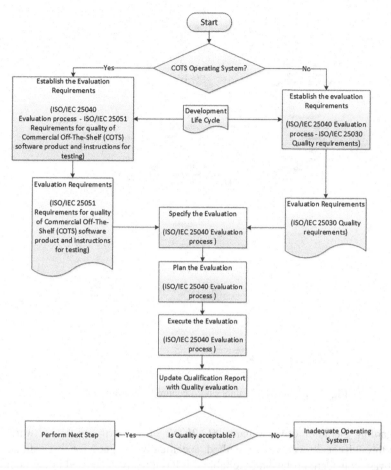

Fig. 2. Quality Evaluation Procedure Domain

4.2 Safety Evaluation

Here, the procedure for the Safety evaluation will be presented both for the railway and the automotive domain.

The procedure for the railway domain, in Fig. 3, is based on the *Software Assessment* defined in EN 50128. The assessment activities determine whether the OS meets the specified requirements and provide a judgment on the suitability of the for the intended purpose. If the OS is not certified EN 50128, the first activity to be performed, according to the standard is *Produce the Software Assessment Plan*, in which the *Software Assessment Plan* (SAP) is elaborated. EN 50128 requires the SAP to be written under the responsibility of the evaluator, that is an entity or a person in charge of carrying out the assessment process. After the *Validation of the Software Assessment Plan and Requirements* is executed (this should be done by an independent entity), the evaluator must perform the necessary actions to verify that the software requirements are met. These actions constitute the *Verify that SAP meets Software Requirements* activity.

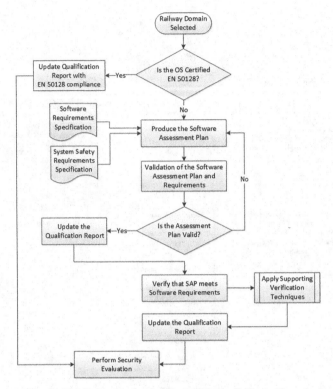

Fig. 3. The Safety Evaluation Procedure for Railway Domain

Regarding the automotive domain, ISO 26262 allows verifying the software compliance through the *Proven in use* method, specifically designed for fast validation of the software considered robust and reliable if it has already been used in the field for a long time without proving any inadequacy. This can be done exploiting the clause 14 of ISO 26262 Part 8, as depicted in Fig. 4. If the SO it is not *Proven in use,* but it is already certified with other standard, it is possible to demonstrate the ISO 26262 compliance with information coming from this different certification, through the application of ISO 26262 Part 8 clause 16. When it is not possible clause 12 should be applied in the *Qualification of Software Components* activity.

4.3 Security Evaluation

This procedure of the security evaluation, reported in Fig. 5, is based on the ISO/IEC 15408 [13] CC (Common Criteria) and foresees considering a Protection Profile (PP) and a Security Target (ST) relating to the Target of Evaluation (ToE), in this case the OS/HV to be evaluated.

The PP is a document that defines the security criteria of a class of IT systems (SW or HW) to satisfy a specific purpose and contains the Security Functional Requirements (SFRs) and the Security Assurance Requirements (SARs). The ST is the document that specifies the security properties of the ToE usually published by the manufacturer. There

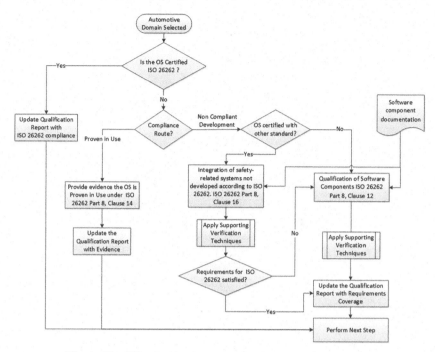

Fig. 4. The Safety Evaluation Procedure for Automotive Domain

are various PPs for available OS/HV (such as [23] suitable for HVs), while sometimes the ST is not produced by the software manufacturer. Hence the procedure proposes to use the OS/HV available security documentation as an alternative of the ST, as long as it is sufficiently detailed. At this point the evaluator can proceed with the *Validation of the Security Documentation consistence with the PP* or *Validation of the ST with the PP* activity, if the ST is available. Hence, the evaluator proceeds with the *Verification of the ToE Conformance with its FSRs and SARs*. This verification checks that the FRSs and SARs of the OS/HV correspond with the expected security level.

5 Qualification of Xen Hypervisor

To verify the effectiveness of the methodology, it has been applied to Xen Hypervisor [9] version 4.6 assuming that Xen has to be integrated in a situational awareness system for the monitoring and protection of a railway infrastructure. This procedure implies that the quality is verified at the same time as the safety, therefore the procedure for the quality evaluation was not carried out intentionally. The safety evaluation has been performed following the procedure in Fig. 3.

For safety evaluation, the SAP has been drawn up which includes safety requirements derived from the particular system to be implemented and the general requirements [9] provided by the manufacturer to integrate Xen in safety-critical contexts. The requirements verification highlighted that Xen complies with all the required requirements

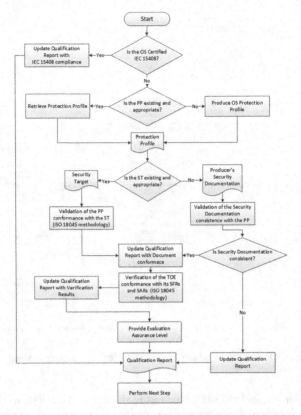

Fig. 5. The Security Evaluation Procedure for Generic Domain

except one in particular: "The hypervisor source code should not contain coding errors or defects and should be implemented in a clear and understandable way". In fact, through the execution of static code analysis, a large number of advisory violations relating to the code readability and 4173 (Fig. 6) violations of required MISRA C rules have been detected.

For security evaluation, not having a CC compliant ST for Xen, manufacturer documentation was considered along with XenServer generic CC certification [22]. This certification was given considering the PP for generic software, not a specific PP for Hypervisor, hence [22] cannot be assumed as valid certification for our purpose. However, the information reported in [22] was used to verify a number of SFRs. All SFRs and SARs, except some that may be justified, have been verified. The results of Xen hypervisor qualification highlight that Xen is not yet fully mature for safety-critical applications such as those considered in the specific railway domain.

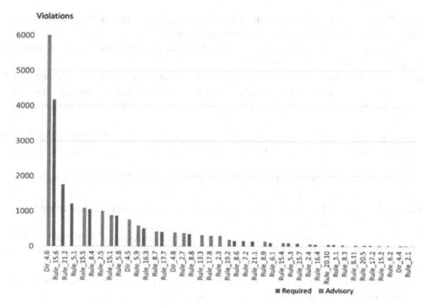

Fig. 6. MISRA C 12 violations per type, detected in Xen Hypervisor by the Understand tool

6 Conclusions and Future Works

The research activity described in this paper explores the reality of IoT technologies starting from its foundations: the OS and HV, which have the difficult task of managing time-critical and safety-critical applications. The methodology for the qualification of OSs and HVs was defined starting from quality, safety and security standards and was applied to Xen Hypervisor demonstrating its applicability and validity. This represents the achievement of an important goal because it is able to bring significant advantages in the design and development phase of critical systems.

However, the methodology has shown a weakness related to the fact that the OSs or HVs do not always have a CC compliant ST, leaving the task of verifying the usability of the software specification provided by the manufacturer instead of the ST. This represents a time-consuming activity that could be mitigated by adopting a simple procedure to translate the software specifications into the format foreseen by CC. This procedure improves the applicability of CC and will be addressed in the near future.

Acknowledgments. The research described in this paper has been supported by the project MAIA "Monitoraggio Attivo dell'Infrastruttura" funded by MIUR PON 14-20 (id code ARS01_00353).

References

1. Knight, J.C.: Safety critical systems: challenges and directions. In: Proceedings of the 24th International Conference on Software Engineering. ICSE (2002)

2. CEI EN 50129. Railway applications - Communication, signalling and processing systems - Safety related electronic systems for signalling (2018)
3. RedHat. Che cos'è l'Internet of Things (IoT)? https://www.redhat.com/it/topics/internet-of-things/what-is-iot. Accessed Aug 2021
4. D2.2 "State of the Art". AMBER Assessing, Measuring, and Benchmarking Resilience (2009)
5. D3.4. "Assessment and analysis guidelines for Off-The-Shelf Product-based Systems Important for Safety" v04, CEMSIS - Cost Effective Modernisation of Systems Important to Safety (2004)
6. Connelly, S., Becht, H.: Developing a methodology for the use of COTS operating systems with safety-related software. In: Proceedings of the Australian System Safety Conference (2011)
7. Pierce, R.H.: Great Britain, and Health and Safety Executive. Preliminary assessment of Linux for Safety related systems (2002)
8. Mazzeo, G., et al.: SIL2 assessment of an active/standby COTS-based Safety-related system. Reliab. Eng. Syst. Saf. **176**, 125–134 (2018)
9. Xen Project. Requirements. https://wiki.xenproject.org/wiki/Automotive_Requirements
10. ISO 25000. The ISO/IEC 25000 series of standards. https://iso25000.com/index.php/en/iso-25000-standards?limit=4&limitstart=0. Accessed Sept 2020
11. CEI EN 50128. Railway applications - Communication, signalling and processing systems - Software for railway control and protection systems (2020)
12. ISO. 26262 "Functional Safety Road Vehicles"
13. Troy, G.: Introduction to the Common Criteria for IT Security (ISO 15408) (1999)
14. Railnova. Access rolling stock data remotely. https://www.railnova.eu/remotely-access-rolling-stock-data/
15. Siemens. SIDOOR - Automatic door control systems for railway applications. https://new.siemens.com/global/en/products/automation/products-for-specific-requirements/sidoor-automatic-door-controls/sidoor-for-railway-applications.html
16. Toshiba Infrastructure Systems & Solutions Corporation. Air Conditioning System. https://www.railnova.eu/remotely-access-rolling-stock-data/. Accessed Aug 2021
17. Veovo. Netherlands Railways Optimizes Operations and Improves Revenue. https://veovo.com/discover/news/netherlands-railways-veovo-technology-to-improve-traveler-experience/
18. Hayashi, A., Ito, Y., Ishikawa, K.: East Japan railway company, "Earthquake disaster prevention and required performance of railway facilities in Japan". In: 17th U.S.-Japan-New Zealand Workshop on the Improvement of Structural Engineering and Resilience (2018)
19. Stadler, J.J., Seidl, N.J.: Software failure modes and effects analysis. General Electric Healthcare (2013)
20. OWASP. Static Code Analysis. https://owasp.org/www-community/controls/Static_Code_Analysis
21. ScienceDirect. Fault Injection. https://www.sciencedirect.com/topics/computer-science/fault-injection
22. CESG Certification Body. Certification Report No. CRP270 Citrix XenServer 6.0.2 Platinum Edition. Issue 1.0. (2012)
23. National Information Assurance Partnership. Protection Profile for Virtualization (2016)
24. Radio Technical Commission for Aeronautics. DO-178B, Software Considerations in Airborne Systems and Equipment Certification (1992)
25. IEC/TR 61508. Functional safety of electrical/electronic/programmable electronic safety-related systems (2011)
26. ISO/IEC 25040. Systems and software engineering—Systems and software Quality Requirements and Evaluation (SQuaRE)—Evaluation process (2011)

Computer-Aided Generation of Assurance Cases

Timothy E. Wang[1]([⊠]), Chanwook Oh[2], Matthew Low[2], Isaac Amundson[3],
Zamira Daw[4], Alessandro Pinto[5], Massimiliano L. Chiodo[1], Guoqiang Wang[1],
Saqib Hasan[3], Ryan Melville[1], and Pierluigi Nuzzo[2]

[1] Raytheon Technology Research Center, Berkeley, CA, USA
timothy.wang@rtx.com
[2] University of Southern California, Los Angeles, CA, USA
[3] Collins Aerospace, Cedar Rapids, IA, USA
[4] University of Stuttgart, Stuttgart, Germany
[5] NASA Jet Propulsion Laboratory, Pasadena, CA, USA

Abstract. Assurance cases (ACs) have gained attention in the
aerospace, medical, and other heavily-regulated industries as a means
for providing structured arguments on why a product is dependable
(i.e., safe, secure, etc.) for its intended application. Challenges in AC
construction stem from the complexity and uniqueness of the designs,
the heterogeneous nature of the required supporting evidence, and the
need to assess the quality of an argument. We present an automated
AC generation framework that facilitates the construction, validation,
and confidence assessment of ACs based on dependability argument patterns and confidence patterns capturing domain knowledge. The ACs
are instantiated with a system's specification and evaluated based on
the available design and verification evidence. Aerospace case studies
illustrate the framework's effectiveness, efficiency, and scalability.

Keywords: Assurance case · contracts · synthesis · validation ·
confidence

1 Introduction

Assurance about certain properties of mission-critical systems, such as safety,
security, and functional correctness, is essential throughout the product development lifecycle. Certification standards (e.g., DO-178C in the aerospace industry) tend to be prescriptive in nature, enforcing a rigid, often costly, evaluation
process. Assurance evaluation is currently performed mostly manually, and due
to the substantial amount of evidence that needs to be examined, can lead to
incomplete or biased assessments.

The trend in research is shifting from a prescriptive certification process to
argument-based certification (e.g., based on overarching properties (OPs) [1]),
which offers more flexibility to certify emerging technologies, including systems
enabled by artificial intelligence (AI). However, this approach expands the scope
of the evidence evaluation process, beyond checking the *sufficiency* of evidence,

© The Author(s), under exclusive license to Springer Nature Switzerland AG 2023
J. Guiochet et al. (Eds.): SAFECOMP 2023 Workshops, LNCS 14182, pp. 135–148, 2023.
https://doi.org/10.1007/978-3-031-40953-0_12

to validating whether the proposed system development activities and outcomes are appropriate to establish safety, security, or standard compliance for a given application. In this context, automated methods and tools that support the creation, maintenance, and evaluation of arguments are deemed as necessary for a streamlined assurance process.

Assurance cases (ACs) are explicit arguments that desired properties have been adequately established for a given system. ACs are typically created manually and, at present, are mostly used to document the argumentation structure. There is a lack of consensus on a systematic approach for creating and validating ACs. Tools for AC visualization and manipulation exist, but notations are often not completely defined, leaving room for interpretation and misunderstanding [2]. For example, the Goal Structuring Notation (GSN) specifies the visual syntax and semantics of its elements, such as goals, strategies, justifications, and solutions. However, the standard [3] primarily relies on natural language for expressing claims, which can be ambiguous and open to misinterpretation. Formalisms and tools that can assist in the creation of rigorous and interpretable arguments are limited to only a few attempts [4–6].

This paper addresses some of the challenges in constructing and validating ACs, including (a) the complexity of modern safety and security-critical systems, (b) the heterogeneous nature of the evidence, and (c) the need to assess the argument quality, i.e., quantify the persuasiveness of the argument given the sources of doubt. We present an *automated, end-to-end* framework that synthesizes and validates ACs. The framework includes (i) an efficient synthesis algorithm that automatically creates AC candidates using a pattern library of *pre-order relations* linking claims with their supporting (sub)-claims and (ii) a validation algorithm that uses logic and probabilistic reasoning to effectively identify a set of *logically valid* and *most persuasive* AC candidates. The framework also includes a visualization tool for traversing the generated ACs in multiple formats at different levels of the argument hierarchy.

Related Work. Several tools [7–10] support manual or partly automated AC creation, instantiation, management, and analysis. Approaches based on the AMASS platform [11–14] use contracts for automated AC creation to enable compositionality and reuse of argumentation patterns. Beyond automated and compositional AC generation with contracts, our framework also provides quantitative assessment of the persuasiveness of an AC, based on design artifacts and evidence, by leveraging Bayesian reasoning [15] to compute confidence values.

A few tools [16,17] also support automated AC generation and confidence assessment, albeit not within a contract-based, compositional framework. A possible limitation of existing approaches to confidence quantification stems from the fact that missing or contrary information may be "masked" by an overall high confidence score at the top-level claim, leading to insensitivity to critical local evidence [18]. We address this issue via a compositional and hierarchical approach that combines local probabilistic reasoning with global logical reasoning to derive the confidence of the top-level claim [19]. Our assessment algorithm, consisting of uncertainty quantification steps followed by decision-making steps, allows for appropriately weighing different evidence items and early discounting of unreliable evidence with low confidence levels, thus making the overall process of propagating confidence values to the top-level claim and determining their sufficiency more robust to inaccuracies in the confidence models.

2   Background

Assurance Cases. An *assurance case (AC)* is an argument constructed to establish that a system satisfies the requirements in its operative environment by means of hierarchical steps that map a *claim* to *evidence* via strategies and intermediary claims [2,6]. ACs are often described using a structured language [20] or graphical notations such as the Goal Structuring Notation (GSN) [21] and the Claims-Arguments-Evidence (CAE) notation [22]. An AC can then be represented as a directed acyclic graph mapping the system specification (the top-level claim) from the root node to the leaf nodes representing the evidence.

Software tools such as AdvoCATE [7] and DS-Bench [23] can be used to specify GSN (or CAE) pattern libraries, providing a limited degree of automation for representation and validation of ACs. However, some semantic elements in these tools are not well-defined in their respective conventions, leaving room for an individual developer to clarify them [2]. The argumentation steps between claims often lack rigor, opening the door for confirmation bias [6]. We address these concerns by leveraging contract operations to solidify the relationship between claims, allied with Bayesian reasoning to assess their strength.

Assume-Guarantee Contracts. Assume-guarantee (A/G) contracts offer effective mechanisms to analyze system requirements in a modular way [24,25]. We use contracts as a specification formalism to represent claims about the system and the development process as well as the contexts under which the claims hold. We represent a contract C as a pair of logic formulas (ϕ_A, ϕ_G), where ϕ_A (assumptions) specifies the context under which the claim holds and ϕ_G (guarantees) specifies the promise of the claim in the context of ϕ_A. We can reason about the replaceability of a contract (or a claim) by another contract via the *refinement* relation. We say that C_2 refines C_1, written $C_2 \preceq C_1$, if and only if C_2 has weaker assumptions and stronger guarantees than C_1. When this is the case, we can replace C_1 with C_2. Contracts C_1 and C_2 can also be combined, e.g., using *composition* (denoted by $C_1 \otimes C_2$) to construct more complex arguments from simpler claims.

3   AC Generation Framework

As shown in Fig. 1, our framework automatically generates and validates ACs given a top-level goal from a pattern library, the evidence database, and the system specification. We refer to the synthesis and validation processes collectively as *generation*. Validation itself coordinates logic and probabilistic reasoning to *select* valid AC candidates and *assess* their confidence level.

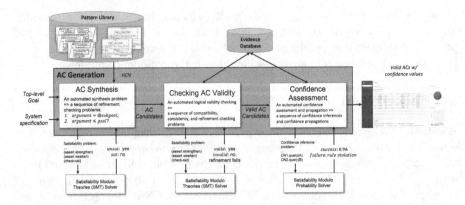

Fig. 1. Overview of the AC generation framework with summary of output candidates.

AC patterns are reusable AC templates that can be instantiated using system specific information to construct larger ACs. The patterns capture, in the form of generic argumentation steps, domain knowledge about what evidence is required to achieve specific goals. We employ hierarchical contract networks (HCNs) to formalize AC patterns and use Resolute [26] as the underlying language for their specification. Uncertainty in assertions is instead modeled using Bayesian networks (BNs). Given a top-level claim from the pattern library and a system under evaluation, the synthesis algorithm automatically selects and instantiates the patterns and assembles the instantiated patterns together into an HCN that represents a set of *AC candidates*.

We denote by *evidence* a set of objective facts collected, for example, via tests, analyses, or proofs, that can be used in support of, or against, a claim. The evidence is maintained according to an *evidence ontology* in a database that is accessible by the AC generation framework. The availability of evidence could be considered by the synthesis algorithm for eliminating certain AC candidates early. However, our framework also targets an assurance-driven development process with objectives (e.g., cost and development time) taken into account during certain stages of the product lifecycle. Particularly, in the early stages of product development, when the system design is incomplete, we are interested in exploring the set of all potential evidence items and assurance arguments, to analyze cost and benefit trade-offs. The *validation* algorithm selects the AC candidates with the lowest number of missing supporting evidence. The selected ACs undergo confidence level quantification, which assesses the ACs' persuasiveness. Finally, our framework returns a set of valid ACs and their confidence scores, ensuring that the most convincing and well-supported ACs are presented to system designers and certification authorities.

Overall, by leveraging our previous results on generic HCN synthesis [27] and AC validation [19], our framework supports the first end-to-end automated methodology that seamlessly integrates contract-based synthesis and validation

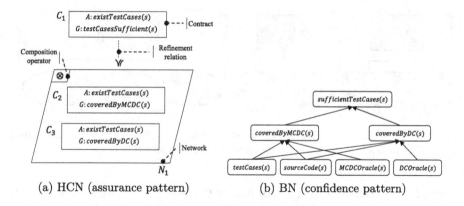

(a) HCN (assurance pattern)   (b) BN (confidence pattern)

Fig. 2. AC pattern for *P2* in Fig. 3.

of ACs, and makes it accessible, via intuitive user interfaces, to system designers and certification authorities.

3.1 AC Pattern Formalization

We formalize an AC pattern as a pair consisting of an HCN (assurance pattern) and a set of BNs (confidence patterns).

Hierarchical Contract Networks. An argumentation step involving a concatenation of claims can be represented as a graph of interconnected contracts, termed *contract network* (CN). A network N of m contracts is equivalent to the contract $C_N = C_1 \parallel \cdots \parallel C_m$, where $\parallel \in \{\otimes, \wedge\}$ denotes a contract operation [24]. Stepwise refinements of higher-level claims into lower-level claims can then be captured by a tree of contract networks, that is, a *hierarchical contract network* (HCN) using contract refinement [19,27]. Figure 2a shows the HCN corresponding to the pattern *P2* in Fig. 3. The patterns in Fig. 3 and 4 are depicted in GSN only for illustrative purposes. Every statement in the pattern is formalized as a logical predicate, which forms the contract assumptions and guarantees. The goal is translated into contract C_1, while the premises are translated into contracts within the contract network N_1.

Confidence Networks. We use *confidence networks* to capture the sources of uncertainty in the claims of an HCN. In this paper, confidence networks are implemented as BNs, which have been used in the past to incorporate subjective notions of probability or belief and quantitatively reason about the confidence in assertions affected by uncertainty [28]. BNs can encompass aleatoric and epistemic uncertainty and tend to produce more compact models in the number of parameters than other probabilistic reasoning frameworks for uncertainty quantification [29]. BNs can be constructed based on domain expert knowledge, e.g., via an elicitation and calibration process, and can leverage notions from Bayesian epistemology to account for lack of knowledge.

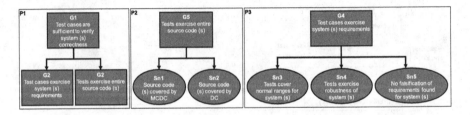

Fig. 3. AC pattern library used in the running example. Evidence items are represented as solution nodes (Sn); claims are represented as goal nodes (G).

Example 1. Assume an AC pattern library that partially addresses the *correctness* goal, shown in Fig. 3. *P1* argues that test cases are sufficient for demonstrating system correctness if the tests exercise all requirements and cover the entire source code. *P2* argues that a set of tests cover the entire source code based on documented coverage metrics. *P3* argues that requirements are covered by a set of test cases if the tests cover the normal and robust ranges of requirements. The BN in Fig. 2b models a *confidence pattern* expressing the key correlations between the outcome of a coverage test and the quality of the artifacts (e.g., source code, test oracle) produced during software development and testing. The BN in Fig. 2b can be associated to pattern *P2* in Fig. 3.

3.2 AC Synthesis Algorithm

Given a contract network N_0, an AC pattern library $\mathcal{L}$, and a set of formulas specifying the context about the system, the synthesis algorithm automatically generates a set of AC candidates in terms of an HCN H with N_0 as the top node. By leveraging the synthesis algorithm first introduced for generic HCNs [27], our synthesis procedure proceeds as follows. The top-level goals N_0 are *instantiated* with the system under evaluation. N_0 is a contract network containing one or more goals. For each instantiated contract $\tilde{C}$ of $\tilde{N}_0$, the algorithm searches the AC pattern library $\mathcal{L}$ for contract networks that are potential refinements. Any contracts that are not refined by any other contract networks in the library are either *evidential*, indicating that they can only be established by evidence from the lifecycle activities, e.g., requirements review, test results, code reviews, formal methods, or undeveloped goals.

The returned refinements are also instantiated with the system under evaluation. After instantiation, the validity of potential refinements is determined by converting contract properties (consistency, compatibility, and refinement) into satisfiability problems that are passed to a satisfiability modulo theory (SMT) solver. The algorithm checks that a refinement holds with respect to the system contexts, which are configurations, properties, and operating contexts of the system, encoded as assertions, e.g., "the software component targets the highest safety integrity level," "the wireless communication in component A is disabled." If the validity of the potential refinement is established, then an edge is added between $\tilde{C}$ and $\tilde{N}$ to form an HCN H. The procedure is recursive, i.e., it starts

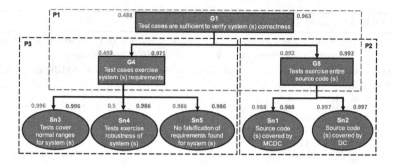

Fig. 4. Generated AC based on the AC pattern library in Fig. 3. Dotted boxes highlight the instantiated pattern. Confidence values when all evidence items are available are shown in green, while red values indicate confidence with missing evidence for Sn4 ("Tests exercise robustness of the system").

again with the contract network $\tilde{N}$ and terminates when all the leaf contracts are either evidential or undeveloped goals. Since a contract could be linked to more than one contract network, the output of the algorithm, a hierarchy of contracts, is a set of one or more AC candidates that connects the top-level claim to evidence items through multiple argumentation levels. An example output AC candidate is shown in Fig. 4.

3.3   AC Validation and Assessment

Among the AC candidates generated from AC synthesis, our selection process prioritizes candidates that are fully supported by evidence items within the evidence library. In addition, we select a set of AC candidates that are partially supported. For these candidates, we determine the minimum number of additional evidence items required to fully support their claims. We then proceed to assess the confidence level associated with each selected candidate, which accounts for the uncertainty associated with the evidence.

Selecting AC Candidates. AC validation and assessment for a realistic system can be time-consuming, particularly when dealing with a large number of candidates (e.g., 10^6), which can also require significant memory. To address this issue, we employ a depth-first-search approach to select AC candidates that can be supported with no or minimum number of additional evidence items. We employ the following completion metric to rank and select the AC candidates:

$$Cpl(H) = \frac{\#\text{ of evidential contracts in } H \text{ with no missing evidence}}{\#\text{ of total evidential contracts in } H}. \quad (1)$$

The completion metric measures the percentage of evidential contracts in H that have complete evidence, thus prioritizing AC candidates with higher completion levels. We then compute the confidence values for these AC candidates.

Algorithm 1: ASSESSCONF(T, $\mathcal{E}$, $\mathcal{W}$, $\mathbf{R}$)

---

input : Top-level refinement $T = (C_r, \varphi_r, N_r)$; library of confidence networks $\mathcal{E}$; library of decision rules $\mathcal{W}$; set $\mathbf{R}$ of HCN refinements.

output: Confidence $\mathcal{P}(C_r)$, $\bot$ if assessment fails; infeasibility certificate *cert*.

1   $cert \leftarrow \bot$ and $\mathcal{P}, Q \leftarrow \bot$
2   **for** $C \in N_r$ **do**
3     $R_{curr} \leftarrow \bot$
4   **for** $R = (C_u, \varphi, N_l) \in \mathbf{R}$ **do**
5 | **if** $C = C_u$ **then** $R_{curr} \leftarrow R$; break;
6   **if** $R_{curr} = \bot$ **then**
7 | $\mathcal{P}(C) \leftarrow$ INFERCONF(C, $\mathcal{E}$)
8   **else**
9 | $\mathcal{P}(C), certificate \leftarrow$ ASSESSCONF(R_{curr}, $\mathcal{E}$, $\mathcal{W}$, $\mathbf{R}$)
10 | **if** $\mathcal{P}(C) = \bot$ **then return** $\bot$, *cert*
11 $Q \leftarrow$ DECIDECONF ($\mathcal{P}$, $\mathcal{E}$, $\mathcal{W}$)
12 **if** $Q = \bot$ **then return** *null*, *cert*
13 **else return** PROPAGATECONF($\mathcal{P}$, R_{curr}), *cert*

Assessing AC Candidates. Given the selected AC candidates as a set of HCNs and a library $\mathcal{E}$ of confidence networks, we employ a combination of probabilistic and rule-based automated reasoning [19] to quantify the confidence associated with an HCN candidate H as summarized by Algorithm 1. The algorithm recursively traverses H using a depth-first-search approach, propagating confidence values up from lower-level CNs to higher-level ones. Specifically, for each evidential contract encountered during traversal, the algorithm uses one or more corresponding networks in $\mathcal{E}$ to calculate its confidence value. If a contract is not evidential, the confidence value is propagated from its lower-level CN by recursively calling ASSESSCONF. However, if any confidence propagation rule is violated (as evaluated by DECIDECONF), the validation process terminates with a failure. For example, the decision-making step in our algorithm can apply a simple rule requiring that the majority of the premises in an evidential contract must have a high confidence level according to a pre-determined threshold. Further details about the AC validation and decision making processes can be found in our previous publication [19].

Example 2. Given the AC pattern library in Fig. 3 and the top-level claim *"Test cases are sufficient to verify system correctness,"* the synthesis algorithm generates the AC in Fig. 4, where the contract networks defined in *P2* and *P3* refine the two premises of *P1*. The logic validity of the AC is established by checking the compatibility and consistency of each claim and the refinement relationships between the claims. The confidence level can be assessed using Bayesian inference on the confidence networks associated with the pattern, such as the one in Fig. 2b. Confidence assessment produces the color-coded values in Fig. 4.

4 Evaluation

In this section, we present two case studies for arguing the security of (1) the Advanced Fail Safe (AFS) module for the ArduCopter rotorcraft [30] given a set of evidence items [31] and (2) an industrial-level aerospace system.

Advanced Fail Safe Module of ArduPilot. ArduPilot is an open source platform for controlling vehicles including rovers, fixed-wing aircraft, and rotorcraft. It is a software stack that performs estimation, control, and communication between the software and hardware. In this experiment, we focus on the ArduPilot modules used for the ArduCopter [30] rotorcraft. We created a library consisting of 17 patterns that incorporate system development best practices for compliance with DO-178C, DO-333, and vetted security arguments from domain experts. For example, Fig. 6 shows a pattern for arguing specification quality via three supporting premises.

Security of an Industrial Aerospace System. Our approach was also validated on an industrial aerospace system to argue that the system meets certain security requirements. The results are provided in Table 1 under the name *Industrial Case Study*.

4.1 AC Generation Framework in Action

Synthesis. Given a top-level argumentation goal, "the ArduCopter software s is acceptably secure", the pattern library, and a set of desired security properties ℓ, with $|\ell|$ as the number of properties, a total of $3^{|\ell|}$ AC candidates were generated, as shown in Table 1. Figure 5 compactly represents the set of all possible ACs for an arbitrary $|\ell|$. The top-level goal is supported by the completeness (C_3 of N_1) and correctness (C_4 of N_1) of the software specification, i.e., the set of requirements that must be satisfied, including a set of security properties, the correctness of the software implementation with respect to the security requirements (C_2 of N_1), and the satisfaction of the security properties of interest, e.g., by eliminating or mitigating certain system-specific security hazards, (C_1 of N_1). Parts of the HCN for supporting C_2, C_3, and C_4 of N_1 are omitted due to the limited space.

AC synthesis considers three methods to assess the satisfaction of a security property $p_i \in \ell$ (C_i of N_2), namely, architecture analysis ($N_{6,1}$), model checking ($N_{6,2}$), and static analysis ($N_{6,3}$). These methods are denoted by the conditional refinements ($R_{2,1,1}$, $R_{2,1,2}$, and $R_{2,1,3}$) represented by dotted lines in Fig. 5. Not all the methods can support every security property. AC synthesis only provides candidates whose conditional refinements connect the properties to the appropriate supporting methods. For example, if a multi-rate, quasi-periodic model of computation is adopted, where processes operate periodically at their individual periods and communicate via bounded latency channels, the satisfaction of a property such as "the processing latency for a message between a pair of

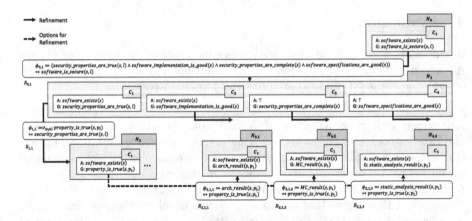

Fig. 5. Compact representation of AC candidates for arguing the security of the ArduCopter software in HCN form.

Table 1. Performance of the AC generation framework for the ArduCopter software and an industrial-level aerospace system.

Case Study	Pattern Library Size	Security Property Count	Total Candidates	Valid Candidates	Average Claims per Candidate	Synthesis (s)	Validation (s)	
							Selection	Assessment
ArduCopter	17	2	3^2	1	43	10	18	69
	17	4	3^4	1	50	12	21	82
	17	6	3^6	1	58	16	26	92
	17	8	3^8	1	66	18	41	102
	17	10	3^{10}	1	73	21	152	119
	17	12	3^{12}	1	81	25	3,143	832
Industrial Case Study	91	N/A	6×10^5	10	652	819	1,683	3,322

communicating AFS subsystems is bounded" can be supported by the evidence generated by an architecture modeling and timing analysis tool geared toward the selected model of computation [32]. On the other hand, the security property that "no denial of service occurs due to triggering of nullness exceptions" can be better supported by evidence generated via static analysis. In our example, with a total of $|\ell| = 4$ properties, it took 12 s to generate 3^4 AC candidates (4 properties with 3 options for refinement), effectively capturing all the possible means of compliance and evaluation strategies.

Validation. To test the selection capability of our framework, we designed the ArduCopter case study to only have one fully supported candidate, out of a total of 81 candidates. However, AC validation also retained 9 AC candidates with the highest completion scores to suggest AC candidates requiring the least additional evidence items. The candidate with the highest completion score was successfully validated with confidence 0.9836 [19]. Its assessment, consisting of 24 refinement steps, took 8 s.

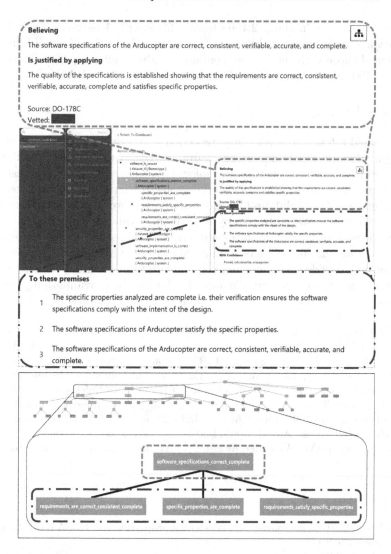

Fig. 6. Detailed view of pattern justification and its instantiation in the generated AC for the ArduCopter platform.

Performance Evaluation. We report the performance and scalability of the AC generation framework by increasing the number of total AC candidates from 9 to 6×10^5 in Table 1. We observed a sub-linear increase in the execution time for the generation and confidence assessment of ACs as the total number of AC candidates increased. The time spent for selecting the ACs grew linearly with the total generated candidates. Larger ACs in the industrial case study resulted in greater execution time for confidence assessment. When applied to an augmented version of the industrial case study, our framework could synthesize

10^{24} AC candidates in about 2,100 s from a library of 91 patterns. Overall, our generation framework was able to generate over 6×10^5 AC candidates and recommend those with the highest confidence values and completion metrics in less than 100 minutes on an Intel Core i3 CPU with 32-GB RAM.

5   Conclusion

We presented a framework for computer-aided generation and validation of ACs leveraging domain knowledge-based assurance patterns. ACs are formalized as hierarchical contract networks, which allow for efficient, modular synthesis and validation of arguments. Empirical results showed that our framework can efficiently generate AC candidates for representative real-world systems in a scalable manner. We intend to improve it by normalizing evidence items from different sources, by ranking candidates using a predictive cost model, and by introducing mechanisms for the elicitation of confidence models. While generating assurance patterns and confidence models may require significant initial effort, we also aim to investigate methods to alleviate this burden by providing templates for computer-aided pattern elicitation, formalization, and validation.

Acknowledgments. Distribution statement "A" (approved for public release, distribution unlimited). This research was developed with funding from the Defense Advanced Research Projects Agency (DARPA), contract FA875020C0508. The views, opinions, or findings expressed are those of the authors and should not be interpreted as representing the official views or policies of the Department of Defense or the U.S. Government. The authors wish to also acknowledge the partial support by the National Science Foundation (NSF) under Awards 1846524 and 2139982, the Office of Naval Research (ONR) under Award N00014-20-1-2258, the Defense Advanced Research Projects Agency (DARPA) under Award HR00112010003, and the Okawa Research Grant.

References

1. Holloway, C.: Understanding the overarching properties, ser. NASA technical memorandum (2019)
2. Rushby, J.: The interpretation and evaluation of assurance cases. Computer Science Laboratory, SRI International, Menlo Park, CA, Technical report. SRI-CSL-15-01 (2015)
3. TACW Group: Goal structuring notation community standard (version 3) (2021)
4. Hawkins, R., Habli, I., et al.: Weaving an assurance case from design: a model-based approach. In: International Symposium High Assurance Systems Engineering, pp. 110–117 (2015)
5. Rushby, J.: Formalism in safety cases. In: Dale, C., Anderson, T. (eds.) Making Systems Safer, pp. 3–17. Springer, London (2010). https://doi.org/10.1007/978-1-84996-086-1_1
6. Bloomfield, R., Rushby, J.: Assurance 2.0. arXiv preprint arXiv:2004.10474 (2020)
7. Denney, E., Pai, G., Pohl, J.: AdvoCATE: an assurance case automation toolset. In: Ortmeier, F., Daniel, P. (eds.) SAFECOMP 2012. LNCS, vol. 7613, pp. 8–21. Springer, Heidelberg (2012). https://doi.org/10.1007/978-3-642-33675-1_2

8. Barry, M.R.: CertWare: a workbench for safety case production and analysis. In: Aerospace conference, pp. 1–10 (2011)

9. Matsuno, Y.: D-case editor: a typed assurance case editor. University of Tokyo (2011)

10. Adelard LLP. Assurance and safety case environment (ASCE) (2011). https://www.adelard.com/asce/

11. Sljivo, I., Gallina, B., Carlson, J., Hansson, H., Puri, S.: Tool-supported safety-relevant component reuse: from specification to argumentation. In: Casimiro, A., Ferreira, P.M. (eds.) Ada-Europe 2018. LNCS, vol. 10873, pp. 19–33. Springer, Cham (2018). https://doi.org/10.1007/978-3-319-92432-8_2

12. Šljivo, I., Uriagereka, G.J., et al.: Guiding assurance of architectural design patterns for critical applications. J. Syst. Architect. **110**, 101765 (2020)

13. de la Vara, J.L., Ruiz, A., Blondelle, G.: Assurance and certification of cyber-physical systems: the AMASS open source ecosystem. J. Syst. Softw. **171**, 110812 (2021). https://www.sciencedirect.com/science/article/pii/S0164121220302120

14. Nešić, D., Nyberg, M., Gallina, B.: Product-line assurance cases from contract-based design. J. Syst. Softw. **176**, 110922 (2021)

15. Neapolitan, R.: Learning Bayesian Networks, ser. Artificial Intelligence. Pearson Prentice Hall (2004)

16. Cârlan, C., Nigam, V., et al.: ExplicitCase: tool-support for creating and maintaining assurance arguments integrated with system models. In: International Symposium on Software Reliability Engineering Workshops (ISSREW), pp. 330–337 (2019)

17. Ramakrishna, S., Hartsell, C., et al.: A methodology for automating assurance case generation. arXiv preprint arXiv:2003.05388 (2020)

18. Graydon, P.J., Holloway, C.M.: An investigation of proposed techniques for quantifying confidence in assurance arguments. Saf. Sci. **92**, 53–65 (2017)

19. Oh, C., Naik, N., Daw, Z., Wang, T.E., Nuzzo, P.: ARACHNE: automated validation of assurance cases with stochastic contract networks. In: Trapp, M., Saglietti, F., Spisländer, M., Bitsch, F. (eds.) SAFECOMP 2022. LNCS, vol. 13414, pp. 65–81. Springer, Cham (2022). https://doi.org/10.1007/978-3-031-14835-4_5

20. Holloway, C.M.: Explicate'78: uncovering the implicit assurance case in DO-178C. In: Safety-Critical Systems Symposium (2015)

21. The GSN Working Group Online, Goal Structuring Notation. http://www.goalstructuringnotation.info/

22. Adelard LLP. Claims, Arguments and Evidence (CAE) (2019). https://www.adelard.com/asce/choosing-asce/cae.html. Accessed 23 Oct 2020

23. Fujita, H., Matsuno, Y., et al.: DS-Bench toolset: tools for dependability benchmarking with simulation and assurance. In: International Conference on Dependable Systems and Networks, pp. 1–8. IEEE (2012)

24. Benveniste, A., Caillaud, B., et al.: Contracts for system design. Found. Trends Electron. Des. Autom. **12**(2–3), 124–400 (2018)

25. Bauer, S.S., et al.: Moving from specifications to contracts in component-based design. In: de Lara, J., Zisman, A. (eds.) FASE 2012. LNCS, vol. 7212, pp. 43–58. Springer, Heidelberg (2012). https://doi.org/10.1007/978-3-642-28872-2_3

26. Gacek, A., Backes, J., et al.: Resolute: an assurance case language for architecture models. In: SIGAda Annual Conference on High Integrity Language Technology, pp. 19–28 (2014)

27. Wang, T.E., Daw, Z., Nuzzo, P., Pinto, A.: Hierarchical contract-based synthesis for assurance cases. In: Deshmukh, J.V., Havelund, K., Perez, I. (eds.) NFM 2022.

LNCS, vol. 13260, pp. 175–192. Springer, Cham (2022). https://doi.org/10.1007/978-3-031-06773-0_9

28. Jensen, F.V.: Introduction to Bayesian Networks, 1st edn. Springer, Heidelberg (1996)
29. Verbert, K., Babuška, R., De Schutter, B.: Bayesian and Dempster-Shafer reasoning for knowledge-based fault diagnosis–a comparative study. Eng. Appl. Artif. Intell. **60**, 136–150 (2017)
30. ArduPilot Dev Team. Arducopter (2023). https://ardupilot.org/copter/
31. Shankar, N., Bhatt, D., et al.: DesCert: Design for certification. arXiv preprint arXiv:2203.15178 (2022)
32. Bhatt, D., Ren, H., Murugesan, A., Biatek, J., Varadarajan, S., Shankar, N.: Requirements-driven model checking and test generation for comprehensive verification. In: Deshmukh, J.V., Havelund, K., Perez, I. (eds.) NFM 2022. LNCS, vol. 13260, pp. 576–596. Springer, Cham (2022). https://doi.org/10.1007/978-3-031-06773-0_31

RACK: A Semantic Model and Triplestore for Curation of Assurance Case Evidence

Abha Moitra[1], Paul Cuddihy[1], Kit Siu[1(✉)], David Archer[2], Eric Mertens[2], Daniel Russell[3], Kevin Quick[2], Valentin Robert[2], and Baoluo Meng[1]

[1] GE Research, Niskayuna, NY, USA
{moitraa,cuddihy,siu,baoluo.meng}@ge.com
[2] Galois, Portland, OR, USA
{dwa,emertens,kquick,val}@galois.com
[3] GE Aerospace, Grand Rapids, MI, USA
daniel.russell@ge.com

Abstract. Certification of large systems requires reasoning over complex, diverse evidential datasets to determine whether its software is fit for purpose. This requires a detailed understanding of the meaning of that data, the context in which it is valid, and the uses to which it may reasonably be put. Unfortunately, current practices for assuring software safety do not scale to accommodate modern Department of Defense (DoD) systems, resulting in unfavorable behaviors such as putting off fixes to defects until the risk of not mitigating them outweighs the high cost of re-certification. In this work, we describe a novel data curation system, RACK, that addresses cost-effective, scalable curation of diverse certification evidence to facilitate the construction of an assurance case.

Keywords: data model · data curation · data provenance · certification · assurance case

1 Introduction

Evidential datasets can come from diverse sources. For example, modern Department of Defense (DoD) platforms are systems of systems from multiple suppliers, each providing evidence in different formats and granularity. There is a need to understand the meaning of the data, the context in which it is valid, and the uses to which it may reasonably be put. This need to precisely understand data semantics is further exacerbated when the users of the data (such as the platform owner applying for qualification or certification) are distinct from, and may be unable to interact with, the providers of the data (such as subsystem suppliers). Certification is a critical tollgate on the path from technology development to approval for use of that technology on a platform for mission purposes. The certification approach generally starts with defining a plan that describes the process to follow, relevant standards to which the system must comply, and the artifacts to produce. These artifacts then become evidence of compliance to the plan.

J. Guiochet et al. (Eds.): SAFECOMP 2023 Workshops, LNCS 14182, pp. 149–160, 2023.
https://doi.org/10.1007/978-3-031-40953-0_13

One way to demonstrate compliance is to assemble an assurance case, which is a structured argument of how, whether, and why the system meets the goal of safe operation. Certification thus requires assimilating not only the system's design artifacts, but also the data regarding how the system was tested or verified to meet those goals. We call this collection of data *assurance case evidence.*

Unfortunately, current practices for assuring software safety do not scale to accommodate the volume and diversity of evidence in modern DoD systems. In 2018 the DoD published a Digital Engineering Strategy [7] to transform linear, document-intensive and stove-piped processes to digital engineering practices that use an integrated, model-based approach. Model curation is mentioned throughout the publication. Our take on the digital engineering revolution is that curation not only involves models but should also include a disciplined approach to data curation. Curating evidence (organize it, assess its quality, and provide easy access to it) manually requires lot of effort and is expensive for current and emerging complex systems. The lack of scalability leads to undesirable behavior: software fixes are not deployed until the risk of not fixing the collection of issues outweighs the cost of re-certification.

In this work, we describe a novel platform, Rapid Assurance Curation Kit (RACK) [8], that is open-sourced and addresses the problem above: cost-effective, scalable curation of certification evidence. RACK curates diverse evidence such as test cases and test results, and relevant requirements and standards. RACK allows for curating metadata as well: its sources, derivation, strength, timeliness, and trustworthiness. This paper expands on [15] which described our initial data model for capturing system development and evaluation.

2   Comparison to Related Works

There are several commercial tools that organize design artifacts. IBM DOORS provides traceability from requirements to tests; Rapita's Verification Suite runs requirements-based tests on embedded software and produces evidence for DO-178C and ISO 26262 certification; Inflectra's SpiraTest provides a repository to manage requirements, defects, and test cases and gives a visualization of the traceability. All these companies offer services to migrate workflows into their integrated environments. Our experience is that the full potential of the vendors' offerings is only realized when projects adopt the entire tool suite. Arguably, this has a disadvantage because of the large amount of data and institutional inertia to switching tools.

The AMASS project (Architecture-driven, Multi-concern and Seamless Assurance and Certification of Cyber-Physical Systems) [17] provides a vision for harmonization, reuse and automation of labor-intensive certification-oriented activities by promoting the use of model-based approaches. The aspirations of AMASS and RACK are similar in that we both aim to lower certification costs. However, our approaches are different in that AMASS provides a reference tool architecture that the users can adopt so they can benefit from seamless tool interoperability. RACK, on the other hand, is a tool agnostic data curation system. We aim to link information from different vendor tools in existing workflows by providing a data curation solution.

It is important to note that RACK is not designed as an assurance case construction tool. However, it can be leveraged to assist in developing assurance cases [14] or building certification artifacts in tools like the Assurance Case Automation Toolset (AdvoCATE) [6]. Requirements can still be managed in DOORS, source code in Git, models in Cameo Teamwork Cloud, and build processes on Jenkins. RACK pulls evidential data from all these sources into a single knowledge graph from which it can be queried and the returned results can be used in reports or to form an assurance case that is compliant with state-of-the-art standards such as Goal Structure Notation (GSN) [13] and Structured Assurance Case Metamodel (SACM) [20].

3   RACK Data Model

RACK is a triplestore with a schema (which we call a data model) tailored for curating certification evidence. The foundation of our data model is an entity-relationship (E-R) model [2]. The E-R model is comprised of entity classes and relationship classes, where entity classes represent real-world concepts or objects, and relationship classes represent the connections between those concepts or objects. In our use of that model, we restrict attributes to be associated only with entity instances. We allow the usual cardinalities on relationship instances.

The quality and trustworthiness of assurance case evidence is determined by the ability to trace and audit its origins. This is provenance information: what activity created the evidence, who participated in that activity, what tools were used to generate those entities, what other entities impacted that evidence, and was that evidence revised over time. We call this data meta-evidence, drawn from the PROV-W3C [16] provenance model (Fig. 1). While PROV-W3C provides a range of ways to say something, we use a constrained subset of it. This meta-evidence model can be applied to evidence for all high assurance systems. Entities represent objects for which meta-evidence can be provided. Activities represent the execution of defined processes that give rise to entities. Agents represent humans, organizations, or tools that cause activities to occur.

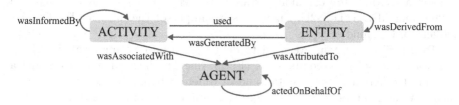

Fig. 1. W3C provenance model.

```
1  THING is a class
2  described by identifier with a single value of type string
3  described by title with values of type string with at most 1 value
4  described by description with values of type string with at most 1 value
5  described by dataInsertedBy with values of type ACTIVITY.
6  ENTITY is a type of THING
7  described by entityURL with values of type string
8  described by wasDerivedFrom with values of type ENTITY
9  described by wasRevisionOf with values of type ENTITY
10 described by wasImpactedBy with values of type ENTITY
11 described by wasGeneratedBy with values of type ACTIVITY
12 described by wasAttributedTo with values of type AGENT
13 described by generatedAtTime with values of type dateTime with at most 1 value
14 described by invalidatedAtTime with values of type dateTime with at most 1 value.
15 AGENT is a type of THING
16 described by actedOnBehalfOf with values of type AGENT.
17 ACTIVITY is a type of THING
18 described by wasAssociatedWith with values of type AGENT
19 described by wasInformedBy with values of type ACTIVITY
20 described by startedAtTime with values of type dateTime with at most 1 value
21 described by endedAtTime with values of type dateTime with at most 1 value
22 described by goal with values of type ENTITY
23 described by used with values of type ENTITY.
```

Fig. 2. Provenance data model expressed in SADL.

We use the Semantic Application Design Language (SADL) [3,9] to capture the provenance model. We developed this language at GE over many years. SADL is a controlled-English language with formal semantics that are automatically translated to OWL, a W3C standard [21]. In addition to being a data modeling language, SADL is also an Eclipse integrated development environment (IDE) that provides text highlighting, hyperlinking between concept definitions and usages, content assist auto-fill, and other features that facilitate model writing and maintenance. Moreover, SADL is very easy for humans to read and write.

To facilitate our meta-evidence, we added several relationships to the ENTITY class from the W3C provenance model (Fig. 2). We also defined data types and added cardinality constraints. These constraints can be expressed inline in the SADL model. For example, Fig. 2, line 2 and line 3 specify two different types of cardinality constraints with obvious meaning. These constraints are important for semantic analysis when we verify the instance data against the data model. We further added to the provenance model concepts (requirements, tests, development activities, etc.) common in standards such as DO-178C, ARP-4764, ISO 26262, and MIL-STD-882E. Figure 3 is a snippet of the data model; the full model can be found in [8].

To describe a system, we need to define a notion of component, interface, hardware and software components (Fig. 3, line 1) which allow us to model a system at different levels of detail and at different points in life-cycle development. We add concepts such as hazards, requirements, and tests that drive the development process (line 2). We introduce the notion of collections and various types of documents (lines 3–4) that are generated during the development process. To support the certification process we added the capability to refer-

```
 1 {SYSTEM, INTERFACE, HWCOMPONENT, SWCOMPONENT} are types of ENTITY.
 2 {HAZARD, REQUIREMENT, TEST, TEST_RESULT} are types of ENTITY.
 3 COLLECTION is a type of ENTITY.
 4 DOCUMENT is a type of COLLECTION.
 5 {PLAN, REPORT, SPECIFICATION} is a type of DOCUMENT.
 6 OBJECTIVE (note "Identifies tasks from a process for which evidence must be provided.")
 7   is a type of ENTITY.
 8
 9 {REQUIREMENT_DEVELOPMENT, TEST_DEVELOPMENT, TEST_EXECUTION} are types of ACTIVITY.
10
11 {PERSON, ORGANIZATION, TOOL} are types of AGENT.
12
13 // properties related to SYSTEM and HAZARD
14 partOf describes SYSTEM with values of type SYSTEM.
15 source describes HAZARD with values of type ENTITY.
16 source is a type of wasImpactedBy.
17
18 // properties for REQUIREMENT, REQUIREMENT_DEVELOPMENT, OBJECTIVE
19 governs describes REQUIREMENT with values of type ENTITY.
20 mitigates describes REQUIREMENT with values of type ENTITY.
21 satisfies describes REQUIREMENT with values of type ENTITY.
22 {governs, mitigates, satisfies} are types of wasImpactedBy.
23 referenced describes REQUIREMENT_DEVELOPMENT with values of type ENTITY.
24 referenced is a type of used.
25 satisfiedBy describes OBJECTIVE with values of type ACTIVITY.
```

Fig. 3. Additional data model concepts and properties.

ence applicable objectives from standards (line 6–7). We also introduce processes to develop requirements (line 9). The development activities are performed by agents which are also defined (line 11). These classes and subclasses are related to each other via properties. For SYSTEM and HAZARD we introduce properties that link them to other entities (lines 14–15; 19–21). Notice also how some properties refine properties from the provenance data model (line 16, 22, 24). Finally, we provide a way to link objectives (like those from standards) to activities (line 25). Together the data models in Figs. 2 and 3 provide the common semantics for data providers to precisely describe the collection of assurance case evidence so that data consumers can find the relevant evidence to build an assurance case.

4   Data Ingestion with Error Checking

Using the data model from the previous section as the foundation, we now describe the process of ingesting data into RACK. Organizing hundreds and thousands of datasets from multiple suppliers requires a well-defined ingestion pipeline. At the end of the pipeline is a triplestore that stores the data for later retrieval through queries to build an assurance case. Layered on top of the triplestore are services for data curation. For this, we leverage SemTK [4,5,10], an open-source Semantic Toolkit that has been in development at GE for several years. SemTK does much of the curation heavy lifting. It provides ingestion templates so that users are decoupled from the nuances of translating their data into triples. It also provides another important aspect of curation which is error checking – making sure that all incoming data matches the types specified by the data model and that all properties and classes are correct. Finally, SemTK provides an expressive query language for use by assurance case developers, which will be discussed in Sect. 7.

RACK provides users with ingestion templates and comma-separated value (CSV) header files which we call Common Data Representation that cover each class in the data model. An ingestion template is a mapping between CSV input files and data model properties (Fig. 4). The left hand side of the figure shows the REQUIREMENT class and the list of properties populated from the data model; the right hand side shows a list of column headers from the CSV file; the middle is the mapping between the column headers and the data model properties. Note how the ingestion template provides various optional text transformations like remove null (rm_null). RACK programmatically generates the common data representations following a pattern of ingestion that targets instance data class with a single unique identifier in "create if missing" mode. In this way, entities are created (and later, looked up) in the triplestore based on identifier. In practice, these identifiers can be those generated by tools in an existing development workflow such as DOORS. Data providers collect evidence and match it to the schema using the ingestion template and common data representation, then SemTK converts the data into triples and ingests them into the triplestore.

Fig. 4. Ingestion template.

The SemTK ingestion process ensures that all instances and object property relationships inserted into the triplestore comply with the model. Further, data type checking is performed on incoming data to verify that types match the range of each data property. Type errors result in error messages that clearly specify which piece of data failed and why.

On large DoD systems where certification evidence can be provided by many distinct organizations contributing data to the same graph in RACK, it is advantageous to avoid a distributed set of rules by which URIs are constructed. To meet this need, SemTK provides automated processes for creation and lookup of the uniform resource identifiers (URIs) for each piece of instance data. Ingestion templates may specify that a particular class is uniquely identified by one or more properties (in the case of RACK, the identifier property), and the URI itself can be a random UUID. Aside from "create if missing" as mentioned before, relationships may be ingested as "error if missing" to prevent broken links, or "error if exists" to prevent duplicates.

In terms of scalability, RACK is able to ingest a data package of 2.5M triples in under 15 min. This ingestion time is inclusive of all the type checking, URI lookups, and verification that all the types and properties are valid.

5   Data Verification

In this section, we describe what it means to do data verification, ensuring that the data is curated correctly before use. There are 3 distinct levels of verification in RACK. The first is verification at ingestion time, which was already described in the previous section. As data is loaded, it is verified against the ingestion template and any inconsistencies are immediately flagged with an ingestion error. Figure 5 gives examples of errors flagged at the ingestion level. The second level of verification is performed against the data model. This verification is to ensure that the loaded evidence adheres to any specified constraints (like cardinality). This can only be done post ingestion and we have built a tool called ASSIST-DV for this purpose. ASSIST-DV is a Prolog module that operates on a specified data model and the associated instance data in the triplestore to perform a number of tests and checks. The final level of verification is domain specific data verification. We can query RACK and verify that the number of returns matches an expected number. For example, DO-178C requires that Level A airborne systems satisfy a certain number of objectives and that a certain subset of these objectives should be satisfied "with independence". That is, software verification activities should be performed by a person other than the developer of the item being verified. ASSIST-DV can also identify disconnected islands of data, check that all the elements of one type have connections to elements of another (e.g. software components connected to some requirements).

On RACK, we perform a data verification query on the ingested dataset and print the results in a report to the end user. Figure 5 gives examples from each of the data verification levels.

6   Data Provenance

RACK curates two important aspects of provenance: 1) origins of data generated by a software development process; 2) traceability of evidence. Support for these distinct aspects allows RACK users to be doubly confident when using the data in a report or building an assurance case. First, it provides a clear understanding of how the software was developed, who created it, when it was created; second, it discerns how that data was curated into RACK itself.

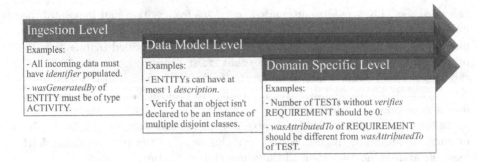

Fig. 5. Levels of data verification.

To support the latter, RACK classes have a uniform *dataInsertedBy* relationship (Fig. 2, line 5) that captures the activity that ingested the data itself into RACK. Queries can use this information to help diagnose discrepancies in the data as well as build up confidence in the fidelity of the results. It becomes possible to relate the data stored in RACK back to specific people running specific tools at specific times (see ACTIVITY properties from Fig. 2 lines 17–23). These relationships enable queries that are restricted to a subset of data providers or generated using tools having certain qualifications without restricting the whole dataset.

7   Use Case: From Query to an Assurance Case

7.1   Query Language

In addition to addressing the cost-effectiveness and scalability of data curation from the ingestion side, RACK also addresses these goals from the data retrieval side. We again leverage SemTK because it provides a user-friendly and expressive query language. Through a graphical interface, SemTK allows users to visually explore the RACK data model (built on Fig. 2 and Fig. 3) and construct SPARQL queries by dragging-and-dropping concepts onto a canvas. This is the construction of a concept called "nodegroup" which is a subgraph of interest. Users build nodegroups by dragging classes from a data model pane onto a canvas and connecting them based on properties. An example of a nodegroup is shown in Fig. 6. This nodegroup finds REQUIREMENTs that mitigate HAZARDs and have verifying TESTs, where the TESTs have confirming TEST_RESULTs that are Passed (which is expressed in a dialog box when clicking on TEST_STATUS). Notice that this nodegroup also returns meta-evidence about the ACTIVITY that inserted the data and its creation date and time. This single nodegroup would return requirements at all levels (high level to low level) thereby improving usability and reducing effort and time required for retrieving data.

Nodegroups are automatically translated to SPARQL. This allows RACK to approach the full capability of SPARQL with much less complexity for data

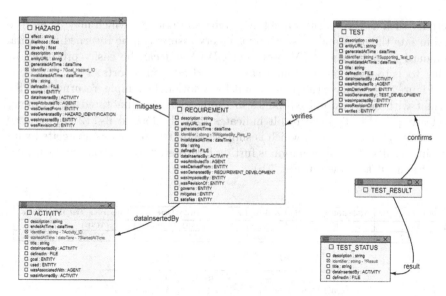

Fig. 6. A nodegroup to retrieve mitigation of hazards.

consumers that will write and read queries. Queries expressed in an intuitive graph pattern makes it easy for a data consumer to make direct connections to the underlying graph nature of the stored data. The resulting visual graph structures give the consumer of a query a clear picture of what data is being extracted from the dataset. Nodegroups as a language is also powerful enough to express the various queries we have encountered for building an assurance case. They can express a range of queries including simple relations, unions, transitive edges, and negative edges. Fields can be filtered with arbitrary predicates and optionally matched. Nodegroups contain query annotations (which properties are returned, custom names, constraints, sort, ...) so that a single nodegroup can automatically generate different types of SPARQL queries such as SELECT, COUNT, DELETE, and INSERT. In fact, the mechanics of data ingestion (mapping CSV data to the ingestion template and converting it into triples, as explained in Sect. 4) are also based on nodegroups.

7.2   Assembling an Assurance Case

An assurance case is a structured argument of how, whether, and why the system meets the goals of safe operation. Several standards exist including Goal Structuring Notation [13]. We demonstrate using a small but illustrative example on how to use the results from running the query in Fig. 6 to build an assurance case fragment, a sub-goal that can be used as part of a more comprehensive assurance case. The result shows the trace from requirements that mitigate hazards, tests that verify the requirements, and test results that confirm the tests. In addition, the results include meta-evidence about the requirement development activity such as the specific time the activity was started, which may be used to instantiate the assurance case context. Query results can be returned in several standard formats (e.g., CSV, json and OWL) and can be easily processed by other tools to assemble assurance cases or certification reports.

Figure 7(a) displays the query result for a notional example, returned in CSV format with user-customized names in the headers (as annotated in the query nodegroup in Fig. 6). The result indicates that the hazard H-1.2 is mitigated by the requirement HLR-1, which is supported by two test cases associated with passing results. This information is further interpreted to construct an assurance case fragment as shown in Fig. 7(b).

Goal_Hazard_ID	MitigatedBy_Req_ID	Activity_ID	StartedAtTime	Supporting_Test_ID	Result
H-1.2	HLR-1	HlrDev1	2023-01-02T18:10:10	TC-1-1	Passed
H-1.2	HLR-1	HlrDev1	2023-01-02T18:10:10	TC-1-2	Passed

(a) RACK Query Results

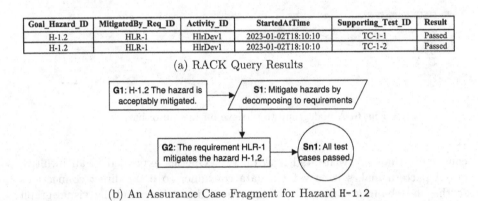

(b) An Assurance Case Fragment for Hazard H-1.2

Fig. 7. Using RACK query results to build an assurance case fragment in GSN format.

In addition to the use case presented above, in previous work we demonstrated how RACK's data model can be used to formalize a software development plan [18] and how RACK can be used to show compliance to safety objectives [12]. While our focus in this work has been on DoD systems, RACK is in general applicable to other non-military systems.

8   Conclusion

We have introduced RACK, a platform for curating evidence, the foundation of which is a data model comprised of classes and properties about entities, their provenance, their interrelationships, and their evolution over time. This model provides a common semantics that enables data providers and data users to communicate complex concepts of system design, verification, and evolution in a non-interactive workflow. RACK is developed under DARPA's Automated Rapid Certification of Software (ARCOS) program and has broad adoption in this research community [11,19] providing evidence of usability of the RACK platform. In addition to being able to interface their tools with RACK, some of the performer teams on ARCOS extended the data model with concepts germane to their own tools and have ingested instance data using the extensions [19]. One of the teams was able to map evidence in RACK into logic programming, which led to research breakthroughs such as target constrained natural query language built on top of RACK's data model within a principled, structured case adhering to Assurance 2.0 methodology [1]. The combination of rich but domain-constrained semantics and future-proofing of evidence seems well-suited to the domain of complex defense systems, beyond ARCOS, with long life cycles that are continually subject to upgrades and refinements over time. Finally, the ARCOS program is structured so that external evaluators will periodically assess effectiveness of all the technologies developed for reducing time and effort needed in constructing persuasive assurance cases. The final assessment will occur at the end of the program in 2024.

Acknowledgements and Disclaimer. Distribution Statement "A" (Approved for Public Release, Distribution Unlimited). This research was developed with funding from the Defense Advanced Research Projects Agency (DARPA). The views, opinions and/or findings expressed are those of the author and should not be interpreted as representing the official views or policies of the Department of Defense or the U.S. Government. The authors would like to give special thanks to John Interrante for ensuring that each RACK release is of highest quality.

References

1. Bloomfield, R.E., Rushby, J.M.: Assurance 2.0. arXiv abs/2004.10474 (2020)
2. Chen, P.P.S.: The entity-relationship model - toward a unified view of data. ACM Trans. Database Syst. (TODS) **1**(1), 9–36 (1976)
3. Crapo, A., Moitra, A.: Toward a unified English-like representation of semantic models, data, and graph patterns for subject matter experts. Int. J. Semant. Comput. **7**(03), 215–236 (2013)
4. Cuddihy, P., McHugh, J., Williams, J.W., Mulwad, V., Aggour, K.S.: SemTK: an ontology-first, open source semantic toolkit for managing and querying knowledge graphs. arXiv preprint arXiv:1710.11531 (2017)
5. Cuddihy, P., McHugh, J., Williams, J.W., Mulwad, V., Aggour, K.S.: SemTK: a semantics toolkit for user-friendly SPARQL generation and semantic data management. In: International Semantic Web Conference (P&D/Industry/BlueSky) (2018)
6. Denney, E., Pai, G., Pohl, J.: AdvoCATE: an assurance case automation toolset. In: Ortmeier, F., Daniel, P. (eds.) SAFECOMP 2012. LNCS, vol. 7613, pp. 8–21. Springer, Heidelberg (2012). https://doi.org/10.1007/978-3-642-33675-1_2
7. Deputy Assistant Secretary of Defense: Digital Engineering Strategy. https://ac.cto.mil/wp-content/uploads/2019/06/2018-Digital-Engineering-Strategy_Approved_PrintVersion.pdf (2018)
8. GE Research: DARPA's Automated Rapid Certification Of Software (ARCOS) project called Rapid Assurance Curation Kit (RACK). https://github.com/ge-high-assurance/RACK. Accessed 28 Apr 2023
9. GE Research: SADL: Semantic Application Design Language. https://github.com/SemanticApplicationDesignLanguage/sadl. Accessed 28 Apr 2023

10. GE Research: SemTK: Semantics Toolkit on GitHub. https://github.com/ge-semtk/semtk. Accessed 28 Apr 2023
11. GrammaTech: A-CERT. https://grammatech.github.io/prj/acert/. Accessed 1 May 2023
12. Herencia-Zapana, H., Russell, D., Prince, D., Siu, K., Cuddihy, P.: Towards compliance to safety objectives using data curation. In: 2023 Annual Reliability and Maintainability Symposium (RAMS), pp. 1–8 (2023)
13. Kelly, T., Weaver, R.: The goal structuring notation-a safety argument notation. In: Proceedings of the Dependable Systems and Networks 2004 Workshop on Assurance Cases, p. 6. Citeseer (2004)
14. Meng, B., et al.: Towards developing formalized assurance cases. In: 2020 AIAA/IEEE 39th Digital Avionics Systems Conference (DASC), pp. 1–9. IEEE (2020)
15. Moitra, A., et al.: A semantic reference model for capturing system development and evaluation. In: 2022 IEEE International Conference on Semantic Computing. IEEE (2022)
16. Moreau, L., Groth, P., Cheney, J., Lebo, T., Miles, S.: The rationale of PROV. J. Web Semant. **35**, 235–257 (2015)
17. Ruiz, A., Gallina, B., de la Vara, J.L., Mazzini, S., Espinoza, H.: Architecture-driven, multi-concern and seamless assurance and certification of cyber-physical systems. In: Skavhaug, A., Guiochet, J., Schoitsch, E., Bitsch, F. (eds.) SAFE-COMP 2016. LNCS, vol. 9923, pp. 311–321. Springer, Cham (2016). https://doi.org/10.1007/978-3-319-45480-1_25
18. Russell, D., Moitra, A., Siu, K., McMillan, C.: Modeling a DO-178C plan and analyzing in a semantic model. In: 2022 Annual Reliability and Maintainability Symposium (RAMS), pp. 1–8 (2022). https://doi.org/10.1109/RAMS51457.2022.9893967
19. Shankar, N., et al.: DesCert: design for certification. arXiv abs/2203.15178 (2022)
20. The Object Management Group: Structured Assurance Case Metamodel (2022). https://www.omg.org/spec/SACM/2.2/About-SACM/
21. W3C: OWL - semantic web standards. https://www.w3.org/OWL. Accessed 28 Apr 2023

2nd International Workshop on Security and Safety Interaction (SENSEI 2023)

2nd International Workshop on Safety-Security Interaction (SENSEI 2023)

Christina Kolb[1], Milan Lopuhaä-Zwakenberg[2], and Elena Troubitsyna[3]

[1] University of Edinburgh, Edinburgh, UK
`christina.kolb2022@gmail.com`
[2] University of Twente, Enschede, the Netherlands
`m.a.lopuhaa@utwente.nl`
[3] KTH Royal Institute of Technology, Stockholm, Sweden
`elenatro@kth.se`

Introduction

Two important criteria in designing high-tech systems are safety (the absence of risk of harm due to technological malfunctioning) and security (the ability to withstand attacks by malicious parties). Safety and security are heavily intertwined, and measures to improve one may have a positive or negative effect on the other. For instance, passwords can secure patients' medical data, but are a hindrance during emergencies. On the other hand, cyberattacks can purposely cause a system to fail, and improving cybersecurity leads to increased safety. To ensure safety and security, it is vital to understand how safety and security interact.

The aim of SENSEI 2023 is to further our understanding of safety-security interaction. For example, two important topics are the co-engineering of safety and security, and integrated safety and security risk assessment. To foster the exchange of concepts, experiences, research ideas, and novel results, we bring together a wide range of researchers in safety and security, from theoretical to practical research. There will be room to present and publish the latest findings in the field, but also for discussion to share experiences and novel ideas.

The first edition of SENSEI was organised last year at SAFECOMP 2022 (Munich). It was a great success, with many participants from both academia and industry, and many interesting contributions. Many participants from last year welcomed the existence of a workshop specific to safety-security interactions, and expressed their desire for SENSEI to become a recurring phenomenon. The discussion session at the end showed that there are many issues still open for research, and for this reason we are eager to organize a new edition.

This year, we have several exciting contributions, including two (co-)authored short papers from the organizers. Like last year, there will be dedicated discussion sessions to discuss the current state of affairs in the study of safety-security interactions.

As chairpersons of SENSEI 2023, we want to thank all authors and contributors who submitted their work, Friedemann Bitsch, the SAFECOMP Publication Chair, Jérémie Guiochet and Erwin Schoitsch, the SAFECOMP Workshop Chairs, the members of the

International Program Committee who enabled a fair evaluation through reviews and considerable improvements in many cases, and Mariëlle Stoelinga for guidance and advice. We want to express our thanks to the SAFECOMP organizers, who provided us the opportunity to organize the workshop at SAFECOMP 2023.

We hope that all participants will benefit from the workshop, enjoy the conference and will join us again in the future!

Acknowledgements. This workshop is partially funded by ERC Consolidator grant 864075 CAESAR.

International Program Committee 2023

Barbara Gallina	Mälardalen University, Sweden
Carlos E. Budde	University of Trento, Italy
Christoph Schmittner	Austrian Institute of Technology, Austria
Gabriel Pedroza	Commisariat à l'Énergie Atomique, France
Georg Macher	Graz University of Technology, Austria
Rajesh Kumar	BITS Pilani, India

Patterns for Integrating NIST 800-53 Controls into Security Assurance Cases

Torin Viger[1]([✉]), Simon Diemert[2], and Olivia Foster[2]

[1] University of Toronto, Toronto, Canada
`torin.viger@mail.utoronto.ca`
[2] Critical Systems Labs, Inc., Vancouver, Canada
{`simon.diemert,olivia.foster`}`@cslabs.com`

Abstract. It is sure that critical systems are appropriately secure and protected against malicious threats. In this paper, we present a novel pattern for Security Assurance Cases that integrates security controls from the NIST-800-53 cyber security standard into a comprehensive argument about system security. Our framework uses Eliminative Argumentation to increase confidence that these controls have been applied correctly by explicitly considering and addressing doubts in the argument.

1 Introduction

Critical systems, such as those in the automotive, rail, aerospace, health, or financial industries, pose risks to those that depend on them. Safety is a principal concern for these systems, and there are many established methods for assuring that a system satisfies a set of safety goals. Assuring system security has also become an increasing concern, but gaining confidence in the security of critical systems remains a challenge.

The NIST 800-53 cybersecurity standard provides a catalog of privacy and security *controls* intended to mitigate threats to a system [2]. The NIST 800-53 catalog is organized into families of controls intended to mitigate specific threats. For example, the family "Access Control" has 25 controls for preventing unauthorized access to privileged information. The catalog also suggests control enhancements that can be used to harden a system's controls. Showing that a system is compliant with NIST 800-53 provides some assurance that specific categories of threats are mitigated. However, since NIST controls are flexible and customizable, simply applying the controls is not sufficient; it is also necessary to reason about them in the context of a specific system.

Assurance Cases (ACs) provide a structured argument, supported by evidence, showing how a system satisfies a particular goal [11]. Security ACs argue that a system has achieved an acceptable level of security, and are increasingly used in critical systems. For instance, ISO 21434 - *Road vehicles - Cybersecurity engineering* requires the creation of an AC [3]. Some authors have incorporated NIST 800-53 controls into their Security ACs [13]. While creating Security ACs helps to assure a system, it is also important to evaluate the confidence in that

© The Author(s), under exclusive license to Springer Nature Switzerland AG 2023
J. Guiochet et al. (Eds.): SAFECOMP 2023 Workshops, LNCS 14182, pp. 165–175, 2023.
https://doi.org/10.1007/978-3-031-40953-0_14

AC, i.e., how confident are the stakeholders that the top-level goal has been achieved? Various methods exist to evaluate confidence, including Assurance Case Points, Bayesian Belief Networks, Dempster-Shafer Theory, and Eliminative Argumentation (EA).

One strength of EA is that it builds confidence by reasoning over doubts in the argument. EA uses defeasible reasoning to increase confidence in an argument by enumerating doubts and showing how they have been mitigated [9]. The incorporation of doubt as a dialectic element of an argument also reduces confirmation bias, a known weakness of ACs. EA has been applied to critical systems [7], and more generally, the role of dialectics in ACs has been recognized by the industrial and academic communities [10]. However, to our knowledge, EA has not been applied to Security ACs to gain confidence in the implementation of NIST 800-53 controls.

In this paper, we propose a pattern for Security ACs that: 1) integrates NIST-800-53's controls into a broader, comprehensive argument showing that a system is appropriately protected against all relevant threats to its correct functionality, and 2) uses EA to increase confidence that these controls have been applied correctly. The pattern is expressed using the Goal Structuring Notation (GSN) pattern notation [11].

2   Assurance Cases

In this section, we provide a short overview of Assurance Cases (ACs) and the Eliminative Argumentation (EA) method and notation.

2.1   Overview of Assurance Cases

ACs are structured arguments intended to show that a system satisfies a high-level goal. While many methods exist for expressing and organizing AC arguments, Goal Structuring Notation (GSN) is most widely used for this purpose [14]. Other methods for expressing arguments include Claims-Argument-Evidence (CAE) notation [5], Toulmin's notation [16], the Friendly Argument Notation (FAN) [12], and EA [9]. Additionally, though it is not a notation, many ACs are expressed using a narrative or essay style that is included as part of a safety report for the system.

Regardless of the approach used to express the argument structure, all of these approaches ground the argument in *evidence* that is generated through various engineering activities. Examples of evidence that might be used to support a security AC include requirement specifications, design reports, test results, static analysis results, inspection records, threat analyses, modelling results and so on. The following quote from ISO 26262 - *Road vehicles - Functional safety* illustrates the relationship between the argument and evidence in an AC; while the ISO 26262 is focused on safety, the relationship between argument and evidence is equally important in the concept of security ACs.

"The safety argument communicates the relationship between the evidence and the objectives. It is possible to present many pages of supporting evidence without clearly explaining how this evidence relates to the safety objectives. Both the argument and the evidence are crucial elements of the safety case. An argument without supporting evidence is unfounded, and therefore unconvincing. Evidence without an argument is unexplained, resulting in a lack of clarity as to how the safety objectives have been satisfied" [1].

ACs are often treated as a "wrapping up" activity and are not created until after the main system development activities have completed, i.e., AC preparation appears on the upper right side of the system development V-model. While it is true that ACs are partially dependent on information and evidence that is only available near the end of development, this does not mean that AC preparation must wait until system development has been completed. In fact, developing an AC during system development can help proactively identify concerns with the system and inform design decisions. In practice, we have found that a "develop early, revise often" approach helps to explicitly document assurance rationale throughout the development lifecycle [7].

2.2 Eliminative Argumentation

For the reasons mentioned above, this paper uses EA to express our security AC patterns. EA is notationally similar to GSN in that the argument is represented as a Directed Acyclic Graph (DAG) and that it resembles a tree. In EA, *claims* (rather than GSN's *goals*) are depicted as rectangular nodes in the graph which assert properties about a system. Claims may be supported by further argumentation through strategies (parallelogram nodes) that decompose a claim into more refined subclaims, or may be directly supported by evidence. Additional contextual information and assumptions may be added using context and assumption nodes respectively. EA also permits the expression of inference rules that describe how the children of a claim should be logically combined to support their parent.

An essential element of EA is the inclusion of *defeaters*, which developers may use to express doubts about their system. EA is founded on the notion of defeasible reasoning, where confidence in a claim is increased as sources of doubt are identified and mitigated [9]. In this way, EA provides a means to assess confidence in an argument and mitigate problems related to confirmation bias. Practitioners often have doubts about systems they develop, and EA provides an avenue to explicitly reason about those doubts in a structured manner.

In EA, there are three types of defeaters:

- **Rebutting Defeaters** express doubt about the validity of a claim directly.
- **Undercutting Defeaters** express doubt about an inference rule or logical step in the argument.
- **Undermining Defeaters** express doubt about the validity of evidence used to support a claim.

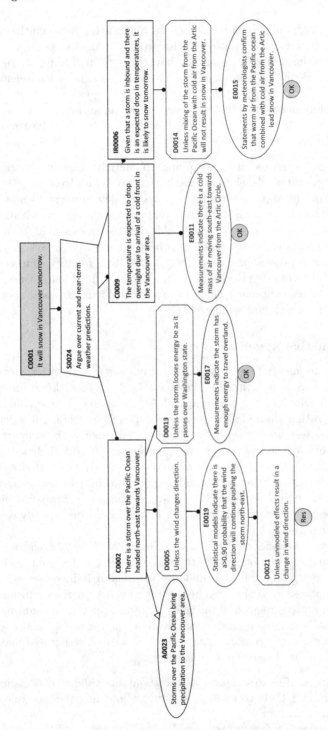

Fig. 1. Example of an EA decomposition asserting that it will snow in Vancouver tomorrow, from [8].

Defeaters are incorporated directly into the logical flow of the argument. Defeaters may be resolved by further argumentation, ideally being supported by additional evidence showing the corresponding doubt is addressed. If defeaters are not resolved, they are marked as *residuals*, indicating that there are unaddressed doubts about the argument. An AC may be accepted by stakeholders even with residual doubt, which suggests that the stakeholders are comfortable with the remaining doubts. One advantage of EA over other notations is that it helps to highlight residual doubts in the AC so that they can be explicitly considered by stakeholders, rather than giving false confidence in a system by omitting doubts [7].

As an example of the EA notation, Fig. 1 presents a small argument about whether it will snow in Vancouver, British Columbia, Canada. This argument was created using *Socrates - Assurance Case Editor* [4]. The strategy (S0024) used to decompose the argument's top-level claim (C0001) is to examine the current and near-term weather predictions. The argument has two main branches. The first branch (rooted in C0002) considers that a storm is moving into the Vancouver area. Two rebutting defeaters challenge this claim (D0005 and D0013) and evidence is presented against these defeaters. In the case of E0019, the evidence is undermined (D0021) on the grounds that the weather models are incomplete; no additional argumentation is available to resolve this defeater, so it is marked as residual. In the other case, the evidence is accepted as adequate to resolve the defeater and is marked as "OK". The second branch of the argument (rooted in claim C0009) considers that the temperature will drop overnight, which is supported directly by evidence (E0011) about an incoming cold front. Finally, an inference rule (IR0006) shows how to logically combine the two main branches of the argument to support the top-level claim about snow. This rule is undercut by another defeater (D0014) questioning whether the rule is a valid inference, which is in turn resolved by evidence (E0015) in the form of expert judgement. In conclusion, based on this argument, it seems reasonable that it will snow in Vancouver; however, the completeness of weather prediction models remains a source of doubt in the prediction.

2.3 Assurance Case Patterns

AC patterns, sometimes called *templates*, express reusable arguments or argument fragments that can be instantiated into a real AC. Patterns were first introduced in Kelly's doctoral thesis [14] and are now regularly used by practitioners and researchers to communicate argument structures [6,8]. When using GSN or EA, patterns are expressed with a notation extension that includes three operators: *optionality*, *multiplicity*, and *choice* [11]. These operators are depicted in Fig. 2 as part of a small example.

The *choice* operator is shown as a diamond and indicates that the user must pick among several nodes/branches in the pattern. In Fig. 2 the choice operator is annotated with "1 of 2" indicating that exactly one of the two branches, either C0003 or C0004, must be selected during instantiation.

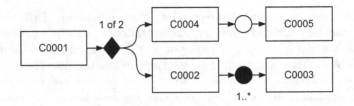

Fig. 2. Example of GSN pattern notation and operators.

The *optionality* operator is shown as an unshaded circle. It indicates that the user instantiating the pattern should pick whether or not to include the nodes below the operator. In Fig. 2, the user has the option to include claim C0005 when instantiating the pattern.

The *multiplicity* operator is shown as a shaded circle and annotated with a multiplicity "m..n". During instantiation, the user must choose the number of times to duplicate the node(s) below the operator between the minimum and maximum numbers given by the multiplicity. In Fig. 2, the user must pick between 1 and * (many) duplicates of node C0003. The patterns in this paper use only the multiplicity operator.

3   Security AC Pattern

Our argument pattern for Security ACs using EA is presented in Fig. 3, 4 and 5, and were rendered using Socrates's pattern creation and rendering feature [4]. To illustrate the different layers of our pattern, we use a running example of a *Maritime Autonomous Surface Ship (MASS)* [17]. The MASS system is intended to transport cargo between locations without requiring direct interaction from humans, and is a representative cyber-physical system where both safety and security are critical. The system includes interconnected subsystems responsible for various functions such as basic steering, navigation, autopilot, chart and information management, collision avoidance and remote control.

Our pattern consists of three decomposition layers: *(i)* decomposition over threat categories, *(ii)* decomposition over individual threats, and *(iii)* decomposition over NIST-800-53 control mitigations. The pattern's top-level claim asserts that some specific functionality F of the system will not be impacted by any malicious interference, i.e., by intentional malicious threats. For the MASS system, one functionality that needs to be protected from threats is the ship's ability to follow its correct heading. The first decomposition layer (shown in Fig. 3) partitions the top-level claim into subclaims asserting that malicious threats will not impact the functionality of subsystems related to F, communication between those subsystems, or their input and output data. The term *"related"* used in nodes *C0004*, *C0005* and *C0006* refers to all subsystems that could impact F if altered. This definition may be refined for a specific system/functionality in context node *X0010*. For example, subsystems related to the MASS system's

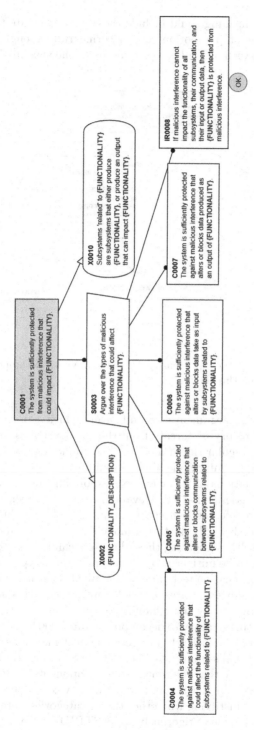

Fig. 3. The first layer of our Security AC pattern, which decomposes over categories of threats.

ability to follow its heading could include those that calculate the ships course, physically cause the ship's motion (e.g., steering rudder/engines), and enable communication between system components (e.g., the system's LAN).

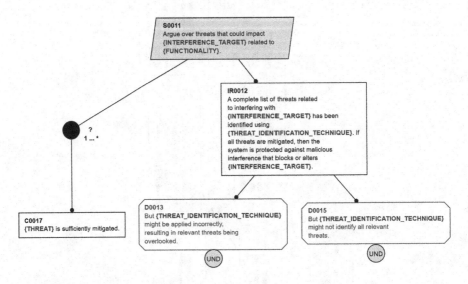

Fig. 4. The second layer of our Security AC pattern, which decomposes a category of threats into individual threats.

Figure 4 gives the argument's second layer, which can be instantiated to decompose each category of threats from the top layer into individual threats identified from a particular threat modeling technique (e.g., STRIDE-LM threat modeling [15]). The circular node above claim *C0017* indicates that there may be multiple instantiations of this claim corresponding to different threats. The inference rule *IR1* asserts that all relevant threats have been identified, and is decomposed by two defeaters reflecting potential doubts in this claim's validity (i.e., failure to correctly apply the threat modeling technique, and incompleteness of the technique itself). Mitigating these defeaters can increase confidence in the argument; *D0013* can be mitigated by describing measures put in place to ensure that the threat identification technique was applied rigorously and correctly, and by justifying why omitted threats are not applicable in this scenario, whereas *D0015* may be mitigated by the reliability of the technique itself.

Consider using this strategy to decompose claim C0004 for the MASS system, i.e., that the system is sufficiently protected against malicious interference that could affect the system's ability to follow its heading. STRIDE-LM modeling may be used to identify that relevant system components could be impacted by spoofing, tampering, repudiation and denial of service threats. Defeater D0013 can be mitigated by justifying why other threat categories were omitted, and by describing measures taken to rigorously apply STRIDE-LM to the MASS system. Defeater D0015 may be mitigated by appealing to the reliability of STRIDE-LM, i.e., by arguing that STRIDE-LM is an established threat modeling framework that has been successfully applied to similar systems in the past.

The final layer of our pattern (shown in Fig. 5) decomposes each threat into its associated mitigating controls from NIST-800-53. Each control that is relevant to a given threat should be included either in a claim asserting that the control is implemented, or in a claim explaining why the control is not applicable for a given system. Inference rule IR0019 asserts that if all relevant controls from NIST-800-53 are either implemented or not applicable to the system, then the threat is mitigated. Our pattern includes the defeater *D0020*, which considers that the controls suggested by NIST may be incomplete. While this defeater is largely mitigated by the reliability of NIST as a continuously updated international security standard, it may be further mitigated by documenting additional efforts made to identify controls/mitigations for the specified threat which are not included in NIST-800-53.

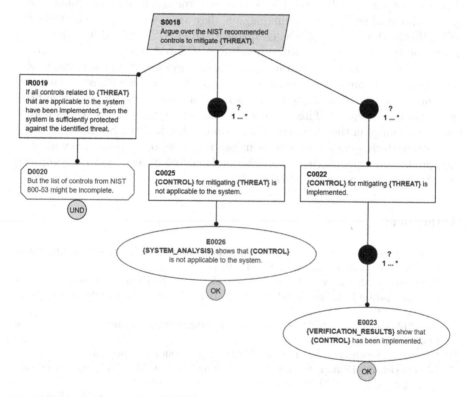

Fig. 5. The third layer of our Security AC pattern, which decomposes individual threats into the NIST-800-53 controls for their mitigation.

In our example, the NIST controls that are relevant to each threat can be easily identified, as the documentation for each control includes the relevant

STRIDE-LM threat(s) that they help mitigate. For each threat, a claim can be added for each relevant control that either asserts that the control has been implemented, or that the claim is not relevant for the system. For example, control AC-4 from NIST on information flow enforcement may be implemented for the MASS system to mitigate the threat of spoofing, but the NIST control PE-3 on physical access control may not be applicable to prevent spoofing for MASS if the system cannot be manually operated.

4   Conclusion

In this paper, we have presented a pattern for Security ACs that uses EA to reason over doubts in the argument. Rather than identifying and addressing threats in an ad-hoc way, our pattern gives a structured approach for enumerating threats and mitigating them in accordance with the established international security standard NIST-800-53. Our patterns are flexible and support any type of threat identification technique, but they are most easily integrated with STRIDE-LM threat modeling as each control from NIST 800-53 includes documentation that explicitly identifies which STRIDE-LM threats they mitigate.

By using EA and incorporating defeaters throughout the argument, AC developers must confront potential doubts related to their identified threats and their mitigation, and explicate their reasoning for why these doubts have been appropriately mitigated. This enables stakeholders to more easily assess potential shortcomings in the argument. Furthermore, developing a Security AC using our pattern during system development can help developers proactively identify the preventative controls that should be implemented in their system to improve security in compliance with NIST-800-53.

References

1. ISO 26262 - Road vehicles—Functional safety. Standard, International Organization for Standardization, Switzerland (2018)
2. NIST 800-53 - Security and Privacy Controls for Information Systems and Organizations. Special Publication SP 800-53, National Institute of Standards and Technology (2020)
3. ISO 21434 - Road vehicles - Cybersecurity engineering. Standard, International Organization for Standardization (2021)
4. Socrates - Assurance Case Editor (2023). https://safetycasepro.com
5. Bloomfield, R., Bishop, P., Jones, C., Froome, P.: ASCAD – Adelard safety case development manual. Technical report, Adelard (1998)
6. Burton, S., Gauerhof, L., Heinzemann, C.: Making the case for safety of machine learning in highly automated driving. In: Tonetta, S., Schoitsch, E., Bitsch, F. (eds.) SAFECOMP 2017. LNCS, vol. 10489, pp. 5–16. Springer, Cham (2017). https://doi.org/10.1007/978-3-319-66284-8_1
7. Diemert, S., Joyce, J.: Eliminative argumentation for arguing system safety - a practitioner's experience. In: 2020 IEEE International Systems Conference (SysCon), pp. 1–7 (2020). iSSN 2472-9647

8. Diemert, S., Goodenough, J., Joyce, J., Weinstock, C.: Incremental assurance through eliminative argumentation. J. Syst. Saf. **58**(1), 7–15 (2023)

9. Goodenough, J.B., Weinstock, C.B., Klein, A.Z.: Eliminative argumentation: a basis for arguing confidence in system properties. Technical report, Carnegie Mellon University-Software Engineering Institute Pittsburgh United (2015)

10. ACW Group: Assurance Case Guidance - Challenges, Common Issues and Good Practice (Version 1.1). Technical report, Safety Critical Systems Club (2021)

11. ACW Group: Goal Structuring Notation Community Standard (Version 3). Technical report, Safety Critical Systems Club (2021)

12. Holloway, C.M.: The Friendly Argument Notation (FAN). Technical report (2020). https://ntrs.nasa.gov/citations/20205002931, nTRS Author Affiliations: Langley Research Center NTRS Document ID: 20205002931 NTRS Research Center: Langley Research Center (LaRC)

13. Jahan, S., et al.: MAPE-K/MAPE-SAC: an interaction framework for adaptive systems with security assurance cases. Futur. Gener. Comput. Syst. **109**, 197–209 (2020)

14. Kelly, T.P.: Arguing safety - a systematic approach to safety case management. Ph.D. thesis, University of York (1998)

15. Muckin, M., Fitch, S.C.: A Threat-Driven Approach to Cyber Security. Lockheed Martin Corporation (2014)

16. Toulmin, S.E.: The Uses of Argument, 2nd edn. Cambridge University Press, Cambridge (2003). https://doi.org/10.1017/CBO9780511840005

17. Wikipedia: Autonomous cargo ship—Wikipedia, the free encyclopedia (2023). https://en.wikipedia.org/wiki/Autonomous_cargo_ship. Accessed 29 Apr 2023

Analyzing Origins of Safety and Security Interactions Using Feared Events Trees and Multi-level Model

Megha Quamara[1]([✉])(iD), Christina Kolb[2]([✉])(iD), and Brahim Hamid[1]([✉])(iD)

[1] IRIT, Université de Toulouse, CNRS, UT2, 118 Route de Narbonne,
31062 Toulouse Cedex 9, France
{megha.quamara,brahim.hamid}@irit.fr
[2] Laboratory for Foundations of Computer Science, School of Informatics,
University of Edinburgh, 10 Crichton Street, Edinburgh EH8 9AB, UK
ckolb@ed.ac.uk

Abstract. Existing approaches to analyzing safety and security are
often limited to a standalone viewpoint and lack a comprehensive mapping of the propagation of concerns, including unwanted (feared events
like faults, failures, hazards, and attacks) and wanted ones (e.g., requirements, properties) and their interplay across different granular system
representations. We take this problem to a novel combination of the Fault
and Attack Trees (FATs) as Feared Events-Properties Trees (FEPTs) and
propose an approach for analyzing safety and security interactions considering a multi-level model. The multi-level model facilitates identifying
safety- and security-related feared events and associated properties across
different system representation levels, viz. system, sub-system, information, and component. Likewise, FEPT allows modeling and analyzing the
inter-dependencies between the feared events and properties and their
propagation across these levels. We illustrate the use of this approach in
a simple and realistic case of trajectory planning in an intersection point
scenario regarding autonomous Connected-Driving Vehicles (CDVs) to
address the potential interactions between safety and security.

Keywords: Safety · Security · Interactions · Antagonism · Fault and
Attack Trees · Feared events trees · Multi-level model

1 Introduction

An ongoing transmission in drone-based applications, when hacked, can be used
to manipulate their functionality, which may impact the safety of other environmental assets like low-flying planes. Autonomous cars may crash into one another
on the manipulation of navigation-related information by a remote attacker.
Important healthcare-related data of a patient is kept a secret; however, in case

This work was partially supported by AISEC Project EP/T027037/1.

J. Guiochet et al. (Eds.): SAFECOMP 2023 Workshops, LNCS 14182, pp. 176–187, 2023.
https://doi.org/10.1007/978-3-031-40953-0_15

of emergencies, it might delay the required treatment of the patient if not accessible. A locked door is more secure because a burglar cannot enter a facility. However, the same is highly unsafe if a fire breaks out and one wants to escape the facility. Thus, safety (protection from accidental failures or the well-being of a person) and security (protection from harmful attacks on a system or a person) are intertwined and must be analyzed in integration. However, analyzing safety and security together when ensuring both might be in a conflict (antagonistic)—for instance [7].

To better understand how safety and security are intertwined, it is important to understand the origin of their interactions. So far, models like Fault and Attack Trees (FATs) combinations are used to capture safety and security interactions [6]. However, it is unclear where exactly the interactions originate from. In alignment with this, several questions are left unaddressed: Which elements of a system cause a safety and security interaction? Is a safety- or security-related measure dependent on another? Is a measure dependent upon a safety- or security-related requirement, or vice versa? An instance can be the fulfilment of safety-related requirements (e.g., application of brakes on detecting an obstacle) in autonomous driving when a security-related measure (e.g., authorized access) is put into place. Likewise, the application of two or more measures may also suffer from conflicting requirements.

In this paper, we aim to comprehend and analyze the origins of safety and security interactions. To this, we consider both the unwanted (viz. faults, failures, hazards, and attacks) and wanted concerns (viz. requirements and properties) from the safety and security perspectives to realize the combination of fault and attack trees as Feared Events-Properties Trees (FEPTs). Moreover, we consider a multi-level system model to capture the safety and security concerns regarding high-level system, sub-systems, information, and component-based representations. We illustrate the approach in the case of autonomous Connected-Driving Vehicles (CDVs), specifically for trajectory planning in an intersection point scenario.

The rest of this paper is organized as follows: Sect. 2 provides a brief background on safety and security interactions, FAT analysis techniques, and a multi-level model supporting the approach development. Section 3 describes our approach to analyzing safety and security interactions. Section 4 presents the approach instantiation regarding a CDVs use case. Section 5 highlights the related works and positions our contribution. Finally, Sect. 6 concludes the paper with future work directions.

2   Background

2.1   Safety and Security Interactions

The authors in [7] introduced the following safety and security interaction types and modeled them using Boolean logic Driven Markov processes (BDMP):

– *Conditional dependency:* Fulfillment of safety requirements conditions security, or vice versa;

- *Mutual reinforcement:* Fulfillment of safety requirements or measures contribute to security, or vice versa;
- *Antagonism:* Safety and security requirements or measures, when considered together, lead to conflicting situations; and
- *Independence:* No interaction.

Although the interactions are identified with respective measures in the case of an industrial pipeline; however, it is still open where exactly the interaction is resulting from. In this paper, we focus on antagonism exemplified by a use case, while the other interaction types will be addressed in future work.

2.2 Fault and Attack Trees

Several models consist of fault and attack tree combinations [6], which will form the basis for analyzing safety and security interactions in this work. FATs merge 1) dynamic attack trees having Sequential AND (SAND) gates to model attacks as a sequence of steps and 2) dynamic fault trees having Priority AND (PAND) gates to model spare components and functional dependencies.

In our extension of FATs, we allow intermediary nodes, unlike in [7] where leaf nodes were used, to be part of a Petri net to model antagonism. The Petri net consists of two nodes, out of which only one is active. We aim to leverage the soundness of FATs, along with the representation capabilities of Petri nets to construct the formalisms in this work.

2.3 Multi-level Model

The engineering process of complex systems typically involves decomposing the system into sub-systems and components, which are further implemented and incorporated into the sub-systems or the whole system [11]. Considering this, the system-related aspects in this paper are rendered at the following levels:

- **Level 3,** *System level,* represents the system as an atomic unit and concentrates on its high-level strategic concerns, like goals and objectives;
- **Level 2,** *Sub-system level,* represents the functional decomposition of the system, wherein different sub-systems have dedicated functionalities that must be integrated to make the whole system;
- **Level 1,** *Information level,* captures the information that facilitates interaction within or between the sub-systems; and
- **Level 0,** *Component level,* focuses on the self-contained computational, communication, and physical elements that make up a sub-system or a system.

3 Proposed Approach

In this section, we describe our approach to analysing the origin of safety and security interactions, including the related artefacts (if any) leveraged or produced throughout. The approach is compliant with the operational concept, design, and analysis phases of the ISO 26262 [5], SAE J3061 [19], and ISO 15288 [4] standards. It comprises the following steps (see Fig. 1):

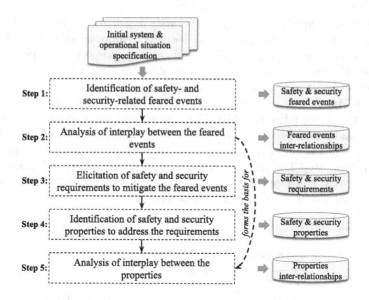

Fig. 1. Proposed approach and related artefacts.

- **Step 1:** *Identification of safety- and security-related feared events.* This step involves unveiling the events that may cause harm to the target of protection (viz., system, sub-system, information, or component) as part of the independent safety and security risk analysis processes. For instance, given an operational situation of a system, a feared event from the safety and security perspectives can be associated with a hazard and threat, respectively [15]. Notably, there may exist feared events that are common to both safety and security domains, with different underlying causes.
- **Step 2:** *Analysis of interplay between the feared events.* This step involves analyzing the potential cause-effect inter-relationships between the feared events belonging to the safety and security domains. It can be envisioned that the feared events identified at one level of safety and security analyses may trigger feared events at another level (see Fig. 2). For instance, a threat associated with a system component may trigger a hazardous situation for the entire system. Likewise, a functional failure at the sub-system level may lead to a security-related feared event at the system level. Antagonism is modeled by assigning intermediary nodes to a Petri net, wherein two or more states of the target element are assigned to the same Petri net. In this case, a token can switch among these states that capture the conflicting situations involving safety- and security-related feared events.
- **Step 3:** *Elicitation of safety and security requirements to mitigate the feared events.* This step involves specifying safety and security requirements drawn out from the underlying feared events and defined on top of the functional requirements. A discrete set of requirements can form the basis to avoid the potential impact of the feared events concerning the target of protection.

– **Step 4:** *Identification of safety and security properties to address the requirements.* In this step, the safety and security requirements identified in the
   previous step are typed by safety and security properties, respectively. In
   essence, the set of requirements can be built upon or influenced by a range of
   properties belonging to the safety and security domains.
– **Step 5:** *Analysis of interplay between the properties.* This step involves analyzing the potential inter-relationships (e.g., mutual reinforcement, antagonism, conditional dependencies) between the safety and security properties
   identified in the previous step. Due to the feared events inter-relationships
   identified in Step 2, a property from the safety domain can influence the one
   from security, and vice versa. Thus, these relationships can form the basis for
   conducting a consistent properties interplay analysis.

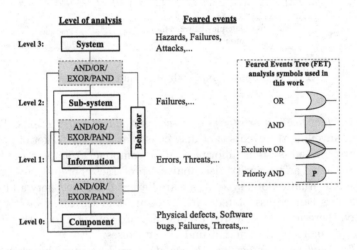

Fig. 2. Multi-level model-based feared events analysis.

4   Use Case: Trajectory Planning for Autonomous Driving at Intersections

In this section, we introduce the use case of autonomous Connected-Driving
Vehicles (CDVs) to illustrate the proposed approach. The choice of this use case
is driven by the safety- and security-critical nature of CDV systems, respectively
due to the potentially hazardous impact of their malfunctioning behaviour and
their highly inter-connected architecture that offers attack surfaces for exploiting
their functionality.

Scenario Description. Herein, we consider a realistic intersection point scenario
inspired by one of our previous works [15]. It comprises three vehicles—two of
which are autonomous (viz. ego vehicles 1 and 2) and a third vehicle (called

merging vehicle), moving towards a non-signalized intersection point [10] with non-negligible speeds, as shown in Fig. 3. The ego vehicles are in driving automation mode above SAE 3 [3], without requiring the human operator to take over the control. In addition, they follow virtual guides to stay in lane. For simplicity, we do not consider any roadside infrastructure and inter-vehicle communication. The instantiation of the approach steps in the context of this use case is detailed as follows:

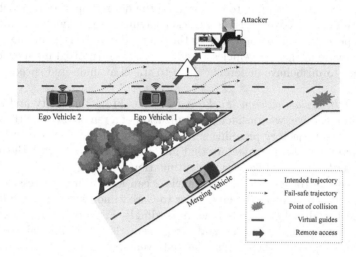

Fig. 3. Combining intersection point scenario with intended and fail-safe trajectories.

Identification of Safety- and Security-related Feared Events. In the considered scenario, the following two safety-related cases may arise:

- **Case 1:** Since the merging vehicle is not within the line of sight of the onboard system of the ego vehicle 1. Therefore, following its intended trajectory, the latter may collide with the former as their future motion path intersects. To address this, the trajectory planning software of ego vehicle 1 computes a fail-safe trajectory [13] to branch off from the intended motion path to end in a safe state.
- **Case 2:** Following its intended trajectory, the ego vehicle 2 determines ego vehicle 1 on its future motion path. Hence, its trajectory planning software computes a fail-safe trajectory to avoid a collision. However, due to case 1, the computed fail-safe trajectory of ego vehicle 2 may intersect with that of ego vehicle 1. In this case, if the speed of the former is not within safe limits concerning the latter, a collision may occur.

Likewise, from the security perspective, we begin with considering the following set of assumptions regarding the capabilities of an attacker upon which the security-related feared events or threats can be derived:

- *Assumption 1:* An attacker can have physical or remote access to the onboard units, as well as remote access to the communication channels of the CDV system through a wireless medium.
- *Assumption 2:* An attacker can intercept and tamper with an ongoing communication within the intra-vehicle network, i.e., among the CDV system modules.

The source of the attack can be an external person or the system's operator with malicious intent, aiming to compromise the desired operation or behaviour of the CDV system. Given this, an attacker having a prior understanding of the system's operation can remotely access the onboard trajectory planning or speed control software of the ego vehicles 1 and 2 in an unauthorized manner, causing the vehicles to misbehave or forcing them to travel at undesired speeds [14].

Analysis of Interplay between the Feared Events. From the safety and security interplay perspective, we consider the realization of a remote access attack by an attacker on the trajectory planning software of the ego vehicle 1, causing its failure to compute a fail-safe trajectory that may lead to a collision with the merging vehicle (refer to Case 1). Likewise, in continuation to Case 1, unauthorized access to the speed control module of ego vehicle 2 can lead to its progressive misbehaviour wherein it changes the lane (refer to Case 2) not within safe limits when ego vehicle 1 is also changing its lane. Accordingly, Fig. 4 presents an excerpt of the feared events tree. The blue nodes represent the safety-related events, the yellow nodes represent the security-related events, and the grey nodes present both safety- and security-related events.

As mentioned in Sect. 2.1, we are interested in one specific interaction type between safety and security, viz. antagonism, in this paper. Figure 5 presents an excerpt of the antagonism regarding Vehicle Speed Sensor (VSS). The node with five edges represents the Petri net node. In this node, a token can switch from one state to another, which models the antagonism. In a remote attack situation, the VSS sensor can be left on or switched off. In the former case, it can communicate with other sensors, but at the same time, lead to providing wrong input. In the latter case, it can avoid interference between sensors, thereby improving security but affecting safety-critical functionality like braking to prevent a collision. This is an example of the antagonism between safety and security. Of course, antagonism may originate from the intra-domain perspective (safety-safety or security-security), which is nonetheless not detailed in this paper.

Specification of Safety and Security Requirements to Mitigate the Feared Events. The safety-related requirement in the considered use case is to prevent a collision between 1) the ego vehicle 1 and the merging vehicle and 2) between ego vehicles 1 and 2. Other specific requirements, in this case, can be to ensure that the VSS software and hardware are working. Likewise, a security-related requirement, in this case, is to prevent an attack on the VSS, specifically involving unauthorized access and tampering with the data from VSS to ensure its correct functionality.

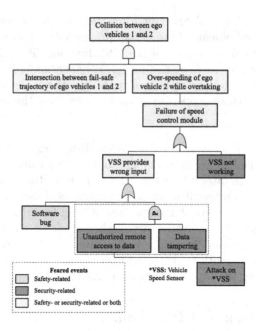

Fig. 4. Feared events tree: Fault and Attack Trees (FATs) combination.

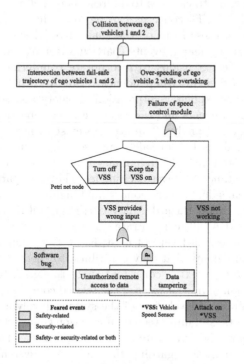

Fig. 5. Feared events tree: Fault and Attack Trees (FATs) combination extended for antagonism.

Identification of Safety and Security Properties to address the Requirements.
Considering the requirements above, safety properties to be ensured in the given
case are *availability* and *integrity* of the VSS functionality. Likewise, from the
security side, the properties to be met include *confidentiality, integrity*, and *availability* of the VSS data. Due to lack of space, we do not depict the tree-based
formalism involving these properties at different levels of the multi-level system
model.

Analysis of Interplay between the Properties. Regarding the interplay, at the
component level, the functional availability of the VSS from the safety perspective conflicts with the integrity of the VSS data from the security perspective
in an attack situation where it needs to be turned off. Likewise, the operational
availability of the VSS data at the component level from the security perspective mutually reinforces the availability of the vehicle speed control module at
the sub-system level from the safety perspective, which is not detailed in the
scope of this work. Essentially, these interactions are drawn out relying on the
knowledge regarding the feared-events relationships.

5   Related Work and Positioning

Integration of fault and attack trees to address modeling and analysis of safety
and security domain-specific concerns can be found in a handful of works in
the literature. Some of these focus on the qualitative [2] and quantitative analysis [8] of the underlying feared events (particularly faults and attacks), while
some [18] also provide extensions to incorporate countermeasures to address
the feared events and their inter-dependencies. However, the analysis process in
these approaches lacks explicit incorporation of safety and security properties
impacted by the feared events and the resulting inter-dependencies.

Regarding the level of analysis, approaches exist to facilitate co-design [16]
and formal-based analysis [17] of safety and security concerns in the context
of a multi-layered system model. Preliminary Hazard Analysis (PHA) [1] in the
safety context, for instance, involves eliciting feared events, particularly hazards,
concerning the system's deployment context and high-level objectives. Similarly,
approaches like Functional Hazard Analysis (FHA) [20] or Failure Mode and
Effects Analysis (FMEA) [9] concentrate on the different sub-systems having
dedicated functionalities. Last yet not least, Fault Tree Analysis (FTA) [9] targets the system components that may contribute to the sub-system or system
failure. In the security context, a consistent analysis, e.g., Attack Tree Analysis
(ATA) or identification of misuse cases of the related concerns [12], often emphasizes a detailed component-level view of the system, involving vulnerable technologies, insecure ports, and unprotected information channels-for instance. Nevertheless, to our knowledge, the state-of-the-art approaches have not addressed
safety and security analysis regarding the multi-level system model, wherein
the feared events associated with one level of analysis may propagate to the

other. Despite the role of the feared events analysis techniques at different system representation levels, an approach needs to be envisioned to address the inter-dependencies between safety and security concerns across these levels.

In contrast to the existing works, the approach proposed herein provides means to analyse the propagation of feared events and their inter-dependencies across different levels of system representation. Notably, we do not change the already existing techniques (namely FTA and ATA) but provide an extension of these techniques to identify and analyze the feared events across different levels. In addition, we enhance the analysis by incorporating properties (and their inter-dependencies) characterizing the desired features a system should have and impacted by the presence of feared events. To this end, the information from the feared events inter-relationships artefacts is used to analyze the properties inter-relationships.

6 Conclusion and Future Work

We presented an approach to analyzing the origins of safety and security interactions in the context of a multi-level system model. The use case of autonomous CDVs was considered to comprehend the origins and the consequences of antagonism between intra-domain (within safety and security) and inter-domain concerns (between safety and security) while modeling antagonism by extending FEPT with Petri net nodes. Our findings are the following:

- The multi-level analysis facilitates understanding of the propagation of concerns, including feared events and properties, and their interplay across different granular representations of the system. Accordingly, horizontal and vertical links can be established between them to analyze their inter-relationships.
- Even if different sub-systems or system components seem independent from one another (e.g., a break looks at first sight independent from an airbag), there can be safety and security interactions among the associated concerns.
- We presented the Petri net as a node with five points to make it different from other rectangular nodes, which helps in further visualizing the antagonism within the entire tree-based formalism.
- We presented the nodes caused by 1) a safety-related event in blue, 2) a security-related event in yellow, and 3) both safety- and security-related events in grey. This node colouring gives a visualization of the origins of safety and security through which one can focus on nodes depending on the analysis needs.

Further work will target investigating other safety and security interaction types, including mutual reinforcement and conditional dependency. In addition, a sequence of models can be considered to switch the Petri net tokens from one state to another. This would present steps of feared events realization via different paths across the tree. We also aim to analyze interactions with probabilities, involving costs or time. For a detailed understanding of the origin of the interactions, other example cases (e.g., industrial control systems) could be of interest.

Acknowledgements. We thank David Aspinall from the University of Edinburgh and a member of the AISEC Project EP/T027037/1 for his support.

References

1. Barr, L.C., et al.: Preliminary risk assessment for small unmanned aircraft systems. In: 17th AIAA Aviation Technology, Integration, and Operations Conference, p. 3272 (2017)
2. Fockel, M., Schubert, D., Trentinaglia, R., Schulz, H., Kirmair, W.: Semi-automatic integrated safety and security analysis for automotive systems. In: Modelsward, pp. 147–154 (2022)
3. International, S.: Taxonomy and definitions for terms related to driving automation systems for on-road motor vehicles. SAE Int. **4970**(724), 1–5 (2018)
4. Iso15288 (2015). https://www.iso.org/standard/63711.html. Accessed March 2023
5. Iso26262 (2018). https://www.iso.org/standard/68383.html. Accessed March 2023
6. Kolb, C., Nicoletti, S.M., Peppelman, M., Stoelinga, M.: Model-based safety and security co-analysis: a survey. ArXiv, abs/2106.06272 (2021)
7. Kriaa, S., Bouissou, M., Colin, F., Halgand, Y., Pietre-Cambacedes, L.: Safety and security interactions modeling using the BDMP formalism: case study of a pipeline. In: Bondavalli, A., Di Giandomenico, F. (eds.) SAFECOMP 2014. LNCS, vol. 8666, pp. 326–341. Springer, Cham (2014). https://doi.org/10.1007/978-3-319-10506-2_22
8. Kumar, R., Stoelinga, M.: Quantitative security and safety analysis with attack-fault trees. In: 2017 IEEE 18th International Symposium on High Assurance Systems Engineering (HASE), pp. 25–32. IEEE (2017)
9. Maier, T.: FMEA and FTA to support safe design of embedded software in safety-critical systems. In: Shaw, R. (eds.) Safety and Reliability of Software Based Systems, pp. 351–367. Springer, London (1997). https://doi.org/10.1007/978-1-4471-0921-1_22
10. Montanaro, U., et al.: Towards connected autonomous driving: review of use-cases. Veh. Syst. Dyn. **57**(6), 779–814 (2019)
11. Nasa, N.: Systems engineering handbook. National Aeronautics and Space Administration (2007)
12. Opdahl, A.L., Sindre, G.: Experimental comparison of attack trees and misuse cases for security threat identification. Inf. Softw. Technol. **51**(5), 916–932 (2009)
13. Pek, C., Althoff, M.: Ensuring motion safety of autonomous vehicles through online fail-safe verification. In: Robotics: Science and Systems-Pioneers Workshop (2019)
14. Petit, J., Shladover, S.E.: Potential cyberattacks on automated vehicles. IEEE Trans. Intell. Transp. Syst. **16**(2), 546–556 (2014)
15. Quamara, M., Pedroza, G., Hamid, B.: Multi-layered model-based design approach towards system safety and security co-engineering. In: 2021 ACM/IEEE International Conference on Model Driven Engineering Languages and Systems Companion (MODELS-C), pp. 274–283. IEEE (2021)
16. Quamara, M., Pedroza, G., Hamid, B.: Facilitating safety and security co-design and formal analysis in multi-layered system modeling. In: 2022 IEEE International Conference on Dependable, Autonomic and Secure Computing, International Conference on Pervasive Intelligence and Computing, International Conference on Cloud and Big Data Computing, International Conference on Cyber Science and Technology Congress (DASC/PiCom/CBDCom/CyberSciTech), pp. 1–8. IEEE (2022)

17. Quamara, M., Pedroza, G., Hamid, B.: Formal analysis approach for multi-layered system safety and security co-engineering. In: Marrone, S., et al. (eds.) Dependable Computing – EDCC 2022 Workshops. EDCC 2022. CCIS, vol. 1656, pp. 18–31. Springer, Cham (2022). https://doi.org/10.1007/978-3-031-16245-9_2
18. Sabaliauskaite, G., Mathur, A.P.: Aligning cyber-physical system safety and security. In: Cardin, M.A., Krob, D., Lui, P., Tan, Y., Wood, K. (eds.) Complex Systems Design and Management Asia, pp. 41–53. Springer, Cham (2015). https://doi.org/10.1007/978-3-319-12544-2_4
19. Saej3061   (2021).   https://www.sae.org/standards/content/j3061_202112/. Accessed March 2023
20. Wilkinson, P., Kelly, T.: Functional hazard analysis for highly integrated aerospace systems. In: IEE Certification of Ground/Air Systems Seminar (Ref. No. 1998/255), pp. 4–1. IET (1998)

Utilising Redundancy to Enhance Security of Safety-Critical Systems

Elena Troubitsyna[✉]

KTH – Royal Institute of Technology, Stockholm, Sweden
elenatro@kth.se

Abstract. For many safety-critical systems, implementing modern cybersecurity protection mechanisms is hindered by legacy design and high re-certification costs. Since such systems are typically designed to be highly reliable, they usually contain a large number of redundant components used to achieve fault tolerance. In this paper, we discuss challenges in utilising redundancy inherently present in the architectures of safety-critical systems to enhance system cybersecurity protection. We consider classic redundant architectures and analyse their ability to protect against cyberattacks. By evaluating the likelihood of a successful cyberattack on a redundant architecture under different implementation conditions, we conclude that redundancy in combination with diversity has better potential to be utilised for cybersecurity protection.

Keywords: Safety-critical systems · Redundancy · Security protection · Cyberattacks · Safety-security interactions

1 Introduction

In the railway domain, CENELEC EN 50126 Standard [1], defines RAMS - Reliability, Availability, Maintainability and Safety as a quantitative and qualitative indicator of the degree to which the system can be trusted to be operating as specified, be available and safe. Safety is the absence of catastrophic consequences on the user(s) and the environment, while reliability is the ability to continuously provide correct service [2]. Safety and reliability are tightly interconnected system properties because safe system behaviour requires both a safety-driven system design process and reliable behaviour of system components during the system operation.

The main means to achieve reliability is to implement fault tolerance [2–4]. Fault tolerance aims at preventing a fault of a component to propagate to the system boundaries and cause a failure [2]. As a result of implementing fault tolerance, a fault of a component can be "masked" [3,4], i.e., compensated by the redundant components or a predictably-degraded behaviour in the presence of faults ensured [2]. Since fault tolerance results in introducing some form of redundancy in the system design, safety-critical systems, including railways, usually have a high degree of redundancy in their architecture.

© The Author(s), under exclusive license to Springer Nature Switzerland AG 2023
J. Guiochet et al. (Eds.): SAFECOMP 2023 Workshops, LNCS 14182, pp. 188–196, 2023.
https://doi.org/10.1007/978-3-031-40953-0_16

Many safety-critical systems, e.g., such as railway systems, have a long lifespan usually lasting over 25 years [5]. Obviously, legacy systems designed over 25 years ago, are not protected against modern cyberthreats. Moreover, introducing security control mechanisms recommended, e.g., by IEC 62443 [6–8] would require significant investments into re-design and re-certification, which is often unfeasible, especially for such large and complex systems as railways. This has motivated our study of whether redundancy, inherently present in safety-critical systems, can be utilized in cybersecurity protection.

In this paper, we consider classic redundant architectures and analyse whether they can be utilized to enhance the cybersecurity protection of safety-critical systems. In our study, we adopt a quantitative approach, i.e., analyse the likelihood of a successful cyberattack on a given redundant architecture. Such an approach is motivated by several factors. On the one hand, an introduction of cybersecurity protection can be prioritized based on the likelihood of a successful attack. On the other hand, when the reuse or insignificant adaptation of a redundant architecture provides sufficient protection against a cyberattack, the investment and time to implement cybersecurity protection can be optimized.

The paper is structured as follows: in Sect. 2, we overview several types of redundant architectures typically used in safety-critical systems. In Sect. 3, we analyse their capabilities to provide cybersecurity protection. Finally, in Sect. 4, we overview the related work and discuss the potential of utilising redundant architectures to enhance the cybersecurity protection of safety-critical systems with legacy design.

2   Redundant Architectures in Safety-Critical Systems

The main goal of fault tolerance is to prevent the propagation of a fault into the system boundaries [2–4]. A fault can be a failure of a hardware component, software bug, memory corruption etc. A fault manifests itself as an error, which should be detected by some error detection mechanism. Once an error is detected it should be confined and error recovery performed.

Let us consider an example of a hardware component fault. Assume that we have a sensor measuring a certain parameter. The measurements are provided as inputs into a controlling component. The controlling component can check whether the received input is within the feasible boundaries and if not then ignore the input. This is an example of error detection and confinement. The controlling device can, e.g., use the last good value to tolerate this fault and switch to the use of spare components for error recovery.

Let us now also consider an example of a software fault. Assume that software contains an error (typically called a bug). Upon executing a faulty code, an exception would be raised. This is error detection and confinement. Consequently, the exception handling procedure is executed to implement error recovery.

Fault tolerance always requires some form of redundancy. In our example of sensor failure, a spare sensor (or several of them) is required. In the example of exception handling, additional time, i.e., time redundancy, is required to execute exception handling.

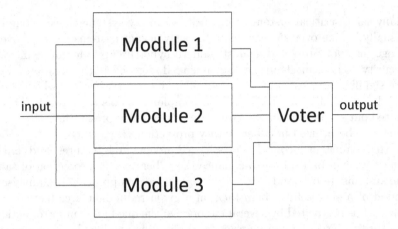

Fig. 1. Triple Modular Redundancy Architecture.

In general, redundancy is the use of some additional elements within the system which would not be required in a system that was free from all faults, i.e. redundancy is the overhead required to tolerate faults [2–4]. It is needed to detect or "mask", i.e., nullify the effect of a fault and continue to operate even if some redundant component failed.

Redundant components usually have the same functionality. Hardware redundancy is the use of additional hardware components, e.g., sensors, controllers, and actuators. Software redundancy is the use of several versions of functionally identical software components.

One of the most frequently used redundant architectures is Triple Modular Redundancy (TMR) [3,4]. The architecture consists of three functionally identical components and a voter. TMR is able to mask a failure of one component, i.e., nullify the effect of a failure of a single component, i.e., the architecture produces the correct output even if one component failed [3,4]. The architecture is presented in Fig. 1.

Depending on the application, a module can be as simple as a single logic gate or as complex as a subsystem of a safety-critical system. The modules receive identical input and produce certain outputs. If none of the modules failed then the outputs should match. If some module failed then its output would differ from the outputs of two other modules. The outputs of the modules are input into the voter, which produces a majority view. If all modules produced identical results then any output is accepted as the output produced by the entire architecture. If one module failed then the majority view, i.e., the output from the other two modules is produced as the output of the entire architecture.

Since TMR architecture prevents a single-point failure, it is often used to mask a failure of a sensor providing critical measurements or a highly-critical module, e.g., power supply. Often cascading arrangement of TMR architectures is introduced to achieve high reliability.

The reliability of a system is characterized by its failure rate or, more generally, by its Mean Time Between Failures (MTBF) [3,4]. MTBF is the inverse of the failure rate in the constant failure rate phase. The probability that the system works correctly for some time t is defined correspondingly as

$$P(t) = e^{-t/MBTF}$$

While evaluating the reliability of a redundant architecture, we are often interested in the probability of the architecture producing a correct result. Implicitly, we consider a certain time instance t and hence, can use the formula above to evaluate the reliability of the components in the architecture at that instance of time. We omit an explicit representation of probability as a function of time.

To assess the reliability of TMR architecture, let R_v be the reliability of a voter, i.e., the probability of providing correct functionality. Let the reliability of each module be $R_i, i = 1..3$. Correspondingly, the unreliability, i.e., the probability of failure for each component be $F_i = 1 - R_i$. Using the basics of probability theory [9], we can compute the reliability of TMR as follows:

$$R_{TMR} = R_v(R_1R_2R_3 + F_1R_2R_3 + F_2R_1R_3 + F_3R_1R_2)$$

If the reliability of each component is the same and equal to R_m. Then the probability of TMR producing correct output is as follows [3,4]:

$$R_{TMR} = R_v(3R_m^2 - 2R_m^3)$$

The result is easy to obtain using basic algebraic manipulations over the general formula of reliability of TMR. Typically, the voter is chosen to be highly reliable, i.e., it is reliability is very close to 1. In this case, the reliability of TMR is as follows:

$$R_{TMR} = R_v(3R_m^2 - 2R_m^3)$$

The most general form of this architecture is N-modular redundancy. The architecture utilizes N modules to tolerate (N-1)/2 rounded to lower integer faults number of faults [3,4].

Static resilient architectures are used when the system cannot tolerate the temporal unavailability of a certain value due to component failure, i.e., component failures should be masked. However, static redundancy is resource-expensive: it requires two additional modules to tolerate one failure, three additional modules to tolerate two failures etc.

Dynamic redundancy relies on the detection of faults and on the system taking appropriate actions to nullify their effects. It does not mask fault but rather tries to confine faults and reconfigure the system to achieve fault tolerance [3,4]. When dynamic resilient architectures are used, an error must be produced before the system can recognize the fault and take action. Hence, it can be used in systems, which can tolerate temporal errors within their operation. An example of a dynamic redundant architecture is a standby spare. It consists of three modules: the main module, a spare and a switch operated by a fault detector.

While no fault is detected the operating module drives output through the switch. When a fault is detected the switch recognizes it and takes output from the standby module. The switch is controlled by a fault detection scheme. Reconfiguring the system causes disruption of the system while outputs are switched. There are two alternatives of the dynamic resilient architecture - a cold standby spare and a hot standby spare.

In hot standby the spare runs continuously in parallel with the active unit. This variant of the architecture minimizes the disruption because the spare module is in the same state as the main one. However, the hot standby resilient architecture increases power consumption (two modules should be powered at the same time) and makes the spare the subject of the same operating stress as the main module. The second variant of the architecture is the cold standby spare. The spare module is unpowered until called into service after the main module fails. The pros and cons of the hot and cold standby spares are opposite to each other.

Often static and dynamic resilient architectures are used in combination and create hybrid redundant architectures. Such architectures use fault masking to prevent errors from being propagated within the system and fault detection and reconfiguration to remove faulty units from the system.

3   Redundant Architectures and Security Protection

By replicating identical hardware components, we can improve the reliability of the corresponding component arrangement. However, replicating identical software modules would not allow us to increase the reliability of the redundant software architecture, because software faults are systematic in nature and hence, have a common mode failure. Software redundancy requires diversity [10].

The distinction between redundancy and diversity lies in the deliberate difference introduced between functionally identical components. This difference aims at protecting against the same design faults. The effect of the use of diversity depends on the degree of dependence between the failure processes of the versions, not only on their individual reliabilities.

It has been demonstrated that software diversification provides efficient protection against such a large class of attacks as code-reuse attacks as well as side-channel attacks [11,12].

For example, let us consider TMR redundant architecture with three identical blocks. Let x be a specific attack. Lets each module has the probability to fail to detect it $F(x)$. Such probability is based on the estimates of such factors as the complexity of the attack, i.e., whether an attacker requires sophisticated equipment and financial investments to plant an attack, whether physical access to the device is required and how easy is to get such access, can the attack be carried out remotely etc. In industrial practice, such probabilities are sometimes simplified and classified as "high, very likely, medium, or remote" with some average values taken to represent each class.

Attacks arrive according to some probability distribution. Such distribution can be constructed from ENISA reports [13] or based on the organization own monitoring data. In case all three modules are identical then the probability of failing to detect the attack is $P(x)$. Such probability is based on the estimates of such factors as the complexity of the attack, i.e., whether an attacker requires sophisticated equipment and financial investments to plant an attack, whether physical access to the device is required and how easy is to get such access, can the attack be carried out remotely etc. If these modules are diverse then the probability of a successful attack (without an additional anomaly detection system):

$$P(successful attack) = \sum_{x \in A} P(x)F(x) \qquad (1)$$

where A is the set of all possible attacks, $P(x)$ is the probability of the attack x to occur according to the given probability distribution, and $P(x)$ over the set A defines the probability distribution of all possible attacks.

Now let us consider the case of diverse modules, i.e. each module has a different probability of failing to detect an attack $F_i(x)$. Then the probability of a successful attack on TMR is as follows:

$$P(successful attack) =$$
$$\sum_{x \in A} P(x)[F_1(x)F_2(x)F_3(x) + (1 - F_1(x))F_2(x)F_3(x)$$
$$+ (1 - F_2(x))F_1(x)F_3(x) + (1 - F_3(x))F_1(x)F_2(x)] \qquad (2)$$

A straightforward comparison of (1) and (2) demonstrates that the use of diverse components in TMR allows us to significantly decrease the probability of a successful attack. For instance, if we consider a side-channel attack. By measuring power consumption, an attacker has a non-zero probability to hack the device. If all devices are the same, i.e., non-diverse, then the same attack succeeds against all of them. However, if the devices are diversified then the attacker should obtain side-channel information at least from the majority of them to succeed.

The ideal diversity would be achieved if under any conditions if one version (or component) fails then another successfully performs the function and vice versa, i.e., the idealistic goal of diversity is to achieve zero probability of common failure [1].

Below are some common strategies used for improving the efficiency of redundancy with respect to fault tolerance:

- isolating redundant subsystems from as many as possible common potential causes of failure;
- diversity and adaptive diversity.

Let us consider an isolation strategy. Assume that we have N servers physically located at different and distant from each other premises. Assume that the attacker aims at physically damaging the servers. Obviously, the probability of success of such an attack is very low - it is very unlikely that an attacker can penetrate all N premises. In this case, the isolation is helpful for enhancing cybersecurity.

Let us consider the effect of diversification strategy. If each server requires its own distinct password then the likelihood of obtaining all N passwords is also low. Hence, the diversification strategy is useful in this case as well.

The main idea behind the adaptive diversity approach is to compose the system from the components which have different failure processes over the different input ranges. This is tightly related to the concept of "defence in depth" [14]. The adaptive diversity requires each successive layer of defence to be increasingly strong against those threats most likely to penetrate the previous layers.

However, if the attacker discovers a vulnerability that creates a back door in all servers then the effect of replication will be nullified. Diversity of software can alleviate this problem though might introduce additional failure modes due to the complexity of maintaining several versions. Obviously, it might also negatively affect the availability of certain control inputs and consequently, safety.

The effect of replication is also minimized in presence of DDoS attack. If the servers are replicated then DDoS attack will result in the unavailability of the entire architecture. A general conclusion can be made that a lack of diversity creates a potential for the propagation of attacks [15].

This observation has been formalized by Littlewood and Strigini [14]. Formally, let us consider a specific attack x and components C_1 and C_2, which are failing to protect against the attack x with probabilities $F_1(x)$ and $F_2(x)$ correspondingly. Assume that the failures to protect are independent. If Q_1 and Q_2 are average values of probabilities to fail to detect an attack as defined by the functions $F_1(x)$ and $F_2(x)$. Then the probability of a successful attack can be defined in terms of covariance between these two functions as follows [14]:

$$P(successful attack) = Q_1Q_2 + cov(P_1(x), P_2(x))$$

where cov is the covariance of the two functions [9]. Intuitively, it designates how similar these functions are.

4 Related Work and Discussion

The main goal of introducing redundancy into the system architecture is to cope with accidental faults [2–4]. Numerous studies evaluating the efficiency of different redundant architectures have been conducted. A comprehensive description of the fault tolerance field can be found, for instance in [4]. However, research investigating how to utilize fault-tolerant architectures to cope with malicious faults is scarce.

The formalization of the problem has been proposed by Littlewood and Strigini [14]. They postulated that diversification is essential for reaping the benefits of redundancy for security. To evaluate the degree of diversity they use the covariance function over the probabilities to fail to detect an attack by the components. Such a formalization allows us to quantitatively assess the impact of diversity and redundancy on cybersecurity protection.

Bain et al. [15] also emphasize the need for diversity based on the field study of cybersecurity incidents. Moreover, they also argue that even diversity can be sometimes insufficient if the components diversified against one type of cyberattack have a common vulnerability against another.

At a more general level, the formalization of safety-security requirements in interactions has demonstrated that a careful analysis of the impact of introducing security protection mechanisms on safety-critical functions is required. For instance, an introduction of secure gateways might delay or block control commands [16]. This also applies to the use of redundant components with identical functional but different real-time properties. At the same time, it is important to identify cybersecurity attacks that might result in safety accidents [17, 18] and prioritise protection against them.

In this paper, we have investigated the problem of utilizing redundant architecture to enhance system cybersecurity. By using the quantitative approach, we have demonstrated that the likelihood of a successful attack decreases when the redundant components are diverse and remains the same if the components are identical. Our result can be seen as an instantiation of a more general result by Littlewood and Strigini [14] that has been formalized using the covariance function over the probabilities of failures of attack detection.

The general conclusion is that if a redundant architecture already employs diversity then it might be a viable option to re-use it in cybersecurity protection. Otherwise, additional investments are required to replace the identical replicated components with diverse ones. Certain simple measures can be implemented for enhancing cybersecurity protection in the case of identical components too, e.g., the use of physical separation of components and communication channels, and the use of different passwords as diversification of input channels and communication paths.

In such safety-critical systems as railways, implementation of all the desirable security protection mechanisms at once is rather unfeasible due to the very large system scale and high complexity as well as the costs and time required. In this paper, we studied whether the potentials already present in the system architecture can be utilized to enhance system cybersecurity. The proposed quantitative approach to evaluating a likelihood of a successful cyberattack combined with the analysis of safety implications of cyberattacks can help to prioritise the implementation of cybersecurity protection mechanisms in industrial practice.

As a future work, it would be interesting to extend the quantitative approach to integrate the monitoring data as well as define the probability bounds for different attacker profiles.

References

1. CENELEC - EN 50126-1. Railway Applications - The Specification and Demonstration of Reliability, Availability, Maintainability and Safety (RAMS) - Part 1: Generic RAMS Process
2. Avizienis, A., Laprie, J.C., Randell, B., Landwehr, C.: Basic concepts and taxonomy of dependable and secure computing. IEEE Trans. Dependable Secure Comput. 1(1), 11–33 (2004). https://doi.org/10.1109/TDSC.2004.2
3. Storey, N.: Safety-Critical Computer Systems. Addison-Wesley, Boston (1996)
4. Koren, I., Mani Krishna, C.: Fault tolerant Systems, 2nd ed. Elsevier, Amsterdam (2007)
5. de Bortoli, A., Bouhaya, L., Feraille, A.: A life cycle model for high-speed rail infra-structure: environmental inventories and assessment of the Tours-Bordeaux railway in France. Int. J. Life Cycle Assess. 25, 814–830 (2020)
6. International Standard., "Industrial communication networks - Network and system se-curity - Part 3–3: System security requirements and security levels," IEC, Edition 1.0 2013–08
7. International Standard, "Security for industrial automation and control systems - Part 2–4: Security program requirements for IACS service providers," IEC, Edition 1.0 2015–06
8. Amendment 1, "Security for industrial automation and control systems - Part 2–4: Security program requirements for IACS service providers," IEC, Edition 1.0 2017–08
9. Oxford Dictionary of Statistics., Oxford University Press (2002)
10. Littlewood, B.: The impact of diversity upon common mode failures. Reliab. Eng. Syst. Saf. 51(1), 101–113 (1996)
11. Tsoupidi, R.M., Lozano, R.C., Troubitsyna, E., Papadimitratos, P.: Securing Optimized Code Against Power Side Channels. arXiv preprint arXiv:2207.02614
12. Tsoupidi, R.M., Troubitsyna, E., Papadimitratos, P.: Thwarting code-reuse and side-channel attacks in embedded systems. arXiv preprint arXiv:2304.13458
13. ENISA Transport Threat Landscape. https://www.enisa.europa.eu/publications/enisa-transport-threat-landscape. Accessed 6 June 2023
14. Littlewood, B., Strigini, L.: Redundancy and diversity in security. In: European Symposium on Research in Computer Security (2004)
15. Bain, C., Faatz, D., Fayad, A., Williams, D.: Diversity as a defense strategy in information systems. In: Gertz, M., Guldentops, E., Strous, L. (eds.) Integrity, Internal Control and Security in Information Systems. ITIFIP, vol. 83, pp. 77–93. Springer, Boston, MA (2002). https://doi.org/10.1007/978-0-387-35583-2_5
16. Troubitsyna, E., Laibinis, L., Pereverzeva, I., Kuismin, T., Ilic, D., Latvala, T.: Towards security-explicit formal modelling of safety-critical systems. In: Skavhaug, A., Guiochet, J., Bitsch, F. (eds.) SAFECOMP 2016. LNCS, vol. 9922, pp. 213–225. Springer, Cham (2016). https://doi.org/10.1007/978-3-319-45477-1_17
17. Vistbakka, I., Troubitsyna, E.: Towards a formal approach to analysing security of safety-critical systems. In: 14th European Dependable Computing Conference (EDCC). Iasi, Romania, 2018, pp. 182–189 (2018)
18. Poorhadi, E., Troubitsyna, E., Dan, G.: Analysing the impact of security attacks on safety using SysML and event-B. In: Seguin, C., Zeller, M., Prosvirnova, T. (eds.) Model-Based Safety and Assessment. IMBSA 2022. LNCS, vol. 13525. Springer, Cham (2022). https://doi.org/10.1007/978-3-031-15842-1_13

1st International Workshop on Safety/Reliability/Trustworthiness of Intelligent Transportation Systems (SRToITS 2023)

1st International Workshop on Safety/Reliability/Trustworthiness of Intelligent Transportation Systems (SRToITS 2023)

SRToITS2023 is in conjunction with SAFECOMP2023

Ci Liang[1], Martin Törngren[2], and Mohamed Ghazel[3]

[1] School of Transportation Science and Engineering, Harbin Institute of Technology, Harbin 150001, China
liangci321@hit.edu.cn
[2] Embedded Control Systems at the Department of Engineering Design, KTH Royal Institute of Technology, Sweden
martint@kth.se
[3] Univ. Gustave Eiffel (ex-IFSTTAR), COSYS/ESTAS, 59650 Villeneuve-d'Ascq, France
mohamed.ghazel@univ-eiffel.fr

1 Introduction

A mix of intelligent transportation systems (ITSs, e.g., the automated car/bus/metro/train, etc.) and regular transportation systems (RTSs) in future traffic networks challenges the safety, reliability and trustworthiness of ITSs, as well as the holistic safety of traffic networks. Hence, it is crucial to understand the risks of such mixed traffic networks where ITSs and RTSs are both involved, with mutual interactions. The risks can be caused by the following aspects: the complexity of operational tasks that ITSs have to deal with has been grossly underestimated, the artificial intelligence (AI) technology-based decision making is not reliable enough, ITSs lack a thorough and correct understanding of human driver behaviors and intentions in mixed scenarios, etc. With this in mind, there are many important issues that need to be investigated to facilitate ITSs performing tasks safely and properly, and assure the safety of traffic networks.

Topics of the Workshop

Contributions are sought in (but are not limited to) the following topics:

- Functional safety of ITSs,
- Safety of the Intended Functionality (SOTIF),

- Reliability/interpretability/trustworthiness of AI based systems,
- Scenario/model based V&V,
- Risk assessment of scenario-based virtual testing,
- Ways to assess the criticality of operational scenarios,
- Safety, security and performance issues of the coordination between automated vehicles and smart infrastructures,
- Understanding of human driver behaviors and intentions,
- Implications from regulatory entities,
- Challenges of road safety considering a mix of automated vehicles and regular ones in future roadways,
- Challenges of intelligent moving block operation in railways.

2   Workshop Format

SRToITS2023 will be a full-day workshop with a mix of keynotes (we plan to host two keynotes), paper presentations and discussion sessions.

Schedule:		
9.00–9.40	**Keynote:** Automated driving safety - when is an automated vehicle ready for the road?	Martin Törngren, (30 min Presentation + 10 min Q&A)
9.40–10.00	Reliability Evaluation of Autonomous Transportation System Architecture Based on Markov Chain	Bingyv Shen, Guangyun Liu, Shaowu Cheng, Xiantong Li, Kui Li and Chen Liang, (15 min Presentation + 5 min Q&A)
10.00–10.30	Coffee Break	
10.30–10.50	Uncertainty Quantification for Semantic Segmentation Models via Evidential Reasoning	Rui Wang, Mengying Wang, Ci Liang and Zhouxian Jiang (15 min Presentation + 5 min Q&A)
10.50–11.10	Research on the Reliability of High-Speed Railway Dispatching and Commanding Personnel with Multi Physiological Signals	Liuxing Hu and Wei Zheng, (15 min Presentation + 5 min Q&A)
11.10–11.30	Research on Brain Load prediction based on machine learning for High-speed Railway dispatching	Dandan Bi, Xiaorong Meng and Wei Zheng, (15 min Presentation + 5 min Q&A)
11.30–13.00	Lunch Break	
13.00–13.40	**Keynote:** Using Monte Carlo and stochastic models to understand rare accident mechanisms and improve safety	Olivier Cazier, (30 min Presentation + 10 min Q&A)
13.40–14.10	HIT Transportation Research Introduction	Ci Liang

Schedule:

14.10–14.30	Towards an Effective Generation of Functional Scenarios for AVs to Guide Sampling	Hugues Blache, Pierre-Antoine Laharotte and El Faouzi Nour-Eddin, (15 min Presentation + 5 min Q&A)
14.30–14.50	Rear-end Collision Risk Analysis for Autonomous Driving	Ci Liang, Mohamed Ghazel, Yusheng Ci, Nour-Eddin El Faouzi, Rui Wang and Wei Zheng, (15 min Presentation + 5 min Q&A)
14.50–15.30	Coffee Break	
15.30–15.50	Improving road traffic safety and performance – barriers and directions towards cooperative automated vehicles	Gianfilippo Fornaro and Martin Törngren (15 min Presentation + 5 min Q&A)
15.50–16.10	Paired Safety Rule Structure for Human-machine Cooperation with Feature Update and Evolution	Satoshi Otsuka, Natsumi Watanabe, Takehito Ogata, Donato Di Paola, Daniel Hillen, Joshua Frey, Nishanth Laxman and Jan Reich, (15 min Presentation + 5 min Q&A)
16.10–16.30	Summary	

3 Acknowledgements

As chairpersons of the SRToITS workshop, we would like to thank all authors, speakers and contributors who submitted their work and reviewed submissions, and the members of Program Committee who enabled a fair evaluation through reviews and considerable improvements in many cases.

Particularly, we want to express our thanks to the SAFECOMP chairpersons and organizers, who provided us the opportunity to organize the workshop at SAFECOMP 2023 as a hybrid event.

We hope that all participants will benefit from the workshop, enjoy the conference and will join us again in the future!

Organization

Workshop Chairs

Ci Liang (liangci321@hit.edu.cn)
Nour-Eddin El Faouzi (nour-eddin.elfassouzi@univ-eiffel.fr)
Mohamed Ghazel (mohamed.ghazel@univ-eiffel.fr)

Workshop Committees

Organization Committee

Ci Liang	Harbin Institute of Technology, China (liangci321@hit.edu.cn)
Mohamed Ghazel	Université Gustave Eiffel (ex IFSTTAR), France (mohamed.ghazel@univ-eiffel.fr)
Guo Zhou	SCANIA, Sweden (guo.zhou@scania.com)

Program Committee

Ci Liang	Harbin Institute of Technology, China
Martin Törngren	KTH Royal Institute of Technology, Sweden
Fredrik Törner	Volvo Car Corporation, Sweden
Christian Berger	Chalmers University of Technology, Sweden
Yusheng Ci	Harbin Institute of Technology, China
Nour-Eddin El Faouzi	Université Gustave Eiffel (ex IFSTTAR), France
Mohamed Ghazel	Université Gustave Eiffel (ex IFSTTAR), France
Thierry Denoeux	Université de Technologie de Compiègne, France
Olivier Cazier	Chez Conseil en Infrastructures de Transport Environnement, Circulation Sécurité, France
Zhanbo Sun	Southwest Jiaotong University, China
Rui Wang	Beijing Jiaotong University, China
Yonggang Wang	Chang'an University, China
Peng Chen	Beihang University, China

Keynotes

Automated Driving Safety - When is an Automated Vehicle Ready for the Road?

Abstract. Automated driving is a fascinating endeavor, representing a big leap in capabilities and complexity. The enormous investments into automated vehicles (AVs) have led to a rapid technological advancement with tremendous impact in the automotive and beyond. Yet, many challenges remain as the hype cycle has taken us through the trough of disillusionment. This talk will address the question of "when an AV is ready for the roads" with respect to acceptable risks, from philosophical, technical and societal viewpoints. In this talk I will attempt to summarize the current state of affairs and discuss some of the key remaining hurdles. Introducing automated vehicles at a somewhat large scale, beyond very limited operational design domains (ODDs), requires the advancement of approaches for cost-effective development, operations and their integration, to pave the way for trustworthy AVs. Key ingredients in development includes new system architectures and methodologies, including for verification and validation where model-based engineering will play an important role. The integration to form "trustworthy DevOps" requires the consideration of the whole life-cycle of activities (beyond primary functions being automated), ODD and operations engineering, and the provisioning of integrated AV and smart infrastructure designs. The talk will also give highlights of research at KTH along these strands including ongoing initiatives towards open research testbeds including AD-EYE (https://www.adeye.se/) and TECoSA (https://www.tecosa.center.kth.se/).

Keynote Speaker: Martin Törngren is a Professor in Embedded Control Systems at the Department of Engineering Design at KTH Royal Institute of Technology since 2002. In 1994 he received the SAAB-Scania award for qualified contributions in distributed control systems, and in 2004 the ITEA achievement award 2004 for contributions to the EAST-EEA project. From 1999 to 2004 he served as the Chairman of the Swedish real-time systems association, and he has represented KTH as a core partner in the EU networks of excellence in embedded systems design, Artist2 and ArtistDesign, and in the Artemis industrial association. He is the director of the TECoSA Swedish national competence center on Trustworthy Edge Computing Systems and Applications. His main research interests lie in safety and complexity management of automated and connected cyber-physical systems.

Using Monte Carlo and Stochastic Models to Understand Rare Accident Mechanisms and Improve Safety

Abstract. Designing an "intelligent" transportation system requires, in order to make it safe, to understand the mechanisms that may lead to relevant accidents. But in a modern transportation system, accidents or even incidents are very rare, and it takes hundreds or thousands of years of observation to be able to confirm that the required safety levels are fulfilled. In addition, if accidents are very rare, it is difficult, almost not impossible, to observe accident mechanisms and to have feedback on safety analyses. However, when we know the overall behavior of a system and its laws of operation, it is possible to model the system by Monte Carlo based models, or in the simplest cases by stochastic models, and use these models to diagnose the causes of the events. A good example of the application of Monte Carlo and stochastic models is the railway crossing: the common belief is that the main cause of accidents is the error or carelessness of the motorized driver. However, a stochastic model shows that this hypothesis is not consistent with accident statistics that the causes resulting in accidents at low-traffic-flow crossings are very different from those at busy crossings and that an effective intelligent accident prevention system will have to be introduced to take into account the various causes. This talk will address the Monte Carlo and stochastic based methodologies and their applications in rare accident/corner case analysis in Railways.

Keynote Speaker: Olivier Cazier is currently the founder of the company Chez Conseil en Infrastructures de Transport Environnement & Circulation Sécurité, specializing in reliability, availability, maintenance and safety for Railway, and a senior consultant for modernizing Railways lines in Eastern France and Occitania. He has been the Head of the Department Technological and Process Innovation of SNCF Network. He has been a member of the Scientific Committee and organization Committee of GeoRail 2011, 2014, 2017. His main interests lie in safety and security of transportation, FDMS, and innovation for intelligent transportation systems.

Reliability Evaluation of Autonomous Transportation System Architecture Based on Markov Chain

Bingyv Shen[1] , Guangyun Liu[1], Shaowu Cheng[1(✉)] , Xiantong Li[1], Kui Li[1], and Chen Liang[2]

[1] School of Transportation Science and Engineering, Harbin Institute of Technology, Harbin 150000, China
csw_h@hit.edu.cn

[2] Shenzhen Urban Transport Planning Centre Co., Ltd, Shenzhen 518000, China

Abstract. Reliability assessment methods are widely used in the reliability evaluation of transportation networks and transportation special equipment. The reliability assessment of Autonomous Transportation System (ATS) architecture can identify possible hidden problems and structural deficiencies before the implementation of ATS. The physical architecture of ATS maps the functional and logical architectures to the real world, hence, reliability assessment of the ATS architecture requires synthesizing information from all the three architectures. However, the current reliability assessment method of ATS architecture only took into account of the logical architecture of ATS. To meet this gap, a Markov chain model of the physical objects of ATS architecture is established, portraying the dynamic evolution of the physical object states, and failure rate and occupancy rate of physical objects is used to describe the reliability of the physical objects of ATS architecture, and the reliability of the physical objects and the importance of the physical objects in the ATS architecture is taken as the reliability index of ATS architecture. The method is applied to the reliability evaluation of the Vehicle Environment Awareness Service (VEAS) architecture, and the results show that the key physical objects that affect the reliability of the ATS architecture can be found by comparing the physical object importance and occupancy rate, and the reliability of the physical objects can be improved by raising the repairable rate and reducing the failure rate, thereby the reliability of the ATS architecture is promoted.

Keywords: Reliability · Failure Rate · Markov Chain · Autonomous Transportation System

1 Introduction

In recent years, with the further improvement of intelligent transportation infrastructure, intelligent transportation systems based on the Internet and other emerging technologies [1] have been developed rapidly, and the autonomous characteristics of the transportation system are becoming more and more obvious, and the transportation system

J. Guiochet et al. (Eds.): SAFECOMP 2023 Workshops, LNCS 14182, pp. 205–217, 2023.
https://doi.org/10.1007/978-3-031-40953-0_17

is transforming into ATS. The ATS architecture can provide specific guidance for the implementation of autonomous transport system. ATS is a complex system with random and self-organizing characteristics, and partial failures may occur during operation, such as system operation failure caused by data loss and network interruption, therefore, reliability assessment of ATS architecture is required, to identify possible hidden dangers and structural deficiencies in the ATS architecture in advance.

The ATS architecture includes functional, logical and physical architectures [2, 3]. The functional architecture is divided into four hierarchical layers: service domain, service, sub-service and function, describing the functions required for ATS services and the relationships between functions. The logical architecture builds a implementation logic of the functions of the functional architecture, which describes relation between system functions and transportation business implementation from the perspective of data flow. The physical architecture maps the functions and their implementation logic to the real world by describing the physical objects that make up the ATS service and the information stream between them. The three types of architectures interact with each other to form the ATS architecture, as shown in Fig. 1.

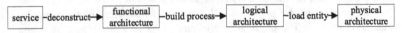

Fig. 1. Autonomous transportation system architecture

Reliability [4] refers to the ability for a system to perform a specified task within a specified time and under specified conditions. Reliability assessment methods can be divided into architecture-based and process-based assessment methods [5]. Architecture-based methods include fault trees [6], decision trees [7], event tree analysis, master logic diagrams, binary decision diagrams [8], reliability block diagrams [9], etc. These methods analyse the causes of a specific type of failure from a logical point of view by experience, estimating the probability of failure and thus reflecting the reliability of the system, and therefore is not universal. The process-based approach evaluates the reliability of a system based on the fault data generated by the system, considering the architecture of the system and the inherent dynamic characteristic of the system, thus reducing the reliance on expert experience and thus having a wider applicability. The methods mainly include Markov chains [10–14], petri nets [15], Bayesian networks [16], neural networks [17], etc.

Within the transportation domain, reliability assessment methods are mainly applied to analyse the reliability of transportation networks [18–20] and specific devices of transportation systems [21–23]. The reliability assessment methodology for ATS architecture has currently concerned only with the logical architecture of the ATS [24], while the ATS architecture has physical and functional architectures in addition to the logical architecture, and the reliability assessment of the ATS architecture needs to integrate information from all the three architectures. Physical objects serve as the material carriers of functionality. By describing the physical objects in the physical architecture, the corresponding relationships between them and the functional architecture can be captured. The data flow in the logical architecture requires transmission media to carry it, and the physical architecture describes these transmission media, known as information exchange pairs. By describing the physical objects and information exchange pairs, the corresponding relationships with the logical architecture can be captured. Therefore, evaluating the physical architecture is equivalent to evaluating the underlying functional and logical architectures together.

Reliability assessment methods based on architectures cannot be used for ATS architectures, because the physical objects that make up an ATS are of different kinds, logically complex and have various types of failures. The state of ATS physical objects can be converted between normal and failure over time, and Markov chain can completely describe the dynamic process of object state change with time [25], which is largely consistent with the ATS physical objects' state characteristics expression.

In this paper, we consider the mapping relationship of functional architecture and logical architecture to physical architecture according to the characteristics of ATS architecture, and obtain the reliability measure of ATS architecture by calculating the failure rate, occupancy rate, and importance of physical objects based on Markov chain model of physical objects of ATS architecture. Finally, the data from the simulation of the VEAS architecture, running on a simulation platform designed based on system dynamics principles, are used to verify the rationality and effectiveness of the method proposed in this paper.

The main contributions of this paper are as follows: 1. Applying the Markov chain model to the field of ATS reliability assessment 2. Synthesizing the physical architecture, functional architecture and logical architecture of the ATS architecture for reliability assessment.

The rest of this paper is organized as follows: Sect. 2 presents the methodology of reliability assessment of ATS architecture. Section 3 conducts a case study and analyses the results. Finally, Sect. 4 elaborates the conclusions.

2 Methodology

2.1 Markov Chains

A Markov chain is a mathematical model describing a stochastic process of a system with discrete time states. The most important property of Markov chains is "posteriority-free", which means that the proceeding state of the system only depends on the current state of the system, independent of the previous state. Based on Markov chains, it is possible to predict the state of the system in the future based on the state of the system at the current moment. Generally, a Markov chain is defined as a quadruple $\{X, S, P, \pi\}$, and each field is detailed as follows:

$X = \{X\alpha, \alpha = 0, 1, 2 \ldots\}$ is a stochastic process with discrete time parameters, called a Markov process, where $X\alpha$ is a state variable, $\alpha \in T$, denoting the state of the system at moment α;

$S = \{1, 2, \ldots, n\}$ is the set of all possible values of the variable $X\alpha$ and is called the state space;

$P^{(\beta)} = \left(p_{ij}^{(\beta)}\right)_{i,j \in S}$ is the β - step transfer probability matrix, where $p_{ij}^{(\beta)} = P\left(X_{\alpha+\beta} = j | X_\alpha = i\right)$ is the β - step transfer probability, representing the probability of the system transferring from state i at moment α to state j via β - step, with $i, j \in S$;

$\pi(\alpha) = [\pi_1(\alpha), \pi_2(\alpha), \ldots, \pi_n(\alpha)]$ is the probability distribution of the state of the system at moment α and is called the state distribution or state vector of the system at moment α. Where $\pi_j(\alpha) = \sum_{i=1}^{n} \pi_i(\alpha - 1)p_{ij}$ is the probability of the system being in state j at moment α, that is, the probability of the system from the initial state to state j via α times state transfer.

2.2 Markov Chains of Physical Objects of ATS Architecture

State Space. Since the states of physical objects of the ATS architecture have only two mutually independent states, normal and failure, and the transfer between the states is random, the state at the future moment is only related to the state at the current moment and has nothing to do with the previous state, therefore, the "posteriority-free" of Markov chains can be satisfied, and a 2-state Markov chain can be formed.

As shown in Fig. 2, the state space is represented as $S = \{X_1, X_2\}$, where X_1 denotes the normal state and X_2 denotes the failure state. p_{12} denotes the probability of the physical object from the normal state to the failure state, p_{21} denotes the probability of the physical object from the failure state to the normal state (repairable rate), p_{11} denotes the probability of the physical object from the normal state to the normal state, and p_{22} denotes the probability of the physical object from the failure state to the failure state.

Fig. 2. State transfer of physical objects of ATS architecture

The failures of the ATS architecture physical object are defined as follows:

- Inventory overflow failure: If the inventory of physical objects exceeds the upper limit of capacity, it is called inventory overflow failure.
- Information stream transmission failure: If the loss of signal token occurs during the operation of the ATS, the inventory change of the physical object is not equal to the difference between the inflow and outflow of the physical object, which is called information stream transmission failure.
- Single connection object failure: The single connection object failure occurs, when the inventory of the physical object without incoming connections increases or the inventory of the physical object without outgoing connections decreases.

State Transfer Probability Matrix. The transfer probability of the physical object from state X_i to state X_j is denoted as p_{ij}, $i, j \in \{1, 2\}$, then the state transfer probability matrix of the physical object is shown as follows:

$$P = \begin{pmatrix} p_{11} & p_{12} \\ p_{21} & p_{22} \end{pmatrix} \tag{1}$$

Assuming that the initial state transfer probability matrix is a unit matrix, the state transfer probability matrix is to be constructed in the following process (as shown in Fig. 3):

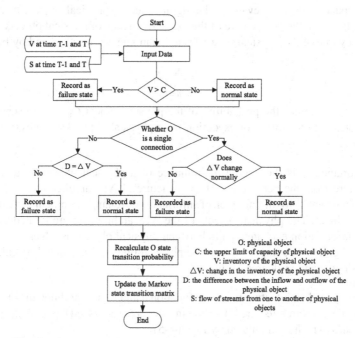

Fig. 3. The process of constructing the state transfer probability matrix

1. Input the upper limit of the capacity and inventory of physical objects, and the flow of information streams between physical objects at time $T - 1$ and T.
2. Determine whether the state of each physical object is a failure state according to the above three failure types.
3. Statistics on the state of all the physical objects at time T so as to obtain the state transfer probability of the physical objects from time $T - 1$ to time T.
4. Update the state transfer probability matrix of the physical objects.

2.3 ATS Architecture Reliability Evaluation Index

In the course of the ATS operation, the failure rate of physical objects, their usage frequency and their position in the ATS architecture all have important effects on the reliability of the ATS architecture.

- Failure rate

    The failure rate is the probability that the physical object O_v does not fail at the moment α and fails per unit time after the moment α, denoted as $\lambda_v^{(\alpha)}$. The failure rate is an important metric for ATS architecture evaluation, and Eq. (2) calculates the failure rate of the physical object O_v at the moment α.

$$\lambda_v^{(\alpha)} = x_1 p_{12}^{(\alpha)} + x_2 p_{22}^{(\alpha)} \tag{2}$$

- Occupancy rate

Occupancy rate is to evaluate the significance of physical objects to the ATS architecture from the perspective of the usage frequency of physical objects, and the occupancy rate of the physical object O_v at the moment α is calculated by Eq. (3).

$$\gamma_v^{(\alpha)} = \sum_{u=1}^{n} b_u p_{uv} \tag{3}$$

where b_u denotes the probability of the physical object O_u being executed and p_{uv} denotes the probability of execution from physical object O_u to physical object O_v, $u \neq v$.

- Importance

Importance I_v is the degree of influence of a physical object O_v to the ATS architecture from the perspective of the structure of ATS architecture itself, which can be represented by the number of information exchange pairs connected to that physical object. The physical objects of the ATS architecture are treated as nodes, and the information exchange pairs between physical objects as edges, which form a directed graph. The importance of the physical object is calculated by calculating the out-degree and in-degree of the node.

- Reliability

The physical architecture maps the functional and logical architectures to the real world, so the ATS architecture reliability metrics are established based on the physical architecture, which is calculated by Eqs. (4–5).

$$R_v(\alpha) = \exp\left(-\lambda_v^{(\alpha)} \gamma_v^{(\alpha)}\right) \tag{4}$$

$$R(R_v, I_v, \alpha) = \prod_{v=1}^{n} \exp\left(-\lambda_v^{(\alpha)} \gamma_v^{(\alpha)} I_v\right) \tag{5}$$

where $R_v(\alpha)$ is the reliability of the physical object O_v at the moment α, $R(R_v, I_v, \alpha)$ is the reliability of the ATS architecture at the moment α, $\lambda_v^{(\alpha)}$ is the failure rate of the physical object O_v, I_v is the importance of the physical object O_v, and $\gamma_v^{(\alpha)}$ is the occupancy rate of the physical object O_v.

3 Case Study

In this case, the proposed method is used to analyse the reliability of the VEAS architecture, with the simulation data of the service generated by the "Autonomous Complex Transportation System Simulation Information Physics Platform" developed based on the system dynamics model. The "Autonomous Complex Transportation System Simulation Information Physics Platform" accurately maps the physical system's state, behavior, and environment into a computer network through information exchange. By adding multi-physics simulation modules and high-performance physics engines, dynamic control and precise scheduling can be achieved, enabling research on simulation of cyber-physical systems.

3.1 Scene Description

In the autonomous driving environment, the VEAS uses the vehicle's positioning system and sensing equipment to provide the vehicle location and driving environment
perception service.

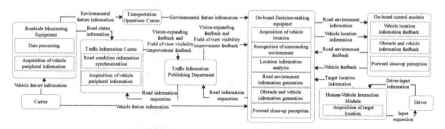

Fig. 4. Physical architecture of the VEAS

- Functional architecture: The functional architecture of the VEAS consists of the sub-
  service layer and the functional layer. The sub-service layer is the VEAS itself, and
  the functional layer is composed of functions that implement the sub-service.
- Logical architecture: The logical architecture of the VEAS further describes the functional architecture of the service, connecting the functions in the functional layer of
  the logical architecture through data flow.
- Physical architecture: The physical architecture of VEAS consists of physical objects
  required for functional implementation and information exchange pairs between physical objects. It maps the functional architecture and logical architecture to corresponding physical objects and information exchange pairs by describing the relationships
  among physical objects and information exchange pairs, as shown in Fig. 4.

3.2 Simulation Data Format

The simulation data of the VEAS provides information about the semantics and the upper
limit of capacity of the physical objects in the physical architecture, the inventory of the
physical objects at each simulation time step, as well as the connection relationship
between the physical objects and the flow of information streams between physical
objects at each simulation time step. Simulation time step refers to the discretization of
continuous time into discrete steps during the simulation process, where each time step
represents a fixed time interval. Within each time step, simulation data is transmitted
and reliability assessment operations are performed. This process is repeated until the
simulation is completed.

The information about the physical object includes the name and the upper limit
of capacity of the physical object. Among them, the upper limit of capacity of the
physical object is used to determine whether the physical object is in the overflow state
when constructing the Markov state transfer probability matrix. When the upper limit
of capacity is −1, it indicates that the physical object has no capacity upper limit, as
shown in Table 1.

The data on the connection relationship between the physical objects is used to describe the name of the information stream between the physical objects and the information about origin and destination objects of the information stream. This data is used to calculate the importance of each physical object when calculating the reliability index of the VEAS, as shown in Table 2.

Table 1. Physical Object.

Physical object name	The Upper Limit of Capacity
Carrier (Carr)	−1.00
Roadside monitoring equipment (Rme)	10000.00
Traffic Information Centre (TIC)	100000.00
Transportation Operations Centre (TOC)	100000.00
Traffic Information Publishing Department (TIPD)	100000.00
On-board decision-making equipment (Ode)	10000.00
On-board control module (Ocm)	10000.00
Human-vehicle interaction module (Him)	10000.00
Driver (Dri)	1000.00

Table 2. Connections between Physical Objects.

Name of the Information Stream	Origin Physical Objects	Destination Physical Objects
Abnormal performance of the vehicle (Apv)	Carr	Rme
Road traffic status information 1 (Rtsi1)	Rme	TIC
Road traffic status information 2 (Rtsi2)	Rme	TOC
Broadcast traffic information 1 (Bti1)	TIC	TIPD
Broadcast traffic information 2 (Bti2)	TIPD	Ode
Traffic control information (Tci)	TOC	Ode
Driving scenario (Ds)	Ode	Ocm
Circumvent result feedback (Crf)	Ocm	Ode
Vehicle Warning Information 1 (VWI1)	Ode	Him
Collision warning (Cw)	Him	Dri

The data of physical object inventory is used to describe the inventory of physical objects at each time step, as shown in Table 3. The data of information stream between physical objects is used to describe the flow of information stream between physical objects at each time step, as shown in Table 4. The inventory data of the physical objects and the flow data of the information stream are used to judge whether the physical objects are in the failure state at each simulation time step.

Table 3. Inventory of Physical Objects.

T	Carr	Rme	TOC	TIC	TIPD	Ode	Ocm	Him	Dri
0	1000.00	5000.00	5000.00	5000.00	0.00	3000.00	1000.00	1000.00	0.00
1	995.00	4995.00	5000.00	5000.00	0.25	3004.25	1000.00	1000.00	5.00
2	990.00	4990.00	5000.00	5000.00	0.75	3009.75	1000.00	1000.00	10.00
...									

Table 4. The flow of Information Stream.

T	Cw	VWI1	Crf	Ds	Bti2	Bti1	Tci	Rtsi1	Rtsi2	Apv
0	5	5	5	5	5	0	5	0	5	5
1	5	5	0	5	5	0	5	0	5	5
2	5	5	0	5	5	0	5	5	5	5
...										

3.3 Result Analysis

To ensure that the VEAS provides a long-term and stable service, simulation data is used to analyse the factors that affect the reliability of the service. The main factors affecting the reliability of the VEAS can be found out by analysing the relationship between the reliability of each physical object and the reliability of the VEAS. Analysing the relationship between the reliability of physical objects and the occupancy rate as well as importance of physical objects helps to adjust the information exchange between physical objects and the operation logic of functions, change the occupancy rate and importance of physical objects, and improve the VEAS reliability. Further, by analysing the relationship between failure rate, occupancy rate, repairable rate and the reliability of physical objects, give solutions to improve the reliability of physical objects, thereby improving the reliability of the VEAS.

The Reliability Trend of the VEAS. In order to analyse the reliability trends of the VEAS, the data throughout 1800 simulation time steps are used to calculate the reliability of the VEAS with formula from (1) to (5), as shown in Fig. 5. The VEAS reliability is low at the beginning of the simulation. The main reason is that at the beginning of VEAS operation, the amount of data used to calculate reliability is small, and when the information transmission between physical objects is unstable, the probability of failure state will be higher. The failure state of a small number of physical objects has a large negative impact on reliability.

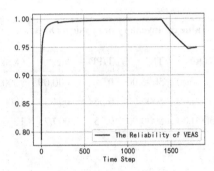

Fig. 5. Reliability trend of the VEAS

The Relationship Between the Reliability of Physical Objects and the Reliability of the VEAS. As can be seen from Fig. 5, the reliability starts to decrease at step 1401. By comparing the failure rate, occupancy rate, importance, and reliability of physical objects at the 1401st time step and the reliability of the VEAS, it can be found that the importance and occupancy rate of the on-board decision-making equipment in the VEAS are the highest, as shown in Fig. 6. As shown in Fig. 7, in the order from left to right and top to bottom, the reliability of physical objects decreases sequentially. It can be seen that the smaller the failure rate, the greater the importance and the occupancy rate, the higher the reliability of the physical object. Therefore, the reliability of the VEAS can be improved by adjusting the importance and occupancy rate of the on-board decision-making equipment.

The Relationship between Failure Rate, Occupancy Rate, Repairable Rate and Reliability of Physical Objects. As we can see from Fig. 8, the repairable rate of the on-board decision-making equipment remains the same from the 1401st time step throughout 1603st time step, but its reliability begins to decline at 1401st time step because the failure rate begins to increase at that time. At time step 1603, while the failure rate continues to rise, the repairable rate continues to decline, so that the reliability declines at an accelerated rate. At time step 1702, the repairable rate, failure rate, and occupancy rate all tend to level off, and reliability also begins to level off. Therefore, the reliability of the on-board decision-making equipment can be promoted by improving the repairable rate or reducing the failure rate, thereby the reliability of the VEAS is improved.

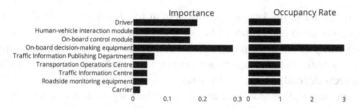

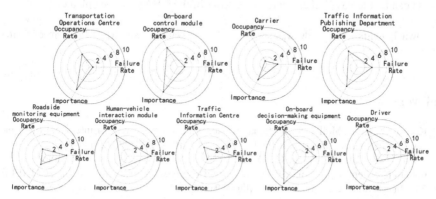

Fig. 6. Importance and Occupancy Rate of Physical Objects of the VEAS at time step 1401

Fig. 7. Failure rate, occupancy rate and importance ranking of the physical objects of the VEAS

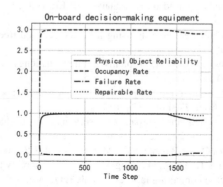

Fig. 8. Parameters of on-board decision-making equipment during simulation

4   Conclusions

This paper proposed a reliability evaluation method for ATS architecture based on Markov chain, with consideration of the multi-dimensional characteristics of ATS architecture. The case study shows that:

In the early stage of system operation, the reliability of the system is low in the short term due to the unstable information transmission between physical objects. Then the system reliability quickly reaches a high level, because the repairability of the failure states of the physical objects. After that, the system maintains a high reliability state for a long time, but in the later stage, the system reliability gradually declines due to functional degradation and failure of physical objects.

The reliability of the system depends on the reliability of the physical objects constituting the system and their importance in the system architecture, the reliability of the physical objects depends on their failure rate and occupancy rate.

The main physical objects that affect the reliability of the system can be found by comparing the importance and occupancy of the physical objects. By improving the repairable rate of physical objects and reducing the failure rate, the reliability of physical objects can be increased, thereby the reliability of the VEAS can be enhanced.

Acknowledgments. This study was sponsored by the National Key R&D Program of China (2020YFB1600400).

References

1. Kolosz, B., Grant-Muller, S.: Sustainability assessment approaches for intelligent transport systems: the state of the art. IET Intel. Transp. Syst. **10**(5), 287–297 (2016)
2. Zhou, Z.-S., Cai, M., Xiong, C., Deng, Z.-l., Yu, Y.: Construction of autonomous transportation system architecture based on system engineering methodology. In: 2022 IEEE 25th International Conference on Intelligent Transportation Systems (ITSC), Macau, China, pp. 3348–3353 (2022)
3. Deng, Z., Xiong, C., Cai, M.: An autonomous transportation system architecture mapping relation generation method based on text analysis. IEEE Trans. Comput. Soc. Syst. **9**(6), 1768–1776 (2022)
4. Schneeweiss, W.G.: Fault-tree analysis using a binary decision tree. IEEE Trans. Reliab. **R-34**(5), 453–457 (1985)
5. Zio, E.: Reliability engineering: old problems and new challenges. Reliab. Eng. Syst. Saf. **94**(2), 125–141 (2009)
6. Kabir, S.: An overview of fault tree analysis and its application in model based dependability analysis. Expert Syst. Appl. **77**, 114–135 (2017)
7. Liu, J.-J., Liu, J.-C.: An intelligent approach for reservoir quality evaluation in tight sandstone reservoir using gradient boosting decision tree algorithm - a case study of the Yanchang Formation, mid-eastern Ordos Basin, China. Mar. Pet. Geol. **126**, 104939 (2021)
8. Wang, C., Liu, Q., Xing, L., Guan, Q., Yang, C., Yu, M.: Reliability analysis of smart home sensor systems subject to competing failures. Reliab. Eng. Syst. Saf. **221**, 108327 (2022)
9. Anantharaman, M., Islam, R., Garaniya, V., Khan, F.: Efficiency, safety, and reliability analysis of turbocharging in a large container vessel. Process Saf. Progress **41**(S1) (2022)
10. Xue, J., Yang, K.: Dynamic reliability analysis of coherent multistate systems. IEEE Trans. Rel. **44**(4), 683–688 (1995)
11. Wang, J.-L.: Markov-chain based reliability analysis for distributed systems. Comput. Electr. Eng. **30**(3), 183–205 (2004)
12. Cui, L., Xu, Y., Zhao, X.: Developments and applications of the finite Markov chain imbedding approach in reliability. IEEE Trans. Rel. **59**(4), 685–690 (2010)
13. Durand, J.-B., Gaudoin, O.: Software reliability modelling and prediction with hidden Markov chains. Stat. Model. **5**(1), 75–93 (2005)
14. Xujie, J., Lirong, C.: A study on reliability of supply chain based on higher order Markov chain. In: 2008 IEEE International Conference on Service Operations and Logistics, and Informatics, Beijing, China, pp. 2014–2017 (2008)

15. Wang, Y., Li, M., Li, L.: The research of system reliability calculation method based on the improved petri net. In: 2013 International Conference on Information Technology and Applications, Chengdu, China, pp. 279–281 (2013)
16. Kabir, S., Papadopoulos, Y.: Applications of Bayesian networks and Petri nets in safety, reliability, and risk assessments: a review. Saf. Sci. **115**, 154–175 (2019)
17. Dave, V.S., Dutta, K.: Neural network based models for software effort estimation: a review. Artif. Intell. Rev. **42**(2), 295–307 (2014)
18. Liu, J., Schonfeld, P.M., Peng, Q., Yin, Y.: Measures of travel reliability on an urban rail transit network. J. Transp. Eng. Part A Syst. **146**(6), 04020037 (2020)
19. Ghodrati, B., Famurewa, S., Hoseinie, S.H.: Railway switches and crossings reliability analysis. In: 2016 IEEE International Conference on Industrial Engineering and Engineering Management (IEEM), Bali, Indonesia, pp. 1412–1416 (2016)
20. Wang, X., Liu, W.: Research on air traffic control automatic system software reliability based on Markov chain. Phys. Procedia **24**, 1601–1606 (2012)
21. Gupta, G., Mishra, R.P., Jain, P.: Reliability analysis and identification of critical components using Markov model. In: 2015 IEEE International Conference on Industrial Engineering and Engineering Management (IEEM), Singapore, Singapore, pp. 777–781 (2015)
22. Li, M., Wang, Y., Limin, J.: A research into the reliability of equipment-integrated system regarding high-speed train based on network model. IEEE Access **7**, 186328–186339 (2019)
23. Prowell, S.J., Poore, J.H.: Computing system reliability using Markov chain usage models. J. Syst. Softw. **73**(2), 219–225 (2004)
24. Guangming, X., Xinyi, L., Linhuan, Z., et al.: Reliability analysis and evaluation of logical architecture for autonomous transportation system. J. Railw. Sci. Eng. 2852–2861 (2022)
25. Muhammad, M., Abd Majid, M.A.: Reliability and availability evaluation for a multi-state system subject to minimal repair. J. Appl. Sci. **11**, 2036–2041 (2011)

Uncertainty Quantification for Semantic Segmentation Models via Evidential Reasoning

Rui Wang[1] 🆔, Mengying Wang[1], Ci Liang[2](✉) 🆔, and Zhouxian Jiang[1] 🆔

[1] Department of Computer and Information Technology, Beijing Jiaotong
University, Haidian District, Beijing 100044, China
[2] Harbin Institute of Technology, Harbin 150001, China
liangci321@hit.edu.cn

Abstract. Deep learning models typically render decisions based on probabilistic outputs. However, in safety-critical applications such as environment perception for autonomous vehicles, erroneous decisions made by semantic segmentation models may lead to catastrophic results. Consequently, it would be beneficial if these models could explicitly indicate the reliability of their predictions. Essentially, stakeholders anticipate that deep learning models will convey the degree of uncertainty associated with their decisions. In this paper, we introduce EviSeg, a predictive uncertainty quantification method for semantic segmentation models, based on Dempster-Shafer (DS) theory. Specifically, we extract the discriminative information, i.e., the parameters and the output features from the last convolution layer of a semantic segmentation model. Subsequently, we model this multi-source evidence to the evidential weights, thereby estimating the predictive uncertainty of the semantic segmentation model with the Dempster's rule of combination. Our proposed method does not require any changes to the model architecture, training process, or loss function. Thus, this uncertainty quantification process does not compromise the model performance. Validated on the urban road scene dataset CamVid, the proposed method enhanced computational efficiency by three to four times compared to the baseline method, while maintaining comparable performance with baseline methods. This improvement is critical for real-time applications.

Keywords: Uncertainty Quantification · Semantic Segmentation · Deep Learning

1 Introduction

Semantic segmentation, as one of the most important tasks in computer vision has been attractive to several safety-critical applications such as medical image analysis and autonomous vehicle control [1, 2]. However, although the performance of such deep learning models has reached or even exceeded human level on many tasks, their outputs are not always reliable [3]. In areas with high safety requirements, failure on the core perceptual decisions based on deep learning may lead to catastrophic consequences [4, 5]. Existing research shows that deep neural networks tend to make overconfident

© The Author(s), under exclusive license to Springer Nature Switzerland AG 2023
J. Guiochet et al. (Eds.): SAFECOMP 2023 Workshops, LNCS 14182, pp. 218–229, 2023.
https://doi.org/10.1007/978-3-031-40953-0_18

predictions [6]. Kendall et al. [3] argue that quantifying the predictive uncertainty of such models is an effective way to improve the reliability of decision-making.

At present, there are mainly two streams of research on predictive uncertainty quantification: Bayesian method and non-Bayesian method. First stream of the existing approaches stems from Bayesian neural networks (BNNs) [7, 8] with the idea of replacing point-estimated parameters of NNs by probabilistic distributions. Recent advances in the variational inference (VI) methods (such as Monte Carlo estimates, stochastic optimization, etc. [9, 10]) help to search for the approximate distributions with minimized Kullback-Leibler divergence, but the VI methods still suffers from prohibitive computational cost, especially for large-scale DNNs [11]. Among the second stream methods, Monte Carlo dropout (MC dropout) [11] adopts one training regularization operation, dropout, at test time to generate predictive distributions. Deep Ensembles [12] increases the performance of uncertainty estimation by assembling the outputs of several DNNs with the same architecture and independently initialized parameters. Inherited from the ensemble method, the training cost of this approach is inevitably enormous for large models.

In this paper, we focus on a non-probabilistic uncertainty theoretical framework belief function theory of evidence, also known as Dempster-Shafer (DS) theory [13, 14]. It is a mathematically generalization of probability theory and often used for reasoning and decision-making under uncertainty. Especially, based on the recently proposed evidential neural networks [15], we propose EviSeg, a predictive uncertainty quantification method for semantic segmentation. Specifically, we extract the parameters and the output features from the last convolution layer of an semantic segmentation model. Subsequently, we map this multi-source evidence to the evidential weights and combine them with Dempster's rule of combination to estimate the predictive uncertainty of the semantic segmentation model. Our proposed method does not require to change the model architecture, training process, or loss function. Thus, this additional component for uncertainty quantification will not affect the performance of segmentation models. Verified on the urban road scene dataset CamVid, the proposed method enhanced computational efficiency by three to four times compared to the baseline method, while maintaining comparable performance with baseline methods. This improvement is critical for real-time applications.

2 Related Work

Recently, numerous studies have been conducted on the uncertainty quantification of deep learning models. These studies primarily fall into two categories: Bayesian-based methods and non-Bayesian approaches.

2.1 Bayesian-Based Methods

Bayesian-based methods are developed based on Bayesian Neural Networks (BNN) [7, 8] that aim to learn the posterior distributions of model parameters, instead of their explicit values. These methods deduce the model uncertainty based on the distributions obtained. To circumvent the computational complexities involved in BNN learning, researchers resort to approximate Bayesian methods. Gal et al. [11] proposed MC dropout, a theoretical framework that leverages the dropout operation to extract information from existing models and estimate their epistemic uncertainty. Kendall et al. [16] introduced the Bayesian SegNet model, which adopts the MC dropout in the testing phase to obtain the predictive uncertainty for the SegNet segmentation model. Krueger et al. [17] presented Bayesian hypernetworks, employing an auxiliary hypernetwork to realize uncertainty quantification. Kendall et al. [3] proposed a Bayesian deep learning framework, which allows the quantification of both aleatoric and epistemic uncertainty. They demonstrated the efficacy of the framework through semantic segmentation and regression tasks. Postels et al. [18] introduced a sampling-free approach to approximate noise injection, thus estimating epistemic uncertainty. However, these quantization techniques of these approximate Bayesian methods are computationally expensive. Most of the methods rely on MC Dropout to quantify uncertainty of deep learning models via multiple MC sampling, leading to a relatively high time complexity.

2.2 Non-Bayesian Methods

Concurrently, numerous researchers have sought to quantify the predictive uncertainty of deep learning models by deploying ensemble learning methods. Lakshminarayanan et al. [12] proposed an alternative to Bayesian neural networks that generates high-quality prediction uncertainty estimations via the incorporation of ensemble learning methods. Malinin et al. [19] introduced a method that employs reverse KL divergence to explicitly learn the model uncertainty, with experimental results suggesting its applicability to more complex, multi-class, large-scale datasets. Wen et al. [20] offered the BatchEnsemble method, characterized by significantly lower computational and memory overheads compared to traditional ensemble methods. Huang et al. [21] proposed an ensemble-based approach for quantifying epistemic uncertainty using influence functions and batches. However, most of these ensemble-based methods necessitate the training of multiple models, leading to computational complexities that are often unsustainable, particularly for large-scale deep models. Sensoy et al. [6] viewed DNN predictions as subjective opinions and formalized them into Dirichlet distributions based on the theory of subjective logic, thereby explicitly quantifying the predictive uncertainty of DNN classifiers. This method, however, requires alterations to the standard training loss function, which may affect the task-specific performance.

Additionally, the Dempster-Shafer (DS) theory, a classical framework for addressing uncertainty, can represent uncertain information more effectively by employing the Basic Probability Assignment (BPA) function and conducting uncertainty reasoning [22]. Denoeux [15] treated the learned parameters and outputs of a neural network layer as evidence. The author proposed transforming the classic network into an evidential one and proved the equivalence of these two models. Final combined mass functions were obtained using Dempster's rule of combination, facilitating the quantification of uncertainty in classification models. Cao et al. [23] formulated a fundamental solution framework for inverse uncertainty quantification based on DS theory. While the theoretical results for uncertainty quantification are significant, an overabundance of evidence may risk exponential explosion.

3 Background

In this section, we introduce the background knowledge on the DS theory and evidential classifier that will be used in the proposed method.

3.1 Prerequisite for DS Theory

Belief function theory of evidence, also known as, evidential theory or Dempster-Shafer (DS) theory, was first proposed by Dempster and Shafer [13, 14] and has now become a complete formalism for reasoning and decision-making on uncertainty.

Mass Function. Let a variable X take values in a finite set $\Omega = \{x_1, \cdots, x_K\}$. The set Ω represents a frame of discernment, which is composed of all the possible states of interest, while 2^Ω denotes the power set of Ω. A mass function on Ω, denoted as $m\Omega$, is a mapping from the power set of Ω to the closed interval [0,1]: $2^\Omega \rightarrow [0, 1]$. It is also called a basic probability assignment (BPA) on the measure space $(\Omega, 2^\Omega)$. Note that, in probability theory, probability masses are always assigned to elements of Ω rather than to subsets. The greater generality of DS theory makes it more suitable to represent states of high uncertainty. A mass function must verify the following property: $\sum_{A \subseteq \Theta} m(A) = 1$. In belief function theory, the mass $m^\Omega(A)$ reflects the level of belief committed to the hypothesis that the truth lies in A and to no subset of it. A subset P of Ω, which meets $m^\Omega(A) > 0$, is a focal set of belief mass m^Ω.

Dempster's Rule of Combination. In practices, the sources of evidence may be different. Under the DS theoretical framework, the independent mass functions from different agents need to be combined, which represents the total trust degree obtained. The Dempster's rule is one of the combination rules. Let m_1, m_2 be two different mass function, assuming that they are independent with each other. $\oplus$ is the sign of the orthogonal sum, which satisfies the commutative and associative laws, and B, C represent subsets from different data sources. The Dempster's combination formula is as follows: $m(A) = (m_1 \oplus m_2)(A) = \frac{1}{1-K} \sum_{B \cap C = A} m_1(B) \times m_2(C)$, where K refers to the *conflict*, which represents the degree of conflict between the two mass functions, that is, the degree of conflict among the evidence. The calculation formula is as follows: $K = $ Badrinarayanan. In extreme cases, if K = 0, it means that there is no conflict among the evidence; if K = 1, it means that there is complete conflict.

3.2 Evidential Classifier

Denoeux [15] offers an evidential interpretation of classical DNN classifiers based on DS theory. In the classification task, each feature vector can be regarded as a piece of evidence for a subset in the sample space. Author converts the input sample or higher-level features into mass functions, then use the Dempster's rule to combine mass functions through evidential reasoning. The traditional neural network classifier generally adopts the softmax function to output the discrimination probability of each class. In an evidential classifier, these outputs can be interpreted with the normalized plausibilities regarding to combined mass functions. The equivalence between these two outputs is proved in this work.

Based on these evidential results, we can easily extract uncertain information, such as the *conflict*, from the more informative mass functions. In this paper, we further proposed an evidential semantic segmentation model to quantify the corresponding predictive uncertainty to assist its reliability of safety-critical applications. Due to the limited space, please refer the inference details to the work [15].

4 EviSeg: Uncertainty Quantification for Semantic Segmentation Models

In this section, we first outline the evidential transformation of semantic segmentation models. Following this, we present our proposed uncertainty quantification method for semantic segmentation models.

4.1 Evidential Interpretation of Semantic Segmentation Models

Semantic segmentation is a pixel-level classification task, that is, assigning one class label to each pixel of the input image. The segmentation result is segmentation maps or masks, in which objects of the same class are marked with the same color in the segmentation maps. Compared with the original image, the segmentation mask is easier to analyze and of more value to exploit in real applications. Generally, fully convolutional neural network (FCN [24]) is used to achieve precise image semantic segmentation. To benefit the results of evidential classifier and transfer them on the semantic segmentation tasks, we firstly study the gap of dataflow dimension between the neural networks classifier and FCN models. The dimension of parameter required in evidential classifier is a two-dimensional parameter matrix. We analysis the model architecture of FCN model and propose the transformation method to build the evidential semantic segmentation model, EviSeg, for uncertainty quantification.

Figure 1 shows the output layer of a vanilla DNN classifier and an FCN architecture for the semantic segmentation task. We take the binary case of classification as examples. Left part of Fig. 1 demonstrates the last hidden layer and output layer of neural network classifier. X, Y and W refer to the feature outputs of the last hidden layer, the output probabilities of the binary classifier and the weight parameters, respectively. The right figure illustrates that the last convolution layer of the FCN network convolutes the input feature maps pixel by pixel in the case of two filter kernels, outputting binary classification output feature maps pixel by pixel. X', Y' and W' refer to the features of the input feature map, the final binary classification probabilities of each pixel and the weights of the filter, respectively. The parameters of the filter in the FCN network are in four-dimensional shapes, which depend on the length and height of the filter. Setting the width and height of the filter to 1 is a common operation to design an FCN model for semantic segmentation. Hence, the parameters of each filter can be regarded as a row of parameters of the weight matrix in the fully connection layer. Then, we can map the parameter into evidence weight and extend the evidential classifier to evidential semantic segmentation model.

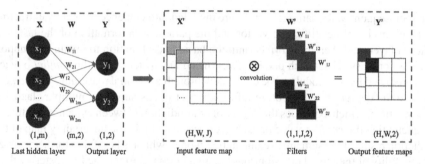

Fig. 1. Illustration for the weights and outputs of DNN and FCN models.

Figure 2 shows the evidence modeling framework of semantic segmentation model. $\varphi_1(x), \varphi_2(x), \ldots, \varphi_J(x)$ are the j feature vectors of the input feature map pixels, β_{jk} and α_{jk} is the parameter obtained from the semantic segmentation model (J = 1, 2, ..., J; k = 1, 2, ..., K). K is to the number of classes. m is the basic mass function containing the feature information of the input sample. They are combined through Dempster's rule. In the process of evidence reasoning, the conflict of each pixel can be calculated [15] to quantify the uncertainty of the prediction result of the semantic segmentation model.

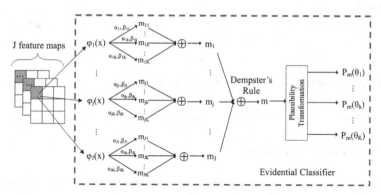

Fig. 2. Integration of evidential classifier with semantic segmentation outputs.

4.2 Uncertainty Quantification Based on EviSeg Models

In this subsection, we propose an uncertainty quantification method of semantic segmentation model based on evidence reasoning. Based on the basic principle of evidence classifier, uncertainty quantification framework of semantic segmentation model is shown in Fig. 3. The backbone network of FCN, constituting convolution, pooling, and up-sampling layers, convert the input data into an intermediate representation and is used as a feature extractor. This process transfers the input data as higher-level feature maps, and then restore the image to the original resolution through the up-sampling layer. Subsequently, the sample features are modeled into evidence weight by extracting the pixel level high-level feature vector and the parameter information of the last convolution layer, and then transformed into the basic mass function to obtain the support of a class or class subset each pixel. Finally, using Dempster's rule, the *conflict* of each pixel predicted by the model can be calculated through evidential reasoning. The *conflict* refers to the degree that the feature information of pixels supports multiple classes at the same time, which expresses the degree of contradiction between evidence (features). By calculating the *conflict* value of each pixel, we can obtain the uncertainty map of the prediction result of the semantic segmentation model, which is helpful to further analyze the reliability of the model decision-making. In addition, through the Dempster's rule, a combined mass function will be obtained, which can be used for decision-making. The research shows that the pixel-by-pixel classification result obtained by this function is equivalent to the output probability of softmax function. Therefore, the *conflict* can be directly used to quantify the uncertainty of model prediction results without affecting the accuracy.

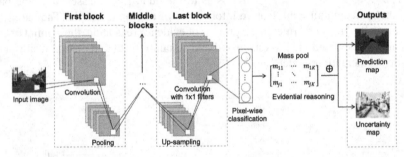

Fig. 3. Evidential uncertainty quantification for semantic segmentation models.

5   Results and Discussion

In this section, we verify the effectiveness of the proposed method through empirical study results. Detailed experiment setup and evaluation metrics are also provided.

5.1   Experiment Setup

Dataset.   The dataset used in this paper is the classic urban road scene dataset released in 2008: CamVid [25]. CamVid dataset is widely used in the field of semantic segmentation. It consists of 367 training set images, 100 verification set images and 233 test set images. The resolution of each image is preprocessed to 360 × 480 pixels. Our experiment used 12 object classes, including a background class (void). The other 11 classes are sky, building, pole, road, sidewalk, tree, sign, fence, car, pedestrian, and bicyclist, respectively.

Models, Baselines, and Hyper-parameters.   In this paper, we adopt the SegNet [26], Bayesian SegNet [16], FCN8 model and FCN32 model [24]. The hyperparametric setting of SegNet model used in this paper is consistent with https://github.com/divamgupta/image-segmentation-keras.git during training, dropout in Bayesian SegNet model is set to 0.5, and the rest are the same as that of SegNet model.

5.2 Evaluation Metrics

Performance Evaluation Metrics of Semantic Segmentation. Semantic segmentation is a pixel-level classification task. and its performance evaluation are mainly statistic metrics: Pixel Accuracy (PA), Class Pixel Accuracy (CPA), and Intersection over Union (IoU).

Uncertainty Metrics. Suppose there are K + 1 classes, including a background class. p_{ij} represents the number of pixels that belong to class i but are predicted into class j. In this paper, the uncertainty metrics used by the selected baseline method MC dropout mainly include the following:

i. Variance. The pixel-by-pixel uncertainty is quantified by calculating the variance of the results of multiple forward calculations. The formula is $\sigma_k^2(p) = \frac{1}{n}\sum_{i=1}^{n}\left(y_k^{(i)}(p) - \mu_k(p)\right)^2$, where, k, n, y, and μ refer to the kth class, the number of forward propagations, the output probability value of the pixel point, and the mean of multiple prediction results, respectively. To quantify the uncertainty of each class of images with variance, we define the class mean variance: $\overline{variance_i} = \frac{\sum_{j=0}^{k}\sigma_{ji}^2}{\sum_{j=0}^{k}p_{ji}}$.

ii. Mutual Information (MI). The formula is $MI(w, y|D, x) \cong H\left[p_{MC}(y|D, x)\right] - \frac{1}{T}\sum_{i=1}^{T}H\left[p(y|w_i, x)\right]$, where x, y, D, p, and H refers to the pixel point, the class label corresponding to the pixel point, the dataset, the predicted distribution, and the pixel-by-pixel entropy value, respectively. To use mutual information to quantify the uncertainty, the formula for class-averaged mutual information is $\overline{MI_i} = \frac{\sum_{j=0}^{k}MI_{ji}}{\sum_{j=0}^{k}p_{ji}}$. In addition, the class-average *conflict* is defined based on the *conflict*, which is used for the experimental analysis later. The formula is $\overline{conflict_i} = \frac{\sum_{j=0}^{k}conflict_{ji}}{\sum_{j=0}^{k}p_{ji}}$.

5.3 Experiment Results

Figure 4 demonstrates the examples of prediction and maps and uncertainty map generated by the proposed method, EviSeg. We visualized the *conflict* degree of pixel-wise predictions with the heatmap. As we can observe that the conflicting areas are consistent with the areas of imprecise prediction (highlighted with bounding boxes), such as the bicyclist in the second row. These areas often focus on the distant visual range and the edges of different objects. In particular, the uncertainty of the object edge is patently obvious. For example, it is easy to recognize the car contour in the uncertainty map of first two images. High uncertainty areas shown by the *conflict* indicate that the pixel-wise predictions in this area are probably incorrect.

Figure 5 presents the relationship between uncertainty and Intersection over Union (IoU) for each class. The class-average *conflict*, variance, and mutual information metrics all demonstrate an inverse relationship with the IoU value. The proposed *conflict*

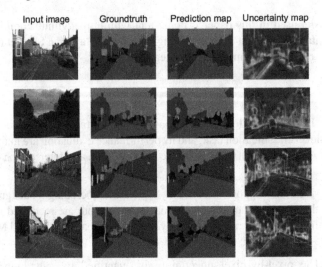

Fig. 4. Visualization of prediction and uncertainty maps.

effectively quantifies the uncertainty of the SegNet model, maintaining a consistent variation trend akin to the baseline methods. Specifically, the class-average *conflict* is higher in all classes that are susceptible to prediction errors (i.e., low-accuracy classes), such as 'pole', 'pedestrian', and 'bicyclist'. For classes that pose high risks in autonomous driving, such as 'pedestrian' and 'bicyclist', alerts triggered by significant predictive uncertainty serve to mitigate the likelihood of severe consequences.

We further investigate the quantitative relationship between our uncertainty measure and the pixel accuracy. Table 1 demonstrates that the degree of prediction confidence (ranging from the 70th percentile to the 0th percentile), as reflected by the least uncertain percentile, correlates strongly with pixel accuracy. Pixels marked as uncertain lead to more prediction errors, while predictions made for pixels deemed confident tend to be reliable. This empirical observation affirms the effectiveness of the proposed *conflict* measure.

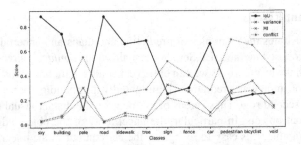

Fig. 5. The relationship between uncertainty index and IoU.

Besides, Fig. 6 presents a scatter plot depicting the relationship between Class Pixel Accuracy (CPA) and class-average conflict on the CamVid dataset. It can be observed

Table 1. Pixel accuracy under different confidence percentile (least uncertain pixels).

Confidence percentile	Pixel accuracy (%)
70	97.96
50	97.54
20	91.50
10	88.16
0	84.61

that there exists a strong inverse correlation between CPA and the class-average conflict. This implies that the SegNet model performs better for classes with lower class-average conflict, such as 'sky' and 'road'. In other words, the model's predictions for these classes are more confident. Conversely, for classes that are more challenging to identify, such as 'pole' and 'bicyclist', the class-average conflict is higher. This suggests that the SegNet model's prediction results for these classes carry a higher level of uncertainty. Thus, we further affirm that the proposed conflict measure is an effective tool for detecting unreliable predictions.

We carried out a comparative experiment to gauge the time consumption between our proposed method and the baseline methods. As seen in Table 2, the time required to quantify the conflict for an image is substantially lower than that required for variance and mutual information (MI). This efficiency is crucial for the real-time application of segmentation models.

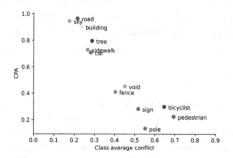

Fig. 6. The relationship between class-average conflict and CPA.

Table 2. Time consumption per image of the proposed and baseline methods

Uncertainty metrics	CPU Time
Conflict	**0.91 s**
Variance	4.91 s
MI	12.33 s

6 Conclusion

In safety-critical scenarios that involve semantic segmentation applications, research on uncertainty quantification is crucial for dependable decision-making. In this paper, we introduce EviSeg, an approach to quantify predictive uncertainty in semantic segmentation models, developed within the framework of an evidential classifier based on Dempster-Shafer theory. First, we affirm the applicability of the evidential classifier to the Fully Convolutional Network (FCN) model used for semantic segmentation. We then implement uncertainty quantification by treating sample features and model parameters as multi-source evidence and combine the extracted evidence using Dempster's rule. Preliminary experiments on the CamVid dataset validate the effectiveness of our proposed method. The results suggest that our proposed uncertainty metrics assign greater uncertainty to highly safety-related classes (such as pedestrians and bicyclists), potentially contributing to the development of safety-oriented decision-making strategies. Importantly, this method does not require modifications to the network structure, training process, or loss function of the semantic segmentation model. Thus, this external way of uncertainty estimation does not sacrifice the model performance. Additionally, the reduced computational overhead compared with baseline approaches endows the proposed method with promising potential for real-time applications.

References

1. Reinhold, J.C., et al.: Validating uncertainty in medical image translation. In: 2020 IEEE 17th International Symposium on Biomedical Imaging (ISBI), pp. 95–98. IEEE (2020)
2. Feng, D., Rosenbaum, L., Dietmayer, K.: Towards safe autonomous driving: capture uncertainty in the deep neural network for Lidar 3D vehicle detection. In: 21st International Conference on Intelligent Transportation Systems (ITSC), IEEE, 2018, pp. 3266–3273 (2018)
3. Kendall, A., Gal, Y.: What uncertainties do we need in Bayesian deep learning for computer vision? Adv. Neural Inf. Process. Syst. **30** (2017)
4. NHTSA, PE 16-007, Technical report: Tesla Crash Preliminary Evaluation Report. U.S. Department of Transportation, National Highway Traffic Safety Administration, Jan 2017
5. NTSB, PB2019-101402, Technical report: Highway Accident Report. National Transportation Safety Board, Nov 2019
6. Sensoy, M., Kaplan, L., Kandemir, M.: Evidential deep learning to quantify classification uncertainty. Adv. Neural Inf. Process. Syst. **31** (2018)
7. Denker, J.S., LeCun, Y.: Transforming neural-net output levels to probability distributions. In: Proceedings of the 3rd International Conference on Neural Information Processing Systems, 1990, pp. 853–859 (1990)

8. MacKay, D.J.: A practical Bayesian framework for backpropagation networks. Neural Comput. **4**(3), 448–472 (1992)
9. Kingma, D.P., Welling, M.: Auto-encoding variational Bayes. arXiv preprint arXiv:1312. 6114 (2013)
10. Louizos, C., Welling, M.: Multiplicative normalizing flows for variational Bayesian neural networks. In: International Conference on Machine Learning, 2017, pp. 2218–2227. PMLR (2017)
11. Gal, Y., Ghahramani, Z.: Dropout as a Bayesian approximation: representing model uncertainty in deep learning. In: International Conference on Machine Learning, pp. 1050–1059. PMLR (2016)
12. Lakshminarayanan, B., Pritzel, A., Blundell, C.: Simple and scalable predictive uncertainty estimation using deep ensembles. In: Advances in Neural Information Processing Systems 30: Annual Conference on Neural Information Processing Systems, 2017, pp. 6402–6413 (2017)
13. Dempster, A.P.: Upper and lower probabilities induced by a multi-valued mapping. Ann. Math. Stat. **38**, 325–339 (1967)
14. Shafer, G.: A Mathematical Theory of Evidence. Princeton University Press, Princeton (1976)
15. Denœux, T.: Logistic regression, neural networks and Dempster-shafer theory: a new perspective. Knowl.-Based Syst. **176**, 54–67 (2019)
16. Kendall, A., Badrinarayanan, V., Cipolla, R.: Bayesian segnet: model uncertainty in deep convolutional encoder-decoder architectures for scene understanding. arXiv preprint arXiv: 1511.02680 (2015)
17. Krueger, D., Huang, C.W., Islam, R., et al.: Bayesian hypernetworks. arXiv preprint arXiv: 1710.04759 (2017)
18. Postels, J., Ferroni, F., Coskun, H., et al.: Sampling-free epistemic uncertainty estimation using approximated variance propagation. In: Proceedings of the IEEE/CVF International Conference on Computer Vision, pp. 2931–2940 (2019)
19. Malinin, A., Gales, M.: Reverse KL-divergence training of prior networks: improved uncertainty and adversarial robustness. Adv. Neural Inf. Process. Syst. **32** (2019)
20. Wen, Y., Tran, D., Ba, J.: Batchensemble: an alternative approach to efficient ensemble and lifelong learning. arXiv preprint arXiv:2002.06715 (2020)
21. Huang, Z., Lam, H., Zhang, H.: Quantifying Epistemic Uncertainty in Deep Learning. arXiv preprint arXiv:2110.12122 (2021)
22. Fu, C., Chang, W., Xu, D., et al.: An evidential reasoning approach based on criterion reliability and solution reliability. Comput. Ind. Eng. **128**, 401–417 (2019)
23. Cao, L., Liu, J., Meng, X., et al.: Inverse uncertainty quantification for imprecise structure based on evidence theory and similar system analysis. Struct. Multidiscip. Optim. **64**(4), 2183–2198 (2021)
24. Long, J., Shelhamer, E., Darrell, T.: Fully convolutional networks for semantic segmentation. In: Proceedings of the IEEE Conference on Computer Vision and Pattern Recognition, pp. 3431–3440 (2015)
25. Brostow, G.J., Fauqueur, J., Cipolla, R.: Semantic object classes in video: a high-definition ground truth database. Pattern Recogn. Lett. **30**(2), 88–97 (2009)
26. Badrinarayanan, V., Kendall, A., Cipolla, R.: SegNet: a deep convolutional encoder-decoder architecture for image segmentation. IEEE Trans. Pattern Anal. Mach. Intell. **39**(12), 2481–2495 (2017)

Research on the Reliability of High-Speed Railway Dispatching and Commanding Personnel with Multi Physiological Signals

Liuxing Hu and Wei Zheng[✉]

The Collaborative Innovation Center of Railway Traffic Safety and National Research Center of Railway Safety Assessment, Beijing Jiaotong University, Beijing, China
{21125030,wzheng1}@bjtu.edu.cn

Abstract. In the event of equipment failure, traffic accident, natural disaster and other abnormal situations, the timely emergency disposal of the traffic dispatcher is required. In order to accurately evaluate the human reliability of the high-speed railway traffic dispatcher in emergency scenarios, this paper proposes a reliability analysis method based on the Phoenix model. In order to eliminate the dependence of the traditional human reliability analysis method on expert experience, a quantification method based on multiple physiological signals is designed. This paper also gives a specific application of this method in the case of inbound signal machine failure. With this human reliability analysis method, the human reliability of the traffic dispatcher and the causative behavior with the highest probability of failure can be accurately calculated, which can provide a reference for the improvement of the emergency handling protocol.

Keywords: Traffic dispatcher · Human reliability analysis · Physiological signals

1 Introduction

In the past decades, a variety of Human reliability analysis (HRA) models and methods have been proposed, and the development of HRA can be divided into 3 phases in chronological order [1]. Some classical methods, such as THERP (Technique for Human Error Rate Prediction) and CREAM (Cognitive Reliability and Error Analysis Method) have been widely used in nuclear power [2,3], mining [4] aviation [5], offshore oil and gas industry [6] and marine transportation [7]. However, in the railway field, there is a general lack of human-caused data in HRA for traffic scheduling and command, which is manifested in the following points: first, the data are extremely difficult to collect, leading to difficulties in model quantification; second, data citability, data from other countries or data from

---

Supported by the Fundamental Research Funds for the Central Universities (Science and technology leading talent team project) (2022JBXT003).

J. Guiochet et al. (Eds.): SAFECOMP 2023 Workshops, LNCS 14182, pp. 230–238, 2023.
https://doi.org/10.1007/978-3-031-40953-0_19

other fields, due to differences in cultural background, social environment and nature of operations and other factors, leading to different human behaviors and habits of thinking, making human-caused data inappropriate to refer to; Third, data reliability, the existing HRA is extremely dependent on expert judgment and subjective opinions of method users, which makes the consistency and accuracy of analysis results poor [8]. Therefore, this paper designs a quantification method for human factors data by selecting physiological signals as objective data for HRA, and establishes an HRA model applicable to railway dispatching command based on PHOENIX.

2   PHOENIX-Based Human Reliability Analysis Model

The Phoenix method is a HRA model proposed by Ekanem [9], which mixes various methods such as event trees, fault trees, and Bayesian networks. Its framework is divided into 3 layers, as shown in Fig. 1.

(1) The top layer is the Human Fault Event Layer (HFE), an event tree model, which aims to identify the HFE and analyze the tasks to be solved by operators in a chronological order to find the risk points that may lead to task failure, which have two states of success/failure and whose probability values of occurrence of the two states are calculated by the middle layer fault tree.

(2) The intermediate layer is the Crew Failure Model layer (CFM), which is a fault tree model, and this layer aims to analyze the HFE retrospectively and per-form deductive reasoning on. Combining the IDAC and SRK models, the cognitive behavior of the dispatcher is divided into: information perception I, rule based diagnostic decision D-1, knowledge-based diagnostic decision D-2, and action execution A, and all failure modes are identified to constitute the CFM set.

(3) The bottom layer is the Performance Shaping Factor layer (PSF), which is a Bayesian network model, mainly reasoning about the probability of occurrence of failure modes, and quantifying and analyzing the occurrence probability of CFM by constructing a causal logic model between PSFs.

3   Human Factors Data Quantification Methods Based on Physiological Signals

3.1   Quantifiable Human Factors Data Collection

Subjects. Data for this experiment were obtained from 20 graduate students, 14 males and 6 females, aged between 22 and 26 years. The subjects were of normal mind, normal or corrected hearing and vision, and had the necessary basic train operation control knowledge. A week-long training was given to them before participating in the experiment, and the training content was the disposal process

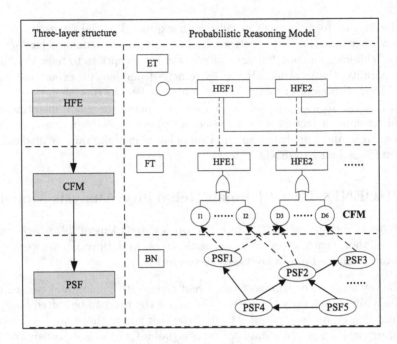

Fig. 1. Model Structure.

summarized by the standard dispatching command process for six emergency scenarios.

Experimental protocol. Stress, attention and workload from the PSF library were selected as quantitative human factors data to design high, medium and low level evoked experiments and dispatching command experiments and to collect Electroencephalogram(EEG), Photoplethysmographic(PPG) and Electrodermal activity(EDA). The stress-induced experiments used a mental arithmetic task, the attention-induced experiments used a game task, and the workload induced experiments used CPT and N-back dual tasks; the dispatching experiments included high wind alarm, incoming signal machine failure, foreign object intrusion limit, automatic train lowering bow, loss of turnout indication and signal closure in open state. Each group of experiments contains three evoked experiments and six dispatching command emergency scenarios, all conducted on the human factors engineering experimental platform shown in Fig. 2.

3.2   Feature Engineering

Preprocessing. Wavelet thresholding is applied to EEG, PPG and EDA for noise reduction, and ICA is used to remove the EOG component of EEG to obtain high-quality physiological signals.

Feature extraction. Through data processing, time domain, frequency domain and nonlinear features are extracted to obtain 224 EEG features of 14 types in 16 channels, 11 PPG features and 8 EDA features.

Fig. 2. Experimental platform.

Feature selection. The RF-SFFS(Random Forest - Sequential Floating Forward Selection) feature selection algorithm constructed in this paper firstly constructs an existing feature subset using the feature importance of RF; then performs SFFS search and uses the classification accuracy of RF as the discriminant criterion of SFFS, traverses the unselected features, and if adding the feature to the feature subset makes the RF classification accuracy higher, then adds the feature to the subset; traverses the selected features, and if adding the If the feature is removed to increase the classification accuracy, the feature is removed, and the search stops when the preset number of features is finally reached, and the optimal feature subsets are obtained as follows: 3 PPG features for pressure level classification, 24 EEG features for attention level classification, and 18 multi-modal features for workload level classification.

Table 1. Classification results.

Status	Classifier	Accuracy(%)	Precision(%)	Recall(%)	F1(%)
Pressure	KNN	60.8	59.6	61.2	60.4
	SVM	65.3	59.8	65.6	62.6
	XGBoost	76.8	77.4	77.1	77.2
Attention	KNN	66.1	66.3	65.9	66.1
	SVM	71.6	73.2	72.3	72.7
	XGBoost	81.2	81.7	81.6	81.6
Workload	KNN	58.4	66.3	65.9	58.7
	SVM	65.5	73.2	72.3	66.7
	XGBoost	79.6	81.7	81.6	79.9

3.3 Status Level Classification

In this paper, three algorithms, KNN, SVM and XGBoost, were selected for multi-level level identification of attention, stress and workload, and the classification model with high accuracy was selected to be applied to state identification and prior probability assignment for scheduling experiments. The identification results are shown in Table 1, and it was found that XGBoost performed better than the first two, and the accuracy rates in the three classifications of stress, attention and workload were 76.8%, 81.2% and 79.6%, respectively, so XGBoost was chosen as the classifier for human factors data quantification.

4 Example Analysis

4.1 Qualitative Analysis

HFE layer. Selecting the home signal failure under the CTCS-3 train control system as the travel scenario, the event tree model shown in Fig. 3

CFM layer. CFM classification of the 14 behaviors in the figure, with the failure behavior as the top event and the failure mode as the bottom event to construct the fault tree model. The CFM classification is shown in the Fig. 4.

PSF layer. Combined with the trained XGBoost model can identify the stress level, attention level and workload of dispatchers in emergency disposal, by counting the present probability of the high and low levels of the three as the prior probability of Bayesian network nodes, accordingly all parent nodes of the three can be eliminated as shown in Fig. 5.

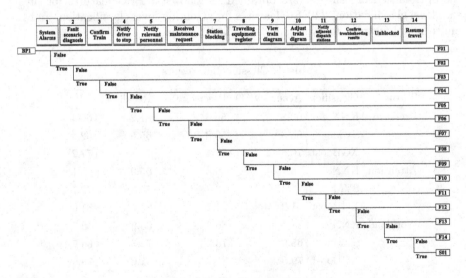

Fig. 3. Event Tree Model.

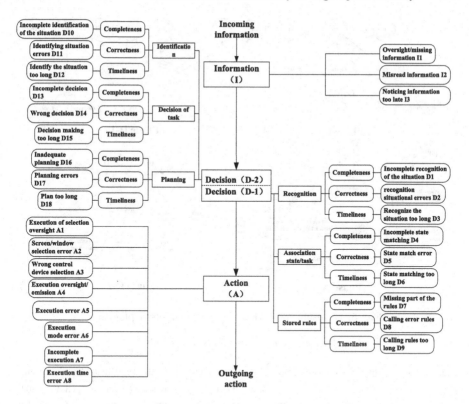

Fig. 4. CFM classification.

4.2 Quantitative Analysis

(1) BN inference. Prior probability assignment, for unmeasurable nodes using D-S evidence theory to fuse the judgment results of different experts, for measurable nodes using XGBoost recognition statistics of high and low levels of present probability as the prior probability of Bayesian network nodes; conditional probability assignment is achieved by fuzzy inference algorithm [10]; the Bayesian network inference results of four cognitive stages are obtained.

(2) CFM occurrence probability calculation. Through the SLIM-BN algorithm [11], the Bayesian network root nodes are all placed in the best and worst states to obtain two SLIs and solve for the values of the unknowns a and b as shown in Eq. 2. Then, the BN inference results in the original state are substituted into Eq. 1 to calculate the probability of CFM occurrence as shown in Table 2.

$$\begin{cases} \lg HEP_{\min} = aSLI_1 + b \\ \lg HEP_{\max} = aSLI_2 + b \end{cases} \tag{1}$$

$$\lg HEP = aSLI + b \tag{2}$$

(3) Event tree inference. The probability of occurrence of various CFM is obtained, so that the cognitive behaviors decomposed in the HEF layer can be

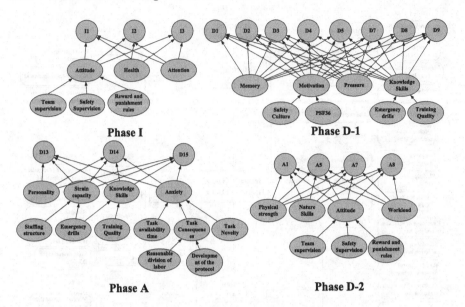

Fig. 5. Bayesian network structure at different phases.

Table 2. CFM occurrence probability.

Phase I	probability	Phase D-1	probability	Phase D-2	probability	Phase A	probability
I1	2.420e−04	D1	8.962e−05	D13	2.982e−02	A1	3.401e−04
I2	2.038e−04	D2	7.598e−05	D14	2.326e−02	A5	4.634e−04
I3	1.903e−04	D3	1.098e−04	D15	2.557e−02	A7	4.184e−04
		D4	8.360e−03			A8	1.851e−04
		D5	6.946e−03				
		D7	1.462e−03				
		D8	2.487e−03				
		D9	8.089e−03				

mapped with CFM as shown in Table 3. Since the task is a tandem task, all behaviors must succeed in order for the task to succeed, so the human reliability of the home signal fault scenario is 0.93265 by event tree inference as shown in Eq. 3, and the causative actions with the highest probability of failure are fault diagnosis, confirming the results of troubleshooting, and registering the traveling equipment register.

$$P(S) = P(HFE1) \times P(HFE2) \times \cdots \times P(HFE14) = 0.93265 \qquad (3)$$

Table 3. CFM occurrence probability.

Behavior number	Possible CFM	Failure probability	Success Probability	Corrected Probability
1	I1\I2\I3	6.3610e−04	0.99936	0.99936
2	D13\D14\D15	0.07865	0.92135	0.96067
3	D1\D2\D3	2.7540e−04	0.99972	0.99976
4	A1\A5\A8	9.8860e−04	0.99901	0.99950
5	A1\A5\A7\A8	0.00141	0.99859	0.99866
6	I1\I2\I3	6.3610e−04	0.99936	0.99936
7	A1\A5	8.0350e−04	0.99920	0.99960
8	D7\D8	0.00395	0.99605	0.99625
9	I2	2.0380e−04	0.99980	0.99981
10	D7\D8\D9	0.01204	0.98796	0.99398
11	A1\A5\A8	9.8860e−04	0.99901	0.99950
12	D4\D5	0.01531	0.98469	0.98546
13	A1\A5	8.0350e−04	0.99920	0.99960
14	A1\A8	5.2520e−04	0.99947	0.99974

5 Conclusion

In this paper, a PHOENIX model-based HRA method is proposed to realize the macro level of dispatcher's error behavior, gradually refine to the possible CFM, and then obtain the influential PSF, and reduce the component of expert judgment in model quantification to make the analysis results objective. The design of a human factors data quantification method based on physiological signals achieves hierarchical identification of stress, attention and workload with average accuracies of 76.8%, 81.2% and 79.6%, which further solving the problem of over-reliance on expert experience. It is also applied to the example analysis to obtain the human factor reliability of the travel dispatcher in this scenario, and gives the highest probability of failure behavior, which provides an improvement direction for the dispatching emergency handling protocol.

References

1. Li, P.C., Chen, G.H., Zhang, L., Dai, L.C.: Research review and development trends of human reliability analysis techniques. At. Energy Sci. Technol. **45**(3), 329–340 (2011)
2. Park, J., Jung, W., Kim, J.: Inter-relationships between performance shaping factors for human reliability analysis of nuclear power plants. Nuclear Eng. Technol. **52**(1), 87–100 (2020)
3. Zou, Y., Zhang, L., Dai, L., et al.: Human reliability analysis for digitized nuclear power plants: case study on the LingAo II nuclear power plant. Nuclear Eng. Technol. **49**(2), 335–341 (2017)
4. Sun, L., Wang, L., Su, C., et al.: Human reliability assessment of intelligent coal mine hoist system based on Bayesian network. Sci. Rep. **12**(1), 21880 (2022)

5. Franciosi, C., Di Pasquale, V., Iannone, R., et al.: A taxonomy of performance shaping factors for human reliability analysis in industrial maintenance. J. Ind. Eng. Manage. (JIEM) **12**(1), 115–132 (2019)

6. Di Bona, G., Falcone, D., Forcina, A., et al.: Systematic human reliability analysis (SHRA): a new approach to evaluate human error probability (HEP) in a nuclear plant. Int. J. Math. Eng. Manage. Sci. **6**(1), 345 (2021)

7. Kandemir, C., Celik, M.: A human reliability assessment of marine auxiliary machinery maintenance operations under ship PMS and maintenance 4.0 concepts. Cogn. Technol. Work **22**(3), 473–487 (2020)

8. Zhang, L., Wang, Y.Q.: Human factors analysis: needs, issues and trends. Syst. Eng. Theory Pract. **6**, 14–20 (2001)

9. Ekanem, N.J., Mosleh, A., Shen, S.H.: Phoenix - a model based human reliability analysis methodology: qualitative analysis procedure. Reliab. Eng. Syst. Safety **145**, 301–315 (2016)

10. Wang, Z.L., Wu, B., Xing, S.R., Guo, J.: Application of fuzzy set-value statistics in the weights of coal mine safety evaluation indexes. China Saf. Sci. J. **1**, 74–76 (2004)

11. Abrishami, S., Khakzad, N., Hosseini, S.M., et al.: BN-SLIM: a Bayesian network methodology for human reliability assessment based on success likelihood index method (SLIM). Reliab. Eng. Syst. Safety (193), 106647 (2020)

Research on Brain Load Prediction Based on Machine Learning for High-Speed Railway Dispatching

Dandan Bi(ID), Wei Zheng(✉)(ID), and Xiaorong Meng(ID)

The Collaborative Innovation Center of Railway Traffic Safety and National Research Center of Railway Safety Assessment, Beijing Jiaotong University, Beijing, China
wzheng1@bjtu.edu.cn

Abstract. In this paper, based on a simulation experiment platform, multimodal physiological data of the operator during emergency scenario processing are collected and processed. Specifically, for the ECG signal acquired by the ECG sensor, the noise is eliminated by using the method of stationary wavelet transform, and then the R-wave labeling is performed by the differential algorithm to obtain the HRV waveform and extract the time-domain, frequency-domain and nonlinear related features; for the multi-channel brainwave signal acquired by the EEG test system, the electrode positioning, potential re-referencing, filtering and noise removal are firstly performed using the eeglab toolkit For the eye-movement data collected by the eye tracker, the subject's fixation behavior was extracted using the position-distance threshold algorithm, and the fixation frequency and mean fixation time were calculated, together with the mean and standard deviation data of the pupil's diameter, as the characteristics of the eye-movement dimension. In the process of regression prediction, a feature selection method based on entropy criterion was proposed in this paper. The results showed that the feature-selected dataset achieved better performance in the regression prediction of the SVR model compared with the original feature set.

Keywords: Brain Load · Machine learning · High-speed railway dispatching

1 Introduction

The improvement of train scheduling automation, on the one hand, reduces the daily operation of dispatchers, which makes them focus on the dynamic changes of the monitoring screen as long as possible; On the other hand, when an emergency occurs, dispatchers need to deal with the emergency quickly and correctly. In this process, the workload of dispatchers fluctuates continuously

Supported by the Fundamental Research Funds for the Central Universities (Science and technology leading talent team project) (2022JBXT003).

J. Guiochet et al. (Eds.): SAFECOMP 2023 Workshops, LNCS 14182, pp. 239–246, 2023.
https://doi.org/10.1007/978-3-031-40953-0_20

with the change of work content and work scene. Excessive or too little workload will have a certain negative impact [1]. Therefore, in order to reduce security incidents caused by human factors and improve the work effect of dispatchers, it is necessary to study the workload of dispatchers.

2   Related Works

Currently, the commonly used workload evaluation methods are subjective evaluation method, task analysis method, physiological measurement method and complexity analysis method, etc. Hart et al. [2] used subjective evaluation method (NASA-TXL scale method) to categorize the influencing factors of workload into six categories, and assigned corresponding weights to weight the workload. The indicators of the physiological assessment method were divided into three major categories according to the functions of the physiological organs involved, namely, those related to the brain, heart, and eyes [3–10]. In an exploratory study of driver mental load, Shimizu et al. [11] used FMRI and FNIRS-related techniques to obtain data on drivers' brain physiological activity in relatively narrow traffic roads, and verified that cerebral blood flow is a physiological indicator for effective evaluation of brain mental load. Tattersall [12] found that the pilot's mental load increased with the increase of the flight task volume, but the LF frequency value in their heart rate variability power spectral density also decreased. Lee et al. [13] used Nocera et al. [14] designed a simulated driving game experiment, the results showed that there were significant differences in the distribution patterns of the test subjects' gaze points at different levels of mental load, and the concentration area of the gaze points shrank as the mental load continued to increase.

It can be seen that the railway field is limited by the invasive of physiological data collection equipment, and there is still room for in-depth research about it. In this paper, based on the high-speed railway dispatching simulation platform, the physiological data of dispatchers in the process of emergency disposal are collected, and the correlation model between physiological data and brain load is constructed to realize the detection and monitoring of brain load of dispatchers.

3   Research Method

3.1   The Experiment Design

The test experiments are conducted based on the human factors engineering experiment system for dispatchers developed independently within the laboratory. The experiment system consists of scenario generation management system, dispatching command simulation system, and data acquisition and analysis system, which can provide functions such as normal and fault scenario generation and management, construction of human-machine interface and related environment for dispatchers, and acquisition and analysis of operational behavior and physiological parameters of the subjects. The graphic workstation, which is the subject's operating object, is also equipped with a desktop vertical radio microphone and a set of keyboard and mouse for interactive operation with the experimental system.

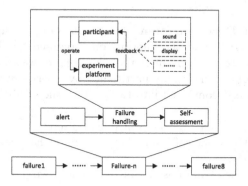

Fig. 1. The experimental process.

The experimental paradigm is shown in Fig. 1. The entire experiment contains a total of eight emergency scenarios, with 10 min between scenes for subjects to rest and adjust the experimental equipment. In the process of failure handling, the experimental platform will give corresponding display or voice feedback after the subject operates on the experimental platform. For example, after the subject calls the driver through the dispatcher's communication simulation subsystem and asks for confirmation of train-related conditions, the communication simulation subsystem will automatically play the corresponding reply voice. The data acquisition analysis marks the above feedback stimuli by recording time stamps and performs timeline alignment and synchronization on the collected physiological data such as ECG, EEG and eye movements. At the end of the disposition process, subjects filled out the NASA-TLX scale to make a self-assessment of the brain load for that contingency scenario.

The physiological data were segmented according to the event markers on the EEG signal, and a total of 120 sets of physiological data were obtained. AHP was used to determine the magnitude of the load induced by each feedback event within the scenario as a percentage of the overall contingency process, thus mapping the subjects' scale scores weighted to the score labels of each group of physiological data.

3.2 Feature Extraction

Data Pre-processing. The EEG data was preprocessed using the eeglab in matlab. (1) Electrode positioning. The channel electrode points are positioned using the standard channel position based on the international 10–20 system. (2) Filtering. Filter 50 Hz industrial frequency interference and use 0.1–30 Hz bandpass filter to filter out high frequency band noise. (3) re-reference. Select the bilateral mastoid as the re-reference channel.

Discrete Wavelet Decomposition. The actual sampled signal is often discrete and finite interval, and the information processed by the computer can only be discrete, hence the introduction of the discrete wavelet transform. The spectrum of any signal can be fully partitioned by a series of wavelet functions and a scale function, decomposed into two parts: scale coefficients and wavelet coefficients.

In this experiment, based on the principle of discrete wavelet decomposition mentioned above, three bands of θ, α and β waves in the EEG signal are extracted as the object of study.

After each frequency band was obtained, its power was calculated separately. In this experiment, excluding the two reference electrodes, a total of 6 channels of EEG signals were acquired, and each channel was decomposed into 3 frequency bands, and a total of 18 power spectrum data were obtained as the characteristics of EEG signals.

Stationary Wavelet Denoising. In wavelet denoising, the multi-level high-frequency noise signal is under thresholding, and the processed detail signal is reconstructed with the approximation signal to obtain an estimate of the noise-contaminated signal. During the processing of ECG data, it was found that the denoised signal produced Gibbs oscillation phenomenon near the singularity point, as shown in Fig. 2(b). To suppress this phenomenon, the cancellation method of stationary wavelet transform is used.

The shape of the Daubechies wavelet family is similar to the QRS wave in ECG signals, and its energy spectrum is concentrated near the low frequency, so db5 in the Daubechies wavelet function family is chosen as the wavelet basis for the experiment in this paper. The results show that the stationary wavelet denoising significantly improves the Gibbs phenomenon at the singularities, as shown in Fig. 2(c).

In this experiment, the R-wave of ECG signal is labeled using the difference method to extract the heart rate variability, and the HRV data are correlated and calculated to obtain a total of 12 features in the time domain, frequency domain, and nonlinearity as the feature dimension of ECG.

3.3 Eye Movement

Fixation is a period of time during which the human eye is continuously focused on an object. The equipment cannot directly output the fixation position and

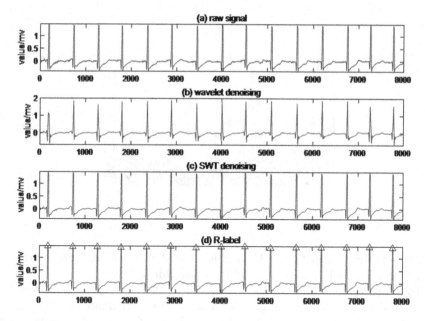

Fig. 2. ECG processing.

time, and an algorithm is needed to extract the fixation from the derived gaze point position and time. In this experiment, a position thresholding algorithm is used, and the points where the difference between the positions of two adjacent gaze points is greater than the threshold are recorded as the end point of the previous segment of fixation and the starting point of the next segment of fixation, respectively, from which the fixation segments are obtained. As shown in Fig. 3. The fixation segments with too short a duration were excluded, and the final fixation data of the subjects were obtained. Based on the fixation and pupil data, four features were extracted to form the feature dimension of eye movements.

3.4 Regression Prediction

Feature Selection. Each feature has a different degree of influence on the brain load prediction. In order to improve feature sensitivity, improve prediction accuracy and model generalization ability, the entropy criterion is used to select the feature set to choose the appropriate and important information.

The entropy measure based on the similarity between objects is constructed to evaluate the importance of the original feature set, so as to filter out the important feature subset.

Regression Method. In the experiment, the SVR model of scikit-learn machine learning toolkit is selected for regression prediction of brain load of

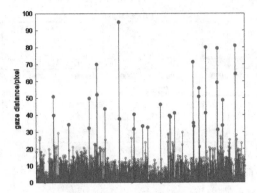

Fig. 3. Fixation extract.

high-speed railway dispatchers. Meanwhile, a ten-fold cross-validation method is used to avoid model overfitting as much as possible.

To compare the prediction accuracy between different regression models, linear regression, random forest regression and SVR regression models with default parameters were trained using the data set before feature selection was performed. The prediction results are shown in Table 1.

Table 1. Error of different model results.

	RMSE	MAE	R^2
Liner regression	53.4744	6.5340	0.6524
Random forest regression	57.506	5.57	0.6262
SVR	10.0921	4.4622	0.7495

Among them, the RMSE of the linear regression and random forest models were 53.4744 and 57.506 respectively, which were much larger than the RMSE of the SVR model; the MAE of the three models were not very different, but the MAE of the SVR model was the smallest among the three; in terms of R^2 value, the SVR model only reached 0.7495, but it was higher than the R^2 of the linear regression and random forest models values. This shows that the SVR model predicts better than the linear regression and random forest regression models on the original data set.

To verify the effectiveness of the above feature selection methods, the SVR model was used for regression prediction based on the original dataset, and the dataset after entropy criterion feature selection, respectively. During the model training, the kernel function is the default rbf Gaussian kernel function, the kernel width parameter gamma of Gaussian kernel is set to 0.1, and the penalty coefficient c is set to 150. The prediction results are shown in Table 2.

Table 2. Error without\with feature selection.

	RMSE	MAE	R^2
Before	9.1602	2.0949	0.7728
After	0.8235	0.5611	0.9280

Compared with the whole features, after entropy criterion feature selection, the R^2 of regression prediction results improved to 0.928, and RMSE and MAE decreased accordingly. The regression results are plotted with the measured value as the independent variable and the predicted value as the dependent variable. As shown in Fig. 4(a) and Fig. 4(b). It can be found that the agreement between the predicted and measured values is significantly improved after feature selection, indicating that the prediction accuracy of the regression model after feature selection is significantly improved and can meet the actual prediction needs.

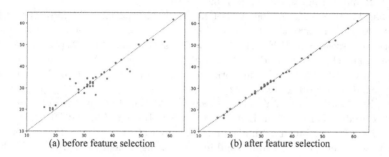

(a) before feature selection   (b) after feature selection

Fig. 4. Predicted values to actual values.

4   Conclusion

In this experiment, a brain load prediction method based on multi-physiological features is proposed for the high-speed railway dispatching under emergency scenarios. Three independent signal processing and feature extraction channels are constructed in this paper for three types of physiological signals, which can be well adapted to the respective data characteristics of different physiological parameters.

However, there are still shortcomings in this experimental study. First, due to the objective conditions, the number of subjects in this experiment is limited, and the randomness of the sample is insufficient. Second, the parameters of the SVR algorithm in this paper are not intelligently optimized, and there is still room for research and improvement.

Next, the model parameters with the best effect will be found with intelligent optimization algorithm. Meanwhile, the feature set can be used as a part of pending variables to participate in the process of SVR intelligent tuning.

References

1. Evans, A.W.: Fatal train accidents on Europe's railways: 1980–2009. Accid. Anal. Prevent. **43**(1), 391–401 (2011)
2. Hart, S.G., Staveland, L.E.: Development of the NASA task load index (TXL): results of empirical and theoretical research. Hum. Mental Workload Amsterdam: Elsevier **52**(6), 139–183 (1988)
3. Waard, D.D., Brookhuis, K.A.: On the measurement of driver mental workload. Rev. Econ. Stat. (1997)
4. Xie, B., Salvendy, G.: Review and reappraisal of modelling and predicting mental workload in single- and multi-task environments. Work Stress. **14**(1), 74–99 (2000)
5. Wickens, C.D.: Multiple resources and performance prediction. Theoret. Issues Ergon. Sci. **3**(2), 159–177 (2002)
6. Glaser, J.I., Benjamin, A.S., Farhoodi, R., et al.: The roles of supervised machine learning in systems neuroscience. Prog. Neurobiol. **175**, 126–137 (2019)
7. Zhang, P., Wang, X., Chen, J., et al.: Spectral and temporal feature learning with two-stream neural networks for mental workload assessment. IEEE Trans. Neural Syst. Rehabil. Eng. **27**(6), 1149–1159 (2019)
8. Zhang, P., Wang, X., Zhang, W., et al.: Learning spatial-spectral-temporal EEG features with recurrent 3D convolutional neural networks for cross-task mental workload assessment. IEEE Trans. Neural Syst. Rehabil. Eng. **27**(1), 31–42 (2018)
9. Chakladar, D.D., Dey, S., Roy, P.P., et al.: EEG-based mental workload estimation using deep BLSTM-LSTM network and evolutionary algorithm. Biomed. Signal Process. Control **60**, 101989 (2020)
10. Jiao, Z., Gao, X., Wang, Y., et al.: Deep convolutional neural networks for mental load classification based on EEG data. Pattern Recogn. **76**, 582–595 (2018)
11. Shimizu, T., Nanbu, T., Sunda, T.: An exploratory study of the driver workload assessment by brain functional imaging using onboard fNIRS. SAE Technical Papers (2011)
12. Tattersall, A.J., Hockey, G.R.J.: Level of operator control and changes in heart rate variability during simulated flight maintenance. Hum. Factors: J. Hum. Factors Ergon. Soc. **37**(4), 682–698 (1995)
13. Lee, Y.C., Lee, J.D., Boyle, I.N., et al.: Visual attention in driving: the effects of cognitive load and visual disruption. Hum. Factor: J. Hum. Factors Ergon. Soc. **49**(4), 721–733 (2007)
14. Nocera, F., Couyoumdjian, A., Ferlazzo, F.: Crossing the pillars of Hercules: the role of spatial frames of reference in error making. Q. J. Exp. Psychol. **59**(1), 204–221 (2006)

Paired Safety Rule Structure for Human-Machine Cooperation with Feature Update and Evolution

Satoshi Otsuka[1](✉), Natsumi Watanabe[1](✉), Takehito Ogata[2], Donato Di Paola[3], Daniel Hillen[4], Joshua Frey[4], Nishanth Laxman[4], and Jan Reich[4]

[1] Research and Development Group, Hitachi Ltd, Ibaraki, Japan
{satoshi.otsuka.hk,natsumi.watanabe.jv}@hitachi.com
[2] European Research and Development Centre, Hitachi Europe, Munich, Germany
takehito.ogata@hitachi-eu.com
[3] European Research and Development Centre, Hitachi Europe, Valbonne, France
donato.di-paola@hitachi-eu.com
[4] Fraunhofer Institute for Experimental Software Engineering IESE, Kaiserslautern, Germany
{Daniel.Hillen,Joshua.Frey,Nishanth.Laxman,
Jan.Reich}@iese.fraunhofer.de

Abstract. Autonomous control systems are used in an open environment where humans exist. Therefore, a safety design needs to be created corresponding to evolutions and changes in the behavior of humans and machines in accordance with an open changing environment. In this study, we propose a structure and derivation method of safety rules based on a pairing structure for the cooperation of humans and machines, which can facilitate feature updates and evolutions in the behavior of humans and machines. For a feature update, feature trees utilizing methods of software product line correspond to the evolution of behavior of a human and a machine by using a pairing safety rule structure.

The results of a case study simulating autonomous driving systems and pedestrians in a city showed that the proposed safety rule structure can facilitate rule switching when features change. The results also showed that human-machine cooperation efficiency could be improved and safety maintained by operation following the change of safety rules in accordance with the proposed structure when the behavior of pedestrians and autonomous vehicles evolved.

Keywords: Safety rule · Human-machine cooperation · Feature update · System and human evolution

1 Introduction

Autonomous control systems have become a solution to alleviate labor shortages in developed countries as well as to reduce accidents due to human errors. Therefore, their application is considered in many business domains (e.g., automotive, factories, construction machinery). However, their safety needs to be ensured to introduce autonomous control systems more widely into society [1].

© The Author(s), under exclusive license to Springer Nature Switzerland AG 2023
J. Guiochet et al. (Eds.): SAFECOMP 2023 Workshops, LNCS 14182, pp. 247–259, 2023.
https://doi.org/10.1007/978-3-031-40953-0_21

As for the symbiosis between humans and machines, thinking in a "human-centered" way is one useful solution and is important as a basic idea. However, if humans are simply assumed to have the highest priority, autonomous control systems will not be able to sufficiently move in a coexistence space due to the system's behavior being too conservative. As a result, autonomous control systems will not be able to be implemented throughout society.

Moreover, autonomous control systems are often not placed in a completely fixed environment. For example, in an open area, the surrounding environment (operational domain) and the surrounding and connected machines (system of systems) change frequently. Another point of view is that as long as humans and machines cooperate, human behavior will also evolve and change with humans' familiarity with and mastery of the environment. Autonomous control systems and surrounding systems may also evolve due to the use of artificial intelligence, for example. Autonomous control systems should be addressed to ensure safety even in such a situation.

Therefore, "safety rules" are needed that can facilitate cooperation between humans and machines. As an example, humans and machines cooperate by following safety rules to maintain safety and improve efficiency at the same time [2], and the system side is safely stopped when a rule is violated [3]. The safety rules are for humans and machines to coexist efficiently. A premise that humans and machines follow their respective rules can ensure human safety.

In these circumstances, existing safety standards, safety rule structures, and safety design reuse methods do not explicitly support both coordination of human-machine cooperation and adaptation to the evolution of human and machines. Therefore, this study proposes a safety design based on safety rules for safely and efficiently coordinating autonomous control systems of human-machine cooperation and a method to facilitate evolutions and changes in the behavior of humans and machines. In a case study, we show an example of the structure of safety rules that can manage evolution and show the effect of changing humans' behavior.

The paper is organized as follows. Section 2 introduces related works. Section 3 explains the proposed safety rule structure and architecture. Section 4 presents how to derive safety rules. Section 5 shows results of a case study. Section 6 discusses key points and enhancements to the proposed method. We conclude in Sect. 7 and present future work.

2   Related Work

The system safety concept is standardized in ISO12100 [4] especially for machinery safety. In this standard, a safety design is implemented with a three-step method that implements safety into a system stepwise. Functional safety (IEC61508 [5], ISO26262 [6]) is focused mainly on failures (random hardware failures and systematic failures) in a control system. In these standards, a human is treated as a system user (operator) or a part of the surrounding environment. No clear procedure has been established to define human-machine cooperation. Therefore, when analyzing a human-machine cooperation system as described above, requirements related to human-machine cooperation are defined as system safety measures or assumptions for such requirements.

There are also other standards about safety design methods for functional and performance insufficiencies and human misuse, such as the safety of the intended functionality (SOTIF) (ISO21448 [7]) in the automotive field. However, besides guidance for safety analysis of human misuse, no definition of safety rules related to the human-machine cooperation can be found in SOTIF. The Systems-Theoretic Accident Model and Processes (STAMP)/System-Theoretic Process Analysis (STPA) [8] method conducts a safety analysis on the basis of interactions between a human and a machine by using a control structure. This method focuses on the safety analysis between humans and machines but does not focus on how to manage or control interactions between them (e.g., safety rules and the structure).

In [9, 10], there are some examples of rule structures. Here, the structure of the rule in the control system is defined as a "rule book". The rule book defines the precedence and description methods, such as a hierarchical structure of the rules. In the automotive field, Responsibility-Sensitive Safety (RSS) [11] is proposed for rules related to how to control a vehicle to avoid collision by assigning responsibility to each vehicle. RSS defines and clarifies the control parameters when vehicles are close and determines the priority of the vehicle when crossing at an intersection (give way). Assumptions for rule parameters are standardized in IEEE2846. In RSS + [12], the idea is extended to forecast vehicles' behavior, but the idea of the rule is based on RSS. In these methods, the rules are mainly for vehicles and are not focused on human-machine cooperation explicitly.

One form of rule is a contract-based design. In particular, ConSert [18] has been proposed in a safety domain. This method guarantees safety by dynamically switching a structure of safety design and arguments in response to changes of the context. However, this method does not explicitly specify structures of safety rules for humans and machines.

For considering feature changes of a system in a software domain, software product line (SPL) [13] methods were developed. The software development phase is separated by a domain and an application, common parts are efficiently designed in the domain development, and the modules are reused and constructed during the application development of individual products. As an idea of applying this method in a safety field, Product-Line Software Fault Tree Analysis (PL-SFTA) [14] is intended to facilitate reuse of safety designs by applying the SPL methods to associate the safety designs and parts of the product. Another SPL application for safety models was introduced in [15], where safety analysis models were dynamically conditioned on the variability of system structure. While this approach reflects changes in a system structure, it does not explicitly consider cooperative systems.

These prior methods did not explicitly consider that humans and machines cooperate, that the behavior of each evolves, and that systems are used in various operational environments. In this study, we propose a structure of safety rules considering these factors. As for an update of features, applying SPL techniques can correspond. As for an evolution of humans and machines, a pair of safety rules can trace the relationships between the rules.

3 Paired Safety Rule Structure and Architecture

The requirements of the proposed method are to (1) correspond to feature changes (e.g., function update, applied business domain change) of the system, (2) respond to evolutions and changes in the behavior of humans and machines, and (3) have an architecture able to update safety rules. These requirements are explained below.

3.1 Overall Structure

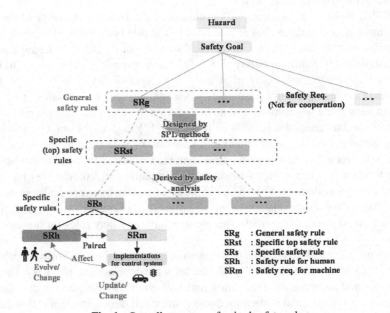

Fig. 1. Overall structure of paired safety rules

The overall proposed safety rule structure is shown in Fig. 1. The top-level general safety rules (safety rules for multi-domain) are derived by deductive analysis (e.g., Fault Tree Analysis (FTA)) from a safety goal derived from hazard analysis. Put simply, safety rules are kinds of safety requirements. However, "requirements" are typically used for some implementations of the system. No requirement can be implemented to humans, so we assume requirements to be safety rules for humans. The overall structure consists of a structure of general and specific rules in which feature changes are taken into account and specific paired safety rules that are for evolutions and changes in the behavior of humans and machines.

To facilitate feature changes in the system, safety rules are decomposed in consideration of the product line structure. When defining a general safety rule, safety rules that can prevent the general hazard should be considered. In an autonomous driving system, a general hazard is, for example, collisions between a human and a machine, and general safety rules are spatial separation and time separation of humans and machines. Specific safety rules are realized by implementing each safety rule for each domain (e.g., signal for an automotive domain, block control for a railway domain).

After the specific (top-level) safety rules are derived, they are decomposed into specific safety rules by carrying out deductive safety analysis (e.g., FTA) from hazards that need to be prevented by implementing the safety rules. In the process, safety rules are decomposed from one cooperative safety rule to paired safety rules for a human and a machine. Performing such a pairing makes it easy to trace the effects of the evolution in behaviors of both humans and machines.

An architecture corresponding to feature changes and evolutions is illustrated in Fig. 2. This architecture refers to a loop structure, such as Dependability Engineering for Open Systems (DEOS) [16]. The project proposed a short-term, fast loop that responds to failures and second loops that respond to long-term changes. As for our proposed architecture, the relationship between the main function and the first Safety Mechanism (SM(1st)) is similar to that between conventional main functions and safety mechanisms. SM(1st) controls the system to stay or move to a safe state after detecting a failure of the main function. The second Safety Layer (SL(2nd)) handles dynamical changes (e.g., evolution of the system). For example, if the layer detects the trigger of an evolution or change in human behavior, the safety layer updates the corresponding safety rules and safety designs in a pre-designed range. The third Safety Layer (SL(3rd)) detects, for example, departures from the pre-designed range (e.g., a new feature being added) and executes a redesign loop.

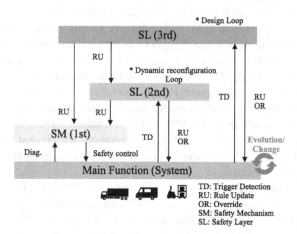

Fig. 2. System architecture for rule updates

4   Procedure for Safety Rule Derivation

In this chapter, we explain how to derive safety rules described in the preceding chapter.

Procedure

1. Organize a high-level concept (general safety rule) in which humans and machines cooperate safely.
2. Create a feature tree (using SPL methods) for system deployment and derive specific (top) safety rules that reflect the structure of the feature tree.
3. Derive specific safety rules to prevent each basic event in the safety analysis results from hazards, which is the opposite concept of the specific top safety rule.
4. Decompose specific safety rules to safety requirements for machines and safety rules for humans (pairing).
5. Clarify each safety requirement for a machine to implement the requirements.

In step 1, a high-level concept (general safety rule) is organized in which humans and machines cooperate safely. For example, general safety rules are spatial separation ("Humans and machines are present in different compartments") and time separation ("In areas where humans and machines need to coexist, each has a separate assigned time") of humans and machines. A general safety rule is created by abstracting a concept that can be used similarly when features change or the behavior of humans and machines evolves.

In step 2, implementations of the general safety rule above are considered to create a feature tree. As shown in Fig. 3, the structure of the system to be implemented is organized using a feature tree [13] (SPL method). In this example, the feature tree organizes implementations of a space separation between humans and machines such as with traffic rules (with or without a signal) or block control (with or without human-machine interaction (HMI)). Then, the structure of the feature tree is transferred to a safety rule structure (to achieve general safety rules, the selected leaf's rules should be satisfied), so the terminal leaves become the specific (top) safety rule.

For the FTA, a structure of PL-SFTA [14] is assumed. The FTA is constructed according to the structure of the variability. In addition, the divided features are not completely independent. Dependencies of feature tree are managed by the SPL technique (require/exclude relationships).

In step 3, as shown in Fig. 4, specific safety rules are derived to prevent each basic event in the safety analysis results (e.g., FTA) from hazards, which is the opposite of the specific top safety rule. In the example in Fig. 4, the safety rule is "At an intersection, a pedestrian and a vehicle do not collide due to time separation with a signal", so the hazard to be analyzed in that case is "A pedestrian and a vehicle collide when crossing an intersection (time separation with a signal)." The basic event is derived by decomposing the hazard by conducting a deductive safety analysis.

In step 4, the specific rules are separated into safety requirements for machines and safety rules for humans. In the example shown in Fig. 4, to prevent accidents due to a human jumping out in front of a machine, the upper speed limit for the human is set and the machine system assumes that the human may jump out in front of it within that speed. Thus, pairing the requirements of the human and the machine enables direct tracing of each change.

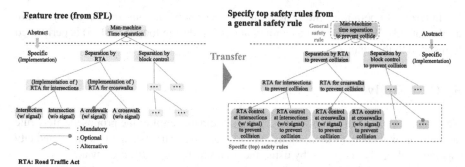

Fig. 3. Deriving specific (top) safety rules from a general safety rule (using feature tree)

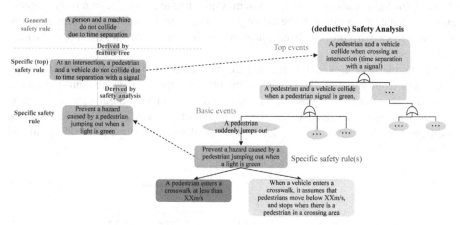

Fig. 4. Derivation of specific rules from a specific top rule

In step 5, the safety requirements for the machine are decomposed, and each requirement is broken down to implement it to a control system. These are basically high-level requirements of the control system, and the requirements are decomposed to each function more finely when implementing the machine.

Thereafter, when the system feature changes, the system is reconfigured and reused in accordance with the structure of the feature tree. If the human side evolves or changes, or if the machine side evolves, pairing rules are updated mutually.

Through these steps, the rule structure for a human-machine cooperative system is created. Along the way, by designing the system design (feature tree) and safety design (FTA) together, a tree of system reusability and safety analysis is fused into the rule structure, and changing the safety rules is compatible with the system reuse and the safety point of view.

Detailed parameters of the safety rules for humans and machines in step 4 should be clarified by iterations. In the iterations, these parameters are determined by balancing bottom-up parameters, such as machine performance constraints, requirements of stakeholders on the human side, and so on.

In terms of operations, the system must detect rule violations and put the system in a safe state [3]. When human behavior changes, a redesign loop (Step1–5) is performed to respond to the changes.

5 Case Study

Next, an example of an autonomous driving system that applies the proposed safety rule structure is explained. (Autonomous) Vehicles and pedestrians exist in a simulated city together and safely cooperate by using the time separation at the crosswalk.

For an example of a feature change in the situation of the system, first, there is no signal in the city (development of autonomous driving system in a special zone), and then a traffic light is installed (or the system is migrated to another region where signals exist). In that case, in step 2 of the above procedure in an application development, it is necessary to switch a previously designed case in the domain development or add a new feature.

Safety rule structures in that situation are shown in Figs. 5 and 6. Figure 5 illustrates an example from safety analysis to the safety rule decomposition where human-machine separation is realized by following the road traffic act (RTA) without signals. Figure 6 illustrates the same structure as Fig. 5, but the part of safety rule structure with signals is different. In this way, rules are decomposed to derive the cooperative safety rule of pedestrians and vehicles.

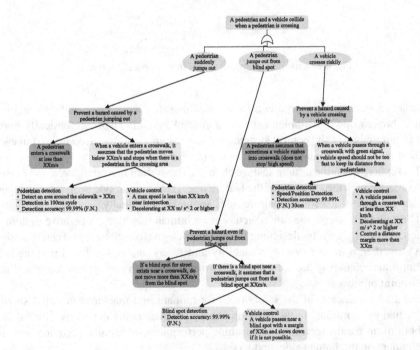

Fig. 5. Example of derivation of specific rules (intersection without signal)

Paired Safety Rule Structure

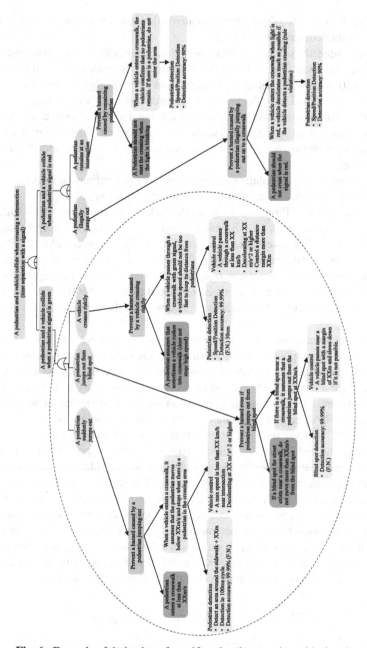

Fig. 6. Example of derivation of specific rules (intersection with signal)

As described in the feature tree in Fig. 3, the case with a signal is an optional structure from the top (denoted by the circle of the branch), and the case without a signal is mandatory (normal branches). Therefore, safety design associated with the safety rule without signals is required during the implementation, and the safety design when there are signals is implemented as an option.

In this example, the safety rule structure in Fig. 5 coincides with the portion enclosed within the dashed line in Fig. 6. The safety rules in the case without a signal are a subset. Here, the safety rules with a signal at an intersection when the signal is green are the same as those without a signal from the viewpoint of safety rule structure. When performing a new implementation of the case where there is a signal, the portion outside of the dashed line is analyzed and designed, and overall safety is verified. Such safety activity can easily focus on differences because it is decomposed by the safety rules derived from the feature tree.

As an example of the evolution of the behavior of pedestrians and vehicles, pedestrians in the area initially do not follow rules about walking speed (e.g., jumping out at crosswalks at 12 km/h). From the situation, the pedestrians come to comply with traffic rules (e.g., moving as fast as 4 km/h) when crossing crosswalks. A corresponding safety rule structure in such a case is the pair structure in Fig. 5 (paired rules of "Prevent a hazard caused by a pedestrian jumping out"). When the speed limit of pedestrians ("A pedestrian enters a crosswalk at less than XX m/s") changes, the corresponding safety requirement ("When a vehicle enters a crosswalk, it assumes that the pedestrian moves below XX m/s and stops when there is a pedestrian in the crossing area") is directly traceable.

The experimental results of the system behavior in this case are shown in Table 1. On the basis of the proposed safety rule structure, the vehicle safety rules are designed to follow the changing parameters of pedestrians. The experiment used a Webots [17] environment (based on city.wbt sample world), in which pedestrians and vehicles were moving along prescribed routes, and sensors of the position and speed were operated without errors. Pedestrians are simulated to run (jump out) with random probabilities. Pedestrians and vehicles intersect at crosswalks. The vehicle calculates the collision potential from the pedestrian's assumed maximum speed. If a pedestrian and a vehicle are likely to collide at a crosswalk, the vehicle stops in front of the crosswalk.

In the results, the traveling efficiency (estimated by average speeds) is improved to 104.9% (calculated as 7.997/7.622) in the case of adapting to the rule change (the vehicles assume the maximum speed of the pedestrians is 4 km/h on crosswalks) compared with the case that it does not follow the parameter change (the vehicles assume the maximum speed of the pedestrians is 12 km/h on crosswalks). Also, no collision occurred after the rule change in each case. In this case, efficiency of the cooperated system can be improved by following changes in the corresponding parameters (rules).

Table 1. Results of case study (efficiency, safety).

	Efficiency (Mileage (m) / s)	Improvement ratio	Safety (No of collisions)
Do not adapt to rule change	7.622	-	0
Adapt to rule change	7.997	104.9%	0

6 Discussion

In this study, safety verification and assurance to system changes are not conducted. When a change is made and the corresponding safety design is done, safety impact analyses and other safety related activities need to be performed. When conducting the analysis in response to various changes, various analyses are to be facilitated to adapt to the changes. In such a situation, our proposed method can trace the impact of changes by the proposed paired structure. There are existing methods such as ConSert [18] to assess the dynamic capability changes and SINADRA [19] to assess dynamic environment changes. In previous work, we enriched a dynamic safety architecture with these approaches [20]. If we combine these methodologies into our proposed method, the behavior of humans and machines can easily evolve while assuring the safety dynamically.

An important point in this study is not to have separate safety rules (requirements) for humans and machines, but to "directly" connect from one superordinate safety rule to another to clarify an easy trace structure and the derivation procedure. In existing methodologies, the relationship between humans and machines is often treated as assumptions in the safety design. The trace relation of the change can become complex when the causal relation becomes indirect. Our proposed approach makes it easier to trace which requirements are required to respond to evolutions and changes in the behavior of humans and machines.

If humans violate a rule, a dangerous event may occur (for example, if a human runs at 12 km/h assuming 4 km/h). Thus, the system needs to monitor whether humans comply with rules. Moreover, if the system detects a rule violation, the system should put machines in a safe state (temporarily reduce efficiency). Then, by redesigning the system to reflect the changed conditions, the system can adapt again to the changed environment.

In particular, quantitative analysis is useful for the safety analysis of our proposed method. When behavior of humans or machines change and the risk is re-determined, quantitative analysis can be used to determine whether the risk is acceptable or not. As a result, if the risk is acceptable, re-design is unnecessary. Thus, a robust safety design for such change is possible.

To improve reusability and interoperability, other methodologies such as safety analysis and assurance also need to be systemized. Therefore, it is desirable to incorporate the proposed method into the open dependability exchange (ODE) meta-model [21] on the basis of the idea of digital dependability identities (DDI) [22] while assuming safety rules as a type of safety requirement. By aligning such standards, safety artifacts related to this design can be made easily reusable and interoperable.

7 Conclusion

We proposed a paired safety rule structure and the derivation procedure that enables humans and machines to cooperate in accordance with safety rules. It can respond to feature changes in systems and evolutions of human and machine behavior that arise from changes in situations. In addition, we conducted a case study of the pedestrians and vehicles following safety rules in a simulated city and showed an example of safety rule structures and results for a situation change and safety rule update by using the proposed safety rule structure. The results showed that the proposed rule structure could increase the efficiency of the system while maintaining safety. Thus, even when humans and machines change and evolve in a cooperated environment, conducting cooperative actions with following safety rules that respond to changes will be possible.

In the future, we will apply a safety certification method (ConSert) in a dynamic safety rule change to this method, execute safety assurance and argumentation on the basis of this structure, and ensure that safety verification and assurance are efficiently adapted to the evolution.

References

1. Tsutsumi, K., van Gulijk, C.: Safety in the future: whitepaper (2020)
2. Drabek, C., Kosmalska, A., Weiss, G., Ishigooka, T., Otsuka, S., Mizuochi, M.: Safe interaction of automated forklifts and humans at blind corners in a warehouse with infrastructure sensors. In: Habli, I., Sujan, M., Bitsch, F. (eds.) Computer Safety, Reliability, and Security, SAFECOMP 2021, vol. 12852, pp. 163–177. Springer, Cham (2021). https://doi.org/10.1007/978-3-030-83903-1_11
3. Ishigooka, T., Yamada, H., Otsuka, S., Kanekawa, N., Takahashi, J.: Symbiotic safety: safe and efficient human-machine collaboration by utilizing rules. In: 2022 Design, Automation & Test in Europe Conference & Exhibition (DATE), pp. 280–281. IEEE (2022)
4. ISO: Safety of machinery -Basic concepts, general ISO12100–1:2003 (2003)
5. IEC 61508 ed2.0, Functional safety of electrical/electronic/programmable electronic safety-related systems (2010)
6. ISO: Road vehicles - functional safety. Standard ISO 26262:2018 (2018)
7. ISO: Road vehicles - safety of the intended functionality. Standard ISO/PAS 21448:2019(E) (2019)
8. Leveson, N.: A new accident model for engineering safer systems. Saf. Sci. **42**(4), 237–270 (2004)
9. Censi, A., et al.: Liability, ethics, and culture-aware behavior specification using rulebooks. In: 2019 International Conference on Robotics and Automation (ICRA), pp. 8536–8542. IEEE (2019)
10. Collin, A., Bilka, A., Pendleton, S., Tebbens, R.D.: Safety of the intended driving behavior using rulebooks. In: 2020 IEEE Intelligent Vehicles Symposium (IV), pp. 136–143. IEEE (2020)
11. Shalev-Shwartz, S., Shammah, S., Shashua, A.: On a formal model of safe and scalable self-driving cars. arXiv preprint arXiv:1708.06374 (2017)
12. Oboril, F., Scholl, K.U.: RSS+: pro-active risk mitigation for AV safety layers based on RSS. In: 2021 IEEE Intelligent Vehicles Symposium (IV), pp. 99–106. IEEE (2021)
13. Pohl, K., Böckle, G., Van Der Linden, F.: Software Product Line Engineering, vol. 10, pp. 3–540. Springer Heidelberg (2005). https://doi.org/10.1007/3-540-28901-1
14. Dehlinger, J., Lutz, R.R.: Software fault tree analysis for product lines. In: Eighth IEEE International Symposium on High Assurance Systems Engineering, 2004. Proceedings, pp. 12–21. IEEE (2004)
15. Bressan, L., et al.: Modeling the variability of system safety analysis using state-machine diagrams. In: Seguin, C., Zeller, M., Prosvirnova, T. (eds.) Model-Based Safety and Assessment, IMBSA 2022, pp. 43–59. Springer, Cham (2022). https://doi.org/10.1007/978-3-031-15842-1_4

16. DEOS white paper. https://www.jst.go.jp/crest/crest-os/osddeos/data/DEOS-FY2011-WP-03E.pdf. Accessed 20 Dec 2022
17. Michel, O.: Cyberbotics Ltd. Webots™: professional mobile robot simulation. Int. J. Adv. Rob. Syst. 1(1), 5 (2004)
18. Schneider, D., Trapp, M.: Conditional safety certification of open adaptive systems. ACM Trans. Auton. Adapt. Syst. (TAAS) 8(2), 1–20 (2013)
19. Reich, J., Trapp, M.: SINADRA: towards a framework for assurable situation-aware dynamic risk assessment of autonomous vehicles. In: 2020 16th European Dependable Computing Conference (EDCC), pp. 47–50. IEEE (2020)
20. Reich, J., et al.: Engineering dynamic risk and capability models to improve cooperation efficiency between human workers and autonomous mobile robots in shared spaces. In: Seguin, C., Zeller, M., Prosvirnova, T. (eds.) Model-Based Safety and Assessment, IMBSA 2022, vol. 13525, pp. 237–251. Springer, Cham (2022). https://doi.org/10.1007/978-3-031-15842-1_17
21. Digital Dependability Identities and the Open Dependability Exchange Meta-Model. https://deis-project.eu/fileadmin/user_upload/DEIS_D3.1_Specification_of_the_ODE_metamodel_and_documentation_of_the_fundamental_concept_of_DDI_PU.pdf. Accessed 20 Dec 2022
22. Schneider, D., Trapp, M., Papadopoulos, Y., Armengaud, E., Zeller, M., Höfig, K.: WAP: digital dependability identities. In: 2015 IEEE 26th International Symposium on Software Reliability Engineering (ISSRE), pp. 324–329. IEEE (2015)

Towards an Effective Generation of Functional Scenarios for AVs to Guide Sampling

Hugues Blache[✉], Pierre-Antoine Laharotte, and Nour-Eddin El Faouzi

Univ. Gustave Eiffel, Univ. Lyon, ENTPE, LICIT-ECO7 UMR T9401,
F-69675 Lyon, France
{hugues.blache,pierre-antoine.laharotte,
nour-eddin.elfaouzi}@univ-eiffel.fr

Abstract. Numerous methods have been developed for testing Connected and Automated Vehicles (CAV). The scenario-based approach is considered the most promising as it reduces the number of scenarios required to certify the CAV system. In this study, we propose a refined six-step methodology that includes two additional steps to compute a critical index for scenarios and use it to guide the sampling process The methodology starts with the generation of functional scenarios using a 5-layer ontology. Next, the driving data is processed to determine the criticality indices of the functional scenarios. This is achieved by using a latent Dirichlet Allocation technique and a Least Means Squares method. Finally, the sampling process is built on a scenario reduction based on clustering and a specific metric related to the a priori criticality indices. Overall, our refined approach enhances the scenario-based methodology by incorporating criticality indices to guide the sampling process, which can reduce drastically the number of scenarios needed for certification of CAV systems.

Keywords: Critical Index Scenario Sampling · Scenario Reduction · CAV scenario testing

1 Introduction

Implementing Connected and Automated Vehicles on the road while ensuring its safety is now a major challenge in the transportation field. However, the deployment of CAV systems can take a considerable amount of time depending on the strategies adopted [1], which challenges their rapid implementation. Therefore, reducing the number of testing scenarios is one of the major issues today in the context of certification and validation for new Automated Mobility Services (AMS). Multiple approaches have been developed for designing the testing process for CAV.

The distance-based approach [2] consists in letting vehicles under test driving until they run into sufficiently traffic situations before validating it. Such an approach remains extremely naïve and inefficient since it might require around 12

J. Guiochet et al. (Eds.): SAFECOMP 2023 Workshops, LNCS 14182, pp. 260–270, 2023.
https://doi.org/10.1007/978-3-031-40953-0_22

years [1] to validate any new service. Alternative approaches were developed in the literature, among others the scenarios-based [2] approach provides promising results and stands as a competitive alternative. This approach groups methodologies to guide the vehicle toward relevant scenarios directly, and works were done to identify the criticality of the scenarios or reduce the number of scenarios to be tested[1] [3,4,15]. However, no procedure exists in the current literature to automatically qualify scenarios at the abstract level with a criticality degree, drastically reducing the number of abstract scenarios under evaluation with a process guided by a priori criticality assessment. The objective pursued in the current study is to detail the main methodological steps to achieve such a result. The paper exposes the main concepts at stake and illustrates key milestones with a potential approach to responding to challenges. The main concepts rely on properly defining, qualifying, grouping, and reducing the set of scenarios to be tested while validating new automation services, according to the definitions of scene and scenario by Ulbrich et al. [13]. Our innovative approach simultaneously reduces the abstract layer of scenarios (functional scenarios) to be tested and analyses them a priori in order to propose experimental designs that exhaustively cover the scope of possibilities of our ontology. This approach aims to drastically reduce the number of scenarios to be tested while maintaining comprehensive coverage of the CAV system's possibilities.

The guiding principles at stake consist in wrapping two alternative approaches from the literature into one. Usually testing scenarios are generated from top-down approaches [7,8] based on ontology or from bottom-up approaches [9,10] based on field-test observation. Both approaches present advantages and drawbacks: with bias due to the modelling framework built by engineers for ontology, or with a sparse coverage of the scenarios for field-test observations. The key concept underlying the introduced methodology is to develop an approach combining both in a complementary way. Initially, the focus is on understanding the relationship between use cases and creating a traffic scene [6], whether in real-world or simulated environments. The objective is to comprehend the logical sequence that connects use cases to an instance of the experimentation. To accomplish this, the proposed approach describes this advance as a graph (or tree), depicted in Fig. 1. When reading the graph from top to bottom, the descending direction can be understood as follows: For a given Operational Design Domain (ODD), its characteristics are converted into a set of q functional scenarios (F_s). Each functional scenario, verbally reported, is depicted by a set of parameters, as a logical scenario (L_s) in a one-to-one relationship. In addition to these logical scenarios, we can identify d actual scenarios (A_s) where $q \leq d$ (relation 1 to n), with q representing the total number of logical scenarios. An actual scenario corresponds to the realization of a logical scenario, akin to the distinction adopted in probability theory between a random variable and its concrete manifestation. The set of actual scenarios consists of p distinct scenes (leaves of the tree) with $m \leq p$, where m represents the total number of actual scenarios, in accordance with a one-to-many relationship. For a given Use Case

---

[1] Pegasus Project and Open Scenario (ASAM).

(U_c), the validation can be performed on a set of j functional scenarios (F_s) with $j \leq i$, where i denotes the total number of Use Cases (U_c), commonly referred to as a one-to-many relationship. Figure 1 provides visual support for bottom-up and top-down approaches. Thus, the current limitations of both approaches are evident: top-down approaches face difficulties in collecting indicators generated at the scene level, while bottom-up approaches only provide fragmented information on the edges of the tree. The main strategy is therefore to bring these two approaches together, which is the subject of this manuscript.

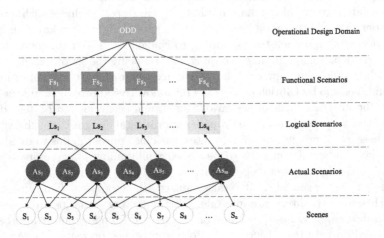

Fig. 1. Hierarchical tree for the identification of scenarios related to an Operational Design Domain. Inspired by [16]

2   Methodology

The objective of the current methodology lies in combining bottom-up and top-down approaches into a unique approach taking advantage of both. Our approach combines an ontology to generate functional scenarios and field-test data to qualify scenarios and generate a prior criticality index. The introduced approach is presented in Fig. 2 and divided into 6 steps.

2.1   Generation of Functional Scenarios by an Ontology

The first step of the process aims at generating a set of potential scenarios to explore while testing any new automated vehicles. As illustrated in Fig. 1, two alternative approaches are usually found in the literature: top-down approach [7,11] based on ontology versus bottom-up approaches [10,12] based on field-test. In our methodology, we initiate the process with an ontology-based description of the set of potential scenarios, while field tests are further used in the following

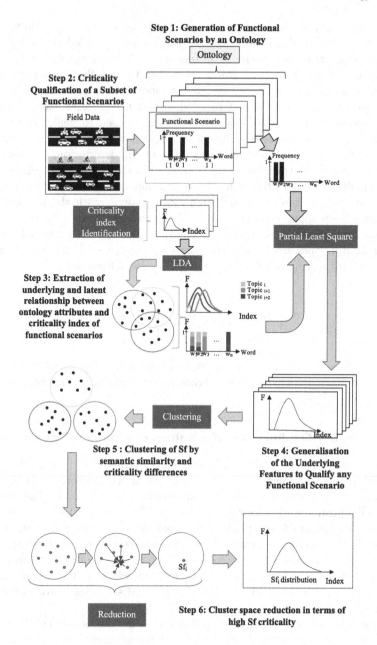

Fig. 2. Methodology in 6 steps

steps to qualify identified scenarios. The building process for ontology requires meticulously detailing and describing the interactions between any component or stakeholder within a scenario. It achieves the description of semantic Functional Scenarios. The ontology used in this study generates a scenario with five independent layers. We assume that the sixth layer, detailed by Weber *et al.* [14], is an integration of systems (*e.g.* telecommunication services) rather than a description of the scenario. Layer 5 represents the weather, Layer 4 pertains to dynamic and static objects, Layer 3 corresponds to temporal changes such as road works, Layer 2 is linked to road infrastructure, and Layer 1 focuses on road topology. The use of "stochastic" term is used to depict the absence of determinism in scenarios description (e.g., precise vehicle movement at time t, exact traffic volume), especially concerning traffic description. It enables the description of generic traffic conditions, instead of specifying each vehicle interaction. Finally, it enables to reach a broader range of functional scenarios. This stochasticity is not purely random; it primarily aligns with the philosophy of traffic simulation tools (especially about using random seeds bringing to semideterminism). Functional scenarios are identified by combining words from each layer, treated independently. This approach will be crucial in the fourth step of the methodology. A functional scenario Sf_i can be defined as:

$$\forall i \in [1, q], \quad S_{f_i} = \begin{pmatrix} \beta_{w_1} \\ \beta_{w_2} \\ ... \\ \beta_{w_n} \end{pmatrix} \tag{1}$$

where $n \in \mathbb{N}, \quad \forall j \in [1, n], \quad \beta_{w_j} \in \{0, 1\}$ is the activation variable associated to ontology attribute w_j. Figure 3 shows an example of a functional scenario generated by our process.

2.2   Criticality Qualification of a Subset of Functional Scenarios

The second step aims at qualifying functional scenarios covered by field observations with criticality indicators. It focuses on the data processing that will assign a criticality distribution to the functional scenarios, and then a critical index. In the modelling framework employed, time series of scenes are utilized to represent field observations, which are subsequently associated with concrete scenarios. By grouping these concrete scenarios, functional scenarios are constructed with a semantic interpretation based on ontology. The objective of this step is to analyze field test data and evaluate the criticality of scenes and scenarios, leading to the identification of critical subsets of functional scenarios. Various datasets, including stationary data, are utilized in this study.

To assess the criticality of functional scenarios, the distribution of the criticality indicator is computed for each available scenario. Each observation is linked to a specific functional scenario $(Sf_i^{qualification})$ following Eq. 2. This allows the characterization of a functional scenario based on a set of field-collected values. An associated histogram, represented by the density $(Sf_i^{qualification})$, is assigned to each functional scenario present in the database. The density distribution is employed to evaluate the criticality of the scenario (Sf).

Layer	Step	Road	Lane	ontology
Layer 1	Junction			T intersection
	Road	Road 1		plane, straight
		Road 2		plane, straight
		Road 3		plane, straight
	Lane	Road 1	Lane 1	traffic, right-hand, r1_l1
			Lane 2	traffic, left-hand, r1_l2
		Road 2	Lane 1	traffic, right-hand, r2_l1
			Lane 2	traffic, left-hand, r2_l2
		Road 3	Lane 1	traffic, right-hand, r3_l1
			Lane 2	traffic, left-hand, r3_l2
Layer 2	Infrastructure			intersectionLight + informationSigns
Layer 3	Temporal Changment			LaneClosed
Layer 4	Special Dynamic element			animal
	Traffic Density			mediumTraffic
	goal ego			r1_l1 to r2_l1
Layer 5	Illuminance			Cloudiness
	Particule			mud
	turbulance			wind
	sky condition			mostlyCloudy
	temperature			medium

Fig. 3. Functional scenario generated by the ontology

$$\forall i \in [1, q], \quad Sf_i^{qualification} = \begin{pmatrix} d^{criticality}(S_{c_1}) \\ d^{criticality}(S_{c_2}) \\ ... \\ d^{criticality}(S_{c_{nb_i}}) \end{pmatrix} \quad (2)$$

where $nb_i \in \mathbb{N}$ is the number of concrete scenarios attached to S_{f_i} into the database and $d^{criticality}(.)$ is the function estimating the degree of criticality associated to a scene. Fig. 4 represents a subset of TTC distributions associated to some S_f.

2.3 Extraction of the Underlying and Latent Relationship Between Ontology Attributes and Criticality Index of Functional Scenarios

The third step prepares the extension of the criticality qualification to any unobserved Functional Scenarios (not part of field data) based on their activated attributes. The goal is to establish the connection between semantic words and global criticality level of the functional scenario. We aim to analyze the semantic words (*i.e.* attributes) used to characterize the functional scenarios and determine their associated criticality level. By incorporating relevant observations, we can obtain a precise evaluation of the criticality of the scenarios. The challenge lies in establishing a connection between the selection of word attributes

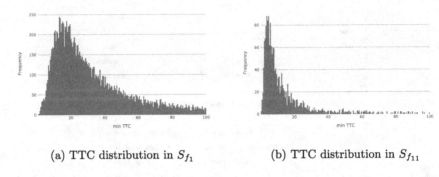

(a) TTC distribution in S_{f_1} (b) TTC distribution in $S_{f_{11}}$

Fig. 4. TTC distribution in of TTC by S_f

in the ontology and the global criticality level of the scenario resulting from the combination of words.

One way to proceed is exposed in Blache *et al.* [6] for a criticality indicator commonly used in the road safety domain: the Time-To-Collision (TTC). Based on the Latent Dirichlet Allocation [5] clustering process, some underlying topics and clusters are generated and enable to associate criticality index degree to ontology attributes generating functional scenarios. The goal is to uncover hidden themes (clusters) by incorporating features that establish a fundamental link between the criticality index, the functional scenario, and the attributes of the ontology. Within this framework: Topics represent latent functional scenarios, defined by time-to-collision (TTC) ranges, which partially contribute to generating the complete set of input functional scenarios. These topics can be utilized to generate TTC profiles for any functional scenario with the same ontology attributes, or semantic vocabulary. It is assumed that a subset of K topics is sufficient to generate criticality profiles for all scenarios (Fig. 5).

2.4 Generalisation of the Underlying Features to Qualify Any Functional Scenario

The fourth step extends the criticality qualification to any unobserved functional scenario. It aims at setting up the predictors to automatically generate a prior criticality value for any given functional scenario based on a set of activated semantic words. We aim to establish a systematic approach that assigns a predetermined criticality level to each functional scenario by considering the presence and activation of specific semantic words associated with the criticality index. This generation of prior criticality values will enable us to prioritize and assess the severity of various functional scenarios in a consistent and efficient manner. By leveraging the activated semantic words, we can establish a reliable framework for evaluating criticality and assisting in both decision-making and resource allocation processes. Based on a least square method, the reconstruction process takes advantage of the formulation of the underlying topics resulting from Latent Dirichlet Allocation (LDA) to predict *a priori* the criticality of any

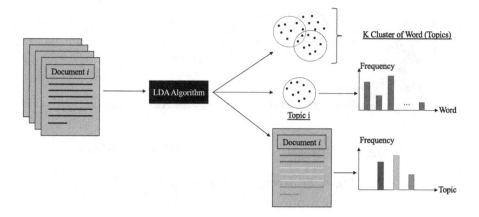

Fig. 5. Latent Dirichlet Allocation (LDA) process

new functional scenario. The topics, representing typical functional scenarios, are expected to exhibit a distribution of ontology attributes. This distribution can be derived for each topic based on their role as generators for criticality profiles. Moreover, it is assumed that these topics could also serve as generators for distributions of ontology attributes associated with S_f. As a result, the prior probability $\theta(i)$, contributing to the topics for S_{f_i}, can be utilized in conjunction with the known attribute distribution for S_{f_i} to reverse the process and generate the attribute distribution for any given topic. This process is illustrated through Eqs. 3 and 4. Additionally, the topics are considered generators for any functional scenario. Determining the contribution of each topic to a new functional scenario involves identifying the appropriate weights or ratios for reconstructing the distribution of ontology attributes associated with the new functional scenario. To address this, a least square method is applied to solve equation 6 and determine the optimal contribution of each topic to the new functional scenario under consideration.

$$\forall \quad topic \quad k \in [1, K], \quad topic^k = (p_{w_1}^k, p_{w_2}^k, ..., p_{w_n}^k) \tag{3}$$

where

$$\forall n \in \mathbb{N}, \forall j \in [1, n], \quad p_{w_j}^k \in [0, 1] and p_{w_j^k} = \frac{\sum_i \theta_k^{(i)} \times \beta_{w_j}^{(i)}}{\sum_i \beta_{w_j}^{(i)}} \tag{4}$$

Figure 6 represents the reconstruction of the two previous scenarios resulting from Blache *et al.* [6].

2.5 Clustering of Scenarios Between Semantic and Criticality Terms

After determining the prior criticality of scenarios, the main step is to reduce the number of functional scenarios. To accomplish this, we believe that gathering

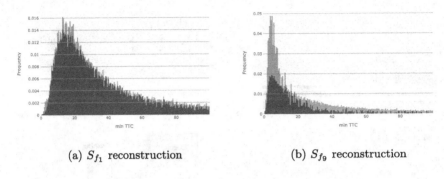

(a) S_{f_1} reconstruction   (b) S_{f_9} reconstruction

Fig. 6. S_f reconstruction according to [6]

scenarios with semantic similarity is crucial in identifying representative scenarios to consider in the testing process. Therefore, choosing clustering approaches becomes an obvious means to achieve this goal. By applying a suitable clustering technique, we can group together functionally similar scenarios, allowing us to select representative scenarios from each cluster for further testing and analysis. This approach not only reduces the overall number of scenarios but also ensures that a diverse range of critical scenarios is included in the final selection, capturing the variability of the system under evaluation.

Multiple clustering-based strategies could be developed to achieve this objective. First, we could conduct preliminary analysis using density clustering (such as DBSCAN) and/or k-means. Then, the functional scenarios are classified based on a metric developed to establish the distance between selected words. However, the previously computed prior criticality difference between scenarios is also taken into account to guide this clustering process, with the aim of maximizing the separation of critical scenarios. The main objective of this clustering of functional scenarios is to identify clusters that demonstrate semantic similarities while minimizing the presence of critical scenarios within the same cluster.

2.6   Reduction of the Number of Functional Scenarios in Each Cluster

The last step is crucial and aims at selecting representative scenarios for each group, where the selection process is guided by the criticality index. When grouping scenarios based on their similarities or using clustering techniques, it is important to identify scenarios that are not only similar in terms of their features but also representative of the criticality levels within each group. By selecting representative scenarios with high criticality, decision-makers can focus their attention on the most impactful and risk-prone situations within each group. These representative scenarios serve as key indicators or archetypal examples that capture the underlying origin of the criticality levels present in the group. However, it is important to note that the selection process should also consider the diversity and coverage of scenarios within each group. In addition to high-criticality scenarios, it may be beneficial to include a range of scenarios covering different dimensions and attribute combinations. This ensures a comprehensive representation of potential risks and critical situations encompassed by the group. The selection of representative scenarios for each group regarding scenario criticality is a balance between capturing the most critical scenarios and maintaining diversity within the group. This approach provides decision-makers with a focused and concise set of scenarios highlighting the criticality levels and potential risks associated with each group, facilitating effective decision-making and risk management strategies.

3 Conclusion

This methodology offers a structured approach for the generation, qualification, and classification of functional scenarios based on their criticality. Based on ontology and clustering techniques such as Latent Dirichlet Allocation, we are able to uncover hidden relationships between ontology attributes and the criticality index of functional scenarios. This enables us to generalize underlying features and predict the criticality of new scenarios. Additionally, the classification and reduction of the number of functional scenarios within each cluster allow us to identify representative scenarios regarding criticality. This methodology provides a comprehensive approach for analyzing and understanding critical functional scenarios, facilitating decision-making and risk assessment processes.

There are multiple potential benefits to our newly proposed reduction methodology. Notably, unlike many functional scenario generation techniques, it prioritizes the stochastic aspect of scenario generation, aligning with the philosophy of simulation tools (e.g., travel demand profile). The literature lacks the prior generation of new functional scenarios that are challenging to observe in the field, despite their potential. Reducing the most critical scenario of a group appears to be a relevant approach due to scenario diversity and its potential hazards compared to other techniques. However, this methodology has some limitations, such as the number of processed data and the profile of "artificially" generated scenarios, leading to the over- or underestimation of criticality for some scenarios. Future steps include gathering more data to reinforce the findings and determine the simulation replication abilities for validating CAV systems.

The next steps of our research expect to focus on the feasibility assessment of individual scenarios. To achieve this, we rely on expert opinions to qualitatively evaluate the functional scenarios. Various techniques, such as the Analytic Hierarchy Process (AHP), can be employed for this purpose. These techniques provide rigorous criteria and methodologies for assessing the feasibility of scenarios, allowing us to prioritize and select the most viable ones for further testing and validation.

References

1. Kalra, N., Paddock, S.M.: Driving to safety: how many miles of driving would it take to demonstrate autonomous vehicle reliability? Transp. Res. Part A: Policy Pract. **94**, 182–193 (2016). https://doi.org/10.1016/j.tra.2016.09.010

2. Riedmaier, S., Ponn, T., Ludwig, D., Schick, B., Diermeyer, F.: Survey on scenario-based safety assessment of automated vehicles. IEEE Access **8**, 87456–87477 (2020). https://doi.org/10.1109/ACCESS.2020.2993730

3. Vater, L., Pütz, A., Tellis, L., Eckstein, L.: Test case selection method for the verification of automated driving systems. ATZelectronics Worldwide **16**(11), 40–45 (2021). https://doi.org/10.1007/s38314-021-0701-0

4. Riedmaier, S., Schneider, D., Watzenig, D., Diermeyer, F., Schick, B.: Model validation and scenario selection for virtual-based homologation of automated vehicles. Appl. Sci. **11**(1), 35 (2020). https://doi.org/10.3390/app110100

5. Blei, D.M., Ng, A.Y., Jordan, M.I.: Latent Dirichlet allocation. J. Mach. Learn. Res. **3**(Jan), 993–1022 (2003)

6. Blache, H., Laharotte, P-A., El Faouzi, N-E.: How to rationalise the sampling of test-scenarios in automated driving based on criticality metrics? In: 2023 International Conference on Models and Technologies for Intelligent Transportation Systems (MT-ITS), Nice, France, 14–16 June 2023 (2023)

7. Bagschik, G., Menzel, T., Maurer, M.: Ontology based scene creation for the development of automated vehicles. In: 2018 IEEE Intelligent Vehicles Symposium (IV), Changshu, China, pp. 1813–1820 (2018). https://doi.org/10.1109/IVS.2018.8500632

8. De Gelder, E., et al.: Towards an ontology for scenario definition for the assessment of automated vehicles: an object-oriented framework. IEEE Trans. Intell. Veh. **7**(2), 300–314 (2022). https://doi.org/10.1109/TIV.2022.3144803

9. Moers, T., Vater, L., Krajewski, R., Bock, J., Zlocki, A., Eckstein, L.: The exiD dataset: a real-world trajectory dataset of highly interactive highway scenarios in Germany. In: 2022 IEEE Intelligent Vehicles Symposium (IV), Aachen, Germany, pp. 958–964 (2022). https://doi.org/10.1109/IV51971.2022.9827305

10. Krajewski, R., Bock, J., Kloeker, L., Eckstein, L.: The highd dataset.: A drone dataset of naturalistic vehicle trajectories on German highways for validation of highly automated driving systems. In: 2018 21st International Conference on Intelligent Transportation Systems (ITSC), Maui, HI, USA, pp. 2118–2125 (2018)

11. Urbieta, I., Nieto, M., García, M., Otaegui, O.: Design and implementation of an ontology for semantic labeling and testing: automotive global ontology (AGO). Appl. Sci. **11**(17), 7782 (2021). https://doi.org/10.3390/app11177782

12. Chao, Q., et al.: A survey on visual traffic simulation: models, evaluations, and applications in autonomous driving. Comput. Graph. Forum **39**, 287–308 (2020). https://doi.org/10.1111/cgf.13803

13. Ulbrich, S., Menzel, T., Reschka, A., Schuldt, F., Maurer, M.: Defining and substantiating the terms scene, situation, and scenario for automated driving. In: 2015 IEEE 18th International Conference on Intelligent Transportation Systems, Spain, pp. 982–988 (2015). https://doi.org/10.1109/ITSC.2015.164

14. Weber, H., et al.: A framework for definition of logical scenarios for safety assurance of automated driving. Traffic Inj. Prev. **20**(sup1), S65–S70 (2019). https://doi.org/10.1080/15389588.2019.1630827

15. Zhang, X., et al.: Finding critical scenarios for automated driving systems: a systematic mapping study. IEEE Trans. Softw. Eng. **49**(3), 991–1026 (2023). https://doi.org/10.1109/TSE.2022.3170122

16. Blache, H., Laharotte, P.A., El Faouzi, N.E.: Evaluation des cas d'usages des véhicules automatisés et connectés: Vers une approche basée sur les scénarios visant à réduire la quantité de tests en simulation ou environnement réel. In 20èmes Rencontres des Jeunes Chercheurs en Intelligence Artificielle (RJCIA), Saint-Etienne, France (2022)

Rear-End Collision Risk Analysis
for Autonomous Driving

Ci Liang[1] , Mohamed Ghazel[2] , Yusheng Ci[1] , Nour-Eddin El Faouzi[3] ,
Rui Wang[4]([✉]) , and Wei Zheng[5]

[1] Harbin Institute of Technology, Harbin 150001, China
`ciyusheng@hit.edu.cn`
[2] Univ. Gustave Eiffel (ex-IFSTTAR), COSYS/ESTAS,
59650 Villeneuve-d'Ascq, France
`mohamed.ghazel@univ-eiffel.fr`
[3] Univ. Gustave Eiffel (ex IFSTTAR), Univ. Lyon, ENTPE, LICIT-ECO7 UMR
T9401, 69675 Lyon, France
`nour-eddin.elfaouzi@univ-eiffel.fr`
[4] Beijing Jiaotong University, Beijing 100044, China
`rui.wang@bjtu.edu.cn`
[5] Collaborative Innovation Center of Railway Traffic Safety and National Research
Center of Railway Safety Assessment,
Beijing Jiaotong University, Beijing 100044, China
`wzheng1@bjtu.edu.cn`

Abstract. Since there will be a mix of automated vehicles (AVs) and
human-driven vehicles (HVs) on future roadways, in the literature, while
many existing studies have investigated collisions where an AV hits an
HV from behind, few studies have focused on the scenarios where an
HV hits an AV from behind (called HV-AV collision). In this paper,
we will investigate the HV-AV collision risk in the Stop-in-Lane (SiL)
scenario. To achieve this aim, a Human-like Brake (HLB) model is proposed first to simulate the driver brake control. In particular, the joint
distribution of *Off-Road-Glance* and *Time-Headway* is originally introduced to simulate the glance distraction of drivers during their dynamic
vehicle control. Sequentially, a case study of HV-AV collisions in the SiL
scenario of autonomous driving (AD) is conducted based on the HLB
model, to reveal how the collision probability changes with respect to
various parameters. The results of the case study provide us with an
in-depth understanding of the dynamic driving conditions that lead to
rear-end collisions in the SiL scenario.

Keywords: Autonomous driving · Risk analysis · Human-like brake
model · Rear-end collision

1 Introduction

In the field of autonomous driving (AD), safety is a core concern. According to the statistics from the National Highway Traffic Safety Administration

J. Guiochet et al. (Eds.): SAFECOMP 2023 Workshops, LNCS 14182, pp. 271–282, 2023.
https://doi.org/10.1007/978-3-031-40953-0_23

(NHTSA) [1], up to May 2022, there are 132 crashes involving AVs reported offi-
cially. In these 132 crashes, 106 crashes reported collisions with other vehicles. 11
crashes involved vulnerable road users (7 with cyclists, 2 with motorcycles and
another 2 with non-motorist electric scooters). NHTSA also stated that collisions
between human-driven vehicles (HVs) and AVs are the main type of collisions
involving AVs, of which collisions that HVs hit AVs from behind (called HV-AV
collisions) make up more than 30% [2–4]. However, few studies investigated HV-
AV collisions. Hence, there is a strong need for effective methods to investigate
risk scenarios where HV-AV collisions may occur.

In the existing studies, using model-based quantitative analyses to help
reduce collisions involving AVs is the mainstream. These models are often
employed to generate driving behaviors further to achieve dynamic driving
tasks [5–7], analyze crash risk [8–10], or respond to warnings and upcoming threats during driving [11–13]. Some existing models adopt end-to-end
approaches based on artificial intelligence technologies to predict driving
responses while ignoring the inherent characteristics of human drivers in reality, which leaves little or no time for surrounding vehicles to react. Meanwhile,
some studies have investigated risky aspects related to AVs [14,15]. Over the
last decades, numerous models have been developed to emulate drivers' steer-
ing/braking to respond to warnings and upcoming threats in various traffic situations [13,16]. These models can be applied to traffic scenarios with a mix
of AVs and HVs. However, most of these models for driver avoidance response
simulation are simply based on the basic kinematics or predetermined intervention profiles; moreover, they adopt an arbitrary assumption that drivers always
keep their eyes on the road. Some works have figured out that drivers decide
their avoidance responses mainly based on visual looming, which describes how
fast the object in front is increasing in size as it is getting closer [13,17]. The
actual visual looming is measured as $P_0(t) = \frac{\theta'(t)}{\theta(t)}$, where $\theta(t)$ represents the
optical size of the lead vehicle on the retina of the driver of the vehicle behind,
reflected by horizontal angle and calculated by $\theta(t) = 2\arctan\frac{W}{2d(t)}$; while $\theta'(t)$
is the expansion rate of the size of the lead vehicle, which can be considered
as the stimulus intensity towards the driver of the following vehicle and cal-
culated by $\theta'(t) = -\frac{Wd'(t)}{d(t)^2+\frac{W^2}{4}}$, where W is the width of the lead vehicle, and
$d(t)$ denotes the longitudinal distance between the lead vehicle's rear bumper
and the following vehicle's front bumper [11,18]. Besides, driver braking control
also depends on the sensory impact of primitive motor actions [19]. With this
in mind, [12,13] developed visual-looming based models that incorporate the
impact of Off-Road-Glance (ORG, see the description in Sect. 2.2) and the sensory impact of primitive motor actions, to simulate the driver braking control.
Nevertheless, the Time-Headway (TH, see the description in Sect. 2.2) between
the lead vehicle and the following one and the joint effect of TH and ORG on
braking control have not been considered in the aforementioned models, which
may lead to an inaccurate brake onset timing.

Therefore, in the present study we seek to solve the aforementioned issues with the proposed HLB model, and also aim for a thorough investigation of the HV-AV collision risk in the Stop-in-Lane (SiL) scenario. The findings from the present study provide a thorough understanding of the dynamic driving conditions which have a significant impact on the HV-AV collision risk in the SiL scenario.

2   Method

2.1   The HLB Model

The developed modeling framework consists of four phases, as shown in Fig. 1:

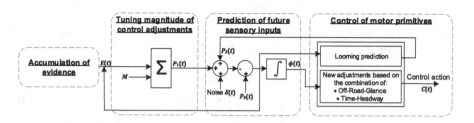

Fig. 1. The modeling framework of HLB.

1) Accumulation of evidence: the HLB model emulates human drivers to react according to the accumulated evidence based on looming. The evidence contains two aspects, namely, the evidence for the need of brake control, and the evidence against the need of brake control.
2) Tuning magnitude of control adjustments: the more severe the driver judges the situation to be, the harder he/she brakes. Accordingly, in the HLB model the magnitude of adjustments is tuned to perceptual inputs.
3) Prediction of future sensory inputs: the HLB model emulates human drivers to predict how the looming will decrease due to each braking action.
4) Control of motor primitives: the driver brakes in steps based on the prediction of future sensory inputs. To generate accurate human-like brake control responses, new adjustments based on the combination of ORG and TH are introduced.

Several variables in the HLB modeling framework are defined as follows:
$P_1(t)$ represents the initial combined perceptual input, which can be defined as follows:

$$P_1(t) = K \cdot E(t) - M, \tag{1}$$

where $E(t)$ denotes the accumulated evidence of looming for or against the need for brake control; specifically, $E(t) > 0$ indicates the need for brake control,

while $E(t) < 0$ is against the need of activating the brake; K is a free model
parameter and corresponds to the weight of the evidence; M, which is a free
model parameter, can be considered as the sum of all non-looming evidence.
Note that the free model parameters K and M can be generated automatically
through a computational fitting process based on the real accident dataset.

$\phi(t)$ is the total accumulated looming predictive deviation, and is defined as
below:

$$\phi(t) = \int \{P_0(t) - [P_1(t) + P_2(t) + \delta(t)]\}, \tag{2}$$

where $\delta(t)$ denotes the Gaussian zero-mean white noise; $P_2(t)$ represents the
looming prediction based on prior braking adjustments. The definition of $P_2(t)$
is given as below:

$$P_2(t) = \sum_{i=1}^{n} \phi'(t_i)H(t - t_i), \tag{3}$$

where n is the number of brake adjustments; t_i denotes to the time of issuing
the ith individual adjustment; $H(t)$ is defined by Eq. (4):

$$H(t) \begin{cases} = 0, & \text{for } t \geq T \\ \to 1, & \text{for } t \to 0^+, \\ \to 0, & \text{for } t \to T^- \end{cases} \tag{4}$$

where T is a free model parameter representing the adjustment duration; $t \to 0^+$
represents t approaching to 0 from the right side of 0; while $t \to T^-$ represents
t approaching to T from the left side of T.

$C(t)$ as defined by Eq. (5) is interpreted as the brake signal generated based
on successive adjustments.

$$C(t) = \sum_{i=1}^{n} w \cdot P_{O,T}(t_i)\phi'(t_i)G(t - t_i), \tag{5}$$

where n is the number of brake adjustments; $P_{O,T}(t_i)$ is the joint distribution of
ORG and TH at the instant t_i; w is the weight of $P_{O,T}(t_i)$; $G(t)$ is interpreted
as the shape of each brake adjustment and is defined as follows:

$$G(t) = \begin{cases} 0, & \text{for } t \leq 0 \\ 1, & \text{for } t \geq T \end{cases}, \tag{6}$$

where T represents the adjustment duration.

2.2 Joint Probability Distribution of ORG and TH

The ORG and TH variables are employed jointly to optimize the control action.
Specifically, ORG emulates the fact that the driver is sometimes looking away
from the road, and thereby not seeing that the lead car is braking, which is

an inherent feature of human driving behavior. The introduction of ORG can make the HLB model more realistic. While TH reflects the distance between the head of the following car and the head of the lead car, which is given as a time quantity. As shown in Fig. 2, the joint probability distribution of ORG and TH is generated based on real data records from the Original Equipment Manufacturer (OEM) in the automotive industry. One can observe that the ORGs shorter than 1 s occur most frequently, which means short glances occur more frequently than long ones. Similarly, the trend of the TH reaches a peak within 1.5 s, which represents the highest frequency of occurrence within a short time. Sequentially, the joint probability distribution[1] is integrated into the HLB model.

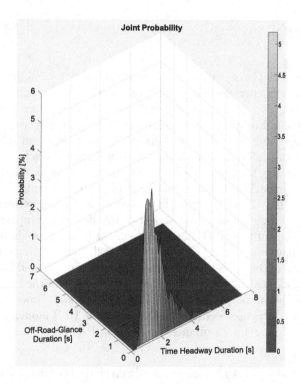

Fig. 2. The joint probability distribution of ORG and TH.

---

[1] The model of the joint probability distribution $P_{O,T}(t_i)$ as shown in Eq. (5) is developed jointly with an OEM, which approximates the Gamma distribution. However, we do not show the mathematical representation of $P_{O,T}(t_i)$ due to the confidentiality of the OEM.

2.3   Validation of Model Performance

The Particle Swarm Optimization (PSO) algorithm [20] is employed to find the optimal parameter values of our HLB model and the initialization ranges of important parameters are given in Table 1. N, r, w, c_1 and c_2 are the population size, maximum number of iterations, inertia weight, cognitive learning rate and social learning rate of PSO, respectively. Meanwhile, K, M, ϕ_0, T_{G0} and T_{G1} are free parameters of HLB model.

Table 1. Initialization ranges of free model parameters.

Free parameters	N	r	w	c_1	c_2	K	M	ϕ_0	T_{G0}	T_{G1}
Initialization range	[4, 40]	[50, 70]	[0, 1]	[0, 2]	[0, 2]	[1, 40]	[0, 10]	[0, 1]	[0.5, 4]	[0.5, 5]

We conducted field-test evaluations to investigate the validity of the HLB model and assess its performance, while considering a rear-end scenario with a lead car issuing a constant brake signal and releasing later. The evaluation results are shown in Fig. 3. One can notice that the lead car is issuing a constant brake signal beginning at $t = 5$ s and its deceleration is about $0.2g$. the HLB model controls the following car to perform braking to react to the braking action issued by the lead car, when the accumulation of braking evidence is sufficient. The comparison between the HLB predicted looming and the actual looming reveals that the HLB model has a sound prediction performance when it comes to simulating human brake control. Besides, the comparison shows a better performance of the HLB model in terms of looming prediction than the relevant model developed in [12] (cf. Figure 2 in [12]). It is worth mentioning that more evaluations of the model performance have been performed by considering t-statistic and Pearson chi-square (PCS) statistic [21] , and the obtained results have confirmed the sound performance of the HLB model. However, due to the limited space, we only discussed the evaluation of the HLB model output signals as an overview of model performance as shown in Fig. 3.

3   Case Study: HAD Car Decelerating to Stop in Lane

Here we will discuss the case study while considering the risky scenario of a lead car decelerating to stop in a lane, which can give raise to rear-end collisions. The opponent (following) car is controlled by the HLB model with reactions based on visual looming depending on the lead car braking, to emulate the human control of the braking response of the following vehicle. Moreover, the lead car is simulated as a High AD (HAD) level vehicle that can fulfill SAE L4 requirements [22]. As we mentioned earlier, the purpose of the case study is to investigate the HV-AV collision risk. That is why in our study, we consider the scenario where an HV is following an AV.

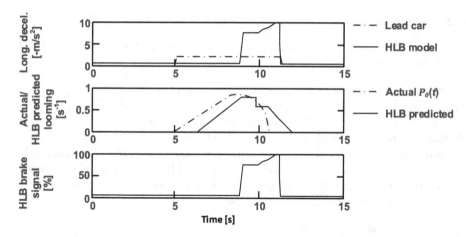

Fig. 3. The performance of the HLB model and comparison with reality: "Long. decel." represents longitudinal deceleration; the deceleration of the lead car is about $0.2g$ (g is the gravitational acceleration).

3.1 Purpose

The purpose of the case study is to investigate the probability of HV-AV collision occurrence in the SiL scenario by considering various collision speeds, initial speeds, decelerations of the opponent car and decelerations of the HAD car, respectively.

Figure 4 illustrates the scenario of the case study. Namely, a HAD (red) car decelerating to stop in a lane with a car-following situation. One can notice that the HAD car is decelerating with a given deceleration level, followed by the opponent (green) car. Meanwhile, the opponent car initiates the braking action depending on the deceleration of the front one.

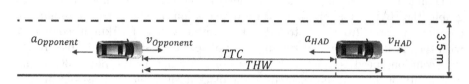

Fig. 4. The scenario illustration: TTC represents Time-To-Collision and the lane width is 3.5 m. (Color figure online)

3.2 Assumptions

In order to facilitate the simulation, several assumptions have been considered and listed below:

Assumption 1: the two cars have the same initial speed[2].

Assumption 2: the deceleration of the opponent car shall fulfill: $a_{Opponent} \leq 1g$[3], where g represents the gravitational acceleration.

Assumption 3: the deceleration of the HAD car shall fulfill: $a_{HAD} \leq 1g$.

Assumption 4: the TH between the opponent car and the HAD car shall fulfill: $TH \leq 7.5$ s. Indeed, a bigger TH value reflects a too long distance separating the two cars, therefore, the driver of the following car is unlikely to trigger a brake as he/she is far from the lead car.

Note that the assumptions above are designed according to the features of the HLB model and conditions in reality, while not restricted by the SiL scenario.

3.3 Results and Discussion

In Fig. 5, through nine charts (sub-figures), we show a detailed analysis of the probability of collision according to different collision speeds, initial speeds and decelerations of the opponent and HAD cars, respectively. In the subsequent part, we will use "R_C_" to define the ID of sub-figures, e.g., R2C1 represents the plot located in the 2nd row and 1st column. Besides, rows reflect the impact of increasing brake capability of the opponent car on the probability of collision by considering different deceleration intensities of the HAD car; while columns reflect the impact of increasing collision speed on the probability of collision by considering different deceleration intensities of the HAD car. Additionally, the Y-axis represents the probability of collision and the X-axis represents the same initial speed of both cars (see **Assumption 1**).

As illustrated in Fig. 5, taking the plot R3C1 for instance, the black dashed line shows that there is 42% probability of collision with collision speeds over 30 km/h if both vehicles travel at an initial speed of 70 km/h and the HAD vehicle is braking at a deceleration of 0.4g, while the opponent car behind brakes with a maximum deceleration of 0.9g. Considering the green solid line in the same graph (the HAD car is braking with a deceleration of 0.5g), the probability of collision increases from 42% to 77% at an initial speed of 70 km/h, compared with the black dashed line at the same initial speed. As shown in the plot R3C2 (the collision speed is >50 km/h instead of >30 km/h in the plot R3C1), the probability of collision represented by the black dashed line decreases from 42% to 2% at an initial speed of 70 km/h, compared with that in the plot R3C1. One can notice that the collision probability goes down at a relatively high collision speed, compared with the probability of collision at a lower collision speed. The

---

[2] The TH introduced to the HLB model only works when the two cars have the same initial speed.

[3] The maximum deceleration of a car, in reality, is about 8 m/s^2.

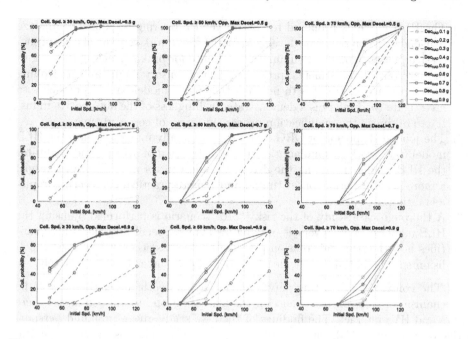

Fig. 5. The probability of collision according to different collision speeds, initial speeds and decelerations of the opponent and HAD cars, respectively.

potential reason lies in the fact that the collision speed ultimately depends on the combination of ORG and TH distributions that less likely leads to a high collision speed as time goes on. Indeed, relatively short ORG and TH time slots occur most frequently as reflected by their significantly high joint probabilities. Furthermore, as shown in the plot R2C1 (the opponent car behind is braking at 0.7g maximum instead of 0.9g in the plot R3C1), the probability of collision represented by the black dashed line soars from 42% to 85% at an initial speed of 70 km/h, compared with that in the plot R3C1. On the other hand, when it comes to the impact of the initial speed represented by the X-axis values, the probability of collision always ascends as the initial speed increases. For instance, the probability of collision goes up from 8% to 42% as the initial speed increases from 50 km/h to 70 km/h (see the black dashed line in plot R3C1).

4   Conclusions

In this paper, we have developed a model called HLB to simulate human drivers' braking control, with the aim of investigating the relation between collision occurrence and various factors in the risky SiL scenario within the Operational Design Domain (ODD) of AD. The parameters considered in our study are respectively: collision speeds, initial speeds, decelerations of cars under test.

The main contributions of our study are as follows:

1) The HLB model is proposed to control vehicle braking responses to analyze rear-end collision risk. The developed model framework consists of a set of successive phases, namely, accumulating evidence for braking, tuning the magnitude of control adjustments, predicting future sensory inputs and controlling motor primitives. It is worth noticing that using model-based approaches to investigate road safety is a demonstrated willingness of the automotive industry to optimize the qualification process in terms of cost and time.

2) The joint distribution of ORG and TH is originally integrated into the HLB model framework to simulate the glance distraction of drivers, and facilitates the HLB model emulating the driver braking control in reality. As a result, a more accurate brake onset timing and a more practical engineering implementation are ensured.

3) A thorough case study of the risky "SiL" scenario is performed by using the HLB model to control vehicle braking behaviors. Specifically, the study quantifies how the rear-end collision probability changes according to various collision speeds, initial speeds, decelerations of cars under test, respectively.

The contributions of this paper provide an in-depth understanding of the mechanism of collision occurrence in the defined "Stop-in-Lane" scenario where AVs and HVs interact. The findings of the case study give a profound perspective on the dynamic driving conditions, namely various collision speeds, initial speeds and decelerations of the following and lead cars, that have a significant impact on collision occurrence in the specific scenario. In addition, the present study can be considered as a base of the Safety of the Intended Functionality (SOTIF) [23] for AD safety analysis. In future work, more risky scenarios of AD will be investigated for SOTIF analysis, by using the HLB model. Moreover, we will introduce Deep Neural Networks to improve the looming prediction of the HLB model.

Acknowledgement. This work was supported by the Fundamental Research Funds for the Central Universities (Science and technology leading talent team project)(2022JBXT003).

References

1. National Highway Traffic Safety Administration: Summary report: Standing general order on crash reporting for automated driving systems. DOT HS 813, 324 (2022)
2. Petrović, D., Mijailović, R., Pešić, D.: Traffic accidents with autonomous vehicles: type of collisions, manoeuvres and errors of conventional vehicles' drivers. Transp. Res. Procedia **45**, 161–168 (2020)
3. Mohammadian, S., Haque, M., Zheng, Z., Bhaskar, A.: Integrating safety into the fundamental relations of freeway traffic flows: a conflict-based safety assessment framework. Anal. Methods Accid. Res. **32**, 100187 (2021)
4. Wang, C., Chen, F., Zhang, Y., Wang, S., Yu, B., Cheng, J.: Temporal stability of factors affecting injury severity in rear-end and non-rear-end crashes: a random parameter approach with heterogeneity in means and variances. Anal. Methods Accid. Res. **35**, 100219 (2022)

5. Chen, J., Zhang, C., Luo, J., Xie, J., Wan, Y.: Driving maneuvers prediction based autonomous driving control by deep Monte Carlo tree search. IEEE Trans. Veh. Technol. **69**(7), 7146–7158 (2020)
6. Xia, Y., Qu, Z., Sun, Z., Li, Z.: A human-like model to understand surrounding vehicles' lane changing intentions for autonomous driving. IEEE Trans. Veh. Technol. **70**(5), 4178–4189 (2021)
7. Yoo, J., Langari, R.: A predictive perception model and control strategy for collision-free autonomous driving. IEEE Trans. Intell. Transp. Syst. **20**(11), 4078–4091 (2018)
8. Arbabzadeh, N., Jafari, M.: A data-driven approach for driving safety risk prediction using driver behavior and roadway information data. IEEE Trans. Intell. Transp. Syst. **19**(2), 446–460 (2017)
9. Strickland, M., Fainekos, G., Amor, H.: Deep predictive models for collision risk assessment in autonomous driving. In: 2018 IEEE International Conference on Robotics and Automation (ICRA), pp. 4685–4692, IEEE (2018)
10. Muzahid, A., Kamarulzaman, S., Rahim, M.: Learning-based conceptual framework for threat assessment of multiple vehicle collision in autonomous driving. In: 2020 Emerging Technology in Computing, Communication and Electronics (ETCCE), pp. 1–6, IEEE (2020)
11. Markkula, G.: Modeling driver control behavior in both routine and near-accident driving. In: The Human Factors and Ergonomics Society Annual Meeting, vol. 58, no. 1, pp. 879–883. SAGE Publications, CA (2014)
12. Svärd, M., Markkula, G., Engström, J., Granum, F., Bärgman, J.: A quantitative driver model of pre-crash brake onset and control. In: The Human Factors and Ergonomics Society Annual Meeting, vol. 61, no. 1, pp. 339–343. SAGE Publications, CA (2017)
13. Svärd, M., Markkula, G., Bärgman, J., Victor, T.: Computational modeling of driver pre-crash brake response, with and without off-road glances: Parameterization using real-world crashes and near-crashes. Accid. Anal. Prev. **163**, 106433 (2021)
14. Leroy, J., Gruyer, D., Orfila, O., El Faouzi, N.E.: Five key components based risk indicators ontology for the modelling and identification of critical interaction between human driven and automated vehicles. IFAC-PapersOnLine **53**(5), 212–217 (2020)
15. Leroy, J., Gruyer, D., Orfila, O., El Faouzi, N. E.: Adapted risk indicator for autonomous driving system with uncertainties and multi-dimensional configurations modeling. In: 2021 IEEE International Intelligent Transportation Systems Conference (ITSC), pp. 2034–2041, IEEE (2021)
16. Markkula, G., Benderius, O., Wolff, K., Wahde, M.: A review of near-collision driver behavior models. Hum. Factors **54**(6), 1117–1143 (2012)
17. Markkula, G., Engström, J., Lodin, J., Bärgman, J., Victor, T.: A farewell to brake reaction times? Kinematics-dependent brake response in naturalistic rear-end emergencies. Accid. Anal. Prev. **95**, 209–226 (2016)
18. Svärd, M., Bärgman, J., Victor, T.: "Detection and response to critical lead vehicle deceleration events with peripheral vision: glance response times are independent of visual eccentricity. Accid. Anal. Prev. **150**, 105853 (2021)
19. Markkula, G., Boer, E., Romano, R., Merat, N.: Sustained sensorimotor control as intermittent decisions about prediction errors: computational framework and application to ground vehicle steering. Biol. Cybern. **112**(3), 181–207 (2018)
20. Clerc, M., Kennedy, J.: The particle swarm-explosion, stability, and convergence in a multidimensional complex space. IEEE Trans. Evol. Comput. **6**(1), 58–73 (2002)

21. Liang, C., Ghazel, M., Cazier, O., El-Koursi, E.M: Developing accident prediction model for railway level crossings. Saf. Sci. **101**, 48–59 (2018)
22. SAE International: Taxonomy and definitions for terms related to driving automation systems for on-road motor vehicles. SAE J3016_202104 (2021)
23. ISO 21448:2022 (E): Road vehicles - Safety of the intended functionality (2022)

Improving Road Traffic Safety and Performance–Barriers and Directions Towards Cooperative Automated Vehicles

Gianfilippo Fornaro(✉) ⓘ and Martin Törngren ⓘ

KTH Royal Institute of Technology, 100 44, Stockholm, Sweden
{fornaro,martint}@kth.se

Abstract. The complexity of deploying automated vehicles (AVs) has been grossly underestimated and vehicles at high levels of automated driving (SAE level 4 and above) have so far only been deployed in very limited areas. Highly automated AVs will face complex traffic, e.g., due to occlusions and unpredictable road-user behaviour, and AVs may shift the distribution of crashes. This has given rise to a renewed interest in connectivity and collaboration, with the need to monitor (emerging) behaviours and risk, and the promise to improve road traffic safety and performance by resolving the "information gap". This motivates further investigations and research in this direction.

In this paper we set out to identify barriers and important directions towards solutions for such collaborative systems, as formed by connected automated vehicles and a supporting cyber-physical infrastructure. Drawing upon a state-of-the art assessment and interactions with experts, we conclude that the current state-of-the art is fragmented, and therefore investigate key topics related to collaboration barriers and propose research questions to address them, hoping that the provided structure can also assist in guiding future research. The topics cover, (i) the socio-technical and system of systems nature of collaborative systems, (ii) the multifaceted design space and architectures with related trade-for such systems including between safety, performance and cost, and (iii) trustworthiness issues, ranging from safety and cybersecurity to privacy and ethics.

Keywords: Cooperative ITS · Connected Automated Vehicles · Connected Road Users · Safety · Security · Dependability

1 Introduction

Enormous investments have been made into automated vehicles leading to significant advances in automated driving technology. However, despite the progress, the complexity of deploying automated vehicles (AVs) was grossly underestimated and vehicles at high levels of automated driving (SAE level 4 and above) have so far only been deployed in very limited areas, see e.g., [1, 2]. In this paper we are mainly concerned with road traffic safety and performance. It has been increasingly realised that AVs may not be able to remove all crashes caused by human driven vehicles, especially those that relate

J. Guiochet et al. (Eds.): SAFECOMP 2023 Workshops, LNCS 14182, pp. 283–294, 2023.
https://doi.org/10.1007/978-3-031-40953-0_24

to inherently complex environments, e.g., due to occlusions and unpredictable road-user behaviour, and moreover, may shift the distribution of crashes [1, 3]. This has given rise to a renewed interest in connectivity and collaboration with the promise to improve road traffic safety and performance [4] by resolving the AVs' "information gap" [5–7]. The concept of information gap is illustrated in Fig. 1A in which actor (C)–vulnerable road users (vRUs) are crossing the road in such a way that the view of (A) is obstructed by the presence of (B) as indicated by the dashed triangle. The red rectangle (E) shows the conflict zone of (A) and (C). A road side camera, (D) can perceive both agents (B) and (C)–indicated by the dashed and dotted triangle –and share this information with (A), thereby resolving the information gap.

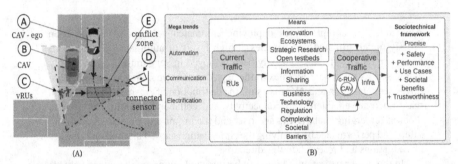

(A)   (B)

Fig. 1. (A) Information gap, adapted from [5]. (B) overall problem formulation. The "means" in (B) are elaborated especially in the Discussion section.

In this paper we look at the cooperative Intelligent Transportation System (C-ITS) where connected automated vehicles (CAVs) are only one of the agents contributing to the overarching system dynamics. While previous efforts towards V2X, V2I and ITS [8] have resulted in little progress in forming collaborative traffic systems, we believe that the motivation has increased with the realization that the complexity of road traffic in some areas will necessitate collaboration to achieve the desired levels of safety and performance. However, several barriers will need to be overcome and the promise of collaboration will require investments in connectivity and digitalized infrastructure support, favouring stakeholder dialog, establishing a governance, stipulating business agreements and responsibilities on how this is to be done robustly, who bears the cost, who is responsible, etc. The corresponding setting for our paper is visualized in Fig. 1B, with the goals to identify barriers and important directions towards collaborative traffic systems.

Drawing upon a state-of-the art (SOTA) assessment and interactions with experts, we discovered that the fragmented SOTA was in need of structure, therefore we investigate and propose key topics related to collaboration barriers and bring forth research questions for them. Section 2 briefly presents our system model, methodology and data sources we used. Section 3 summarizes SOTA perspectives, emphasizing CAVs' surveys. Section 4 presents our findings, and an analysis combining them and the SOTA perspectives. In Sect. 5, we provide a discussion and present our considerations on the identified research questions and directions.

2 System Model and Methodology

System. We describe the collaborative system formed by C-ITS actors in Fig. 2A, involving heterogenous types of road-users with different capabilities and a supporting physical infrastructure such as roads and barriers, but also cyber-physical systems (CPS) such as connected sensors, communication and computation infrastructure.

Cooperative and Collaborative are two concepts used in the context of C-ITS, which tend to be used interchangeably in the literature; we will take them as synonymous. Etymologically, *co-* means *with* or *together*, and *opera-* means *work* or *artifact*, while *labor-* means *work*. Another closely related term is that of a System of Systems (SoS), where one essential characteristic is that of independent evolution of the individual (or constituent), systems, [9]. We use the ETSI definition of road user [10], whereas we refer to a "cooperative agent" in the C-ITS context as an operationally independent entity such as RUs (from now own cooperative RUs, C-RUs) and CPS entities in the infrastructure, e.g., network systems, endowed with certain capabilities and goals that together elicit cooperative behaviours. Capabilities involve functions such as communication, sensing and computation, (encompassing information fusion, automation and cooperation - goal-oriented interaction), that can evolve over time and are manifested with different degrees (levels), see Fig. 2B. The behaviour of the C-ITS will emerge based on the interactions and behaviours of the constituent actors, i.e., RU's and the infrastructure, see Fig. 2A. SAE J3016 and J3216 define levels of automation and cooperation for CAVs.

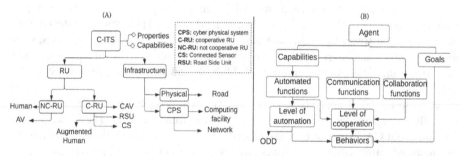

Fig. 2. (A) C-ITS collaborative system and communication abstract models. (B) Agent model.

Methodology. The paper draws upon two data sources, the results of a workshop with experts (SCSSS) [11] and a SOTA survey. The workshop saw the participation of 40 experts mainly from the safety and automotive fields (11 from academia and research, 29 from industry), representing automotive OEMs, chip makers, software, telecommunication, and consultancy. The workshop invited the participants to reflect on aspects of (i) Problems and Barriers, (ii) Safety and Cybersecurity, and (iii) research questions and new directions for C-ITSs, and collected their contributions in digital post-it forms, (using "Lucidspark"). Thematic analysis was used to analyse the collected opinions. For the SOTA survey, we used "google scholar" with relevant keywords. Firstly, we used combinations of key1 = ["CAV" OR "C-ITS"] AND key2 = ["survey" OR "barriers" OR "safety" OR "security"], secondly, we used key1 AND ["concept" or "theme"] where "concept", "theme" are the ones derived from the coding of the primary data source. Lastly, we applied backward snowballing, i.e., using the reference lists of the found articles, and expanding the research by using the similarity engine "www.connectedpap ers.com".

3 State-of-The Art

Cooperative Connected Automated Mobility (CCAM) is an umbrella term encompassing Connected Automated Mobility (CAM), i.e., CAV, and Cooperative ITS (C-ITS), as the cyber physical space where connected road users generate, exchange, and use data. C-RUs and C-ITS cover a broad spectrum of themes such as mobility, traffic, automation, connectivity, computing, safety, and cybersecurity. Much of AV research focuses on Automated Driving (AD) aspects [12] with an ego-vehicle centric view on topics such as safety [13], and cybersecurity [14]. With CAVs, the paradigm shifts from the single ego AV system to an SoS and expands to connectivity by encompassing communication technologies [8], e.g., Dedicated Short Range Communications (DSRC) and Next Generation V2x (NGV), cellular networking (e.g. 5G) and computing infrastructures such as edge computing [15]. There are several surveys looking at technology development, impacts, legal aspects, and application of CAVs. Opportunities, such as, improvements to road networks and society, new services and uncertainties, e.g., adoption rate and effectiveness are summarized in [16]. An extensive review of technology enabling AV and CAV capabilities such as cooperative sensing and control is presented in [17]. Telecommunication technologies and applications require considerations of network performances, security privacy authentication and protocol design w.r.t nodes mobility and density, [8]. CAV cybersecurity is extensively investigated in [18], while [19] focuses on the security of over the air software updates, essential for the CAVs' lifecycle. CAV use cases, such as, cooperative manoeuvres [20], are presented in [21] and a survey on legal issues and CAV usage implications is found in [22]. Multiple stakeholders relate to CAV's, [23, 24].

A socio technical analysis investigating who will drive the transition, along with the different stakeholder's viewpoints on CAVs is found in [25]. The Czech public opinion about CAV societal benefits expectations and concerns, includes expectations on enhanced traffic safety (e.g., fewer and less severe crashes) and performance (e.g., fewer congestions), [26]. Concerns include safety, i.e., CAVs faults, interaction with non-AVs, software hacking/misuse, performance under diverse operational design domains (ODDs), and legal and data privacy aspects [27]. The challenges that CAVs pose to the road infrastructure in terms of redesign, dedicated asset provisioning and investments are discussed in [28]. Changes to legislation (traffic rules), controlling methods (law enforcement), standards and organizational frameworks are suggested in [29], along with a list of priority challenges such as users' safety, liability issues, merging of national and supernational regulatory authority. An introduction to CAVs' opportunities and challenges is given in [4]. Whereas a broad and high-level survey on CAVs and shared and electrical vehicles drivers and barriers is provided by [30]. Trustworthiness is of specific relevance in C-ITS encompassing classical dependability attributes as well as ethics and privacy, [31]. The European Commission [32], and UK [33], proposes ethical recommendations to follow, while raising concerns over privacy topics. Wang et al. [34], shortly surveys relevant generic and specialized automotive cybersecurity frameworks and proposes a systematic risk assessment framework with an AV focus, while Alam et al. [23], looks at how safety and cybersecurity affect CAV's stakeholders due to their interactions. Diverse system viewpoints are necessary to describe the complexity of CAVs'. Safety and security represent large field, that encompasses generic methods (e.g., HARA and TARA) and methodologies (such as SAHARA and STAMP/STPA), generic standards (such as IEC 61508 for functional safety), as well as domain specific standards and regulations, such as the automotive domain functional safety standard (ISO26262) and cybersecurity standard (ISO21434) and regulation (UNECE155) [23].

The presented survey papers depict technological, safety and security aspects, applications, and legal frameworks regarding CCAM and CAVs. To the best of our understanding, an analysis of the barriers and means to improve traffic safety and performance in a collaborative setting is still missing, motivating further research.

4 Findings and Analysis

In the following section we analyse the themes and the concepts identified through the workshop and SOTA, see Table 1. We formulate related research questions (RQ) and directions (RD) and finally discuss them in terms of barriers and means to overcome in the Discussion section.

Collaborative System. The SoS nature of a C-ITS implies that many non-technical aspects (business, organizational collaborations, etc.) will be crucial for accomplishing

Table 1 Themes, concepts, and research questions and directions.

Themes	Definition	SCSSS concepts	Research questions and directions
Collaborative system	System of systems [9]	System of systems, legacy assets, vehicle automation mix, maintenance, business case, cost, barrier free market, political barriers, Intellectual Property (IP) protection, lack of regulations and authorities	(RD1)"Business models and regulatory frameworks to incentivise the introduction of C-ITS." (RQ1)"How can the C-ITS innovation processes better address social aspects instead of purely technological innovation?" (RQ2) "How can we bridge between innovation and policy makers?" (RD2) "What are suitable operational models for a traffic SoS to ensure continuous (risk) management?
Architecture	Fundamental organisation of a system and the principles governing it (shortened from [49])	Configuration (centralized/decentralized); interfaces; monitoring, ownership; graceful degradation; self-diagnosis	(RQ2)"At what level of distributed sensing, communication and information sharing, do the benefits outweigh the costs?" (RD3)"Composability of C-ITS as CPS in order to avoid unintended effects and to facilitate integration"; (RD4) "Architecture frameworks and engineering tools to support the design and operation C-ITS"
Communication	The capability of transferring data between C-RUs, and between C-RUs and the infrastructure	Latency, reliability, deterministic, protocol, secure, standards, fail safe	(RQ3)"Defining the constraint on end-to-end latencies according to diverse situations", (RQ4)"Defining the maximum time an agent can wait for a message before decision making". (RQ5) "Which are key design parameters and their relations, and how to analytically model communication in safety critical situations?"
Interoperability, Interfaces and Standards	Shared boundary between two functional units, defined by functional characteristics, established by consensus and approved by a recognised body [49]	Lack of: regulations and standards, standard technologies and protocols, system interface	(RQ6)"How to handle the independent evolution of the various agent's technology while maintaining the same metrics, e.g., dependability and performance?" (RD5) "How to deal with the coexistence of diverse communication technology stacks, w.r.t. deployment complexity and resource sharing?
Ethics and Privacy	Set of moral principles dealing with accepted standards of conduct	Ethical concerns, liability	(RD6)"How can we align CAV decision making with human ethics and value systems?" (RD7)"It seems necessary to define a cooperative ODD with a clear contract between the parties w.r.t. ethics and privacy." (RD8) "How do CAVs advance sustainability?" (RQ7)"How to provide decision making transparency for cooperative agents in the context of C-ITS?"
Safety cybersecurity and Risk	The degree to which (malicious) harm is prevented, detected, and reacted to. The degree relates to the risk in terms of consequence and probability of occurrence. [50]	Anomaly detection, dynamic safety case, metrics for hazard detection, false positive, minimal risk conditions, safety cooperative solutions. Attack vector, cyber-attack, malicious actor.	(RD9)"How do we manage and provide end-to-end safety for cooperative traffic systems, encompassing functional safety, safety of the intended functionality and cybersecurity in an SoS setting? (RQ8)"How do we measure the cooperative risk?" (RQ9)"How do we estimate the residual risk for CAVs, fleets of CAVs and specific traffic situations?" (RQ10)"How do we anticipate, and predict emerging risks, for an evolving C-ITS?"
Trust	Trust is "a key element in the development of effective relationships", including between humans–automation, affecting safety, performance, and use rate. [51]	Consumer trust, information correctness and fusion, system and technology trust, stakeholders trust, actual system behaviours (e.g., statistics on accidents and their relation to traffic scenarios)	(RD10)"The issue of certification for evolving C-ITS needs to be investigated, beyond approval for individual systems". (RD11)"CAVs must integrate trustworthy concepts in their architecture w.r.t the reliability of the information source and the correctness of sensed data (e.g., confidence). Architectures and methods such as fault detectors and safety monitors are directions to follow." (RD12)"Investigate the user understanding when interacting with CAVs and explore mismatches." (RQ11)"Which mechanisms could be adopted to solve the responsibility partitioning problem by design?"

the transition depicted in Fig. 1B. A C-ITS is characterised by a plurality of stakeholders driven by diverse motivations with often conflictual interests and different system viewpoints. The lack of a "central" designing actor to initiate the processes to enable connected cooperative RUs in C-ITS is often seen as a chicken and egg problem involving industrial (e.g., automotive OEMs and telecommunication operators) as well as societal stakeholders. The presence of major communication technology options such as DSRC and cellular networks (4G, 5G and beyond) complicates business investments. At the same time policy makers should maintain a neutral position not to hinder competition and technological advancement, see the EU technology neutral approach [35]. When involved in cooperative actions, multiple actors could potentially be liable for accidents resulting from malfunctioning systems or cyberattacks. Related to this, the division of responsibilities needs to be clear both from a liability and operational management points of view (who monitors what, who acts proactively or when things go wrong)? Regarding AV liabilities, legislations vary by country. For example, the UK has appointed the vehicle automaker as liable for automated cars accidents when operating in AD [36], whereas in USA this may differ from state to state [30]. There are various reasons why a technology gets adopted, for instance, the presence of a stakeholder industrial dominant design, regulatory compliance, or municipal, national, or supranational directives and policies. This is most often the subject of controversy due to the stakeholder interest-power relationship and linked to the risk of the investment [37]. The unregulated environment does not facilitate business investments as uncertainty hinders the development of strategic planning and leaves room only for speculation with the risk for companies to take all the costs upon themselves.

Architecture. The architecture, as the overall organization of collaborative systems, closely relates to the design space, legacy constraints, trade-offs between (potentially conflicting) properties such as safety and performance, and how the system can be managed and allowed to change such that the intended properties can be maintained/enhanced while avoiding unintended side effects. A C-ITS encompasses infrastructure and RUs (recall Fig. 2A) and is at the same time evolving, (e.g., due to new RUs, increased capabilities, or new technologies), leading to new and emerging behaviours. Regulations and other societal frameworks are also evolving but at a slower pace. The multifaceted design space inherits legacy investments that technically constrain what can be achieved thus exacerbating the challenge of the traffic transformation. If we want to improve traffic safety and performance through connectivity and collaboration, we should at least consider: (i) where to deploy–i.e. what are critical traffic areas and ODDs where collaboration would make sense, (ii) what perception to deploy - what sensing capabilities should be deployed in such critical areas both in terms of vehicle and infrastructure sensors (w.r.t. performance, reliability, quality and cost), (iii) what (sets of) communication technology to deploy - to achieve a desired level of collaboration including information sharing, (iv) what additional risks are introduced–e.g. relating to new failure modes, cybersecurity and unintended use, and (v) what are the costs–safety–and performance trade-offs involved, e.g. "at what level of distributed sensing, communication and information sharing, does the benefits outweigh the costs?" The architectural principles and patterns should be chosen such that a C-ITS can evolve and with monitoring incorporated to understand the emerging behaviours in real-time (e.g., for detection of critical scenarios/anomalies) and for off-line analytics. A C-ITS should be designed to be resilient, i.e., robust to failures/attacks while preferably feature graceful degradation in the presence of failures. Beyond monitoring, these properties will require some sort of adaptability, and humans in the loop to handle (foreseen and unforeseen) events. Finally, to handle all the above aspects, there is a need for (e.g., modelling and simulation tools) and architecture frameworks, i.e., organized collections of adequate models describing different system views and their interrelations, [38].

Communication. Communication includes considerations over the desired functional and extra-functional requirements. The functional aspects concern the design of the abstraction needed for the delivery of the cooperative services (e.g., information sharing, computing offloading, cooperative sensing). They encompass a technological layer, i.e., wireless technologies, with low level protocols and principles and concepts for application-level semantics, e.g., cooperative awareness message (CAM), cooperative perception message (CPM) [37]. The extra-functional requirements involve the definition of qualities of service (QoS) based on metrics such as performance and dependability. A fundamental characteristic of safety critical application is end-to-end latency (Le2e), measured as the latency between sending and receiving a semantically relevant application-level packet between two agents. Le2e is highly dependent on availability, reliability and robustness quality factors as it accounts for the principal causes of delays e.g., propagation, channel condition, queuing, processing, etc. Le2e relates to QoS as higher QoS levels fulfil more stringent requirements and offer lower Le2e at the expense of a higher cost. Le2e directly impacts the Age of Information (AoI) [6], i.e., how fresh the received information is, and in safety critical situation, influencing the safety performance trade-off. Recalling Fig. 1A, Le2e constraints CAV (A) speed and how far from a (potential) conflict zone (E) it must receive information about (C).

Interoperability, Interfaces and Standards. Two concepts were identified. (i) Technological interfaces and adaptabilities, i.e., coexistence of different HW/SW stacks as seen by the diverse stakeholders. C-ITS presents a heterogeneous landscape of communication technologies that will force c-RUs producers to install multiple hw/sw stacks to be interoperable with others and maintain communication capabilities in diverse geographical contexts. (ii) Application-level design, i.e., software design patterns and data semantics. At the application level the cooperation will involve at least two choices, the protocol used to exchange information and the protocol used to perform cooperation (e.g., CAM vs. protocols for cooperative manoeuvres [20].)

Ethics and Privacy. Considering the UN SDG goals for ethical transportation systems 11.2, 3.6, 9.3., 9.5, there are several ethical issues CAVs should address [32, 33]. The coexistence of hybrid actors could cause fairness issues, for example, more evolved agents could limit the performances of legacy ones. If vehicle OEMs release specific cooperative mechanisms for their models, this might also privilege cooperation amongst themselves. Cooperative behaviours should be based upon clear openly accessible engagement rules and every agent should be guaranteed to have its requests equally accepted or negated. Risk assessment and decision making for safety manoeuvres should not optimize nor prioritize over human or vehicle's attributes e.g., age, health state, assets value. This provides further arguments for CAV and infrastructure algorithms to be known and transparent. Another ethical issue concerns the extent to which agents are bound to abide to agreed cooperation rules, also with relation to collateral damage. Cooperation cost involves the trade-off between individual and group benefits, where cooperation promoting safety should be incentivized against own goals. In the presence of a cooperation tradable credit scheme, the governing credit mechanism, i.e., how credit is exchanged, should not prevent cooperation in the presence of safety risk. AVs are rapidly becoming datacentres on wheels with high increases in energy consumption [39]. Additional dedicated power is used by the infrastructure layer (telecommunication, computing) to support cooperation, raising concerns regarding sustainable energy consumption. Finally, C-RUs will exchange sensitive information, e.g., location and intentions that could be exploited. Despite the EU GDPR guidelines, new compliance challenges emerge in the form of data acquisition and management, informed consent practices and user control over data.

Safety, Cybersecurity and Risk. The C-ITS casts new safety and risk challenges as failures can happen at the connectivity, individual system or collaborative systems level. Due to the heterogeneity of the involved systems, a common prescription in the event of failure is missing. CAVs will need to elicit strategies that do not only consider local failures. This is further exacerbated by emergent behaviours stemming from independent evolution, ODD complexity and perception challenges. In light of this, both leading and lagging metrics for safety and risk need to be adopted and managed operationally to ensure that actual risks remain acceptable [40]. Cooperative safety mechanisms need to be well understood to attain cooperative safety goals. For this reason, C-RUs and in particular CAVs should be able to communicate and agree upon minimal risk conditions when involved in cooperation. An interesting direction is to consider sharing information of failures via a cooperative safety interface to make the other systems aware of how a system will degrade performance in an event of fault during cooperative interactions, i.e., manoeuvres. In principle, at design time there should be a common understanding of what are the admissible failures, with consequent failure modes, in a certain cooperative scenario. Then, at run-time, during "handshake", there should be an exchange of information to understand the current failure capabilities (capabilities and failure modes can evolve) of the involved parties and to agree upon safe states, [13]. Communication exposes the C-ITS agent to an increased attack surface. Literature offers already concrete examples of malicious actors exploiting potential C-RU vulnerabilities, for instance attacks on the CAM protocol [41] and asymmetric attacks, [42]. Furthermore, perceptive systems are vulnerable to (physical, and/or cyber) attacks aiming at degrading the performance to the point of generating system failures. In general, attacks may introduce errors and/or failures with direct relevance for safety and, in so doing, cybersecurity threats can become security hazards for the C-RUs. Frameworks like CRAF, SAHARA, STPA-SEC (generic) and HTARA (automotive specific) [23] can be used to understand such implications. Achieving trustworthiness is further aggravated by the multiple aspects of safety including SOTIF, functional and system safety aspects.

Trust. Agents need to trust other agents. Having agent identities well defined would facilitate the division of responsibility and liability, and detection of faulty and malicious agents. Agents may be not aware of being in a faulty state and other agents could report it; malicious agents need to be identified to take countermeasures. Information trust is deeply linked to information accuracy and agent trustworthiness, i.e., ability to generate correct information. We can distinguish between "information fusion" (deciding how to treat information from other agents based on the receiver prior belief on the sender trustworthiness), and "content or sensor fusion" (actually making use of the information content, assuming it is trusted). The information fusion process is characterized by, (i) Reliability of the information source; despite cryptography, integrity and authenticity, wrong information can still be generated, e.g., through a malicious or faulty sender; (ii) Information content uncertainty characterized by measurement errors; and (iii) Time of the measurement and information order of processing as neither perfect clock synchronization not ordering can be fully assumed (logical clock and concept of precedence). Trust from C-ITS's human users will derive from the belief that CAVs will follow reasonable and ethical steps, acceptable to society when making decisions under critical situations. It is essential that the conditions under which CAVs can operate and their limits within a specific ODD, are made publicly known. Lack in terms of CAV knowledge could be the source of switching costs in the form of human drivers retraining [36, 43] (point 8.6), increased CAV costs to improve human-machine interaction [44], litigations due to the liability problem where responsibility is unclear [43] (point 8.72) and "over trust" [45], which tends to distort the perceived risk and lower the user attention.

5 Discussion

Connectivity represents an enabler for a multitude of traffic opportunities and corresponding services. It is thus not surprising that many visions, use-cases and interpretations have been provided for connected and collaborative traffic, as by the plurality of names used to describe it, e.g., C-ITS, CAM, CCAM and SoS.

In this paper, our primary purpose was to investigate barriers and directions towards improving traffic safety and performance in the context of CAVs supported by a cyber-physical infrastructure. The identified themes (recall Table 1) are not independent and can be overall structured into collaborative systems, architectures, communication and interoperability aspects, and trustworthiness related concerns. These themes can be seen as both C-ITS's deployment barriers and enablers, and correspond to a hierarchy of concerns, conceptually similar to (parts of) established risk management frameworks [46]. C-ITS span multiple dimensions, from the operational technical layer including sensing, communications, and assumptions about faults/failures and attacks, to upper "layers" corresponding to sociotechnical considerations. The dimensionality requires to select and establish appropriate modelling abstractions and frameworks, and ways of dealing with dependencies across models. Further, relevant metrics of traffic performance and safety need to be established together with incentives and requirements for gathering and sharing data.

An architecture design capable to harness an evolving SoS structure involving stakeholders' concerns and hybrid technologies, while balancing performance, trustworthiness and cost, will play a crucial role to harmonise business drivers, societal concerns and a supporting legal framework. Automated and collaborative systems acting in open environments clearly belong to Snowden's view of "complex domain", in which new knowledge and methodologies need to be developed and systems engineering tools such as the Cynefin framework [47] holds some guidance on how to proceed forward. For instance, by leveraging both technical/engineering and social/humanitarian "means" to foster research through innovation eco-systems, open testbeds by forming new coalitions, and engaging stakeholders including the general public in a debate on acceptable risks and trustworthiness concerns. This will help to promote an inclusive and risk aware introduction of new technologies such as C-ITS, as opposed to an "innovation and tech-driven" approach, [48].

When it comes to introducing C-ITS, we believe that the inherent inertia and difficulties in an SoS, will require proactive approaches to promote the transition. The industry faces the challenge of reconciling business models and intellectual properties as cooperation implies interoperability and open interfaces and should anticipate users and regulatory demands that could arise post deployment, especially in terms of data privacy, security, and ethics. Market penetration rate has been seen as a potential barrier in order to reach a critical mass of cooperative traffic [4]. However, considering traffic statistics, e.g., regarding accidents, it becomes clear that deployments focused on the most difficult traffic environments would be a way forward. For example, it is known that a subset of all intersections in cities stand for a very large percent of critical accidents, [1]. The technical and societal challenges motivate further research, the creation of open research testbeds, the formation of private-public partnerships, and knowledge and data sharing. Research and stakeholder collaboration can inform in evaluating and providing inputs to adequate business models and regulatory frameworks that incentivize the introduction of trustworthy C-ITS.

Acknowledgments. We acknowledge support from KTH Digital Futures (the PERCy project), and the Swedish Innovation Agency, Vinnova (the Entice project and the TECoSA centre for Trustworthy edge computing systems and applications).

References

1. Shetty, A., et. al.: Automated vehicle safety and deployment: lessons from human crashes. In: ICCVE 2022 - IEEE International Conference on Connected Vehicles and Expo (2022)
2. Schiegg, F.A., et al.: Collective perception: a safety perspective. Sensors 21(1), 159 (2020)
3. Mcdonald, A.: Crash themes in automated vehicles: a topic modeling analysis of the california department of motor vehicles automated vehicle crash database (2020)
4. Shladover, S.E.: Opportunities and challenges in cooperative road vehicle automation. IEEE Open J. Intell. Transp. Syst. 2, 216–224 (2021)
5. Shetty, A., et al.: Safety challenges for autonomous vehicles in the absence of connectivity. Transp. Res. Part C: Emerg. Technol. 128, 103133 (2021)
6. Arvin, R., et al.: Safety evaluation of connected and automated vehicles in mixed traffic with conventional vehicles at intersections. J. Intell. Transp. Sys. Technol. Plan. Oper. 25(2), 170–187 (2020)
7. Bischoff, D., et. al.: Impact of imperfect communication on cooperative vehicular maneuvering at intersections. In: IEEE Vehicular Technology Conference (2020)
8. Siegel, J.E., et al.: A survey of the connected vehicle landscape - architectures, enabling technologies, applications, and development areas. IEEE Trans. Intell. Transp. Syst. 19(8), 2391–2406 (2018)

9. Maier, M.W.: Architecting principles for systems-of-systems. Syst. Eng. **1**(4), 267–284 (1998)
10. ETSI (2020) TS 103 300–3 - V2.1.1 - Intelligent Transport Systems (ITS)
11. Workshop on Automated and connected driving at SCSSS 2022: http://safety.addalot.se/2022/program. Accessed 10 May 2023
12. Watzenig, D., Horn, M.: Automated Driving: Safer and More Efficient Future Driving. Springer, Cham (2016)
13. Gyllenhammar, M., et. al.: Holistic Perspectives on Safety of Automated Driving Systems - Methods for Provision of Evidence
14. Sommer, F., et. al., (2019) Survey and classification of automotive security attacks. Information (Switzerland), 10 (4)
15. Mao, Y., et al.: A survey on mobile edge computing: the communication perspective. IEEE Commun. Surv. Tutorials **19**(4), 2322–2358 (2017)
16. Shiwakoti, N., et al.: Investigating the state of connected and autonomous vehicles: a literature Review. Transp. Res. Procedia **48**, 870–882 (2020)
17. Eskandarian, A., et al.: Research advances and challenges of autonomous and connected ground vehicles. IEEE Trans. Intell. Transp. Syst. **22**(2), 683 (2020)
18. Sun, X., et al.: A survey on cyber-security of connected and autonomous vehicles (CAVs). IEEE Trans. Intell. Transp. Syst. **23**(7), 6240–6259 (2022)
19. Halder, S., et al.: Secure over-the-air software updates in connected vehicles: a survey. Comput. Netw. **178**, 107343 (2020)
20. Hafner, B., et al.: a survey on cooperative architectures and maneuvers for connected and automated vehicles. IEEE Commun. Surv. Tutorials **24**(1), 380–403 (2022)
21. Montanaro, U., et al.: Towards connected autonomous driving: review of use-cases. Veh. Syst. Dyn. **57**(6), 779–814 (2019)
22. Crane, D.A., et al.: A survey of legal issues arising from the deployment of autonomous and connected vehicles recommended citation. Michigan Telecommun. Technol. Law Rev. **23**, 191 (2017)
23. Alam, S., et al.: Safety and security analysis of connected and automated vehicles: a methodology based on Interaction with stakeholders (2023)
24. Petit, J.: Automated vehicles cybersecurity: summary avs'17 and stakeholder analysis. In: Meyer, G., Beiker, S. (eds.) Road Vehicle Automation 5 Lecture Notes in Mobility, Springer, Cham, pp. 171–181 (2019). https://doi.org/10.1007/978-3-319-94896-6_15
25. Marletto, G.: Who will drive the transition to self-driving? A socio-technical analysis of the future impact of automated vehicles. Technol. Forecast Soc. Change **139**, 221–234 (2019)
26. Gabrhel, V., et al.: Public opinion on connected and automated vehicles: the Czech context. Trans. Transp. Sci. **10**(2), 42–52 (2019)
27. Kyriakidis, M., et al.: Public opinion on automated driving: results of an international questionnaire among 5000 respondents Transp. Res. Part F: Traffic Psychol. Behav. **32**(127), 140 (2015)
28. Saeed, T.U., et al.: Preparing road infrastructure to accommodate connected and automated vehicles: system-level perspective. J. Infrastruct. Syst. **27**(1), 0602003 (2021)
29. Gaitanidou, E., et. al.: Stakeholders' survey on the introduction of connected and automated vehicles in Greece. pp. 406–419 (2023). https://doi.org/10.1007/978-3-031-23721-8_35
30. Mahdavian, A., et al.: Drivers and barriers to implementation of connected, automated, shared, and electric vehicles: an agenda for future research. IEEE Access **9**, 22195–22213 (2021)
31. European Commission. AI High Level Expert Group. Ethics guidelines for trustworthy AI (2019). https://digital-strategy.ec.europa.eu/en/library/ethics-guidelines-trustworthy-ai
32. Danaher, J.: Ethics of Connected and Automated Vehicles: Recommendations on Road Safety, Privacy, Fairness, Explainability and Responsibility (2020)
33. Centre for Data Ethics and Innovation (2022) Responsible Innovation in Self-Driving Vehicles. UK Policy Paper

34. Geisslinger, M., et al.: An ethical trajectory planning algorithm for autonomous vehicles. Nat. Mach. Intell. **5**(2), 137–144 (2023)

35. Wang, Y., Wang, Y., Qin, H., Ji, H., Zhang, Y., Wang, J.: A systematic risk assessment framework of automotive cybersecurity. Automot. Innov. **4**(3), 253–261 (2021). https://doi.org/10.1007/s42154-021-00140-6

36. EU Commission supplementing Directive 2010/40/EU of the European Parliament and of the Council with regard to the deployment and operational use of cooperative intelligent transport systems

37. Great Britain. Law Commission., and Scottish Law Commission. (2022) Automated Vehicles: joint report

38. Executive Summary of 5GAA Board Feedback on C-ITS Delegated Regulation

39. Ramli, M.R., et al.: Towards reference architectures for trustworthy collaborative cyber-physical systems: reference architectures as boundary objects (2021)

40. Ansari, M.R., et. al.: V2X Misbehavior and Collective Perception Service: Considerations for Standardization. https://doi.org/10.48550/arXiv.2112.02184

41. Fraade-Blanar L., et. al.: Measuring automated vehicle safety: forging a framework. RAND Corporation (2018). https://www.rand.org/pubs/research_reports/RR2662.html

42. Sawade, O., et al.: Robust communication for cooperative driving maneuvers. IEEE Intell. Transp. Syst. Mag. **10**(3), 159–169 (2018)

43. Sudhakar, S., et al.: Data centers on wheels: emissions from computing onboard autonomous vehicles. IEEE Micro **43**(1), 29–39 (2023)

44. Calvert, S.C., et. al.: Designing Automated Vehicle and Traffic Systems towards Meaningful Human Control

45. Pattinson, J.A., et al.: Legal issues in automated vehicles: critically considering the potential role of consent and interactive digital interfaces. Human Soc. Sci. Commun. **7**(1), 1–10 (2020)

46. Rasmussen & Svedung. Proactive risk management in a dynamic society. Swedish Rescue Services (2000)

47. Snowden, D.J., Boone, M.E.: A Leader's Framework for Decision Making. Harvard Business Review, Nov. 2017 (2007)

48. Stilgoe, J., Cohen, T.: Rejecting acceptance: learning from public dialogue on self-driving vehicles. Sci. Public Policy **48**(6), 849–859 (2021)

49. ISO/IEC/IEEE 24765, (2017) Systems and software engineering-Vocabulary

50. Firesmith, D.G.: Common Concepts Underlying Safety, Security, and Survivability Engineering, Technical Note CMU/SEI-2003-TN-033 (2003)

51. Schaefer, K.E.: Measuring trust in human robot interactions: development of the "trust perception scale-HRI." In: Mittu, R., Sofge, D., Wagner, A., Lawless, W.F. (eds.) Robust Intelligence and Trust in Autonomous Systems, pp. 191–218. Springer, Boston, MA (2016). https://doi.org/10.1007/978-1-4899-7668-0_10

6th International Workshop on Artificial Intelligence Safety Engineering (WAISE 2023)

6th International Workshop on Artificial Intelligence Safety Engineering (WAISE 2023)

Simos Gerasimou[1], Orlando Avila-García[2], Mauricio Castillo-Effen[3], Chih-Hong Cheng[4], and Zakaria Chihani[5]

[1] Department of Computer Science, University of York, Deramore Lane, York
YO10 5GH, UK
simos.gerasimou@york.ac.uk
[2] Arquimea Reserch Center, Spain
oavila@arquimearesearchcenter.com
[3] Lockheed Martin, USA
mauricio.castillo-effen@lmco.com
[4] Fraunhofer IKS, Germany
chih-hong.cheng@iks.fraunhofer.de
[5] CEA LIST, CEA Saclay Nano-INNOV, Point Courrier 174,
91191 Gif-sur-Yvette, France
zakaria.chihani@cea.fr

1 Introduction

Empowering *Artificial Intelligence (AI)* to achieve its full potential and delivering the anticipated technical, societal and economic benefits mandates the provision of strong guarantees about its compliance with the expected levels of safety, also addressing issues like conformance to ethical standards and liability for accidents involving AI-enabled systems. Employing AI-enabled systems that operate close to and/or in collaboration with humans mandates that current *safety engineering* and legal mechanisms ensure that individuals –and their properties– are not harmed and that the desired benefits outweigh the potential unintended consequences. Accordingly, researchers, engineers and policymakers with complementary expertise must work closely together to address these major challenges.

The increasing interest in developing approaches to enhance AI safety cover not only practical and engineering-focused aspects of autonomous systems and safety engineering but also pure theoretical concepts and topics, including uncertainty analysis, AI integrity levels, and fair decision making. These two sides of AI safety must be examined in tandem. To this end, engineering safe AI-enabled autonomous systems demands bringing together philosophy and theoretical science with applied science and engineering. Through the adoption of a truly multi-disciplinary and cross-disciplinary approach, it is possible to amalgamate these seemingly disparate viewpoints and contribute to the engineering of safe AI-enabled systems underpinned by ethical and strategic decision-making capabilities.

Increasing levels of AI in "smart" sensory-motor loops allow intelligent systems to perform in increasingly dynamic, uncertain, complex environments with increasing degrees of *autonomy*, with the human being progressively removed from the control loop. *Machine Learning (ML)* methods enable adaptation to the environment rather than more traditional engineering approaches, such as system modelling and programming. The enormous progress achieved by deep learning, reinforcement learning, and their combination in challenging real-world tasks such as image classification, natural language processing and speech recognition raises the expectation for their seamless incorporation into safety-critical applications. However, the *inscrutability* or opaqueness of their statistical models for perception and decision-making is a major challenge. Also, the combination of autonomy and inscrutability in these AI-based systems is particularly challenging in safety-critical applications, such as autonomous vehicles, personal care or assistive robots and collaborative industrial robots.

The Sixth *International Workshop on Artificial Intelligence Safety Engineering (WAISE)* explores new ideas on AI safety, ethically-aligned design, regulations, and standards for AI-based systems. WAISE brings together experts, researchers, and practitioners from diverse communities, such as AI, safety engineering, ethics, standardisation, certification, robotics, cyber-physical systems, safety-critical systems, and application domain communities such as automotive, healthcare, manufacturing, agriculture, aerospace, critical infrastructures, and retail. The sixth WAISE edition was held on September 19, 2023, in Toulouse (France) as part of the 42nd International Conference on Computer Safety, Reliability, & Security (SAFECOMP 2023).

2 Programme

The Programme Committee (PC) received 17 submissions (13 full papers, 3 short papers and 1 doctoral paper). Each paper was peer-reviewed by at least three PC members, following a single-blind reviewing process. The committee decided to accept 12 papers (8 full papers, 3 short papers, and 1 doctoral paper) for oral presentation.

The WAISE 2023 programme was organised into thematic sessions, adopting a highly interactive format. In particular, each session was structured into paper presentations and talks, with each presentation/talk followed by a discussion session. The theme of the community debate session was "How can AI support the safe engineering of AI-enabled systems" and encouraged plenary discussion between participants.

The specific roles that were part of this format included session chairs, presenters and session discussants.

- *Session Chairs* introduced sessions and participants. The Chair moderated the session, took care of the time and gave the word to speakers in the audience during discussions.
- *Presenters* gave a paper presentation in 15 minutes and then participated in the discussion.
- *Session Discussants* prepared the discussion of individual papers and gave a critical review of the session papers.

The mixture of topics has been carefully balanced, as follows:

Session 1: AI Uncertainty & Monitoring

- Contextualised Out-of-Distribution Detection using Pattern Identification Romain Xu-Darme, Julien Girard-Satabin, Darryl Hond, Gabriele Incorvaia and Zakaria Chihani
- Conformal Prediction and Uncertainty Wrapper: What Statistical Guarantees Can You Get for Uncertainty Quantification in Machine Learning? Lisa Jöckel, Michael Klaes, Janek Groß and Pascal Gerber
- Towards Deep Anomaly Detection with Structured Knowledge Representations Konstantin Kirchheim

Session 2: Assurances for Autonomous Systems

- AERoS: Assurance of Emergent Behaviour in Autonomous Robotic Swarms Dhaminda Abeywickrama, James Wilson, Suet Lee, Greg Chance, Peter Winter, Arianna Manzini, Ibrahim Habli, Shane Windsor, Sabine Hauert and Kerstin Eder
- Safety Integrity Levels for Artificial Intelligence Simon Diemert, Laure Millet, Jonathan Groves and Jeffrey Joyce
- A Reasonable Driver Standard for Automated Vehicle Safety Philip Koopman and William Widen

Session 3: AI Safety

- Evaluating and Increasing Segmentation Robustness in CARLA Venkatesh Sambandham, Konstantin Kirchheim and Frank Ortmeier
- AIMOS: Metamorphic Testing of AI - An Industrial Application Augustin Lemesle, Aymeric Varasse, Zakaria Chihani and Dominique Tachet
- A Group-Level Learning Approach Using Logistic Regression For Fairer Decisions Marc Elliott and Deepak Padmanabhan

Session 4: Assurances for Autonomous Systems 2

- Towards Safe Machine Learning Lifecycles with ESG Model Cards Thomas Bonnier and Benjamin Bosch
- Can Large Language Models assist in Hazard Analysis? Simon Diemert and Jens Weber
- Structuring Research Related to Dynamic Risk Management for Autonomous Systems Rasmus Adler, Jan Reich and Richard Hawkins

3 Acknowledgements

As chairpersons of WAISE 2023, we want to thank all authors and contributors who submitted their work to the workshop. We also congratulate the authors whose papers were selected for inclusion in the programme and proceedings. We would also like to thank Friedemann Bitsch, the SAFECOMP Publication Chair, Erwin Schoitsch, the general workshop co-chair, and the SAFECOMP organisers, who provided us with the opportunity to organise the WAISE workshop at SAFECOMP 2023.

We especially thank our distinguished PC members, for reviewing the submissions and providing useful feedback to the authors:

- Vincent Aravantinos, Argo AI, Germany
- Markus Borg, CodeScene, Sweden
- Simon Burton, IKS Fraunhofer, DE
- Radu Calinescu, University of York, UK
- Javier Cámara, University of Malaga, Spain
- Krzysztof Czarnecki, University of Waterloo, Canada
- Huascar Espinoza, KDT JU, Belgium
- John Favaro, INTECS, Italy
- Jérémie Guiochet, LAAS-CNRS, France
- Nico Hochgeschwende, Bonn-Rhein-Sieg University, Germany
- Bettina Könighofer, Technical University of Graz, Austria
- Philip Koopman, Carnegie Mellon University, USA
- Nicholas Matragkas, CEA LIST, France
- Adedjouma Morayo, CEA LIST, France
- Chokri Mraidha, CEA LIST, France
- Vladislav Nenchev, BMW Group, Germany
- Jonas Nilsson, Nvidia, USA
- Philippa Ryan Conmy, University of York, UK
- Mehrdad Saadatmand, RISE SICS, Sweden
- Ioannis Sorokos, Fraunhofer IESE, Germany
- Andrea Stocco, Technical University Munich, Germany
- Mario Trapp, Fraunhofer IKS, Germany
- Meine van der Meulen, DNV, Norway
- Xingyu Zhao, University of Liverpool, UK

We also would like to thank the following researchers who participated as subreviewers in the research paper review process:

- Fabio Arnez, CEA LIST, France
- Sondess Missaoui, University of York, UK
- Prajit T Rajendran, CEA LIST, France
- Ioannis Stefanakos, University of York, UK

A Group-Level Learning Approach Using Logistic Regression for Fairer Decisions

Marc Elliott$^{(\boxtimes)}$ ⓘ and Deepak P.ⓘ

School of Electronics, Electrical Engineering and Computer Science,
Queen's University Belfast, Belfast, UK
melliott22@qub.ac.uk, deepaksp@acm.org

Abstract. Decision-making algorithms are becoming intertwined with each aspect of society. As we automate tasks which result in outcomes that affect an individual's life, the need for assessing and understanding the ethical consequences of these processes becomes vital. With bias often originating from the datasets imbalanced group distributions, we propose a novel approach to in-processing fairness techniques, by considering training at a group-level. Adapting the standard training process of the logistic regression, our approach considers aggregating coefficient derivatives at a group-level to produce fairer outcomes. We demonstrate on two real-world datasets that our approach provides groups with more equal weighting towards defining the model parameters and displays potential to reduce unfairness disparities in group imbalanced data. Our experimental results illustrate a stronger influence on improving fairness when considering binary sensitive attributes, which may prove beneficial in continuing to construct fair algorithms to reduce biases existing in decision-making practices. Whilst the results present our group-level approach achieving less fair results than current state-of-the-art directly optimized fairness techniques, we primarily observe improved fairness over fairness-agnostic models. Subsequently, we find our novel approach towards fair algorithms to be a small but crucial step towards developing new methods for fair decision-making algorithms.

Keywords: Algorithmic Fairness · Group-Level Learning · Logistic Regression · Imbalanced Data

1 Introduction

Algorithmic decision-making tools are being increasingly woven into society, producing outcomes which impact human lives. Consequently, concerns are growing towards errors produced by these tools negatively impacting sensitive groups of people. In the education sector, data-driven algorithms have been increasingly implemented in recent years to improve education experience [16]. The implementation of these algorithms range from providing personalised learning to students, assisting in shortlisting admission applications, and predicting student performance [13,23,24]. These tools are typically trained using attributes

© The Author(s), under exclusive license to Springer Nature Switzerland AG 2023
J. Guiochet et al. (Eds.): SAFECOMP 2023 Workshops, LNCS 14182, pp. 301–313, 2023.
https://doi.org/10.1007/978-3-031-40953-0_25

302 M. Elliott and D. P.

corresponding to their academic achievements, such as exam scores and qualifications acquired. However, many datasets used for these tasks also include demographic and more personal characteristic attributes such as their gender, race or area of residency [15]. Interestingly, inclusion of sensitive information in combination with education analytics for data-driven tasks has shown increased accuracy performance for the final models produced [19]. Though including these attributes may improve classification accuracy, we are left questioning the fairness and legitimacy of algorithms that parameterize their decisions on such attributes [7,9]. With algorithms deployed to classify whether students will pass their studies or in shortlisting admission applications, including data attributes outside of their academic records opens greater possibilities of furthering extant structural inequalities. This can perpetuate unfairness towards minority groups and often negatively impact those from lower socioeconomic backgrounds [17]. Whilst unfairness may originate from unintentional preexisting discriminative views which appear in historic data, it can often be difficult to pinpoint the cause of the bias. Barocas [2] provides crucial insight into the harmful impact imbalanced group representation can cause when utilized by decision-making tools; often resulting in bias and skewed conclusions being drawn. Therefore, before continuing to further entangle these algorithms into aspects of society, exploring methods of mitigating existing biases and assessing the fairness of such methods should take priority.

In this paper, we nudge the logistic regression (LR) training process to learn parameters at a group-level, through employing aggregation methods in training to tailor the learned model towards more equal treatment for underrepresented groups. We illustrate that our approach reduces fairness disparities regardless of group imbalances in the datasets. We deviate from the standard approach of directly integrating the fairness measure into the training objective to improve fairness and move towards an approach of providing minority groups a greater say in the algorithmic training process, so the eventual decision-making process does not directly make use of sensitive group memberships. Specifically, our technical modification of the traditional LR algorithm adapts the training process to derive coefficient values associated with each considered sensitive group. We then utilize the median group coefficient values with the motive of forming algorithmic parameters that better represent all considered sensitive groups opposed to constructing parameters that primarily align with the majority group.

2 Related Work

2.1 AI Fairness

Mehrabi [14] defines fairness in decision-making as "the absence of any prejudice or favoritism toward an individual or group based on their inherent or acquired characteristics". AI solutions which do intentionally or unintentionally produce predicted outcomes influenced by acquired characteristics are categorized as biased or unfair algorithms. As fairness is a complex concept with various notions that can be interpreted as fair treatment, similarly, there are a range of algorithmic measurements that quantify the fairness of decisions produced by an algorithm. Dependent on the choice of fairness notion implemented, this can result in sensitive groups receiving different quality of predictions and often incompatibility issues occur when considering multiple fairness notions simultaneously [10]. One of the most commonly implemented notions of fairness in the relevant literature is demographic parity (DP) [25]. For a decision-making tool to be fair in regard to DP, the proportion of positive outcomes is equalized across the given sensitive groups:

$$DP \Rightarrow P(\hat{y} = 1|S = 0) \approx P(\hat{y} = 1|S = 1) \tag{1}$$

This represents that the probability of an algorithm predicting the positive outcome ($\hat{y} = 1$) for the disadvantaged group ($S = 0$) is the same as the advantaged group ($S = 1$) when DP has been satisfied. With imbalanced classifications between sensitive groups, enforcing this notion of fairness would require incorrect predictions to be made to reduce the disparity, which may conflict with other fairness metrics such as error-rate parity [10].

Another notion of fairness which we incorporate into this paper is equal opportunity (EO) [6,14]. A decision-making tool is considered fair with regard to EO when the proportion of correctly predicted positive outcomes is equal independent of sensitive group status:

$$EO \Rightarrow P(\hat{y} = 1|S = 0, Y = 1) \approx P(\hat{y} = 1|S = 1, Y = 1) \tag{2}$$

From a technical perspective, achieving EO would ensure that advantaged and disadvantaged groups would receive equal true positive rates (TPR) in the decision-making process. Whilst both DP and EO are measured through the quality of positive predictions, they can correlate to two different treatments to the individuals involved.

If we consider bias arising from disproportionate group representations, decision-making on imbalanced group distributions can increase the disparate impact [4]. For an algorithm with no awareness to demographic groups, the training process unintentionally learns parameters that primarily reflect the majority group in an imbalanced dataset, resulting in biases appearing via skewed group distributions. Therefore, by providing underrepresented groups with an equal representation in the training process could reduce disparities.

2.2 Fairer AI Solutions

In fair AI literature, a common approach taken towards designing in-processing fair algorithms is through modifying the algorithms' training objective towards a selected fairness notion that results in learned attributes being more strongly aligned with fairness than maximizing accuracy [8,22,25]. When utilizing such fairness nudges (in the form of additional objectives or constraints), these approaches can reduce fair classification to a sequence of cost-sensitive problems between the chosen fairness metric and a classification accuracy metric. As seen in Agarwal's paper [1], the reductions approach can utilize cost-sensitive learning to produce an AI solution with the desired trade-off between fairness and accuracy. The constraints approach has previously been implemented with the LR model to minimize the empirical error-rate utilizing a regularizer value to enforce fair classification [8]. Although these approaches have become common, our paper takes inspiration from the technique presented in Roh's FairBatch [20], which approaches improving fairness by adaptively optimizing batch selection during model training. If the models current training iteration achieves a lower accuracy for a given sensitive group, the following iteration will contain a batch-size with a greater ratio for the disadvantaged group. In the same spirit, but in a substantially different way, our technique adapts the LR learning process through each training iteration handling each sensitive group's data as independent batches. Unlike the method used in FairBatch [20], we use the entire training data at each learning iteration and utilize group-level training to provide minority groups with a greater contribution towards the learned attributes through aggregation of attribute coefficients.

2.3 Sensitive Attribute Visibility at Training vis-à-vis Decision Making Time

When discussing the usage of sensitive attributes in the training process, a decision-making algorithm which incorporates sensitive attributes during model learning is often referred to as 'fairness through awareness', whereas excluding these attributes from the model is 'fairness through unawareness'. Due to the possibility of sensitive attributes being deduced from non-sensitive attributes, it has been shown that unawareness is a less efficient approach to fairness in comparison to awareness [5]. As such, many of the fair in-processing approaches require that sensitive attributes are accessible during training and prediction when utilized for the input data [26]. For real-world deployment of fair algorithms, due to existing privacy laws, sensitive attributes may be unavailable for the input attribute set. Though our approach utilizes the sensitive attributes in model training, these are excluded from the learned attributes and as such are not required for producing predictions from the final model. Despite requiring training data that has access to sensitive characteristics, having the capability to produce fairer classifications with the final model without access to personal characteristics is advantageous from a real-world deployment perspective, making it applicable to a wider variety of decision-making scenarios.

3   Methodology

3.1   Group-Level Logistic Regression

The LR is a commonly utilized classification algorithm, its simple and intuitive structure makes it inherently explainable via interpreting the relative weights of the features. These factors position it as a more suitable algorithm for tasks which impact individuals' lives as opposed to black-box alternatives [21]. The

LR algorithm utilizes coefficient values that are associated with each of the input attributes, where the optimal coefficient values minimize the logistic loss function:

$$LogLoss = -(y\ log(\hat{y}) + (1-y)log(1-\hat{y})) \qquad (3)$$

Algorithm 1. Group-Level LR Training

Input: Training data values X and target value Y, sensitive attribute S
Output: Trained Weights W and Bias B

1: **function** FIT(X, Y, S)
2:     Initialise learning rate a
3:     Initialise Weights W and Bias B
4:     **for** Number of training iterations **do**
5:         Initialise empty list $groupWeights$ and $groupBias$
6:         **for** group g in S **do**
7:             Xg, Yg = Subsample of X, Y corresponding to attribute value g
8:             dWg, Bg = compute gradients of Xg with respect to W and B
9:             Add dWg to list $groupWeights$
10:             Add Bg to list $groupBias$
11:         **end for**
12:         $newDW = median(groupWeights)$
13:         $newB = median(groupBias)$
14:         Update $W = W$ - (a * $newDW$)
15:         Update $B = B$ - (a * $newB$)
16:     **end for**
17:     **return** W, B
18: **end function**

Where y represents the actual target value and $\hat{y}$ represents the predicted probability value which is calculated through a weighted sum of the input values (X) with the corresponding coefficients. The sigmoid function is then applied to scale the weighted sum to a predicted probability of the target task between 0 and 1. The LR algorithm optimizes the logistic loss function through stochastic gradient descent optimization. This optimization results in obtaining derivative coefficient values and a derivative intercept (or bias) value, which are applied for updating the LR parameters (θ). Producing a derivative value for each coefficient influences how these values are updated to minimize the logistic loss function. The following describes how parameters are updated at each training iteration:

$$\theta_i = \theta_i - \alpha\left(\frac{X(\hat{y}-y)}{n}\right) \qquad (4)$$

For updating θ, value α represents the learning rate and n represents the number of training samples. The updated θ is calculated by subtracting it from the learning rate multiplied by the coefficient derivative values. This traditional

approach obtains derivative values across all training samples, whereas our approach, outlined as pseudo-code in Algorithm 1, adapts the derivative function
to compute at a group-level. Our approach splits training data X according to
their sensitive attribute S. This training process considers each sensitive group
independently to produce coefficient derivative values (dW) for each group:

$$dW_{\mathrm{Si}} = \frac{X_{\mathrm{Si}}(\hat{y}_{\mathrm{Si}} - y_{\mathrm{Si}})}{n_{\mathrm{Si}}} \tag{5}$$

where X_{Si} represents the batch of input values corresponding to the sensitive
group. This represents the compute gradients process in Algorithm 1. Processing
each sensitive group independently results in a collection of derivative coefficient
values that uniquely correspond to each sensitive group ($dW_{\mathrm{S0}}, \ldots, dW_{\mathrm{Si}}$), which
requires aggregation for producing the values to be used for updating θ for
the following training iteration. Therefore, our modified LR updates parameters
using the following form, where f is an aggregation function:

$$\theta_i = \theta_i - \alpha(f(dW_{\mathrm{S0}}, \ldots, dW_{\mathrm{Si}})) \tag{6}$$

Our group-level learning approach utilizes median aggregation as our function
f. At each training iteration, θ_i is updated with the median derivative coefficient
value across groups. The median ensures that each training iteration selects a
derivative coefficient value that aligns with one of the sensitive group's data.
Algorithm 1 represents how the training process of the LR has been updated
to accommodate for group-level learning. In contrast, if we were to enforce a
mean aggregation, the mean value has the possibility to be far from accurately
representing any group's independent value (especially, if the values are all far
apart numerically, the mean could lie in a valley where it is not representative
of any group) and could negatively impact each sensitive group, especially when
considering extreme or outlier values. Although the median value may not consistently align with all sensitive groups, it provides a stronger basis for achieving
centrality between the groups through the attribute learning process.

Irrespective of aggregation function selected, the motivation for our group-
level LR adaptation provides sensitive groups, which may encompass a smaller
data distribution, a more significant contribution towards defining the algorithm's parameters without requiring data resampling techniques. This positions
our approach towards designing decision-making models that improve group representation through the attribute learning process as opposed to learnt attributes
aligning with majority represented groups in imbalanced data.

If we compare our approach to a fairness-agnostic model, the latter may
discover a correlation between an input feature and the positive outcome. This
feature may then obtain a high weight value and have a significant impact on the
predicted outcome. However, given an imbalanced dataset, this correlation might
exist only for the majority group, therefore the minority groups may have little
impact on influencing the model parameters in training. Minority groups would
be subjected to predictions that place substantial importance on features that
strongly correlate with the majority group but do not accurately represent the

minority groups. Instead our approach restrains such circumstances occurring, which likely reduces model accuracy but has potential to incur greater fairness. Utilizing our approach could reduce the weighting provided to the feature that had a strong correlation between the majority group and the positive outcome. Reducing the weight of this feature may lower the success-rate of the majority group and group-level training could reveal a correlation between a feature and the target outcome that is more suitable for all groups. Whilst this approach may not be as beneficial for predicting the majority group, it could improve correlation collectively for all groups and therefore could benefit in improving DP. The approach is motivated towards defining parameters that better reflect all groups and ensuring that all considered groups are provided a similar quality of prediction. For imbalanced group distributions, receiving similar quality of predictions could improve EO, however, with notable group classification imbalances there may be conflicts between being able to improve both EO and DP.

3.2 Datasets

Two datasets have been used for the experiments conducted in this paper, the Adult Income dataset [11] and the Open University Learning Analytics (OULA) dataset [12]. The Adult Income is a commonly utilized binary classification dataset for predicting whether an individual's annual salary is greater than 50K. The data was pre-processed having samples with missing values removed, categorical attributes being encoded and converting the hours worked attribute to binary. Resulting in 45,222 samples and 25 attributes, with an 80/20 split used for obtaining training and test sets. This real-world dataset has been applied due to containing several sensitive attributes with substantial class distribution imbalances and group representation imbalances. Notably, the majority race group 'White' encompasses over 80% of all samples, similarly a greater number of the majority group receive the positive outcome than most of the minority groups. Specifically, our experiment will consider race groups as the sensitive attribute due to providing the opportunity to evaluate multiple sensitive groups in aggregation. Additionally, this dataset will form a secondary experiment where the race attribute will be transformed to a binary value of whether their race is 'White' or 'Non-White', as the white race group is the majority group for this dataset. These two experiments will be beneficial in analyzing fairness between a non-binary and binary sensitive attribute setting.

The OULA dataset collected students' interactions from a virtual learning environment across 22 university courses over a 2 year period. The dataset was gathered with the purpose of student prediction and course structure analysis scenarios in mind [12]. We utilise this dataset for binary prediction on academic performance, to classify whether the student will pass their course. The attributes encompass student click-stream and exam submission details, with their final result value determining their classification attribute. Standard pre-processing practices were employed to handle missing values, with ordinal encoding being applied to categorical attributes and a min-max attribute scaling function was applied. Resulting in 32,593 samples with 23 input attributes, with a 70/30 split used for obtaining training and test sets. The dataset contains sensitive attributes on gender and disability, although the class distribution is reasonably balanced, there exists large group distribution imbalances within the dataset, with students with disabilities accounting for under 10% of the data samples. Our experiment will consist of two tests, first considering a single binary sensitive attribute (disability) and then a combination of attributes (disability and gender).

3.3 Experiment Setup

This initial experiment aims to identify how group-level aggregated algorithm training alters the fairness of the predicted outcomes. Therefore, a classical LR model will be trained as a baseline comparator to the proposed modified LR variations. The baseline LR will be constructed using Scikit-Learn [18], with the 'liblinear' solver applied. The learnt baseline model will be fairness-agnostic and have the sole objective of predictive accuracy, therefore, it is expected to achieve the highest accuracy and higher levels of unfairness. Additionally, two fairness orientated algorithms will be implemented as baseline fairness comparators. Using the Fairlearn fairness toolkits [3], the reduction technique detailed in Agarwal's paper [1] will be deployed on the experiment. This state-of-the-art approach can be applied to any formalized fairness notion (such as DP and EO) and does not require access to sensitive attributes at decision-making time, making it a suitable fair comparator to our own approach. The Fairlearn toolkit allows for a fairness metric to be selected and a constraint regularizer value to be adjusted. To adequately assess our group-level LR, a DP constrained model and an EO constrained model will both be implemented. As our objective focuses on maximizing fairness, the regularizer has been adjusted to maximize the constrained fairness metric. Specifically, the implementation utilizes the grid search reduction method detailed by Agarwal, where a LR has been implemented as the estimator algorithm for the grid search and the 'constrained weight' parameter has been set to 1 (maximum constraint to the provided fairness metric). This returns directly optimized fairness models for selecting a desired trade-off between accuracy and fairness. The selected final models will represent the lowest difference in constrained fairness metric between the considered sensitive groups, irrespective of the loss of predictive accuracy. For both tests, the sensitive attribute is employed to split the training data but is not utilised at decision-making time for the group-level LR. For determining the algorithmic fairness of the trained models, we will measure DP (Eq. (1)) and EO (Eq. (2)). As the experiments contain scenarios with multiple sensitive groups (non-binary race or gender-disability), the fairness metrics will be determined by the difference between the most advantaged group (highest score) and the least advantaged (lowest score). For example, assessing fairness on the OULA dataset, where the sensitive groups considered are gender and disability status, DP will be measured via difference between the predicted highest success-rate group and lowest success-rate group from the final model on the test data. A difference of 0 represents parity being achieved and treats all considered groups fairly with respect to the given fairness notion, whereas 1 would represent maximum disparity. The same assessment applies to the EO metric with regard to assessing the difference in TPR between sensitive groups. The experiments will be conducted on the datasets previously described, where each model implemented will use the training data for model learning. The test data will then be used to evaluate the final model, which will report the predictive performance accuracy and both considered fairness metrics (DP and EO). The group-level LR utilizes early-stopping functionality to continue training iterations until there is no further improvement in accuracy over the training data. For each experiment the group-level algorithm will be trained three times and the average results will be recorded.

4   Experimental Results

4.1   Adult Income Dataset Results

Our experiments on the Adult Income dataset considered the race sensitive group and we applied our model to two different scenarios. Firstly, we considered the race attribute as non-binary, therefore examining the five demographic race values. Secondly, we utilize the same experiment but treat the sensitive attribute as a binary attribute, where the majority race 'White' is considered as one value and the four remaining minority groups collectively form our other binary value.

Table 1. Adult dataset results.

Algorithm	Non-Binary Attribute			Binary Attribute		
	ACC	DP	EO	ACC	DP	EO
Baseline LR	**0.8084**	0.1057	0.1687	**0.8084**	0.0312	0.0118
Fairlearn DP	0.7982	**0.0240**	0.1478	0.8011	**0.0059**	0.0502
Fairlearn EO	0.7563	0.0795	**0.0576**	0.8043	0.0255	**0.0028**
Group-Level LR	0.7535	0.0798	0.2370	0.7733	0.0230	0.0215

In both cases, as we expected, the fairness-agnostic baseline LR achieves the highest predictive accuracy at the cost of comparatively lower levels of fairness in regard to both DP and EO. Similarly, for maximizing a given fairness metric, the constraint optimized Fairlearn models achieve the closest results to parity for their constrained metric. The group-level LR approach does not return optimal fairness results, particularly, in the case of the non-binary attribute it achieves worse EO than the baseline LR model, but when applying it to the binary race attribute we observe considerable improvements in DP and EO for this model (Table 1). Notably, even though the group-level LR never achieves the best fairness results, if we consider both DP and EO simultaneously the group-level LR achieves greater levels of fairness in the metrics Fairlearn are not optimized towards. For example, FairlearnDP for binary race is 0.59% from DP but at the cost of EO being 5.02% from parity. Comparatively, the group-level LR is

1.71% further from DP than the FairlearnDP, but is 2.87% closer to parity in EO than the FairlearnDP; a similar pattern is present between the FairlearnEO and group-level LR models.

4.2 OULA Dataset Results

Table 2. OULA dataset results.

Algorithm	Non-Binary Attribute			Binary Attribute		
	ACC	DP	EO	ACC	DP	EO
Baseline LR	**0.8441**	0.0933	0.0843	**0.8441**	0.0899	0.0708
Fairlearn DP	0.8284	**0.0458**	0.0488	0.8331	**0.0488**	0.0343
Fairlearn EO	0.8062	0.1036	**0.0381**	0.8294	0.0514	**0.0286**
Group-Level LR	0.7875	0.0881	0.0501	0.7807	0.0501	0.0290

Two tests were completed with the OULA dataset. Firstly the disability attribute was monitored as it provides the opportunity to assess how the model variations are influenced by an imbalanced binary group. Secondly, we considered multi-sensitive attributes by including gender and disability. This test contained four demographic groups, male and females with disabilities and male and females with no disabilities. Similar to the experiments on the Adult Income dataset, we observe that the baseline LR achieves the best accuracy in both tests (Table 2), whereas the constrained Fairlearn models achieve the greatest levels of fairness towards their given constrained fairness notion. The group-level LR presents a considerable drop in predictive accuracy, however, in comparison to the baseline LR model it presents fairer DP and EO for both binary and non-binary sensitive attribute experiments. The improvement in fairness between the baseline and group-level LR models is particularly apparent for the binary student test. Additionally, the group-level LR demonstrates competitive fairness levels to the Fairlearn counterparts in the binary student test, where the FairlearnEO is marginally fairer by 0.04% in EO than the group-level LR, in contrast to the group-level LR being 0.13% fairer than FairlearnEO with regards to DP. In the binary test, although the group-level LR is not optimal, it is competitive in fairness to state-of-the-art fair algorithms that are strictly constrained to their given fairness metrics. Similarly to the Adult test, the group-level LR moderately underperforms in comparison to the Fairlearn models in the non-binary test. For considering disability-gender as the sensitive group for the OULA dataset, introducing an additional sensitive attribute increases disparities across each model (with the exception of DP for FairlearnDP). Whilst each fair-aware model achieves a higher degree of fairness than the baseline LR, the group-level LR is outperformed by the Fairlearn models, specifically the FairlearnDP achieves fairer DP and EO than the group-level LR in this scenario.

4.3   Discussion

The results from both experiments demonstrate that the group-level approach to fairer decision-making is not consistently as beneficial as the state-of-the-art fair approaches, but exemplifies that in imbalanced datasets at the cost of accuracy we can improve fairness over a fairness agnostic algorithm. In the OULA experiment, our group-level LR improves DP and EO in binary and non-binary test cases against the baseline LR model. Thus demonstrating that providing minority groups more control over weight values can result in a more similar quality of prediction for all groups. However, in both Adult experiments our approach improves DP but fares worse in EO comparatively to the baseline LR, notably in the non-binary experiment. The increase in EO disparity may originate from the notable classification imbalance between groups. In the Adult dataset, three of the five race groups have a notably lower true success-rate than the other two groups. As the group-level approach provides groups equal contribution towards the weight values, with the majority of groups having true lower success-rates this will be represented in the trained model's predictions. This presents a conflict between EO and DP in this case, where our group-level approach has constructed weights primarily aligning to the majority of groups (which have a lower success-rate), thus we achieve fairer DP in obtaining similar success-rates. Achieving this would require more false negative predictions from the higher success-rate groups ('White' and 'API') which will obtain a lower TPR than the other three groups thus increasing the EO disparity. For the OULA dataset, classification imbalances are less significant than that seen in the Adult data and both fairness metrics are improved over the baseline LR, providing groups with similar levels of predictive performance. Thus for group-level learning, considering both dataset distribution and classification imbalances across sensitive groups is important to how the trained group-level model performs.

5   Conclusion and Future Directions

Our motivation towards the group-level LR approach was to focus on deriving fairness through providing unrepresented demographic groups a more significant role in forming the algorithmic models which are being developed and integrated into society. Those algorithmic models have previously been seen to treat these minority groups unfairly in their predictive outcomes, so our motive pursued improving fairness by providing minority groups the opportunity to impact the algorithmic parameters learnt during model training. The experiment results presented that the group-level approach to fairness is primarily not as advantageous as enforcing fairness constraints into the training objective as demonstrated by the Fairlearn models. However, whilst the group-level LR maintained the lowest predictive accuracy, it also showed to improve both DP and EO over the baseline LR in the majority of experiment scenarios. Additionally, in the binary sensitive attribute experiments, the group-level LR attains DP and EO values that can be competitive to the Fairlearn approaches which utilized the maximum fairness constraint possible in the model implementation to maximize their fairness.

The group-level algorithm may not yield the greatest fairness returns in one fairness direction but points towards how fairness has the potential to be improved through harnessing imbalanced data at the group-level. Where we observe issues arising is when we consider non-binary or multiple sensitive groups and groups which encompass a particularly small sample of the data. Although our approach aims to provide all considered sensitive groups an equal contribution towards the final model parameters, increasing the number of sensitive groups incorporated can ultimately perpetuate unfairness as presented in our non-binary experiments. Given the student example, the disability sensitive group initially represented a small portion of the data, by further segmenting this group into disability-gender it produced coefficient values that represented an exceedingly small minority group and resultantly aggregated towards parameters that did not accurately represent those minority groups in the testing samples.

The group-level approach to fairness shows potential as a promising direction to take future developments of fair AI. Integrating the current approach with a fairness constrained training objective as seen in other work may provide greater consistency to the group-levels fairness performance. The current technique had been applied to the LR model, however, due to the technical simplicity of the approach it could be adapted to other gradient-based models and be a more generalizable approach to fairer classifications. As we identified that attempting to accommodate to a larger number of minority groups resulted in less fair outcomes, further work should be conducted to investigate methods to mitigate unfairness arising from groups with few data samples producing outlier or extreme coefficients that may not fairly represent that group.

References

1. Agarwal, A., Beygelzimer, A., Dudík, M., Langford, J., Wallach, H.: A reductions approach to fair classification (2018). https://doi.org/10.48550/arXiv.1803.02453
2. Barocas, S., Selbst, A.D.: Big data's disparate impact. Calif. Law Rev. **104**(3), 671–732 (2016)
3. Bird, S., et al.: Fairlearn: a toolkit for assessing and improving fairness in AI. Technical report, Microsoft (2020). https://www.microsoft.com/en-us/research/publication/fairlearn-a-toolkit-for-assessing-and-improving-fairness-in-ai
4. Farrand, T., Mireshghallah, F., Singh, S., Trask, A.: Neither private nor fair: impact of data imbalance on utility and fairness in differential privacy. In: Proceedings of the 2020 Workshop on Privacy-Preserving Machine Learning in Practice, pp. 15–19. ACM, New York (2020). https://doi.org/10.1145/3411501.3419419
5. Gajane, P., Pechenizkiy, M.: On formalizing fairness in prediction with machine learning (2018). https://doi.org/10.48550/arXiv.1710.03184
6. Hardt, M., Price, E., Price, E., Srebro, N.: Equality of opportunity in supervised learning. In: Proceedings of the 30th International Conference on Neural Information Processing System, pp. 3323–3331 (2016)
7. Jiang, W., Pardos, Z.A.: Towards equity and algorithmic fairness in student grade prediction. In: Proceedings of the 2021 AAAI/ACM Conference on AI, Ethics, and Society, New York, pp. 608–617 (2021). https://doi.org/10.1145/3461702.3462623

8. Kamishima, T., Akaho, S., Asoh, H., Sakuma, J.: Fairness-aware classifier with prejudice remover regularizer. In: Flach, P.A., De Bie, T., Cristianini, N. (eds.) ECML PKDD 2012. LNCS (LNAI), vol. 7524, pp. 35–50. Springer, Heidelberg (2012). https://doi.org/10.1007/978-3-642-33486-3_3

9. Kizilcec, R.F., Lee, H.: Algorithmic fairness in education (2021). https://doi.org/10.48550/arXiv.2007.05443

10. Kleinberg, J., Mullainathan, S., Raghavan, M.: Inherent trade-offs in the fair determination of risk scores (2016). https://doi.org/10.48550/arXiv.1609.05807

11. Kohavi, R.: Scaling up the accuracy of Naive-Bayes classifiers: a decision-tree hybrid. In: Proceedings of the Second International Conference on Knowledge Discovery and Data Mining, pp. 202–207. AAAI Press (1996)

12. Kuzilek, J., Hlosta, M., Zdráhal, Z.: Open university learning analytics dataset. Sci. Data 4 (2017). https://doi.org/10.1038/sdata.2017.171

13. Maseleno, A., Sabani, N., Huda, M., Ahmad, R., Jasmi, K.A., Basiron, B.: Demystifying learning analytics in personalised learning. Int. J. Eng. Technol. 7, 1124–1129 (2018). https://doi.org/10.14419/ijet.v7i3.9789

14. Mehrabi, N., Morstatter, F., Saxena, N., Lerman, K., Galstyan, A.: A survey on bias and fairness in machine learning. ACM Comput. Surv. 54, 1–35 (2021). https://doi.org/10.1145/3457607

15. Mihaescu, C., Popescu, P.: Review on publicly available datasets for educational data mining. Wiley Interdisc. Rev. Data Min. Knowl. Discov. 11 (2021). https://doi.org/10.1002/widm.1403

16. Nafea, I.: Machine learning in educational technology, pp. 175–183. IntechOpen, London (2018). https://doi.org/10.5772/intechopen.72906

17. O'Neil, C.: Weapons of Math Destruction: How Big Data Increases Inequality and Threatens Democracy. Crown Publishing Group, USA (2016)

18. Pedregosa, F., Varoquaux, G., Gramfort, A., Michel, V., Thirion, B.: Scikit-learn: machine learning in Python. J. Mach. Learn. Res. 12, 2285–2830 (2012)

19. Riazy, S., Simbeck, K., Schreck, V.: Fairness in learning analytics: student at-risk prediction in virtual learning environments. In: Proceedings of the 12th International Conference on Computer Supported Education, Prague, pp. 15–25 (2020). https://doi.org/10.5220/0009324100150025

20. Roh, Y., Lee, K., Whang, S.E., Suh, C.: FairBatch: batch selection for model fairness (2021). https://doi.org/10.48550/arXiv.2012.01696

21. Rudin, C.: Stop explaining black box machine learning models for high stakes decisions and use interpretable models instead. Nat. Mach. Intell. 1, 206–215 (2019). https://doi.org/10.1038/s42256-019-0048-x

22. Shen, A., Han, X., Cohn, T., Baldwin, T., Frermann, L.: Optimising equal opportunity fairness in model training (2022). https://doi.org/10.48550/arXiv.2205.02393

23. Sweeney, M., Lester, J., Rangwala, H., Johri, A.: Next-term student performance prediction: a recommender systems approach. J. Educ. Data Min. 8(1), 22–51 (2016). https://doi.org/10.5281/zenodo.3554603

24. Waters, A., Miikkulainen, R.: GRADE: machine learning support for graduate admissions. AI Mag. 35, 64–75 (2014). https://doi.org/10.1609/aimag.v35i1.2504

25. Zafar, M.B., Valera, I., Gomez-Rodriguez, M., Gummadi, K.P.: Fairness constraints: a flexible approach for fair classification. J. Mach. Learn. Res. 20(75), 1–42 (2019)

26. Zhao, T., Dai, E., Shu, K., Wang, S.: Towards fair classifiers without sensitive attributes: exploring biases in related features. In: Proceedings of the 15th ACM International Conference on Web Search and Data Mining, pp. 1433–1442 (2022). https://doi.org/10.1145/3488560.3498493

Conformal Prediction and Uncertainty Wrapper: What Statistical Guarantees Can You Get for Uncertainty Quantification in Machine Learning?

Lisa Jöckel[✉], Michael Kläs[✉], Janek Groß, and Pascal Gerber

Fraunhofer Institute for Experimental Software Engineering IESE, Fraunhofer Platz 1, 67663 Kaiserslautern, Germany
{lisa.joeckel,michael.klaes,janek.gross, pascal.gerber}@iese.fraunhofer.de

Abstract. With the increasing use of Artificial Intelligence (AI), the dependability of AI-based software components becomes a key factor, especially in the context of safety-critical applications. However, as current AI-based models are data-driven, there is an inherent uncertainty associated with their outcomes. Some in-model uncertainty quantification (UQ) approaches integrate techniques during model construction to obtain information about the uncertainties during inference, e.g., deep ensembles, but do not provide probabilistic guarantees. Two model-agnostic UQ approaches that both provide probabilistic guarantees are conformal prediction (CP), and uncertainty wrappers (UWs). Yet, they differentiate in the type of quantifications they provide. CP provides sets or regions containing the intended outcome with a given probability, UWs provide uncertainty estimates for point predictions. To investigate how well they perform compared to each other and a baseline in-model UQ approach, we provide a side-by-side comparison based on their key characteristics. Additionally, we introduce an approach combining UWs with CP. The UQ approaches are benchmarked with respect to point uncertainty estimates, and to prediction sets. Regarding point uncertainty estimates, the UW shows the best reliability as CP was not designed for this task. For the task of providing prediction sets, the combined approach of UWs with CP outperforms the other approaches with respect to adaptivity and conditional coverage.

Keywords: Dependable AI · Benchmarking Study · Traffic Sign Recognition · Automated Driving · Model Agnostic Uncertainty Estimation · Reliability

1 Introduction

The use of AI based on data-driven models (DDMs), particularly deep neural networks, has enabled significant improvements in perception tasks. The application of these models in safety-critical contexts poses challenges due to their hard-to-predict behavior. Especially, it cannot be guaranteed that a DDM provides the intended outcome for

© The Author(s), under exclusive license to Springer Nature Switzerland AG 2023
J. Guiochet et al. (Eds.): SAFECOMP 2023 Workshops, LNCS 14182, pp. 314–327, 2023.
https://doi.org/10.1007/978-3-031-40953-0_26

every possible input. To address this issue, dependable uncertainty quantification (UQ) approaches that provide statistical guarantees and that can be checked by experts for plausibility are required. In this paper, we compare three kinds of UQ approaches: in-model UQ, model-agnostic uncertainty wrappers (UWs) [1], and UQ using conformal prediction (CP) [2, 3]. In-model UQ is model-specific or applies specific UQ techniques when building the model. Resulting uncertainty estimates commonly do not provide statistical guarantees and are very difficult to verify due to the complexity of the underlying DDM. CP-based UQ is a popular alternative due to the promise of statistical guarantees and due to being applied as a post-processing step like calibration approaches [4]. A further alternative with statistical guarantees is the use of UWs, which explicitly address all three sources of uncertainty stated in the onion shell model [5] and can provide transparent estimates based on semantically interpretable factors.

To the best of our knowledge, there is not yet a comparison of the benefits and limitations of these approaches. Therefore, our research questions are:

RQ1 How do the characteristics of in-model, UW-based, and CP-based UQ approaches compare and what are their key differences?
RQ2 Can we combine the capabilities and strengths of UW and CP?
RQ3 How can the performance of in-model, UW, and CP-based UQ approaches be compared for (a) point uncertainty estimates and (b) prediction sets?

Our contributions to answering these questions include a list of characteristics comparing the different kinds of UQ approaches and a side-by-side comparison to discuss their key differences, a method to get prediction sets for UQ approaches designed for providing point uncertainty estimates, and a method to get point uncertainty estimates from CP. Applying the approaches on a traffic sign recognition DDM, we perform an empirical evaluation with metrics for both tasks, providing point uncertainty estimates and prediction sets. We propose a UQ approach that combines UW and CP to be inherently applicable for both tasks and compare its performance with the existing ones.

Overall, this paper aims to provide insights into the strengths and limitations of different approaches to quantify DDM uncertainty and to contribute to the development of more dependable and transparent models for safety-critical applications.

The paper is structured as follows: Sect. 2 provides background and related work on the investigated UQ approaches. Section 3 gives a structured comparison based on key characteristics. Section 4 introduces an approach to combining UW with CP. Section 5 describes the study design and execution. Section 6 presents and discusses the study results, and Sect. 7 concludes the paper.

2 Background and Related Work

This section outlines in-model UQ, outside-model UQ, as well as conformal prediction.

In-Model UQ. Often, UQ is integrated into the DDM itself. Certain classes of DDMs (e.g., logistic regression, Naïve Bayes, support vector machines) provide a numerical preference value along the outcome, which ranges from zero to one. For UQ, these values are commonly interpreted as probabilities, which we refer to as 'in-model' UQ and is limited as they are usually determined based on training data, thus tending to be overconfident. Calibration methods like isotonic regression can be applied to the preference values to counteract these limitations in a post-processing step [6].

Outside-Model UQ. An approach that follows the separation of concerns principle is the Uncertainty Wrapper (UW) [1, 7]. It considers the DDM as a black box and addresses all three sources of uncertainty considered in the onion shell model, which includes uncertainty related to model fit, input quality, and scope compliance [5].

The UW models input quality-related and scope-compliance-related factors in a quality and scope model, respectively. Within a traffic sign recognition use case, factors such as haze or motion blur, which can impair visibility, could constitute input-quality factors, while the location based on coordinates provided by GPS can be utilized as a scope factor indicating a DDM application outside its target application scope.

Using a decision-tree-based approach, the target application scope – we refer to as operational design domain (ODD) [8] in the following – is decomposed into areas of similar uncertainties (μODDs) based on the input-quality factors. The decision tree uses information from the input-quality factors as independent variables and the correctness of the DDM as the dependent variable. A leaf in the decision tree represents a μODD, which is associated with its respective uncertainty. Considering a requested statistical confidence level, the uncertainties of the μODDs can be safeguarded. In a separate model, the scope compliance model, the scope factors are evaluated to estimate the probability of the DDM being used outside its ODD.

Conformal Prediction. An approach to provide prediction sets or prediction regions for classification or regression tasks, respectively, is conformal prediction (CP). In the following, we focus on classification, where CP provides prediction sets containing the intended outcome with a requested level of certainty, given by a probability value, on average (cf. Marginal coverage). Based on a heuristic concept of uncertainty, a conformity score function ($s(x, y)$) must be defined, with larger scores representing larger conformity of an input x to the intended outcome y (i.e., class label). For classification neural networks, a naïve scoring might use the preference value for a specific class of the softmax layer, or alternatively, an adaptive prediction set (aps) scoring can be used, which considers additionally the classes that are considered as more likely being the intended class by the DDM based on the softmax values [3, 9].

Next, the conformity score function needs to be applied to calibration data. On the resulting scores, an empirical quantile $\hat{q}$ is determined for a requested level of certainty. To create a prediction set, all classes are added to the prediction set that have a conformity score higher or equal to $\hat{q}$.

3   Structured Comparison on UQ Approach in ML (RQ1)

In the following, we compare three classes of UQ approaches for DDM predictions with a focus on approaches with probabilistic or statistical guarantees. Figure 1 gives an overview of the data flow for each class of approaches with characteristics that help to structure our comparison of similarities and dissimilarities.

Input. In-model UQs are based on input the DDM uses for its predictions and are usually determined on the training dataset. Independent calibration data is needed if

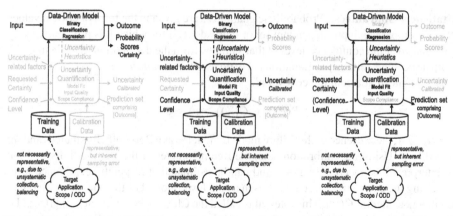

Fig. 1. Three variants of UQ. In-model predictions (left), uncertainty wrapper (middle) and conformal prediction (right) are compared.

a post-processing calibration is done. UWs are trained but not calibrated on training data. UW and CP both need calibration data. Input for the UW at runtime are quality factors (QFs). QFs can be derived from the DDM input as well as separate data sources. Additionally, a confidence level, at which the uncertainties are estimated, is specified for the UW. CP takes as input a conformity score which is commonly calculated based on outputs of the DDM. Additionally, an expected certainty is required for CP.

Outcome. Our working definition of uncertainty is the probability of a specific failure mode. The presence of a failure mode is modeled as a binary random variable, and the probability of the failure mode being present is the uncertainty. The outcome of in-model UQ is the uncertainty of the failure mode "the model prediction is incorrect". The outcome of the UW is also an uncertainty. However, the UW can be adapted for the UQ of any failure mode that can be derived from the model outcome. The CP outcome is a prediction set or region that is intended to cover the correct outcome on average with the probability specified by the requested certainty.

Separation of Concerns. In-model UQ is not separated from the DDM per definition. Modular subcomponents simplify the assurance of components with DDMs and reduce the risk of dependent failures. Therefore, the UW is designed to produce uncertainty estimates separately from the DDM. CP is applied separately after the DDM. However, the DDM outcome and their certainty are confounded in the CP outcome, which consists of a prediction set or interval.

Statistical Assumptions. In-model UQ does not provide formal guarantees. Softmax pseudo-probabilities, which they commonly provide, can be overconfident. The application of isotonic regression can improve the reliability of the estimated probabilities. However, it also does not provide formal guarantees for their correctness. Statistical guarantees for a random variable $\mathbb{Y}$ require several statistical assumptions. For both, CP and UW, it is assumed that the datapoints are stochastically independent and identically distributed (iid) [3], which can be relaxed to only require the weaker exchangeability [2] condition.

Statistical Guarantees. Probabilistic guarantees are given in the form of critical values that encompass an input-dependent set or interval $C(\mathbb{X})$ for which it is probabilistically guaranteed at the confidence level cl that samples from the distribution of $\mathbb{Y}$ lie in $C(\mathbb{X})$ with a specified certainty c. Equation (1) expresses that a *marginal coverage* at certainty c is guaranteed at a confidence level cl.

$$P(P(\mathbb{Y} \in C(\mathbb{X})) \geq c) \geq cl \qquad (1)$$

For the UW, the presence of the failure mode is modeled as a Bernoulli distributed random variable $\mathbb{Y}$. Using the calibration data, the free parameter of the Bernoulli distribution is interpreted as uncertainty $1 - c$ and can be estimated at a specific confidence level cl. Using the calibration data, c is chosen as the lower bound of the one-sided binomial confidence interval $C(\mathbb{X})$. This interval is called the Clopper-Pearson interval [10] and it can be calculated exactly using the respective binomial distribution. Formal guarantees can also be calculated for CP. The inclusion of the true label in the prediction set C is also modeled as a Bernoulli distributed random variable $\mathbb{Y}$. The free parameter of the Bernoulli distribution is interpreted as the certainty c that CP receives as input. Using the Beta distribution as the conjugate prior for the free parameter of the Bernoulli distribution a cl confidence interval for the certainty c of CP predictions can be calculated [3]. Reducing the specified certainty c to reflect this error margin at a specified confidence level cl could lead to strict marginal statistical guarantees on the correctness of the prediction sets. Although theoretically possible, this approach is not commonly applied [4].

A stronger statistical guarantee is the *conditional coverage* at confidence level cl

$$P(P(\mathbb{Y} \in C(\mathbb{X})|\mathbb{X}) \geq c) \geq cl \qquad (2)$$

Hereby we require that $\mathbb{Y}$ lies within the confidence interval $C(\mathbb{X})$ at certainty c not just on average but for all possible input conditions $\mathbb{X}$. In practice, this condition is hardly achievable. However, partial conditional coverage can be achieved by focusing only on selected input conditions. The UW uses QFs to identify input regions [1]. Thereby, a weaker form of conditional coverage with the respective input region as conditions is achieved. Within each of these regions, still, only marginal coverage can be guaranteed.

Evaluation. Different metrics are required for the evaluation of the different UQ outcome types. Considering uncertainty estimates as probabilities, they can be evaluated with the Brier score and its components [11, 12]. Furthermore, overconfidence measures the validity of the uncertainty predictions [13]. For the evaluation of prediction sets, different metrics are required. CP is mainly evaluated using metrics for efficiency, adaptivity, and validity of the prediction sets [3].

Considered Uncertainty Types. There are several sources of uncertainty in DDM predictions: model fit, input quality, and scope compliance [5]. The UW was explicitly created to address all three sources [1]. Monitoring of scope compliance is not possible for in-model predictions from DDMs trained only on data from the ODD. Some CP methods allow for the monitoring of scope compliance because empty prediction sets can indicate outliers in the conformity score and model out-of-scope application.

Interpretability. Dependability and assurance of DDMs require interpretability. A verifiable UQ approach should use a transparent model [14] for UQ. The interpretability of in-model UQ depends on the transparency of the specific DDM. Since black box models are very common, this property is usually not fulfilled. CP is interpretable in terms of the generation of the outcomes. It can be explained and visualized using histograms. However, the generation of the softmax outcomes of black box models, which are often used to build conformity scores, is not semantically interpretable. The UW uses a transparent decision tree model with limited depth for the generation of its outcomes. The inputs to the decision tree are semantically understandable QFs. Therefore, UQs from UWs are humanly understandable and can easily be verified by experts.

DDM Task. The suitability of the compared methods varies depending on the task of the DDM. In-model UQ and UW are suitable for binary and multiclass classification tasks. For continuous variables, in-model UQ is rather uncommon since most regression models are not suited for UQ. To apply the UW for regression DDMs, a binary failure mode needs to be derived from the continuous DDM outcome. CP is most suitable for regression tasks since the prediction sets form meaningful intervals. Additionally, it can be applied to classification tasks. However, in the case of binary classification, the prediction sets are not very informative.

Uncertainty Handling. While there is a lot of research with a focus on UQ, the handling of the outcome of these methods currently receives less attention. It is often unclear how prediction sets and point uncertainty estimates should be treated on the system level. Handling of uncertainty estimates is applied for dynamic risk management [15], and corresponding software architecture patterns [16] were proposed.

4 UWccp: Uncertainty Wrapper with Conditional Conformal Predictions (RQ2)

As shown in our comparison, UWs are not intended to provide set predictions but transparent and situation-aware uncertainties for a given DDM outcome. On the other hand, the key purpose of CP is to provide prediction sets with marginal coverage guarantees based on a given certainty requirement, but it is not directly applicable to get uncertainty estimates for a single DDM outcome or binary decision. To provide a more universal UQ approach, we propose a hybrid named *uncertainty wrapper for conditional conformal predictions* (UWccp). The approach builds on the UW framework [7] by extending the decision tree (DT) approach that is used to derive input quality-related uncertainties. As illustrated in Fig. 2, for each leaf of the DT, which can be understood as an individual μODD, the UWccp uses the subset of data points in the calibration dataset that satisfy the criteria of the leaf for two complementary purposes: (a) determine an uncertainty estimate for a given point prediction with conditional probabilistic guarantees considering the leaf criteria as proposed in the UW framework, i.e., how UQs are commonly determined using UWs, and (b) determine a prediction set C using CP on a requested certainty c with conformity scoring heuristic s.

From CP, additionally, a point uncertainty estimate can also be derived as the maximum certainty for which the prediction set contains only one class.

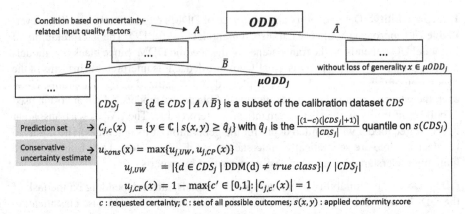

Fig. 2. The quality impact model of UWccp can provide both prediction sets and uncertainties.

There are two key advantages beyond the isolated application of UW and CP. First, when we determine *prediction sets* on a requested certainty, we can use the disjunct decomposition of the ODD into μODDs provided by the DT leaves to give, instead of marginal coverage guarantees for the provided prediction sets over the overall ODD, conditional probabilistic guarantees considering individual μODD. For example, if the DT separates between situations with and without haze, the prediction sets will not only be valid on average over all kinds of situations but conditional for both situations, with and without haze. Second, when determining the uncertainty of a DDM outcome, we can get *conservative uncertainty estimates* u_{cons}, which are less likely conditionally overconfident. We get them by considering the larger of both uncertainty values, the one estimated by the UW considering relevant quality factors (u_{UW}) and the one additionally considering the conformity score (u_{CP}). u_{CP} is derived from CP considering the subset of calibration data points associated with the leaf (cf. Figure 2).

5 Study Design and Execution

This chapter describes the study design, including the study context and datasets, and explains the study execution, including DDM construction, considered UQ approaches, and evaluation metrics.

Context. In our use case, the DDM is tasked with correctly classifying traffic signs on images. The ODD of the DDM is 'roadworthy passenger cars driving on German streets under different operating conditions like rain or dirt on the camera lens'. The interest in this study is on investigating the uncertainty quantification associated with the DDM outcome, not on the performance of the DDM with respect to its primary outcome.

Datasets. We use *training data* to build the DDM and differentiate between degrees of uncertainty associated with different μODDs, *calibration data* to quantify uncertainties without bias, and representative *test data* to evaluate the UQ approaches. Our datasets are based on the datasets from the German Traffic Sign Recognition Benchmark (GTSRB) [17], containing images of traffic signs together with their ground truth sign types.

To provide further information on factors that might influence the uncertainty (e.g., weather), we augmented the GTSRB data with selected realistic quality deficits using the data augmentation framework described in [18]. We considered 9 types of quality deficits in varying intensities: rain, darkness, haze, natural backlight, artificial backlight, dirt on the traffic sign, dirt on the sensor lens, steamed-up sensor lens, and motion blur. For further information on the generated augmented datasets, see [13].

DDM Training and Calibration. The DDM uses a convolutional neural network based on [19] in a variant, which is described in [13]. For in-model UQ, the DDM was calibrated on the calibration data by applying the scikit-learn implementation of Isotonic Regression as an optional post-processing step.

UQ Approaches. We consider the UQ approaches that were compared in Sect. 3 and the combined method from Sect. 4. This paper focuses on UQ approaches providing some kind of statistical guarantees. A detailed comparison of uncertainty wrappers with calibration and deep ensembles can be found in [13].

As an in-model UQ approach, we consider one minus the preference values from the softmax layer of the DDM as uncertainties (*softmax uncal*). An optional calibration step transforms these pseudo-probabilities into more reliable prediction probabilities (*softmax isotonic*). For *CP*, we examine *naïve* and *aps* conformity scoring, respectively. The calibration scores are determined on the calibration data. We built an *UW* using only *semantic* quality factors, i.e., all nine types of augmented deficits, and the size of the traffic sign image. The decision tree used by the UW was trained on the training data with no pruning. After training, the leaf uncertainties were calibrated on the calibration data and all leaves containing less than 500 calibration data points were pruned. The UW considers a confidence level of 0.9999. A scope compliance model was not included as we focus on the input quality-related uncertainty in this study and all data points are considered inside the ODD. For *UWccp*, we use the UW with semantic quality factors and enhance its decision tree leaves with conformal predictors as described in Sect. 4, which either use *naïve* or *aps* scoring.

UQ Tasks. We differentiate between two types of UQ tasks: For single-valued outcomes of the DDM (i.e., point predictions), UQs are provided in the form of estimates on the possibility that the DDM outcome is not the intended outcome, i.e., *uncertainty estimation (T1)*. For a requested certainty of 0.95 and 0.99, *prediction sets (T2)* are provided that include the intended outcome on average with the probability given by the requested certainty.

Regarding T1, we use the (calibrated) softmax-based UQ as well as the UW-based uncertainty estimates. To compare CP, we consider the largest certainty for which the prediction set is a singleton to estimate the uncertainty. For UWccp, we only consider the conservative estimates as they are more relevant in a safety-critical context.

For T2, the prediction sets provided by CP and UWccp are considered. To compare the in-model UQ (i.e., softmax uncal and isotonic), prediction sets are constructed by adding classes to the set that are associated with high softmax values (in descending order) until the sum of their softmax values reaches the requested certainty. The UW is not considered for T2.

Evaluation of UQs. The performance in *T1 (uncertainty estimation)* is evaluated using the Brier score (*bs*) as a measure of the mean squared difference between the predicted outcome probability and the actual outcome [11]. Using variance (*var*), resolution (*res*), and unreliability (*unr*), the *bs* can be decomposed with $bs = var - res + unr$ [12]. Hereby, *var* solely depends on the error rate of the DDM. The extent to which case-specific uncertainty estimates differ from the overall uncertainty is expressed by *res*. As *var* is bounding the values of *res*, and high values of *res* are preferred, we define *unspecificity* as $var - res$. The calibration quality of the uncertainty estimates on the observed error rate of the DDM is described by unreliability (*unr*). Lower values are preferred, as they are associated with high reliability. To measure the part of unreliability which is caused by underestimating the actually observed error rate, we defined *overconfidence* [13].

To evaluate the performance in *T2 (set predictions)*, we considered *validity, efficiency, adaptivity,* and *conditional coverage*. *Validity* is examined by calculating the proportion of test data for which the prediction set contains the intended outcome, which should be close to the requested certainty. *Efficiency* assesses the informative use of prediction sets, which is high when only a small number of classes are contained therein. For the evaluation, average and median set sizes were calculated. *Adaptivity* assesses the degree to which prediction sets vary in their size. Here, we evaluated the variance of the set sizes. A high adaptivity is desired as we intend to provide smaller prediction sets for easier DDM inputs and larger sets for harder inputs. Lastly, we evaluated (partial) *conditional coverage*, which is a stronger property than the marginal coverage that CP ensures. The partial conditional coverage consists of evaluating the coverage for subsets on the test data [2, 3]. We considered the subsets of the test dataset in which a certain quality factor is present and the subsets constituted by the 69 district μODDs identified from the decision tree approach considering all quality factor.

6   Study Results and Discussion

This section presents and discusses evaluation results obtained for RQ3a and RQ3b.

6.1   Evaluation of Point Uncertainty Estimates (RQ3a)

We compare UQ approaches concerning T1 using the Brier score and its components.

The unreliability component can be further examined using the reliability plot in Fig. 3. As Table 1 shows, the softmax-based approaches provide good Brier scores, but with high unreliability, overconfidence, and no statistical guarantees. The softmax calibrated with isotonic regression performs slightly better. CP can theoretically be applied to get uncertainties for point estimates, yet the Brier score is not as good, and the reliability is low. Although CP provides statistical guarantees for prediction sets, they do not hold when applying the approach to determine point uncertainty estimates (cf. Corresponding curves in Fig. 3).

The UW with semantic quality factors has a worse degree of unspecificity, but instead a high reliability and low overconfidence. Moreover, we get statistical guarantees for uncertainty on point estimates. The UWccp still provides statistical guarantees due to the conservative way of combining uncertainty estimates as described in Sect. 4. Please

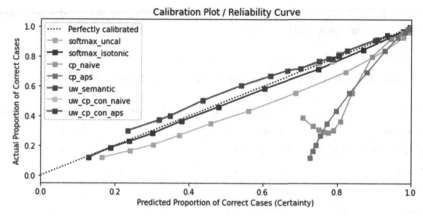

Fig. 3. Reliability plot showing the over- and underconfidence of uncertainty estimates for different approaches. Sorted certainty estimates (1-uncertainty) are grouped into quantiles and plotted against their actual correctness. Points below the line indicate overconfidence. Curves for the semantic UW strongly overlap with *UWccp* for *naïve* scoring and is identical for *aps*.

Table 1. Study results on the performance of UQ approaches for point uncertainty estimates.

Approach	Brier Score	Variance	Unspecificity	Unreliability	Overconfidence
Softmax uncal	.09481	.19946	.00164	.09317	.06087
Softmax isotonic	.09049	.19553	.00001	.09048	.04534
CP naïve	.17531	.19946	.07003	.10528	.10332
CP aps	.17209	.19946	.06103	.11106	.10971
UW semantic	.16489	.19946	.16339	.00150	.0
UWccp cons naïve	.16484	.19946	.16046	.00438	.00212
UWccp cons aps	.16489	.19946	.16339	.00150	.0

note, that the UWccp with aps scoring provides the same uncertainty estimates as the UW without extension as $u_{UW} \geq u_{CP}$ for all test data. The UWccp versions provide better overall performance than pure CP versions.

6.2 Evaluation of Prediction Sets (RQ3b)

For T2, we consider *validity* by investigating coverage for a requested certainty of 0.95 and 0.99, as well as *efficiency* by average and median set size. *Adaptivity* is considered by the variance in the set size. *Conditional coverage* is examined for the presence of QFs in isolation and for 69 distinct μODDs based on the decomposition of the complete ODD provided by the semantic UW.

Validity. As Table 2 shows, the coverages for both requested certainties are quite well for most investigated approaches. Only using the uncalibrated softmax results in a relevant difference between requested certainty and marginal coverage on the test dataset (0.008 and 0.014 less than expected).

Table 2. Study results on the performance of UQ approaches for prediction sets.

Approach	Certainty	Coverage	Set Size Avg.	Set Size Median	Set Size Variance
Softmax uncal	.95	.94234	4.30	1	30.15
Softmax isotonic	.95	.97470	5.96	1	53.38
CP naïve	.95	.95047	4.43	1	25.85
CP aps	.95	.95032	4.65	1	35.45
UWccp naïve	.95	.94995	4.83	1	42.58
UWccp aps	.95	.95055	4.99	1	46.89
Softmax uncal	.99	.97559	6.30	1	62.82
Softmax isotonic	.99	.99348	8.86	3	97.96
CP naïve	.99	.99070	8.36	3	96.89
CP aps	.99	.99074	8.58	3	102.06
UWccp naïve	.99	.99173	8.66	3	105.35
UWccp aps	.99	.99161	8.76	2	107.55

Efficiency. Average and median set size grows with determined coverage. In general, there is a tradeoff between average set size and adaptivity, i.e., the ability to vary set size in relation to the degree of uncertainty that is expected for a specific prediction [3].

Adaptivity. Variance in set sizes increases when using aps instead of naïve scoring, as well as the UWccp version instead of the plain CP version. Using softmax without calibration results in a rather low variance compared to the other approaches.

Conditional Coverage. As shown in Fig. 4 (left), for a requested certainty of 0.95, both UWccp appear stable for most QFs. Yet, for darkness and even more for rain, there is a drop in coverage that leads to overconfidence. The calibrated softmax – although providing no statistical guarantees – reaches a higher than requested coverage for each quality factor. Other approaches, especially the uncalibrated softmax, appear systematically overconfident for almost all investigated QFs. For a requested certainty of 0.99, the variation in conditional coverage caused by different QFs appears insignificant for all approaches except for the uncalibrated softmax. Based on Fig. 4 (right), conditional coverage concerning μODDs seems mostly stable for both UWccps. Calibrated softmax appears to be underconfident for most but the most difficult μODDs for which it gets overconfident. Strong overconfidence can be observed for the other approaches in case of a requested certainty of 0.95. In general, we observe increasing overconfidence with an increasing error rate for the μODD. The uncalibrated softmax is systematically overconfident with requested certainty of 0.99.

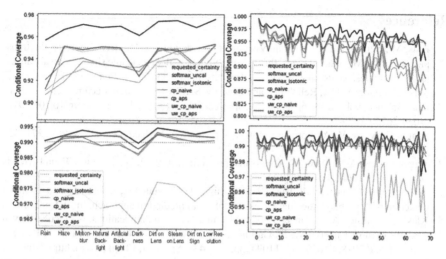

Fig. 4. Conditional coverage for different approaches wrt. Presence of quality factors (left), and 69 distinct μODDs (right), with requested certainty of 0.95 (top), and 0.99 (bottom). The μODDs are ordered by increasing error rate of the DDM on the test data.

7 Conclusion

We compared UQ approaches, which provide statistical guarantees, i.e., CP and UWs, with baseline in-model UQ approaches without statistical guarantees. Further, we introduced a hybrid model of UWs with CP (UWccp), combining the benefits of both approaches. Our study focused on the UQ tasks of providing (a) uncertainty estimates for point predictions, and (b) prediction sets for the use case of traffic sign recognition.

To summarize our conclusions on the research questions: CP and UW approaches were designed for different UQ tasks. For *providing point uncertainty estimates*, UWs or conservative UWccps perform best regarding reliability and overconfidence, which are relevant in a safety-critical context. The softmax-based approaches reach a better overall Brier score but are not suited for safety-critical applications as they do not provide statistical guarantees and perform poorly regarding reliability and overconfidence. Despite CP providing statistical guarantees for prediction sets, they do not hold for point uncertainty estimates as reflected by their poor performance for reliability and overconfidence.

For the task of *providing prediction sets*, most investigated approaches reach good coverage. Concerning adaptivity of set sizes, aps is more adaptive than naïve scoring, and UWccp is more adaptive than CP. UWccp versions and the calibrated softmax-based approach seem to provide stable conditional coverage.

In the future, we want to consider regression tasks. Further topics concern using CP for out-of-distribution detection, and uncertainty handling.

Acknowledgments. Parts of this work have been funded by the project "LOPAAS" as part of the internal funding program "ICON" of the Fraunhofer-Gesellschaft, and by the Federal Ministry for Economic Affairs and Energy in the project "SPELL".

References

1. Kläs, M., Sembach, L.: Uncertainty wrappers for data-driven models – increase the transparency of AI/ML-based models through enrichment with dependable situation-aware uncertainty estimates. In: Romanovsky, A., Troubitsyna, E., Gashi, I., Schoitsch, E., Bitsch, F. (eds.) Computer Safety, Reliability, and Security. SAFECOMP 2019. Lecture Notes in Computer Science, vol. 11699, pp. 358–364. Springer, Cham (2019). https://doi.org/10.1007/978-3-030-26250-1_29
2. Shafer, G., Vovk, V.: A tutorial on conformal prediction. J. Mach. Learn. Res. **9**(3), 371–421 (2008)
3. Angelopoulos, A.N., Bates, S.: Conformal prediction: A gentle introduction. Found. Trends Mach. Learn. **16**(4), 494–591 (2023)
4. de Grancey, F., Jean-Luc, A., Alecu, L., Gerchinovitz, S., Mamalet, F., Vigouroux, D.: Object detection with probabilistic guarantees: a conformal prediction approach. In: WAISE (2022)
5. Kläs, M., Vollmer, A.M.: Uncertainty in Machine Learning Applications: A Practice-Driven Classification of Uncertainty. In: Gallina, B., Skavhaug, A., Schoitsch, E., Bitsch, F. (eds.) SAFECOMP 2018. LNCS, vol. 11094, pp. 431–438. Springer, Cham (2018). https://doi.org/10.1007/978-3-319-99229-7_36
6. Guo, C., Pleiss, G., Sun, Y., Weinberger, K.: On calibration of modern neural networks. In: ICML (2017)
7. Kläs, M., Jöckel, L.: A framework for building uncertainty wrappers for AI/ML-based data-driven components. In: Casimiro, A., Ortmeier, F., Schoitsch, E., Bitsch, F., Ferreira, P. (eds.) SAFECOMP 2020. LNCS, vol. 12235, pp. 315–327. Springer, Cham (2020). https://doi.org/10.1007/978-3-030-55583-2_23
8. Koopman, P., Osyk, B., Weast, J.: Autonomous vehicles meet the physical world: RSS, variability, uncertainty, and proving safety. In: Romanovsky, A., Troubitsyna, E., Bitsch, F. (eds.) Computer Safety, Reliability, and Security. SAFECOMP 2019. Lecture Notes in Computer Science, vol. 11698, pp. 245–253. Springer, Cham (2019). https://doi.org/10.1007/978-3-030-26601-1_17
9. Amoukou, S.I., Brunel, N.J.B.: Adaptive conformal prediction by reweighting nonconformity score. arXiv:2303.12695 (2023)
10. Clopper, C.J., Pearson, E.S.: The use of confidence or fiducial limits illustrated in the case of the binomial. Biometrika **26**(4), 404–413 (1934)
11. Brier, G.W.: Verification of forecasts expressed in terms of probability. Mon. Weather Rev. **78**(1), 1–3 (1950)
12. Murphy, A.H.: A new vector partition of the probability score. J. Appl. Meteorol. **12**(4), 595–600 (1973)
13. Jöckel, L., Kläs, M.: Could we relieve AI/ML models of the responsibility of providing dependable uncertainty estimates? A study on outside-model uncertainty estimates. In: Habli, I., Sujan, M., Bitsch, F. (eds.) Computer Safety, Reliability, and Security. SAFECOMP 2021. Lecture Notes in Computer Science, vol. 12852, pp. 18–33. Springer, Cham (2021). https://doi.org/10.1007/978-3-030-83903-1_2
14. Arrieta, A.B., et al.: Explainable artificial intelligence (XAI): concepts, taxonomies, opportunities and challenges toward responsible AI. Inf. Fusion **58**, 82–115 (2020)
15. Kläs, M., Adler, R., Sorokos, I., Jöckel, L., Reich, J.: Handling uncertainties of data-driven models in compliance with safety constraints for autonomous behaviour. In: EDDC (2021)
16. Groß, J., Adler, R., Kläs, M., Reich, J., Jöckel, L., Gansch, R.: Architectural patterns for handling runtime uncertainty of data-driven models in safety-critical perception. In: Trapp, M., Saglietti, F., Spisländer, M., Bitsch, F. (eds.) Computer Safety, Reliability, and Security. SAFECOMP 2022. Lecture Notes in Computer Science, vol. 13414, pp. 284–297. Springer, Cham (2022). https://doi.org/10.1007/978-3-031-14835-4_19

17. German Traffic Sign Benchmarks. http://benchmark.ini.rub.de/?section=gtsrb. Accessed 11 May 2023
18. Jöckel, L., Kläs, M.: Increasing trust in data-driven model validation – a framework for probabilistic augmentation of images and meta-data generation using application scope characteristics. In: Romanovsky, A., Troubitsyna, E., Bitsch, F. (eds.) Computer Safety, Reliability, and Security. SAFECOMP 2019. Lecture Notes in Computer Science, vol. 11698, pp. 155–164. Springer, Cham (2019). https://doi.org/10.1007/978-3-030-26601-1_11
19. Arcos-García, Á., Alvarez-Garcia, J., Soria Morillo, L.: Deep neural network for traffic sign recognition systems: an analysis of spatial transformers and stochastic optimisation methods. Neural Netw. **99**, 158–165 (2018)

AIMOS: Metamorphic Testing of AI - An Industrial Application

Augustin Lemesle[1]([✉]), Aymeric Varasse[1], Zakaria Chihani[1],
and Dominique Tachet[2]

[1] Université Paris-Saclay, CEA, List, 91120 Palaiseau, France
{augustin.lemesle,aymeric.varasse,zakaria.chihani}@cea.fr
[2] Production Engineering Industrial System Renault, 78280 Guyancourt, France
dominique.tachet@renault.com

Abstract. In this paper, we present the AIMOS tool as well as the results of its application to industrial use cases. Relying on the widely used Metamorphic testing paradigm, we show how the process of verification and validation can benefit from the early testing of models' robustness to perturbations stemming from the intended operational domain.

Keywords: metamorphism · testing · artificial intelligence · neural networks · support-vector machines · verification and validation

1 Introduction

Advocating for the added value of AI in many industrial applications is becoming as unnecessary as justifying the usefulness of computer science itself. Indeed, while the jury is still out on the future of some aspects such as Artificial General Intelligence, the stakeholders in general and the AI community in particular seem convinced that AI winters are a thing of the past. As a matter of fact, the recent developments, particularly in the subfield related to Neural Networks (NN), have shown a phenomenal ability to assist humans in numerous, albeit specific, tasks such as image recognition and some limited forms of command and control.

While the efficiency in these tasks is far from sufficient to completely replace all existing systems, they can still be of great value as subcomponents in more traditional cyber-physical systems such as vehicles and electronic devices. In some of these systems, reliability is more than a desirable feature, it can be a critical *sine qua non* for the adoption of an AI-based component. This makes any method and tool able to aid in the verification and validation process a necessary commodity to ensure, on top of its accuracy, the reliability of an AI model in different scenarios.

In this paper, we report on one such tool, AIMOS, specialized in metamorphic testing for AI, and its application on two industrial use cases.

J. Guiochet et al. (Eds.): SAFECOMP 2023 Workshops, LNCS 14182, pp. 328–340, 2023.
https://doi.org/10.1007/978-3-031-40953-0_27

1.1   Our Contribution

Our contributions can be summed up by the following:

1. We propose a tool to assess the stability of an AI system on a given dataset based on the specification and the test of metamorphic properties without the need of a labelling process.
2. We provide a model-agnostic tool that implements and automates the entire process of applying these metamorphic properties on the inputs and outputs of an AI model, and of comparing and compiling the result of the subsequent test into a stability score which can then be presented in a graphical way.
3. We apply our method and tool to two industrial use cases with different metamorphic properties to show their usefulness.

1.2   Related Work

Invented by T.Y. Chen and others in a technical report in 1998, later republished [2], metamorphic testing was then applied to many domains, from embedded systems [15] to bioinformatics [10], including machine learning [4]. A comprehensive survey [11] of these applications was conducted, closely followed by another [3], this time by the original authors.

As traditional testing methods are inherently limited when applied to machine learning models, metamorphic testing has been considered as a viable alternative, particularly for critical uses of AI-based components. One of the predominant use case where metamorphic testing has been used is autonomous driving, with [5], which focuses on identifying what is defined as implementation bugs in machine learning based applications, [14] and [16] that concentrate on deep neural networks for autonomous driving and [17] that uses metamorphic testing on Apollo (Baidu's self-driving vehicles on-board software).

From there, various other use cases have also been tackled, such as autonomous drones, in [9], where metamorphic testing is used in combination with model based testing to test autonomous drones. Another use case is neural machine translation (NMT) models, where in [7], another metamorphic testing approach is proposed, called structure-invariant testing, specially designed for NMT models. In [13] mutation is combined with metamorphic testing to detect inconsistency bugs in NMT models, to provide tests for real-world machine learning translation models and repair the mistranslations found during the testing phase.

While also based on metamorphic properties, and more specifically on geometric transformations, the work in [1], specific to neural networks, tries to formally verify a neural network against these metamorphic transformations. By computing linear relaxations for these transformations, they are able to prove, by using external formal verification tools, the robustness of the model around a set of selected inputs.

Overall, while there are plenty methods and tools to apply metamorphic testing to AI models, all of them have been designed either for a specific use case or for a specific technology (*e.g.* deep neural networks built with Keras), and therefore they lack adaptability for other AI systems or metamorphic properties.

In contrast to these methods, the tool presented here is self-sufficient, does not rely on other provers and is completely task agnostic (classification, control-command, detection, ...). In a sense, AIMOS allows to rapidly test a much larger set of inputs in a much shorter time, which offers a simple and rapid early problem detection mechanism. In layman's terms, our testing is useful to cover a much larger ground surface, detecting unwanted mines, so to speak, with little cost and in little time, whereas the formal verification techniques such that of [1] can verify at a much deeper level a much smaller space.

2   Background

2.1   AI in This Document

As the aim of AIMOS is to be as agnostic as possible of the AI model used, the necessary background to understand it and the work presented in this paper is henceforth quite small. In this document, we simply consider any type of AI model to be a function $p : \mathcal{X} \to \mathcal{Y}$ with $\mathcal{X}$ its input space and $\mathcal{Y}$ its output space. We call this function the inference function of the AI model. In that sense, we consider any AI model such as Neural Networks, Support Vector Machines (SVM), Decision Trees, ... as a black box to be tested by AIMOS. The inherent specificities of each model type will not impact our testing procedure.

2.2   Metamorphic Property

Simply stated, the main idea behind metamorphic testing is that certain relationships (*e.g.*, R_1, R_2) on some inputs (*e.g.*, a, b, c) should induce, in a sound software S, other relationships (*e.g.*, R_1', R_2') on the outputs. For example:

$$\forall a, b, c, R_1(a, b) \wedge R_2(b, c) \to R_1'(S(a), S(b)) \vee R_2'(S(b), S(c))$$

Consider the most common example: a software S that computes the minimal cost of travel between two points, a and b, in an undirected graph. Even if the actual result of this operation is not known, it is possible to generate an arbitrary number of tests using the knowledge that the result should be impervious to symmetry. Here, the relation between the inputs (a, b) and (b, a) is the symmetry, and the relationship on the outputs $S(a, b)$ and $S(b, a)$ is the equality. Such a process can be considered a generalization of the data translations techniques mentioned above (rotations, flip, *etc.*,), since they can all be mathematically described, making them a subset of metamorphic properties. Crucially, focusing on metamorphic properties opens the possibility of more general data generation. Indeed, the relationships can be more complex. Consider an evolution S' of the software S above, that takes as input a point of origin o and a list L of points and computes the lowest cost for package delivery to all of them and come back to the origin. One can generate numerous partitions of L into lists $L_1, L_2, ...,$

and the sum of the results of calls $S'(o, L_i)$ should be greater or equal than the result of $S'(o, L)$. (For the mathematically inclined: $\forall L_1, \ldots, L_n, L = \bigoplus_{i=1}^{n} L_i \rightarrow S'(o, L) \leq \sum_{i=1}^{n} S'(o, L_i)$, where $\bigoplus$ is the list concatenation).

A metamorphic property will rely on the following set of functions:

- the input transformation $f_i : \mathcal{X} \rightarrow \mathcal{X}$, (*e.g.*, if f_i is used for R_1 above, then $f_i(a) = b$)
- the output transformation $f_o : \mathcal{Y} \rightarrow \mathcal{Y}$,
- and the inference transformation $f_{pred} : (\mathcal{X} \rightarrow \mathcal{Y}) \rightarrow (\mathcal{X} \rightarrow \mathcal{Y})$.

In that definition, f_i will be a transformation on the input space. This can be seen as a function that produces a perturbation on the inputs, either through adversarial attacks, symmetries, rotations, noise, ... Similarly, f_o represents the expected transformation on the outputs which could be the identity (*e.g.*, when checking for an unchanged classification), a symmetry, *etc.* These two functions are completed by a transformation on the inference function of the model, as this function can also depend on the setting (see the ACAS Xu use case in Sect. 5.3). We note $p' = f_{pred}(p)$ to ease the notation, most of the time, however, f_{pred} will be the identity function as we infer the result keeping the same function. This function only targets specific use case with multiple decision models. From there, this metamorphic property can be applied to any given subset of $\mathcal{X}$ and a model as defined by its inference function $p(x)$.

3   Metamorphic Testing

As mentioned, our approach aims at testing a given AI model on a dataset using metamorphic properties. As such, we present a tool named AIMOS, standing for AI Metamorphism Observing Software. This approach and tool are black-box as we do not use in any way the intrinsic characteristics of an AI model, we are treating the model as an inference function.

Our approach with AIMOS improves the usual approaches which only test a model against a perturbation without considering potential change to the output. Indeed, a transformation on the input space can also be linked to a transformation on the output space, *e.g.*, a symmetry on the input can mean a symmetry on the outputs as well (*e.g.*, a left arrow becoming a right arrow). A rough schema of the principle behind AIMOS is shown in Fig. 1.

AIMOS is implemented in Python as it is the most commonly used language for AI nowadays to allow an easy interface with numerous AI frameworks, such as TensorFlow/Keras, PyTorch, scikit-learn, and others. By default, AIMOS supports different format for inputs (*e.g.*, .png, .jpg, .csv, *etc.*) and for models (.h5, .pb, .onnx, .nnet) and implements different classical metamorphic properties (rotation, noise, symmetry, *etc.*,). It can be easily extended with specific loader or properties with simple Python functions.

Figure 2 shows an example configuration file of AIMOS to launch a simple test on CIFAR-10 easily. AIMOS aims to allow the user to provide a more flexible and complete framework for property testing thus specific efforts were made in

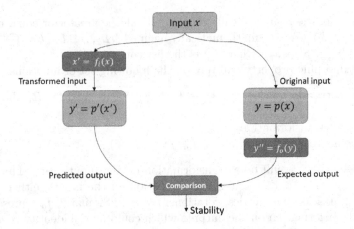

Fig. 1. AIMOS' principle

order to simplify the various APIs in AIMOS such as this config file. In the same figure we show a simple developed graphical interface for AIMOS, once again to ease its usage.

Fig. 2. AIMOS user interfaces: a configuration file (left) and its GUI (right)

As we are agnostic of the model type used, AIMOS can compare different types of models or architectures and, in turn, provide incentives for a choice between one type or another. As such, this permits comparisons between similar models types but with different architectures (*e.g.,* one Convolution vs two Convolution layers) but also between very different architectures (*e.g.,* Neural Networks vs SVMs vs Decision Trees) in similar settings, or also of simply differently trained models.

The aim of this approach is to rapidly and widely test a given AI model on a given dataset. This testing can serve to exhibit inefficiencies of the models, compare them to gauge the most stable ones, *etc.* Thus, while being far from a panacea for validation (but, indeed, no tool can pretend to that status) AIMOS can be an important part of an AI development process, providing a framework to facilitate and automate a rapid testing procedure. The metamorphic properties themselves, as part of the testing procedure, should be carefully selected to provide a good criterion of evaluation for the model when tested with AIMOS. For instance, if the problem represented by the AI model does not present any axe of symmetry, it would be of little value to test it against that.

4   Use Cases

4.1   Welding Use Case

The first use case considered for the testing of AIMOS is the control of the conformity of welds of rear axles on a vehicle production line of Renault at a factory in Le Mans. This control is realized by the analysis of the image of the weld by an algorithm which has been trained on weld images labelled by a professional operator.

In Renault's quality process, the need was expressed to test the performance of the algorithm beyond its accuracy. To assist in this task, test cases have to be defined in which the initial test images will be degraded following some specific criteria. These degradations were selected by Renault by analyzing their Operational Design Domain (ODD) for this system. Defined initially in the context of autonomous vehicles in the standard J3016, ODD can be extended to any autonomous system such as this algorithm. Therefore, the ODD defines the operating conditions under which a given system is designed to function, including, but not limited to, environmental, geographical, and time-of-day restrictions, and any other characteristic of interest.

In Fig. 3, we can see the result of Renault's context analysis on the problem with both the fixed input parameters (AD) and the ODD parameters to take into account for testing.

Renault aims to gauge with AIMOS the performance of a given AI model on degraded images but also to define the tolerance of the system with a confidence indicator. This tolerance will then be used in collaboration with other works in the monitoring of each characteristic of the ODD. Indeed, it is worth repeating that such metamorphic testing is far from being a comprehensive answer to all validation processes, and the properties it tests are not the be-all and end-all of safety assurances. But such a process remains an essential part of software validation and its extension to AI is actively pursued by industrial and academic actors alike.

	Image	
1	Dimension	AD
2	Size	AD
3	Blur	ODD
4	Colorimetry	ODD
5	Rotation	ODD
6	Translation	ODD
7	Transport noise	ODD
8	Number of colors (RGB)	AD
9	Transparency (A)	AD
10	Image format	AD
11	Histogram	ODD
12	Zone of interest	ODD

Fig. 3. Operation Design Domain on the Welding use case from Renault

Two models are currently being used by Renault depending empirically on where they achieve the best results:

– Models generated automatically through Google's AutoML framework.

– Specific models created by data scientists at Renault internal research and development lab, henceforth named RD.

These models have different architectures. The AutoML models are using a succession of 52 convolution layers including 17 depth-wise convolution and some residual connections. The RD models are built by combining a pre-trained mobilenet-v1 neural network on the ImageNet dataset to work as a feature extractor and Support Vector Machine (SVM) trained on the output of the first NN. Both models take the image as input after a resizing and have two outputs: whether the weld is OK or it needs to be reworked.

4.2   ACAS Xu Use Case

The second use case we will tackle is the widely known ACAS Xu as presented by [8] as an Airborne Collision Avoidance System for unmanned vehicles. As opposed to regular and large lookup tables producing advisory, this system uses a deep neural network to produce the advisory to avoid midair collisions. The approach was partly introduced to reduce the memory requirements for hardware of the original 2 GB tables down to 3 MB. The authors in [8] express concerns on the certification of such a system based on neural networks and, indeed, in such safety critical systems a basis of trust in those systems should be built.

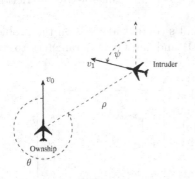

Fig. 4. ACAS Xu setting

Figure 4 shows the different parameters of the problem. Two additional parameters, τ (s), the time until loss of vertical separation and a_{prev} (°/s) the previous advisory, complete the 7 input parameters of this use case. Five advisories are possible for the system: "Clear-of-Conflict", "Weak right", "Strong right", "Weak left", or "Strong left", corresponding respectively to the heading rates 0°/s, −1.5°/s, −3.0°/s, 1.5°/s and 3.0°/s. By discretizing the last two inputs τ and a_{prev} with respectively 9 and 5 values, 45 networks are created, one for each combination. Each network is composed of five inputs and 6 hidden layers of 50 neurons each with ReLU activation functions. We denote their respective inference functions as $p_{\tau,a_{prev}}$.

As mentioned, the concerns on such a system are related to certification and how to show that the DNNs are well representing the properties of the original problem and tables. For example, the setting and the original tables in this use case are symmetric alongside the ownship heading direction. In that sense, we should observe here the same symmetry on the DNNs trained from the tables.

5   Experimentation

As AIMOS does not require more than the inference function of the selected AI model and its execution in terms of computing power, it can be run on a similar architecture as the one normally used for the inference of the model. In this section, all the experimentations were run on a 16 cores and 64 GB RAM server.

5.1   Renault Welding Use Case

For the Renault Welding use case, we will consider 3 different production lines called C10, C20 and C34 and their corresponding weld. They represent different welds on different parts of a car in the factory. As seen in Fig. 5, each weld has different characteristics such as lighting conditions, orientation, or even position in the image. All the images are initially Full HD images which are then resized for the inference with the models. Our test set is composed of several hundreds of images depending on the weld (898 for C10, 1069 for C20 and 1070 for C34).

Fig. 5. Welds C10, C20 and C34 of a rear axles production line. (from left to right)

For the purpose of this use case, we compare the two available types of models on each of these production lines with five different AutoML trained models (TFLite) and one Renault own in-house model (pickle format). The accuracy of all models is on average over 97% and is thus sufficient to be able to correctly consider their stability to metamorphic properties.

For each of these models, we will focus on the blur perturbation as it is included in the ODD defined by Renault. The range chosen to test this perturbation is purposefully quite large to include the ODD of Renault but also show results outside this zone. The resulting perturbations can thus also imply that the image should not be recognizable by the human or the model. Following this, the metamorphic property tested is the absence of classification change after applying the perturbation and are defined more formally as follows:

- $f_i(x) = blur(x, k)$ where blur is a convolution by a kernel with $k \in [1, 20]$ the kernel size chosen for the blur with a step of 1.
- $f_o(x) = x$ and $f_{pred}(x) = x$

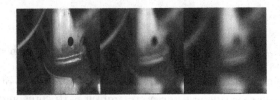

Fig. 6. Example of blur applied on a C34 weld image. Left is original image, middle has a kernel size of 10 and right of 20.

The blur modification is created using a normalized box filter which is convoluted to our original image through the OpenCV library. This implementation corresponds to the one used by Renault. The effect on the intensity of the blur can be seen on Fig. 6. In Renault's ODD, this blur can come either from the sensors themselves, *i.e.*, the camera settings are slightly off, or from vibrations caused by the production line operation. A more precise validation of the consistency with the real blur observed should be pursued in case of further testing on Renault's side in order to evaluate a meaningful perturbation.

5.2   Results on the Renault Welding Use Case

As shown in Fig. 7, the different AutoML models, which have the same architecture, present a similar trend in their response, *i.e.*, the stability of the model drops quickly for low perturbation then plateaus at a lower level. Some variations can nevertheless be seen between the models, such as with the first and third

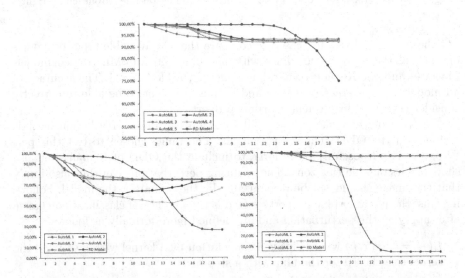

Fig. 7. Stability of the models on the C10, C20 and C34 welds for the blur property with kernel size ranging from 1 to 20. Value points are linked *only* for aesthetic consideration to improve readability as AIMOS does not perform interpolation.

model of C20 or the fifth of C34, showing the differences here that the training can bring even at similar accuracy.

On the contrary the RD model on each weld presents greater stability than AutoML models up until a certain point, then drops drastically in stability. This drop, at varying kernel sizes for each weld, shows the limit of the model before it fails to even identify the weld and thus infers a rework is needed for everything (here the test set presents a majority of OK labelled welds). This clearly contrasts with the AutoML models which tend to classify everything as OK at high blur values. After further discussion with Renault, the results of the AutoML models is indeed problematic as it is overly robust and is not desirable for them. Indeed, at high blur level, which are not recognizable by a human, the default action should be to ask for a rework and not the validate the weld.

The different models' responses between the different welds also vary in intensity, showcasing that the setting of each weld can bring different responses. C10 drops in stability are the most moderate with AutoML models staying above 90% whereas it goes down as low as 53% for C20's fourth model and 80% for C34's third model. A possibility here is that the blur is more present in the training dataset for certain production lines as it occurs more frequently there, leading to a better stability.

With these results from AIMOS, metrics can be defined on the stability at a given blur kernel and thus include this indicator in a quality process at Renault to validate a model or not. This could be further linked with other results on different perturbations such as brightness, rotation, etc. Of course, all of this should remain coupled with some performance indicator like the accuracy of the model to avoid selecting models outputting constant values (which would always be stable).

As a preliminary work, further testing were also made with AIMOS to compare different type of robust training for the models. Randomized smoothing or 1-Lipschitz models were thus compared to original models. Nevertheless, no clear conclusion was found as some of them appear overly robust like the AutoML models and other present varying degree of stability. A more complete study should be pursued and linked to the full ODD of Renault.

Overall, the chosen perturbation for this paper was kept simple for pedagogical concerns, and more complex perturbation (rotation on top of blur, etc.) could be used. Even so, we already see here some notable differences between the various model types and architectures in the way they respond to these metamorphic properties. In fact, the results on these properties have shown the utility of this tool to Renault. We are currently collaborating to extended our work on the rest of the control elements as defined in Renault's Operational Design Domain. AIMOS would then be able to be integrated in Renault's quality process.

5.3   ACAS Xu Use Case

For the ACAS Xu use case, we tested the symmetry of all 45 models to a symmetry alongside the ownship heading axis. The models are available under the NNet format and AIMOS is able to directly read and infer from this format.

For our tests, we defined two test scenarios on different ranges of input. The first one is defined on the full range of the five inputs, and we pick 100 000 test points uniformly on this range. We remarked that more than 85% of these points' output was "Clear-of-conflict". As such while it should remain unchanged by the symmetry it did not allow to fully test this transformation on the output right and left. We then defined a second scenario and selected 100 000 uniformly on a more restricted part of the input space. This subspace was chosen so that a majority of the inputs in that subspace are predicted as either "Strong right" or "Strong left" or if τ is high as "Clear-of-conflict". For smaller τ, around 95% of the inputs is for each network either "Strong right" or "Strong left"

Finally, as the 45 networks were discretized through the previous advisory when considering a symmetry on the system, the previous advisory should also be symmetrized. This leads to inferring the result with a *different* network. This is the incentive behind the extension of metamorphic testing from the usual transformations on inputs and outputs to include also transformations on the models themselves. In that sense, we defined the metamorphic property tested here as follows:

- $f_i((\rho,\ \theta,\ \psi,\ v_{own},\ v_{int})) = (\rho,\ -\theta,\ -\psi,\ v_{own},\ v_{int})$
- $f_o(a) = -a$ with a in $^\circ/s$
- $f_{pred}(p_{\tau,a_{prev}}) = p_{\tau,-a_{prev}}$.

5.4   Results on the ACAS Xu Use Case

Overall, the stability of the models *w.r.t.* to our defined symmetry metamorphic property is quite high on the full input space as the average stability over all 45 networks is above 97%, even the worst network drops only to 94%. Nevertheless, on a more restricted space we can see more difference *w.r.t.* to the previous advisory. Indeed, on average over the previous advisory we are at 89.7% stability with "Clear-of-Conflict" and with Left advisories we are at 95% while we are above 99.6% for Right advisories. This shows a clear imbalance between the models of left and right previous advisory. On the other hand, there does not seem to be any correlation between τ and the stability.

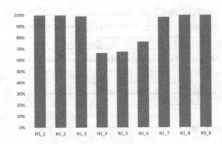

Fig. 8. Stability of the ACAS Xu models with ordered by τ with previous advisory being "Clear of Conflict" on the restricted space.

Figure 8 shows the differences between networks in function of τ when the previous advisory is "Clear-of-conflict", where the stability is the lowest. In fact, this comes from the 3 models with intermediate values of τ that show only 66%, 67% and 76% of stability to the symmetry. As the network should have trained on fully symmetrical tables, this results shows a discrepancy between the networks and the table and that further training might be necessary for these networks.

This second use case and the metamorphic property tested with AIMOS are presenting more complex and essential properties that one can test using our tool. Indeed, such considerations, like the symmetry of the model trained, should certainly be considered when the dataset and what it represents are also symmetrical. In the same idea, rotation or translation properties can also be considered by AIMOS. In turn, they can help design a more comprehensive dataset for further training if needed, $e.g.$, in case some configurations were underrepresented. As an additional note, such properties have also been tested in two other settings in maritime and avionics use cases ($e.g.$, with our Technip Energies partners, as a part of a larger reliability assessment, mentioned in [12]).

6   Conclusion

We presented AIMOS, a metamorphic testing tool specialized in AI applications, as well as the results of its usage in industrial contexts. Through these results, we hope to advocate for the inclusion of such tools in the verification and validation process of AI-based components. AIMOS will be made freely available for teaching and research purposes as a part of an ongoing effort to increase the awareness of reliability issues in the future generations of AI practitioners. It will also be integrated in more holistic open-source platforms for characterizing safety in AI systems such as CAISAR [6].

This participation in a greater effort for validation will allow AIMOS to collaborate more closely with other tools, such as formal provers. By integrating in a wider platform, we also hope to facilitate the application of AIMOS to the AI-based components of software products that also have non-AI-based components, which is essential for system-wide verification and validation.

Finally, we are investigating application to another type of use cases, very prevalent in the industry, which is time series. Here again, several partners are particularly interested in time-series-specific transformations and this is part of our medium-term plans.

Acknowledgments. This work has been supported by the French government under the "France 2030" program, as part of the SystemX Technological Research Institute. The AIMOS tool is also funded under the Horizon Europe TRUMPET project grant no. 101070038 and the European Defence Fund AINCEPTION project grant no. 101103385.

References

1. Balunović, M., Baader, M., Singh, G., Gehr, T., Vechev, M.: Certifying geometric robustness of neural networks. In: Advances in Neural Information Processing Sys-

tems 32, vol. 20, pp. 15234–15244. Curran (2020). https://doi.org/10.3929/ethz-b-000395340

2. Chen, T.Y.: Metamorphic testing: a simple method for alleviating the test oracle problem. In: Proceedings of the 10th International Workshop on Automation of Software Test, AST 2015, pp. 53–54. IEEE Press (2015)

3. Chen, T.Y., et al.: Metamorphic testing: a review of challenges and opportunities. ACM Comput. Surv. (CSUR) **51**(1), 1–27 (2018)

4. Ding, J., Hu, X.H., Gudivada, V.: A machine learning based framework for verification and validation of massive scale image data. IEEE Trans. Big Data **7**(2), 451–467 (2017)

5. Dwarakanath, A., et al.: Identifying implementation bugs in machine learning based image classifiers using metamorphic testing. In: Proceedings of the 27th ACM SIGSOFT International Symposium on Software Testing and Analysis. ACM (2018). https://doi.org/10.1145/3213846.3213858

6. Girard-Satabin, J., Alberti, M., Bobot, F., Chihani, Z., Lemesle, A.: CAISAR: a platform for characterizing artificial intelligence safety and robustness. In: AISafety. CEUR-Workshop Proceedings (2022). https://hal.archives-ouvertes.fr/hal-03687211

7. He, P., Meister, C., Su, Z.: Structure-invariant testing for machine translation (2020)

8. Julian, K.D., Lopez, J., Brush, J.S., Owen, M.P., Kochenderfer, M.J.: Policy compression for aircraft collision avoidance systems. In: 2016 IEEE/AIAA 35th Digital Avionics Systems Conference (DASC), pp. 1–10 (2016). https://doi.org/10.1109/DASC.2016.7778091

9. Lindvall, M., Porter, A., Magnusson, G., Schulze, C.: Metamorphic model-based testing of autonomous systems. In: 2017 IEEE/ACM 2nd International Workshop on Metamorphic Testing (MET), pp. 35–41 (2017). https://doi.org/10.1109/MET.2017.6

10. Pullum, L.L., Ozmen, O.: Early results from metamorphic testing of epidemiological models. In: 2012 ASE/IEEE International Conference on BioMedical Computing (BioMedCom), pp. 62–67. IEEE (2012)

11. Segura, S., Fraser, G., Sanchez, A.B., Ruiz-Cortés, A.: A survey on metamorphic testing. IEEE Trans. Softw. Eng. **42**(9), 805–824 (2016)

12. Serge, D., Augustin, L., Zakaria, C., Caterina, U., François, T.: ReCIPH: relational coefficients for input partitioning heuristic. To be Presented at ICML's Workshop on Formal Verification of Machine Learning (WFVML 2022) (2022)

13. Sun, Z., Zhang, J.M., Harman, M., Papadakis, M., Zhang, L.: Automatic testing and improvement of machine translation (2019)

14. Tian, Y., Pei, K., Jana, S., Ray, B.: DeepTest: automated testing of deep-neural-network-driven autonomous cars (2018)

15. Tse, T., Yau, S.S.: Testing context-sensitive middleware-based software applications. In: Proceedings of the 28th Annual International Computer Software and Applications Conference, COMPSAC 2004, pp. 458–466. IEEE (2004)

16. Zhang, M., Zhang, Y., Zhang, L., Liu, C., Khurshid, S.: DeepRoad: GAN-based metamorphic testing and input validation framework for autonomous driving systems. In: 2018 33rd IEEE/ACM International Conference on Automated Software Engineering (ASE), pp. 132–142 (2018). https://doi.org/10.1145/3238147.3238187

17. Zhou, Z.Q., Sun, L.: Metamorphic testing of driverless cars. Commun. ACM **62**, 61–67 (2019)

AERoS: Assurance of Emergent Behaviour in Autonomous Robotic Swarms

Dhaminda B. Abeywickrama[1(✉)], James Wilson[1,2(✉)], Suet Lee[1],
Greg Chance[1], Peter D. Winter[1], Arianna Manzini[1], Ibrahim Habli[3],
Shane Windsor[1], Sabine Hauert[1], and Kerstin Eder[1]

[1] University of Bristol, Bristol, UK
{dhaminda.abeywickrama,j.wilson,suet.lee,greg.chance,peter.winter,
arianna.manzini,shane.windsor,sabine.hauert,kerstin.eder}@bristol.ac.uk
[2] Dyson Institute of Engineering and Technology, Malmesbury, UK
[3] University of York, York, UK

Abstract. The behaviours of a swarm are not explicitly engineered. Instead, they are an emergent consequence of the interactions of individual agents with each other and their environment. This emergent functionality poses a challenge to *safety assurance*. The main contribution of this paper is a process for the safety assurance of emergent behaviour in autonomous robotic swarms called *AERoS*, following the guidance on the Assurance of Machine Learning for use in Autonomous Systems (AMLAS). We explore our proposed process using a case study centred on a robot swarm operating a public cloakroom.

Keywords: Assurance · Safety · Emergent behaviour · Guidance · Swarms

1 Introduction

Swarm robotics provides an approach to the coordination of large numbers of robots inspired by swarm behaviours in nature. The overall behaviours of a swarm are not explicitly engineered in the system [1,12]. Instead, they are an emergent consequence of the interactions of individual agents with each other and the environment, we call this emergent behaviour (EB) [1]. EB can be difficult to model and characterize and this property of swarms poses a critical challenge to *assurance* [2]. Assurance tasks comprise conformance to standards, verification and validation (V&V), and certification. Assurance criteria for autonomous systems (AS) include both functional and non-functional requirements such as safety [2].

Existing standards and regulations of AS are either implicitly or explicitly based on the V lifecycle model [4]. However, this model is unlikely to be suitable for systems with EB; for example through interaction with other agents and the environment, as is the case with swarms. ISO standards have been developed for the service robotics sector (non-industrial) (e.g. ISO 13482, ISO 23482-1), and

J. Guiochet et al. (Eds.): SAFECOMP 2023 Workshops, LNCS 14182, pp. 341–354, 2023.
https://doi.org/10.1007/978-3-031-40953-0_28

the industrial robotics sector (e.g. ISO 10218-1, ISO/TS 15066) [1]. However, although these standards focus on ensuring the assurance of robots at the individual level, they do not cover safe or unsafe behaviours at the swarm level that may arise through emergence which is the focus of this study.

Related Work. There are several standards and guidance related to machine learning (ML) in aeronautics, automotive, railway and industrial domains [8], for example the guidance on the Assurance of Machine Learning for use in Autonomous Systems (AMLAS) [3], the European Union Aviation Safety Agency (EASA) concept paper, the DEpendable and Explainable Learning (DEEL) white paper [10], the Aerospace Vehicle System Institute (AVSI) report, the Laboratoire National de Métrologie et d'Essais (LNE) certification, and the UL 4600 standard. However, none of these approaches targets robot swarms. In this work we used AMLAS [3] as the foundation for developing an assurance process for autonomous robotic swarms. AMLAS provides guidance on how to systematically integrate safety assurance into the development of the ML components based on offline supervised learning. AMLAS contains six stages where assurance activities are performed in parallel to the development activities. AMLAS has the advantage of ensuring safety assurance for complex AS where the behaviour of the system is controlled by ML algorithms. Our study takes inspiration from AMLAS, but adapts it to focus on emergence as the driver for complexity, rather than learning.

Main Contribution and Paper Outline. In this work, we propose a process for the safety assurance of EB in autonomous robotic swarms (AERoS), adapted from AMLAS [3]. AERoS covers six EB lifecycle stages: safety assurance scoping, safety requirements elicitation, data management, model EB, model verification, and model deployment. The AERoS process is domain independent and therefore can be applied to any swarm type (e.g. grounded, airborne). In particular, a system of components can be considered as analogous to a swarm if the system is decentralized with local interactions between components. AERoS may be applicable in such cases as well. In this paper, we explore the AERoS process using a case study centered on a robot swarm operating a public cloakroom at events with 50 to 10000 attendees [5]. In the cloakroom, a swarm of robots assist attendees to deposit, store, and deliver their belongings (e.g. jackets) [5]. As the swarm operates in a public setting, the system must prioritise public safety (e.g. avoid harm from collisions, fire hazards caused by blockages). The rest of the paper is organised as follows. In Sect. 2, we discuss the six stages of AERoS. Section 3 provides a brief discussion and concludes the paper.

2 The AERoS Process

This section discusses the six main stages of AERoS targeting autonomous robot swarms. AERoS is iterative by design, and the assurance activities are performed in parallel to EB development (see Fig. 1). For each stage, we describe its inputs and outputs, main assurance activities and their associated artefacts.

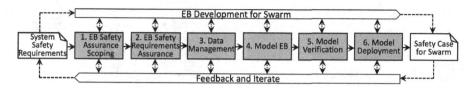

Fig. 1. The AERoS process with the six stages adapted from AMLAS.

2.1 Stage 1: EB Safety Assurance Scoping

Stage 1 contains two activities which are performed to define the safety assurance scope for the swarm (see Fig. 2).

Activity 1. Define Assurance Scope for the EB Description and Expected Output. The goal of Activity 1 (Fig. 2) is to define the safety assurance scope for the EB and expected output. The requirements defined in this stage are independent of any EB technology, which reflects the need for the robot swarm to perform safely regardless of emergence.

[A] System Safety Requirements: The system safety assessment process generates the safety requirements of the swarm, and covers the identification of hazards (e.g. the blocking of critical paths in the cloakroom) and risk analysis. Figure 3 illustrates how individual robot failures propagate through the neighbourhood to swarm-level hazards: we can then derive safety requirements in the form of concrete failure conditions at the level of the whole swarm which capture, implicitly, all levels of the swarm. Failure propagation might include a faulty sensor on an individual agent (e.g. odometry readings). This could mean that an individual or multiple agents may not detect other robots in its or their neighbourhood, leading to a high density of agents accumulating and blocking critical areas such as a fire exit.

[B] Environment Description: It is essential to consider the system environment when allocating safety requirements to the swarm. In the cloakroom, a swarm of robotic agents collects and delivers jackets, which are stored in small box-like containers. The agents are required to navigate a public space between collection and delivery points.

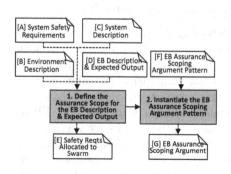

Fig. 2. Stage 1: The AERoS emergent behaviour assurance scoping process.

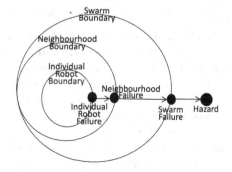

Fig. 3. Failure conditions in a swarm adapted from DO-178C and AMLAS.

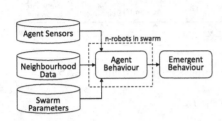

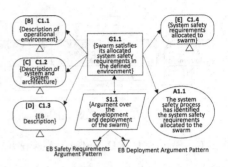

Fig. 4. Inputs fed into individual agent behaviour producing overall swarm emergent behaviour.

Fig. 5. Emergent behaviour safety assurance scoping argument pattern.

[C] System Description: In the cloakroom, we can consider three inputs: sensor availability, neighbourhood data (used because there is no access to global data in real-world deployments), and swarm parameters (see Fig. 4). The *sensors* available to agents can be cameras and laser time-of-flight sensors. The neighbourhood data of the swarm can be specified through the communication systems available to agents, in this case Bluetooth. Through the use of this short-range communication, agents can access neighbourhood data, such as approximate position or current state of local agents. As for the swarm-level parameters, we can consider options specified by a user, that is, the number of agents deployed, and the maximum speed of agents. Once defined, the three inputs are then fed to the individual agents to instruct their behaviour. This behaviour enacted by multiple agents then produces a swarm-level EB as the individuals interact with one another and their environment.

[D] EB Description and Expected Output: By expected output, we refer to the gains that can arise from the system by deploying multiple agents. In the cloakroom, the output is a collaborative system capable of collecting, sorting, and delivering jackets in a public setting. To achieve this, the EB of the system needs to arise from the available behaviours of the individual agents, their interactions, and the constraints outlined in the system description. The safety requirements generated from Activity 1 for the swarm need to be documented [E].

Activity 2. Instantiate EB Assurance Scoping Argument Pattern. Each stage of the AERoS process includes an activity to instantiate a safety argument pattern based on the evidence and artefacts generated in that stage. *Argument patterns* [3], which are modelled using the Goal Structuring Notation, can be used to explain the extent to which the evidence supports the relevant EB safety claims. In Activity 2, we use the artefacts generated from Stage 1 (i.e. [A–E]) to instantiate the EB Assurance Scoping Argument Pattern ([F] - see Fig. 5). The instantiated argument [G] along with other instantiated arguments resulting from the other five stages of AERoS constitute the safety case for the swarm. The activities to instantiate argument patterns of the other stages follow a very similar pattern so are not shown due to space limitations.

2.2 Stage 2: EB Safety Requirements Assurance

Stage 2 contains three activities (Fig. 6), which are performed to provide assurance in EB safety requirements for the swarm.

Activity 3. Develop EB Safety Requirements. We define EB safety requirements to specify risk controls for the swarm-level hazards by taking into account the system architecture defined and the operating environment.

Taking inspiration from AMLAS, the EB safety requirements are primarily safety focussed, but we go beyond the performance and robustness safety concerns of ML systems which are considered in AMLAS. The swarm behaviours or the properties of the swarm emerge from the robot interactions with each other, the environment and the humans. Their use in the real world is typically measured using performance and their ability to adapt. Therefore, to drive this emergence, we consider four types of requirements: *performance, adaptability, environment,* and *human safety* ([H] – see Table 1). These example requirements have been derived following three main considerations: the hazards for each safety requirement type, the metrics [9] available to assess these hazards, and the realistic thresholds [6] given the specification of the system. The requirements have been formulated using 'shall' statements. As the robot swarm is composed of many agents, there is potential for a large number of faults to occur at any given time [9]. This motivates three further sub-categories for each of the performance, adaptability, and human-safety requirements: *faultless operations, failure modes (graceful degradation),* and *worst case.* The environment requirements capture the need for the system to be robust to variation in the operative space. Scalability of the swarm in particular is captured by requirement 3.1 specifying for correct operation at given environmental density.

We consider several safety metrics under each requirement category: (i) performance: low-impact and high-impact collisions (the swarm should operate below a *critical number* of such collisions); (ii) adaptability: percentage of swarm stationary outside of the delivery site, number of stationary agents, time since last agent moved; (iii) environment: sum of objects in an area (the density of objects in the environment should not block swarm operation); and (iv) human safety: velocity or average velocity of agents, swarm size, rate of humans encountered, proximity to humans.

Activity 4: Validate EB Safety Requirements The required input to Activity 4 is the EB Safety Requirements [H]. These are validated by both review and simulation. Firstly, the requirements derived for the cloakroom have been reviewed by a safety-critical systems engineering expert to ensure that the specified EB safety requirements for the swarm will deliver its intended safe operation. Secondly, we will validate all safety requirements for the cloakroom system in a simulator environment. We use both low-fidelity 2D simulators and high-fidelity 3D Gazebo simulator to replicate the 4 m × 4 m lab environment [6] used for hardware implementation (see Fig. 7). Replication of the real lab environment takes into account robot and arena dimensions as well as the sensors, actuators and communication available to each robot. In our case, validation will be per-

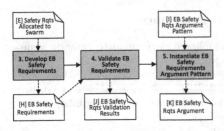

Fig. 6. Stage 2: The AERoS emergent behaviour safety requirements assurance.

Fig. 7. 3D simulation created to validate several emergent behaviour safety requirements.

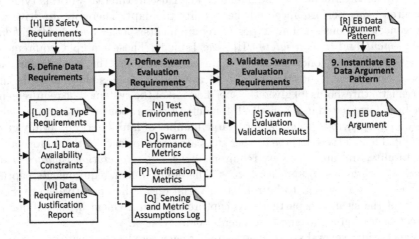

Fig. 8. Stage 3: The AERoS data management process.

formed in Gazebo as it allows for the immediate transfer of the same validated code for robot control from high-fidelity simulation to the real world. In **Activity 5**, the artefacts generated in this stage are used to instantiate the EB Safety Requirements Argument Pattern [I].

2.3   Stage 3: Data Management

When designing EB, input data for training an algorithm comes from local sensing of individual agents, both onboard the agent itself and in its local environment. The activities and outputs in this stage take into account the complexities of interactions between multiple agents.

Activity 6. Define Data Requirements. We take the EB Safety Requirements [H] outlined in Stage 2 as an input (see Fig. 8) which guide the data requirements in this activity, feeding into the data specification outlined here. We split the data requirement outputs into two multi-agent focused requirements: [L.0] Data Type Requirements and [L.1] Data Availability Constraints.

Table 1. Examples of performance, adaptability, environmental, and human-safety safety requirements for the cloakroom scenario.

RQ	Performance Requirements
1.1	The swarm *shall* experience < **1 high-impact (V > 0.5 m/s)** collisions across a **day** of **faultless** operation
1.2	The swarm *shall* experience < **0.1%** increase in **high-impact** collisions across a **day's** operation with **full communication faults** occurring in **10%** of the swarm
1.3	The swarm *shall* experience < **0.1%** increase in **high-impact** collisions across a **day's** operation with **half-of-wheels motor faults** occurring in **50%** of the swarm
1.4	The swarm *shall* experience < **2 high-impact (V > 0.5 m/s)** collisions across a **day** of **faulty** operation
1.5	The swarm agents *shall* **weigh** < **3 kg** and shall have **acceleration** < **4 m/s** so that the **maximum collision force** in the swarm is within acceptable bounds
1.6	The swarm agents *shall* only carry objects of **weight** < **2 kg**

	Adaptability Requirements
2.1	The swarm *shall* have < **10%** of its agents **stationary*** outside of the **delivery site** at a given time. *Agents are considered stationary once they have not moved for > **10 s**
2.2	All agents of the swarm *shall* move at least every **100 s** if outside of the **delivery site**
2.3	The swarm *shall* experience < **10%** increase in the **number of stationary agents** at any time with **half-of-wheels motor faults** occurring in **50%** of the swarm
2.4	The swarm agents *shall* experience < **10%** increase in **stationary time** with **half-of-wheels motor faults** occurring in **50%** of the swarm
2.5	The swarm *shall* experience < **10%** increase in **number of stationary agents** at any given time with **full communication faults** occurring in **10%** of the swarm
2.6	The swarm agents *shall* experience < **10%** increase in **stationary time** with **full communication faults** occurring in **10%** of the swarm

	Environmental Requirements
3.1	The swarm *shall* perform as required in environmental density levels **0–4 p_o** of **objects** (sum of boxes and agents per m^2) in the environment
3.2	The swarm *shall* perform as required when **floor incline** is **0–20°**
3.3	The swarm *shall* perform as required in a **dry environment**

	Human-Safety Requirements
4.1	The swarm agents *shall* travel at speeds of less than **0.5 m/s** when within **2 m** distance of a **trained human** (a worker who has received relevant training)
4.2	The swarm agents *shall* travel at speeds of less than **0.25 m/s** when within **3 m** distance of an **attendee**
4.3	The swarm agents *shall* only come within **2 m** distance of a **human** < **10** times collectively across **1000 s** of **faultless** operations
4.4	The swarm *shall* experience < **10%** increase in **human encounters** across **1000 s** of operation with **full communication faults** occurring in **10%** of the swarm
4.5	The swarm *shall* experience < **10%** increase in **human encounters** across **1000 s** of operation with **half-of-wheels motor faults** occurring in **50%** of the swarm
4.6	The swarm agents *shall* only come within **2 m** distance of a **human** < **20** times collectively across **1000 s** of **faulty** operations.

Table 2. Examples of requirements for output [L.0].

RQ	Relevance Requirements Examples
5.1	All simulations *shall* include environments with ranges of incline between 0–20°
5.2	All simulations *shall* be conducted in a dry environment
	Completeness Requirements Examples
6.1	All simulations *shall* be repeated to include occurrences of faults representative of full communication faults
6.2	All simulations *shall* be repeated a number of times to ensure results are statistically representative of typical use
6.3	All simulations *shall* be repeated in various test environments representative of the operating conditions that will be experienced in each environment expected in the real-world use of the system
	Accuracy Requirements Examples
7.1	All boxes *shall* only be considered 'delivered', if all four of the boxes' feet are positioned within the delivery zone
7.2	All boxes *shall* only be considered 'delivered', once they are no longer in direct contact with a swarm agent
	Balance Requirements Examples
8.1	All simulations *shall* be repeated to obtain representative evaluations for each possible mode of failure (defined under performance, adaptability and human-safety reqts. in Stage 2)
8.2	All simulations *shall* be repeated equally across each test environment

[L.0] Data Type Requirements: This element focuses on the *relevance, completeness, accuracy,* and *balance* of the information that will be used to construct the swarm behaviour (see examples in Table 2), and subsequently, to test the EB of the system before deployment. The *relevance* of the data used in the development of the EB specifies the extent to which the test environment must match the intended operating domain of the robot swarm. The *completeness* of the data specifies the conditions under which we test the behaviour, that is, the volume of tests that will be run, the variety of tests executed, and the diversity of environments (i.e. different room configurations) expected to be used in the testing process. The aim is to cover a representative sample of conditions for testing. *Accuracy* in this context relates to how well the data captures the parameter space defining the performance of the robot swarm. *Balance* refers to the evenly distributed trials executed in the testing process of the EB algorithm. By considering balance, we expect the number of tests conducted for failure modes or environments to be justified, ensuring that there is not an unrealistic bias in testing towards a particular scenario.

[L.1] Data Availability Constraints: With the introduction of multiple agents comes the issue of data availability. Distributed communication is a key feature found in emergent systems. As such, it is crucial to define how much information each agent is expected to hold, how easily data may transfer between agents, and across what range agents should be able to transfer information between one

another. Feasible constraints include *storage capacity, available sensors, communication range* and *operator feedback* [6].

[M] Data Requirements Justification Report: This report is an assessment of the data requirements, providing analysis and explanation for how the requirements and constraints ([L.0] and [L.1]) address the EB Safety Requirements [H].

Activity 7. Define Swarm Evaluation Requirements. Taking the outputs [L.0] and [L.1] from Activity 6, the evaluation requirements consider how the EB of the swarm will be assessed, specifying the testing environment and the metrics to be used to assess the test results.

[N] Test Environment: This takes into consideration the requirements specified in Activity 6, and defines the environment in which the EB will be tested. In most cases this will be multiple simulation environments featuring diverse sets of the terrain, environmental conditions, and obstacle configurations. There may also be instances in which this test environment is specified as a physical environment operating under laboratory conditions, with a hardware system acting as a test bed to observe designed behaviours.

[O] Swarm Performance Metrics: This output is used to quantify how well the system is performing. While there may be multiple performance metrics, these metrics should be defined with respect to the primary function of the robot swarm. Metrics that might feature in this output could include: the delivery rate in a logistics scenario, the rate of area coverage in an exploration task, or the response time in disaster scenarios.

[P] Verification Metrics: These metrics should be derived from the EB Safety Requirements [H] specified in Stage 2. They are intended to be used as the criteria for success within the verification process. For example, swarm density, which is used in verifying environmental safety specifications such as RQ3.1, maximum collision force experienced by agents, which could be used to verify that the swarm meets performance requirements such as RQ1.1 and RQ1.2, or the current speed of all agents, a metric relating directly to the human-safety requirements RQ4.1 and RQ4.2. Identifying [P] early, ideally during the requirements assurance stage, allows consideration of [P] during the design and development of the swarm to facilitate verification.

[Q] Sensing and Metric Assumptions Log: This log serves as a record of the details and decisions made in Activities 6 and 7. It should contain details of the choices made when producing the Test Environment [N], Swarm Performance Metrics [M], and the Verification Metric [P].

Activity 8. Validate Evaluation Requirements. Taking into account outputs [N], [O], and [P] from Activity 7, this activity aims to validate these components with respect to the requirements specified in Activity 6. Should any discrepancies exist between the data requirements and the evaluation requirements, they should be fully justified and recorded in the output Swarm Evaluation Validation Results [S]. The artefacts generated in this stage are used to instantiate the EB Data Argument Pattern [R] in **Activity 9**.

2.4   Stage 4: Model Emergent Behaviour

In the design of an EB algorithm, the challenge is in selecting behaviours at the individual level of the agents which give rise to the desired EB at the swarm level. We step away from the ML paradigm to allow consideration for all possible optimisation algorithms which may attain the target EB.

Activity 10. Create EB Algorithm. This can be nature inspired, hand designed, or evolved from a relatively simple set of instructions for individual behaviour, which takes into account agent-to-agent and environmental interactions [7]. These instructions when given to a large number of agents, create a synergistic behaviour for the swarm that is more powerful than the sum of the individual agent's performance. The EB algorithm is engineered at the level of the individual agent behaviours for the Test Environment output [N] from Stage 3. The resultant EB must meet the Safety Requirements [H] defined in Stage 2 (see Fig. 9) and this will be tested in the following activity. In the cloakroom case study, the target EB for the swarm must ensure that items are stored and retrieved by individuals as quickly as possible. An example control algorithm for the individual which produces the desired collective navigation and transport behaviours is a simple random walk [11]. The swarm engineer may adjust parameters such as robot velocity to optimize for rate of task completion. However, the EB Safety Requirements [H] should eliminate parameter choices which give rise to safety hazards. For example, performance requirements RQ1.1 and RQ1.2 specify an upper bound on the low/high-impact collisions that a swarm shall experience in a given time frame. These requirements may be fulfilled by constraining the maximum velocity of individual robots or by ensuring that a robot has one or more sensory devices, such as a camera, enabling it to detect obstacles. The key output from this activity is the Candidate EB [U] for testing.

[V] Model Development Log: This should log the rationale in the design process of the EB algorithm, in particular how all Safety [H] and Data Type Requirements [L.0] have been met given the Data Availability Constraints [L.1].

Activity 11. Test EB Algorithm. In this activity, the candidate EB algorithm will be tested against the Swarm Performance Metrics [O] produced in Stage 3. Testing ensures that the Candidate EB Algorithm [U] performs as desired with respect to the defined metrics and in the case where performance passes accepted thresholds, the EB Algorithm [W] will be produced as the output of the activity. If testing fails Candidate EB Algorithm [U] can be iteratively modified and tested until it passes successfully.

[Y] Internal Test Results: This output provides a degree of transparency in the testing procedure as the results may be further examined to ensure tests have run correctly. In **Activity 12**, the artefacts generated in this stage are used to instantiate the EB Argument Pattern [X].

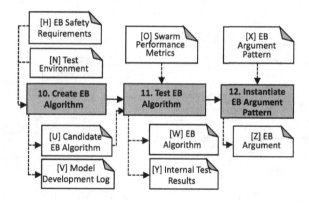

Fig. 9. Stage 4: The AERoS model learning process.

2.5   Stage 5: Model Verification

Activity 13. Verify EB. The inputs to the verification process are the EB Safety Requirements [H], Verification Scenarios (Test Generation) [P], and the EB Algorithm [W] (see Fig. 10). The verification method and assessment process within that method will be largely determined by the specifics of the safety requirements. Some safety specifications lend themselves towards certain assessment methods due to the scenarios they prescribe. For example, to assess that the robot swarm meets the requirements for performance given a motor-fault occurrence (see RQ1.3), it may be easier to realise this in physical or simulation-based testing approaches rather than attempting to construct a formal model of robot behaviour given the complex physical dynamics of a faulty wheel. However, when considering the adaptability requirements, a formal, probabilistic verification technique of the EB Algorithm [W] is more suitable. For example, in RQ2.1, analysis using a probabilistic finite state machine of the swarm behaviour could identify the dwell period within states. Monitors could be used to observe when agents enter a stationary state, for example, `agent_velocity=0` $\land$ `t_counter` $\geq$ `100`, and identify if time within that state exceeds some fixed value, and ascertain a probabilistic value to this metric.

Simulation-based validation of swarms may exhibit non-determinism, which needs to be managed. For debugging, the simulation environment should expose all sources of non-determinism to the end user, so that the simulation becomes repeatable. For gaining insight into swarm behaviour using simulations of the real world, however, the parameters in the simulation should be sampled from data obtained in real-world experiments during model characterisation. This reduces the reality gap that would otherwise exist between the real world and the simulation.

[P] Verification Scenario (Test Generation): In most cases there will be multiple, valid verification scenarios (test cases) applicable for each of the safety specifications. An example of a test case could include a scenario of the swarm in a hazardous environment where too many boxes create an obstacle.

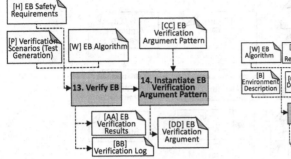
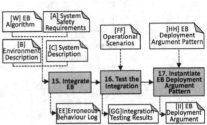

Fig. 10. Stage 5: The AERoS verification process.

Fig. 11. Stage 6: The AERoS model deployment assurance process.

Verification Results [AA] from individual assessments form entries in the Verification Log [BB]. The Verification Log identifies assessments where assurance of the EB Algorithm [W] is acceptable with respect to the Safety Requirements [H] and can be used as a set of evidence for building an assurance case. The artefacts generated in this stage are used to instantiate the EB Verification Argument Pattern [CC] in **Activity 14**.

2.6 Stage 6: Model Deployment

Activity 15. Integrate EB. With the EB verified, the next step is to take [W], [A], [B] and [C] as inputs, and integrate the EB with the system to be deployed (see Fig. 11). In this activity, we use the inputs to this stage to inform the implementation of the EB and anticipate errors we might expect in the interactions between agents and the overall EB. Despite the rigorous validation and testing conducted in previous stages, there will still be a gap between the test environment and the intended, everyday-use, deployed scenario. The output, [EE] Erroneous Behaviour Log, captures these anticipated gaps between testing and reality and the differences in behaviour that may surface.

Activity 16. Test the Integration. Once the initial integration is complete, the physical implementation should undergo additional testing in which the system will be observed in multiple operational scenarios, as specified in [FF].

[FF] Operational Scenarios: These scenarios should reflect the environment descriptions specified in [B], offering real-world situations to examine the behaviour of the integrated system. The testing of the integrated system in these true-to-operation environments should be conducted in a safe manner, ensuring that the entire multi-agent system can be shut down in an emergency. In the cloakroom, an example of [FF] may take the form of a deployment of agents in a controlled storage area that will not interfere with emergency services.

[GG] Integration Testing Results: Results from the integration testing will be reported here, detailing how the system performs against the EB Safety Require-

ments [H] specified in Stage 2. The artefacts generated in this stage are used to instantiate the EB Deployment Argument Pattern [HH] in **Activity 17**.

3   Conclusion

Using AMLAS [3] as a foundation, we proposed the six-stage development process AERoS. This process acts as guidance for those looking to construct swarm robot systems, particularly those that exhibit emergent behaviour through environmental and agent-to-agent interaction. The stages of AERoS break down the design of these systems to ensure that fundamental safety requirements are adhered to, even in instances of system degradation and compounded failures that should be expected, and managed, in robot swarms. We achieve this with an approach that allows for iteration of and feedback to the previous stages as issues of safety are encountered and investigated. We combine this iteration with repeated specification at each stage, observing the issue of safety through the lens of: data, modelling/behaviour design, verification, and deployment. While the iterative nature of AERoS is a key advantage, the scope of this work has been limited to investigating inherent swarm qualities and the emergent properties that arise from these. However, one can expand on this, and consider adaptation of individual robots through techniques such as ML (e.g. by applying AMLAS). A parallel process to AERoS can identify hazards of individual robots using standards like ISO 13482. Managing uncertainty of the system and the assurance process can be considered as well following standards like ISO 21448 and UL 4600. Also, we can broaden the evaluation by considering additional swarm use cases (e.g. monitoring fires in a natural environment, and also a social swarm), and by providing a worked example of the entire AERoS process. While the focus of AERoS is to ensure the safety assurance of EB in swarms, the trustworthiness of an AS can be dependent on many factors other than safety, such as ethics and regulation, which we will investigate as part of future work.

Acknowledgements. The authors would like to thank Alvin Wilby, John Downer, Jonathan Ives, and the AMLAS team for their fruitful comments. The work presented has been supported by the UKRI Trustworthy Autonomous Systems Node in Functionality under Grant EP/V026518/1. I.H. is supported by the Assuring Autonomy International Programme at the University of York.

References

1. Abeywickrama, D.B., Bennaceur, A., Chance, G., et al: On specifying for trustworthiness (2022). http://arxiv.org/abs/2206.11421
2. Cheng, B.H.C., et al.: Using models at runtime to address assurance for self-adaptive systems. In: Bencomo, N., France, R., Cheng, B.H.C., Aßmann, U. (eds.) Models@run.time. LNCS, vol. 8378, pp. 101–136. Springer, Cham (2014). https://doi.org/10.1007/978-3-319-08915-7_4
3. Hawkins, R., Paterson, C., Picardi, C., Jia, Y., Calinescu, R., Habli, I.: Guidance on the assurance of machine learning in autonomous systems (AMLAS). Guidance Version 1.1, University of York (2021)

4. Jia, Y., McDermid, J., Lawton, T., Habli, I.: The role of explainability in assuring safety of machine learning in healthcare. IEEE Trans. Emerg. Top. Comput. **10**(4), 1746–1760 (2022)
5. Jones, S., Milner, E., Sooriyabandara, M., Hauert, S.: Distributed situational awareness in robot swarms. Adv. Intell. Syst. **2**(11), 2000110 (2020)
6. Jones, S., Milner, E., Sooriyabandara, M., Hauert, S.: DOTS: an open testbed for industrial swarm robotic solutions (2022)
7. Jones, S., Studley, M., Hauert, S., Winfield, A.: Evolving behaviour trees for swarm robotics. In: Groß, R., et al. (eds.) Distributed Autonomous Robotic Systems. SPAR, vol. 6, pp. 487–501. Springer, Cham (2018). https://doi.org/10.1007/978-3-319-73008-0_34
8. Kaakai, F., Dmitriev, K., Adibhatla, S., et al.: Toward a machine learning development lifecycle for product certification and approval in aviation. SAE Int. J. Aerosp. **15**(2), 127–143 (2022). https://doi.org/10.4271/01-15-02-0009
9. Lee, S., Milner, E., Hauert, S.: A data-driven method for metric extraction to detect faults in robot swarms. IEEE Robot. Autom. Lett. **7**(4), 10746–10753 (2022)
10. Mamalet, F., Jenn, E., Flandin, G., Delseny, H., Gabreau, C.: White paper machine learning in certified systems. Technical report HAL-03176080, IRT Saint Exupery (2021)
11. Milner, E., Sooriyabandara, M., Hauert, S.: Stochastic behaviours for retrieval of storage items using simulated robot swarms. Artif. Life Robot. **27**(2), 264–271 (2022). https://doi.org/10.1007/s10015-022-00749-8
12. Winfield, A.F.T., Nembrini, J.: Safety in numbers: fault-tolerance in robot swarms. Int. J. Model. Identif. Control. **1**(1), 30–37 (2006)

A Reasonable Driver Standard for Automated Vehicle Safety

Philip Koopman[1](✉) and William H. Widen[2]

[1] Carnegie Mellon University, Pittsburgh, PA, USA
koopman@cmu.edu
[2] University of Miami – School of Law, Miami, FL, USA
wwiden@law.miami.edu

Abstract. Current "safe enough" Autonomous Vehicle (AV) metrics focus on overall safety outcomes such as net losses across a deployed vehicle fleet using driving automation, compared to net losses assuming outcomes produced by human driven vehicles. While such metrics can provide an important report card to measure the long-term success of the social choice to deploy driving automation systems, they provide weak support for near-term deployment decisions based on safety considerations. Potential risk redistribution onto vulnerable populations remains problematic, even if net societal harm is reduced to create a positive risk balance. We propose a baseline comparison of the outcome expected in a crash scenario from an attentive and unimpaired "reasonable human driver," applied on a case-by-case basis, to each actual loss event proximately caused by an automated vehicle. If the automated vehicle imitates the risk mitigation behaviors of the hypothetical reasonable human driver, no liability attaches for AV performance. Liability attaches if AV performance did not measure up to the expected human driver risk mitigation performance expected by law. This approach recognizes the importance of tort law to incentivize developers to continually work on minimizing driving negligence by computer drivers, providing a way to close gaps left by purely statistical approaches.

Keywords: Automated vehicles · safety · liability · regulation

1 Introduction

Discussions about autonomous vehicle (AV) safety requirements historically have two major themes: claiming that human drivers are bad, and a statistical/utilitarian argument of reduced net harm. However, neither ensures acceptable safety across relevant stakeholders. In this position paper we argue that a third approach based on a comparison of AV performance to a "reasonable driver" is required. While one might parlay a "Positive Liability Balance" into an AV deployment standard based on lower net liability than human drivers, we argue that the statistical approach must be combined with practical accountability for negligent AV driving behavior assessed crash-by-crash.

© The Author(s), under exclusive license to Springer Nature Switzerland AG 2023
J. Guiochet et al. (Eds.): SAFECOMP 2023 Workshops, LNCS 14182, pp. 355–361, 2023.
https://doi.org/10.1007/978-3-031-40953-0_29

Industry promotional narratives over-emphasize the first theme of human driver frailties, while promising that computer drivers will necessarily improve safety because computers do not have problematic human behaviors like drunk driving [1]. This narrative ignores potential AV crashes caused by software defects.

The second theme uses an engineering-based narrative that makes utilitarian arguments claiming improved safety from AV deployment—the Positive Risk Balance (PRB) label favored in Europe and, the Absence of Unreasonable Risk (AUR) label more favored in the US [2]. Reducing overall harm is a worthy goal, but the devil is in the details for PRB, which posits a comparison of AV safety outcomes to some notional average human driver safety outcome. To the degree that the AUR label uses a metric of "better than a human driver," both labels end up in the same place.

Whether PRB losses involving automation are comparable to losses generated by human drivers depends on operating conditions, passive safety features, active safety features, risk due to geographic location, risk due to driver age, and so on. Accurately predicting risk outcomes for novel technology before deployment is a significant challenge which raises serious ethical concerns because the technology may cause harm not only to vehicle occupants, but also to other road users who did not volunteer for this grand AV experiment by purchasing an AV or electing to ride in a robotaxi.

Fully autonomous AV proponents complain that, though deployment will (they presume) save many lives, their crusade to improve road safety will be impeded both by regulation and imposition of liability on their technology for every crash [3].

Previous approaches to managing risk and regulating technology propose pursing insurance-based solutions, enhancing information sharing, technology regulation, and making significant changes to product liability approaches [4]. While these approaches can all provide value in the long term, we see a need for a minimalist intervention that can substantially improve the safety situation right away, thereby providing time for realignment of industry business and regulatory models as technology matures.

We argue that blaming automated vehicle technology for *each crash a competent human driver might reasonably have avoided* – regardless of net safety outcomes – is a safety promoting feature, not a public policy mistake. In fact, it is the most efficient and effective strategy to resolve many liability claims that will follow deployment, while at the same time providing a non-regulatory approach to motivate the industry to make responsible deployment decisions for this still-immature technology.

2   Limits to Statistical Safety Approaches

A rhetorical approach claiming that AVs will be safe because "computers don't drink and drive" has convinced some state legislators to allow AVs on the road and to gather limited statistical data in the process. However, it will be many years before the hundreds of millions of miles required for statistical significance will accumulate. Even then, statistical approaches will have issues beyond the challenges of performing a like-for-like comparison to an appropriate human driver baseline [5].

Even if net statistical parity were achieved overall between AVs and humans, the shift to AVs might be unacceptable due to risk redistribution. This is especially true if vulnerable and disadvantaged populations (likely vulnerable road users) have increased risk exposure, while safety benefits accrue to economically advantaged AV users.

Consider a thought experiment in which all cars instantly turn into AVs, decreasing annual US road fatalities from 40,000 to 20,000 per year. We would rightfully celebrate this Positive Risk Balance victory. But some hypothetical outcomes might still prove problematic. (Baseline comparison numbers below are 2020 data from NHTSA [6].)

- All 20,00 fatalities are pedestrians and cyclists. This increase almost triples the 2020 numbers of 6,516 pedestrian and 938 cyclist fatalities (7,454 total).
- The number of fatalities related to school transportation increased to 1000—a nine-times increase over the average of 113 per year.
- Fatalities correlated with people having darker skin color due to a prevalence of light-colored skin in pedestrian training data.
- Technology updates necessitate continuing large-scale road-testing, with residents in testing areas at a significantly increased risk of harm compared to human-driven vehicles, while road users elsewhere enjoy increased safety.
- Every crash was due to a design defect that would likely have been caught by following industry best practices for design quality and validation, but was not.
- Every crash was due to a software defect that was known but not fixed by the manufacturer, due to a rationalization that there was a moral imperative to ship "good enough" software to improve net statistical safety as soon as possible.

We make no judgement as to which of these hypothetical outcomes would be morally justifiable or acceptable by society if they were to occur. However, it is reasonable to anticipate that at least some stakeholders would be unhappy, especially if they were personally affected by increased risk, or even a loss event.

Harm is especially problematic if associated with a risk redistribution, in which some segments of road users suffer increased risk while others enjoy decreased risk. One might devise a fine-grain framework for assessing Positive Risk Balance (a net decrease in risk) to account for risk redistribution. But it is unrealistic to expect this to happen immediately for at least the following reasons: (1) we do not yet know what risk redistribution will actually occur, (2) there will not be enough data to evaluate risk redistribution until after enough harm has been done to build up a statistically valid set of samples. Addressing this topic is essential – but it will take years to do this, while deployment decisions require action now.

3   The Reasonable Driver vs. The Tyranny of Net Risk

One key aspect of statistical statements of safety is that an individual who has been harmed did not benefit from the safety improvement. Even if we solve justice and fairness concerns surrounding statistical risk redistribution, the specifics of each crash still matter for attribution and allocation of liability.

Saying: "We're sorry Widow Smith, but please know that your husband's completely preventable death was part of a statistical 10% improvement in safety. The world is a safer place even as we are meeting our quarterly revenue goals" provides cold comfort to the victim's families. But it would be a shame to lose a potential safety benefit because different people will be harmed by AVs than would be harmed (in greater numbers) by human drivers. (Pareto optimality approaches to resolve this issue are not a viable basis for social decision-making because every choice disadvantages somebody in practice.)

Current AV capabilities do not support a vaccination-type argument to justify ignoring the specifics of each case—a situation in which it is appropriate to ask everyone to take a small risk for the overall public good. Imposing AV risk on the public (including those who do not directly benefit from using AVs at all) might only become compelling when the number of people harmed is reduced by orders-of-magnitude compared to the status quo. Vehicle automation technology is nowhere near such a capability.

Equipment regulation on a statistical basis should continue. Recalls for obvious patterns of harm can be accomplished under existing regulatory frameworks to keep known harms from continuing unabated. Test-based regulations and star-based rating systems can increase pressure on basic safety performance. But we need more.

We propose to add an additional safety approach to risk management and safety standard conformance, which moves from the statistical to the specific: *In every loss event, to avoid liability AV performance must not be negligent as measured by the performance standard we require of human drivers.*

3.1   A Lay Summary of Tort Law

Civil tort law provides a method to compensate a claimant who has suffered loss proximately caused by the negligence of another party. "Negligent driving" refers to unacceptably hazardous behavior by a vehicle (whether human or computer driven). In contrast, "product liability" refers to a manufacturing defect, design defect, or other product characteristic proved to cause unacceptably hazardous behavior.

Pursuing product liability claims typically costs more than pursuing negligence claims because expert engineering evidence proving a design defect or other technical cause of a crash can cost hundreds of thousands of dollars or more. The manufacturer also incurs significant defense costs. Costs and long time-scales render pursuit of product liability claims impractical for a run of the mill traffic accident.

Proving a negligence claim is more straightforward, with the plaintiff claiming that the defendant owed her a duty of care which was breached by failure to act as a reasonable person would have acted, and that this breach caused harm—the legal standard used to determine negligence liability. Breaking traffic laws likely amounts to negligent behavior. If an AV runs a red light, the driver likely is negligent.

Significantly tort law liability can be based solely on negligent behavior without proof of a product defect. Absent a recognized excuse, such as an Act of God, if conduct falls short of the performance we expect of a reasonable person, the defendant has liability. If an AV behaves in a dangerous way, the law should infer AV negligence proximately caused any harm, just as the law infers liability of a human driver. In a rear-end collision, for example, the law tends to infer negligent driving of the rear vehicle.

A crash victim needs a straightforward recovery method in addition to complex product liability claims in AV accident cases, because manufacturers have asymmetric access to data recordings, design expertise, and a war chest to pay lawyers. We must supplement the status quo to better incentivize manufacturers to strive for safety.

3.2 Safety by Comparison to a Reasonable Driver

Using a negligence-based approach to evaluate AV safety changes the baseline for comparison from "anything non-human is better" or "better than a statistically average driver" (Positive Risk Balance) to a human-centric standard. The baseline for liability is the legal construct of a "reasonable" person/driver.

Courts have crafted the concept of "reasonable driver" as a hypothetical ideal person over time for use in resolving human-to-human driver negligence cases. This is not an "average" driver or an expert driver. Rather, this is a driver who can handle situations in a reasonably competent way, without lapses in judgement. For example, if a ball rolls into the street near a school playground, many would agree that a reasonable driver should anticipate a child will soon appear to chase after it and start slowing down before the child appears. This is not a technical standard, but a flexible yet objective standard that has proven its worth for use by courts and lay juries.

Our specific use of this principle is that the actions of an AV should be compared to a hypothetical reasonable human driver with regard to liability for causing harm or failing to mitigate reasonably avoidable harm. If a reasonable human driver would have avoided causing harm, so too should an AV's computer driver. If it were unreasonable to expect a human driver to avoid harm in a particular situation, then the AV driver is blameless – even if a theoretically better design might have avoided the harm. (A claimant still might pursue a product defect claim, but not ordinary negligence.)

On a situation-by-situation basis, an AV should be as safe as a reasonable human driver. Any instance in which the AV displays negligent driving behavior means that it is in practice unsafe, just as a human driver would have been unsafe in that situation.

3.3 Case-by-Case Liability

We propose that tort laws at the US state level should be modified to recognize the concept of negligence for the legal fiction of a computer driver. The idea is that whenever a driving automation system is in control of a vehicle, it should be treated the same as a human driver regarding negligence on a case-by-case basis for every time it might have inflicted harm. The manufacturer should be the responsible party (with the manufacturer perhaps being a system integrator, depending on the specifics) [7].

This approach transforms many highly technical product defect cases into much simpler negligence cases with lower transaction costs to resolve, and more direct access to common-sense outcomes. If an AV makes a mistake and runs a red light when a reasonable human driver in that situation would likely have stopped, the AV manufacturer should be responsible for negligent driving by the computer driver it produced, and incur any burden of proof that exigent circumstances (if any) excused the driving behavior. This is the same burden the law places on a human driver.

AV proponents and engineers in general might argue that exposure to negligence liability creates too great a burden because it might prevent them from making design tradeoffs that reduce overall harm at the cost of increasing redistribution of harm. We argue that such tradeoffs should bear their full social cost. A reasonable design decision should be able to compensate victims while leaving excess manufacturer benefits.

If a human driver with a perfect lifetime driving record crashes while driving the wrong direction on a one-way street, that driver will have negligence liability for losses. A judge might consider the driving record in criminal sentencing, but liability remains. Even the best drivers don't get a "free crash" exclusion from negligence. Computer driver liability should be the same, even if AVs make streets statistically safer.

An added benefit to this approach is that it lowers the bar to reasonable claims by parties harmed by negligent AV behavior. Negligence lawsuits are much less expensive and much more predictable for both parties involved than product liability lawsuits.

Our approach does not require AVs to have perfect, loss-free safety records. Even if they crash, if the technology achieves a "reasonable driver" level of harm mitigation, negligence liability will not attach. Aspirational or factual claims to improved statistical safety should not give AVs a free pass to exhibit driving behavior that would be considered negligent if performed by a human driver.

Requiring behavior that is at least as good as that of a "reasonable driver" raises the question of how to define such behavior in a way that is amendable to deriving engineering requirements. While a reasonable driver is considered well defined from a legal point of view, a precise engineering requirement definition would likely require analysis of case law to account for liability outcomes involving human drivers in a variety of circumstances. While each specific crash might have some aspect of "it depends" involved in assessing liability, there will be common fact patterns that predispose determinations that some computer driver behaviors are reasonable, and some are negligent. For example, a major traffic rule violation such as running a red light in a way that causes a crash is likely to be negligent unless there is significant mitigating circumstance. For borderline cases, the ultimate legal process to determine negligence is via the court system. Engineering audiences might be uncomfortable with a requirement that is not immediately amenable to a prescriptive, deterministic, and complete set of rules. However, they should be able to cope with yet another aspect of vehicle automation which might be addressed via data mining of past court cases to learn what behavior is reasonable.

A technical model might be created that bounds some aspects of reasonable driver behavior. A candidate for some aspects of negligence that might be evaluated is Waymo's "non-impaired human with their eyes on the conflict" (NIEON) model [8].

4 Conclusion

If an AV runs a red traffic light and kills a pedestrian, the victim's family should not suffer through years of uncertainty nor be forced to identify a law firm willing to fund a million-dollar-plus legal effort to hunt for a defect in a machine learning system that caused the vehicle to miss both the red light and the pedestrian in the cross-walk. A much simpler approach presents itself and should be used: simply hold computer drivers to the same standards of negligence as human drivers, with the manufacturer named as the responsible party.

We do not expect AVs to be perfect. But to achieve broadly acceptable safety there needs to be a check and balance mechanism that is both more practical and more immediate than equipment regulation and product defect lawsuits. Tweaking tort law to explicitly support the legal fiction of computer driver negligence provides just such a mechanism.

It also introduces a new constraint on AV manufacturers: it is not sufficient to be statistically safe. One must also avoid harm in each situation in which a competent "reasonable driver" would also have avoided harm – the same as human drivers must.

This approach can be extended to encompass not only fully autonomous vehicles, but any vehicle automation technology that is prone to inducing automation complacency or otherwise resulting in a situation in which automation misbehavior is prone to causing mishaps [9]. This includes any vehicle with sustained automated steering, even if a human driver is tasked with supervising automation safety.

This paper concentrates on US tort law. Extending analysis to other legal systems would require future work. However, other legal systems could likely benefit from an alternative to a product defect approach to addressing many loss events that will eventually occur involving automated driving capabilities. Core principles might be introduced to other legal frameworks by defining appropriate equivalents of a duty of care for a computer driver, and a notion of synthetic negligence for computer drivers, with the responsible party being manufacturers.

This same principle of synthetic negligence for computer drivers might be extended to other areas in which automated systems supplant humans who previously owed a duty of care to others. That might help avoid such a duty being swept away or hidden behind the opacity of a product's "artificial intelligence" branding.

References

1. NHTSA, Automated Driving Systems 2.0: A Vision for Safety, DOT HS 812 442 (2017)
2. Favaro, F.: Exploring the relationship between 'positive risk balance' and 'absence of unreasonable risk', 20 October 2021. https://arxiv.org/abs/2110.10566
3. Augustin, F.: Elon Musk says Tesla doesn't get 'rewarded' for the people its Autopilot technology saves, but instead gets 'blamed' for the people it doesn't. Business Insider (2021)
4. Smith, B.W.: Regulation and the risk of inaction. In: Maurer, M., Gerdes, J.C., Lenz, B., Winner, H. (eds.) Autonomous Driving, pp. 571–587. Springer, Heidelberg (2016). https://doi.org/10.1007/978-3-662-48847-8_27
5. Koopman, P.: How Safe Is Safe Enough (2023). ISBN: 979-8846251243
6. NHTSA, Traffic safety Facts. https://crashstats.nhtsa.dot.gov/Api/Public/ViewPublication/813369. Accessed 6 June 2023
7. Widen & Koopman: Winning the Imitation Game, April 2023. https://papers.ssrn.com/sol3/papers.cfm?abstract_id=442969
8. Waymo: Benchmarking AV Safety. https://waymo.com/blog/2022/09/benchmarking-av-safety.html. Accessed 6 June 2023
9. Widen & Koopman: The Awkward Middle for Automated Vehicles: Liability Attribution Rules When Humans and Computers Share Driving Responsibilities, May 2023. https://papers.ssrn.com/sol3/papers.cfm?abstract_id=4444854

Structuring Research Related to Dynamic Risk Management for Autonomous Systems

Rasmus Adler[1]([✉]) [iD], Jan Reich[1] [iD], and Richard Hawkins[2]

[1] Fraunhofer IESE, Kaiserslautern, Germany
{rasmus.adler,jan.reich}@iese.fraunhofer.de
[2] University of York, York, UK
richard.hawkins@york.ac.uk

Abstract. Conventional safety engineering is not sufficient to deal with Artificial Intelligence (AI) and Autonomous Systems (AS). Some authors propose dynamic safety approaches to deal with the challenges related to AI and AS. These approaches are referred to as dynamic risk management, dynamic safety management, dynamic assurance, or runtime certification [4]. These dynamic safety approaches are related to each other and the research in this field is increasing. In this paper, we structure the research challenges and solution approaches in order to explain why dynamic risk management is needed for dependability of autonomous systems. We will present 5 research areas in this large research field and name for each research area some concrete approaches or standardization activities. We hope the problem decomposition helps to foster effective research collaboration and enables researchers to better navigate the challenges surrounding dynamic risk management.

Keywords: Dynamic Risk Management · Dynamic Assurance · Safety · Autonomous Systems · Artificial Intelligence

1 Introduction

Artificial Intelligence (AI) and Autonomous Systems (AS) have the potential to significantly contribute to the current ecological, social, and economic challenges. However, safety is often a major obstacle to unlocking the full potential of AI and AS. Several approaches to deal with these safety challenges refer to 'dynamic' or 'runtime' approaches, such as dynamic risk management [1], dynamic safety management [2], dynamic assurance [3], or runtime certification [4], which are collectively referred to as dynamic risk management (DRM) in this paper. In order to structure the large research field of DRM and make a first step towards a taxonomy to support efficient discussions, this paper will clarify different notions of DRM that relate to AS, as well as present related work that proposes ways to integrate the different DRM aspects. Finally, conclusions will be drawn with respect to the DRM research community and safety standardization.

© The Author(s), under exclusive license to Springer Nature Switzerland AG 2023
J. Guiochet et al. (Eds.): SAFECOMP 2023 Workshops, LNCS 14182, pp. 362–368, 2023.
https://doi.org/10.1007/978-3-031-40953-0_30

2 Notions of Dynamic Risk Management for AS

AS have no single accepted definition, but many definitions refer to their situation-specific behavior, self-sufficient behavior, and the complexity of their mission and environment when characterizing AS. Moreover, collaboration and the ability to remain up-to-date with changes such as the evolution of the operational environment and regulatory requirements are defining features of AS. To further illustrate AS and its related notions of DRM, Fig. 1 in our study depicts five aspects of AS in its upper part and five corresponding notions of DRM in its lower part. In this section, we will explain each of these DRM notions and associated AS aspects in detail.

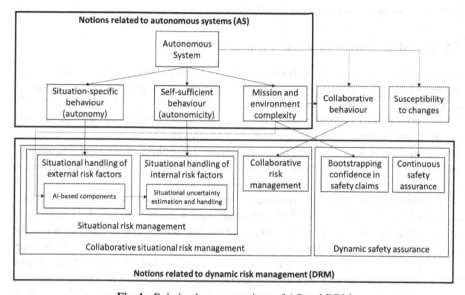

Fig. 1. Relation between notions of AS and DRM

2.1 Situational Handling of External Risk Factors

Popular definitions of AS refer to **situation-specific behavior**. Kagermann et al. [5] defines that a system can be described as autonomous if it is capable of independently achieving a predefined goal "*in accordance with the demands of the current situation...*" [6] describes autonomy as the concept of having "*flexibility in decision-making to reach its goals...*".

A related notion of DRM is that the AS is aware of the risks in the current environmental situation and that it behaves so that the risks will not become unacceptable. In contrast to conventional safety functions, this risk management function requires reasoning about the current environmental situation and potential harm scenarios [7], i.e. the **situational handling of external risk factors**. To this end, safety supervisors are used to monitor the nominal behavior (cf. German application rule VDE-AR-E 2842-6 part 3 clause 12.4), and evaluate the risks on different time horizons such as operational, tactical and strategic. Physics-based approaches like Time-To-Collision (TTC) and Responsibility-Sensitive Safety Model [8] are used to identify risks. However, these physics-based approaches are not sufficient for developing human-like defensive driving capabilities, and thus, expert systems that imitate human risk reasoning must be developed. For example, the SINADRA framework [9] uses Bayesian Networks to model the influences of situation-specific risk metric parameters. Ultimately, as AI-based perception is often necessary for situational handling of external risk factors, the direct relationship between AI and situational risk is represented in Fig. 1. Unsolved challenges in this research area are the identification of relevant risk factors as well as the definition of a risk criterion combining these factors to express the border between safe and unsafe situations on different time horizons.

2.2 Situational Handling of Internal Risk Factors

Another AS notion is its **self-sufficiency**, its autonomicity or its capability to maintain its operation [6], i.e. achieving a goal without human control [5]. The degree of human independence is promoted in problem structuring frameworks like SAE J3016 or ALFUS [10]. The related DRM notion is that the AS dynamically handles *internal* risk factors, i.e. all kinds of component failures including failures due to functional insufficiencies or limitations like limited sensor range. **Situational handling of internal risk factors** enhances error detection and handling approaches by considering the risks of detected errors, which vary in different operational situations.

Challenges in this research area emerge from the complexity in detecting all relevant errors and handling them so that the best possible functionality is provided. The approach in [11] proposes how to identify component degradation variants and considers the reconfiguration sequences for transitioning from one system configuration to another [12]. Trapp et al. [2] enhances this approach with respect to the risk-oriented handling of errors and proposes to shift parts of a functional safety engineering lifecycle to runtime. Further challenges emerge from components based on Machine Learning (ML), because their output is subject to uncertainty, which we understand as the likelihood that the actual output deviates in a particular way from the correct output. This likelihood depends on the current operational situation and leads to the challenge of situational estimation and handling of uncertainties (cf. Figure 1). DIN SPEC 92005 [24] will provide a terminology for distinguishing between different notions of uncertainty. Henne et al. [13] proposes to handle uncertainty in perception by switching to a verified-low-performance safety channel. Kläs et al. [14] and Groß et al. [15] propose to handle uncertainty by increased safety margins.

2.3 Collaborative Risk Management

Some AS missions can only be achieved by many collaborating systems. For instance, the mission to realize the flow of material in a warehouse may require several vehicles. A related notion of DRM is that systems and components flexibly collaborate to realize a safety function. For instance, warehouse infrastructure systems like cameras and the vehicles collaborate to realize a collision avoidance function. In addition to situational risk management, a key feature of this DRM is that systems or components can enter and leave a composition without requiring time-consuming recertification. This requires a commonly accepted format for dynamically exchanging safety-relevant information such as the level of confidence in the information. Research has already proposed some formats but it is still a long path to wide-spread adoption in industry. The ConSerts approach [16] uses a simple guarantee-demand interface based on safety requirements with Safety Integrity Levels (SILs). The Open Dependability Exchange (ODE) meta-model [17] and its instances called Digital Dependability Identities (DDI) provide a more flexible approach.

2.4 Bootstrapping Confidence in Safety Claims

Achieving high confidence for complete AS product lifetimes is very challenging in complex environments in combination with immature technology. Thus, a related DRM notion is the bootstrapping of confidence in safety claims by means of field feedback. The idea of bootstrapping confidence is to use field data to generate additional evidence collected during operation to create a stronger argument. At initial deployment, the safety argument and evidence may only be strong enough for a limited mission time, number of AS and with operators in the loop. During this limited mission time, field data is collected with the goal to substantiate supporting evidence for a stronger argument and therefore "bootstrap" the next operation/evidence collection period, potentially with more AS or with less operator involvement. This bootstrapping approach is described in Sect. 5.4.1 in [18] and in [19]. An approach to identify which field data should be collected during operation to enhance the safety case is based on the use of dialectic arguments [20].

2.5 Continuous Safety Assurance

Even after a sufficiently safe initial deployment, unforeseeable changes such as changing situation distributions or new traffic actors with new behaviors will likely increase the operational risk, as AS were not specifically designed for these changes. In addition, security loopholes identified post deployment and new regulatory requirements call for systematic methods to continuously monitor safety case validity and if necessary realize system modifications through updates. A related DRM notion is continuous assurance and engineering of safety. This focusses on the challenge that safety claims or assumptions may become invalid after deployment as a result of change. Avionics, railway and mining are promising application domains [3, 21]. The German project *AutoDevSafetyOps* develops a reference process for automotive continuous safety assurance. In this context, Safety Performance Indicators (SPI) first defined in the safety standard UL 4600 play a critical role. A SPI is a metric and a related threshold that measures the validity of a safety claim. SPIs can be used to engineer field data types to be monitored during operation, which allow to monitor the assurance case validity of an AS fleet.

3 Related Work

In the following we will discuss related work, which aims at structuring DRM research based on different but related structuring schemes. In [2], it is stated that "the approach described in this paper combines and extends different existing puzzle pieces as a first step towards an overall dynamic safety management framework". The scope of the paper is limited to the situational handling of internal risk factors. Schneider and Trapp present in [22] an approach for collaborative risk management. It focuses on situational collaborative realization of simple safety functions such as *self-acceleration must not occur during standstill*. The topic of risk metrics and criterion to derive which behavior is required for managing risks is not discussed. In [23] is also motivated by inconsistently used terminology found in literature. It presents a continuous assurance process that reflects some of the notions presented in Fig. 1. It distinguishes clearly between the notions of (collective) situational risk management and the notion of dynamic safety assurance by distinguishing between a runtime system (performing situational risk management) and a design-time system (for dynamic assurance). It does work out all the DRM notions that we presented and it does derive the notions from definitions of AS. While the presented notions are similar to ours, the used terms for these notions are different. S. Saidi [6] charts AS design as new discipline involving AI, cyber-physical systems and Automation. It presents similar notions of AS. It considers the difference between autonomy and autonomicity and it puts emphasis on AS as collaborating agents. It proposes a new safety-assured, verification-aware design process showing required enhancements for AS design with a strong focus on situational handling of internal risk factors. Through this examination of related work, it can be seen that our proposed structure contributes to existing work for structuring research around DRM.

4 Conclusion and Future Work

Conventional safety engineering and assurance is not sufficient for AS. Several approaches propose approaches that refer to more dynamicity and automation in safety and risk management. An issue in this regard is that the terms are used differently. This hinders the research community to effectively move forward by developing new or alternative puzzle pieces and by puzzling different pieces together. We proposed several notions that we think are worth to distinguish from a problem perspective. This shall serve as a basis for discussions in research collaborations such as the LOPAAS project [25] and it shall be a first step towards standardization.

We focused on the presentation of the notions and did not share our rationales for the terms that we used for these notions. We plan to do this in another paper that involves more researchers from this research area and probably in context of the next workshop on Dynamic Risk managEment for AutonoMous Systems (DREAMS) [26]. This will include a discussion about the issue that the term dynamic risk management is heavily used in context of financial risks and security risks. For instance, the security-related standard ISO/IEC FDIS 23894 [27] uses the term dynamic risk management.

Acknowledgments. This work has been funded by the project "LOPAAS" (Layers of Protection Architecture for Autonomous Systems) as part of the internal funding program "ICON" of the Fraunhofer-Gesellschaft.

References

1. Kurd, Z., Kelly, T., McDermid, J., Calinescu, R., Kwiatkowska, M.: Establishing a framework for dynamic risk management in 'intelligent' aero-engine control. In: Buth, B., Rabe, G., Seyfarth, T. (eds.) SAFECOMP 2009. LNCS, vol. 5775, pp. 326–341. Springer, Heidelberg (2009). https://doi.org/10.1007/978-3-642-04468-7_26
2. Trapp, M., et al.: Towards safety-awareness and dynamic safety management. In: 2018 14th European Dependable Computing Conference (EDCC), Iasi, Romania (2018)
3. Asaadi, E., Denney, E., Menzies, J., Pai, G.J., Petroff, D.: Dynamic assurance cases: a pathway to trusted autonomy. Computer 53(12), 35–46 (2020)
4. Rushby, J.: Runtime certification. In: Leucker, M. (ed.) RV 2008. LNCS, vol. 5289, pp. 21–35. Springer, Heidelberg (2008). https://doi.org/10.1007/978-3-540-89247-2_2
5. Kagermann, H., et al.: Das fachforum autonome systeme im hightech-forum der bundesregierung –chancen und risiken für wirtschaft, wissenschaft und gesellschaft. Final report, Berlin (2017)
6. Saidi, S., Ziegenbein, D., Deshmukh, J.V., Ernst, R.: Autonomous systems design: charting a new discipline. IEEE Design Test. 39(1), 8–23 (2022)
7. Feth, P., Schneider, D., Adler, R.: A conceptual safety supervisor definition and evaluation framework for autonomous systems. In: Tonetta, S., Schoitsch, E., Bitsch, F. (eds.) SAFECOMP 2017. LNCS, vol. 10488, pp. 135–148. Springer, Cham (2017). https://doi.org/10.1007/978-3-319-66266-4_9
8. Shalev-Shwartz, S., Shammah, S., Shashua, A.: On a formal model of safe and scalable self-driving cars. ArXiv abs/1708.06374 (2017)
9. Reich, J., Wellstein, M., Sorokos, I., Oboril, F., Scholl, K.U.: Towards a software component to perform situation-aware dynamic risk assessment for autonomous vehicles. In: European Dependable Computing Conference - EDCC 2021 Workshops (2021)
10. Huang, H.-M., et al.: Autonomy levels for unmanned systems (ALFUS) framework: an update. In: Proceedings of the 2005 SPIE Defense and Security Symposium, Orlando, Florida (2005)
11. Adler, R.: A Model-based approach for exploring the space of adaptation behaviors of safety-related embedded systems. Dissertation. Fraunhofer Verlag (2013)
12. Trapp, M., Adler, R., Forster, M., Junger, J.: Runtime adaptation in safety-critical automotive systems (2007)
13. Henne, M., et al.: Benchmarking uncertainty estimation methods for deep learning with safety-related metrics. In: SafeAI Workshop@AAAI Conference (2020)
14. Kläs, M., et al.: Handling uncertainties of data-driven models in compliance with safety constraints for autonomous behavior. In: 2021 17th European Dependable Computing Conference (EDCC), Munich, Germany, pp. 95–102 (2021)
15. Groß, J., et al.: Architectural patterns for handling runtime uncertainty of data-driven models in safety-critical perception. In: Trapp, Saglietti, Spisländer, Bitsch (eds.) SAFECOMP 2022. LNCS, vol. 13414, pp. 284–297. Springer, Cham (2022). https://doi.org/10.1007/978-3-031-14835-4_19
16. Schneider, D., Trapp, M.:. Conditional safety certification of open adaptive systems. ACM Trans. Auton. Adapt. Syst. 8(2), 1–20 (2013). Article 8
17. Zeller, M., et al.: Open dependability exchange metamodel: a format to exchange safety information. In: Annual Reliability and Maintainability Symposium (RAMS), USA (2023)
18. Rushby, J.: The interpretation and evaluation of assurance cases (2015). http://www.csl.sri.com/users/rushby/papers/sri-csl-15-1-assurance-cases.pdf30T
19. Bishop, P., Povyakalo, A., Strigini, L.: Bootstrapping confidence in future safety from past safe operation. In: 2022 IEEE 33rd International Symposium on Software Reliability Engineering (ISSRE), Charlotte, NC, USA, pp. 97–108 (2022)

20. Hawkins, R., Conmy, P.: Identifying runtime monitoring requirements for autonomous systems through the analysis of safety arguments. In: Proceedings of 42nd International Conference on Computer Safety, Reliability and Security (Safecomp 2023) (2023, to appear)
21. Denney, E., Pai, G., Habli, I.: Dynamic safety cases for through-life safety assurance. In: 2015 IEEE/ACM 37th IEEE International Conference on Software Engineering, Florence, Italy, pp. 587–590 (2015). https://doi.org/10.1109/ICSE.2015.199
22. Schneider, D., Trapp, M.: B-space: dynamic management and assurance of open systems of systems. J. Internet Serv. Appl. **9**, 15 (2018). https://doi.org/10.1186/s13174-018-0084-5
23. Schleiss, P., Carella, F., Kurzidem, I.: Towards continuous safety assurance for autonomous systems. In: 2022 6th International Conference on System Reliability and Safety (ICSRS), Venice, Italy, pp. 457–462 (2022). https://doi.org/10.1109/ICSRS56243.2022.10067323
24. DIN Spec homepage, DIN SPEC 92005 Artificial Intelligence - Uncertainty quantification in machine learning. https://www.din.de/de/forschung-und-innovation/din-spec/alle-gescha eftsplaene/wdc-beuth:din21:360097552. Accessed June 2023
25. Press Release "LOPAAS project". https://www.iese.fraunhofer.de/en/media/press/pm-2021-10-18-paradigmenwechsel-se.html. Accessed June 2023
26. DREAMS workshop homepage. https://www.iese.fraunhofer.de/en/seminare_training/edcc-workshop.html, visited 06.2023
27. ISO/IEC FDIS 23894: Information technology—Artificial intelligence—Guidance on risk management (2022)

Towards Safe Machine Learning Lifecycles with ESG Model Cards

Thomas Bonnier[(✉)] and Benjamin Bosch

Société Générale, Paris, France
{thomas.bonnier,benjamin.bosch}@socgen.com

Abstract. Machine Learning (ML) models have played a key role in many decisions that can affect society. However, the inductive and experimental nature of ML exposes it to specific risks. If the latter are not controlled, ML has the potential to wreak havoc by impacting people and the environment. In that context, Environmental, Social and Corporate Governance (ESG) is an approach used to measure a company's sustainable behavior along those three dimensions. To develop responsible behavior, an organization should employ an ESG framework within its structure. In this paper, we propose a risk-based approach which aims to produce safe ML lifecycles. Its objective is to smoothly implement the ESG strategy throughout the ML process by identifying and mitigating risks. Based on that analysis, we present the ESG model card, a concrete tool to report the ESG impacts of the ML lifecycle, along with the actions used to reach that outcome.

Keywords: Model card · Safe Machine Learning · Risk-based approach · ESG impacts

1 Introduction

Environmental, Social and Corporate Governance (ESG) is an approach to assess a company's responsible behavior. The term was coined in 2004 in a United Nations report where several financial institutions developed recommendations on ESG investment [35]. Its three pillars can be seen as measuring performance based on certain factors: (i) Environmental impacts: e.g., climate change and related risks. (ii) Social impacts: e.g., workplace health and safety. (iii) Corporate governance: e.g., accountability and transparency. Thus, to improve its ESG position, it is key for an organization to adopt some best practices within its structure. In the same vein, our objective is to show how the ESG approach can spread throughout the Machine Learning (ML) lifecycle (data, model design, implementation, use and monitoring). ML has become a dimension underlying many daily life decisions and current societal challenges, such as chatbot triage systems for incoming patients in hospitals [32]. During these critical tasks, ML algorithms aim at generalizing the decisions based on prior data. However, the inductive and experimental nature of ML exposes it to ESG risks. For instance,

J. Guiochet et al. (Eds.): SAFECOMP 2023 Workshops, LNCS 14182, pp. 369–381, 2023.
https://doi.org/10.1007/978-3-031-40953-0_31

a language model like GPT-3 has more than 175 billion abstract parameters [1]. The carbon footprint of its lifecycle is undoubtedly significant (environmental impact), and its reproducibility and explanation remain a challenge (transparency impact). ML models such as neural networks are also prone to adversarial attacks [6] (social impact). When ML models can be used for good, the negative effects of the ML lifecycle should not cancel out the benefits. If these risks are not controlled, ML has the potential to wreak havoc by impacting people (e.g., model users, individuals), society (e.g., subgroup, organization), and the environment throughout its whole lifecycle. In that context, we propose an approach which identifies the environmental, social, and transparency risks and suggest mitigating actions for each aspect of the ML modeling lifecycle. This approach aims to meet the following criteria:

- **Environmental** pillar: Efficient, Environmentally-friendly ML.
- **Social** pillar: Secure, Fair, Unbiased, Robust ML.
- **Governance** pillar: Transparency, Accountability, Auditability, Compliance throughout the ML lifecycle.

Some of the risks covered here are not specific to ML lifecycles but are exacerbated by its ecosystem. Further, that selection of risks and mitigations is not exhaustive but indicative of some critical threats and potential solutions in the ESG context. The ESG net impacts of a given ML lifecycle are thus assessed after applying mitigation techniques and can be estimated via safety metrics. Some examples of such indicators are the number of cyber-security vulnerabilities or the quality of model explanations. The next stage is then to report these impacts in the ESG model card, along with the actions employed to reach that result. Our main contribution is thus to propose standardization in deploying safe ML by presenting a risk-based approach and a reporting tool considering the ESG impacts.

2   ESG Risk Identification and Mitigation Through the ML Lifecycle

2.1   The Data Layer

Fitted Data Size (E Pillar). Big data has brought volume and variety to the training datasets of ever-improving ML models. On the other hand, data ingestion, storage and processing require power draw. This produces carbon emissions responsible for global warming, which threatens biodiversity and human welfare. It is estimated that 0.5% of US GHG emissions are due to data centers [33]. For a comprehensive estimate of the carbon footprint, it is relevant to consider the manufacturing, transportation, and recycling of infrastructure, such as servers and buildings. With the big data era, there is a clear tendency to collect data in excess. This trend exacerbates the need for ever more storage capacity. Indeed, data is a valuable asset, but it may not always be fit for purpose. To mitigate these risks, we advise applying the *principles of proportionality and minimization*. Proportionality rule is popular in law and reflects that the means should be proportionate to the end. Minimization removes superfluous dependencies. Therefore, collecting all the data may not be required. Data ingestion must be commensurate with the pursued objective: will the data be used for a critical application or to industrialize a secondary process? As explained in the next paragraphs, the security or regulatory stakes can also initiate downscaling.

Protected Data Area (S Pillar). An uncontrolled number of external data sources exposes an organization to security breaches as there is no guarantee of quality. For instance, using pre-trained models, which is a common practice for Transformers and other big neural network architectures [27], is relevant for rapidly transferring learned knowledge to a child model that will be fine-tuned. However, loading training data or model weights from an uncertain provenance favors poisoning attacks or biases [19]. This could result in corrupt decision-making and affect in some cases the reputation and viability of an organization. The underlying guideline we propose here is the *Know Your Data (KYD) principle*: we advise using reliable or independently certified sources, exploring the datasets, and sanitizing or pre-processing them before fitting a model.

Transparent Data Flows (G Pillar). The terms specifying permissions and limitations to use third-party libraries or external data should be thoroughly verified. For instance, any unauthorized extraction of web data could have negative consequences for an organization. Further, personal data must be processed in a legitimate and transparent fashion to comply, for instance, with the Article 5 of the General Data Protection Regulation (GDPR) in European Union [9]. The *right to be forgotten* can drive data governance in firms where owners of sensitive data must be accountable and follow the *principles of proportionality and minimization* for personal information retention. For instance, keeping sensitive data for fraud detection may be required for a company, whereas storing it for several years for marketing purposes might seem excessive. Internally, lack of transparency regarding sources and data usage could hamper the deployment of valuable ML applications in the future.

In the first place, a streamlined data lineage with all the data sources connected to their related end-user applications safeguards traceability. This graph turns out to be beneficial to pinpoint shadow sources and prune superfluous inputs. Secondly, implementing a reliable ESG data framework requires defining reference datasets with their associated limitations. For instance, bias detection controls performed by the data owner should be documented, and identified biases should be communicated to potential data users. Dataset consumers can make informed choices when the dataset lifecycle is transparent. This can be achieved through datasheets documented by dataset creators [12]. By answering a set of questions, the latter reflect on each milestone of the ML dataset lifecycle, from the motivation behind the creation of the dataset to its recommended uses and maintenance process. To conclude, the *KYD principle* turns out to be valuable here as well to serve the transparency goal.

2.2   The Model Design Layer

Design Rethinking (E Pillar). Computationally demanding models have a significant carbon cost. During the modeling process, time and space complexity depends on the hypothesis space and the optimization phase. The former includes the set of observations, the feature space, and the modeling method set: this is the structural cost. The latter embraces the constraints on the model architecture, the learning algorithm and the hyperparameter optimization (HPO). It searches for the hypothesis space subset which reaches the objective function optimum under constraints: this forms the algorithmic cost. Three levers stand out to lessen the computational burden: reducing the hypothesis space (e.g., transfer learning [28]), lightening the model structure (e.g., quantization [4]), and speeding up the optimization (e.g., cost-frugal optimization [36]). However, the generalization error should remain reasonable. In other words, we allocate a computational budget, and remove complexity without sacrificing the variance bias trade-off. In fact, it has been evidenced that large neural networks can reveal lightweight structures which generalize just as well [10]. Most importantly, even if model packing does not curb the computational debt during training, it will pave the way for a faster inference. We thus suggest applying the *principle of parsimony*.

Treatment for Model's Achilles' Heel (S Pillar). While a model displays good overall performance, some population subgroups may be inclined to higher error rates. This situation might be due to lack of representativeness in the modeling data. For instance, gender imbalance in chest X-ray imaging datasets can generate biased classifiers. For some diseases, the best-performing models for women proved to be better at diagnosing men than women [21]. To treat the lack of fairness, we suggest investigating data pre-processing, model in-processing or prediction post-processing techniques, such as the reject option classification [17].

With respect to security and privacy, ML models are prone to adversarial attacks which have various facets depending on the attacker's goals [6]. Model extraction and membership inference attacks jeopardize the confidentiality dimension. They respectively threaten the intellectual property of an organization through API probing or put individual privacy at risk. In particular, membership inference attacks target a model by determining whether a given record belongs to the training dataset. To prevent the leakage of sensitive information, differential privacy can be leveraged during training [8]. In the case of deep learning models, differentially private stochastic gradient descent (DPSGD) adds noise to the gradient updates [30]. As this deteriorates the model performance, the best trade-off between utility and privacy should be decided depending on the targeted application.

With regard to the integrity aspect, evasion attacks happening during inference exploit models' weak spots. Small perturbations in the inputs will lead the model to misclassify. The Fast Gradient Sign Method (FGSM) is a white box attack method with a misclassification goal [13]. It uses the gradients of the neural network to create an adversarial example of an input image:

$$adv\_img = img + \epsilon * sign(\nabla_{img} J(\theta, img, y))$$

where img denotes the input image, y the original input label, and ϵ the perturbation factor. θ stands for the model parameters and J the loss function. This method can be used to evaluate a neural network's robustness against adversarial threats. The feasibility of all these exploits strongly depends on the attacker's access: contexts such as insider access, open-source model or API are more vulnerable. Various types of adversarial attacks could be considered depending on the adversary's knowledge of the target model [7]: white box attacks (e.g., FGSM) rely on the access to detailed information on the model such as the architecture or the gradients of the loss w.r.t the inputs; transfer-based blackbox attacks assume the access to training data to create adversarial instances on a surrogate model; score-based black-box attacks (e.g., prior guided random gradient free method) suppose that the attacker can get the output probabilities of the target model; decision-based black-box attacks (e.g., boundary attack) rely only on the predicted labels and are far more challenging for the attacker. In response, some defenses exist. An innovative view is to consider the context of competitive games, where both the model and the attacker confront each other to have an edge [6]. Incremental learning is one of the suggested solutions, so that the model interactively learns based on the adversary's new exploits. In addition, human intervention during the design cycle (e.g., feature selection) can be a way out. To sum up, the *principle of proportionality* turns out to be useful for a fair and secure model design: the remediation should be proportionate to the threat magnitude.

Scientific Evidence (G Pillar). The mechanisms of the model decision-making must be explainable. Prototypes are relevant to reveal archetypes of model errors. Those are data instances representative of a whole dataset [3]. This can be achieved by minimizing the squared Maximum Mean Discrepancy (MMD^2) between the distributions of the data and selected prototypes [14]:

$$MMD^2 = \frac{1}{n^2} \sum_{i,j=1}^{n} k(x_i, x_j) - \frac{2}{nm} \sum_{i,j=1}^{n,m} k(x_i, z_j) + \frac{1}{m^2} \sum_{i,j=1}^{m} k(z_i, z_j)$$

where k denotes a kernel function, m is the number of prototypes z and n is the number of original data points x. The algorithm first requires setting a number of prototypes before greedily searching for the data point that minimizes MMD^2 at each iteration. Displaying the final set of prototypes, along with the related model error, helps to find prototypes of errors.

Further, the Local Interpretable Model-agnostic Explanations [31] method (LIME) makes it possible to explain why single model predictions were made.

It relies on the training of an interpretable model (e.g., LASSO regression) to locally approximate the prediction of a black-box model:

$$\xi(x) = argmin_{g \in G}(\mathcal{L}(f, g, \pi_x) + \Omega(g))$$

where G is a class of potentially interpretable models (e.g., linear model), f the model being explained, π_x the neighborhood of x, $\mathcal{L}$ a measure of the approximation of f by g in the locality defined by π_x, and Ω a complexity measure (e.g., the number of non-zero weights). Other eXplainable AI (XAI) methods such as the ones based on Shapley values [23], can be used to address the need for transparency and explanations of the decisions for ML models. Such explanations consolidate accountability and the confidence of subject matter experts in the model.

Local (e.g., LIME) and global (e.g., surrogate models) post-hoc explainability methods come with some caveats. In fact, the outputs of different techniques can disagree with each other. Krishna et al. define the notion of consistency between the outcomes of local post-hoc explanation methods by suggesting various metrics to measure disagreement [18]. The main criteria to define disparity between explanation methods are the differences between the set of top-k features, and whether the signs of contributions and the ordering among the top-k features are different. The authors experimentally notice that disagreement often occurs, but resolving it remains an open question. To conclude, we thus suggest using the *Know Your Model (KYM) principle* for a transparent model design: the model mechanism and limitations should be human-understandable and documented.

2.3 The Model Implementation Layer

Low-Carbon Code (E Pillar). Code with redundancies, inadequate data structure and algorithm choice might generate bottlenecks, and thus increase the environmental havoc. We thus recommend performing code profiling in order to identify potential bottlenecks. This best practice is strongly advised for the inference code that is frequently run. Further, to evaluate the future carbon footprint at inference, we recommend assessing the average inference time and the number of queries per day, in order to check whether the model needs to be optimized a bit more or not.

Lastly, implementation is also about infrastructure. The data center location and Power Usage Efficiency (PUE) are both consequential. Areas like the Nordics in Europe offer a good mix of free cooling and renewable energy. Even if geographical distance impacts the latency when demand is far away, the carbon footprint might be more advantageous. Next, recycling plays a role too. For instance, hardware lifespan could be extended if used in optimal conditions up to that point. To conclude, *re-usability* is the key principle for an efficient model implementation both on the software and hardware sides.

Catch Exceptions (S Pillar). Unsecured model implementation strategy leads to irrevocable user experience; worse, it exposes users' personal data. When repeated, this would impact the confidence of people in algorithmic decision-making. In fact, an organization can rapidly be overwhelmed with ML models developed by inexperienced data scientists. In that case, the risk of shadow APIs can surface, with potential vulnerabilities that may lead to sensitive data leakage. To overcome this problem, a good practice is to make an inventory of models and related status, and to review and certify them before implementation according to their materiality (*principle of proportionality*). In addition, the introduction of third-party packages might weaken the robustness of the implementation. Awareness of the packages' limitations is a pre-requisite for trustworthy use. Testing of edge cases or adversarial testing is thus highly recommended. For instance, floating point overflow or *Not A Number* values during inference could result in crash, silent failure, or loss of precision [34]. Implementation risks can also be reduced by regularly checking the Common Vulnerabilities and Exposures (CVE) listed by MITRE (MIT Research and Engineering) [26]. In any case, it is critical to report any error, flaw, security breach, or data leakage to the stakeholders. In a nutshell, the *principle of continuous robustness* is useful to deal with all these pitfalls: do not cause a solid model to fail because of a weak implementation.

Reproducibility at Every Stage (G Pillar). ML pipelines can be intricate, which may question the trust we place in the decision-making mechanism. Therefore, the ML pipeline architecture must be transparent at any data transformation and modeling stage. For instance, the software and hardware infrastructure used to run experiments should be specified. Replicability paves the way for the re-usability of the pipeline and code for similar tasks. It saves experimental time, and thus lessens the carbon footprint. Further, code documentation is of paramount importance to facilitate auditability and knowledge transfer. It helps the developers to structure the script and makes the handover to future code owners easier. The *principle of re-usability* is thereby efficient in that context too.

2.4   The Model Use and Monitoring Layer

Ongoing Monitoring (E Pillar). Once the model has been deployed, it is of the utmost importance to ensure that it behaves as expected. For instance, it is key to monitor that the model is being used on the scope and for the objective it was designed for. To this end, the governance must define clear roles and responsibilities for this task, as well as metrics and critical cut-off points. We call it the *principle of continuity*: the model lifecycle does not stop once implemented. The continuous monitoring ensures that no deviation in performance or use is looming, and that the model meets the objectives. For instance, the annual carbon footprint due to inference is assessed before implementation by using the number of queries' annual estimate and the average inference time. Once the model is in production, it is key to report actual values and verify that no critical gap is emerging. Otherwise, corrective actions ought to be decided such as reducing the scope of use or changing the model. Human intervention, or human-on-the-loop, is thus required to check the metrics and act.

Vulnerability Monitoring (S Pillar). Beyond model prediction accuracy, specific attention should be placed on monitoring security. Two aspects are important to track once the model is in use: actual incidents and hidden vulnerabilities. The first aspect must be reported and corrected. For example, in case of sudden surge in API queries, an attempt of model extraction must be investigated. In case of sensitive data breach, the relevant Data Protection Authority should be notified. The second aspect could take the form of uncovered exploits in third party packages. Once again, we recommend regularly checking the new CVE, and sharing them with the ML community.

Distribution shifts and hidden biases in black-box models can increase the model uncertainty in specific areas of the feature space. During the monitoring phase, quantifying and visualizing the model uncertainty on unlabeled data is thus a way to reduce potential harmful effects. For instance, conformal prediction for classification and regression is a useful method to construct prediction sets or intervals [29]. The Non-Conformity Analysis leverages conformal prediction and a tree representation in order to identify the most uncertain regions in classification tasks [2]. Actions such as human-in-the-loop can help to reduce possible adverse effects when model predictions are very uncertain [5].

To conclude, the *principle of continuous monitoring* is relevant here: one should prevent any deterioration in the model behavior over time.

Trust but Verify (G Pillar). Algorithm aversion and untrustworthy model decisions are challenges that can affect the implementation of ML algorithms. Direct users (e.g., an employee) and end users (e.g., a private individual) may thus experience dehumanization feelings. In contrast, automation bias and over-reliance on a model can lead to alienation and loss of critical ability. Setting the right degree of decision automation requires considering the direct user's expertise and the model limitations. When the system is not fully automated, direct user mistrust is detected by the rate of overridden decisions. In that case, the override rationale helps to understand the reasons for the user concerns. The risk of model misuse can be thus thwarted by training direct users on the model scope and weaknesses. In that case, human-in-the-loop, with arbitration in the decision process, mitigates the risk of harming end users, especially when the model is uncertain. To sum up, we advise using the *principle of proportionality*: in fact, the magnitude of human intervention must be commensurate with the model stakes and risks.

To conclude, the main risk identification and mitigation strategies are summarized in Fig. 1, along with the related caveats. Its content is not exhaustive and should be adapted to each use case. We also emphasize that the very purpose of the model needs to be ESG compatible. Every organization can use ML to perform optimizations that are socially or environmentally beneficial.

ML life cycle	Angle	E pillar	S pillar	G pillar
Data	Risk	Carbon emissions due to excessive storage, processing, and related infrastructure.	Using unchecked external data. Lack of transparency of pre-trained models. Embedded biases.	Inadequate personal and sensitive information retention. Lack of dataset transparency. Illegal collection of data.
	Mitigation	Proportionality rule based on use case. Data minimization. Reduced storage time.	Using reliable certified sources. Data exploration and pre-processing. Reweighing.	Data lineage. Documenting data limitations. Proportionality rule and data minimization.
	Limitation	Reduced availability of data resources for users.	Checking entire dataset is unachievable. Access to sensitive attributes for monitoring.	Detecting data bias in multidimensional settings is complex.
Design	Risk	Carbon cost due to feature engineering and model optimization, training, and inference.	Model bias in decision-making. Adversarial attacks.	Lack of transparency of model decision process.
	Mitigation	Model compression. Parsimonious feature selection. Cost-frugal optimization. Knowledge transfer.	Diagnostic tools: fault tree analysis, causal graph. Human oversight. Incremental learning. Differential privacy. In-processing techniques.	Model documentation. ESG model card. Auditing. XAI methods.
	Limitation	Bias amplification due to model compression. Lack of transparency of pre-trained models.	Utility vs. privacy. Disagreement between bias detection metrics. Fault tree in multidimensional settings.	Disparate quality of XAI methods across subgroups. Disagreement in XAI. Computational and storage cost of XAI.
Implementation	Risk	Carbon footprint of inefficient coding practices and data centers.	Shadow APIs. Flaws in third-party packages. Data leakage.	Lack of pipeline reproducibility.
	Mitigation	Sharing benchmarks. Code profiling. Optimizing data center location.	Model review, certification, and inventory. Adversarial testing. Reporting security breaches. Checking CVE.	Code documentation. Specifying software and hardware characteristics. Randomness control.
	Limitation	Performance/latency trade-off.	Exhaustive list of edge cases. Hidden vulnerabilities.	External package dependency. Difficult to achieve reproducibility with certain libraries or online learning.
Use & Monitoring	Risk	Deviation in the expected carbon footprint.	Deviation in bias detection metrics. Hidden vulnerabilities. Incidents. Increase in model uncertainty.	Algorithm aversion. Automation bias. No feedback from model users.
	Mitigation	Continuous monitoring: number of queries, average inference time, data size. Human-in-the-loop.	Human oversight. Monitoring bias detection metrics. Corrective actions. Checking new CVE. Reporting data breaches. Explaining model uncertainty.	Monitoring usage, user feedback, and rationale for model overrides. Training users on limitations. Human comprehensible explanations.
	Limitation	Complexity of carbon cost measurement in decentralized systems.	Disagreement between bias detection metrics. Patch deployment time frame.	Sparsity of explanations in multidimensional settings.

Fig. 1. ESG risk reduction strategies with related limitations throughout the ML lifecycle.

3   The ESG Model Card

3.1   Motivations Behind the ESG Model Card

Model cards have been suggested to concisely and systematically report ML models' main information [25]. They provide valuable insights about the model, such as its context, performance metrics across population subgroups, the representativeness of the evaluation data, and potential model limitations. On the other hand, the ESG model card concentrates on reporting the ESG net impacts of the ML lifecycle, along with the actions used to reach that outcome. The ESG model card can thus help to launch new initiatives and prompt model developers to build frugal, secure, and transparent ML systems.

As the example displayed in Fig. 2, the ESG model card is composed of five layers. The first layer includes the model details, its intended use, and three key risk metrics: the application stakes (low/medium/high), the automation level of the decision process (low/medium/high), and the adverse impact strength (low/medium/high). The model details and intended use sections were already proposed in the original model card [25]. The application stakes depend on the use case. For instance, using the model for triaging incoming patients in a hospital could be considered as a high-stake application. The automation levels low/medium/high mean that the decision is not/partially/fully automated, respectively. Lastly, the adverse impact strength is a qualitative evaluation of the whole ML lifecycle footprint, based on the ESG impacts described in the next layers. An organization might want to prevent fully automated models with strongly adverse impacts from being used for high-stakes applications. The next layers are used to report the ESG impacts throughout the ML lifecycle.

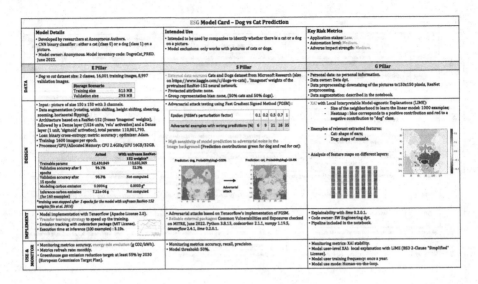

Fig. 2. ESG model card - Image classification.

For instance, in the data layer, we will report the environmental impacts due to data collection and processing, along with the mitigating actions which led to that result (e.g., the data center location). The content of these layers reflects the outcomes of the risk-based approach described previously.

3.2   Example: Image Classification

Image classification is a specific task of the object recognition process, which is required in applications such as autonomous driving [11] or crop maturity assessment [16]. To illustrate the relevance of the ESG model card, we present a simple example: the purpose of our model is to classify whether pictures contain either cats or dogs [24]. The first row in Fig. 2 provides general information about the model, its intended use and its key risk metrics. In the first column of the ESG model card, we point out the relevance of the transfer learning strategy using a pre-trained ResNet-152 [15], based on the accuracy level achieved after a few epochs and the low carbon emission level of the overall training process, as measured by CodeCarbon package [20,22]. Regarding the S pillar, we note the high sensitivity of model predictions to adversarial noise in the image background. We could recommend putting in place defense methods against such threats in order to improve the robustness of the model. In the Governance column, we highlight the use of LIME to understand the predictions of the model. This eXplainable AI method (XAI) seems also useful to pinpoint the effect of the FGSM adversarial attack on the pixels of the image and to extract some relevant features such as the characteristic shapes of a dog's muzzle or a cat's ear.

4 Conclusion

In this paper, we presented a risk-based approach to standardize safe ML deployment. Several practical principles have been suggested: proportionality, parsimony, or continuity, just to name a few. By carefully using its ML assets, an organization spreads positive ESG effects in its whole ecosystem. This initiative prompts innovators to develop safe ML systems: this is a virtuous circle. We also proposed the ESG model card for fairly reporting the model impacts and remediations across the ML lifecycle. Practitioners can make the most of the risk-based approach and ESG model card by adapting them to the use case at hand. Future collaborative work could focus on the design of an ESG MLOps tool. It would scale ESG principles by applying the best practices on the whole model portfolio of an organization. Such system would undoubtedly have to balance competing objectives with active human oversight.

References

1. Bender, E.M., Gebru, T., McMillan-Major, A., Shmitchell, S.: On the dangers of stochastic parrots: can language models be too big? In: Proceedings of the 2021 ACM Conference on Fairness, Accountability, and Transparency, pp. 610–623 (2021)
2. Bonnier, T., Bosch, B.: Engineering uncertainty representations to monitor distribution shifts. In: NeurIPS 2022 Workshop on Distribution Shifts: Connecting Methods and Applications (2022)
3. Burkart, N., Huber, M.F.: A survey on the explainability of supervised machine learning. J. Artif. Intell. Res. **70**, 245–317 (2021)
4. Cheng, Y., Wang, D., Zhou, P., Zhang, T.: Model compression and acceleration for deep neural networks: the principles, progress, and challenges. IEEE Signal Process. Mag. **35**(1), 126–136 (2018)
5. Cranor, L.F.: A framework for reasoning about the human in the loop. In: Proceedings of the Usability, Psychology, and Security, UPSEC 2008, San Francisco, CA, USA, 14 April 2008. USENIX Association (2008)
6. Dasgupta, P., Collins, J.B., Mittu, R.: Adversary-Aware Learning Techniques and Trends in Cybersecurity. Springer, Heidelberg (2021). https://doi.org/10.1007/978-3-030-55692-1
7. Dong, Y., et al.: Benchmarking adversarial robustness on image classification. In: Proceedings of the IEEE/CVF Conference on Computer Vision and Pattern Recognition, pp. 321–331 (2020)
8. Dwork, C., McSherry, F., Nissim, K., Smith, A.: Calibrating noise to sensitivity in private data analysis. In: TCC 2006. LNCS, vol. 3876, pp. 265–284. Springer, Heidelberg (2006). https://doi.org/10.1007/11681878_14
9. E.U.: General data protection regulation (GDPR) (2016). https://eur-lex.europa.eu/eli/reg/2016/679/oj. Accessed 01 June 2022
10. Frankle, J., Carbin, M.: The lottery ticket hypothesis: finding sparse, trainable neural networks. In: 7th International Conference on Learning Representations, ICLR 2019, New Orleans, LA, USA, 6–9 May 2019 (2019)
11. Fujiyoshi, H., Hirakawa, T., Yamashita, T.: Deep learning-based image recognition for autonomous driving. IATSS Res. **43**(4), 244–252 (2019)

12. Gebru, T., et al.: Datasheets for datasets. Commun. ACM **64**(12), 86–92 (2021)
13. Goodfellow, I.J., Shlens, J., Szegedy, C.: Explaining and harnessing adversarial examples. In: 3rd International Conference on Learning Representations, ICLR 2015, San Diego, CA, USA, 7–9 May 2015, Conference Track Proceedings (2015)
14. Gurumoorthy, K.S., Dhurandhar, A., Cecchi, G.A., Aggarwal, C.C.: Efficient data representation by selecting prototypes with importance weights. In: 2019 IEEE International Conference on Data Mining, ICDM 2019, Beijing, China, 8–11 November 2019, pp. 260–269. IEEE (2019)
15. He, K., Zhang, X., Ren, S., Sun, J.: Deep residual learning for image recognition. In: Proceedings of the IEEE Conference on Computer Vision and Pattern Recognition (CVPR) (2016)
16. Horng, G.J., Liu, M.X., Chen, C.C.: The smart image recognition mechanism for crop harvesting system in intelligent agriculture. IEEE Sens. J. **20**(5), 2766–2781 (2019)
17. Kamiran, F., Karim, A., Zhang, X.: Decision theory for discrimination-aware classification. In: 2012 IEEE 12th International Conference on Data Mining, pp. 924–929. IEEE (2012)
18. Krishna, S., et al.: The disagreement problem in explainable machine learning: a practitioner's perspective. arXiv preprint arXiv:2202.01602 (2022)
19. Kurita, K., Michel, P., Neubig, G.: Weight poisoning attacks on pre-trained models. In: Proceedings of the 58th Annual Meeting of the Association for Computational Linguistics, pp. 2793–2806. Association for Computational Linguistics, Online (2020)
20. Lacoste, A., Luccioni, A., Schmidt, V., Dandres, T.: Quantifying the carbon emissions of machine learning. In: Workshop on Tackling Climate Change with Machine Learning at NeurIPS 2019 (2019)
21. Larrazabal, A.J., Nieto, N., Peterson, V., Milone, D.H., Ferrante, E.: Gender imbalance in medical imaging datasets produces biased classifiers for computer-aided diagnosis. Proc. Natl. Acad. Sci. **117**(23), 12592–12594 (2020)
22. Lottick, K., Susai, S., Friedler, S.A., Wilson, J.P.: Energy usage reports: environmental awareness as part of algorithmic accountability. In: Workshop on Tackling Climate Change with Machine Learning at NeurIPS 2019 (2019)
23. Lundberg, S.M., Lee, S.I.: A unified approach to interpreting model predictions. In: Advances in Neural Information Processing Systems, vol. 30 (2017)
24. Microsoft: Cats and dogs dataset (2022). https://www.kaggle.com/c/dogs-vs-cats. Accessed 01 Jan 2023
25. Mitchell, M., et al.: Model cards for model reporting. In: Proceedings of the Conference on Fairness, Accountability, and Transparency, FAT* 2019, Atlanta, GA, USA, 29–31 January 2019, pp. 220–229. ACM (2019)
26. MITRE: CVE (1999). https://cve.mitre.org/. Accessed 01 June 2022
27. Neyshabur, B., Sedghi, H., Zhang, C.: What is being transferred in transfer learning? In: Advances in Neural Information Processing Systems, vol. 33, pp. 512–523 (2020)
28. Pan, S.J., Yang, Q.: A survey on transfer learning. IEEE Trans. Knowl. Data Eng. **22**(10), 1345–1359 (2010)
29. Papadopoulos, H., Proedrou, K., Vovk, V., Gammerman, A.: Inductive confidence machines for regression. In: Elomaa, T., Mannila, H., Toivonen, H. (eds.) ECML 2002. LNCS, vol. 2430, pp. 345–356. Springer, Heidelberg (2002). https://doi.org/10.1007/3-540-36755-1_29

30. Rahman, M.A., Rahman, T., Laganière, R., Mohammed, N.: Membership inference attack against differentially private deep learning model. Trans. Data Priv. **11**(1), 61–79 (2018)

31. Ribeiro, M.T., Singh, S., Guestrin, C.: "Why should i trust you?": explaining the predictions of any classifier. In: Proceedings of the 22nd ACM SIGKDD International Conference on Knowledge Discovery and Data Mining, KDD 2016, pp. 1135–1144 (2016)

32. Sezgin, E., Sirrianni, J., Linwood, S.L.: Operationalizing and implementing pretrained, large artificial intelligence linguistic models in the us health care system: outlook of generative pretrained transformer 3 (GPT-3) as a service model. JMIR Med. Inform. **10**(2), e32875 (2022)

33. Siddik, M.A.B., Shehabi, A., Marston, L.: The environmental footprint of data centers in the united states. Environ. Res. Lett. **16**(6), 064017 (2021)

34. Stevens, R., Suciu, O., Ruef, A., Hong, S., Hicks, M., Dumitraş, T.: Summoning demons: the pursuit of exploitable bugs in machine learning. arXiv preprint arXiv:1701.04739 (2017)

35. UNEP-FI: Who cares wins: Connecting financial markets to a changing world. UN GlobalCompact (2004)

36. Wu, Q., Wang, C., Huang, S.: Frugal optimization for cost-related hyperparameters. In: Proceedings of the AAAI Conference on Artificial Intelligence, vol. 35, pp. 10347–10354 (2021)

Towards Deep Anomaly Detection with Structured Knowledge Representations

Konstantin Kirchheim[✉]

Computer Science, Otto-von-Guericke University Magdeburg, Magdeburg, Germany
konstantin.kirchheim@ovgu.de

Abstract. Machine learning models tend to only make reliable predictions for inputs that are similar to the training data. Consequentially, anomaly detection, which can be used to detect unusual inputs, is critical for ensuring the safety of machine learning agents operating in open environments. In this work, we identify and discuss several limitations of current anomaly detection methods, such as their weak performance on tasks that require abstract reasoning, the inability to integrate background knowledge, and the opaqueness that undermines their trustworthiness in critical applications. Furthermore, we propose an architecture for anomaly detection models that aims to integrate structured knowledge representations to address these limitations. Our hypothesis is that this approach can improve performance and robustness, reduce the required resources (such as data and computation), and provide a higher degree of transparency. As a result, our work contributes to the increased safety of machine learning systems. Our code is publicly available. (https://github.com/kkirchheim/sumnist)

Keywords: Anomaly Detection · Out-of-Distribution Detection · Deep Learning · Machine Learning Safety · Hybrid Models

1 Introduction

Anomaly detection is a well-established field with numerous applications [20]. Some argue that anomalies play a fundamental role in driving scientific progress as they can expose flaws in our models of reality [12]. In recent years, anomaly detection methods have attracted increasing attention in the area of machine learning (ML) safety, as they can help to identify observations that are so dissimilar from the training data that a machine learning agent can not be expected to handle them reliably. In this paper, we propose to equip an anomaly detection model with abstract reasoning capabilities by using a hybrid architecture that combines Deep Neural Networks (DNNs) [13,22] with a structured knowledge representation. Our hypothesis is that structured modeling of human-understandable concepts in the representation learned by the DNN and directly

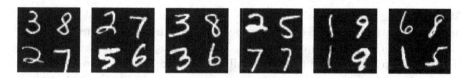

Fig. 1. Sample of the SuMNIST benchmark dataset created from MNIST. For normal examples, the numbers sum to 20. State-of-the-art anomaly detectors fail to solve this task. For details, see Sect. 5.

imposing constraints about which observations are considered *"normal"* can decrease the amount of data and computation required to train a good anomaly detection model to such an extent that learning a model for extremely high-dimensional streaming data becomes feasible with contemporary means. Furthermore, we argue that this architecture offers a higher degree of transparency compared to fully neural systems.

2   Motivation

A common assumption in anomaly detection is that *"normal"* data is drawn from some unknown probability distribution. The goal is then to identify *"anomalous"* samples that lie in low probability regions under this distribution. The prevalent approach in anomaly detection is to build a model of "normality", such that anomalies can be detected based on their deviation from this model [20]. Closely related fields are Novelty Detection [19], Out-of-Distribution (OOD) Detection [25] and Open-Set Recognition [6].

What Is the Problem? Despite their remarkable performance on high-dimensional inputs, current anomaly detection methods based on DNNs suffer from several drawbacks. For instance, it is surprisingly simple to construct anomaly detection problems that current models are unable to solve. Consider Fig. 1. State-of-the-art anomaly detection methods fail at this task, even when equipped with a large, pretrained Vision Transformer [3] (for details, see Sect. 5). Identifying the anomalous image based on only a few examples without additional information can be challenging, even for humans who possess extensive prior knowledge, e.g., on the representation of numbers by symbols. However, as soon as we introduce the constraint that the sum of the numbers corresponding to the depicted symbols should be constant, the task becomes trivial for humans.

Current DNN architectures seem to lack the kind of abstract reasoning capabilities required to solve tasks where the anomalousness arises on a semantic level, and they do not provide a straightforward way to directly integrate such constraints. Furthermore, their predictions are opaque: even if a DNN could solve the task perfectly, we would be unable to determine if it has actually learned what we see as the underlying semantic structure of the data or is just acting on spurious statistical patterns.

Will Scaling Solve the Problem? It has been argued that the largest advances in artificial intelligence have been brought by scaling general-purpose algorithms with more computation [23]. While scaling Large Language Models (LLM), researchers noticed emergent abilities that the models were not directly trained for [24]. For anomaly detection, similar trends can be observed [5]. For example, Fig. 2 depicts the classification accuracy and the corresponding anomaly detection performance of a ResNet architecture [26] with varying depth and height, using the MSP baseline method [10] on a common CIFAR10 OOD detection benchmark [16]. As we can see, higher model capacity is generally associated with better anomaly detection capabilities, even though the models are trained for the classification of normal data. Is solving anomaly detection just a matter of dataset size and model capacity?

Recent studies on Vision Transformers concluded that the performance of DNNs on large-scale anomaly detection tasks seems to have reached the limits of currently available data and computation [8]. Furthermore, a study of LLMs on a dataset with mathematics problems found that scaling models up seems to be surprisingly ineffective in improving performance, which suggests that the kind of abstract reasoning required for this task might be difficult to learn from scratch with current algorithms [9].

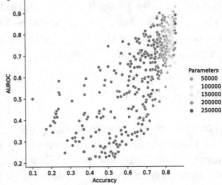

Fig. 2. Classification and anomaly detection performance of the MSP baseline on a common benchmark on CIFAR10.

3   Limitations of Current Approaches

In this section, we will briefly outline the shortcomings of contemporary methods for anomaly detection in real-world applications and consider their safety implications.

Classification. Detecting unusual inputs is a well-researched topic in ML because classifiers can make egregiously wrong predictions with high confidence when faced with such inputs [18,25]. In real-world use cases, there may be additional information about the classification task that restricts which inputs are considered normal. When classifying objects, humans can rely on rich structured background knowledge, such as hierarchical relations (e.g., *"A sheep is a mammal."*) or attributes associated with particular types of objects (e.g., *"All German stop signs are red octagons."*). Intuitively, such constraints provide additional information about the structure of the underlying data-generating distribution, including low-density regions or regions with no support. However, such knowledge is seldom utilized in current anomaly or OOD detection methods.

(a) Misclassified   (b) Biased   (c) Undetected

Fig. 3. Predictions of a Mask R-CNN-based object detector [7] trained on the COCO dataset [15] illustrate common failure modes of object detection models that are confronted with anomalies. In Fig. 3a, a deer (unknown class) is misclassified as a *dog*. In Fig. 3b, a sheep (known class) remains undetected, presumably because of its unusual color. In Fig. 3c, a moose (unknown class) is not detected.

Object Detection. While anomaly detection in object detection settings has recently received some attention, the topic has not yet been exhaustively studied [4]. The anomaly detection problem can be seen as having two aspects: *structural* and *logical* (or *semantic*) anomalies [2]. Structural anomalies could be objects of unknown categories or unusual variations of objects that otherwise belong to known categories. In safety-critical applications, such anomalies have to be localized. For example, Fig. 3a depicts a number of structural anomalies. Logical anomalies, on the other hand, can arise, e.g., from the arrangements of objects in an image [2]. SuMNIST (Sect. 5) can be seen as a logical anomaly detection problem.

Again, we hypothesize that prior knowledge, which is currently underutilized, can be used to facilitate the localization of both structural and logical anomalies. Such priors could include part-of-relations, which imply that two objects tend to co-occur (e.g., *"A human face is part of a human."*), or information about the relative position or orientation of objects in space (e.g., *"Humans usually stand on the ground."*).

Temporal Dynamic. In dynamic environments, there might be sequences of observations such that each observation is normal when considered in isolation while the sequence is anomalous as a whole. Anomalies in high-dimensional sequential data, such as videos or lidar streams, have, to the best of our knowledge, not yet been extensively studied in the context of ML safety. With more autonomous agents operating in dynamic environments, one could expect this topic to become increasingly important in the future. Again, humans possess certain prior knowledge, such as time evolution laws (e.g. *"A dog is unlikely to become a cat."*, or *"There is a limit to the velocity of objects."*) that constrains the space of probable sequences and that might be difficult to learn from scratch. However, it remains unclear how such priors could be integrated into DNNs.

Structure Learning. Up until here, we have assumed that knowledge about the world is provided to the detector. However, in some applications, it is conceivable that there are some known semantic concepts, but the rules that govern the relations between those concepts are unknown or subject to change over time. For example, we might expect that the presence of an object of type A implies the presence of another object of type B. Such associations might be inferred from a dataset. Yet, it remains unclear how structured knowledge, once integrated into DNNs, could be extended or updated.

4   Hybrid Models for Deep Anomaly Detection

To address the shortcomings of current anomaly detection systems, as outlined above, we propose a hybrid anomaly detection architecture that combines a DNN-based perception system with a reasoning system that verifies that the observations are compatible with knowledge of the domain. While it has been argued that integrating structured knowledge by using hybrid models could increase the robustness and performance of DNN-based models in general [17], to our knowledge, such approaches have not yet been explored for anomaly detection.

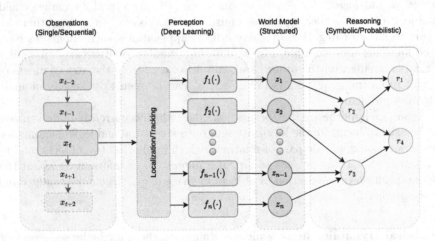

Fig. 4. Structure of our proposed architecture for deep anomaly detection with hybrid models: the DNN-based perception component localizes and tracks objects and updates the state of a structured world model from the observations. The reasoning component then draws inferences about the consistency of the world model with some background knowledge in order to detect anomalies.

The general architecture is depicted in Fig. 4. The task of the DNN-based perception system is to process the high-dimensional input to update the state of a *"world model"*, which represents the current observation on a semantic level, and that is designed to be human-interpretable. The perception system is necessary to close the gap between raw observations and human understandable concepts on which formal constraints can be defined. On top of this world model, we can then build a reasoning system that uses symbolic (e.g. logical/mathematical constraints, logic programming) or probabilistic models (e.g., probabilistic graphical models) that explicitly encode domain knowledge, such as constraints that impose restrictions on the space of probable worlds (or on transitions between world-states).

With the proposed design, it is possible to inspect the world model of the detector at any given time, since the structured model is by design human interpretable, which renders the system transparent. As described in Sect. 2, abstract reasoning capabilities, while possibly emergent from scaling general-purpose algorithms, are computationally expensive to learn from scratch. We argue that integrating prior knowledge in the proposed fashion could enable anomaly detection applications that are unattainable with the computational resources and data currently available.

5 Proof of Concept

In this section, we demonstrate that a simple variant of our proposed model can outperform state-of-the-art approaches on our example dataset. Our implementation is based on PyTorch-OOD [11].

Dataset. We present SuMNIST, a new anomaly detection benchmark dataset with 60,000 training examples. For each training image, we select four different random numbers $\in [0, 9]$ that sum to 20 and concatenate corresponding randomly sampled images from the MNIST training set. The resulting images have a size of 56×56. For the test set, we follow the same process, but sample images from the MNIST test set to avoid target leakage. In addition to the 7500 normal test images, we generate 2500 anomalous images for which the numbers do not sum to 20.

Model. As perception system ϕ, we use a Faster R-CNN with a ResNet-18 backbone which we train to detect and classify the numbers. For some input $x \in \mathbb{R}^{56 \times 56}$, the corresponding world model $\phi(x)$ is the tuple of detected numbers that were classified with confidence > 0.8. We then propose two kinds of reasoning systems: (1) *Hybrid Memory* stores a set $\mathcal{V}$ of all world models encountered during training $\mathcal{V} = \{\phi(x) : x \in \mathcal{D}_{train}\}$. At inference time, some input x is marked as anomalous if and only if $\phi(x) \notin \mathcal{V}$. Note that this approach, which is effectively a lookup table that checks if the current class configuration has been observed during training, does not require knowledge of the numbers corresponding to each MNIST class. (2) *Hybrid Sum* calculates the sum over all number in the world model and checks if it is equal to 20. As this hard-coded rule reflects the true underlying semantic structure of the data, we would expect the performance to be close to optimal.

Results. Results can be found in Tab. 1. As we can see, our domain-specific models achieve almost perfect scores, outperforming all other approaches by far. Only the Deep Nearest-Neighbor model slightly outperforms random guessing.

Table 1. Results for several shallow and deep anomaly detectors. ↑ indicates that higher values are better, while ↓ indicates the opposite. All values in percent.

Method	Backbone	AUROC ↑	AUPR-IN ↑	AUPR-OUT ↑	FPR95 ↓
Nearest Neighbor	–	50.00	59.18	90.82	100.00
Deep Nearest Neighbor [1]	ViT-L/16	51.19	18.81	82.21	94.34
Mahalanobis	–	50.00	59.18	82.31	100.00
Deep Mahalanobis [14]	ViT-L/16	50.00	59.18	84.58	100.00
Deep SVDD [21]	–	49.32	18.07	81.28	95.14
Hybrid Memory (**Ours**)	ResNet-18	95.30	82.72	99.29	9.26
Hybrid Sum (**Ours**)	ResNet-18	**98.41**	**92.69**	**99.76**	**2.98**

6   Conclusion

In this paper, we discussed the shortcomings of deep anomaly detection methods and their safety implications and illustrated the problem by presenting a simple benchmark task that current methods can not solve due to their lack of reasoning abilities. Furthermore, we provided evidence that, at least in the near future, such abilities will not emerge from simply scaling current architectures. We then proposed an architecture for anomaly detection systems that can solve these problems, which we demonstrate on our benchmark dataset. Future work should extend the presented architecture and investigate its applicability to larger, real-world datasets.

References

1. Bergman, L., Cohen, N., Hoshen, Y.: Deep nearest neighbor anomaly detection. arXiv preprint arXiv:2002.10445 (2020)
2. Bergmann, P., Batzner, K., Fauser, M., Sattlegger, D., Steger, C.: Beyond dents and scratches: logical constraints in unsupervised anomaly detection and localization. Int. J. Comput. Vision **130**(4), 947–969 (2022)
3. Dosovitskiy, A., et al.: An image is worth 16x16 words: transformers for image recognition at scale. In: International Conference on Learning Representations (2021)
4. Du, X., Wang, Z., Cai, M., Li, Y.: VOS: learning what you don't know by virtual outlier synthesis. In: International Conference on Learning Representations (2021)
5. Fort, S., Ren, J., Lakshminarayanan, B.: Exploring the limits of out-of-distribution detection. In: Advances in Neural Information Processing Systems, vol. 34 (2021)
6. Geng, C., Huang, S.J., Chen, S.: Recent advances in open set recognition: a survey. IEEE Trans. Pattern Anal. Mach. Intell. **40**, 3614–3631 (2020)

7. He, K., Gkioxari, G., Dollár, P., Girshick, R.: Mask r-CNN. In: Proceedings of the IEEE International Conference on Computer Vision, pp. 2961–2969 (2017)
8. Hendrycks, D., Basart, S., Mazeika, M., Mostajabi, M., Steinhardt, J., Song, D.: Scaling out-of-distribution detection for real-world settings. arXiv preprint arXiv:1911.11132 (2019)
9. Hendrycks, D., et al.: Measuring mathematical problem solving with the math dataset. arXiv preprint arXiv:2103.03874 (2021)
10. Hendrycks, D., Gimpel, K.: A baseline for detecting misclassified and out-of-distribution examples in neural networks. In: International Conference on Learning Representations (2017)
11. Kirchheim, K., Filax, M., Ortmeier, F.: PyTorch-OOD: a library for out-of-distribution detection based on pyTorch. In: Proceedings of the IEEE/CVF Conference on Computer Vision and Pattern Recognition (CVPR) Workshops, pp. 4351–4360 (2022)
12. Kuhn, T.S.: The structure of scientific revolutions, vol. 111. Chicago University of Chicago Press, Chicago (1970)
13. LeCun, Y., Bengio, Y., Hinton, G.: Deep learning. Nature **521**(7553), 436–444 (2015)
14. Lee, K., Lee, K., Lee, H., Shin, J.: A simple unified framework for detecting out-of-distribution samples and adversarial attacks. In: Advances in Neural Information Processing Systems, vol. 31 (2018)
15. Lin, T.-Y., et al.: Microsoft COCO: common objects in context. In: Fleet, D., Pajdla, T., Schiele, B., Tuytelaars, T. (eds.) ECCV 2014. LNCS, vol. 8693, pp. 740–755. Springer, Cham (2014). https://doi.org/10.1007/978-3-319-10602-1_48
16. Liu, W., Wang, X., Owens, J., Li, Y.: Energy-based out-of-distribution detection. In: Advances in Neural Information Processing Systems, vol. 33 (2020)
17. Marcus, G.: The next decade in AI: four steps towards robust artificial intelligence. arXiv preprint arXiv:2002.06177 (2020)
18. Nguyen, A., Yosinski, J., Clune, J.: Deep neural networks are easily fooled: high confidence predictions for unrecognizable images. In: Proceedings of the IEEE Conference on Computer Vision and Pattern Recognition, pp. 427–436 (2015)
19. Pidhorskyi, S., Almohsen, R., Adjeroh, D.A., Doretto, G.: Generative probabilistic novelty detection with adversarial autoencoders. In: Advances in Neural Information Processing Systems, vol. 31 (2018)
20. Ruff, L., et al.: A unifying review of deep and shallow anomaly detection. Proc. IEEE **109**, 756–795 (2021)
21. Ruff, L., et al.: Deep one-class classification. In: International Conference on Machine Learning, pp. 4393–4402. PMLR (2018)
22. Schmidhuber, J.: Deep learning in neural networks: an overview. Neural Netw. **61**, 85–117 (2015)
23. Sutton, R.: The bitter lesson. In: Incomplete Ideas vol. 13, no. 1 (2019)
24. Wei, J., et al.: Emergent abilities of large language models. In: Transactions on Machine Learning Research (2022). Survey Certification
25. Yang, J., Zhou, K., Li, Y., Liu, Z.: Generalized out-of-distribution detection: a survey. ArXiv abs/2110.11334 (2021)
26. Zagoruyko, S., Komodakis, N.: Wide residual networks. In: British Machine Vision Conference 2016. British Machine Vision Association (2016)

Evaluating and Increasing Segmentation Robustness in CARLA

Venkatesh Thirugnana Sambandham[✉], Konstantin Kirchheim,
and Frank Ortmeier

Department Computer Science, Otto-von-Guericke University, Magdeburg, Germany
{venkatesh.thirugnana,konstantin.kirchheim,frank.ortmeier}@ovgu.de

Abstract. Model robustness is a crucial property in safety-critical applications such as autonomous driving and medical diagnosis. In this paper, we use the CARLA simulation environment to evaluate the robustness of various architectures for semantic segmentation to adverse environmental changes. Contrary to previous work, the environmental changes that we test the models against are not applied to existing images, but rendered directly in the simulation, enabling more realistic robustness tests. Surprisingly, we find that Transformers provide only slightly increased robustness compared to some CNNs. Furthermore, we demonstrate that training on a small set of adverse samples can significantly improve the robustness of most models. The code and supplementary results for our experiments are available online (https://github.com/venkatesh-thiru/weather-robustness).

Keywords: Deep Learning · Robustness · Simulation · Segmentation

1 Introduction

Robustness is a crucial property of Deep Learning (DL) models, enabling them to generalize well to data with significant variance or domain drift. Model robustness is particularly important in safety-critical applications such as autonomous driving [17] and medical diagnosis [1] to ensure the safety of DL model-dependent systems [18]. While current research often focuses on adversarial robustness, where an adversary intentionally alters the model inputs [1,8,22], adversarial examples usually do not occur naturally. Previous works that evaluated the robustness of Convolutional Neural Network (CNN) models for image classification [10], object detection [16], and semantic segmentation [12] tasks estimated the robustness by overlaying images from existing datasets with synthetic perturbations such as noise, rain, snow, and fog. However, these overlays may not capture the complexities of natural environments accurately. Furthermore, Vision Transformers (ViT) [5] recently outperformed CNN-based models on many computer vision tasks; however, their robustness has not been evaluated.

Supplementary Information The online version contains supplementary material available at https://doi.org/10.1007/978-3-031-40953-0_33.

Unlike previous works, we use CARLA to apply environmental conditions directly to the simulation that generates the data instead of modifying existing images. This approach allows us to simulate more realistic environmental conditions - including realistic reflections in water or changing shadows - and renders the modifications more consistent. We evaluate the robustness of several state-of-the-art semantic segmentation models, including various CNNs and a Vision Transformer [20], with different backbones.

In addition to testing model robustness, we demonstrate that training on a small set of samples with adverse weather conditions can significantly improve the robustness of most models.

2   Related Works

Several studies have examined the robustness of transformer architectures in various contexts, comparing them with other architectures. [11] found no clear advantage of transformers over Multilayer Perceptrons (MLPs) in terms of robustness for Lane Departure Warning systems. [2] compared transformers and CNN models for image classification and found that CNNs can exhibit comparable robustness. [3] observed that Vision Transformers tend to outperform ResNet models in terms of robustness and performance for image classification. For semantic segmentation, [12] benchmarked the robustness of various CNN architectures to adversarial attacks and adverse weather conditions. [15] demonstrated that convolution-based models are significantly more robust than transformer-based models on artificially corrupted data in segmentation, object detection, and classification tasks. While some works benchmarked CNN and transformer models on adverse weather conditions [3,12], the adverse weather corruptions are overlaid onto the images. In this work, we generated a testing dataset by inducing different weather and lighting parameters to extract identical scenarios in combinations of different conditions.

3   Dataset and Architectures

We generated our dataset using the CARLA simulation environment, which allowed us to precisely control the environmental conditions. The generated images and segmentation masks have a resolution of 1280 × 720 and include 23 classes, such as road, green cover, car, and pedestrian.

(a) Training   (b) Rain   (c) Fog   (d) Sun

Fig. 1. Example images from our test dataset depicting identical scenes under diverse environmental conditions.

Training Dataset. To create our training dataset, we simulated a 60-min (in-simulation) drive at 30 frames/s and captured every 40th frame, resulting in 2700 images. For the validation set, we selected a different world map and simulated a 15-min (in-simulation) drive, resulting in 750 images. For both sets, the environment was set to a clear noon scenario, with no rain or fog and a solar angle of $90°$.

Test Data. We created a test dataset consisting of a challenging 10-second scenario at a crossroads. The scenario, which we recorded on a different map to avoid target leakage, includes, among others, pedestrians crossing the street, cars, and motorbikes. We created several versions of this scene, where we varied the rain and fog intensity between $\{0, 25, 50, 75, 100\}$ and the solar altitude angle between $\{-60°, 0°, 90°\}$, corresponding to *night*, *dawn*, and *noon*, respectively, which resulted in 75 different scenarios with 300 test images each. A sample of images can be found in Fig. 1.

Architectures and Training. We tested three commonly used fully convolutional architectures, namely UNet [6], FPN [14], and PSPNet [21]. Each of these architectures was trained with four different feature extraction backbones: ResNet-50 and ResNet-101 [9], EfficientNet [19], and SegFormer [20] (MiT-B3, 44M parameters). Each backbone was pre-trained on the ImageNet-1K dataset [7]. We trained the models with the Adam optimizer [13] for 100 epochs with a

Table 1. Performance under synthetic image perturbations. All values in percent.

Decoder	Backbone	Clear (mIoU)	Noise		Blur	
			G	PD	G	M
UNet	ResNet-50	88.42	45.21	23.55	85.39	82.08
	ResNet-101	88.02	30.75	19.82	85.37	82.54
	EfficientNet B6	**88.91**	51.34	17.06	82.91	81.52
	MiT-B3	88.84	57.64	18.92	86.22	83.62
FPN	ResNet-50	87.54	74.37	37.60	84.45	80.17
	ResNet-101	88.42	62.0	31.87	86.09	81.52
	EfficientNet B6	88.81	76.34	59.17	82.82	79.69
	MiT-B3	88.84	**83.75**	61.38	**86.69**	**84.03**
PSPNet	ResNet-50	87.35	67.34	12.86	82.61	78.86
	ResNet-101	87.44	47.41	17.49	81.57	80.45
	EfficientNet B6	87.91	40.22	37.74	78.55	79.31
	MiT-B3	87.74	81.93	**62.09**	85.87	83.16

batch size of 5, minimizing the cross-entropy. The initial learning rate of 0.001 was reduced by a factor of 0.75 if no improvements in the validation loss were observed over 10 epochs. We validated the models at the end of each epoch and subsequently tested the model with the best validation loss.

4 Robustness Testing

We measure the performance of models in terms of their mean Intersection over Union (mIoU) on the test set. The dataset consists of multiple classes, so the IoU of all the classes is balanced based on the support of each class on each ground truth mask. Under good conditions, the models performed similarly.

Synthetic Image Perturbations. We evaluated the robustness against four different synthetic perturbations: Gaussian Noise (G), Pixel Dropout Noise (PD), Gaussian Blur (G), and Motion Blur (M). We test the models' robustness by applying different perturbations to the input images. Results are given in Table 1.

The FPN architecture with a SegFormer backbone performed significantly better on the Gaussian noise than other models. We also observe that the UNet models, regardless of the backbone, perform very poorly under both noise perturbations. Regarding the PD noise, all models show a significant drop in performance. In contrast, Blurring does not seem to have as much of an impact.

Table 2. Mean Intersection over Union (mIoU) under simulated environmental conditions. All values in percent.

Decoder	Backbone	Rain									Fog					
		night ($-60°$)			dawn ($0°$)			noon ($90°$)			night		dawn		noon	
		0	50	100	0	50	100	0	50	100	50	100	50	100	50	100
UNet	ResNet-50	05.9	04.9	04.7	06.2	05.3	05.3	88.0	86.0	50.4	06.5	04.5	06.5	04.5	69.6	60.9
	ResNet-101	06.5	05.6	05.5	07.0	06.2	06.6	88.4	86.3	52.8	06.6	04.9	06.6	04.9	70.3	65.2
	EfficientNet-B6	26.4	16.4	07.1	40.3	25.2	11.4	**88.9**	87.1	66.7	32.1	29.4	32.1	29.4	**73.8**	**69.8**
	MiT-B3	05.5	05.3	05.0	05.5	05.2	05.3	88.8	86.7	46.9	04.9	04.7	04.9	04.6	72.0	66.7
FPN	ResNet-50	30.2	23.7	21.7	28.8	22.8	20.3	87.5	85.7	67.7	27.6	25.4	27.6	25.4	70.4	64.9
	ResNet-101	34.4	23.4	24.2	33.2	23.8	23.3	88.4	87.4	68.8	33.3	31.8	33.3	31.8	72.3	64.7
	EfficientNet-B6	47.3	35.0	28.0	46.6	34.8	26.8	88.8	87.4	73.9	**44.3**	42.5	**44.3**	42.5	71.4	67.2
	MiT-B3	**48.1**	**42.4**	**40.1**	**46.8**	**35.9**	**24.7**	88.8	**87.8**	**75.2**	44.2	**43.3**	44.2	**43.4**	73.6	69.4
PSPNet	ResNet-50	35.4	25.3	03.9	41.1	33.5	05.6	87.4	85.3	66.8	33.9	33.8	33.9	33.8	68.8	61.1
	ResNet-101	07.7	05.0	02.7	08.5	06.0	03.5	87.4	85.7	65.4	07.6	06.4	07.6	06.4	68.0	58.0
	EfficientNet-B6	40.7	19.7	04.1	37.0	17.9	08.4	87.9	84.5	64.9	31.6	29.8	31.6	29.8	71.8	67.8
	MiT-B3	26.1	20.7	27.0	25.7	22.4	17.0	87.7	84.6	65.3	22.0	21.8	22.1	21.8	68.7	60.6

Adverse Weather Conditions. The performance of different models under adverse environmental conditions is listed in Table 2. All models exhibit a significant performance drop when tested on adverse light conditions, even without adverse weather, regardless of the backbones and architectures. Although the UNet with EfficientNet B6 encoder performed best in the clear scenario, the model performance drops drastically for adverse lighting conditions. Similar to the experiments with synthetic perturbations, the FPN models with EfficientNet B6 and SegFormer appear significantly more robust in many scenarios, with only slight differences between both models. Additional results for combinations of weather and lighting conditions are provided with our supplementaries.

Overall, our findings suggest that ViT-based architectures might offer slightly better robustness than some CNN-based architectures. However, given their higher computational and memory requirements, using smaller models like EfficientNet might prove beneficial in scenarios where slightly lower robustness is preferred to increased latency.

5   Improving Robustness via Fine-Tuning

Our second objective is to investigate the potential of fine-tuning models to improve their performance under adverse environmental conditions. A combination of five fog and rain intensity levels and three different lighting conditions yields 75 distinct scenarios to achieve complete coverage. To systematically identify the best scenario that maximally increases the training dataset coverage, we used the 2-projection coverage metric [4].

We iteratively generated additional training and validation scenarios, achieving 100% coverage after 26 iterations. This was done by calculating the 2-projection coverage (equally weighted rain, fog, and solar angle parameters), identifying the best scenario, and adding 35 training and 5 validation samples for each configuration. More details about this process can be found in the supplementaries.

The performance of the FPN architecture with MiT-B3 and EfficientNet B6 backbones over the course of this process is provided in Fig. 3. Interestingly, the performance for both models converges fast. To identify this behavior, we took the base model trained on the training dataset and fine-tuned it on every scenario. We noticed that the model's performance improved significantly due to the configuration of the first generated scenario, wherein the rain level was set at 25, the fog level at 50, and the solar angle at $-60°$. From Fig. 2,

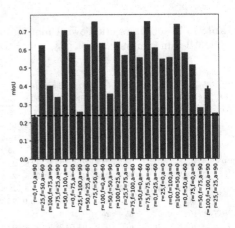

Fig. 2. Comparison of mIoU under extreme weather conditions {rain(r) = 100; fog(f) = 100; solar angle(a) = $-60°$} of the base model before and after fine-tuning on different scenarios.

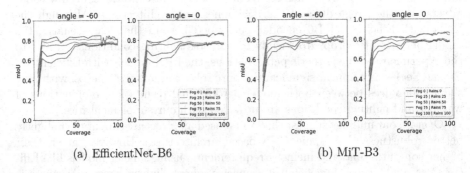

(a) EfficientNet-B6   (b) MiT-B3

Fig. 3. mIoU of the FPN model with Efficientnet B6 and MiT-B3 backbones, at different weather conditions on each iteration of finetuning. The performances of both models drastically increase on the first iteration of fine-tuning.

we could observe that there were no significant improvements in the mIoU of some models even after fine-tuning, such scenarios are very close to the actual training dataset with low fog/rain intensity and noon conditions.

6 Conclusion and Future Work

In this work, we used the CARLA simulator to evaluate the robustness of several state-of-the-art segmentation architectures with CNN and Vision Transformer-based feature extractors. Our experimental results suggest that the transformer-based backbones are comparably robust to different perturbations and weather conditions. However, we found that the EfficientNet B6 model also exhibited competitive performance while being far more resource-efficient, which aligns with other related works. Additionally, we demonstrated that fine-tuning with a few training examples (compared to the size of the training dataset) with adverse conditions can drastically improve model robustness.

In this work, we used hybrid segmentation models with a transformer-based feature extractor and a CNN-based decoder. Future research should investigate whether our findings hold for fully transformer-based models, CNNs with dilated convolutions and CNNs inspired by the design of ViTs. Moreover, further research is necessary to explore the trade-offs between model size, robustness, and performance in various application domains. Replicating our experiments in field tests with real-world data could reveal if our conclusions generalize to real world conditions.

References

1. Apostolidis, K.D., Papakostas, G.A.: A survey on adversarial deep learning robustness in medical image analysis. Electronics 10(17), 2132 (2021)
2. Bai, Y., Mei, J., Yuille, A.L., Xie, C.: Are transformers more robust than CNNs? In: Ranzato, M., Beygelzimer, A., Dauphin, Y., Liang, P., Vaughan, J.W. (eds.) Advances in Neural Information Processing Systems, vol. 34, pp. 26831–26843. Curran Associates, Inc. (2021)
3. Bhojanapalli, S., Chakrabarti, A., Glasner, D., Li, D., Unterthiner, T., Veit, A.: Understanding robustness of transformers for image classification. In: Proceedings of the IEEE/CVF International Conference on Computer Vision, pp. 10231–10241 (2021)
4. Cheng, C.-H., Huang, C.-H., Yasuoka, H.: Quantitative projection coverage for testing ML-enabled autonomous systems. In: Lahiri, S.K., Wang, C. (eds.) ATVA 2018. LNCS, vol. 11138, pp. 126–142. Springer, Cham (2018). https://doi.org/10.1007/978-3-030-01090-4_8
5. Dosovitskiy, A., et al.: An image is worth 16 × 16 words: transformers for image recognition at scale. In: International Conference on Learning Representations (2021). https://openreview.net/forum?id=YicbFdNTTy
6. Falk, T., et al.: U-Net: deep learning for cell counting, detection, and morphometry. Nat. Methods 16(1), 67–70 (2019)
7. Fei-Fei, L., Deng, J., Li, K.: ImageNet: constructing a large-scale image database. J. Vis. 9(8), 1037–1037 (2009)

8. Goodfellow, I.J., Shlens, J., Szegedy, C.: Explaining and harnessing adversarial examples. In: International Conference on Learning Representations (2015)

9. He, K., Zhang, X., Ren, S., Sun, J.: Deep residual learning for image recognition. In: Proceedings of the IEEE Conference on Computer Vision and Pattern Recognition, pp. 770–778 (2016)

10. Hendrycks, D., Dietterich, T.: Benchmarking neural network robustness to common corruptions and perturbations. In: Proceedings of the International Conference on Learning Representations (2019)

11. Hsuan-Cheng Liao, B., Cheng, C.H., Esen, H., Knoll, A.: Are transformers more robust? Towards exact robustness verification for transformers. arXiv e-prints, pp. arXiv-2202 (2022)

12. Kamann, C., Rother, C.: Benchmarking the robustness of semantic segmentation models. In: Proceedings of the IEEE/CVF Conference on Computer Vision and Pattern Recognition, pp. 8828–8838 (2020)

13. Kingma, D.P., Ba, J.: Adam: a method for stochastic optimization. arXiv preprint arXiv:1412.6980 (2014)

14. Lin, T.Y., Dollár, P., Girshick, R., He, K., Hariharan, B., Belongie, S.: Feature pyramid networks for object detection. In: Proceedings of the IEEE Conference on Computer Vision and Pattern Recognition, pp. 2117–2125 (2017)

15. Liu, Z., Mao, H., Wu, C.Y., Feichtenhofer, C., Darrell, T., Xie, S.: A convnet for the 2020s. In: Proceedings of the IEEE/CVF Conference on Computer Vision and Pattern Recognition, pp. 11976–11986 (2022)

16. Michaelis, C., et al.: Benchmarking robustness in object detection: autonomous driving when winter is coming. In: Machine Learning for Autonomous Driving Workshop, NeurIPS 2019, vol. 190707484 (2019)

17. Nesti, F., Rossolini, G., Nair, S., Biondi, A., Buttazzo, G.: Evaluating the robustness of semantic segmentation for autonomous driving against real-world adversarial patch attacks. In: Proceedings of the IEEE/CVF Winter Conference on Applications of Computer Vision, pp. 2280–2289 (2022)

18. Schwalbe, G., Schels, M.: A survey on methods for the safety assurance of machine learning based systems. In: 10th European Congress on Embedded Real Time Software and Systems (ERTS 2020) (2020)

19. Tan, M., Le, Q.: EfficientNet: rethinking model scaling for convolutional neural networks. In: International Conference on Machine Learning, pp. 6105–6114. PMLR (2019)

20. Xie, E., Wang, W., Yu, Z., Anandkumar, A., Alvarez, J.M., Luo, P.: SegFormer: simple and efficient design for semantic segmentation with transformers. In: Neural Information Processing Systems (NeurIPS) (2021)

21. Zhao, H., Shi, J., Qi, X., Wang, X., Jia, J.: Pyramid scene parsing network. In: Proceedings of the IEEE Conference on Computer Vision and Pattern Recognition, pp. 2881–2890 (2017)

22. Zhou, X., Kouzel, M., Alemzadeh, H.: Robustness testing of data and knowledge driven anomaly detection in cyber-physical systems. In: 2022 52nd Annual IEEE/IFIP International Conference on Dependable Systems and Networks Workshops (DSN-W), pp. 44–51 (2022). https://doi.org/10.1109/DSN-W54100.2022.00017

Safety Integrity Levels for Artificial Intelligence

Simon Diemert$^{(\boxtimes)}$, Laure Millet, Jonathan Groves, and Jeff Joyce

Critical Systems Labs Inc., Vancouver, Canada
simon.diemert@cslabs.com

Abstract. Artificial Intelligence (AI) and Machine Learning (ML) technologies are rapidly being adopted to perform safety-related tasks in critical systems. These AI-based systems pose significant challenges, particularly regarding their assurance. Existing safety approaches defined in internationally recognized standards such as ISO 26262, DO-178C, UL 4600, EN 50126, and IEC 61508 do not provide detailed guidance on how to assure AI-based systems. For conventional (non-AI) systems, these standards adopt a 'Level of Rigor' (LoR) approach, where increasingly demanding engineering activities are required as risk associated with the system increases. This paper proposes an extension to existing LoR approaches, which considers the complexity of the task(s) being performed by an AI-based component. Complexity is assessed in terms of input entropy and output non-determinism, and then combined with the allocated Safety Integrity Level (SIL) to produce an AI-SIL. That AI-SIL may be used to identify appropriate measures and techniques for the development and verification of the system. The proposed extension is illustrated by examples from the automotive, aviation, and medical industries.

Keywords: Artificial Intelligence · Machine Learning · Safety Integrity Levels · Safety-Critical Systems

1 Introduction

Artificial Intelligence (AI), including Machine Learning (ML), methods are widely used in many applications. These methods are especially effective when the task is too complex to be reasonably implemented by conventional software but is still constrained enough to permit learning at a manageable scale [1]. As such, many systems combine AI and conventional methods such that the AI performs a task and then provides the results to the conventional software/hardware for further processing. We refer to these systems as AI-based systems. Even though the system is not entirely implemented by AI, its function(s) would be impossible (or severely limited) without the use of AI methods. We use the term "AI" to broadly refer to software intended to mimic human intelligence to perform a task that, when performed by a human being, requires some combination of perceiving, knowing, synthesizing, reasoning, and decision-making [2], these are also referred to as 'cognitive systems' [3].

Safety-critical systems are systems where the consequences of failure might cause injury, loss of life, damage to equipment/property, or environmental damage. There

J. Guiochet et al. (Eds.): SAFECOMP 2023 Workshops, LNCS 14182, pp. 397–409, 2023.
https://doi.org/10.1007/978-3-031-40953-0_34

are established engineering methods for managing risk associated with these systems. Such approaches are captured in domain-specific safety standards such as: ISO 26262 automotive systems; IEC 61058 and IEC 61511 industrial control systems; MIL-STD-882 defense systems, EN 50126 rail systems; and DO-178C for aviation. These standards adopt a "level of rigour" (LoR) approach to risk management where more demanding engineering activities are required as the level of risk increases.

AI-based systems are now used in safety-critical applications and are subject to these safety standards. We have observed limitations of existing risk assessment methods and LoR approaches for AI-based systems. First, existing risk assessment methods are not well-calibrated for AI-based systems and sometimes fail to differentiate between systems that, from a common-sense point of view, pose different levels of risk. For instance, in ISO 26262, many AI-based systems are (unnecessarily) assigned ASIL D (highest level of criticality) because they remove an opportunity for a human supervisor to intervene [3]. Second, to our knowledge, there is no framework that integrates the growing body of knowledge on AI assurance in a manner that is compatible with the LoR approach used by existing standards. While some recent standards partially address AI (such as ISO 21448:2022 and UL4600 2nd Edition), there is a gap in terms of connecting the standards guidance and knowledge from other academic and industrial resources [3–9] with existing LoR approaches.

This concept paper addresses this gap by proposing the notion of an Artificial Intelligence Safety Integrity Level, i.e., an AI-SIL (Sect. 3). Our approach extends existing SIL determination practices with two new criteria (input entropy and output nondeterminism) that assess the complexity of a task performed by an AI-based system. Importantly, our method focuses on the task performed by AI, not its implementation. These new criteria are combined with an existing SIL to produce an AI-SIL that may then be used to guide AI-specific LoR activities in addition to activities already covered by the existing SIL. We show how an AI-SIL can be used to grade LoR activities (Sect. 4) and then, illustrate the method on six example systems (Sect. 5).

2   Background on Level of Rigour Methods

This section provides a short introduction to risk assessment methods from industrial standards for conventional software, and how the results of the assessment are used to drive LoR engineering activities.

Risk Assessment. A pre-requisite to risk assessment is identifying hazardous events. Once hazards are identified, risk assessment methods typically combine various factors (often severity and likelihood) to determine a measure of risk or risk ranking. Assessment methods consider among other factors severity and likelihood, and can be performed quantitatively or qualitatively. The choice of method depends on the system, availability of data to support the assessment, and applicable standards. In general, methods for risk assessment are based on purely functional or 'black box' views that disregards whatever might be known about the design or implementation of the system.

After the initial risk assessment, functional safety standards have different methods for using the result. For instance, IEC 61508 adopts the perspective that an additional safety-related system (e.g., a safety monitor) should be used to reduce the level of risk associated with the 'plain system' to a tolerable level. The magnitude of risk reduction determines the SIL.

Other standards use the initial risk assessment result to directly determine a SIL. For example, ISO 26262 uses a qualitative approach for ASIL (Automotive Safety Integrity Level) determination that takes account of severity, exposure, and controllability of a hazardous event [10]. Given rankings for each factor, a tabular method is used to determine the ASIL for each hazard. For example, a high severity, low probability of exposure, and uncontrollable hazard corresponds to ASIL B.

Level of Rigour. Once a SIL (or equivalent) is determined it is used to select an appropriate combination of engineering methods to mitigate the risk of a hazardous event occurring, we refer to this as a "Level of Rigour" (LoR) approach. As the SIL (now a proxy for risk or risk reduction) increases, more demanding engineering activities are prescribed. The LoR approach is particularly useful for software, where the probability of failure cannot easily be quantified. It is frequently used as a basis for decisions about the allocation of resources, imposing constraints on the development process, and establishing criteria to measure the adequacy of work products. For example, consider software unit verification, an activity required by ISO 26262. As the ASIL increases, more demanding verification activities are required: ASILs A and B (lower criticalities) "Data flow analysis" is only "recommended" but at ASILs C and D (higher criticality) it is "highly recommended". Similarly, "Formal verification" is highly recommended for ASIL D.

Limitations. Conventional risk assessment methods used in multiple application domains/industries do not help differentiating risk levels for systems that make use of AI. This is evident in the case of fully autonomous systems where there is limited opportunity for intervention by a human supervisor [3]. For example, many new vehicles include some form of Collision Avoidance System (CAS), which reduce the risk of an imminent collision with a forward vehicle. It may be reasonable to suppose that CAS is 'less complex' than a path planning function in a fully autonomous vehicle. However, the method used in ISO 26262 for road vehicles would yield the same (A)SIL, due to the consideration of 'controllability' criterion. As in the case of CAS, there might not be any way for the human driver to "cancel" an unsafe emergency braking action initiated by the automation.

The lack of differentiation afforded by existing LoR approaches for systems that depend on AI motivates our search for a method that accounts for the complexity of tasks performed by AI and that is compatible with existing LoR approaches.

3 AI Safety Integrity Levels (AI-SILs)

Given the challenges of LoR methods discussed above, this section introduces a new method for assessing the criticality of AI-based functions. This method builds on the existing SIL assessment methods used by industrial standards. Different industries use different terminology; for example, DO-178C for airborne systems uses a Design Assurance Level (DAL) and ISO 26262 for automotive systems uses Automotive Safety Integrity Level (ASIL). While recognizing that there are nuances to each of these risk grading systems, for generality we use "SIL" with the expectation that our method can be tailored to a specific industry or risk management approach.

The output of the method is an AI Safety Integrity Level (AI-SIL) that can be used as input to subsequent engineering activities, such as an LoR-based AI-development process. The method is summarized in Fig. 1 where activities (performed by an analyst) are shown in boxes and arrows showing control flow.

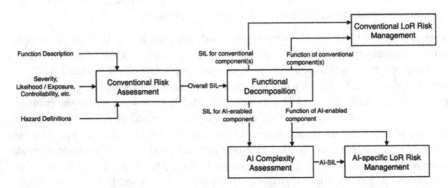

Fig. 1. Overview of AI-SIL assessment method.

The method begins with a Conventional Risk Assessment using the appropriate measures for the given application area. For example, for automotive systems severity, exposure, and controllability are used to determine an (A)SIL per ISO 26262; other application areas might use different methods such as hazard rate calculations or risk graphs. Regardless of method, the output is a SIL for system of function.

Next a Functional Decomposition step is used to partition the overall function into conventional (non-AI-based) components and AI-based components. This step might also involve SIL decomposition or apportionment activities. For instance, ISO 26262 permits certain higher ASILs to be decomposed into lower ASILs [10]. Functions allocated to conventional software components are subject to conventional risk management activities (from appropriate standards) at the assigned SIL.

Functions that are to be realized by AI-based components are subjected to an AI Complexity Assessment that takes account of the complexity of the function to be performed by AI and its assigned SIL from the functional decomposition. The details of this assessment are described below in Sect. 3.1. The output is an AI-SIL that informs AI-specific risk management activities using a LoR approach.

In terms of the overall method, there are two additional points to consider. First, though Fig. 1 depicts the Functional Decomposition step as dividing the function into two parts (a conventional component and an AI-based component), this is not strictly required, any decomposition might be appropriate. Note that if the overall function does not depend on AI, the method 'collapses' into the typical risk management process recommended by existing standards that employ an LoR-based approach. Second, when performing the Functional Decomposition, it is important to limit the definition of AI-based components to a singular function (or task). For instance, an automotive perception system that classifies objects might have several conventional components that perform pre- and post-processing and an AI-based component that executes the neural network's model to perform classification; in this case, only the neural network itself should be subject to the AI Complexity Assessment and the pre- and post-processing components should be managed using a conventional approach.

3.1 Assessment of AI-Based Components

The primary contribution of this paper concerns the "AI Complexity Assessment" step that follows Functional Decomposition, as shown in Fig. 1. Our approach uses a novel method to assess the complexity of the task performed by the AI-based component.

The assessment method has two steps. First, the complexity of the task performed by the AI is assessed on a two-axis scale that considers the complexity of the input (entropy) and the complexity of the output (non-determinism). Second, these factors are combined using with the assigned SIL to determine the AI-SIL. When assessing the AI-based component, analysts should consider the component from a functional ('black-box') perspective and should focus on the complexity of the task performed by the AI rather than the underlying algorithm(s) used to realize the function.

We have considered how the same assessment of complexity could be made for a human expert performing the same task as the AI-based component (disregarding the limited "processing speed" and capacity of humans compared to software). First, a human expert needs to "make sense" of the inputs to obtain a "mental model" of some situation. For example, the driver of a car maintains a mental model of visible objects such as pedestrians, bicyclists, and vehicles. Next, the human expert uses this mental model to make a decision, such as steering left or right to avoid a collision.

In our method, the difficulty of the "making sense" step of human cognition corresponds to the evaluation of "input entropy, and the difficulty of making a conclusion or decision corresponds to the evaluation of "output non-determinism" (Fig. 2).

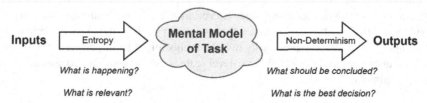

Fig. 2. Role of entropy and non-determinism.

Input Entropy. The input entropy evaluates the dimensionality and variability of the AI-based function's input space. Input spaces with higher levels of entropy are likely to be more challenging for AI methods to handle. For instance, the variability associated with classifying hand-written digits (from the MNIST dataset) is much lower than the variability associated with classifying objects around an autonomous vehicle. Similarly, AI-based functions that consume highly dimensional data (e.g., from multiple independent sensors) have a more sophisticated input space.

When using our approach to evaluate the input entropy of an AI-based component, we imagine a group of human experts independently performing the same task. Disregarding human performance limitations, we consider how likely this group are likely to independently derive a similar model of the situation from the same input. A three-level scale is used to qualitatively assess input entropy:

- **E1 (Low)** – Low input dimensionality with relatively little variability within each dimension. Independent human experts would likely derive (nearly) identical mental models of the situation.
- **E2 (Medium)** – Moderate number of input dimensions with a high degree of variability within each dimension. Independent human experts might derive different mental models of the situation but, after discussion, would likely agree about a mental model of the situation.
- **E3 (High)** – Many input dimensions where each dimension has a high-degree of variability. Independent human experts might derive different mental models of the situation and, even after discussion, might disagree on the correctness of each other's mental models of the situation.

Output Non-Determinism. The output non-determinism assesses the size and variability of an AI-based function's output space. A function that performs binary classification has a small output space whereas a function that produces a vehicle trajectory has a much larger (potentially infinite) output space. The assessment of non-determinism also takes account of whether it is feasible to decide whether an output is 'correct' or 'incorrect'. For a given input, there might be many correct (or nearly correct) outputs and determining which output is the 'best' is non-trivial task. For this purpose, the assessment uses the standard of agreement between multiple independent human experts. Tasks where experts are less likely to agree on the correct output have a higher level of non-determinism.

Importantly, the assessment of output non-determinism does not consider knowledge of the input space. When assessing non-determinism, analysts should assume 'perfect' knowledge of the situation and focus on the complexity of the output space. Complexity of the inputs, including the possibility that the inputs might be imperfect is considered by the input entropy assessment. A three-level scale is used to qualitatively assess output non-determinism:

- **N1 (Low)** – Given perfect knowledge of the situation, independent human experts performing this task will produce the same result.
- **N2 (Medium)** – Given perfect knowledge of the situation, independent human experts performing this task might produce different results, but they are likely to agree that each other's conclusions are acceptable.
- **N3 (High)** – Given perfect knowledge of the situation, independent human experts performing this task might produce different results, and they might will disagree on the acceptability of each other's result or the level of confidence of the results.

Selecting the AI-SIL. The input entropy, output non-determinism, and the allocated SIL for the AI-based component are combined using a table-based method to produce an AI-SIL, see Table 1. The AI-SIL is a number between 1 and 4 where 1 represents a lowest criticality and 4 is the highest criticality.

In Table 1, as the level of complexity of the AI-based function increases (increasing entropy and non-determinism) and as the component's assigned SIL increase, the AI-SIL increases. Also observe key relationships between the SIL and the AI-SIL. For AI-based components allocated SIL 1, the most complex tasks (E3, N3) are assigned AI-SIL 2, and for AI-based components allocated SIL 2, only the simplest tasks (E1, N1) are allocated AI-SIL 1.

Table 1. Tabular approach for determining AI-SIL.

SIL	Entropy	Non-Determinism		
		N1 (low)	N2 (med)	N3 (high)
SIL 1	E1 (low)	1	1	1
	E2 (med)	1	1	1
	E3 (high)	1	2	2
SIL 2	E1 (low)	1	2	2
	E2 (med)	2	2	2
	E3 (high)	2	2	3
SIL 3	E1 (low)	2	3	3
	E2 (med)	3	3	3
	E3 (high)	3	3	4
SIL 4	E1 (low)	3	4	4
	E2 (med)	4	4	4
	E3 (high)	4	4	4

4 Level of Rigour Activities for AI-SILs

By considering both the complexity of the task performed by the AI (as measured by entropy and non-determinism) and the criticality (as measured by a SIL), the assigned of AI-SIL reflects both the level of difficulty of developing and assuring an AI-based component and the level of safety risk associated with the function performed by the AI-based component. The focus of this paper is to introduce the concept of AI-SILs. Prescribing the complete list activities for each AI-SIL is beyond the scope of this paper. We expect that an effort to identify a suitable set of activities for each AI-SIL would require serious deliberation amongst academic and industry experts to arrive at a list that reflects the current state-of-the-art in terms of AI/ML assurance and is also practical in terms of industrial use.

In this section, our intent is more modest. We offer an interpretation of each AI-SIL and suggest activities that might be appropriate at each level for a generic AI-based component whose functionality is implemented by a ML algorithm. Though this list is based on our theoretical and practical knowledge of AI-based systems for safety-critical applications, we make no claims about the completeness of this list.

AI-SIL 1. These AI-based components require the lowest level of engineering rigor. For AI-SIL 1 the focus is on establishing the necessary performance requirements for the AI-based component and demonstrating they are satisfied through an appropriate combination of verification and validation (V&V) activities. The performance requirements should be specified using well-defined performance metrics that are appropriate for the task at hand; for instance, a measure such as false-negative rate is suitable for classification tasks. Once the AI-based component is deployed, a monitoring program should be undertaken to ensure that the 'in-field' performance continues to satisfy the performance requirements [11]. Finally, tools, libraries, and scripts used to assess the AI-based component's performance should be qualified.

AI-SIL 2. At AI-SIL 2 additional rigour is applied in four areas: engineering process, operational domain definition, requirements, and detailed design. First, a systematic development process should be defined. In the case of ML, this includes phases like data collection/cleaning, training, model validation, and verification [4]. Second, the operational domain for the component should be specified using a structured method [12]; for example, the operational domain for an object perception component of an autonomous vehicle likely includes pedestrians and their variants. A field monitoring program should be established to detect changes in the operational domain that might impact the component's performance. Third, the requirements should cover a range of topics, and in the case of ML, requirements address performance, robustness, and data quality (relevance, balance [4]). Fourth, detailed design choices should be documented. For ML, this includes a rationale for the chosen algorithm(s), hyperparameters (e.g., number of layers in a neural network).

AI-SIL 3. At AI-SIL 3 even more rigour is applied with a focus on V&V. From a verification perspective, the artifacts produced at each phase of the engineering process should be subject to increased scrutiny by independent entities. For instance, the specification of the operational domain (as discussed for AI-SIL 2 above) should be subject to independent review to verify that it adequately reflects the real-world. From a V&V perspective, more rigorous test and simulation methods are applicable. For instance, combinatorial testing should be used to show that combinations of operational conditions are handled by the AI-based component [13, 14]. Other applicable methods include assessment of domain and structural coverage assessments [15], surprise adequacy [16], and metamorphic testing [17].

AI-SIL 4. If AI-SIL 4 is assigned, then the use of AI (or ML) should re-considered. Note that only the most critical (SIL 3 and SIL 4) components are assigned AI-SIL 4 (see Table 1). Given the criticality, it is prudent to question whether the use of AI is an appropriate design choice. When AI-SIL 4 is assessed, there are three courses of action for a system developer. First, the developer could revise the functional decomposition (see Fig. 1) to reduce the SIL allocated to the AI-based component (e.g., by using a safety monitor architecture). Second, reducing the complexity of the task assigned to the AI-based component (e.g., by adopting a narrower operational domain) might reduce the input entropy. Similarly, reducing the number of output options for the AI-based component (e.g., from an n-class to a binary classification problem) might reduce the output non-determinism. Finally, if the developer must proceed at AI-SIL 4, then very demanding activities are required. For instance, formal methods should be used to demonstrate the correctness and robustness of the algorithm [6, 18].

5 Examples of AI-SIL Assessment

This section applies the proposed method for AI-SIL determination to four automotive examples of increasing complexity and criticality, one example for an air traffic control system, and one example for medical radiation therapy.

Example: Vehicle Occupancy Detection. One relatively simple application of AI is to turn off the interior lights in a vehicle when it is no longer occupied. In this example, the input to the system is the ambient volume measured by a single microphone, which is used to detect human presence. This application would likely be a SIL 1 system, as a turning the lights off is expected to be low risk. The input entropy of this system would likely receive an E1 ranking, as the inputs originate from a single simple sensor. The non-determinism of this system would likely receive an N1 ranking, as occupancy of the vehicle is a binary value; it is unlikely that experts would disagree on if the vehicle is occupied or not. The combination of SIL 1, E1, and N1 results in AI-SIL 1.

Example: Engine Health Analysis. A more complex and higher risk application is to assess the health of a combustion engine. The output can be used to turn on (or off) a 'check engine light' on the vehicle's instrument cluster. Several sensors provide inputs, including temperature, sound intensity, and signals from various engine control components. Suppose the AI-based component is assigned a SIL 2. The input entropy for this task would likely receive an E1 ranking since there are a modest number of inputs with a constrained range of values. The output non-determinism for this task would likely receive N2 ranking, because even though the output is binary whether a specific set of measurements indicate a problem with the engine health might be matter of some debate between experts. For example, when sensors provide seemingly conflicting inputs, how would these cases be interpreted? The combination of SIL 2, E1, and N2 results in AI-SIL 2.

Example: Lane Change Assist. Another potential application is a "lane change assist" warning system. The AI-based component uses camera and radar data to identify whether there is an object within a blind spot and raises audio and visual warnings to the driver. The AI-based component must distinguish between objects to avoid (e.g., other vehicles, barriers, and pedestrians) and objects that can be reasonably driven over (e.g., newspapers). Suppose that this AI-based component is allocated SIL 3: this is an assistive system, but there are potentially severe consequences if this system fails, and lane changes are a common occurrence. The input entropy might be ranked as E2 as there are only two inputs (camera, radar) but each of these has reasonably high variability due to the environmental conditions and variability in the objects. The non-determinism might be ranked as N1 since it is expected that experts would readily agree. Overall, this combination results in AI-SIL 3.

406 S. Diemert et al.

Example: Autonomous Vehicle Path Planning. The typical processing pipeline for a fully autonomous vehicle includes perception, prediction, and planning tasks [11]. For this example, we consider just the planning task. The AI-based component's task is to generate a trajectory for the vehicle such that, 1) progress towards the objective is achieved, 2) driving rules/laws are obeyed, and 3) no collisions occur. Suppose the AI-based component performing this task is assigned SIL 4; this is reasonable given the severity of potential accidents, exposure to hazardous conditions, and a lack of human oversight. There is a significant amount of variability in the environment including the diversity of object types and behaviours, driving rules, and environmental conditions. For this reason, we the input entropy might be ranked as E3. From an output perspective, there are many (potentially infinite) possible trajectories that could be produced, many of which will trade off progress, safety, and rule-following. The well-known 'trolley problem' illustrates well that humans often disagree on the best choice for path planning [19]. The output non-determinism is likely to be ranked as an N3. Overall, this results in AI-SIL 4.

Example: Air Traffic Conflict Resolution. Air traffic controllers must ensure that each flight within their area of responsibility is separated from other flights. This task is governed by a complex set of "separation rules". When a "conflict" exists, i.e., a violation of the rules for separating aircraft, the controller must find a way to resolve the conflict which, for example, might involve clearing an aircraft to a different altitude or flight level. An AI-based function is being developed that will identify the "best" resolution to a conflict and issue the change to clearances without approval from a human controller, though a human controller could still intervene and override the clearance if necessary. Suppose the AI-based component performing this task is SIL 4; this is reasonable given the severity of a mid-air collision due to an erroneous clearance. While there is some variability in the input, aircraft follow defined flight paths in controlled airspaces; for this reason, we rank the input entropy E1. However, we rank the output non-determinism at N3 since there are many valid potential resolutions, but determining which one is "best" is a very difficult task that experts might disagree on, especially when considering downstream effects that changing one aircraft's clearances might have on clearances for other nearby aircraft. Overall, this results in AI-SIL 4.

Example: Radiation Treatment Planning. When a patient is treated using radiation therapy a treatment plan consisting of many parameters used to control the location and dose of radiation is created and provided to the radiation therapy machine. Developing these plans requires knowledge of both medicine and physics and is typically performed by experts such as radiation oncologists or medical physicists. An AI-based function is being developed to automatically generate radiation treatment plans based on medical imaging data (e.g., CT scans) and the nature of the malignant tissue. Suppose this function is evaluated at SIL 2; this is reasonable since it is only generating a plan which will be reviewed by a human expert, but the plan might be complex enough that the expert might miss an error. Medical images are complex in both variability and dimensionality. Therefore, we rank the input entropy as E3. The output is also complex, and experts might disagree about the whether a given treatment plan will be effective, so we rank the output non-determinism as N3. Overall, this results in AI-SIL 3.

6 Related Work

Assurance of AI-based systems is a very active area of research, with many notable projects and results, a full review of this field is beyond the scope of this paper. Recent work in this area includes the AMLAS framework [5], UL 4600 2nd Edition and ISO 21448:2022, Ashmore et al.'s survey of "desirata" (assurance criteria) for each phase of an ML engineering lifecycle [4], and EASA's latest concept paper on AI [8].

Part D of EASA's concept paper identifies LoR activities for AI-based systems where the LoR is increased based on the role of the AI (e.g., "human augmentation" or "supervised advanced automation") combined with the criticality of the overall system incorporating the AI or ML [8]. Like the EASA guidance, our approach considers the criticality of the overall system. However, our approach differs from the EASA guidance in two ways. First, rather than assessing the human-AI relationship, we use the difficulty of the task being performed as measured by input entropy and output non-determinism. Second, we use a combined AI-SIL to determine the required LoR.

The Safety-Critical System Club (SCSC) has also published guidance on the assurance of autonomous systems that incorporate AI and ML [9]. The guidance identifies assurance objectives for autonomous systems and includes considerations for "tailoring" the guidance based on the criticality of the system, i.e., a LoR approach. However, the SCSC's tailoring does not use the difficulty of the task being performed by the AI-based system to determine what assurance objectives are applicable.

Remarkably, the notion of a dedicated SILs for AI appears to be an under-explored area in the literature, with two exceptions. Suman *et al.*, point out the need for SILs for AI, but do not offer a concrete proposal to address the gap [20]. Second, Lohn suggests that failure rates assigned by various standards (e.g., IEC 61508 SIL 1 permits one failure in 10^5 of continuous hours operation) as a standard for AI performance [21]. Lohn points out that even the top-performing ML models do not achieve this performance. While we agree with Lohn that modern ML models have limited performance, the performance limitations of ML models do not appear to have stopped the rapid uptake of AI for safety-critical applications, such as perception in autonomous vehicles.

Though it has not been published, the draft version of MIL-STD-882F includes a notion of an "Artificial Intelligence Category" that might be used as part of an LoR approach to assurance for defense systems. However, the current draft does not include any details on how to assess AI or the associated LoR activities. Other guidance being developed that address AI/ML include ISO/AWI PAS 8800 – *Road Vehicles – Safety and artificial intelligence* and ISO/IEC CD TR 5469 – *Artificial intelligence – Functional safety and AI systems*. Our hope is that this paper can help to guide the on-going development of these standards.

7 Discussion and Future Work

The proposed method combines the established notion of a SIL with two measures of AI task complexity (input entropy and output non-determinism) to produce an AI-SIL that grades the LoR required for development of an AI-based component.

Applying the method to determine AI-SILs for several simple examples suggests that it helps to distinguish between tasks of varying complexity. However, further evaluation is required to demonstrate its feasibility for real-world applications. First, the method should be assessed for *repeatability*. Second, the method should *generalize* to a range of AI tasks. Of particular interest is whether (or not) the method captures the range of complexity inherent in tasks performed by AI in modern systems. This could be demonstrated by applying the method to tasks that are common in other domains, e.g., medical images/data analysis. Finally, the method should be demonstrated to be *useful* in the context of existing LoR approaches in various industries: does the method help engineers building AI-based systems grade the LoR in a manner that appropriately mitigates risk? Case study methods, where the application of the method is observed by researchers in a real-world setting might be applicable.

One important concept we have not addressed in this paper, is the notion of an assurance case (i.e., an evidence-based structured argument that a system has achieved an acceptable level of safety, security, etc.). As novel technologies are increasingly used in critical systems, assurance cases are recognized as providing a 'goal-oriented' perspective that complements 'process-oriented' approaches taken by existing standards. One might regard the extension of LoR-based activities (which are inherently process-oriented) as 'in tension' with goal-oriented approaches. However, this is not our intent! We view the preparation of assurance case as an essential activity for critical systems development [22] and see process-oriented assurance as strongly complementary to goal-oriented assurance. If an LoR approach existed for AI-based systems, it would be necessarily generic. Any organization applying its guidance would still make use of engineering judgement, which should of course be reflected in the assurance case.

Finally, while this paper has made some suggestions about LoR activities at each AI-SIL, these are by no means definitive. As noted above, it will be a significant undertaking to consolidate the existing knowledge of AI and ML assurance into an LoR framework or standard that is appropriate for industrial use.

References

1. Darwiche, A.: Human-level intelligence or animial-like abilities? Commun. ACM **61**(10), 56–67 (2018)
2. Russell, S., Norvig, P.: Artificial Intelligence - A Modern Approach, Third Edition. Prentice Hall, Hoboken (2010)
3. Rueb, H., Burton, S.: Safe AI - How is this possible? Fraunhofer Institute for Cognitive Systems (2022)
4. Ashmore, R., Calinescu, R., Paterson, C.: Assuring the machine learning lifecycle: desiderata, methods, and challenges. ACM Comput. Surv. **54**(5), 111:1–111:39 (2021)
5. Hawkins, R., Paterson, C., Picardi, C., Jia, Y., Calinescu, R., Habli, I.: Guidance on the Assurance of Machine Learning in Autonomous Systems (AMLAS), University of York (2021)
6. Huang, X., et al.: A survey of safety and trustworthiness of deep neural networks: verification, testing, adversarial attack and defence, and interpretability. Comput. Sci. Rev. **37**, 100270 (2020)
7. European Union Aviation Safety Agency, "Concepts of Design Assurance for Neural Networks," 2020
8. European Union Aviation Safety Agency, "EASA Concept Pper: First usable guidance for Level 1 & 2 machine learning applications," 2023

9. Safety of Autonomous Systems Working Group, "Safety Assurance Objectives for Autonomous Systems," Safety Critical Systems Club, 2022
10. International Organization for Standards, "ISO 26262 - Road vehicles - functional safety," 2018
11. Koopman, P.: How Safe is Safe Enough?: Measuring and Predicting Autonomous Vehicle Safety, Independently Published (2022)
12. Czarnecki, K.: Operational design domain for automated driving systems - taxonomy of basic terms. Waterloo Intelligent Systems Engineering (WISE) Lab (2018)
13. Kuhn, R., Kacker, R., Lei, Y.: NIST Special Publication (SP) 800-142 - Practical Combinatorial Testing, National Institute of Standards and Technology (2010)
14. Diemert, S., Casey, A., Robertson, J.: Challenging autonomy with combinatorial testing (forthcoming). In: Proceedings of the International Workshop on Combinatorial Testing, Dublin, Ireland (2023)
15. Sun, Y., Huang, X., Kroening, D., Sharp, J., Hill, M., Ashmore, R.: Structural test coverage criteria for deep neural networks. ACM Trans. Embed. Comput. Syst. 18(5s), 1–23 (2019)
16. Kim, J., Feldt, R., Yoo, S.: Guiding deep learning system testing using surprise adequacy. In: International Conference on Software Engineering (ICSE), vol. 41, pp. 1039–1049 (2019)
17. Xie, X., Ho, J., Murphy, C., Kaiser, B., Xu, B., Chen, T.Y.: Testing and validating machine learning classifiers by metamorphic testing. J. Syst. Softw. 84(4), 544–558 (2011)
18. Urbank, C., Mine, A.: A Review of Formal Methods applied to Machine Learning," arXiv, (2021)
19. Awad, E., et al.: The moral machine experiment. Nature 563(7729), 59–64 (2018)
20. Suman, S.K., Bhagyalakshmi, R.L., Shrivastava, L., Shekhar, H.: On a safety evaluation of artificial intelligence-based systems to software reliability. In: Multi-Criteria Decision Models in Software Reliability, CRC Press (2022)
21. Lohn, A.: Estimating the Brittleness of AI: Safety Integrity Levels and the Need for Testing Out-Of-Distribution Performance, arXiv, (2020)
22. Diemert, S., Joyce, J.: Eliminative argumentation for arguing system safety - a practitioner's experience. In"IEEE SysCon, Montreal (2020)

Can Large Language Models Assist in Hazard Analysis?

Simon Diemert[✉][iD] and Jens H. Weber[iD]

University of Victoria, Victoria, Canada
sdiemert@uvic.ca

Abstract. Large Language Models (LLMs), such as GPT-3, have demonstrated remarkable natural language processing and generation capabilities and have been applied to a variety tasks, such as source code generation. This paper explores the potential of integrating LLMs in the hazard analysis for safety-critical systems, a process which we refer to as *co-hazard analysis (CoHA)*. In CoHA, a human analyst interacts with an LLM via a context-aware chat session and uses the responses to support elicitation of possible hazard causes. In a preliminary experiment, we explore CoHA with three increasingly complex versions of a simple system, using Open AI's ChatGPT service. The quality of ChatGPT's responses were systematically assessed to determine the feasibility of CoHA given the current state of LLM technology. The results suggest that LLMs may be useful for supporting human analysts performing hazard analysis.

Keywords: Hazard Analysis · Artificial Intelligence · Large Language Models · Co-Hazard Analysis

1 Introduction

So called Large Language Models (LLMs), such as GPT-3 [1] and BERT [2], have shown remarkable abilities in processing and generating text documents and images. Applications include software development support (e.g., OpenAI's Codex model that powers GitHub Co-Pilot). The quality of text generated by LLMs is even high enough to cause legitimate academic integrity concerns in secondary and post-secondary settings [3]. However, there are concerns that, despite their ability to generate seemingly coherent text, LLMs do not understand the meaning of text and simply predict the next word/phrase using statistical models learned from very large training corpora [4].

Safety-critical systems often pose complex challenges for analysts. Many industrial standards provide guidance to practitioners in this area, such as ISO 26262 for automotive systems. *Hazard analysis* (HA) is a pivotal activity prescribed in these standards. At their core, HA methods provide a structured approach to reasoning about how an event or condition (which we call a 'hazard cause') can result in a loss. HA methods involve some manner of brainstorming that relies on the judgement and creativity of analysts. This means that outcomes are sensitive to factors such as an analyst's level of experience, attentiveness, creativity, and knowledge of the system's underlying technical principles

J. Guiochet et al. (Eds.): SAFECOMP 2023 Workshops, LNCS 14182, pp. 410–422, 2023.
https://doi.org/10.1007/978-3-031-40953-0_35

and operating environment. Failure to perform an adequate HA can lead to increased risk arising from unknown (and unmitigated) hazard causes.

This paper proposes a co-operative method where a human analyst and an LLM both participate in HA. This is like the approach taken by Microsoft's GitHub Co-Pilot tool, which assists software developers by generating source code based on text prompts. However, instead of generating source code, our approach uses an LLM to suggest lines of inquiry for consideration by a human analyst thus providing a secondary source of ideas for the creative and error prone tasks related to HA. More specifically, the contribution of this paper is three-fold. First, a new co-operative hazard analysis (CoHA) process is introduced. Second, the feasibility, utility, and scalability of CoHA is studied in an experiment where an LLM (GPT-3 accessed through ChatGPT) is used to support an STPA for multiple versions of a water heater system.

2 Co-hazard Analysis

HA is the process of *identifying, assessing,* and *controlling* hazards in safety-critical systems, where a hazard is defined as a potential condition of the system that, given worst case assumption about the state of the system or its operational environment, may contribute to the occurrence of a loss (accident or mishap) [5]. Many HA methods exist, including Failure Modes and Effects Analysis (FMEA), Hazard and Operability Study (HAZOP), System-Theoretic Process Analysis (STPA) [6].

Given recent advances in the field of artificial intelligence (AI), particularly LLMs, there has been an increasing interest in exploring the use of AI in system engineering processes. LLMs have already shown promise in assisting system engineering tasks [7]. We propose that conversational AI services like ChatGPT also have the potential to participate in hazard analysis as part of a human-AI team, for example during brainstorming sessions. We refer to this vision as Co-Hazard Analysis (CoHA).

Figure 1 summarizes this preliminary vision, where human analysts provide the LLM with a preliminary description of the system (and related information, such as losses to be avoided) and then converse with it to identify hazardous conditions that may contribute to the occurrences of such losses. In Fig. 1 the 'conversation' with the LLM is depicted as "queries", perhaps of the form: *"Can {condition X} contribute to {hazard Y} occurring?", "How might a failure of {X} contribute to {hazard Y} occurring?",* or even *"Suppose {property Z}, can {condition X} still lead to {hazard Y}?".* The human analyst(s) review the responses of the LLM and then formulate the HA results.

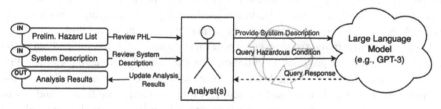

Fig. 1. Overview of CoHA method.

The role of the LLM is not to replace the human analysts. The AI is not even required to always provide "correct" answers. We believe that responses that may initially be seen as "incorrect" may in fact be useful to indicate problems with the system description, such as implicit (unstated) assumptions and ambiguities. However, involving the AI should add, on average, value to the HA process.

3 Experiment

This section explores the feasibility of CoHA with a preliminary experiment, focusing on the task of identifying unsafe control actions (UCAs) and causal (loss) scenarios as part of an STPA for a simple water heater system. The quality of the LLM's responses were assessed by two human analysts who are practiced with STPA.

STPA was chosen because: 1) it is a widely adopted hazard analysis method; 2) it includes an explicit system modelling step, which is helpful for structuring the input to the LLM; and 3) its UCA identification process uses explicit guide phrases (e.g., "not provided" or "stopped too soon") to assess how system behaviours might contribute to hazard occurrences, such phrases are readily used to build queries for an LLM. In this preliminary experiment we aim to answer the following research questions:

RQ1 (Feasibility) – *Can an LLM, when used for CoHA, produce results that are useful to human analysts identifying UCAs and causal scenarios for STPA?*
RQ2 (Utility) – *What proportion of responses from an LLM are useful and correct v. incorrect v. not useful for UCA and causal scenario identification?*
RQ3 (Scalability) – *Does the response quality of an LLM degrade as system under analysis increases in complexity?*

3.1 Method

To answer the research questions above, a four-phase experimental protocol was used: 1) system selection, 2) system encoding, 3) querying the LLM, and 4) manual response review and coding. This study used Open AI's ChatGPT platform (running GPT-3).

System Selection. The system for this experiment was chosen based on the following criteria. First, it should be expressible as a STAMP control structure, the modelling method for STPA. Second, it should be describable with simple terminology to avoid the case where the LLM's performance is degraded by niche terms or specialized concepts that might not appear in the training data for a general-purpose LLM. Third, the complexity should be scalable to assess performance on increasingly complex systems.

Per the criteria above, this experiment used a simple water heater with a simple feedback controller that aims to match the temperature of the water flowing out of a tank with a setpoint. In the simplest version of this system, water flows in and out of the tank and the controller provides a continuous 'enable' signal to a heating element that heats the water in the tank. A single thermometer provides temperature feedback to the controller. Complexity is increased by adding valves to control the flow in and out of the tank and by incorporating a secondary feedback loop within the physical ('plant') system, e.g., a heat exchanger. See Fig. 2 for depictions of these systems.

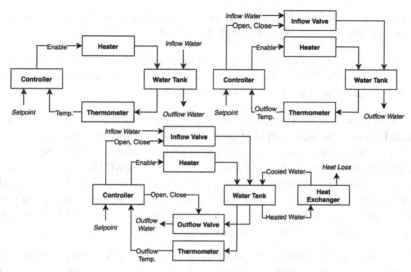

Fig. 2. Three STAMP control structures for the water tank system with increasing complexity: top-left – lowest, top-right – moderate, bottom-middle – highest.

System Encoding. Since ChatGPT allows a user to interact in a 'session' that stores context, the system description can be provided independently of and before the queries. A systematic approach was used to create a system description with four parts:

1. Elements - In an in-sentence list, name all system elements. Each block in the control structure should appear in this paragraph. For example: *"Consider a system consisting of a <u>Controller</u>, <u>Heater</u>, <u>Water Tank</u>, and <u>Thermometer</u>"*.
2. Relationships – Using short sentences, state the relationships between the elements listed in the first part. Every arrow between elements in the control structure should be represented in this paragraph. Template sentences are used to simplify statements and improve repeatability (e.g., "{The|While|When|If} Element X provides Y [to Element Z]..."). For the simple water heater, the description was:

   > *The Controller provides the enable signal to the Heater to maintain a temperature setpoint. While the Controller is providing the enable signal to the Heater, the Heater heats the water in the Water Tank. When the Controller stops providing the enable signal to the Heater, the Heater does not heat the water in the Water Tank. The Thermometer measures the current water temperature inside the Water Tank. The Thermometer provides the current temperature of the water flowing out of the Water Tank to the Controller.*

3. Assumptions and Constraints – Statements describing additional constraints or assumptions are expressed in a third part. Short simple sentences are used like "The Element X does not Y" or "Property W is never greater than V". There are many constraints and assumptions that could be specified, even for a simple water heater system. For this experiment, some constraints and assumptions

were intentionally not specified to allow us to observe how ChatGPT responds to under-specified systems. For the simple water heater, this part was:

> *The water flowing into the tank has variable temperature between 5 and 60 degrees Celsius. The ambient temperature is above 0 degrees Celsius. Water flows in and out of the tank at the same rate.*

4. Hazard Definition(s) – The definition of one or more hazards from the preliminary hazard list are provided in the last part. We adopt Leveson's definition of a hazard, i.e., a "system state or set of conditions that, together with a particular set of worst-case environment conditions, will lead to an accident (loss)" [6]. However, to avoid confusion with other definitions of 'hazard' that the LLM might have learned from the training data, the term "dangerous event" is used. Each dangerous event is expressed in a single sentence, for example: "*A dangerous event occurs if the temperature of the water flowing out of the tank is greater than 90 degrees Celsius.*"

Depending on the intent of the analysis, it is necessary to provide an additional statement about whether there are other unidentified dangerous events, i.e., does the analysis make a 'closed world' or 'open world' assumption. For this study, we adopted the closed world assumption and added the sentence: "*There are no more dangerous events*" to the final part of the system description. Preliminary experiments that omitted this sentence resulted in ChatGPT describing other potentially dangerous events for the water heater, like the water in the tank freezing.

Querying the LLM. Once the system description was provided to ChatGPT, queries were formulated using STPA's standard guidewords for identifying UCAs: "provided", "not provided", "too early", "too late", "stopped too soon", "applied too long". For brevity, we omitted the "out of sequence" and "wrong order" guidewords that are also considered in STPA. Queries were formulated for each of the controller's control actions crossed with each identified dangerous event. Each query had the form: "`Could < Element X > < doing guideword+ control action > result in < dangerous event > ?`". For example: "*Could the Controller providing the enable signal too early to the Heater result in the temperature of the water flowing out of the tank exceeding 90 degrees C?*" Queries were provided one at a time to ChatGPT. For each query, the first response was recorded. Though the ChatGPT user interface provides options to pre-maturely halt response generation and re-generate responses, neither were used. Furthermore, beyond issuing the query as described, no further information was provided to ChatGPT. For example, we did not provide further inputs to clarify the intent of the query if ChatGPT responded as if it had "misinterpreted" the question.

Response Review and Coding. The text of response was independently reviewed by two human analysts (the authors) who are both experienced users of the STPA method. Each word in the response (typically whole sentences) was coded into one of three categories based on how well the response would support a human analyst determining whether the candidate guideword-action pairing is relevant for hazard analysis.

- Correct and useful – The text is correct in that it: 1) accurately describes whether the guideword-action pairing correctly identifies a condition that precedes a hazard occurrence or correctly determines that a hazard does not occur; and 2) it does not contain any incorrect statements or invalid inferences. Text that provides a credible rationale to support a conclusion about hazard occurrences was also included.

- Correct but not useful – The text does not contain any incorrect statements or inferences but is not directly useful for a human analyst performing STPA. Such text might be regarded as 'noise' in the response. This includes text with repeated information (e.g., previously coded "useful and correct", or restated constraints or assumptions).
- Incorrect – The text contains incorrect statements, invalid inferences, and/or the response might be misleading to a human analyst.

We initially considered sentence-level coding, but then found that some sentences contained clauses that might be coded differently, e.g., see the third sentence in Fig. 3.

Coding was first performed independently. Then the reviewers met to discuss their assigned codes. During discussion, reviewers were permitted to modify their codes to reflect an updated understanding of ChatGPT's response. Agreement between reviewers was measured after discussion using Cohen's Kappa agreement statistic. Agreement was measured at the word level such that complete agreement exists if both reviewers assigned the same code to each word. Agreement was computed for each response independently and again across the entire set of responses.

To answer the RQs, a 'final coding' was produced where each word in all responses is assigned a single code (i.e., a combination of the two reviewer's codes). In cases where both reviewers agreed, the agreed upon code was chosen. In cases of disagreement, the final code for the word was selected using the following protocol:

1. If one reviewer assigned the code "Correct and useful" and the other reviewer assigned the code "Correct but not useful", then the word was marked "Correct and useful" in the final coding. This is because 'usefulness' is subjective, and it is possible that an arbitrary CoHA analyst would also find the word useful.
2. If one reviewer assigned the code "Correct but not useful" and the other reviewer assigned the code "Incorrect", then the word was marked as "Incorrect".
3. If one reviewer assigned the code "Correct and useful" and the other reviewer assigned the code "Incorrect", the finding was indeterminate and the word was not included as part of the analysis used to answer the RQs.

Reviewers were also permitted to annotate ChatGPT's responses with additional observations. Themes that emerged from these comments are discussed below.

3.2 Results

To perform the STPA for all three system versions, a total of 78 queries were posed to ChatGPT. Summary statistics are shown in Table 1. The results are presented in terms of the research questions posed above. The overall Cohen's kappa statistic was $\kappa = 0.89$, , which represents significant (post-discussion) agreement between the reviewers.

RQ1 – Feasibility. For CoHA to be feasible, the LLM must return responses that (at a minimum) contain both correct and useful information for the human analyst. Even if only a portion of the response is correct and useful, it can still provide value

Table 1. Results by system version (standard deviation in parentheses).

Complexity	# Queries	Words per Response	Total Words	Agreement
Lowest	6	143.7 (34.4)	862	0.77
Moderate	28	122.7 (51.1)	3436	0.91
Highest	44	116.0 (48.5)	5016	0.89
Overall	78	120.6 (48.6)	9404	0.89

to an analyst. Therefore, to answer RQ1 the number of responses that contain some information (at least one word) coded as 'Correct and useful' are considered. In total, across all system versions considered, 50 out of 78 (64%) of all responses contained some useful information (minimum number useful words was 23 words). See Table 2 for details.

Table 2. Number of responses with at least one word coded in each category.

Complexity	Correct and Useful	Correct but not useful	Incorrect
Lowest	5 (83%)	5 (83%)	3 (50%)
Moderate	20 (71%)	23 (82%)	14 (50%)
Highest	25 (56%)	32 (72%)	29 (70%)
Overall	50 (64%)	60 (77%)	46 (59%)

To further contextualize the results, an example query and response is shown in Fig. 3. The response contains samples of correct and useful (green), correct but not useful (blue), and incorrect (red) information. First, ChatGPT replies with a correct answer to the query. Then, it makes an incorrect statement about the relationship between the water temperature in that it neglects the role of inflowing water in cooling the tank's overall temperature; reviewers felt that the phrase "…primarily determined by…" was too strong. The next sentence has a mix of correct and incorrect information. While it is true that the inflow valve controls the flow rate into the tank, it is incorrect to say that it does not affect the temperature. The second last sentence is about the tank's water level and is not related to the query and is thus marked as 'correct but not useful'. Finally, the last two sentences offer observations about the system's behaviour, but they are not directly useful for answering the query.

Based on the above results, RQ1 is answered as follows:

> **Query:** *Could the Controller providing the open command to the Inflow Valve too early result in the temperature of the water flowing out of the tank exceeding 90 degrees C?*
>
> **Response:** No, providing the open command to the Inflow Valve too early will not cause the temperature of the water flowing out of the tank to exceed 90 degrees C. The temperature of the water in the tank is primarily determined by the heater and the ambient temperature. The inflow valve controls the water flow rate into the tank, it does not affect the temperature of the water flowing out of the tank. The water level in the tank will increase due to the water flow rate. If the controller is monitoring the water level, it can adjust the inflow valve and the heater accordingly to maintain the

Fig. 3. Sample query and response from ChatGPT for highest complexity system. Key: green – correct and useful, blue – correct but not useful, red – incorrect. (Color figure online)

> ***Answer to RQ1*** *– When used for CoHA with STPA, ChatGPT's responds to queries about potentially unsafe control actions with useful and correct information with moderate frequency (64% of the time). Therefore, it is feasible to use ChatGPT to support STPA. However, ChatGPT's responses are likely to also contain correct but not useful and incorrect information and so responses must be scrutinized by a human analyst.*

RQ2 – Utility. As shown in Table 1, responses from ChatGPT contain a mix of correct and useful, not useful, and incorrect information. For CoHA to be useful in broad sense, a human analyst must be able to easily use the LLM's responses. This is only possible if a meaningful proportion of each response is both useful and correct, and the proportions of not useful (i.e., 'noise') and incorrect information are relatively low. To answer RQ2 the proportion of words coded into each category is considered. Table 3 shows the distribution of codes in terms of total number and average number of words per response for each system version. Figure 4 visualizes the overall proportion of words (across all responses for each system version) assigned to each code.

Table 3. Word-level codes applied to each system.

Complexity	Correct and useful		Correct but not useful		Incorrect	
	Count	Avg (SD)	Count	Avg (SD)	Count	Avg (SD)
Lowest	420	70.0 (39.0)	343	57.2 (47.1)	93	15.5 (19.7)
Moderate	1461	52.2 (40.1)	1296	46.3 (36.0)	553	19.8 (24.4)
Highest	1430	32.5 (32.5)	1832	41.6 (46.1)	1828	41.5 (42.3)
Overall	3311	44.4 (37.3)	3471	44.5 (42.5)	2474	31.7 (36.9)

It is observed that a meaningful proportion of ChatGPT's responses (especially for the lowest and moderate complexity systems) are correct and useful. Overall, across all

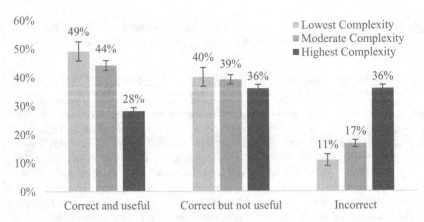

Fig. 4. Proportion of codes assigned by system complexity (95% CI shown).

system versions, 35% of words returned by ChatGPT were coded as 'correct and useful'. However, the proportion of correct and useful information appears to decline as the system complexity increases while the proportion of 'incorrect' information increases (see further analysis for RQ3). Interestingly, the amount of 'correct but not useful' information (overall 38%) is relatively consistent, even as the complexity increases.

Based on these results, RQ2 is answered as follows:

> ***Answer to RQ2** – When used for CoHA with STPA, between one quarter to one half of the content in ChatGPT's responses is correct and useful information. The remaining content is either correct but not useful to an analyst or simply incorrect. So, even though correct and useful information is available, human analysts performing CoHA with ChatGPT will have to sift through responses to find it. Therefore, in terms of correct and directly useful information, ChatGPT's responses are moderately useful.*

RQ3 – Scalability. As the complexity of the system increases, intuition says that the analysis should be harder (for either an AI or a human). RQ3 focuses on whether ChatGPT's responses degrade in quality as the complexity increases. Two word-level measures are of interest: 1) the proportion of incorrect words in ChatGPT's responses, and 2) amongst correct words in ChatGPT's responses, the proportion of useful words. Six pair-wise statistical (two-tailed) tests for significance between population proportions ($\alpha = 0.01$) for different system complexities are used. Since multiple concurrent tests are performed, the Bonferroni correction is used to reduce the probability of a Type I error (i.e., incorrectly rejecting the null hypothesis). This resulted in a modified $a_0 = \alpha/6 = 0.00167$. The results are shown in Table 4.

As an example, consider the first row in Table 4, which corresponds to testing the null hypothesis, H_0, that the proportion of words coded as 'incorrect' is equal between the lowest and moderate complexity systems, $\hat{p}_{low}$ and $\hat{p}_{mod}$ respectively. From Table 3 above, the proportion of words coded as 'incorrect' for the lowest complexity system is computed as $\hat{p}_{low} = 93/(420 + 343 + 93) = 0.11$, similarly the proportion of 'incorrect' words for the moderate complexity system is $\hat{p}_{mod} = 0.17$. The difference between these proportions is $\hat{p}_{mod} - \hat{p}_{low} = 0.06$, which is a small increase in the proportion of incorrect words. The corresponding test statistic is $Z = 4.21$, which is larger than the critical value ($Z_{\alpha_0} = 3.14$). Therefore, the null hypothesis is rejected in favour of the alternative that the proportion of words coded as incorrect are different. The corresponding p-value is $p = 0.0000256$. From this test, it can be concluded that between the low and moderate complexity systems, the proportion of 'incorrect' words increased.

Table 4. Tests for significance between different system complexities.

Measure	$H_0 : \hat{p}_x = \hat{p}_y$	$\hat{p}_x$	$\hat{p}_y$	$\hat{p}_y - \hat{p}_x$	Outcome
Proportion of Incorrect Words in Responses	$\hat{p}_{low} = \hat{p}_{mod}$	0.11	0.17	0.06	Reject H_0 ($p < 0.01$)
	$\hat{p}_{mod} = \hat{p}_{high}$	0.17	0.36	0.19	Reject H_0 ($p < 0.01$)
	$\hat{p}_{low} = \hat{p}_{high}$	0.11	0.36	0.25	Reject H_0 ($p < 0.01$)
Proportion of Useful Words in Responses	$\hat{p}_{low} = \hat{p}_{mod}$	0.55	0.53	−0.02	Do Not Reject H_0
	$\hat{p}_{mod} = \hat{p}_{high}$	0.53	0.44	−0.09	Reject H_0 ($p < 0.01$)
	$\hat{p}_{low} = \hat{p}_{high}$	0.55	0.44	−0.11	Reject H_0 ($p < 0.01$)

Inspecting the results in Table 4 shows that as the system complexity increases the proportion of words coded as incorrect increases. Additionally, amongst the correct words, the proportion that are useful words decreases with increased complexity, but only between the moderate and highest complexity systems (and therefore also the lowest to highest); the difference between the lowest and moderate complexity systems is inconclusive. Further quantification of the relationship between complexity and usefulness is not possible since we have not quantified the complexity of the systems.

Based on the above results, RQ2 is answered as follows:

> ***Answer to RQ3** – When used for CoHA with STPA, the quality of ChatGPT's responses declines as the system complexity increases. Specifically, for the example water heater systems, the proportion of incorrect information in ChatGPT's responses increases as system complexity increases. Additionally, for systems above a certain complexity, the proportion of correct and useful information declines.*

4 Summary and Discussion

This paper has introduced Co-Hazard Analysis (CoHA), a method where an LLM such as ChatGPT, assists a human analyst during HA. The results of our experiment allowed us to derive preliminary answers to our RQs. They indicate that CoHA, when used for

STPA on simple systems, is a feasible and moderately useful method. However, it is also apparent that the performance of ChatGPT degrades as the system complexity is increased. We see that CoHA has potential to support analysts and warrants further investigation. The remainder of this section offers additional observations, discusses threats to validity, and proposes avenues for future work.

Observations. ChatGPT's responses always contained a supporting rationale. In some cases, this rationale was incorrect, but in others it was both correct and concise. Indeed, even when it was incorrect, ChatGPT's rationale was more useful than just a binary assertion about whether a hazard might occur. We found that reviewing the rationale prompted us to think critically, often leading to further insights about the system. This suggests that the utility of CoHA might have been under-represented in our analysis above. Ultimately, we are interested in whether CoHA 'adds value' to the HA process, and so future studies might use methods that adopt a more wholistic notion of utility that includes the value of critical thinking prompted by an LLM's response.

Though the queries posed were binary in nature, we noted that ChatGPT sometimes 'hedges' and produces less-than-definitive responses. For example, instead of responding with "*No, X cannot happen*", it might reply with "*It is unlikely that X can happen*". Though we did not conduct a systematic analysis, ChatGPT appears to use "no" and "unlikely" (and similar terms) as synonyms, and it does not appear that it is able to grade the likelihood of specific events occurring so as to ascribe meaning to these words. Understanding whether LLM's are capable of 'fuzzy' reasoning in this manner would be an interesting line of future work.

During coding we noted that many responses from ChatGPT included suggestions for how to mitigate risk. For example, ChatGPT's responses often contained some variant of the sentence: "... *It's important for the controller to monitor the water temperature in the tank ..., and also to have safety mechanisms in place to prevent dangerous events...* ". While this is not an incorrect statement, it is also not useful in terms of answering the CoHA query about whether a specific condition could cause a hazard. Therefore, we marked these parts of the response as 'correct but not useful'. Regardless, it is interesting that ChatGPT is capable suggesting mitigations as part of its response. Using LLM's to synthesize mitigations might be a fruitful area of future research.

Threats to Validity. A threat to the study's internal validity arises from the inherent ambiguity of natural language, which might have impacted the study in three ways. First, the system description provided to ChatGPT was necessarily incomplete and did not specify behaviour for all operational scenarios. This was intentional since a human analyst can make reasonable assumptions about how a simple system will behave. The study method (partially) mitigated this concern, by adopting a template-based approach for describing the system to ChatGPT. Second, for similar reasons, there might have been ambiguity in the queries issued to ChatGPT. Third, the responses from ChatGPT were reviewed by humans who have differing interpretations. Indeed, this occurred many times, most of which were resolved during discussion.

There are four notable threats to external validity. First, the study was performed using ChatGPT (Jan 9th version). It is possible that other LLM's or even other versions of ChatGPT will produce different results. Second, the study used STPA, so we cannot directly infer that CoHA is feasible or useful for other HA methods. However, our overall impression is positive: we hypothesize that CoHA will be feasible and useful for other HA methods as well. Third, the systems used for this study, even the highest complexity variant, are simple both in terms of the principles of their operation and in terms of the number of components and interactions between them. It is not clear how Chat-GPT would perform on a real-world system that is significantly more complex. Finally, the terminology used to describe the water heater systems is relatively simple ("tank", "heater", "valve", etc.) and likely well represented in the LLM's training data. Indeed, our experiment protocol included criteria to select systems that could be described using common language. However, real-world systems often contain niche concepts and terms that might be difficult or impossible to substitute. It is possible that LLM performance will degrade if more sophisticated terminology is used.

Future Work. Since LLMs are a new technology, their potential as productivity aids is largely unexplored. There is an opportunity for researchers to demonstrate and validate the application for LLMs to support HA using methods such as CoHA. However, since this is preliminary work, many questions remain.

First, our preliminary results suggest performance degrades with increasing complexity. Scalability of CoHA to increasingly complex systems should be investigated further. However, the extent and rate of degradation is not currently known: perhaps LLM and human-only performance converge as complexity grows? Moreover, using different approaches to describing the system or structuring the queries might permit more complex systems to be analyzed. Indeed, this preliminary study used a restrictive query structure that limited the LLM to "yes" or "no" responses. Future work might explore how different querying strategies impact LLM performance for CoHA. For example, more open-ended queries might be issued to the LLM such as *"why might <component> performing <UCA> result in a dangerous event occurring?"*.

Second, this experiment used STPA as the HA method. However, STPA is one of many HA methods available to practitioners. Future work might explore using CoHA with other HA methods, such as FMEA, HAZOP, or even FTA. Perhaps one of these methods is more amenable to LLM-based analysis? A control trial that compares LLM results across different HA methods might be a fruitful activity. Similarly, future work might explore how LLMs can assist with other HA activities such as hazard identification, risk assessment, or even generating/selecting control measures.

Third, further work is necessary to validate the hypothesis that CoHA adds value to HA. The present study focused mainly on "correctness" of LLM responses, but work is also required to establish the usefulness of as part of a large HA activity. One category of studies would be controlled trials where the results of human-only HA (the control group) is compared to the results of CoHA (the intervention group). The analysis might compare both the number and quality of the HA results generated by both groups. However, since the overall goal of CoHA is to support human analysts in practice, experimental results should be complemented by "field studies" that investigate CoHA when used by real practitioners on real-world systems. Future case studies might report the performance and utility of CoHA when used on real-world systems. An important contribution of such studies would be whether practitioners perceived CoHA as adding value to their HA activities; for example, did CoHA help analysts identify hazards or hazard causes that might have been otherwise missed?

Fourth, even if LLMs (eventually) achieve acceptable performance for HA tasks, methods should be developed that aid humans in interpreting the LLM's outputs. Of particular concern is supporting a human to understand whether an output (like a proposed UCA) is credible. For simple systems, such as our water heater example, it is easy for a human to make this judgement. However, results output by LLMs for more complex systems might be harder to understand.

Finally, experts in HA methods might partner with experts from the machine learning community to tailor a general-purpose LLM (such as GPT-3) to a specific application area or HA method such that the LLM has awareness of domain-specific terminology. For example, tailoring might result in an LLM specifically trained to produce results for STPA in the automotive sector or HAZOP results for the process-control applications. An even more ambitious project might aim to train an LLM to "understand" commonly occurring artifacts, such that, rather than a human transcribing a system description, the LLM consumes documents and then performs HA.

References

1. Brown, T., et al.: Language models are few-shot learners. In: Advances in Neural Information Processing Systems, pp. 1877–1901. Curran Associates, Inc. (2020)
2. Devlin, J., Chang, M.-W., Lee, K., Toutanova, K.: BERT: pre-training of deep bidirectional transformers for language understanding. In: Proceedings of 2019 Conference of the North American Chapter of the Association for Computational Linguistics. Human Language Technologies, pp. 4171–4186. Association for Computational Linguistics (2019)
3. Hristova, B.: Some students are using ChatGPT to cheat—here's how schools are trying to stop it (2023). https://www.cbc.ca/news/canada/hamilton/chatgpt-school-cheating-1.6734580
4. Bender, E.M., Gebru, T., McMillan-Major, A., Shmitchell, S.: On the dangers of stochastic parrots: can language models be too big? In: Proceedings of the 2021 ACM Conference on Fairness, Accountability, and Transparency, pp. 610–623. Association for Computing Machinery, New York (2021)
5. Ericson, C.: Hazard Analysis Techniques for System Safety. Wiley, Hoboken (2005)
6. Leveson, N.G.: Engineering a Safer World: Systems Thinking Applied to Safety. The MIT Press, Cambridge (2012)
7. Lim, S.C.: A case for pre-trained language models in systems engineering (2022). https://dspace.mit.edu/handle/1721.1/147405

Contextualised Out-of-Distribution Detection Using Pattern Identification

Romain Xu-Darme[1,3]([envelope]), Julien Girard-Satabin[1], Darryl Hond[2],
Gabriele Incorvaia[2], and Zakaria Chihani[1]

[1] Université Paris-Saclay, CEA, List, 91120 Palaiseau, France
`{romain.xu-darme,julien.girard-satabin,zakaria.chihani}@cea.fr`
[2] Thales UK, Research, Technology and Innovation, Reading, UK
`{darryl.hond,gabriele.incorvaia}@uk.thalesgroup.com`
[3] Univ. Grenoble Alpes, CNRS, Grenoble INP, LIG, 38000 Grenoble, France

Abstract. In this work, we propose CODE, an extension of existing work from the field of explainable AI that identifies class-specific recurring patterns to build a robust Out-of-Distribution (OoD) detection method for visual classifiers. CODE does not require any classifier retraining and is OoD-agnostic, *i.e.*, tuned directly to the training dataset. Crucially, pattern identification allows us to provide images from the In-Distribution (ID) dataset as reference data to provide additional context to the confidence scores. In addition, we introduce a new benchmark based on perturbations of the ID dataset that provides a known and quantifiable measure of the discrepancy between the ID and OoD datasets serving as a reference value for the comparison between OoD detection methods.

Keywords: Out-of-distribution detection · Explainable AI · Pattern identification

1 Introduction

A fundamental aspect of software safety is arguably the modelling of its expected operational domain through a formal or semi-formal specification, giving clear boundaries on when it is sensible to deploy the program, and when it is not. It is however difficult to define such boundaries for machine learning programs, especially for visual classifiers based on artificial neural networks (ANN) that process high-dimensional data (images, videos) and are the result of a complex optimisation procedure. In this context, Out-of-Distribution (OoD) detection - which aims to detect whether an input of an ANN is In-Distribution (ID) or outside of it - serves several purposes: 1) it helps characterise the extent to which the ANN can operate outside a bounded dataset; 2) it constitutes a surrogate measure of the generalisation abilities of the ANN; 3) it can help assess when an input is too far away from the operational domain, which prevents misuses of the program and increases its safety. However, one crucial aspect missing from current OoD detection methods is the ability to provide some

© The Author(s), under exclusive license to Springer Nature Switzerland AG 2023
J. Guiochet et al. (Eds.): SAFECOMP 2023 Workshops, LNCS 14182, pp. 423–435, 2023.
https://doi.org/10.1007/978-3-031-40953-0_36

form of explanation of their decision. Indeed, most approaches are based on a statistical model of the system behaviour, built upon an abstract representation of the input data, sometimes turning OoD detection into an opaque decision that may appear arbitrary to the end-user. While it would be possible to generate a visual representation of the abstract space using tSNE and to highlight ID data clusters for justifying the OoD-ness of a given sample, tSNE is extremely dependent on the choice of hyper-parameters, sometimes generating misleading visualisations [25]. In this regard, methods from the field of Explainable AI (XAI), which are typically used to provide some insight about the decision-making process of the model, can be adapted to build models for OoD detection that provide some context information to justify their decision. In the particular task of image classification, XAI methods can help extract visual cues that are class-specific (*e.g.*, a bird has wings), and whose presence or absence can help characterise the similarity of the input image to the target distribution (*e.g.*, an object classified as a bird that shows neither wings nor tail nor beak is probably an OoD input). Therefore, in this work we make the following contributions:

1. We introduce a new benchmark based on perturbations of the ID dataset which provides a known and quantifiable evaluation of the discrepancy between the ID and OoD datasets that serves as a reference value for the comparison between various OoD detection methods (Sect. 3).
2. We propose CODE, an OoD agnostic detection measure that does not require any fine-tuning of the original classifier. Pattern identification allows us to provide images from the ID dataset as reference points to justify the decision (Sect. 4). Finally, we demonstrate the capabilities of this approach in a broad comparison with existing methods (Sect. 5).

2   Related Work

Out-of-Distribution Detection. In this work, we focus on methods that can apply to pre-trained classifiers. Therefore, we exclude methods which integrate the learning of the confidence measure within the training objective of the model, or specific architectures from the field of Bayesian Deep-Learning that aim at capturing uncertainty by design. Moreover, we exclude *OoD-specific* methods that use a validation set composed of OoD samples for the calibration of hyper-parameters, and focus on *OoD-agnostic* methods that require only ID samples.

In this context, the maximum softmax probability (MSP) obtained after normalisation of the classifier logits constitutes a good baseline for OoD detection [8]. More recently, ODIN [15] measures the local stability of the classifier using gradient-based perturbations, while MDS [13] uses the Mahalanobis distance to class-specific points in the feature space. [16] proposes a framework based on energy scores, which is extended in the DICE method [21] by first performing a class-specific directed sparsification of the last layer of the classifier. ReAct [20] also modifies the original classifier by rectifying the activation values of the penultimate layer of the model. [6] proposes two related methods: MaxLogit - based on the maximum logit value - and KL-Matching which measures the KL divergence between the output of the model and the class-conditional mean softmax values. The Fractional Neuron Region Distance [9] (FNRD) computes the range of activations for each neuron over the training set in order to empirically characterise the statistical properties of these activations, then provides a score describing how many neuron outputs are outside the corresponding range boundaries for a given input. Similarly, for each layer in the model, [18] computes the range of pairwise feature correlation between channels across the training set. ViM [24] adds a dedicated logit for measuring the OoD-ness of an input by using the residual of the feature against the principal space. KNN [22] uses the distance of an input to the k-th nearest neighbour. Finally, GradNorm [10] measures the gradients of the cross-entropy loss $w.r.t.$ the last layer of the model.

Evaluation of OoD Detection. All methods presented above are usually evaluated on different settings (*e.g.,* different ID/OoD datasets), sometimes using only low resolution images (*e.g.,* MNIST [2]), which only gives a partial picture of their robustness. Therefore, recent works such as [6,21] - that evaluate OoD methods on datasets with higher resolution (*e.g.,* ImageNet [1]) - or Open-OoD [27] - which aims at standardising the evaluation of OoD detection, anomaly detection and open-set recognition into a unified benchmark - are invaluable. However, when evaluating the ability of a method to discriminate ID/OoD datasets, it is often difficult to properly quantify the margin between these two datasets, *independently* from the method under test, and to establish a "ground truth" reference scale for this margin. Although [27] distinguishes *"near-OoD datasets [that] only have semantic shift compared with ID datasets"* from *"far-OoD [that] further contains obvious covariate (domain) shift "*, this taxonomy lacks a proper way to determine, given two OoD datasets, which is "further" from the ID dataset. Additionally, [17] generates *"shifted sets"* that are *"perceptually dissimilar but semantically similar to the training distribution"*, using a GAN model for measuring the *perceptual* similarity, and a deep ensemble model for evaluating the *semantic* similarity between two images. However, this approach requires the training of multiple models in addition to the classifier. Thus, in this paper we propose a new benchmark based on gradated perturbations of the ID dataset. This benchmark measures the correlation between the OoD detection score returned by a given method when applied to a perturbed dataset (OoD), and the intensity of the corresponding perturbation.

Part Detection. Many object recognition methods have focused on part detection, in supervised (using annotations [28]), weakly-supervised (using class labels [14]) or unsupervised [4,26,29] settings, primarily with the goal of improving accuracy on hard classification tasks. To our knowledge, the PARTICUL algorithm [26] is the only method that includes a confidence measure associated with the detected parts (used by the authors to infer the visibility of a given part). PARTICUL aims to identify *recurring patterns* in the latent representation of a set of images processed through a pre-trained CNN, in an unsupervised manner. It is, however, restricted to homogeneous datasets where all images belong to the same macro-category. For more heterogeneous datasets, it becomes difficult to find recurring patterns that are present across the entire training set.

3   Beyond Cross-Dataset Evaluation: Measuring Consistency Against Perturbations

In this section, we present our benchmark for evaluating the consistency of OoD detection methods using perturbations of the ID dataset.

Let $f : \mathcal{X} \to \mathbb{R}^N$ be a classifier trained on a dataset $X_{train} \sim \mathcal{P}_{id}$, where $\mathcal{P}_{id}$ is a distribution over $\mathcal{X} \times \mathbb{R}^N$ and N is the number of categories learned by the classifier. We denote $\mathcal{D}_{id}$ the marginal distribution of $\mathcal{P}_{id}$ over $\mathcal{X}$. For any image $x \in \mathcal{X}$, f outputs a vector of logits $f(x) \in \mathbb{R}^N$. The index of the highest value in $f(x)$ corresponds to the most probable category (or *class*) of x - relative to all other categories. Without loss of generality, the goal of an OoD detection method is to build a class-conditional[1] confidence function $C : \mathcal{X} \times \mathbb{R}^N \to \mathbb{R}$ assigning a score to each pair (x, y), where y can be either the ground truth label of x when known, or the prediction $f(x)$ otherwise. This function constitutes the basis of OoD detection, under the assumption that images belonging to $\mathcal{D}_{id}$ should have a higher confidence score than images outside $\mathcal{D}_{id}$.

A complete evaluation of an OoD detection method would require the application of the confidence function C on samples representative of the ID and OoD distributions. However, it is not possible to obtain a dataset representative of all possible OoD inputs. Instead, **cross-dataset OoD evaluation** consists in drawing a test dataset $X_{test} \sim \mathcal{D}_{id}$ (with $X_{test} \neq X_{train}$), choosing a different dataset $D_{ood} \not\sim \mathcal{D}_{id}$, then measuring the *separability* of $C(X_{test})$ and $C(D_{ood})$, where $C(X)$ denotes the distribution of scores computed over dataset X using C. Three metrics are usually used: Area Under the ROC curve (AUROC); Area Under the Precision-Recall curve (AUPR), False Positive Rate when the true positive rate is 95% (FPR95).

In this work, in addition to cross-dataset evaluation, we propose to *generate* an OoD distribution $\mathcal{D}_{ood}$ by applying a perturbation to all images from $\mathcal{D}_{id}$. Although image perturbation is a standard method for evaluating the robustness of classifiers [7], our intent differs: rather than trying to capture the point of failure of a classifier, we monitor how the various confidence scores evolve when applying a perturbation of increasing intensity to the ID dataset. In practice, we use four transformations: Gaussian noise, Gaussian blur, brightness changes and rotations. More generally, a perturbation P_α is a function that applies a transformation of magnitude α to an image $x \in \mathcal{X}$ (*e.g.*, a rotation with angle α). When applying P_α over $\mathcal{D}_{id}$, we define the expected confidence as

$$E(P_\alpha, C) = \mathbb{E}_{x \sim \mathcal{D}_{id}}\big[C\big(P_\alpha(x), f(P_\alpha(x))\big)\big] \tag{1}$$

which is evaluated over the test set X_{test}. Although it would again be possible to measure the separability of ID and OoD confidence distributions, perturbations

---

[1] Class-agnostic methods simply ignore the image label/prediction.

of small magnitude would result in almost identical distributions. Instead, we evaluate the correlation between the magnitude of the perturbation and the average confidence value of the perturbed dataset as the Spearman Rank Correlation Coefficient (SRCC) r_s between α and $E(P_\alpha, C)$, using multiple magnitude values $(\alpha_0, \ldots, \alpha_n)$. $r_s = 1$ (resp. -1) indicates that the average confidence measure increases (resp. decreases) *monotonically* with the value of α, *i.e.*, that the measure is correlated with the magnitude of the perturbation. The key advantage of the SRCC resides in the ability to compare the general behaviour of various OoD detection methods that usually have different calibrations (*i.e.*, different range of values). Assuming that the discrepancy between $\mathcal{D}_{id}$ and $P_\alpha(\mathcal{D}_{id})$ is correlated to the magnitude of the perturbation α (ground truth), this benchmark measures the *consistency* of the OoD methods under test.

4   Contextualised OoD Detection Using Pattern Identification

In this section, we present CODE, our proposal for building a *contextualised* OoD detector. CODE is an extension of the PARTICUL algorithm described in [26], which is intended to mine recurring patterns in the latent representation of a set of images processed through a CNN. Patterns are learnt from the last convolutional layer of the classifier f over the training set X_{train}, in a plug-in fashion that does not require the classifier to be retrained. Let v be the restriction of classifier f up to its last convolutional layer, *i.e.*, $f = l \circ v$, where l corresponds to the last pooling layer followed by one or several fully connected layers. $\forall x \in \mathcal{X}$, $v(x) \in \mathbb{R}^{H \times W \times D}$ is a convolutional map of D-dimensional vectors. The purpose of the PARTICUL algorithm is to learn p distinct $1 \times 1 \times D$ convolutional kernels $K = [k_1, \ldots, k_p]$ (or *detectors*), such that $\forall x \in X_{train}$: 1) each kernel k_i strongly correlates with exactly one vector in $v(x)$ (*Locality* constraint); 2) each vector in $v(x)$ strongly correlates with at most one kernel k_i (*Unicity* constraint).

Learning Class-Conditional Pattern Detectors. While PARTICUL is an unsupervised approach restricted to fine-grained recognition datasets, CODE uses the training labels from X_{train} to learn p detectors *per class*. More precisely, let $K^{(c)} = [k_1^{(c)}, \ldots k_p^{(c)}]$ be the set of kernel detectors for class c. Similar to [26], we define the normalised activation map between kernel $k_i^{(c)}$ and image x as:

$$P_i^{(c)}(x) = \sigma\big(v(x) * k_i^{(c)}\big) \in \mathbb{R}^{H \times W} \tag{2}$$

where σ is the *softmax* normalisation function. We also define the cumulative activation map, which sums the normalised scores for each vector in $v(x)$, *i.e.*,

$$S^{(c)}(x) = \sum_{i=1}^{p} P_i^{(c)}(x) \in \mathbb{R}^{H \times W} \tag{3}$$

Then, we define the *Locality* and *Unicity* objective functions as follows:

$$\mathcal{L}_l = - \sum_{(x,y) \in X_{train}} \sum_{c=1}^{N} \sum_{i=1}^{p} \mathbb{1}_{[c=y]} \times \max\big(P_i^{(c)}(x) * u\big) \tag{4}$$

$$\mathcal{L}_c = \sum_{(x,y) \in X_{train}} \sum_{c=1}^{N} \mathbb{1}_{[c=y]} \times \max\left(0, \max\left(S^{(c)}(x)\right) - t\right) \quad (5)$$

where $\mathbb{1}$ is the indicator function, and u is a 3×3 uniform kernel that serves as a relaxation of the Locality constraint. Due to the softmax normalisation of the activation map $P_i^{(c)}(x)$, $\mathcal{L}_l$ is minimised when, for all images x of class c, each kernel $k_i^{(c)}$ strongly correlates with one and only one 3×3 region of the convolutional map $v(x)$. Meanwhile, $\mathcal{L}_c$ is minimised when, for all images x of class c, the sum of normalised correlation scores between a given vector in $v(x)$ and all kernels $k_i^{(c)}$ does not exceed a threshold $t = 1$, ensuring that no vector in $v(x)$ correlates too strongly with multiples kernels. The final training objective is $\mathcal{L} = \mathcal{L}_l + \lambda_u \mathcal{L}_u$. Importantly, *we do not explicitly specify a target pattern for each detector*, but our training objective will ensure that we obtain detectors for p different patterns for each class. Moreover, since patterns may be similar across different classes (e.g., the wheels on a car or a bus), we *do not treat images from other classes as negative samples* during training.

Confidence Measure. After training, we build our confidence measure using the function $H_i^{(c)}(x) = \max_{v^* \in v(x)} (v^* * k_i^{(c)})$ returning the maximum correlation score between kernel $k_i^{(c)}$ and $v(x)$. Assuming that each detector will correlate more strongly with images from $\mathcal{D}_{id}$ than images outside of $\mathcal{D}_{id}$, we first estimate over X_{train} the mean value $\mu_i^{(c)}$ and standard deviation $\sigma_i^{(c)}$ of the distribution of maximum correlation scores $H_i^{(c)}$ for $(x, c) \sim \mathcal{P}_{id}$. Then, we define

$$C^{(c)}(x) = \frac{1}{p} \sum_{i=1}^{p} C_i^{(c)}(x), \text{with } C_i^{(c)}(x) = sig\left(\left(H_i^{(c)}(x) - \mu_i^{(c)}\right)/\sigma_i^{(c)}\right) \quad (6)$$

as the *class confidence score* for class c. Though it could be confirmed using a KS-test on empirical data, the logistic distribution hypothesis used for $H_i^{(c)}$ - rather of the normal distribution used in PARTICUL - is primarily motivated by the computational effectiveness[2] and the normalisation effect of the sigmoid sig that converts a raw correlation score into a value between 0 and 1. During inference, for $x \in \mathcal{X}$, the confidence measure $C(x)$ is obtained by weighting each class confidence score by the probability that x belongs to this class:

$$C(x) = \sum_{c=1}^{N} C^{(c)}(x) \times P(Y = c \mid X = x) \quad (7)$$

where the categorical distribution $P(Y \mid X = x)$ is obtained from the vector of normalised logits $n = \sigma(f(x))$, as shown in Fig. 1. Note that it would be possible to build $C(x)$ using only the confidence score of the most probable class $c = \arg\max(f(x))$. However, using the categorical distribution allows us to mitigate the model (in)accuracy, as we will see in Sect. 5.

---

[2] Although good approximations of the normal CDF using sigmoids exist [3].

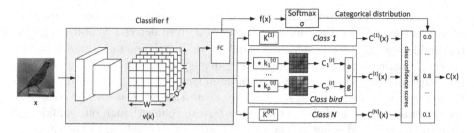

Fig. 1. CODE inference overview. When processing a new sample x, the confidence measure sums up the average contribution of the detectors from each class weighted by the probability of x belonging to that class.

(a) Out-of-distribution image.   (b) Inside-Of-Distribution image.

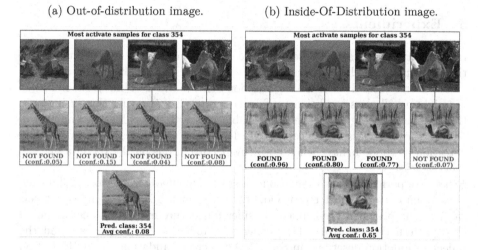

Fig. 2. Explanations generated by CODE for ID and OoD samples. For each image, the classification as ID/OoD rely on the presence/absence of class-specific visual cues extracted from the training set.

Extracting Examples. One of the key advantages of CODE over existing OoD detection methods resides in the ability to provide a visual justification of the confidence measure. For each detection kernel $k_i^{(c)}$ for class c, we first identify the sample $(x, c) \in X_{train}$ that most faithfully represents the distribution of correlation scores $H_i^{(c)}$ across the training (in practice, we select the sample whose correlation score is closest to $\mu_i^{(c)}$). Then, as in [26], we locate the pattern associated with this detector inside image x using the SmoothGrads [19] algorithm. This operation anchors each detector for each class to a part of an image in the training set. Moreover, the ability to visualise patterns can also serve as a sanity check to verify that our method has indeed learned unique and *relevant* patterns *w.r.t.* to the class object.

For each new image, as shown in Fig. 2, we first identify the predicted class $c = \arg\max \left(f(x) \right)$ returned by the classifier. Then, we use the individual confidence scores $C_i^{(c)}(x)$ for each detector of class c to infer the presence or absence of each pattern. When the confidence score of a given detector is above a given threshold (*e.g.*, $C_i^{(c)}(x) > 0.3$), we highlight the corresponding pattern inside image x (again using SmoothGrads) and display the most correlated sample from the training set as a reference. In summary, *we justify the OoD-ness of the new image by pointing out the presence or absence of class-specific recurring patterns that were found in the training set.* Note that although our confidence measure is computed using *all* class confidence scores (weighted by the categorical distribution, see above), we believe that an explanation built solely on the most probable class can provide enough justification for the decision, while being sufficiently concise to be understandable by the user.

5   Experiments

In this section, we start by describing the experimental setup designed to answer the following research questions: 1) How does CODE fare against other detection methods on a cross-dataset OoD evaluation benchmark? 2) What is the influence of weighting all class-condition confidence scores (Eq. 7) rather than using only the confidence score of the most probable class? 3) How does the number p of detectors per class influences CODE detection capabilities? 4) How do OoD detection methods behave when applying perturbations on the ID dataset?

Setup. We performed our evaluation using the OpenOoD framework [27], which already implements most recent OoD detection methods. For each ID dataset, we used the provided pre-trained classifier for feature extraction and trained 4 or 6 pattern detectors per class, using the labels of the training set and the objective function described in Sect. 4. After cross-validation on a CIFAR10 v. CIFAR100 detection benchmark, we set $\lambda_u = 1$, putting equal emphasis on the locality and unicity constraints. Although CODE trains a high number of detectors, the learning process remains computationally efficient since the classifier is not modified and only the detectors of the labelled class are updated during the back-propagation phase. Additionally, for large datasets such as ImageNet, detectors from different classes can be trained *in parallel* on chunks of the dataset corresponding to their respective class. We trained our detectors with RMSprop (learning rate 5×10^{-4}, weight decay 10^{-5}), for 30 epochs (ImageNet) or 200 epochs (all other ID datasets). As a comparison, we also implemented a class-based FNRD [9], extracting neuron activation values at different layers of the classifier.

Cross-Dataset OoD Evaluation. The cross-dataset evaluation implemented in OpenOoD includes a OoD detection benchmark and an Open Set Recognition (OSR) benchmark. For the OoD detection benchmark, we use the ID/Near-OoD/Far-OoD dataset split proposed in [27]. For the OSR benchmark, as in [27], M-6 indicates a 6/4 split of MNIST [2] (dataset split between 6 closed set classes used for training and 4 open set classes), C-6 indicates a 6/4 split

Table 1. Comparison of AUROC scores between CODE and state-of-the-art methods on a cross-dataset benchmark. Results with * are extracted from [27] - keeping only OoD-agnostic methods. We also add results of our implementation of a class-based FNRD [9]. Experiments on ImageNet using 6 CODE detectors have not yet been conducted due to limited ressources (denoted ⊙). For readability, AUPR and FPR95 are omitted but available upon request.

	OSR					OoD Detection (Near-OoD / Far-OoD)				
	M-6	C-6	C-50	T-20	Avg.	MNIST	CIFAR-10	CIFAR-100	ImageNet	Avg
MSP* [8]	96.2	85.3	81.0	73.0	83.9	91.5/98.5	86.9/89.6	80.1/77.6	69.3/86.2	81.9/87.9
ODIN* [15]	98.0	72.1	80.3	**75.7**	81.8	92.4/99.0	77.5/81.9	79.8/78.5	73.2/94.4	80.7/88.4
MDS* [13]	89.8	42.9	55.1	57.6	62.6	**98.0**/98.1	66.5/88.8	51.4/70.1	68.3/94.0	71.0/87.7
Gram* [18]	82.3	61.0	57.5	63.7	66.1	73.9/**99.5**	58.6/67.5	55.4/72.7	68.3/89.2	64.1/82.3
EBO* [16]	**98.1**	84.9	82.7	75.6	85.3	90.8/98.8	87.4/88.9	71.3/68.0	73.5/92.8	80.7/87.1
GradNorm* [10]	94.5	64.8	68.3	71.7	74.8	76.6/96.4	54.8/53.4	70.4/67.2	75.7/95.8	69.4/78.2
ReAct* [20]	82.9	85.9	80.5	74.6	81.0	90.3/97.4	87.6/89.0	79.5/80.5	79.3/95.2	84.2/90.5
MaxLogit* [6]	98.0	84.8	82.7	75.5	85.3	92.5/99.1	86.1/88.8	**81.0**/78.6	73.6 / 92.3	83.3/89.7
KLM* [6]	85.4	73.7	77.4	69.4	76.5	80.3/96.1	78.9/82.7	75.5/74.7	74.2/93.1	77.2/86.7
ViM* [24]	88.8	83.5	78.2	73.9	81.1	94.6/99.0	88.0/92.7	74.9/**82.4**	79.9/**98.4**	84.4/**93.1**
KNN* [22]	97.5	**86.9**	**83.4**	74.1	**85.5**	96.5/96.7	**90.5/92.8**	79.9/82.2	**80.8**/98.0	**86.9**/92.4
DICE* [21]	66.3	79.3	82.0	74.3	75.5	78.2/93.9	81.1/85.2	79.6/79.0	73.8/95.7	78.2/88.3
FNRD [9]	59.4	68.2	58.4	54.3	60.1	84.8/97.1	70.2/71.5	54.6/58.5	75.4/87.5	71.3/78.7
- This work										
CODE (p = 4)	74.7	86.7	76.5	62.4	75.1	81.8/99.5	87.8/90.7	73.9/72.4	76.6/84.4	80.0/86.8
most probable class only	73.7	86.4	74.6	61.3	74.0	80.5/99.5	87.4/90.3	72.2/71.0	73.7/77.3	78.5/84.5
CODE (p = 6)	73.7	86.0	76.1	61.5	74.3	82.2/99.2	88.5/92.4	73.0/76.4	⊙	
most probable class only	72.8	85.7	73.9	60.4	73.2	81.8/98.7	87.8/91.8	70.9/74.5	⊙	

Table 2. Summary of the perturbations, with definition of α and its range.

Perturbation P	Description	Range for α
Blur	Gaussian blur with kernel 3×3 and standard deviation $\sigma = \alpha$	$\alpha \in [0.0, 10]$
Noise	Gaussian noise with ratio α	$\alpha \in [0, 1.0]$
Brightness	Blend black image with ratio $1 - \alpha$	$\alpha \in [0.1, 1.0]$
Rotation forth (R+)	Rotation with degree α	$\alpha \in [0, 180]$
Rotation back (R−)	Rotation with degree α	$\alpha \in [180, 360]$

of CIFAR10 [11], C-50 indicates a 50/50 split of CIFAR100 [11] and TIN-20 indicates a 20/180 split of TinyImageNet [12]. The AUROC score is averaged over 5 random splits between closed and open sets.

The results, summarised in Table 1, show that CODE displays OoD detection capabilities on par with most state-of-the-art methods (top-10 on OSR benchmark, top-8 on Near-OoD detection, top-9 on Far-OoD detection). Moreover, as discussed in Sect. 4, using the categorical distribution of the output of the classifier to weight class confidence scores systematically yields better results than using only the confidence score of the most probable class (up to 7% on

432   R. Xu-Darme et al.

Table 3. Comparison of OoD methods on our perturbation benchmark. For each perturbation, ↑ (resp. ↓) indicates that the average confidence on the perturbed dataset should increase (resp. decrease) with α, *i.e.*, that the sign of the SRCC should be positive (resp. negative). Results in red indicate either a weak correlation (absolute value lower than 0.3) or an unexpected sign of the correlation coefficient, *e.g.*, the average Gram confidence score increases with the noise ratio on CIFAR100 ($r_s = 1.0$) when it should be decreasing. Results in **bold** indicate a strong expected correlation (absolute value greater than 0.9). The last column represents the average correlation score, taking into account the expected sign of the correlation (results with * are partial average values). ⊕ indicates a timeout during the experiments.

	CIFAR10					CIFAR100					ImageNet					Avg.
	Noise↓	Blur↓	Bright.↑	R+↓	R-↑	Noise↓	Blur↓	Bright.↑	R+↓	R-↑	Noise↓	Blur↓	Bright.↑	R+↓	R-↑	
MSP	-0.22	-0.88	**0.98**	-0.55	0.56	0.33	-0.78	**0.99**	-0.32	0.31	0.71	**-1.0**	**1.0**	-0.77	0.85	0.54
ODIN	-0.85	-0.7	0.18	-0.15	0.13	-0.15	-0.77	0.75	-0.22	0.21	0.12	-0.87	0.2	-0.81	0.81	0.45
MDS	**-1.0**	0.41	0.84	-0.03	0.19	**-1.0**	0.68	0.84	-0.03	0.2	**-1.0**	0.98	-0.35	-0.16	0.11	0.20
Gram	1.0	**-1.0**	**1.0**	-0.15	-0.02	1.0	-0.83	**1.0**	-0.23	0.25	⊕	⊕	⊕	⊕	⊕	0.24*
EBO	-0.62	-0.88	0.96	-0.33	0.29	-0.32	-0.78	**0.99**	-0.22	0.22	0.63	**-0.93**	**1.0**	-0.78	0.75	0.56
GradNorm	0.05	-0.69	-1.0	-0.04	-0.01	-0.71	-0.78	0.88	-0.32	0.31	0.75	**-0.93**	**1.0**	-0.47	0.41	0.32
ReAct	-0.44	-0.88	0.96	-0.37	0.33	-0.75	-0.78	**0.99**	-0.22	0.21	-0.25	**-0.95**	**1.0**	-0.66	0.66	0.63
MaxLogit	-0.62	-0.88	0.96	-0.33	0.33	0.0	-0.78	**0.99**	-0.22	0.22	0.65	**-0.93**	**1.0**	-0.78	0.78	0.54
KLM	-0.1	**-0.93**	0.95	-0.53	0.44	-0.01	-0.83	**0.99**	-0.27	0.26	⊕	⊕	⊕	⊕	⊕	0.53*
ViM	-0.78	-0.83	0.92	-0.29	0.3	**-1.0**	-0.88	**1.0**	-0.18	0.38	**-1.0**	**-1.0**	**1.0**	-0.43	0.43	0.69
KNN	-0.36	-0.88	0.99	-0.46	0.4	-0.02	-0.79	**1.0**	-0.26	0.35	**-0.99**	**-1.0**	**1.0**	-0.5	0.5	0.63
DICE	**-0.97**	-0.88	0.92	-0.46	0.37	**-0.99**	-0.78	**0.99**	-0.32	0.22	0.65	**-0.93**	**1.0**	-0.74	0.74	0.64
FNRD	**-1.0**	0.58	-0.99	-0.11	0.08	**-1.0**	0.49	-0.88	-0.21	0.13	**-1.0**	-0.85	0.99	-0.35	0.35	0.21
CODE	-0.69	-0.88	**1.0**	-0.5	0.35	**-0.95**	-0.78	**0.99**	-0.3	0.29	-0.85	**-0.93**	**1.0**	-0.85	0.83	**0.75**

the Far-OoD benchmark for ImageNet). Interestingly, increasing the number of detectors per class from 4 to 6 does not necessarily improve our results. Indeed, the Unicity constraint (Eq. 5) becomes harder to satisfy with a higher number of detectors and is ultimately detrimental to the Locality constraint (Eq. 4). This experiment also shows that the choice of Near-OoD/Far-OoD datasets in OpenOoD is not necessarily reflected by the average AUROC scores. Indeed, for CIFAR100, most methods exhibit a higher AUROC for Near-OoD datasets than for Far-OoD datasets. This observation highlights the challenges of selecting and sorting OoD datasets according to their relative "distance" to the ID dataset, without any explicit formal definition of what this distance should be. In this regard, our proposed benchmark using perturbations of the ID dataset aims at providing a quantifiable distance between ID and OoD datasets.

Consistency Against Perturbations. We also evaluated all methods on our perturbation benchmark (see Sect. 3), measuring the Spearman Rank correlation coefficient (SRCC) between the magnitude of the perturbation (see Table 2) and the average confidence measured on the perturbed dataset. The results, shown in Table 3, reveal that, on average, *CODE seem to correlate more strongly to the magnitude of the perturbation than all other methods.* Moreover, some OoD methods sometimes display unexpected behaviours, depending on the choice of dataset and perturbation, as shown in Fig. 3. In particular, MSP tends to increase with the noise ratio, hence the success of adversarial attacks [5,23]. Additionally, by construction, any perturbation reducing the amplitude of neuron activation values (blur, brightness) has the opposite effect of increasing the FNRD. Gram also increases with the noise ratio and is highly sensitive to rotations, although we do not have a satisfactory explanation for this particular behaviour. We also notice that - contrary to our expectations - the average confidence does not monotonously decrease when rotating images from 0 to 180°: all methods show periodic local maximums of the average confidence that may indicate a form of invariance of the network *w.r.t.* rotations of specific magnitude (45° for CIFAR10, 90° for CIFAR100/ImageNet, 180° for MNIST). This effect seems amplified for CIFAR100 (see Fig. 3). Finally, we notice that the top-3 methods for Near-OoD detection (KNN, ViM and ReAct) also strongly correlate with the magnitude of the perturbation, which opens the door to a more in-depth analysis of the relationship between the two benchmarks.

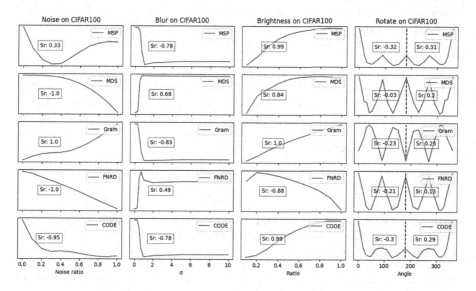

Fig. 3. Evolution of the average confidence score v. magnitude of the perturbation. Curves in red indicate anomalous behaviours. Since all methods have different calibration values, we omit the units on the y-axis, focusing on the general evolution of the average confidence score over the perturbed dataset.

6   Conclusion and Future Work

In this paper, we have demonstrated how the detection of recurring patterns can be exploited to develop CODE, an OoD-agnostic method that also enables a form of visualisation of the detected patterns. We believe that this unique feature can help the developer verify visually the quality of the OoD detection method and therefore can increase the safety of image classifiers. More generally, in the future we wish to study more thoroughly how part visualisation can be leveraged to fix or improve the OoD detection method when necessary. For instance, we noticed some redundant parts during our experiments and believe that such redundancy could be identified automatically, and pruned during the training process to produce a more precise representation of each class. Additionally, providing a form of justification of the OoD-ness of a sample could also increase the *acceptability* of the method from the end-user point of view, a statement that we wish to confirm by conducting a user study in the future. Our experiments show that CODE offers consistent results on par with state-of-the-art methods in the context of two different OoD detection benchmarks, including our new OoD benchmark based on perturbations of the reference dataset. This new benchmark highlights intriguing behaviours by several state-of-the-art methods (*w.r.t.* specific types of perturbation) that should be analysed in details. Moreover, since these perturbations are equivalent to a *controlled covariate shift*, it would be interesting to evaluate covariate shift detection methods in the same setting. Finally, note that CODE could be applied to other part detection algorithms, provided that a confidence measure could be associated with the detected parts.

Acknowledgements. Experiments presented in this paper were carried out using the Grid'5000 testbed, supported by a scientific interest group hosted by Inria and including CNRS, RENATER and several Universities as well as other organisations (see https://www.grid5000.fr). This work has been partially supported by MIAI@Grenoble Alpes, (ANR-19-P3IA-0003) and TAILOR, a project funded by EU Horizon 2020 research and innovation programme under GA No 952215.

References

1. Deng, J., Dong, W., Socher, R., Li, L.J., Li, K., Fei-Fei, L.: ImageNet: a large-scale hierarchical image database. In: CVPR 2009, pp. 248–255 (2009)
2. Deng, L.: The MNIST database of handwritten digit images for machine learning research. IEEE Signal Process. Mag. **29**(6), 141–142 (2012)
3. Eidous, O.M., Al-Rawash, M.: Approximations for standard normal distribution function and its invertible. ArXiv (2022)
4. Han, J., Yao, X., Cheng, G., Feng, X., Xu, D.: P-CNN: part-based convolutional neural networks for fine-grained visual categorization. IEEE Trans. Pattern Anal. Mach. Intell. **44**(2), 579–590 (2022)
5. Hein, M., Andriushchenko, M., Bitterwolf, J.: Why RELU networks yield high-confidence predictions far away from the training data and how to mitigate the problem? In: CVPR 2019, pp. 41–50 (2019)
6. Hendrycks, D., Basart, S., Mazeika, M., Mostajabi, M., Steinhardt, J., Song, D.X.: Scaling out-of-distribution detection for real-world settings. In: ICML 2022 (2022)
7. Hendrycks, D., Dietterich, T.G.: Benchmarking neural network robustness to common corruptions and perturbations. ArXiv (2018)
8. Hendrycks, D., Gimpel, K.: A baseline for detecting misclassified and out-of-distribution examples in neural networks. In: ICLR 2017 (2017)
9. Hond, D., Asgari, H., Jeffery, D., Newman, M.: An integrated process for verifying deep learning classifiers using dataset dissimilarity measures. Int. J. Artif. Intell. Mach. Learn. **11**(2), 1–21 (2021)

10. Huang, R., Geng, A., Li, Y.: On the importance of gradients for detecting distributional shifts in the wild. In: NeurIPS 2021 (2021)
11. Krizhevsky, A.: Learning multiple layers of features from tiny images. Technical report (2009)
12. Krizhevsky, A., Sutskever, I., Hinton, G.E.: ImageNet classification with deep convolutional neural networks. In: NIPS (2012)
13. Lee, K., Lee, K., Lee, H., Shin, J.: A simple unified framework for detecting out-of-distribution samples and adversarial attacks. In: NeurIPS (2018)
14. Li, H., Zhang, X., Tian, Q., Xiong, H.: Attribute mix: semantic data augmentation for fine grained recognition. In: 2020 IEEE International Conference on Visual Communications and Image Processing (VCIP), pp. 243–246 (2020)
15. Liang, S., Li, Y., Srikant, R.: Enhancing the reliability of out-of-distribution image detection in neural networks. In: ICLR 2018 (2018)
16. Liu, W., Wang, X., Owens, J., Li, Y.: Energy-based out-of-distribution detection. In: NeurIPS 2020, pp. 21464–21475 (2020)
17. Mukhoti, J., et al.: Raising the bar on the evaluation of out-of-distribution detection. ArXiv (2022)
18. Sastry, C.S., Oore, S.: Detecting out-of-distribution examples with gram matrices. In: ICML (2020)
19. Smilkov, D., Thorat, N., Kim, B., Viégas, F.B., Wattenberg, M.: SmoothGrad: removing noise by adding noise. ArXiv (2017)
20. Sun, Y., Guo, C., Li, Y.: ReAct: out-of-distribution detection with rectified activations. In: NeurIPS 2021 (2021)
21. Sun, Y., Li, Y.: DICE: leveraging sparsification for out-of-distribution detection. In: ICCV 2021 (2021)
22. Sun, Y., Ming, Y., Zhu, X., Li, Y.: Out-of-distribution detection with deep nearest neighbors. In: ICML 2022 (2022)
23. Szegedy, C., et al.: Intriguing properties of neural networks. In: ICLR 2014 (2014)
24. Wang, H., Li, Z., Feng, L., Zhang, W.: ViM: out-of-distribution with virtual-logit matching. In: CVPR 2022 (2022)
25. Wattenberg, M., Viégas, F., Johnson, I.: How to use t-SNE effectively. Distill (2016).http://distill.pub/2016/misread-tsne
26. Xu-Darme, R., Quénot, G., Chihani, Z., Rousset, M.C.: PARTICUL: part identification with confidence measure using unsupervised learning. In: XAIE: 2nd Workshop on Explainable and Ethical AI - ICPR 2022 (2022)
27. Yang, J., et al.: OpenOOD: benchmarking generalized out-of-distribution detection. NeurIPS 2022 - Datasets and Benchmarks Track (2022)
28. Zhao, X., et al.: Recognizing part attributes with insufficient data. In: ICCV 2019 (2019)
29. Zheng, H., Fu, J., Mei, T., Luo, J.: Learning multi-attention convolutional neural network for fine-grained image recognition. In: ICCV 2017 (2017)

Author Index

J. Guiochet et al. (Eds.): SAFECOMP 2023 Workshops, LNCS 14182, pp. 437–438, 2023.
https://doi.org/10.1007/978-3-031-40953-0

Printed in the United States
by Baker & Taylor Publisher Services